THE NEW KEY TO COSTA RICA

THE NEW KEY TO COSTA RICA

Nineteenth Edition

BEATRICE BLAKE

DEIDRE HYDE
Illustrator

DAVID GILBERT
Photographer

Ulysses Press

Published by: Ulysses Press
P.O. Box 3440
Berkeley, CA 94703
www.ulyssespress.com

ISSN 1098-7398
ISBN 978-1-56975-696-6

Printed in Canada by Transcontinental Printing

20 19 18 17 16 15

Managing Editor: Claire Chun
Copyeditor: Emma Silvers
Editorial Associates: Elyce Petker, Lauren Harrison, Abigail Reser, Katy Loveless
Typesetting: Judith Metzener
Interior maps: XNR Productions except map on pages xviii–xix by Pease Press
Color map: Stellar Cartography
Indexer: Sayre Van Young
Front cover photography: © Pep Guasch Photography (white-faced monkey)
Back cover photography: *top:* © istockphoto.com/Lawren Graf (green macaw);
    middle: © istockphoto.com/Peter Gile (iguana); *bottom:* © istockphoto.com/
    Antonio Roldan (zipline)

Corcovado hiker and leaf-cutter ant photographs in color insert © Margaux Gibbons. Other photographs in insert © David Gilbert.

Illustrations on pages 105 and 106 by Anabel Maffioli

Part of Chapter Two was compiled by Sorrel Downer and J. Patrick O'Marr, and
    originally published by *Costa Rica Today*

Distributed by Publishers Group West

For peace with justice in harmony with nature

Table of Contents

Maps

Acknowledgments

Many thanks to Kyra Cruz, Eva Arauz, Karine Chardon and all the members of ACTUAR for facilitating much of my research.

Much thanks goes out to Eladio Salazar of Coopesavegre, Hernan Ramirez of Nacientes Palmichal, Daniel and Dominique of Sueño Celeste, and Roy Meza of ACTUAR. Each of you greatly expanded my knowledge of your areas and provided great companionship during my research. It was also fun to travel with Joan and George Packard while they were producing a fascinating video about ACTUAR destinations. Alex Murray of Casa Mañana and Emma Harrison, scientific director of the Caribbean Conservation Corps, generously took time to orient me with their expertise.

Thanks also to old friends Deirdre Hyde, Robert Lee, John and Sue Trostle, and Margaret Smith Adelman for fun and companionship. This edition could not have happened without the collaboration and friendship of Heidi Daub and Elena Arias. I can't thank you enough!

Thanks to all the readers who sent me their comments. Your feedback is a boon to all your fellow travelers.

Happy 52nd anniversary to the *Tico Times*, one of the bravest little papers on the planet, for their in-depth coverage of political, social, and environmental issues in Costa Rica.

The year 2008 marks the 32nd anniversary of *The Key to Costa Rica*, which my mother, Jean Wallace, started in 1976. Bless her for her joyful and generous spirit and the love of Costa Rica that inspired this book. This year also marks the 22nd anniversary of my collaboration and redesigning of this book with Anne Becher. Even though she was not involved in this edition, her words, spirit, and values still pervade the book, and we wish her well in her busy life as mother, professor, and freelance writer.

Thanks to my family for their love and support while I put out yet another edition.

Thanks to the staff at Ulysses Press for their ability to whip this manuscript into a user-friendly guide.

Beatrice Blake
October 2008

Innovative Communities and Your Vacation

In many of the projects highlighted in this edition, organic agriculture, appropriate energy technology, and preservation of forests and rivers are combined with tourism in a way that holds great promise for the future. By visiting these communities, you will not only meet some lovely people, but you will be inspired by their ability to put innovative principles into practice. You will also see the results of the intelligent, dedicated work of the United National Development Program, COOPRENA, ACTUAR, and individual social entrepreneurs, who, in a time of worldwide chaos, are faithfully sowing the seeds of peace.

THE EVOLUTION OF CONSERVATION AND ECOTOURISM IN COSTA RICA

Because it contains 4 percent of global biodiversity in its very small territory, Costa Rica has been a mecca for tropical biologists and ecologists for the last 50 years. These scientists worked with visionary Costa Ricans to establish the famous National Parks Service in the 1970s. As protected areas were established and research was carried out, biologists observed that most animals migrate from one altitude to another during the year. Researchers discovered that many wild felines like panthers, jaguars, and pumas need hundreds of square miles of habitat in order to hunt and reproduce successfully. In fact, they have found that, in order for large cats to sustain their populations, each species requires a preserve big enough to support at least 500 to 5000 individuals of each species. If, through careless development, the original habitat is degraded into small, isolated pieces, the cats, and less charismatic animals, birds and insects, rapidly face extinction.

This awareness led to the creation of more and more parks and protected areas during the 1980s. The National Parks Service began a concerted effort to teach environmental education in the schools. Costa Rica also made a decision to rely on its biodiversity to attract tourism, instead of becoming yet another fun-and-sun tropical destination. Word spread, and soon Costa Ricans were seeing that their commitment to the protection of nature was providing jobs and opportunities for advancement.

At the same time, farmers who were struggling to make ends meet saw the tourism boom around them, and often decided to sell their farms in order to get funds to build tourist lodging, or to sell to foreigners who were paying exaggerated prices for land. Often foreigners knew how to establish and publicize nature tourism to people in North America and Europe, making for successful businesses. Setting up a B&B or an ecolodge became a dream for many foreigners who migrated here. Costa Rican families with large tracts of land also set up reserves to preserve wildlife habitats and gain government protection against squatters. Conservationists, farmers, and loggers often found themselves in a bitter race to gain control of the country's remaining unprotected forests.

In the early 1990s, area governments entertained the idea of the *Paseo Pantera* (Panther's Path): an unbroken strand of protected forest lands stretching along the Caribbean coast of Central America which would guarantee the range that wild animals need in order to survive. Although this project was funded by a consortium of conservation organizations, it floundered in the face of opposition from indigenous and *campesino* groups. Indigenous lands often have extensive forests, and governments have rarely been concerned with giving native people legal title to them. Poor farmers often lacked title as well. Both groups were aware of Central American history, in which elites have taken the most desirable land and pushed native people out. They feared a land grab that would banish them, once again, from their homes.

With time, even strict conservationists came to see that it was unnecessary to prohibit all human activity in order to preserve nature. They also began to understand that large tracts of land could never be assembled if the needs of local residents were not met.

In 1994, Costa Rica conducted a thorough survey of its richest ecosystems to determine how to conserve its remaining biodiversity. But the government, with 25 percent of national territory under some kind of protection, could not afford to buy and maintain more land. The government acknowledged that many privately owned reserves supported conservation by forming buffer zones and biological corridors around and between existing national parks. In 1995, the National System of Conservation Areas (SINAC) was formed. This divides the country into 11 conservation areas, ignoring provincial boundaries and concentrating on related ecosystems. In each area, private- and state-owned conservation activities are interrelated. SINAC's goals are to manage and promote the sustainable use of natural resources along with economic and social development.

Costa Rica's 1997 biodiversity law authorized a tax on gasoline in order to compensate the owners of forested land for the environmental services that their forests offer to society. These services are:

- reduction of greenhouse gases
- protection of drinking water
- protection of rivers that can be harnessed for hydroelectric power
- protection of biodiversity and its sustainable use for pharmaceuticals and science
- protection of ecosystems, life forms and scenic beauty.

Article 50 of the Costa Rican Constitution states: "All people have the right to a healthy and ecologically balanced environment." Citizens have lived with environmental education, conservation, and ecotourism for a generation, and today it is rare to find Costa Ricans who are not wholeheartedly in favor of protecting nature. At the same time, poverty and lack of jobs still lead to illegal poaching, and land speculation and greed on the part of developers and corrupt officials lead to overdevelopment (see Chapter Two). The struggle between exploiting nature and conserving forests and wildlife continues.

COSTA RICAN COMMUNITIES AND CONSERVATION

Costa Rica's vital grassroots democracy lends itself to innovation. In contrast to most Latin American countries, Costa Rica celebrated its first democratic election in 1889. Elections have continued almost uninterrupted through the present day. But what is truly impressive is the level of community organization.

In the 1970s, President Daniel Oduber (1974–78) said, "Humans must not be the object, but the subject of their own development." He believed that the wellbeing of rural communities was intimately linked to the health of the nation. He formed the National Directorate for Community Development (DINADECO) to help communities organize themselves to address their needs for water, electricity, health care, and cultural activities. Advisors would travel by jeep, motorcycle, or horseback to make sure that communities had the tools they needed to form successful organizations. Today, DINADECO is no longer very active, but the culture of community involvement persists.

Building on its traditions of grassroots democracy, the Ministry of the Environment has encouraged citizens to form Natural Resource Vigilance Committees (COVIRENAS). These volunteer groups are active in almost every rural area of the country, educating their neighbors about illegal logging, poaching, fishing, trade in endangered species, water protection, and how each person's actions can make a difference. They work with art and theater to encourage children's awareness, carry out clean-up campaigns, and report environmental infractions to the authorities. They are given official ID cards as environmental inspectors *ad honorem*.

COMMUNITY-BASED ECOTOURISM

Through its Small Grants Program, the United Nations Development Program has funded COVIRENAS groups, local conservation and development associations, and farmers' cooperatives so that rural communities with limited resources can have their own ecotourism businesses. This supports farmers in conserving their forests and rivers, keeping their families on the land, and supplementing their farming incomes. Many are turning to organic agriculture and are planting crops that provide habitat for a diversity of birds and wildlife.

At the same time, there are many noteworthy efforts by foreigners who have brought green technologies to Costa Rica and shared them with the local communities.

In each chapter of this book, you will learn about the tourism destinations that are combining innovative ideas, green practices and community self-sufficiency throughout Costa Rica, and you'll find highlighted reports on our adventures traveling to these communities.

Costa Rica still has the dreamy ecolodges that made it famous, where, after your massage and your yoga class, you can sit sipping rum-laced tropical smoothies and nibbling on delicate fish *carpaccio* while gazing out over the ocean. The extensive rainforest reserves owned by many of these lodges are also part of the conservation system.

Equally vacation worthy are the places that are putting innovative ideas into practice and building strong communities that can confront the challenges posed by tourism, and the land speculation and overdevelopment it brings. For assistance in planning itineraries that include both kinds of ecotourism, see keytocostarica.com.

We all know that clean air, water, soil, and forests are limited, and thus our most precious assets. Costa Rica is leading the way in valuing these resources and finding ways for humans to live in harmony with nature. Just by vacationing, adventuring, and learning at Costa Rica's innovative ecotourism communities, you will be contributing to this world-changing work.

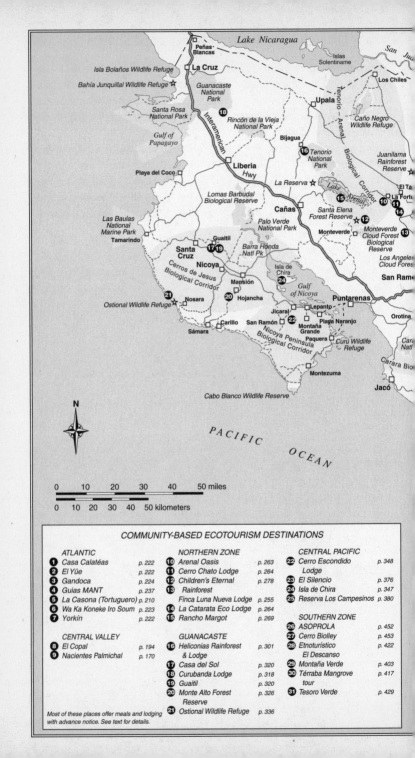

COMMUNITY-BASED ECOTOURISM DESTINATIONS

ATLANTIC
1 *Casa Calatéas* p. 222
2 *El Yüe* p. 222
3 *Gandoca* p. 224
4 *Guias MANT* p. 237
5 *La Casona (Tortuguero)* p. 210
6 *Wa Ka Koneke Iro Soum* p. 223
7 *Yorkín* p. 222

CENTRAL VALLEY
8 *El Copal* p. 194
9 *Nacientes Palmichal* p. 170

NORTHERN ZONE
10 *Arenal Oasis* p. 263
11 *Cerro Chato Lodge* p. 264
12 *Children's Eternal Rainforest* p. 278
13 *Finca Luna Nueva Lodge* p. 255
14 *La Catarata Eco Lodge* p. 264
15 *Rancho Margot* p. 269

GUANACASTE
16 *Heliconias Rainforest & Lodge* p. 301
17 *Casa del Sol* p. 320
18 *Curubanda Lodge* p. 318
19 *Guaitil* p. 320
20 *Monte Alto Forest Reserve* p. 326
21 *Ostional Wildlife Refuge* p. 336

CENTRAL PACIFIC
22 *Cerro Escondido Lodge* p. 348
23 *El Silencio* p. 376
24 *Isla de Chira* p. 347
25 *Reserva Los Campesinos* p. 380

SOUTHERN ZONE
26 *ASOPROLA* p. 452
27 *Cerro Biolley* p. 453
28 *Etnoturístico El Descanso* p. 422
29 *Montaña Verde* p. 403
30 *Térraba Mangrove tour* p. 417
31 *Tesoro Verde* p. 429

Most of these places offer meals and lodging with advance notice. See text for details.

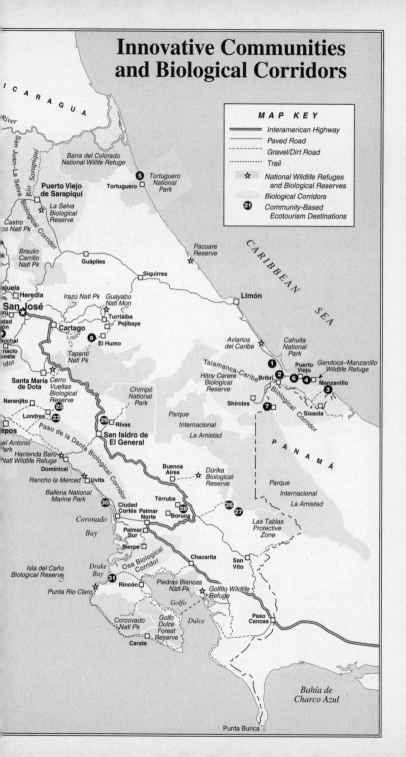

Innovative Communities and Biological Corridors

MAP KEY

≡≡≡ Interamerican Highway
— Paved Road
‐‐‐ Gravel/Dirt Road
⋯⋯ Trail
☆ National Wildlife Refuges and Biological Reserves
▨ Biological Corridors
㉑ Community-Based Ecotourism Destinations

NICARAGUA

River
San Juan–La Selva Biological Corridor
Río Sarapiquí

Barra del Colorado National Willife Refuge

Puerto Viejo de Sarapiquí

La Selva Biological Reserve

⑤ Tortuguero
Tortuguero
Tortuguero National Park

Castro co Natl Pk

Braulio Carrillo Natl Pk

Guápiles

Siquirres

ajuela Heredia
Irazú Natl Pk
Guayabo Natl Mon

zú dad ón
San José
Cartago
Turrialba
Pejibaye

Pacuare Reserve

CARIBBEAN SEA

Limón

nichal nacio osta

⑧ El Humo

Tapantí Natl Pk

Aviarios del Caribe

Cahuita National Park

Gandoca–Manzanillo Wildlife Refuge

Santa María de Dota

Cerro Vueltas Biological Reserve

Talamanca-Caribe
Hitoy Cerere Biological Reserve

① Bribri
② Puerto Viejo
⑥ ④
③ Manzanillo

Naranjito

Chirripó National Park

Shiroles

Biological Corridor

Sixaola

⑦

Londres ㉓

㉕

㉙ Rivas

Parque Internacional La Amistad

PANAMÁ

epos

Paso de la Danta Biological Corridor

San Isidro de El General

el Antonio Park
Hacienda Barú Natl Wildlife Refuge

Dominical

Rancho la Merced Uvita

Ballena National Marine Park

Buenos Aires

Dúrika Biological Reserve

Parque Internacional La Amistad

㉚ Ciudad Cortés
Palmar Norte
Térruba
㉘ Boruca

㉖ ㉗

Coronado Bay

Palmar Sur

Sierpe

Chacarita

San Vito

Las Tablas Protective Zone

Isla del Caño Biological Reserve

Drake Bay
Osa Biological Corridor

㉛ Rincón

Piedras Blancas Natl Pk

Golfito Wildlife Refuge

Punta Río Claro

Golfo

Corcovado Natl Pk

Golfo Dulce Forest Reserve

Dulce

Paso Canoas

Carate

Bahía de Charco Azul

Punta Burica

Sustainable Ecotourism Rating

A Sustainable Ecotourism Rating had been a feature of our book from 1992 to 2002. In fact, *The New Key to Costa Rica* was the first guidebook to use a green rating system.

In more recent editions, we relied on our personal observation of ecotourism businesses over the years, and a pattern began to emerge. Parts of Costa Rica are being destroyed by tourism. In other parts, tourism is a vital support for innovation. Often the challenges of tourism development bring out the worst rather than the best in the relationships between residents, developers, conservationists, government, business, workers, foreigners, locals, etc. Tourism challenges communities to confront it in a united way. In this edition we are calling your attention to communities that have stepped up responsibly to this challenge, using ecotourism to support economic and energy self-sufficiency.

Even though the lodges we used to rate on our Sustainable Ecotourism list have been largely a positive force in Costa Rican society and culture, we can no longer ignore the fact that the majority of these ecolodges are owned by foreigners. There is hardly any beach property in Costa Rican hands, except for beaches protected by national parks. Prices of farmland are often out of the range of farmers, but easily accessible to foreigners. This neo-colonialism does not fit with Costa Rican history and values, and shows that it is very difficult for Costa Ricans to make a living from the land, as they have traditionally.

On the other hand, there are quite a few foreigners who are working together with their Costa Rican neighbors to create the innovative communities highlighted in this edition.

Over the last 30 years, we have observed how the conservation ethic has permeated the country. The most interesting thing Costa Rica has to share with tourists today is a network of rural communities that are devoted to sustainability: in agriculture, in the use of alternative energy, in learning how to work together, and in providing fascinating and beautiful experiences in nature.

We call your attention to these special communities on the map on pages xviii–xix.

ONE

Costa Rica: A Brief History

To understand the unique character of the Costa Rican people today, it helps to know something of their history. Over the centuries, Costa Rica has taken some decidedly different turns from her Central American sister states.

PRE-COLUMBIAN COSTA RICA

The largest and most developed pre-Columbian population in Costa Rica was that of the Chorotegas, whose ancestors had migrated from Southern Mexico to the Nicoya Peninsula, probably in the 13th century. They were running away from enemies who wanted to enslave them—their name translates as "fleeing people."

Much of the information we have about the Chorotegas was collected by Gonzalo Fernández de Oviedo, a Spanish explorer who lived with them for a short period in 1529.

Outstanding farmers, the Chorotegas managed three harvests of corn per year. They also grew cotton, beans, fruits, and cacao, which they introduced to Costa Rica and whose seeds they used as currency. Land was communally owned and the harvest was divided according to need, so that old people and widows with children could be cared for.

The Chorotegas lived in cities of as many as 20,000 people, which had central plazas with marketplaces and religious centers. Only women could enter the market. Women wore skirts, the length of which depended upon their social level. Men could go naked, but often wore a large cloth or a woven and dyed sleeveless cotton shirt.

Women worked in ceramics, producing vessels painted in black and red, decorated with plumed serpents (the symbol for unity of matter and

1

spirit), jaguars, monkeys, and crocodiles. They carved stylized jade figures in human and animal shapes. The figures may have been used in fertility ceremonies or to bring good luck in the hunt. They wrote books on deer-skin parchment and used a ritual calendar.

War was institutionalized. A permanent military organization fought to obtain land and slaves, who were used as human sacrifices. Eating some-one who had been sacrificed to the gods was a purification rite. The Choro-tegas also sacrificed virgins by throwing them into volcano craters.

The Chibcha people from Colombia migrated to the South Pacific re-gion of Costa Rica, where they lived in permanent, well-fortified towns. Their concern with security could have arisen from their possession of gold—which they fashioned into human and animal figures (especially tur-tles, armadillos, and sharks). Both women and men fought for the best lands and for prisoners, who were used as slaves or as human sacrifices. They believed in life after death; vultures performed a vital role in trans-porting people to the other world by eating their corpses.

These people probably made the granite spheres that lie in linear for-mations in the valley of the Río Térraba and on the Isla del Caño off the coast of the Osa Peninsula. These spheres range in diameter from 7.5 cen-timeters (the size of an orange) to 2.5 meters. Their almost-perfect round-ness and careful placement make them one of Costa Rica's pre-Columbian mysteries.

Peoples from the jungles of Brazil and Ecuador migrated to the lowland jungles of the Costa Rican Atlantic Coast. They lived semi-nomadically, hunting, fishing, and cultivating *yuca* (manioc), *pejibaye* (small cousin to the coconut), pumpkin, and squash. Their chief's nobility was hereditary, passed down through the female line of the family.

Social prestige was gained by good warriors. Apparently, decapitated heads of enemies were war trophies. Their stone figurines represent war-riors with a knife in one hand and a head in the other.

They worshiped the sun, the moon, and the bones of their ancestors and believed that all things had souls. During religious festivals there was a rit-ual inebriation with a fermented *chicha* made from *yuca* or *pejibaye.* The burial mounds of these people have yielded the greatest number of pre-Columbian artifacts in the country.

COLONIAL COSTA RICA

On September 18, 1502, during his fourth and last voyage to the New World, Christopher Columbus anchored in the Bay of Cariari (now Limón) after a violent tempest wrecked his ships. During the 17 days that he and his crew were resting and making repairs, they visited a few coastal villages. The native people treated them well, and they left with the impression that Veragua (a name that Columbus used for the Caribbean Coast between Honduras and Panama) was a land rich in gold, whose gentle and friendly inhabitants could be easily conquered.

A few years later, in 1506, King Ferdinand of Spain sent a governor to colonize Veragua. Governor Diego de Nicuesa and his colonizers received a different welcome. First, their ship went aground on the coast of Panama, and they had to walk up the Atlantic shore. Food shortages and tropical diseases reduced the group by half. Then they met the native people, who burned their crops rather than feed the invaders. The Spanish realized that their task was not going to be easy. There was no centralized empire to conquer and sack, and the scattered tribes were at home in a climate and terrain that the explorers found devastating. This first attempt at colonization was a miserable failure.

After Vásco Núñez de Balboa "discovered" the Pacific Ocean in 1513, the Spaniards started exploring the west coast of Veragua. In 1522, an exploratory land expedition set out from northern Panama. Despite sickness, starvation, and tropical weather, the survivors of the long, hazardous trip called it a success: They had obtained gold and pearls, and their priest claimed he had converted more than 30,000 of the native people to Catholicism between Panama and Nicaragua.

More explorers and would-be colonizers arrived. There were attempted settlements on both coasts, but they ended in tragedy for the settlers, who died of hunger, were driven out by the native people, or fought among themselves and dissolved their communities.

Juan Vásquez de Coronado arrived as governor in 1562. He found a group of Spaniards and Spanish *mestizos* living inland from the Pacific Coast. Coronado explored Costa Rica, treating the native people he met more humanely than had his predecessors. He decided that the highlands were more suitable for settlement, so he moved the settlers to the Cartago Valley, where the climate was pleasant and the soils were rich from the lava deposited by Volcán Irazú. In 1563, Cartago was established as the capital of Costa Rica.

In contrast to most other Spanish colonies, there was no large exploitable workforce in Costa Rica. The indigenous population had been decimated early on by war and disease. Because it had no riches and was difficult to reach from Guatemala, the seat of Spain's Central American empire, Costa Rica was left free from foreign intrusion. Forgotten by its "mother country," Costa Rica was almost self-sufficient in its poverty. At one point, even the governor was forced to work his own small plot of land to survive.

While some Costa Ricans were slaveholders, they owned few compared to other countries. Most slaves tended cacao plantations in the Atlantic Coast town of Matina, or served in Central Valley homes. The Calvo Chinchilla household held 27 slaves, more than any other family in colonial Costa Rica. Their case illustrates a tendency that was common in colonial times. Son Miguel had five children with his parents' slave Ana Cardoso. He acknowledged them, and his parents eventually freed her and their grandchildren. The tendency of slaveowners to have children with their slaves—mostly by force, though not in this case—contributed to the "bleaching" of African roots in the Central Valley population. Historian and genealogist Mauricio Meléndez Obando identified several causes for African slaves not maintaining a strong identity: 1) forced and accelerated racial mixing; 2) a relatively small black population; 3) the heterogeneous nature of the slave population, since they were from various parts of Africa; and 4) their integration with other constituents of the population, including poor Spaniards, *mulattos*, *mestizos* (one parent Spanish and the other indigenous), and Zambos (one parent indigenous, the other black).

Costa Rica's Spanish population remained small and its lifestyle humble through the 17th century. In 1709, Spanish money became so scarce that settlers used cacao beans as currency, just like the Chorotegas. Women wore goat-hair skirts; soldiers had no uniforms. Volcán Irazú erupted in 1723, almost destroying Cartago. Nevertheless, the Spanish survived, and the area settled by Spaniards actually increased during the 1700s. Three new cities were founded in the Meseta Central (Central Valley): Cubujuquí (Heredia) in 1706, Villanueva de la Boca del Monte (San José) in 1737, and Villa Hermosa (Alajuela) in 1782.

INDEPENDENCE

In October 1821, word arrived from Guatemala that Spain had granted independence to its American colonies on September 15th. It had taken the news one month to travel through the mountains and valleys to Costa Rica. After a period of internal strife between conservative elements in Cartago who wanted to continue the monarchy and a more liberal faction in San José who wanted to join South America's liberation movement, Costa Rica declared itself a state in the short-lived Federal Republic of Central America, and the capital was moved from Cartago to San José.

The first president of free Costa Rica, Juan Mora Fernández, built roads and schools and gave land grants to anyone who would plant coffee, the most profitable export crop at the time. This epoch was one of the most influential in the evolution of Costa Rican democracy, because small farmers were encouraged to grow coffee and sell the beans to wealthier farmers, who would prepare the beans for export. Thus, rich and poor each had an important place in the coffee-growing process, and mutual respect was developed.

By the mid-1800s, coffee was Costa Rica's principal export, and coffee growers were a powerful and wealthy elite. They built a road to transport coffee from the Meseta Central to Costa Rica's port, Puntarenas. They exported first to Chile, then later to Germany and England. By mid-century, European money was entering the pockets of Costa Rican coffee growers, and Europeans were arriving en masse at this tropical frontier. Costa Rica was becoming cosmopolitan. A university was founded in 1844 to disseminate European thinking, and Costa Rican politicians sported European liberal ideologies.

By 1848, the coffee elite was influential enough to elect its own representative for president, Juan Rafael Mora. He was a self-made man who had become one of the most powerful coffee growers in the country. He was charismatic, astute, and respected by the coffee elite and the campesinos alike. He became a veritable national hero by leading an "army" of Costa Ricans to defend his country when it was invaded by one of the most detested figures in Central American history, the North American William Walker.

THE SAGA OF WILLIAM WALKER

A study of William Walker's early life gives one little indication of how he would later come to be the scourge of Central America. Walker graduated from the University of Nashville at the age of 14. By the time he was 19, he held both a law and a medical degree from the University of Pennsylvania. He followed this memorable academic record with two years of postgraduate study in Paris and Heidelberg.

His success stopped there. Returning from Europe, Walker quickly failed as a doctor, lawyer, and journalist. He had an ill-fated courtship with a beautiful deaf-mute New Orleans socialite, then in 1849 turned up as a gold miner in California. He didn't fare well in this occupation either, and soon started working as a hack writer in several California cities.

At this point, something happened in the mind of William Walker, and he launched himself on a career as a soldier of fortune. From then on, he succeeded in creating chaos wherever he took his five-foot, three-inch, 100-pound frame.

In the early 1850s, Walker sailed with several hundred men on a "liberating expedition" to the Baja California Peninsula and Mexico. The expedition was financed by the Knights of the Golden Circle, a movement bent on promoting the "benefits" of slavery. Walker spent a year in Mexico, during which time he awarded himself the military title of colonel and proclaimed himself "President of Sonora and Baja California."

Back in the United States after several encounters with the Mexican Army, he was arrested for breaking the Neutrality Act of 1818. His acquittal of the charge gained him fame and followers. His next expedition was to Nicaragua.

Walker went with two main goals. One was to convert Central America into slave territory and annex it to the southern United States; the other was to conquer Nicaragua and ready it for the construction of a transisthmic canal. The new riches that were being discovered in California attracted many Easterners, but crossing the United States by land was slow and difficult. Walker had made contacts with a group of economically powerful North Americans who thought that a sea route could be more efficient and profitable. Southern Nicaragua would be a perfect site for the isthmus crossing; ships could sail up the San Juan River, which formed the Nicaragua–Costa Rica border, cross Lake Nicaragua, then pass through a to-be-built 18-mile canal from the lake to the Pacific Ocean.

Walker's contacts arranged for an invitation from the Liberal Party of Nicaragua, which at the time was embattled with the Conservatives. In June 1855, he landed in Nicaragua with 58 men. After losing his first encounter with the Conservatives, Walker managed to hold out until several hundred reinforcements arrived from California, bringing new model carbines and six-shooters. They soon overpowered the Conservatives, and, after an "open" election, Walker became "President of the Republic of Nicaragua."

Central Americans from throughout the isthmus rose to fight Walker and his band of *filibusteros*. In February 1856, President Juan Rafael Mora of Costa Rica declared war on Walker, but not on Nicaragua. Mora raised an Army of 9000 in less than a week. This "army," led by Mora and his brother-in-law José María Cañas, was composed of *campesinos*, merchants, and government bureaucrats ill-dressed for combat and armed only with farm tools, machetes, and old rifles. They marched for two weeks to Guanacaste, where they found 300 *filibusteros* resting at the Santa Rosa hacienda (now a national monument in Santa Rosa National Park). Having invaded Costa Rica, the *filibusteros* were preparing to conquer San José. The Costa Rican Army, by then diminished to 2500 men, attacked the *filibusteros*, who fled back to Nicaragua after only 14 minutes of battle.

Two thousand Costa Ricans followed Walker up to Nicaragua and, in a generally masterful campaign, fought him to a standstill. The turning point came in Rivas, Nicaragua. Walker and his band were barricaded in a large wooden building from which they could not be dislodged. Juan Santamaría, a drummer boy, volunteered to set fire to the building and succeeded in forcing Walker's retreat. In his action, Santamaría lost his life, and became Costa Rica's national hero.

Walker's attempt to convert Nicaragua and the rest of Central America into slave territory was backed by U.S. president James Buchanan, and his failure angered the president. When Walker confiscated the transisthmic transportation concession that U.S. financier Cornelius Vanderbilt had already started installing, Vanderbilt began to finance some of Walker's enemies. This was the beginning of the end of Walker's career.

After another engagement in late 1856 on Lake Nicaragua, where the Costa Rican Army brilliantly cut Walker off from his support troops, the rag-tag *filibustero* forces were near defeat. On May 1, 1857, Walker surrendered to a U.S. warship.

The adventurer traveled to Nicaragua again in late 1857, but this time he was taken prisoner before he could wreak any havoc. When he was released in 1860, he sailed to Honduras, where, upon landing, he seized the custom house. This brought a British warship to the scene, upon which Walker, pursued by the Hondurans, eventually took refuge. Offered safe

La Casona,
scene of Walker's defeat

conduct into U.S. hands by the British commander, Walker insisted he was the rightful president of Honduras. The British therefore put Walker ashore again, where he was taken by the Hondurans and promptly shot.

The net result of Walker's Central American marauding was the death of some 20,000 men. The inscription on William Walker's tombstone reads, "Glory to the patriots who freed Central America of such a bloody pirate! Curses to those who brought him and to those who helped him."

Juan Rafael Mora is now acclaimed for having saved Central America from Walker and the interests he represented, but he wasn't that popular when he returned from battle. People accused Mora of having been too ambitious and blamed him for an epidemic of cholera that infected Costa Rican soldiers in Nicaragua and spread to kill almost ten percent of the population.

Mora manipulated the 1859 election to win despite massive opposition. In August 1859, his enemies overthrew him. A year later, Mora led a coup d'etat against the new president, also a member of the coffee elite. His attempt failed, and he was shot by a firing squad in 1860—an inglorious end for a man who is now a national hero. All through the 1860s, quarrels among the coffee growers helped to put presidents in power and later depose them. Nevertheless, most presidents during these years were liberal and intellectual civilians. Despite the political instability of the decade, the country managed to establish a well-based educational system. This was a time when new schools were founded, European professors were brought over to design academic programs, and the first bookstores in San José opened their doors.

THE ATLANTIC RAILROAD AND UNITED FRUIT

By the mid-1800s, Costa Rica realized it needed an Atlantic port to facilitate coffee export to Europe. When Tomás Guardia declared himself Chief of State in 1871, he decided to build a railway to Limón. He contracted Henry Meiggs, a North American who had built railways in Chile and Peru. Meiggs went to England to secure loans for the project. He obtained 3.4 million sterling pounds, of which only one million actually arrived. These loans created the first foreign debt in Costa Rica's history.

Costa Rica's population wasn't large enough to provide the project with the necessary labor force, so thousands of Jamaican, Italian, and Chinese workers were recruited. After an optimistic start, it soon became evident that it was going to be a slow, dangerous, and costly process. Construction of the railroad claimed some 4000 workers' lives, cost the equivalent of $8 million and lasted 19 years. The jungle proved itself a formidable and deadly barrier.

Meiggs' nephew, Minor C. Keith, became the director a few years after the project started. The railroad he inherited was constantly beleaguered by severe shortages of funds, so he started experimenting with banana production and exportation as a way to help finance the project. When he realized that the banana business could yield very profitable results, Keith made a deal with the new president, Bernardo Soto, in 1884. In return for a grant from the Costa Rican government of 323,887 hectares of untilled land along the tracks, tax-free for 20 years, and a 99-year lease on the railroad, Keith would renegotiate the project's pending debts to England, and complete construction at his own expense.

By 1886, Keith had settled the financial problems with England. He spent the next four years laying the last 52 miles of track that climbed through the steep, treacherous valley of the Reventazón River. Relations between Keith and the labor force weren't good. In 1888, Italian workers organized the first strike in Costa Rica's history, demanding prompt payments and sanitary working and living conditions.

The railroad was completed in 1890. Until 1970, it was the only route from the Meseta Central to Limón. And, until the line was closed in late 1990, it was still the major means of transportation for many of the people who lived in the tiny towns it passed. Children took the train to school; it served as an ambulance for the sick and as a hearse for the dead.

After they finished the railway, many Italian workers settled in Costa Rica's highlands. Chinese workers settled in various parts of the country. The Jamaicans stayed on the Atlantic Coast and started working on the banana plantations that Keith established on his free acres. The development of banana plantations where there had once been jungles forced the native peoples to move up into the mountains.

In 1899, Keith and a partner founded the United Fruit Company. La Yunai, as it was called, quickly became a legendary social, economic, political, and agricultural force in many Latin American countries. Costa Rican author Carlos Luis Fallas describes work conditions on the steamy plantations in his book *Mamita Yunai*, and Gabriel García Márquez tells what it did to the imaginary town of Macondo in *One Hundred Years of Solitude*. Although Costa Rica was the smallest country where it operated, United possessed more land here than anywhere else. Costa Rica became the world's leading banana producer.

Keith ended up a very wealthy man and married the daughter of one of the presidents of Costa Rica. Most profits from the banana industry went to the foreign owners of the production, shipping, and distribution networks that made export possible.

United's peak year in Costa Rica was in 1907. By 1913 the company was facing serious problems. Panama disease had infected banana trees, and United's employees were protesting unfair working conditions. A 1913 strike was broken by the Costa Rican government—two strike leaders were chased into the plantations and killed.

United initiated a new policy: it would lease company land to independent growers and buy bananas from them. Tensions with workers grew; a 1934 strike led by two young San José communists, Manuel Mora and Jaime Cerdas, finally brought better working and living conditions. They maintained the original demands of 1913 and added to the list regular payment of salaries, free housing, medical clinics on plantations, and accident insurance. United wouldn't talk with the strikers, but the planters leasing land from United did, and convinced United to sign an agreement.

In the late 1930s, a new disease, *Sigatoka*, infected banana trees up and down the coast. In 1938, United decided to pick up and move west to the Pacific lowlands around Golfito, where banana remained king until violent labor conflicts and dwindling Pacific markets compelled the company to abandon its installations in 1985. Now bananas are again big business on the Atlantic lowlands, and you can tour large plantations or smaller organic farms as part of your trip to Costa Rica.

LIBERALISM ARRIVES IN COSTA RICA

The 1880s saw an increasing split between a traditional, conservative church and a liberalizing state. The bishop of Costa Rica criticized the European ideas that were becoming popular with the elite and the politicians. The bishop was summarily expelled from the country in 1884, and in 1885 there was an official denouncement of an earlier church-state concord that had declared Catholicism the state religion. Public outcry at the government's treatment of the church was minimal.

The first truly democratic election, characterized by real public participation (male only), took place in 1889. Liberals saw it as the result of their efforts to educate and raise democratic consciousness in the people. In fact, their efforts worked so well that the public gave their overwhelming support to the liberals' opposition. Supporters of the liberals threatened not to recognize the new president, so 10,000 armed opposition members flooded the streets of San José. The liberals then demonstrated their firm commitment to democracy by recognizing the new, rightfully elected president.

Costa Rica's democratic tradition has endured until today, with only a few exceptions. One was in 1917, when the Minister of War and the Navy,

Federico Tinoco, overthrew an unpopular president. Tinoco's brutal and repressive dictatorship lasted through 30 months of widespread opposition. Finally, Tinoco fled the country. A provisional president held office for a year until normalcy was reached, and Costa Rica resumed its democratic tradition with a fair presidential election.

ROOTS OF THE 1948 CIVIL WAR

In 1940, Dr. Rafael Angel Calderón Guardia was elected president. Calderón was a very religious Catholic who had studied medicine in Belgium and was convinced that the social guarantees available to Europeans should be instituted in Costa Rica. He initiated many social reforms that still exist today, including social security, workers' right to organize, land reform, guaranteed minimum wage, and collective bargaining. These reforms, plus the fact that he wanted to raise taxes, alienated him from the elite. However, he found support in the Catholic archbishop, Monseñor Victor Manuel Sanabria, and in Manuel Mora of the Costa Rican Communist Party.

Although Calderón enjoyed great popularity among the poor, many educated, middle-class Costa Ricans were suspicious of the alliance between the Church, the government, and the Communist Party. Calderón's most vocal opponent, José "Pepe" Figueres, also wanted to improve conditions for the poor, but he was adamantly opposed to communism. "Social revolutionaries and bourgeois conservatives," he declared, "you fight under the same flag: antagonism." Figueres felt that laissez faire capitalism created an arbitrary class division, pitting owners against their competition, and owners and workers against each other. In reality, he maintained, both management and workers are needed in order for production to take place, so they should have a cooperative relationship. He also was convinced that "in the large industrialized countries, sheltered in the idealists' camps, supposed redeemers set up their tents, only to become vampires of the weakest classes, extortionists of the privileged classes, and impediments to production."

After the 1944 presidential election, suspicions began growing that Calderón's party had manipulated the ballots in order to elect Calderón's successor, Teodoro Picado. The opposition fanned the flames of these suspicions until many citizens were convinced that Calderón and the communists were not going to relinquish power if their party lost the next election. When the police shot some demonstrators at an opposition rally in Cartago in July 1947, the opposition mobilized the shocked populace into a nationwide strike that shut down schools, banks and businesses for 12 days. The government responded by bringing 3000 banana union workers from the

Atlantic coast to reinforce the 300-man army. The armed banana workers were stationed on street corners in the capitol. Because they were unaccustomed to the cool highland weather, the government gave them blankets, which they wore across their shoulders. The communist banana workers looked like stereotypical Mexican peasants with their blankets and their ammunition belts, so the *josefinos* called them "mariachis." That became a generalized derogatory term referring to Calderón and his allies.

The next presidential election in February 1948 was won by Otilio Ulate of the opposition party. But Calderón called the election a fraud, and a fire in the schoolhouse where the ballots were stored destroyed many voting records. The legislative assembly, controlled by Calderón's party, annulled the election. This was the final straw for Figueres and his allies, who had been preparing for this eventuality for months beforehand. He had already been training an army to fight for "electoral purity" and to attack what he called "Caldero-Communism." On March 12, 1948, Figueres took over the airport in San Isidro de El General, in the southern part of the country, and moved his troops north toward Cartago, east of San José. Figueres and his soldiers then captured the Atlantic port of Limón.

Through astute military planning and strategy, and widespread popular support, Figueres managed to bring Calderón's government to the bargaining table in just over a month. In a historic clandestine meeting, Catholic priest Benjamin Nuñez negotiated an agreement between Mora of the Communist Party and Figueres in which Figueres agreed that he would implement Calderón's social guarantees if Calderón would honor the rightful election results.

Figueres took over the government for 18 months in order to formulate a new constitution. He gave voting rights to women and blacks, established an independent branch of the government to oversee elections, imposed an income tax, and nationalized the banking system. To neutralize opposition and to channel funds to social priorities like education, he abolished the army.

Figueres, a clear-eyed observer of history, saw that armies in Latin America had only sapped government resources and acted as tools of the elites to prevent positive change. He had also been impressed that the United States, newly in Cold War mode after its alliance with Russia in World War II, had begun to amass troops in Panama to come to the aid of his rebels who were thought to be fighting communism. Calderón and Mora, fearful of more bloodshed if the U.S. entered the fray, had been more receptive to negotiating an end to the hostilities because of this. Figueres reasoned that if the United States was so bent on policing its "backyard" against communist incursions, it wasn't really necessary for Costa Rica, a U.S. ally, to waste her limited resources on her own army.

After 18 months, Figueres turned the government over to Otilio Ulate, the rightful winner of the 1948 election. Since then, elections have happened every four years without a hitch.

In the years after 1948, Figueres and his fellow revolutionaries formed the National Liberation Party (PLN), which is a member of Socialist International. The Costa Rican government nationalized the electric, telephone, water, insurance, and health care industries, reasoning that only government-owned services would promote development at all levels of society. They also promoted Solidarismo, a cooperative bargaining arena for workers and business owners. Their audacious reforms ushered in an era of economic growth and upward mobility for many Costa Ricans, and by the 1960s a strong middle class was forming. This kept Costa Rica free of the civil unrest that plagued the rest of Central America in the 1970s and '80s, in which many countries became unfortunate pawns in the Cold War.

Figueres was elected president in 1953 and again in 1970. "Don Pepe" died on June 8, 1990, and was mourned by people of all political persuasions as a defender of Costa Rican democracy and development.

SINCE 1948

Costa Rica fortified its progressive social policies during the three decades following 1948, and enjoyed a gradual upward economic trend. The policy of the 1960s and 1970s was to try to become more self-sufficient agriculturally and industrially, which actually led to a heavier dependence on imported pesticides, fertilizers, raw materials, machinery, and oil. Costa Rica and many other Third World countries accepted large First World loans for infrastructure projects like bridges, hydroelectric dams, and roads. When the price of oil rose in the early 1970s, the economy could no longer do without it. Then coffee, banana, and sugar prices went down on the world market, the loans came due, and Costa Rica found itself entering the 1980s with its economy in shambles.

The instability of neighboring countries like Nicaragua and El Salvador impeded cooperation in the Central American Common Market and made Costa Ricans feel insecure. From 1978 to 1979, under President Rodrigo Carazo, northern Costa Rica served as a virtual base for Sandinista operations. Costa Ricans had no sympathy for the Somoza dynasty and were hopeful that the Nicaraguans could make a go of democracy. But after Somoza was deposed, the Sandinista arms build-up and Marxist-Leninist doctrine disillusioned many Costa Ricans. Although the government had an official policy of neutrality, PLN president Luis Alberto Monge (1982–1986) lent tacit support to the Contras, who were operating out of the northern jungles of Costa Rica.

Costa Rica elected a president in February 1986 from the younger generation of the PLN. Oscar Arias, an economist, lawyer, and author of several books on the Costa Rican economy and power structure, campaigned on the promise to work for peace in Central America. The first part of his task was to enforce Costa Rica's declared neutrality policy, and to stand up to the United States and the politicians within his own party who were supporting Contra activity in Costa Rica (such as the secret airstrip that figured in the Iran-Contra scandal).

As the world knows by now, Arias' untiring efforts to fulfill his promise won him the 1987 Nobel Peace Prize. While the peace process met with much opposition at home, plus skepticism and even ennui in the First World press, for many Central Americans it signified a coming of age—a chance to unite and shape their future in a new way. The first democratic elections in Nicaragua's history, held February 25, 1990, were largely a result of the peace plan and saw the Sandinistas defeated.

Rafael Angel Calderón Fournier, son of Rafael Angel Calderón Guardia (who "lost" the 1948 Civil War), succeeded Arias in 1990. Calderón Fournier was inaugurated as president 50 years to the day after his father assumed power. In 1994, José María Figueres, son of Don Pepe, took over from "Junior" Calderón, becoming one of the youngest presidents in history. Following in his father's footsteps, he initiated some truly novel policies, like the sale of "carbon-sequestering" bonds. He built on Costa Rica's reputation for having a well-educated populace to attract software giant Intel, which opened a 400,000-square-foot plant in April 1998 and promptly became one of the country's number-one exporters. Costa Rica's progressive labor codes have ensured that this has meant decent jobs, unlike the *maquiladoras* (sweatshops) NAFTA has produced in the Mexican border area.

As mentioned in the introduction, Costa Rica has been a world-leader in fostering the notion that forested areas perform a service for the planet, and that the owners of these areas (public or private) should be compensated for this service. In Costa Rica, 87 percent of the water for hydroelectric generation comes from protected forests. Replacing it with fossil fuel generation would be financially impossible. With money from a 15 percent fuel tax, the Figueres administration initiated the National Fund for Forest Financing, which pays landowners for the environmental services provided by their forests.

The 1998 election was won by a wealthy and well-educated economist and businessman, Miguel Angel Rodriguez. His administration allowed thousands of forest giants to be cut down in the Osa Peninsula and Talamanca. The government then announced plans to deregulate environmental building controls, and to abolish laws that halted building permits when archaeological sites were unearthed during construction projects. In general, the Rodriguez administration did little to further the far-sighted environmental and social policies that have made Costa Rica famous.

Abel Pacheco of National Unity became president in 2002. He is a psychiatrist who for many years was a fatherly television commentator. During the previous presidential term, then-president Miguel Angel Rodriguez (1998–2002) had granted Harken Oil (the company in which George W. Bush and Dick Cheney figured prominently) exclusive oil exploration rights off Costa Rica's beautiful Caribbean coast. The area includes a RAMSAR wetlands site, is recognized by the U.N. as a World Heritage Site, and is considered by The Nature Conservancy to be a critical bird migration area. Communities all over Costa Rica organized against the decision, and the Environmental Ministry also ruled against the drilling project, but Harken persisted. One of Abel Pacheco's first acts when he took office in May 2003 was to ban open-pit mining and oil exploration, ordering Harken to leave Costa Rica. In September 2003, the company filed for international arbitration in Washington, D.C., seeking to recover $57 billion in "lost potential" because it was prevented from drilling an estimated 2.3 billion barrels of oil and 6 trillion cubic feet of natural gas. Fifty seven billion dollars is about four times Costa Rica's gross domestic product. The oil company withdrew its arbitration request in October 2003, but they reinitiated their suit in 2006.

In 2004, former presidents Miguel Angel Rodriguez (1998–2002) and Rafael Angel Calderón (1990–94) ended up in prison for accepting kickbacks from government financial deals during their administrations, and former president José María Figueres (1994–98) was accused of similar actions but so far has refused to return to Costa Rica from his present home in Switzerland to face charges. That such action could be taken against powerful members of his own party is anther tribute to President Abel Pacheco (2002–2006).

COSTA RICA TODAY

Because of the presidential corruption scandals, the legislature changed the constitution in order to allow former president (1986–90) and Nobel Peace Prize winner Oscar Arias to run again. He won the 2006 presidential election by a very narrow margin. Much of the debate in the election was about CAFTA, the Central American Free Trade Agreement, known locally as the *Tratado de Libre Comercio*, or TLC, which Arias favors. Because of fierce internal opposition to CAFTA, Costa Rica has been the only Central American country to delay signing of the agreement. Soon after Arias took office, the country had its first nation-wide referendum on whether Costa Rica should join CAFTA or not. After an intense campaign, the Yes vote won in October 2007, and the legislature is proceeding to change Costa Rican laws to conform to CAFTA requirements.

CAFTA opponents see the Costa Rican Electricity Institute (ICE) as a key force behind the country's development for the past 50 years. Opening this and other government-owned monopolies to competition as CAFTA mandates is seen as a step backward. Many Costa Ricans don't want to see the success of their unique system thrown away for a one-size-fits-all economic scheme imposed from without. On the other hand, ICE and other state-owned monopolies are inefficient and lack customer service, prompting many Costa Ricans to favor change.

The large foreign-owned hotel and condo projects that are turning the Central Valley and the beaches of Jacó and Guancaste into a concrete jungle also created opposition to CAFTA. Locals watch massive amounts of money being invested in luxury second homes and time shares that don't bring economic benefits to local people. President Arias proposes a tax on houses worth more than $192,000. The tax would be used to create housing for poor people. Even though the economy in general has improved greatly under Arias, the gap between rich and poor continues to grow, with nearly half of the country's GDP going to the richest fifth of the population.

Women in Costa Rica reach higher education levels than men and occupy high positions in government and business. Almost a third of President Arias's cabinet members are women, as are his two vice presidents. The Legislative Assembly has the third highest percentage of female legislators in the world.

The Arias administration pays poor families to keep their kids in school, and has increased the small pension to the elderly, widows, orphans and invalids living in poverty. Because of Costa Rica's national health care and social security systems, life expectancy (78.5 years) is the same as in countries where income is four times that much, and health care is on par with that of industrialized nations.

President Arias promotes what he calls the "Costa Rica Consensus," based on the idea that third-world countries which invest in health, education, and housing for their people should be rewarded with debt forgiveness and international aid. In 2008, Costa Rica won a seat on the UN Security Council, from which it advocates for disarmament and progressive environmental policies.

Arias also decreed the Peace with Nature program, calling on a group of environmental experts to propose solutions to the country's environmental problems. Ecotourism is central to the program, because it brings greater earnings to Costa Rica than other kinds of tourism due to greater inclusion of Costa Rican–owned businesses and products.

Costa Ricans' love for the beauty and freedom of their country is almost palpable. At 6 p.m. each September 14, the eve of their Independence Day, everyone drops what they are doing to sing the national anthem. In corner stores and homes across the country, everyone joins in. It's a rousing hymn in tribute to peace, hard work, and the generosity of the earth, but it's also a warning that if these things are threatened, Costa Ricans will "convert their rough farming tools into arms," as they did when William Walker tried to invade in the 19th century.

TWO

The Ecological Picture

Costa Rica measures only 185 miles across at her widest point, but four mountain ranges divide her like a backbone. Mount Chirripó, at 12,000 feet, is the highest point in southern Central America. It is part of Costa Rica's oldest and southernmost mountain range, the Cordillera de Talamanca, which extends into Panama. The Central Volcanic Range is made up of volcanoes Turrialba, Irazú, Barva, and Poás. More than half of Costa Rica's almost four million inhabitants live in the Central Valley, whose fertile soil was created by the activity of these volcanoes over the last two million years. To the northwest is the Tilarán range, which reaches 5500 feet at Monteverde and includes the active Volcán Arenal. Farthest northwest, toward the Nicaraguan border, is the Guanacaste Range, which boasts five active volcanoes, including Rincón de la Vieja and Miravalles (now being used to generate geothermal energy). The most ancient rocks in the area are more than 100 million years old and occur in the "Nicoya complex," low mountains that crop up here and there along the Pacific.

Costa Rica may be one of the smaller countries in the Americas, but it boasts the most diverse selection of flora and fauna in the hemisphere. There are several reasons for this diversity: Costa Rica's topography ranges from the bleak, treeless paramo, 12,000 feet above sea level, to rainforests on the coasts only 50 miles away, with countless microclimates in between. Costa Rica's latitude contributes steady temperatures year-round, and abundant precipitation creates hospitable conditions for many forms of life. Perhaps most important is Costa Rica's position between the Americas: a land bridge between North and South, where migrating animals and plants meet. North American white-tailed deer sniff at South American brocket deer and northern rattlesnakes slide by southern bushmasters. There are animals here that have evolved nowhere else in the world: *pacas* and *agoutis* (cousins of guinea pigs), *dantas* (huge tapirs), and prehensile-tailed porcupines, to name a few. The ecology of Costa Rica is so complex and fascinating that this brief chapter should only be considered a very elementary and anecdotal survey.

ECOSYSTEMS

From high, dry mountains to verdant rainforests, Costa Rica is home to a wide range of ecosystems. Following are descriptions of some of the most common.

The **paramo**, related to the Andean ecosystem of the same name, covers the summits of Costa Rica's southern Talamanca mountain range. Just as the foliage is tough and small, which protects it from the elements and conserves energy, the animals that live here are mostly small rodents and tiny lizards activated by strong sun. There is paramo at Cerro de la Muerte, Chirripó, and the high mountain peaks in Parque Internacional La Amistad (visit through Dúrika Biological Reserve above Buenos Aires or through ASOPROLA and ASOMOBI near the Altamira entrance to the Park).

The highest rainforests, blanketing the slopes of the Continental Divide, are called **cloud forests** because they are nearly always veiled in clouds. Clouds pause momentarily at the Divide after ascending the Atlantic slope, and the forest soaks up their moisture. Scientists postulate that global warming is making the clouds rise higher over the divide, depriving cloud forests of their mist. They think that this subtle drying effect might be responsible for the disappearance of moisture-sensitive frogs and toads.

These forests provide a crucial watershed for areas below. Monteverde is Costa Rica's most famous cloud forest. There are many others as well, some of which are easier to reach from San José: Bosque de Paz and the ancient oak forests near Copey, Providencia, San Gerardo de Dota, and Siberia near Los Quetzales National Park on Cerro de la Muerte.

The lower elevations have what most of us think of when we hear the word "**rainforest**": tremendously tall trees with vines twisting up their girth, hanging roots of philodendrons whose leaves are high above. Rainforest pilgrims can visit the many reserves in the Sarapiquí area, like the Tirimbina Wildlife Refuge, Selva Verde, La Selva, and Rara Avis, or the forests of the Atlantic coast and the Osa Peninsula. The Heliconias Reserve, north of Cañas on the road to Upala, and Tenorio and Rincón de la Vieja National Parks in Guanacaste also have extensive rainforests. Carara and Manuel Antonio National Parks are the most (over) visited rainforests in the country, due to their easy accessibility. There are many smaller rainforest reserves, mentioned throughout the text.

The characteristic that most differentiates tropical rainforests from their temperate counterparts is their diversity. Year-round warm temperatures and abundant rain have produced a plethora of species, each with a high degree of specialization. There are insects that blend in perfectly with the type of leaves they eat. Some of the most fragrant flowers only release their scent at night, to attract nocturnal, nearly blind, bats.

The forest has several levels, from ground-covering ferns and mosses, to short bushes and tree ferns, to canopy species stunted by a lack of light, to shade-loving trees that reach a certain height and provide a mid-canopy, to the canopy trees, which, depending upon the life zone (determined by altitude and precipitation), can reach up to 180 feet in height. Seeds are eaten or unwittingly carried by birds or monkeys that travel through the forest and drop them along the way, often far from the mother tree. Many seedlings flourish in the shade at ground level. Species that demand much light will flounder in the relatively dark forest floor until an old tree dies or falls, and leaves a "light gap." At that point, the light-demanding species will shoot up until one reaches the canopy and fills the hole.

A true rainforest is evergreen: Trees will never all lose their leaves at once. The **dry pacific forest** is deciduous, shedding its leaves during the severe dry season to conserve water. The canopy is significantly lower than in the rainforest. When the trees are bare, it is often easier to see wildlife here. Many of the animals that frequent the dry pacific forest are seasonal visitors from other ecosystems. Tropical dry forests occur only in Guanacaste. Santa Rosa protects a large tract, and Lomas Barbudal and Palo Verde are home to others.

Mangroves are found in intertidal zones at river mouths and estuaries where fresh water and saltwater meet. Comprising the various species of tree that are virtually the only flora that can live half the time submerged in salty water, the other half in nearly airless mud, the different types of mangroves (red, black, white, tea, and buttonwood) are actually from four unrelated families, each having developed ways of coping with these challenging conditions. They resist osmosis by maintaining a higher concentration of salt in their tissues than in the seawater, and secrete excess salt from their leaves or roots. To aerate, as well as to survive in a natural flood zone, mangroves have aerial roots with multiple buttresses. By preventing large predators from entering, their tangle of roots provides a habitat for many species of marine life at their most vulnerable stages of development. Baby oysters and sponges attach to the roots. Algae generated in the nutrient-rich mud is abundant food for young crabs, lobsters, shrimp, and barnacles.

Some types of mangroves gradually turn a wet intertidal zone into dry land. As their leaves drop onto silt collected in the roots, a layer of soil slowly develops. Eventually, the mangroves, which can't live outside their tidal habitat, are stranded on dry land and die. At the same time that this curious suicidal behavior occurs, however, unique floating seedlings with weighted bottoms are carried in the water until they can lodge in the mud. Because seeds germinate while still on the tree, they quickly take root, in a never-ending quest for new territory.

Some of the best areas to observe mangroves include the estuaries of the Pacific Coast, the Río Térraba delta, the Río Sierpe boat trip to Drake Bay, the Atrocha route between Golfito and Zancudo, the canals just north of Moín on the way to Tortuguero, and near the Isla Chira in the Gulf of Nicoya.

Mangroves filter sediment-rich river water so that much clearer water flows into the ocean. In some areas off the coast, where the water is very clear, **coral reefs** develop. Coral reefs are animals, plants, and geologic formations all in one. They create habitats of rich biological gardens populated by life forms as diverse as those found in the rainforest, from unicellular organisms such as algae to fish like the damselfish. (The damselfish actually tends her garden, plucking undesirable sea grasses from her seascape.)

The coral structure is formed by unique plantlike animals that live within it, filtering water to obtain nutrients then excreting calcium carbonate, which becomes the coral skeleton. The coral reef itself breaks waves, creating a calm interior thick with sea grasses, and important nutrients for turtles, manatees, and other marine animals.

Manuel Antonio's third beach has calm waters and a lovely reef. The point at Cahuita has, too, although sediment carried downriver from banana plantations is diminishing its growth. The Manzanillo Reef south of Puerto Viejo has only recently been mapped, and we hear it is spectacular. The reef in Bahía Ballena National Marine Park south of Dominical is shaped like a whale's tail. One of the best places to dive and snorkel is Isla del Caño, 20 kilometers off Drake Bay, which has five coral platforms.

FLORA

Costa Rica is home to an incredibly diverse selection of flora, each type adapted for life in a particular ecosystem. At forest floors, the predominant color is green, but at eye level there are brightly colored and fragrant flowers. Especially common in rainforests are species of the heliconia flower—large red, yellow, or orange bursts of tropical exuberance. Fragrant orchids, too, are common here, as are a spectacular array of ferns. From the lowliest lichen to the towering *ceiba* tree, the Costa Rican landscape offers a rich display of plant life.

EPIPHYTES   Whether in the ghostly, fog-draped cloud forests or the towering lowland rainforests, branches and treetops look impossibly top-heavy, covered as they are with orchids, mosses, ferns, lichens, bromeliads, and other families of epiphytes (plants whose roots grasp tree branches and absorb their nutrients from leaf matter and water dripping off the canopy).

Among the tiniest epiphytes are the mosses found growing on leaf surfaces and the lichens clinging to tree bark. They are restricted to areas that are moist year-round. Because they can hinder a plant's ability to photosynthesize, many plants have developed a variety of techniques for getting rid of these pesky hangers-on. "Drip tip" leaves will drain water collected on them so that their surface is dry, making it difficult for mosses to colonize. Some trees slough off their bark regularly, shedding lichens as well.

Ferns are a diverse category of flowerless epiphyte. Notable species among the 800 types found in Costa Rica include the primordial-looking tree fern (an upright fern with prickly spines) and the resurrection fern, which dries and curls up during periods of drought, only to spring back to life with the return of the rains.

The 1500 species of orchids that are found in Costa Rica are the showiest epiphytes, with intricate and spectacular flowers. Orchids appear on every continent except Antarctica, but are most diverse in the tropics, where they range in size from half an inch to more than 25 feet. About 350 orchid species are found only in Costa Rica. Because they do not have edible pollen to offer their pollinators, orchids rely either on an alluring strong scent or mimicry to deceive insects into believing they are something they are not.

Bromeliads are epiphytes that collect and store water in their tightly joined leaf bases, or trap tiny droplets in their hairlike trichomes. This water is rendered nutrient-rich when particles fall into it or when mosquitoes and other insects that breed in it die and decompose there. The 170 species of bromeliads found in Costa Rica provide niches for up to 250 forms of life.

FLOWERS   Costa Rica offers a variety of flowering plants, many of which have developed very specific traits for survival. For instance, the angel's trumpet tree produces pendulous white flowers that open only at night and are just the right shape for a bat snout. They exude an almost dizzying smell. The aristolchia flower, which attracts one particular bat as its pollinator, mimics the genitalia of the female of that species of bat to attract the males. The dracontium flower depends on feces-loving flies as pollinators and has a distinct stench almost everyone recognizes.

TREES   The diversity of the tropical forest is evident in the trees that make it up. In just two and a half acres, there can be over 90 species of trees. Following are descriptions of just a few of the many unusual types of trees you may encounter during your visit to Costa Rica.

Coconut trees lean out over the beach to reach more sunlight and to drop their nuts where the waves will pick them up. Coconuts can float in the ocean for several months and land on another beach thousands of leagues away before they sprout. The infant plant is nourished by the rich coconut milk and meat, and once leaves emerge and photosynthesis begins, thousands of roots emerge from the nut and anchor the young tree to the beach. Biologists have observed this colonization process on new volcanic islands. Coconuts are what have made human habitation possible on otherwise inhospitable islands. New leaves grow and old ones are shed about once a month. So, in order to calculate the age of a coconut tree in years, count the number of leaves and leaf scars on a coconut tree trunk, and divide by twelve.

Recognizable by its prominent orange-red roots, the milk or cow tree is common in the rainforest of Corcovado National Park. Its Latin name is *Brosimum utile*, and useful it is. Through the trunk flows a drinkable white latex. The tree's sweet fruit is edible, and its wood is useful for construction. The indigenous people of the area used its bark to stay warm: They would cut a portion of bark from the tree, soak it, then dry it and beat it to make a warm, soft blanket.

Indio desnudo ("naked Indian," also known as the "sunburned gringo"), with bright orange bark, is another easily recognizable tree found mostly in dry Pacific forests. The leaves fall off during the dry season, but chloroplasts under the bark's surface allow photosynthesis to continue. Each tree produces a bounty of between 600 and 6000 fruits, which are savored by white-faced monkeys. When the monkeys accidentally drop fruit-laden branches onto the forest floor, collared peccaries eat them, too.

Considered sacred by Costa Rica's indigenous people, the *ceiba* or kapok tree is one of the fastest-growing trees known, climbing as much as 13 feet a year to a maximum recorded height of 198 feet. This makes it a prime pioneer, quickly colonizing fields allowed to regenerate. Its seed pods contain envelopes of cottony fibers that enclose the seeds. The envelopes are carried by the wind and eventually the seed falls out. Kapok fiber has long been used as stuffing for pillows, saddles, and clothing. The wood is too light for construction, but is used for canoes and coffins.

Strangler figs are parasitic tree-like plants that begin as epiphytes on a tree limb when a seed from a bird dropping takes root in a hospitable nook. Once the seedling is established, it sends roots that surround the host tree trunk in a close embrace, and branches reach to cover the upper branches of the host tree. The host tree eventually dies, probably not because of strangulation, but because the fig's branches block the host tree's light source.

FAUNA

As rich and varied as is Costa Rica's flora, you'll find the fauna that use it as a habitat equally diverse.

FROGS AND TOADS   Rainforest amphibians generally have toxins in their skin. The mildest poisons just taste bad, while the strongest can kill predators (including humans) by causing vasoconstriction, respiratory paralysis, hypertension, and other mortal conditions. The toxin may be ingested through the mucous membranes of the mouth or throat, or through the pores in the skin. The message: Don't touch these guys. (Ironically, they may be the source of lifesaving antibacterial and antiviral compounds that scientists are still researching.) Big bullfrogs that are common near beaches can even shoot toxin a distance of up to six and one half feet, so be wary of them, too.

So named because indigenous warriors poisoned their arrow tips with its venom, the vermilion-colored **poison dart frog** spends its entire life high above the rainforest floor. Bromeliad water vessels serve as the frog's breeding grounds, protecting the developing tadpoles from predators. At the end of the two-month gestation period, an adult dart frog emerges from the plant shelter with a fully developed defense system: Its skin glands exude a poison that rolls off its back like drops of sweat. Any animal taking a poison dart frog into its mouth is poisoned. The frog's brilliant red color serves as warning.

Other toxic amphibians warn predators with "flash colors"—brightly colored legs or groin areas, which are revealed only when the animal jumps. This startles the predator, and might dissuade it from attacking. The U.S.-based *National Wildlife* magazine lists the **golden toad**, which disappeared from Monteverde in 1989, as the "first species extinction attributed to global warming." According to biologist Allan Pounds of the Tropical Science Center, another 18 species of highland frogs have not been sighted for two decades. Luis Diego Marin of the Association for the Preservation of Wild Flora and Fauna (APREFLOFAS) says that amphibians are the species most susceptible to global warming because of their sensitive skin and their incubation process, which takes place in water that pools between the leaves of cloud forest plants. Other species, like lizards, are less sensitive to climate change because of their protective scales. Frogs and toads are particularly vulnerable to chytrid fungus, a skin disease prevalent now in tropical frogs.

SEA TURTLES   Three kinds of **sea turtles** nest on Costa Rica's shores: the Pacific or olive ridley at Playa Nancite in Santa Rosa National Park and at Ostional near Playa Nosara; the green turtle at Tortuguero; and the leatherback at Playa Grande near Tamarindo, Tortuguero, the Pacuare Reserve near Parismina, and the Gandoca–Manzanillo Wildlife Refuge in Talamanca.

Playa Grande, famous for being the nesting site of huge leatherback turtles, is the subject of a bitter land dispute between developers and turtle conservationists. Although the government declared that the park extends 125 meters above the high tide line and began the process of expropriating land within that area, landowners are fighting the case in the International Arbitration Court in Washington, DC, so expropriation has been delayed. In the 1980s, up to 200 leatherbacks nested at Playa Grande per night during the season. That plummeted to three per night in 1994. There were 75 nesting females in the whole three-month 2007-08 season, up from only 57 in 2006-7.

An estimated 40,000 sea turtles die each year due to long-line fishing. A new U.N. resolution calls for the closure of fishing in areas of elevated turtle activity in international waters. This could take years to implement because it would require diplomatic work. More than 1000 scientists around the world agree that leatherback turtles could disappear within 5 to 15 years if action isn't taken to reduce the dangers that threaten them. According to the *Tico Times*, commercial Costa Rican fishermen use fishing lines of up to 800 hooks that can extend 15 to 20 miles during their two-week fishing expeditions. Around the world, international fleets from Asia, Spain, and Norway drag lines with up to 5000 hooks that extend more than 100 miles, posing an even larger threat to turtles and other species. Often the sea animals become tangled or caught on the lines, and die when fishermen rip the hooks from their mouths. PRETOMA (tortugamarina.org) is continuing to work for a long-line moratorium.

Although scientists are blaming the diminishing numbers on irresponsible fishing practices, studies have shown that the presence of humans affects turtle reproduction. The thin line of light on the ocean horizon guides turtle hatchlings as they scramble towards the sea, and the illumination of human development, either on the beach or in the hills behind it, can confuse them, preventing them from reaching the water before their limited energy stores are depleted. The glare of unbridled development in Tamarindo, across the bay from Playa Grande, must have had an effect. Peaceful Playa Grande is the scene of a battle to protect the venerable and voiceless turtles' right to nest where their instincts demand. For more information, see www. leatherback.org. Because of the overdevelopment struggles in this area, we don't recommend visiting Playa Grande to see turtles at this time.

Global warming is also affecting sea turtle reproduction. The temperature of the sand determines gender during the turtle gestation process. The hotter the sand, the more females will be born. Turtle protectors in Playa Junqillal are moving the nests to shady places so that the eggs can hatch at normal temperatures.

CROCODILES   Two kinds of **crocodiles** are found in Costa Rica. The smaller ones, called caymans, which grow no longer than three feet, live in creeks, ponds, mangrove swamps, and beach lowlands. What are commonly called crocodiles are the larger animals, reaching up to 13 feet in length. We have seen them lounging in the muddy banks of rivers in the Northern Zone, on the boat trip to Tortuguero, in the mangroves near Isla Chira, on the Río Sierpe, and at the Carara National Park near Playa Jacó.

SNAKES   Due to their camouflage and wariness of humans, you are not likely to see snakes in a brief visit to the forest, but it is worth knowing which ones are dangerous. Non-poisonous **boa constrictors** are long (reaching 18 feet in length), fat snakes with dark squares on a light brown or gray background. They sit and wait until a likely prey appears (they have been known to eat lizards, tanagers, opossums, young porcupines, deer, and even ocelots), and then they strike, impale the animal on their fangs, lift it, strangle it, then swallow it head first. Because they have few recorded pred-

ators, boas are believed to be at or near the top of the food chain. When a boa feels threatened, its body fills with air along its entire length, and it emits a deep, ghostly roar.

Of the 136 species of snakes in Costa Rica, 18 are lethal. **Fer-de-lance** *(terciopelo)* snakes are venomous residents of rainy jungles, large rivers, and overgrown fields. They are brown and black with a white "X" pattern running down their back, which make them almost impossible to see among the twigs and leaves. When disturbed, this aggressive six-and-a-half-foot-long snake bites anything that moves, and its bite can be fatal to humans. Its usual diet consists of mammals and birds. At Parque Viborana in Turrialba, we observed snake expert Minor Camacho walking in a cage of angry *terciopelos*. When they prepared to strike, he stood completely still until they calmed down. Then he would take a step, they would rear their heads again, he would stand still again and they would relax. He did this several times, demonstrating how knowledge of this snake's behavior can keep people from getting bitten, and also keep snakes from being killed by fearful humans.

The dreaded **eyelash vipers** are so named for a visor-like scale that extends beyond their eyes. These snakes are small, less than three feet in length, and come in green, brown, rust, gray, or light blue, with a darker diamond pattern on the back, although some are gold, without the pattern. They hang in trees. Three to six people per year in Costa Rica die after being bitten by this highly venomous snake.

Costa Rica has its own species of **rattlesnake** as well, with stripes on its neck and diamonds on its back. They are mostly found in Guanacaste. Their venom can cause blindness, paralysis, and suffocation.

These are the poisonous snakes. You can look them in the eye at one of the country's many serpentaria. Hopefully, those will be the only snakes you will encounter on your trip. See "Health Precautions" in Chapter Three to find out what to do if bitten by a snake.

BIRDS   Costa Rica's most famous cloud-forest bird is the **resplendent quetzal**, a large, brilliant green bird whose males sport a two-foot-long, wispy tail. They migrate to forests more than 3600 feet above sea level, where they nest from February to April in the hollows of the tallest and oldest trees. Males and females share the incubation of eggs and the feeding of hatchlings. The females sit on the eggs at night and at midday, and the male sits with his beautiful green tail hanging out of the nest during the rest of the day. Quetzals cannot live in captivity, a poetic quality that has made them a symbol of freedom for the people of Central America.

Other birds that follow ripening fruits up and down the mountains include the **three-wattled bellbird**, which gets its name from its bell-like voice and the three wattles or wormlike pieces of skin that flop over its beak. This bird eats the same avocado-like fruits as the quetzal, and also migrates to much lower elevations after breeding in the cloud forest.

There is also the **bare-necked umbrella bird**, whose males are large and black with big fluffy pompadour headdresses and bright red featherless throats that they inflate to attract the much less ornate females. Females are usually much less conspicuous and camouflage their young while nesting.

Other, more notable birds include the liquid-voiced **oropéndolas**. These large, dull-colored birds with yellow tails weave long, sac-like nests on dead tree branches. Visitors from temperate climes enjoy sighting **parrots**, abundant in the tropics. Sixteen species of this raucous family inhabit Costa Rica, from tiny parakeets and parrotlets, to giant scarlet macaws. **Scarlet macaws**, which are monogamous and mate for life, used to live throughout the lowlands of Costa Rica, but massive deforestation and poaching have restricted the few remaining birds to Carara National Park and the Osa Peninsula.

Green macaws used to range through the entire Atlantic lowland region of Costa Rica, nesting in giant *almendro* trees. Until recently, these trees were left by lumbermen because their wood was too hard to process as lumber. However, new technology has been developed and the trees are being cut at an alarming rate. The habitat for green macaws has been reduced by 95 percent, but projects like the Costa Rican Bird Route are working to provide income from birdwatching for landowners and communities that conserve green macaw nesting areas (see Chapter Nine).

Of the 330 species of **hummingbirds** known to exist in the world, almost one-fifth are found in Costa Rica. These tiny nectar-eaters have unusual wings that can rotate at the shoulders, allowing them to fly in any direction or hover over a flower while they fit their beak into the floral tube and suck out the nectar. Almost any pink, red, or orange flower attracts hummingbirds. A great place to get to know hummingbirds is La Paz Waterfall Gardens on the eastern slopes of Poás volcano, because they have large signs that identify the different species. But you will see hummingbirds all over Costa Rica.

Among the many waterbirds frequenting Costa Rica are the **frigate bird** (pterodactyl-like with a six-and-a-half-foot wingspan, whose primitive body type makes landing and taking off difficult) and the six species of **kingfishers** (short-necked, large-headed, and sharp-billed divers who dwell at rivers and coasts).

About a quarter of Costa Rica's 850 species of birds are seasonal visitors from North or South America. They fly to the tropics to escape scarcity during harsh winters, making long, arduous journeys over land and sea. Among the most amazing feats is the first leg of the **ruby-throated hummingbird**'s annual trip south: a nonstop 500-mile flight over the Gulf of Mexico. The **raptors** (hawks, falcons, and eagles) fly over Costa Rica on their way south every October. Traditionally, they have sought temporary shelter in the Atlantic Zone. The Kekoldi indigenous tribe has built a raptor observation tower in the hills above Puerto Viejo de Talamanca. Birds that summer in North America and winter in Costa Rica include warblers, swallows, thrushes, finches, orioles, flycatchers, and tanagers.

The classic *Guide to the Birds of Costa Rica* by Stiles and Skutch is still a birding heavyweight, but it has been supplanted by *The Birds of Costa Rica, a Field Guide* by long-time birding guides Richard Garrigues and Robert Dean. The new book measures 5 by 7 inches and weighs much less than the two-pound classic, so is much easier to carry into the field. Excellent illustrations and notes on habitat, behavior, key identifying marks and calls are all noted opposite the picture of each bird, as well as the best months and locations in which to see them. It's available online or in bookstores throughout Costa Rica and North America. For less serious birders, a series of laminated cards with bird species for various areas of the country is available in most souvenir shops.

MAMMALS   Even though you must have a lot of patience and be accompanied by an experienced guide to see birds in the forest, they are still easier to observe than most other animals. Mammals such as the jaguar and the tapir are part of the hype that is attracting so many ecotourists to the rainforest. However, they are rarely seen by visitors because they flee from humans and are nocturnal.

Jaguars, the largest Costa Rican carnivores, are most common in areas where there has been little human penetration. Each jaguar adult requires a forest-covered hunting ground one hundred miles in size. As humans colonize their territories, the jaguars recede, crowding into areas too small for them. A reduced gene pool leads to weakened animals and mutations; this might eventually lead to their extinction. The Mesoamerican Biological Corridor, hopes to link protected areas throughout Central America in order to create one unbroken reserve the length of the isthmus for large cats and other animals who need vast amounts of space to roam.

Huge vegetarian **tapirs** have long been considered one of the finest delicacies a Costa Rican hunter can bring home, so these mammals are also in danger of extinction. Currently, they can be found only where hunting has been prohibited. Their immense size does not prevent them from being swift runners. Their feet have an interesting adaptation that aids them when running through the muddy forest floor. Their feet spread out as they step down, then their toes draw together to make pulling out of the mud easier.

With a keen eye, you might see a **sloth** hanging from a tree limb. Most vegetarian animals must eat berries or nuts to generate the energy they need to survive. Sloths just eat leaves, so they need to carry out a low-maintenance lifestyle. They have little muscle tissue, compared to other animals. Their upside-down position hanging from tree limbs is ideal for scooping hanging leaves into their mouths. Algae-shrouded fur camouflages them in the treetops, and their meat does not taste good. When attacked by one of their few predators, their slow metabolism allows them to survive wounds that would kill other animals. Still, habitat loss and injuries are taking their toll on these loveable animals. Your can learn about their fascinating natural history and support efforts to help take care of them at the Sloth Sanctuary, near Cahuita on the Atlantic coast (slothrescue.org).

Monkeys are the most sociable forest dwellers. Intensely attached to their family group or troupe, they are among the most intelligent animals. Although white-faced and howler monkeys are still fairly easy to spot in some areas, an alarming report released in 2007 indicates that their numbers are in serious decline. There are four types of monkeys in Costa Rica. The diminutive, insect-eating **white-faced monkey** (*mono cariblanco*) inhabits the Caribbean lowland rainforest, Manuel Antonio National Park, Monteverde premontane forest, the Osa Peninsula, and the dry forests of Guanacaste. It's estimated that the number of *cariblancos* has diminished from about 95,000 in 1995 to 54,000 in 2007. Large **howler monkeys** (*mono congo*), audible if not always visible throughout Costa Rica, are so named because their bellows resonate through the forest, making them sound like much more terrifying animals than the vegetarians they are. They live in many parts of Costa Rica below 7500 feet. Their numbers have gone down 64% in the last 12 years. Blond-chested **spider monkeys** (*mono colorado*) have long, prehensile tails with a fingerprint-like imprint at the end, adapted for gripping. Their increased agility allows them to leap up to 30 feet. Preferring primary forest, the population of spider monkeys is estimated to have gone down 72% in the last twelve years. Tiny **squirrel monkeys** (*mono tití*) live in the Pacific lowland area and are highly social, living in bands up to 30 strong. Their population is estimated to have declined from about 7300 in 1995 to 4200 in 2007. University of Costa Rica biologist Gustavo Gutierrez, who reported on the study at the Conference on Costa Rica's Primates in July 2007, says that monkey populations have become increasingly isolated by the onslaught of development, leading to inbreeding and genetically weak populations that are highly susceptible to disease and climatic variations. This is one reason that we are leaving the overdeveloped beaches of Guanacaste out of this edition, and including information on those places that are creating biological corridors.

Coatis (*pizotes*), which look like jungle raccoons with long, slightly bushy, monkeylike tails, are diurnal and easily seen in open areas. Agile in trees, they are competent ground dwellers as well. They live in every habitat in Costa Rica, and eat everything from fruit and mice to tarantulas and lizards. Females and young live in bands that can number 30 (this contributes to their being easy to spot); adult males are solitary.

Another community-oriented mammal is the pig-like **collared peccary**. Living in groups of three to 30, they greet one another by rubbing their heads to the scent glands near their tails, and sleep together to conserve heat. They have long hair covering their gray-black skin; a band of white rings their neck. They are the favorite food of jaguars, so their populations must be healthy in order for wild felines to survive.

Some mammals that are receiving renewed attention in Costa Rica are dolphins and whales. Several species of **dolphin** are visible on both the Atlantic and Pacific coasts. Special dolphin-watching tours are offered in Drake Bay on the Osa Peninsula, in Parque Marino Ballena just above the Osa, in Manuel Antonio and in Manzanillo on the Caribbean. Those who have come to know and love the intelligent and friendly dolphin are noting a decrease in the populations and are becoming increasingly concerned that the "dolphin-safe" fishing methods used by tuna fish companies are not really allowing dolphins to escape.

Humpback and pilot **whales** are visible off the Pacific coast, especially at Ballena National Marine Park in Uvita de Osa and in Drake Bay, where they come to give birth between mid-December and mid-April. Because the baby whales can't stay submerged for too long, the whales are easier to see here than in more northern climes. Humpback whales are shyer, while pilot whales seem to like people.

INTERACTIONS

Even more fascinating than the individual species in the forest is how they interact. Nature's most intimate and complex relationships involve what biologists call "mutualisms." In mutual relationships, each actor provides a necessary service for the other, and often neither can survive alone. Following are a few intriguing examples of nature's interdependencies.

Tiny tree frogs, which never touch ground, have one of the most intimate relationships with bromeliads. The female vermilion poison dart frog lays a few eggs in damp humus, but when they hatch she carries them on her back to her "nursery": bromeliad water vessels. In this secluded habitat, they develop virtually unthreatened. The mother visits daily, locating them easily because they wiggle their tails to make ripples in the water. She lays unfertilized, protein-rich eggs, which the tadpoles perforate and suck. Two months after birth, they are fully developed, two-centimeter-long adult frogs. The frogs' waste products decompose in the bromeliad's stored water, making absorbable nutrients for the plant.

Ants participate in some of the most complex and perfect mutualisms. One example is the azteca ant/cecropia tree relationship. Cecropias are medium-sized, weak-limbed rainforest trees. Azteca ants live in the hollow trunk and stems of the cecropia and obsessively scour the limbs for epiphyte seeds and seedlings, which they dump off the side. This act is crucial for the cecropia because the weight of epiphytes would break its limbs. Cecropias produce fat and protein-packed capsules at their leaf tips, which nourish the ants. Azteca ants appreciate sweet nectar, too, but since the cecropia doesn't produce flowers, the ants tend masses of aphids inside the tree. The aphids do not harm the cecropia, but produce a sweet honeydew, which the ants eat.

Sometimes a mutual relationship can appear quite exploitative. Cowbirds and *oropéndolas* have a very intricate relationship that puzzled scientists for many years until biologist Neal Smith, working at his research site in Panama, discovered what was really happening. *Oropéndolas* are bird artisans that craft long, sacklike nests which hang from bare-limbed trees in the forest. Cowbirds are parasitical, laying their eggs in *oropéndolas'* nests and then leaving the *oropéndola* to incubate and raise the cowbird hatchling. Although cowbird chicks do preen *oropéndola* chicks, cowbird chicks are aggressive and develop faster than *oropéndola* chicks and can deprive *oropéndolas* of food. Sometimes *oropéndolas* tolerate this, sometimes they don't. It wasn't until another threat to *oropéndolas* was discovered that the *oropéndolas'* decision-making process was revealed. *Oropéndola* chicks are born without a protective downy coat of feathers, and are particularly vulnerable to botflies burrowing into them and killing them. When wasps and bees are present in the area, they prevent a botfly population from developing. *Oropéndola* mothers allow the cowbirds to lay their eggs only if the nest is located in an area with no wasp or bee populations to control the botflies, so the cowbirds' preening is appreciated. If there are wasps or bees around, the *oropéndola* will chase away the cowbird mother or dump her egg out of the nest.

CONSERVATION EFFORTS

The interactions of species that are so fascinating to observe in Costa Rica forests are a lesson for humans in how to live cooperatively with nature, rather than exploiting, exterminating, and controlling it. Despite the steps that the country has taken to conserve nature, it had one of the highest deforestation rates in Latin America in the late 20th century. Now, according to former Environment Minister Carlos Manuel Rodriguez, deforestation is slowing and forest cover is increasing by about 5 percent per year. Although only about 15 percent of Costa Rica's original forest cover still stands, today about 51 percent of the country is covered in some kind of forest, including the 25 percent that is planted in tree farms, mostly of the foreign species gmelina and teak. Since 1999, more wood has come from these tree farms than from the nation's forests. But monoculture tree crops cannot support the biodiversity of rainforests, so the projects creating biological corridors are reforesting with a variety of native species.

BANANAS   A green seal for bananas (ECO-O.K., known as "Better Bananas" in Europe) has been developed by the New York-based Rainforest Alliance and the Costa Rican Fundación Ambío, in collaboration with scientists, environmentalists, and banana growers. It gives a marketing incentive to growers who make the effort to protect workers and produce bananas away from rivers and with less dangerous pesticides. About 15,000 hectares of banana-cultivated land in Costa Rica has passed the test so far, including all of Chiquita's Costa Rica–based operations, and Chiquita has brought all of its Latin America plantations up to ECO-O.K. standards. Look for ECO-O.K. coffee, oranges, and chocolate, too (ra.org).

SMART WOOD   The Rainforest Alliance also has the Smart Wood Program, to certify wood products that were harvested from forests managed in compliance with environmentally sound principles.

GLOBAL WARMING RESEARCH IN COSTA RICA   According to a study by the San José–based Regional Water Resources Committee, in Costa Rica, temperatures are expected to increase by 2°F by 2030, and 6.1°F by 2100. Using a moveable tower that reaches up to 44 meters, scientists at La Selva Biological Station in Sarapiquí have been able to study the effects of global warming on all levels of the forest canopy and in 50 different locations within the reserve. According to the *Tico Times*, "increased temperatures [could] mean that the forest is respiring more, which in turn would mean that the forest is absorbing less and releasing more of the greenhouse gas, carbon dioxide. . . . The possibility of the forest no longer absorbing carbon dioxide at the present rate is a threat that could have considerable impact." In the tropical forest, species that require high humidity may die as temperatures increase. According to biologist Allan Pounds of the Tropical Science Center, "Changes in birds, reptiles, and plants correlate to climatic change. Species in the foothills are moving up mountain slopes, seeking lower temperatures." He said that a study of more than 1000 species from around the world predicts that one-fourth could disappear because of global warming.

HOW MUCH IS WATER WORTH?   In 2005, Costa Rica became the first country in the world to protect its nationwide water supplies by giving an economic value to the water itself. Water costs went up from their formerly low levels, providing $20 to $25 million for watershed conservation through 2015. According to former minister of energy, Carlos Manuel Rodriguez, "The idea is to put a cash value on the worth of water as a raw material, rather than quantifying only the infrastructure and administration it takes to capture the natural resource." This is a boon for the national park system, which will receive $5 to $7 million dollars a year, doubling their budget, for their role in water production. Private, indigenous, and government-sponsored water conservation projects will benefit, too.

THE MARITIME ZONE   Only 15 percent (137 out of a total of 910 coastal miles) of Costa Rica's shores have primary (or "old-growth") forests. The Maritime Zone (Zona Maritimo-Terrestre) is the first 200 meters of land from the high tide line. It belongs to the state by law. The first 50 meters are considered public terrain and cannot be developed. The remaining 150 meters previously had been given concessions by municipalities to be developed privately for hotels, restaurants, or homes. Forested areas in the Maritime Zone have been decreed part of the national patrimony and are now overseen by the Ministry of the Environment. Concessions can no longer be granted in the Maritime Zone where forest exists, thus ending the power of municipalities to determine what should happen in this zone. This is why you won't find many hotels, besides very large and rich ones, who can pay the concessions, right on the beach. Towns (like Jacó) that were already developed before the promulgation of the 1975 Zona Maritimo law are grandfathered in and can have buildings on the beach.

TOURISM AND THE ENVIRONMENT

Costa Rica transformed itself from an agricultural to a tourism-based economy between 1985 and 1990, and development was, and still is, poorly planned. Now that Costa Rica is a prime tourism destination, growth keeps increasing at the expense of environmental and community concerns. Although unbridled growth and real estate speculation is happening all over the country, it is at its most alarming at the famous beaches in the northwestern province of Guanacaste.

According to the Costa Rican Chamber of Builders, in 2006, construction in Guanacaste increased by 107%, largely due to new condos and private luxury residences in the Tamarindo and Flamingo areas (*Tico Times*, Feb. 23, 2007). In 2007, construction in Guanacaste increased by 1.6 million meters (*TT*, April 11, 2008). In a random survey done by the Federation of Engineers and Architects of 217 Guanacaste hotels, condominiums and private residential developments, 45 were found to lack even the most basic government permits (*TT*, March 16, 2007).

In March 2007, developments in Playa del Coco, Playa Hermosa and Playa Panamá became the subject of a lawsuit by residents who demanded a moratorium on construction until their water supply is secured and appropriate sewage treatment facilities are in place. The 300-room Hotel Allegro Papagayo was found to be pumping sewage into the estuary beside the hotel and was shut down by the Ministry of Health in February 2008. It was later allowed to open, but at only half of its capacity. Neighboring Hotel Gran Papagayo was also under investigation for improper sewage disposal.

In September of 2007, the life guards at the famous surfer mecca Tamarindo were dismissed because hotels in the community would not pay them. After a US tourist drowned there in January 2008, efforts were made to reinstate the program. Tamarindo, lost its Blue Flag designation in 2008, after high levels of contamination were found in its waters. Although sanitary conditions have improved, multistory condos and hotels are constantly under construction in this former fishing village, now Costa Rica's third largest tourism destination.

In May 2008, President Arias proclaimed that the construction of buildings over five stories would not be permitted anywhere in Guanacaste, but the new guidelines will only apply to permits granted six months after the proclamation takes effect. This does nothing to address the overabundance of hotels and condos that already have permits, not to mention those that are building without them. The decree will be effective until 2012, by which time, communities are expected to have their own sewage treatment plants and zoning laws. While there are residents working very hard to improve conditions and implement zoning plans and water treatment plants, Guanacaste is in the grips of a struggle that may take years to resolve.

HOW TO HELP

Fortunately, many Costa Ricans and international conservationists have good ideas about how to turn the tide toward restoration and preservation of the country's natural resources. Below, you can read about their efforts, as well as their suggestions for how you as a tourist can help.

VISIT COMMUNITY-BASED ECOTOURISM PROJECTS

At the same time as overdevelopment flourishes at the beaches of Northern Guanacaste, other parts of Costa Rica are making many efforts toward integrating sustainable agriculture, conservation, and ecotourism. You can be part of this by spending time at the small, locally owned reserves that are mentioned throughout this book. Almost everyone who consults me about planning their trip (keytocostarica.com) starts out wanting to go to Arenal volcano, Monteverde, Manuel Antonio, and Tortuguero. These places are beautiful, it's true, but they can be combined with interesting and rewarding trips that are off the beaten track. Community-based ecotourism projects are often more isolated and difficult to get to, but the chance to experience this new way of travel is worth it. If logistics are too complex, consider taking a tour with **ACTUAR CONSERVacations** (keytocosta rica.com). You'll bathe in waterfall pools, see birds and other wildlife, and be inspired by the dedication of these citizen conservationists. There is no better way to get to know the culture, support local communities and, in the long run, make tropical conservation work.

CARBON NEUTRAL AIR TRAVEL

Just by visiting the community-based destinations mentioned above, you are contributing to the preservation of the rainforest. ACTUAR member organizations protect over 25,000 acres of forest, and many are actively doing reforestation projects. A donation of $10 to any of these projects will help them plant five trees, and you can often participate in the planting. It is estimated that, besides offering habitat to animals and birds, thus promoting biodiversity, one tree will neutralize one metric ton of carbon during its lifetime. If you are moved to contribute to conservation in Costa Rica, making donations to these grassroots community efforts is a great way to do it.

If you would like to calculate the carbon produced by one person traveling by air to Costa Rica, there are several websites that can help you. One of the easiest carbon calculators is found at **terrapass.com**. For instance, one flight from Boston to Costa Rica and back (4756 miles roundtrip) produces about one metric ton of carbon dioxide emissions, the principal cause of global warming. At TerraPass you can purchase **carbon offsets** equal to the amount of carbon dioxide emitted during your trip. Purchasing offsets means that you are contributing money to organizations that counteract global warming. The efforts made by all the carbon off-setters on Terrapass are independently verified.

One of our favorite carbon offset purveyors is **Trees, Water and People** (1-877-606-4TWP, treeswaterpeople.org). They help communities in Guatemala, Honduras and El Salvador plant trees to supply their needs for fruit and furniture. TWP also teaches people to build fuel efficient cook stoves that reduce the use of firewood 50 to 70% relative to traditional open cooking fires.

BE AN ETHICAL TRAVELER

Here are some simple guidelines for ethical ecotourism:

- Dispose of waste properly.
- Stay on trails.
- Ask permission before entering private property or indigenous reserves, and pay fees if required.
- Dress appropriately. In Costa Rica, this means no skinny dipping.
- Coral reefs, caves, and petroglyphs are easily damaged, so be careful not to touch them.
- Monkeys and other wild animals should not be fed because this alters their diet and behavior.
- Keep your distance from wildlife so that it is not compelled to take flight. Animal courtship, nesting, or feeding of the young should not be interrupted. Birds and their nests should be observed from a safe distance through binoculars, and nesting sea turtles should be observed only with a trained guide.
- Photographers should keep their distance. Leave foliage around nests, and be careful not to bother animals for the sake of a picture.
- Make sure that natural products you buy are commercially grown, and that archaeological artifacts are reproductions.

• Hire local guides. You'll see more, and you'll be supporting the local economy.

The year 2002 was the United Nations International Year of Ecotourism. Over 1000 delegates from 133 countries met in Quebec in May 2002 to draft guidelines for ecotourism to be used at the Johannesburg Summit on Sustainable Development in August 2002. Their final Declaration reflects a deep understanding of the importance and impact of ecotourism on rural communities: " . . . Ecotourism development must consider and respect the land and property rights, and, where recognized, the right to self-determination and cultural sovereignty of indigenous and local communities, including their protected, sensitive, and sacred sites as well as their traditional knowledge. . . . Many of these areas are home to peoples often living in poverty, who frequently lack adequate health care, education facilities, communications systems, and other infrastructure required for genuine development opportunity. . . . Small and micro businesses seeking to meet social and environmental objectives are key partners in ecotourism and are often operating in a development climate that does not provide suitable financial and marketing support for ecotourism. . . ." We strongly support this worldwide effort to make ecotourism a force for good.

ASK QUESTIONS

When you want to buy hardwood souvenirs or stay in a hotel built with precious woods, ask about the materials, and how the business has contributed to conservation and reforestation efforts. Most beautiful hardwoods are not "sustainably harvested" but are mined right from the rainforest. One rainforest tree can be used to make dozens of coffee tables or hundreds of bowls. Since the wood is much more valuable when used in this way, the hope is that its value will generate more respect. While it is not necessarily unconscientious to use endangered woods, those who use them should recognize their endangered status and contribute to efforts to reforest with these types of trees. If nothing else, your questions might sensitize the handicraft dealer or hotelier.

WRITE LETTERS

Tourism is Costa Rica's largest industry, and officials need to maintain the country's image as a tourist's eco-paradise. Letters from travelers worried about environmental destruction, unbridled growth of megatourism projects, and abuses by police or bureaucrats all serve to inform and pressure the government about these problems. Your experience in Costa Rica is of interest to policymakers. Write to the president of Costa Rica (Hon. Oscar Arias, Presidente de Costa Rica, Apdo. 520, Zapote, San José, Costa Rica; fax: 2253-9078, presidente@casapres.go.cr) or call the ICT at 1-866-COSTARICA. It's a good idea to send a copy of your letter to the media as well (*Tico Times*: Apdo. 4632, San José; ticotimes.net, ttimes@racsa.co.cr; or in Spanish, *La Nación*: Apdo. 10138-1000, San José; nacion.co.cr).

VOLUNTEER

Volunteering opportunities exist all over Costa Rica. You'll find them outlined in the regional sections of the book, complete with websites and e-mail addresses. Volunteers almost always have to pay for their own room and board, usually $15-$20 per day, and usually have to make a definite time-commitment to the project they work on.

There are three different turtle protection projects on the Atlantic Coast: **ANAI** in the Gandoca–Manzanillo Wildlife Refuge, the **CCC** in Tortuguero, and the **Reserva Pacuare** in Parismina. ANAI also takes volunteers at its experimental farm in Gandoca.

PRETOMA (2241-5227; tortugamarina.org) works to stop pelagic long-line fishing practices that threaten sea turtles with extinction.

In the Northern Zone, the **Sarapiquí Conservation Learning Center** and **Rainforest Biodiversity Group** work with local communities on reforestation and building of trails and bridges. **Monteverde Institute** coordinates a number of volunteer projects ranging from trail maintenance to working in health clinics to organizing women's groups. Also in Monteverde, the **Centro Panamericano de Idiomas** includes volunteer work with its Spanish classes. At **Ecolodge San Luis**, people with a strong background in biology and ecology can help with research.

In Guanacaste, volunteers can work protecting turtles at Playa Grande, Playa Langosta, or Santa Rosa (see ASVO, below).

In the Central Pacific, volunteers are needed at the **Karen Mogensen Reserve** and **ASEPALECO** on the Nicoya Peninsula. In Manuel Antonio, **Coope El Silencio** needs help with its macaw release and endangered orchid-raising projects.

In the Southern Zone, **Proyecto Campanario** works in rainforest ecology.

Through **ASVO** (Association of Volunteers for Service in Protected Areas; Calle 36, Avenidas 3/5; 2258-4430; asvocr.org), visitors at least 18 years old can donate support services to the severely understaffed national parks and reserves. Volunteers must adapt themselves to work in all kinds of weather, and they should be willing to do everything that a normal park ranger would do. Initiative and willingness to learn are more important than previous experience. Volunteers should speak Spanish and make a minimum one-month commitment.

NOTE: Sometimes it is possible to just walk up to a national park or reserve and volunteer without going through an organization. Try it!

There are several interesting projects in which you can learn about organic farming, sustainable living, permaculture and agricultural experimentation. Among them are **Finca IPE** (fincaipe.com) near Dominical, **Finca La Flor** (la-flor-de-paraiso.org) in Paraiso de Cartago, **Punta Mona** (puntamona.org) in the Gandoca Manzanillo Wildlife Refuge on the Southern Atlantic, and **Rancho Mastatal** (ranchomastatal.com) in the mountains between the Central Valley and the Pacific. Also see Finca Luna Nueva and Rancho Margot in the Northern Zone Chapter.

THREE

Planning Your Trip

CALLING COSTA RICA

In this book, Costa Rica numbers are listed without the country code, which is 506. To call Costa Rica from North America, dial 011, then 506, then the number. All Costa Rican phone numbers have eight digits. A 3 or an 8 at the beginning of a number indicates a cell phone while phone number with 2, 4, 6, 7 and 9 indicate land lines.

SURFING THE WEB

There is a lot of information on the internet about Costa Rica, but nothing truly comprehensive, and not a lot about community-based ecotourism and other low-cost accommodations, so your trusty guidebook is not yet obsolete. Most websites charge the hotels that appear on them, so you will only see the hotels that have paid to be on that site. We have tried to list websites in the text whenever possible, so with the combination of our recommendations and the websites, you should be able to make very good choices. New websites are springing up every day, so if you want to find out more about a hotel that has no website in the book, type its name and "Costa Rica" after it, and you might well find it on the web. Here are some of the websites we think can be the most helpful in planning your trip:

keytocostarica.com, our website, has links to our favorite ecolodges, and samples of the customized tours we plan. If you would like our help with your travel plans, e-mail beatrice@keytocostarica.com (fee). Please put "Costa Rica" in the subject of your e-mail.

costaricainnkeepers.com has information on inns and B&Bs in all price ranges

costa-rica-guide.com offers comprehensive travel-planning advice, as well as the most detailed and comprehensive map of Costa Rica that we have found. And it's waterproof!

Some of the best sites are created by community-minded groups of tourism people from the areas you are interested in visiting, like **arenal. net**, **monteverdeinfo.com**, **nosara.com**, **greencoast.com** (an excellent site about the Talamanca region on the Atlantic coast), **soldeosa.com** (about the Osa Peninsula), **tortuguerovillage.com**, and **nicoyapeninsula.com**. These websites often put you in direct contact with the hotels, and the group that puts the website together provides quality control.

WHEN TO GO

In Costa Rica, the tourist season has traditionally been December through April, which corresponds to the dry season. You can almost depend on clear, sunny weather, but there are occasional unseasonal storms from the north that can last for several days. The rainy season usually takes a while to get started in May, and often diminishes for a couple of weeks in June or July. The rains dwindle in December. In Guanacaste, the only really rainy months are October and November. On the Atlantic side, the only predictably dry months are September and October.

Now that Costa Rica has become so popular, July and August are also considered the high season, and popular hotels charge high-season rates despite the rain. There are certain advantages to going during the "green" season: The mornings are almost always clear and warm. The scenery is fresher and greener. The days are cooled by the rains, which can be a blessing, especially at the beach. The clouds usually clear in time for a magnificent sunset. Many hotels now consider May 1 to June 15 and September 1 to November 15 to be the off-season, and offer substantial discounts, sometimes as much as 50 percent.

You really need to plan ahead for Christmas week and the week before Easter. Hotel rooms are booked six to ten months in advance, and popular hotels are often booked several months in advance during the January to April dry season as well. If you want to try less frequented beaches, like Zancudo in the Southern Zone or the beautiful beaches of Talamanca on the Atlantic, you can take a "let's just explore and see what happens" vacation, and you'll almost always find a place to stay. Airlines are usually booked far in advance from about December 10 to January 10, so make your plane reservations early if you want to go during that time. The same goes for the weeks before and after Easter.

CLIMATE

Given Costa Rica's latitude—between 8° and 12° north of the equator—day length and temperature do not change drastically with the seasons. The sun rises around 5 a.m. and sets around 6 p.m. year-round. Temperature differences are experienced by changing altitude. The misty highlands are in the 10°–13°C (50°–55°F) range, while the Central Valley, at 3800 feet, averages 26°C (78°F). At sea level, the temperature is 30°–35°C (85°–95°F), tempered by sea breezes on the coast. Slight variations occur in December, January, and February, due to cold winds from the North American winter. These cooler temperatures bring on the dry season or "summer," as Central Americans call it, which lasts from December through April. Temperatures start to rise as the sun approaches a perpendicular position over Costa Rica. This causes increased evaporation and brings on the rainy season, or "winter," which lasts from May through November, except for a two-week dry season, a time called *el veranillo de San Juan* (the "little summer"), which occurs sometime in June or July.

Costa Rica's weather pattern is changing and is not as predictable as it used to be. Now there are many dry days during the "winter" and a few storms during the "summer." Here's a new rule of thumb: The more gloriously sun-drenched the morning during the rainy season, the harder it will rain in the afternoon. Conversely, on a cloudy morning there will be less evaporation, and thus a generally drier day.

The Atlantic Coast has always been an exception to the rule. Trade winds laden with moisture from the Caribbean approach Costa Rica from the northeast. As the moisture rises to the chilly heights of the Cordillera, it condenses into rain on the eastern slopes. For this reason, there is no definite dry season in the Atlantic zone, but the beaches tend to be sunnier than the mountains. Residents insist that the rainiest months in the rest of Costa Rica, September and October, are the driest on the Caribbean coast. Often you can see Arenal volcano best in September and October. In a similar phenomenon, trade winds from the southeast discharge their moisture against the mountains that separate the Osa Peninsula from the rest of the country. The Atlantic plains and the Osa both receive 150 to 300 inches of rain a year, compared to an average of 100 inches in the Central Valley.

One of the most surprising things for newcomers to the Central Valley is that it's not as warm as they expected. December, January, and February are usually rain-free, but the weather can be downright chilly, especially at night or if a wind is blowing. During the rainy season, May to November, the days tend to start out warm and sunny but cloud over by noon. The downpour usually starts around 2 or 3 p.m. and it can get pretty cold then, too. Usually a sweater and long pants are enough to keep you warm. When it rains, it *really rains*, but afternoon downpours are usually short-lived. If you go down in altitude from San José's 3800 feet, you'll be able to wear the kind of clothes you hoped you could wear in the tropics.

HOLIDAYS

Costa Rica has 11 official *feriados* (holidays) per year, and they are taken quite seriously. Do not expect to find government offices, banks, professional offices, or many stores open on *feriados*. Twice during the year, the whole country shuts down completely. These are *Semana Santa* (the week before Easter) and the week between Christmas and New Year's Day. Transportation stops totally on Holy Thursday and Good Friday, making Wednesday's buses very crowded. If you are on a tour or driving during Holy Week, don't worry—gas stations will be open, and life will go on.

Easter week is the time to see picturesque religious processions in the countryside. There are large nonreligious parades in San José on Labor Day, Independence Day, and during Christmas week. The *Tico Times* (tico times.net) will tell you where the most interesting events are. It's best to avoid visiting the beach during Easter week because it's often the last holiday young Ticos have before school starts, and they're all there with their boom boxes.

Following is a list of Costa Rica's *feriados*:

January 1   New Year's Day
April 11   Anniversary of the Battle of Rivas
Holy Thursday through Easter Sunday
May 1   Labor Day
July 25   Annexation of Guanacaste Province
August 2   Our Lady of the Angels (Costa Rica's patron saint)
August 15   Assumption Day, Mother's Day
September 15   Independence Day
October 12   Día de la Raza (Columbus Day, Carnival in Limón)
December 24 and 25   Christmas Eve and Christmas Day

CALENDAR OF EVENTS

JANUARY

San José: Top junior tennis players from around the world compete in the week-long **Copa del Café**.

Santa Cruz: Tico-style bullfights and lively regional folk dancing are the main attractions at the **Santa Cruz Fiestas**.

FEBRUARY

Liberia: The **Liberia Festival** is held the last week in February, hosting Guanacastecan folklore, concerts, and horsemanship.

Puntarenas: The yearly **Carnaval** takes place with 10 days of parades, fireworks, sports, and dancing in the streets.

San Isidro de El General: A cattle show, agricultural and industrial fair, and orchid show highlight this town's **fiestas**.

San José: The **Open-Air Festival** at the National Center for Culture offers free theater, concerts, and dance shows on weekends all month.

MARCH

Countrywide: **Holy Week** processions throughout the country. The best processions are at the Church of San Rafael de Oreamuno near Cartago, and in San Joaquín de Flores near Heredia.

San Antonio de Escazú: A parade of brightly colored carts and the blessing of the animals and crops mark **Día del Boyero** (Ox-Cart Driver's Day), the second Sunday in March.

Monteverde: **Monteverde Music Festival** features Costa Rica's best jazz, flamenco, and *trova* musicians on weekends in March and April.

San José: March is a busy month in San José. You'll find the **National Orchid Show**, featuring more than 1500 species, as well as the **Bonanza Cattle Show**, the year's biggest event for cattlemen (but many visitors come for the Wild West fun of the rodeos and horseraces). An **International Arts and Music Festival** (festivaldelasartes.com) brings musicians and theater groups from all over the world to perform. The **Carrera de la Paz** marathon attracts as many as a thousand runners.

Ujarrás: The ruins of the first colonial church in Costa Rica, in Ujarrás, is the destination of a **religious procession**.

Playa Chiquita: The **Music of South Caribbean Coast Festival** runs in March and April.

APRIL

Alajuela: Fiestas are held in honor of Costa Rica's national hero in this, his hometown, for the whole week near April 11, **Juan Santamaría Day**.

Cartago: In late April, visit the Cartago Social Club for the **Cartago Orchid Show**.

San José: The University of Costa Rica marks **University Week** with parades, dances, and cultural events the last week in April.

MAY

Limón: May 1, celebrated as **International Labor Day** all over Costa Rica, is a day for picnics, dances, and cricket matches.

San Isidro: Any town of this name—and there are several—is likely to be celebrating **San Isidro Labrador** on May 15 (this saint's day) with festivities that include a blessing of the animals.

San José: San Juan Day sees the running of the **Carrera de San Juan**, the year's biggest marathon.

JUNE

Countrywide: On June 29, **Saint Peter and Saint Paul's Day** is celebrated throughout the country. The third Sunday of the month is **Father's Day**.

JULY

Liberia: Parades, rodeos, concerts, and Tico-style bullfights are the highlights of the celebration commemorating the **Annexation of Guanacaste** to Costa Rica on July 25, 1824.

Puntarenas: Don't miss the regatta of beautifully decorated fishing boats and yachts celebrating the **Fiesta of the Virgin of the Sea**, on the Saturday closest to the 16th.

San José, mountain and beach hotels: The **International Music Festival** features renowned artists from around the world in July and August.

AUGUST

Countrywide: **Mother's Day** is August 15 in Costa Rica.

Cartago: On August 2, the old capital is the destination of an annual national pilgrimage honoring Costa Rica's patron saint, the **Virgin of Los Angeles**, known for her miracles. Over a million people make the pilgrimage each year.

San José: **International Black Peoples' Day** is the focal point of **Semana Cultural Afro-Costarricense** (Afro–Costa Rican Culture Week), and features lectures, panels, and displays on black culture.

San Ramón: On August 31, all the saints from neighboring towns are brought on a pilgrimage for **Día De San Ramón** in the towns named for this saint. Fiestas follow the parade.

SEPTEMBER

San José: **Independence Day** is celebrated with parades in the capital and the rest of the country. The Freedom Torch is passed from Guatemala and throughout the isthmus until it crosses the Nicaraguan border to relay runners who deliver it to the president in the old colonial capitol of Cartago at 6 p.m. on September 14. Children parade with homemade paper lanterns and everyone sings the national anthem. Schoolchildren present drumming parades the next day.

OCTOBER

Limón: The weeklong **Carnaval** resembles Mardi Gras in Rio, with brightly costumed dancers parading through the streets all night, concerts, and general merrymaking.

NOVEMBER

Countrywide: An **International Surf Tourney** is held at beaches on both coasts. In honor of **All Soul's Day**, families gather in the cemeteries all across the country on November 2. The last weekend in November, ox-cart drivers camp in La Sabana, sing folk songs, and parade down Paseo Colón on Sunday.

DECEMBER

Countrywide: Christmas celebrations begin early in the month everywhere in Costa Rica, with music, special foods, *rompope* (eggnog), *chicha* (home-made corn liquor), and tamales. There are three **Audubon Christmas Bird Counts**, each in a different part of the country.

Boruca: **Fiesta de Los Negritos** celebrates the week of December 8 with costumes, music, and dance. Then on the 30th, see a re-creation of the struggle between the Indians and the Spaniards at the time of the conquest during the **Fiesta of the Diablitos**, held in this small Indian village near Buenos Aires in the Southern Zone.

Guanacaste: Nicoya is the site of **Fiesta de la Yegüita**, with a procession, foods made from corn, music, bullfights, and fireworks on the week of the 12th.

San José: December 15 is the start of **Las Posadas**, a Christmas tradition in which children, musicians, and carolers go door-to-door re-creating Mary and Joseph's search for lodging. The week between Christmas and New Year's Day offers San José's biggest celebration of the year. There are Tico-style bullfights, a giant parade with floats, and *El Tope*, a huge equestrian parade in the Sevillian tradition in which elegantly clad riders show off their purebred steeds. The fairground in Zapote turns into an amusement park. Choirs from around the country perform at the National Theater for the **Christmas Choir Festival**. The **International Dance Festival** is held the first two weeks of the month.

COMING AND GOING

ENTRY REQUIREMENTS

When traveling with a passport, citizens of the United States, Canada, and most Latin American and European countries are entitled to stay in Costa Rica for 90 days. They must enter the country with a departure ticket and a valid passport that does not expire within 30 days of their arrival in Costa Rica. If you don't have a ticket out of the country, you might be prevented from boarding a plane *to* Costa Rica because airlines can be fined if they let passengers board without the required travel documents. Citizens of some Latin American, Asian, African, and East European countries must obtain a visa from a Costa Rican consulate and pay a deposit upon entering the country, refundable when they leave. Check with the consulate nearest you for the latest information or see costarica-embassy.org/consular/visa.

Always carry your ID: While in Costa Rica, if you don't want to carry your passport with you, get a copy of it made. The copy must include the page that was stamped when you entered the country. Don't go anywhere without identification. You can have your passport copy *emplasticado* (laminated) at various street stands in San José. You *will* need your passport, not a copy, to change money at banks.

Passport theft and emergency consular information: Unfortunately, Costa Rica has one of the highest rates of passport theft in the world. U.S. citizens can get their passports replaced at the **U.S. Consulate** in Pavas, west of San José. Call 2519-2000. The consular section is open weekdays and closed on Costa Rican and U.S. holidays. For emergencies outside office hours, call 2519-2280 or 2519-2279, fax: 2220-2455. If your passport is stolen, it really helps if you have a copy or know your passport number. You might also want to register with the U.S. Embassy through the State

Department's travel registration website before you travel abroad. The **Canadian Embassy** is in Sabana Sur (2242-4400; after hours call toll-free in Costa Rica: 0 800 015-1161). The **British Embassy** is in Centro Colon (2258-2025, emergency pager: 2225-4049).

EXIT AND EXTENDED VISAS

All tourists must pay an airport tax of $26 when they leave. If you overstay your 30- or 90-day visa, you will have to pay an extra $20 fine upon departure and may be delayed at the airport.

You can stay legally by leaving the country for a few days after your first three months and coming back in with a new tourist visa. *Be sure that your passport is stamped as you re-enter Costa Rica.* If your passport is not stamped correctly on re-entry, your efforts to renew your visa will have been in vain. Don't depend on leaving the country every three months as a way to remain in Costa Rica indefinitely. Immigration officials start becoming suspicious after you have done this three times. They could deport you. If you are deported, you can't return to Costa Rica for 10 years. Longer stays are granted only to those applying for student visas or residency.

Be sure to confirm your departure flight 72 hours in advance. Get to the airport at least two hours ahead of flight time. Flights are often overbooked.

ENTRY AND EXIT REQUIREMENTS FOR TRAVELING WITH CHILDREN UNDER THE AGE OF 18

In an effort to prevent international child abduction, many governments have initiated special procedures for minors at entry and exit points. These often include requiring documentary evidence of the child's relationship to the accompanying parents and, if one of the parents is not traveling with the child, permission from the non-traveling parent for the child's travel. For instance, if you are traveling with your child, and the child's other parent is not traveling with you, you need a notarized letter from the absent parent stating that he or she gives permission for the child to travel on certain dates with you. This can be the case even if both parents have been traveling together but one has to leave Costa Rica earlier than the rest of the family. Getting a signed letter from the absent parent can save you a lot of hassle when you leave the country. This also applies if you are traveling with someone else's children.

Non–Costa Rican parents of minors who obtained Costa Rican citizenship through birth in Costa Rica or to a Costa Rican parent should be aware that these children may only depart Costa Rica upon presentation of an exit permit issued by the Costa Rican immigration office. Parents of dual-citizen children are advised to consult with the Costa Rican embassy or consulate in the U.S. about entry and exit requirements before travel to Costa Rica.

TRANSPORTATION

AIRLINES SERVING COSTA RICA

LACSA, Costa Rica's international airline, is part of Grupo TACA, the alliance of Central America's airlines. It flies from Chicago, Houston, Dallas, San Francisco, Oakland, Los Angeles, New York City (JFK), Miami, Washington (IAD), and Toronto.

American Airlines, **United**, **US Airways, Delta, Continental**, and **Mexicana** have flights to Costa Rica with package connections to all major American cities. Discounted rates are offered several times a year, especially in the off-season.

You can fly to either Juan Santamaría International Airport (SJO) in the town of Alajuela, about half an hour west of San José, or to Daniel Oduber Quiros International Airport (LIR) in Liberia, Guanacaste. If you just want to visit Arenal volcano and the beaches in Guanacaste or the Nicoya Peninsula, and want to avoid driving on winding mountain roads, this airport is for you. It is possible to get an "open-jaw" ticket that lands you in SJO and lets you depart from LIR, or vice versa. Go to kayak.com to see which airline gives you the best prices for the dates and routes you want. If you are working with a travel agent, try to get one who is experienced in sending people to Costa Rica because there are many alternatives. I recommend **Earthroutes** (in the U.S.: 207-326-8635; earthroutes.com).

Whatever airline you take, book several months ahead if you are going during the dry season, especially for Christmas or Easter, and confirm your reservation 72 hours in advance. Get to the gateway airport at least two hours before flight time. Check-in lines are lengthy and documentation checks and payment of airport taxes may take time.

LOCAL TRANSPORTATION

See Chapter Four for information on buses and car rentals.

DRIVING TO COSTA RICA

If you're driving from the U.S., allow about three weeks from the time you enter Mexico until the time you reach Costa Rica, ten days if you don't want to sightsee on the way. Avoid the highlands of Guatemala and El Salvador, drive only during the day, and do not plan to camp. You may drive your car in Costa Rica tax-free for up to six months as a tourist. You pay $40 when you enter the country and another $40 to renew your visa after three months. After that you have to pay hefty import taxes or pay to have the car stored.

SAMPLE ITINERARIES

These few sample itineraries are designed to accommodate particular interests, with as much efficiency in routing as possible. We've tried to include off-the-beaten track destinations in these suggestions. Combine several circuits for a longer vacation. These itineraries work best if you have your own car, or have hired a naturalist guide/driver (see keytocostarica.com).

OLD ROUTE TO LIMÓN, WITH RAINFOREST AND BEACHES

Day 1	San José
Day 2	Drive to Turrialba, go white-water rafting or go birding at El Copal Reserve
Day 3	Drive from Turrialba to Talamanca
Day 4	Talamanca beaches
Day 5	Do the river trip to the indigenous village of Yorkín in a dugout canoe, and learn how chocolate is grown and processed.
Day 6	Rainforest visit in Sarapiquí or tour Tortuguero
Day 7	Back to San José

CENTRAL HIGHLANDS, ARENAL, AND SOUTHERN GUANACASTE BEACH

The most efficient way to include beaches, rainforests, and volcanoes.

Day 1	Central Valley hotel
Day 2	Early-morning visit to Poás and La Paz Waterfall Gardens; drive to Sarapiquí
Day 3	Rainforest visit in Sarapiquí
Day 4	Drive to Volcán Arenal
Day 5	Visit volcano and hot springs
Day 6	Drive to Samara or Nosara
Days 7 & 8	Stay at beach
Day 9	Return to Central Valley

NICOYA PENINSULA AND GUANACASTE

A one-week rainforest and beach trip off the beaten track.

Day 1	Drive to Puntarenas, take a ferry to Playa Naranjo, continue to Jicaral. Ride horses to Karen Mogensen Reserve
Day 2	Hike in the reserve, swim at Bridal Veil Falls
Day 3	Drive to Playas Carrillo, Samara or Nosara
Days 4 to 6	Stay at beach, see turtle nesting at Ostional between June and December
Day 7	Back to Central Valley

NORTHERN GUANACASTE AND ARENAL

Eight days with volcano, national park and beach visits; a good route in the rainy season.

Day 1	From Liberia airport, drive to Rincón de la Vieja; camp or lodge nearby
Day 2	Rincón de la Vieja National Park and canopy or tubing tours
Day 3	Santa Rosa National Park
Day 4	Visit beaches of northern Guanacaste, like Bahía Junquillal Wildlife Refuge
Day 5	Drive through Cañas, Tilarán, and around Lake Arenal. Stay near Volcán Arenal
Day 6	Visit volcano and Tabacón Hot Springs or Ecotermales
Day 7	Back to Liberia

SOUTHERN ZONE

This area is still off the beaten track for most visitors, but tourism is definitely increasing.

Day 1	San José; leave early afternoon for Copey, Quetzal Paradise, or San Gerardo de Dota
Day 2	Drive south to San Isidro after a morning birding hike, drive east to San Gerardo de Rivas and Chirripó, or go west to visit the beaches of Dominical or Uvita
Day 3	Explore previous day's destination
Day 4	Continue south to Sierpe, take boat to Drake Bay
Days 5 to 7	Tour Isla del Caño, Corcovado, watch dolphins or whales
Day 8	Head back to San José

QUETZALS, BEACH, AND RAINFOREST

A multi-altitude loop off the beaten track in the Southern Zone.

Day 1	Go to Palmichal de Acosta, a lovely mountain town about an hour south of the San José airport
Day 2	Hike, visit local farms, see how coffee is processed
Day 3	Drive through the Los Santos area to Copey de Dota
Day 4	Look for quetzals in the morning, drive south across Cerro de la Muerte to San Isidro and then west to Dominical, and south again to Uvita
Day 5	Visit the beaches of Ballena National Marine Park
Day 6	Visit Isla Ballena or go kayaking in the mangroves of the Rio Terraba
Day 7	Return to Central Valley via the coast

PACKING

Tourists are permitted to bring binoculars, two cameras, and electrical items that are for personal use only, like a small radio, a hairdryer, a laptop, a video camera, etc. The most important thing to remember is that the items should not be in their original boxes and not look too new. The government doesn't want tourists to "import" electronic items for resale. We do not recommend bringing a laptop if you are on vacation. There is too much risk of it getting stolen, and you can check your e-mail at almost any hotel. Most towns have internet cafés.

In San José during the rainy season, people usually carry umbrellas— brightly colored *sombrillas* for women and black *paraguas* for men. In the mountains, a lightweight rain poncho is usually more convenient except for those who wear glasses. You'll be glad to have high rubber boots if you go hiking in the rainforest, especially in Corcovado or Sarapiquí. You can buy good ones in Costa Rica for under $7 at San José's Mercado Central and at provincial supply stores, and many places rent them to visitors or include them as part of a tour. Bring boots from home only if you wear an especially large size.

When you go to the beach or rainforest, bring at least one shirt for each day. You're bound to get sweaty. Lightweight cotton or cotton-mix clothing is best, protected inside a plastic bag in case of sudden downpours. Even if you are going to the steamy lowlands, you often have to pass through high mountains to get there—Cerro de la Muerte on the way to the Osa, Braulio Carrillo or Vara Blanca on the way to Sarapiquí. You'll be happier if you have a windbreaker, long pants, and socks that can be peeled off as you get to lower altitudes.

Most hotels will let you store excess luggage while you venture off. You can usually fit everything needed for a trip to the countryside in a day pack so bring lightweight daypacks that you can roll up inside your luggage, so you can leave your larger suitcases in storage and travel light. Plus:

Two bathing suits	Socks for each day of your trip
Three pairs of lightweight pants and shorts	Shirts for each day
	Sleepwear
A cotton overshirt	Books
A cover-up to wear at the beach	An umbrella or rain poncho

A lightweight, one-layer, hooded nylon windbreaker, especially the kind that folds up into a handy little pouch made out of the front pocket. If you are traveling during the dry season and not planning to spend a lot of time atop volcanoes, it's all you'll need to keep warm and to ward off occasional raindrops. If you are going to Irazú, Poás, Chirripó, or other high-altitude areas, you'll need a lined jacket and warm socks.

Plenty of memory, rechargeable batteries, recharger and a waterproof case for your camera	Sandals that won't slide off your feet
	Beach sandals or waterwalkers
Binoculars	Sunscreen
Pocket alarm clock or watch with alarm	Sunglasses
	Hats with visors for sun or rain protection
Valid passports for all members of your party, including children	Insect repellent
	Anti-itch ointment
Drivers licenses if you plan to rent a car	SteriPen UV water purifying device
Pocket calculator	Small first-aid kit
Waterproof, lightweight hiking boots or two pairs of tennis shoes with good treads. If one pair gets wet, use that pair whenever you are likely to get your feet wet again; plastic bags to store them in.	Metal water bottle
	Contact lens solution or an extra pair of glasses
	Toothbrush, toothpaste, shampoo, and other toiletries in a plastic bag to comply with airline carry-on regulations
	Birth control items

Vitamins or medications
Earplugs
A universal plug for bathroom
  sinks
Beach towel
Washcloth
Your own plastic cup
Flashlight with rechargeable
  batteries and extra bulb

String and clothespins for hanging laundry
Battery-operated reading lamp
  for late-night readers
Plastic bags for storing wet
  clothes and protecting dry
  clothes and equipment

ELECTRICITY

The electrical current used in Costa Rica is 110 volts, AC. The sockets are American-style, but budget places usually don't have a place for a grounding prong. Appliances whose plugs don't have grounding prongs should work, but it's always a good idea to check with your hotel about the voltage *before* you plug anything in, especially if your lodge uses solar electricity.

TRAVELING EXPENSES

Costa Rica is not as inexpensive for travelers as other Central American countries. Still, you can take a bus to anywhere in the country for under $8, meals cost from $3 to $10, and you can usually find decent hotels for under $50 for two people. If you are determined to spend as little money as possible, visit in May, June, September, or October and take advantage of the off-season rates. Fancy rooms at the beach are often $75 and up. Groceries cost about two-thirds as much as in the United States. According to Tourism Institute statistics, most visitors spend between $75 and $116 per day. However, two penny-pinching people can travel for about $25 a day each, including bus transportation, comfortable lodging (double occupancy), and eating at local *sodas*. Camping out is cheaper still, but you have the inconvenience of hauling around equipment and making sure your tent is guarded at all times. Yet another advantage of visiting community-based lodges is their extremely reasonable prices—usually $25-$45 per person including meals and tours.

CURRENCY

The currency unit is the *colón* (¢). Bills come in denominations of ¢500 to ¢10,000, and coins from 5 to 100 *colones*. The exchange rate as of October 2008 is ¢550 to ¢560 per U.S. $1. The value of the *colón* has been in reference to the U.S. dollar for many years, but if the dollar continues to lose strength compared to the euro, that could change.

CHANGING MONEY

The *tipo de cambio*, the rate at which dollars are being bought and sold on a particular day appears in the daily newspaper.

Traveler's checks: It is increasingly difficult to cash traveler's checks outside banks. So don't forget to cash your traveler's checks when you are in towns that have banks. You must have your passport with you to change travelers checks or cash at banks.

Before you get there: There is no advantage to trying to change dollars to *colones* before you get to Costa Rica.

At the airport: You can change money at the airport banks from 5 a.m. to 8 p.m. There are two ATMs there as well. Ask for the *cajera automática*. You will see money-exchange booths in the baggage claim area at the airport, but they charge hefty commissions. You will get a better rate at the Banco de San José, upstairs in the departure area.

At your hotel: Hotels are authorized to change money for their guests; sometimes their rates are less favorable than the bank rate, but only by a few cents on the dollar and the time you save is worth it.

ATMs: ATMs that work with debit cards are located all over Costa Rica. If you don't have a debit card, order one several weeks before you leave, so that your bank has time to mail it to you.. Be sure you know your PIN, and find out your daily withdrawal limit before you depart. To protect themselves from theft, credit card companies sometimes limit the amount that can be withdrawn abroad, so let them know you will be traveling. You can get the official exchange rate using an ATM, but banks impose a fee every time a card is used at an ATM in a different city or bank, and the bank from which you withdraw cash may charge its own fee. Still, the time you save by using an ATM rather than travelers checks (which also have fees attached) might be worth it.

In the provinces: There are banks in virtually every tourist destination now, with ATMs. Often the provincial banks' process is faster for changing travelers checks.

At San José banks: Banks are open from 9 a.m. to 3 p.m., and some branches stay open until 5 p.m. State-owned banks (Banco de Costa Rica, Banco Nacional de Costa Rica, Banco Popular, Banco de Crédito Agrícola) are more crowded. The many private banks such as Banex, Scotiabank and BAC are quicker, and the money-changing process is simpler.

On the street: Don't risk changing money on the street. A common changer's scam is to pretend to panic and run because "the police are coming"—before you have time to count the *colones* they give you. They're experts in folding bills so that the stack appears larger.

CREDIT CARDS

Most, though not all, tourism businesses accept major credit cards. Visa seems to be the most widely accepted. There is often a surcharge for credit card transactions.

American Express credit cards are often not accepted, but only American Express traveler's checks are accepted at banks.

Credomatic is the agency that issues credit cards in Costa Rica. For stolen cards, call them at 2295-9000, or contact your company directly. For **Visa** cards, call 0-800-011-0030. For **MasterCard**, call 0-800-011-0184.

Special note for Canadians: All branches of **Banco de Costa Rica** (Avenidas 2/Central, Calles 4/6; 2287-9000) and **Banco Nacional de Costa Rica** (Calles 2/4, Avenidas 1/3; 2223-2166) accept cash or traveler's checks in Canadian dollars.

HEALTH PRECAUTIONS

INOCULATIONS

See your doctor before taking any foreign journey to be sure you're up to date on your regular vaccinations (tetanus, polio, measles, pertussis and so on). It's recommendable to get hepatitis A and B. These shots must be started a few months before you go. Check for current recommendations by calling the **Centers for Disease Control** hotline in Atlanta at 877-FYI-TRIP (877-394-9747), or visit cdc.gov/travel.

TRAVELER'S INSURANCE

It's a very good idea to get traveler's insurance before you leave home. These policies are not too expensive and cover medical expenses, trip cancellations, and theft (if you have a police report or a letter from the hotel where you were staying verifying that you were robbed). See insure my trip.com.

WATER

Water is safe to drink in most parts of Costa Rica, but if you feel safer drinking bottled water, it is sold in most supermarkets throughout the country. A handy gadget to have is the SteriPen, a flashlight-sized gizmo that purifies water with UV light. You can stick it in whatever you want to drink, swirl it around for 90 seconds, and all organisms will be gone.

AMOEBAS AND PARASITES

Even though Costa Rica's water is good in most places, visitors traveling in the provinces sometimes have intestinal problems. If symptoms are persistent, they might be due to *amibas* or *giardia*. If you get a strong attack of diarrhea, it's wise to take a stool sample to a local lab to have it analyzed. Put it in a clean glass jar, and deliver it immediately, or just appear at the lab and they will give you the appropriate receptacles to take a sample then and there. Amoebas can't be found in samples that are a few hours old. Your results will be ready the same day, especially if you bring your sample before noon ($6-$8 in advance). If results are negative, take up to three samples. Sometimes the offending organisms are not found the first time. The most dangerous one is *entamoeba histolytica*. This can migrate to your liver and cause damage later.

We have not found that natural methods cure amoebas. Even if you get over your diarrhea, the organisms can still be doing damage to your system unless you've taken the proper medicine. Symptoms often show up as a tendency toward constipation and a feeling of depression and low energy. It's best to take the chemicals and be done with the bugs. Be sure to ask for the literature that goes with the medicine so you'll know about possible side effects.

To avoid bugs when traveling outside San José, stay away from drinks made with local water or ice, and fruits and vegetables that cannot be peeled. See SteriPen info above.

DEHYDRATION

Dehydration can be a problem at the beach and other steamy lowland areas where you sweat a lot, and equally problematic if you suffer from excessive diarrhea or vomiting. Bring a drinking bottle of good water if you hike. The water in green coconuts (*agua de pipa*) is both pure and full of the very same minerals that you lose when you sweat or vomit. *Caldo*, a clear soup with vegetables and chicken or meat, can also help you regain lost liquid and salt, and it is one of the easier foods to get down when you're not feeling well.

DENGUE FEVER

The disease that has caused the most trouble in the last few years is dengue fever, a virus carried by mosquitoes. It begins with a sudden fever of 102° or higher that can last for as long as seven days. Acute pain in the head, muscles, joints, and eyes, and a rash on the chest and back can accompany the fever. Symptoms start five to seven days after being bitten by an infected mosquito of the species *aedes aegypti*, active between dawn and dusk, not after dark. *Aedes aegypti* is a rather large mosquito and has black and white stripes on its legs and back. You should seek medical treatment as soon as symptoms appear. People usually recover from dengue, but if you catch the disease twice it can be life-threatening.

MALARIA

Malaria is not a danger for most travelers to Costa Rica. If you are going to an area where you have heard there has been malaria, you can pick up chloroquine in any Costa Rican pharmacy. Sometimes North American doctors prescribe prophylactic doses of Lariam or Mephaquine, the trade names for mefloquine, which has been known to produce neuropsychiatric effects like panic attacks, convulsions, headaches, and visual and auditory hallucinations that persist months after the last dose. Find out more at geocities.com/thetropics/6913/lariam.htm. The CDC actually recommends chloroquine for visitors to Costa Rica.

SWIMMING POOLS AND RIVERS

Look for any visible signs of pollution before you jump into a river or pool, and always be sure to wash well with soap and water after you come out. To avoid fungus infections in the ears, clean them with rubbing alcohol and a swab after swimming.

INSECTS

Mosquitoes can be a problem, even in breezy San José at night during the dry season. A natural repellent that has been tested to be effective for up to six hours against mosquitoes, sandflies, and *purrujas* is **Cactus Juice Skin and Insect Protectant** (in the U.S.: 877-554-5222; cactusjuicetm.com). If you want DEET, **Repel Insect Repellent Family Formula** (in the U.S.: 800-558-6614; repel.com) is 23% DEET.

Most hotels located where mosquitoes are a problem have screened windows and/or mosquito nets.

On the Atlantic Coast, beware of **sandfly** bites that seem to become infected and grow instead of disappearing. This could be a sign of *papalomoyo* (Leishmaniasis), a disease that can be life-threatening if untreated. See a tropical disease specialist immediately.

Purrujas (no-see-ums) are perhaps the most aggravating of Costa Rican insects. They bite you without your even seeing or feeling them, then the bite itches for days. *Purrujas* like to hang out at the edge of the beach where the sand meets the trees. They seem to be more active at dusk. That means you should wear shoes and socks on the beach for your sunset walk AND apply insect repellent.

Eating lots of garlic and brewer's yeast tablets purportedly makes your blood unpalatable to mosquitoes, flies, and no-see-ums.

Some people have serious allergic reactions to **ant** bites. A person having an allergic reaction might begin to itch all over, then turn red and swell up. If that happens, get to a hospital as soon as possible. In the worst scenario, a person's throat swells up, causing asphyxiation. To avoid ant bites, wear closed shoes whenever you're in the jungle or on the beach.

Africanized bees have worked their way north from Brazil, and can attack humans with fatal results if the bees' nests are disturbed. Bee colonies are ten times denser in hot, dry areas than in rainforests. If attacked, run as fast as you can in a zigzag direction, or jump into water. Bees don't see well over distances. Never try to take cover; don't crawl or climb into a precarious position from which you cannot make a quick exit. Throw something light-colored over your head to protect your eyes and nose; keep your mouth closed. If you know you are allergic to bee stings, talk with your doctor before you go to Costa Rica and carry the proper medication with you. You might want to buy a self-injector kit for bee stings, available in pharmacies in the U.S. with a prescription.

SNAKES

Although not all snakes in Costa Rica are dangerous, a few are potentially deadly: fer-de-lance, eyelash vipers, bushmasters, and rattlesnakes. To recognize these snakes should you run across one in the wild, visit the serpentariums in Turrialba, Monteverde, Sarapiquí, Grecia, La Fortuna and El Castillo, Dominical, or Buena Vista Lodge in Guanacaste. If you are bitten, stay calm and head to the nearest health post for a series of antivenin shots. According to the *Tico Times*, you shouldn't waste time trying to suck the venom out cowboy-style; experts say it doesn't help. And definitely don't use a knife or razor to enlarge an opening in your skin: Bleeding and risk of infection will only make matters worse. You have four hours to get to a clinic from when you were bitten before tissue loss sets in. To avoid bites, wear thick hiking boots (even when crossing streams) and do not touch branches or plants without looking first.

ACCOMMODATIONS IN COSTA RICA

How we list hotel rates: Our hotel rates are based on double occupancy (unless otherwise indicated) and include a 16.4 percent government tax. Most hotels give their rates without the taxes, so amounts in this book might appear to be more than those stated in hotel advertising or on their websites. At the bottom of most website price lists, it will say whether taxes are included or not. Prices change; although we try to be as accurate as possible, don't take it on faith that a hotel still charges what we said it charges—always ask. Rates will vary if you are alone or in a group, or if meals are included.

Reservations: Make reservations three months ahead at Christmas or Easter. Most hotels require that you guarantee your reservation with a credit card or a deposit.

Rates to expect: You can find clean, fairly comfortable rooms almost anywhere for $20 to $30 for two. Atmosphere costs more, getting you into the $50-$150 range. If you can afford them, there are plenty of places with great atmosphere, equipment, and service.

Noise pollution: Our main complaint about many hotels, even some expensive ones, is that you're often subjected to noise pollution from somebody's high-powered sound system. The usual source is a nearby dance hall or neighbors with a loud radio. A place can seem perfectly *tranquilo* when you arrive during the day; the thumping disco across the river only comes on at night. The best solution is to get up and dance. The sounds of trucks and motorcycles rumbling by during the day might not be a problem, but it can keep you awake at night, so be aware of your hotel's distance from the road.

How many words for hotel are there in Spanish? We should clarify the meaning of various terms referring to lodging.

Hotels usually have more than one story, though not always. *Cabinas* are the most common form of lodging at the beach or in the mountains. They are usually connected in rows or duplexes, roughly corresponding to what a North American would call a "motel." However, here *motel* refers to a small number of establishments that couples use for clandestine romantic trysts. Motels rent by the hour. *Villas, bungalows, cabañas,* and *chalets* are fancy cabinas, usually separate from one another. *Pensiones* and *hospedajes* are usually converted houses, and often serve family-style meals. A *posada* is an inn. An *albergue* is a lodge, usually in the forest or the mountains, and most often oriented toward ecotourism.

Youth hostels are also called *albergues* or, less commonly, *hostales*. Most of them are simply hotels and lodges that give substantial discounts to International Youth Hostel Federation members. Homestays offer the opportunity of a more authentic Tico experience. If you study Spanish in San José or at schools in beach or mountain locations, you can choose to live with a Tico family fairly inexpensively. See the listings for Spanish schools near the end of this chapter. **Bell's Home Hospitality** (2225-4752; home stay.thebells.org, homestay@racsa.co.cr) is another great way to hook up with Tico families and get comfortable accommodations in the $40-$50 price range. See their listing near the end of the San José chapter (Chapter Six). If you have young children, homestays might be a good alternative because many Tico homes have children of their own. Homestays and inexpensive locally owned lodgings in northern Costa Rica can be found at costaricanruraltours.com.

Discounts: Beach and mountain hotels often give discounts in the green season (May to November). Weekly and monthly rates are common as well.

House or villa rentals: See the *Tico Times* for listings, or ask at a local *pulpería*; make sure that you understand what the security situation is at any place you rent on your own. For listings of vacation rentals in Costa Rica: vrbo.com (Villa Rental By Owner), greatrentals.com, unusualvilla rentals.com, villascostarica.com. stayincostarica.com, haciedapinilla.com, and bosquedelcabo.com. Villas on these sites usually range from $1000 to $5000 per week. Less expensive beach and jungle rentals can be found on the Caribbean coast at caribesurrealestate.com.

Shower temperature: We have four categories for telling you about water temperature in the shower when we describe a hotel.

Cold water means just that—no hot water. However, showers at places near the beach are often "solar-heated" naturally, and it feels good to take a cool shower instead of a hot one.

Heated water refers to an electric device that warms the shower water as it comes out of the showerhead. *Note:* These contraptions are usually set to come on when the water is turned on. You should not have to turn them on yourself. Check how yours works while you are dry and have your shoes on. You don't want to be fooling around with it while you are wet and barefoot in the shower. If there is too little water pressure, the little buggers become too hot and can burn out, so be careful; the more you open the tap, the cooler they get. Usually they make for pretty limp, lukewarm showers.

Hot water refers to water heated by a hot-water tank.

Solar-heated water indicates the use of solar-heating devices, often something as simple as black tubing on the roof, which will mean heated showers in the afternoon. A real solar heating system will have hot water 24/7.

Natural ventilation refers to places at the beach that, because of their location or construction, take advantage of ocean breezes and don't need fans.

NOTES FOR SENIOR TRAVELERS

Older travelers will certainly be able to find good company, comfortable traveling conditions and lodging, with the assurance that excellent health care is available if they should need it.

Note: The bad condition of the sidewalks is a real problem in many towns, and much care must be taken by pedestrians.

Elderhostel (800-454-5768; elderhostel.org), an American organization that sponsors inexpensive and interesting trips for people 55 years of age or over, includes Costa Rica in its itinerary.

NOTES FOR TRAVELERS WITH DISABILITIES

In 1996, activists for disabled rights won a victory when legislation was enacted that guarantees education, social services, and jobs for all disabled people in Costa Rica. Because of the 1996 legislation, many recently constructed or remodeled rooms do have features that make them at least somewhat accessible. Hotels usually will mention accessibility on their websites. These rooms used to be a rarity in Costa Rica, but now there are too many to list here.

The following three categories classify tours and lodging for travelers with disabilities:

1. *Adapted:* a person with a disability could use the installations without any help. The only place that fits this category is the **Hotel Real Com-**

fort in Santa Ana. All rooms have signs in Braille, and offer the choice between an adapted room with a bath or a rolling shower. A phone for deaf people is also available.

2. *Accessible:* no steps (ramped) and enough space to go everywhere without help: **Poás Volcano, La Selva Biological Station** in Puerto Viejo de Sarapiquí, **TuRuBaRi Adventure Park** near Turrucares and Orotina, and **INBio Park** in Santo Domingo de Heredia. Many hotels claim to be accessible, but you have to be specific with them to make sure they have what you need.

3. *Accessible with help*: one or two steps at the entrance, steep ramps, but enough space to get to bathrooms and rooms for a person in a wheelchair.

The following tourist attractions are in this third category:

SAN JOSÉ MUSEUMS   **Gold Museum** (steep ramp); **Museo Nacional** (one step in one of the exhibition rooms); **Museum of Costa Rican Art**, La Sabana Park (one step)

TOURS AND TOURIST ATTRACTIONS   **Café Britt**, Heredia; **Parque Central and church**, Heredia; **Zoo Ave**, La Garita; **Oxcart Factory** and souvenir shop, Sarchí; **Central Park and Basílica**, Cartago; **Lankester Gardens**, Cartago; **Irazú Volcano**, near Cartago; **Rainforest Aerial Tram**, Braulio Carrillo; **Tabacón Resort** (using the left-hand side entrance), La Fortuna; and **Arenal Observatory Lodge**, La Fortuna; **Restaurant Ram Luna**, above San José.

Vaya con Silla de Ruedas (8391-5045, phone/fax: 2454-2810; gowith-wheelchairs.com, vayacon@racsa.co.cr) is a transportation and tour company with an ADA-approved van with elevator, three wheelchair stations, front and back air conditioners, and room for friends and companions. They custom-design trips to accessible places and their website has many links to other interesting sites for disabled travelers.

Unfortunately, very little has been done to make the streets easier for people with disabilities and parents pushing strollers. Sidewalks are often in deplorable condition, some curbs are more than a foot high, and many roads do not have sidewalks at all, forcing everyone into the street. Despite all this, several people with disabilities have told us that they felt conditions were better for them here than in the U.S. because of the climate, the relatively low cost of quality health care and hospitalization, and the low cost of maids and other helpers. Many neighborhoods do have sidewalks and downtown San José has some sidewalk ramps at intersections, but they are often too high to be helpful.

NOTES FOR TRAVELING WITH CHILDREN

Ticos love children. You won't get dirty looks for bringing them along—only smiles and a helping hand when needed. Both men and women seem to be naturally sensitive to the needs of children, whether it is to spontaneously help you lift them on or off the bus, or to include the kids in conversation. If you have a baby (especially a fair-haired one), be prepared to be stopped in the street while people admire your little treasure.

Entry/exit parental authorization letters: If you are traveling with a child 18 or under, one or both of whose parents will not be in the country, you must get a notarized letter from the absent parent(s) giving you permission to enter Costa Rica and take the child out of Costa Rica again. (Even if you are one of the parents, you need a letter from the other if he or she is absent.) If the child was born in Costa Rica, you must present a variety of documents, even if the child has a foreign passport. To check on these regulations, call the Costa Rican embassy nearest you.

What to bring: When preparing for your trip here, you should pack a junior first-aid kit with baby aspirin, thermometer, vitamins, diarrhea medicine, oral rehydration solution in case of serious dehydration, sunblock, bug repellent, tissues, wipes, cold medicine, aloe vera for sunburns, and anti-itch cream.

Pack extra plastic bags for dirty diapers, cloth diapers for emergencies, baby sunscreen, a portable stroller and papoose-style backpack, easy-to-wash clothes, swimsuits, a floppy hat to wear in the water, a life jacket, beach toys, and picture books relating to Costa Rica. Some car rental agencies, like Adobe (adobecar.com) provide car seats.

Travel tips: Try to plan a flight during your child's nap time, but feed a baby during take-off and landing to relieve pressure in the ears. If you are pregnant or breast-feeding, be sure to stay well hydrated during the flight. Bring everything you need on board—diapers, food, toys, books, and extra clothing for kids and parents alike. It's also helpful to carry a few new toys, snacks, and books as treats if boredom sets in.

Pace your trip so your child can adapt to all the changes in routine. Don't plan exhausting whirlwind tours, and keep travel time to a minimum. You'll be a lot more comfortable if you splurge on a rental car rather than taking buses, at least until your kids are over seven. Our seven- and nine-year-olds did great on bus trips. The thing that really bothered them was getting too hot, so we'd try to take early-morning or late-afternoon rides. Seek out zoos, parks, plazas, outdoor entertainment, and short excursions to amuse your child. Bathrooms are hard to find sometimes, and it is perfectly acceptable for little ones to pee in the bushes or even against a building if you are in the city. Disposable diapers are readily available for trips, but you won't find many places with changing tables. A portable changing pad comes in handy. People will help you find the best place to do what has to be done.

Activities: During the Costa Rican summer (January to March), there are "summer" activities for children at the **Simon Bolivar Zoo** (2256-0012) and its sister institution, the **Santa Ana Conservation Center** (2282-8434), **INBioparque** in Santo Tomas de Heredia (2507-8107), and the **National Museum** (2257-1433 ext. 223). There are children's theater performances in San José on Sundays and some arts-and-crafts stuff in the parks. Playgrounds, like Central American plumbing, seem to get trashed and ruined overnight. The Friday and Sunday editions of the daily *La Nación*'s *"Viva"* section and the "Weekend" section of the *Tico Times* list whatever is happening for children over the weekend.

One place most kids will enjoy is the **Parque Nacional de Diversiones** (open daily November through February, 9 a.m. to 7 p.m.; Wednesday to Sunday the rest of the year, 9 a.m. to 5 p.m.; 242-9200), a large, clean, and well-run amusement park in La Uruca, west of San José. It has many rides, including a small Ferris wheel, two rollercoasters, and the *Pacuare*, where six "rafters" in a round, inflatable boat go down a 150-foot slide into a tranquil lagoon. Expect to get wet. About $8.50 will entitle your kid to all the rides he or she can take in a day, as well as admittance to **Pueblo Antiguo**, a model of old-time Costa Rican life, where dance and theater performances are often held on weekends; actors wear traditional *campesino* attire and become the citizens of Pueblo Antiguo. All proceeds go to support the Children's Hospital. There are plenty of places to eat there, but they are all of the greasy fast-food variety, so bring your own snacks and juices.

The park is located two kilometers west of Hospital México, the large building you see on the left as you leave the western suburbs of San José heading for Puntarenas. To find it, you must get off the main highway at the Juan Pablo II rotunda and take the access road that runs parallel to the highway directly in front of the hospital. Or take the "Hospital México" bus.

San José converted its castle-like penitentiary into a well-designed **Children's Museum** (open weekdays, 8 a.m. to 4:30 p.m.; weekends, 9:30 a.m. to 5 p.m.; closed Monday, Christmas, and Holy Week; admission $2, children under 18, $1.50; at the extreme north end of Calle 4; 2258-4929; museocr.com). There is a genuine airplane cockpit to play in, and a couple of flight simulators. Another large room has been turned into a rainforest. There are many other exciting interactive exhibits. (You have to cross a pretty bad neighborhood to get there, so spring for a cab.) You can read about the excellent Gold, Jade, Natural and Art Museums in the San José chapter.

Our favorite **beaches for kids**—those that are shady and have gentle waters—include: Bahía Junquillal Recreation Area in northern Guanacaste and Carrillo in southern Guanacaste, Ballena National Marine Park in Uvita, and the third beach at Manuel Antonio (though it's a 20-minute walk through the park to get there). The beaches are beautiful and lined with palms in Talamanca, but the currents can be so strong that nothing more than wading or playing in knee-deep water is suggested. At low tide in Playa Chiquita (south of Puerto Viejo), Drake Bay, Dominical, Playa Santa Teresa, and Montezuma, there are tidepools that are fun for kids to play in.

To prepare your six- to twelve-year-olds, order *Let's Discover Costa Rica*, a bilingual, 64-page book full of activities like cut-out-and-assemble mobiles, mazes, and paint-by-number pictures, all woven into a story of intercultural friendship. Order from Avie Gingold ($7, including shipping; dylanandpaco@aol.com).

NOTES FOR WOMEN

Costa Rica is one of the safest countries for women travelers in Latin America, given its peaceful nature and well-developed tourism industry. Although domestic violence is, unfortunately, all too common, the sexual assault rate is much lower than in the U.S. However, as in any area, women traveling alone must use caution, especially at night. Be aware of which neighborhoods have a reputation for trouble. Take advantage of programs like **A Safe Passage** (8365-9678; costaricabustickets.com, rchoice@racsa.co.cr).

This is a country where *machismo* is still considered normal male behavior even though the Costa Rican National Assembly has the second highest percentage of female legislators in the world. An unaccompanied woman should disregard the flirtatious comments many Tico men will call out, such as *mi amor* (my love), *machita* (if you are a blond), or *guapa* (pretty). If they are farther away, they hiss as a woman passes by. It's annoying, but not dangerous. The best policy is to ignore them and keep walking.

Ticos can be compelling in their professions of eternal devotion. Whether they are married or single does not seem to have much to do with it. Take anything that is said with a grain of salt. Ticos often regard foreign women as easy conquests. But, as in most other Latin countries, they look for *la Virgen Purísima* when making a lasting commitment.

NOTES FOR MEN

Prostitution is legal in Costa Rica, and prostitutes are given medical tests on a regular basis. Some prostitutes have been found to be carrying AIDS. Prostitutes have been known to gang up on men in the street and rob them. There have also been cases of men being drugged and robbed after having invited women to their apartment or room—or just for a drink. Be careful, guys.

Sexual exploitation of minors has also become a problem in the last ten years, and Costa Rica has enacted severe laws to punish anyone caught paying or giving any kind of economic benefit to underage persons for sexual favors. Call Patronato Nacional de la Infancia (PANI, 2221-1212) for more information.

Costa Rican women are known for their loveliness and intelligence. Ticas are also good at being *chineadoras*, i.e., taking care of men as if they were babies. Many foreign men have sought out Costa Rican women for relationships. Although we know of many successful intercultural marriages, we urge our readers to pay close attention to deeply ingrained cultural differences that can cause major communication problems when the idyllic glow wears off. Also divorce is much more complicated legally and financially than in the U.S.

NOTES FOR TRAVELING WITH PETS

Dogs are not regarded with the same affection as they are in North America and Europe, and are used as guards rather than as pets. Most Costa Ricans are scared to death of dogs.

Another problem might be finding a temporary place to stay with your pet. In general, bed and breakfasts are more willing to take animals.

To learn the current requirements for bringing pets to Costa Rica, go to costarica.com and search for "pets."

NOTES FOR STUDENT TRAVELERS

If you are interested in adventure, plus the opportunity to understand the interface between conservation, community development, and ecotourism, or tropical biology and ecology, there could be no more interesting place to visit than today's Costa Rica. The community-based ecotourism projects, mentioned in the introduction and throughout the text, are inexpensive to visit, give you a real taste of the culture, and are small enough for you to really connect with people. You might be able to find a way to get credit for your stay. Many universities and colleges offer study/travel options in Costa Rica.

See "Accommodations in Costa Rica" section earlier in this chapter for details on youth hostels, and check out the study-abroad options near the end of this chapter. The U.S. **Peace Corps** and **Habitat for Humanity** also have projects here. Volunteer opportunities are mentioned throughout the book.

NOTES FOR GAY AND LESBIAN TRAVELERS

Costa Rica continues to enjoy a steady increase in gay and lesbian visitors. This is in part due to the social tolerance exhibited here, at least when compared to other Latin American countries. But keep in mind, this is a small, mostly Catholic country and the gay lifestyle is primarily discreet in nature.

Gay rights have only recently been allowed out of the closet. After a 1995 police raid on the popular gay disco Deja Vu, the owners filed suit and, with a legal victory, opened the door for a more public gay rights movement. In 1999, protesters blocked the arrival of a bus of gay tourists who were headed for a festival in Manuel Antonio. After a lot of press coverage and apologies by key officials, the controversy faded away.

However, both gay and straight men are vulnerable to crime that can occur when they pick up people. In February 2003, Richard Stern, director of the Costa Rica–based Agua Buena Human Rights Association, issued a statement warning visiting gay men about the possible violence against gays in Costa Rica. "While 99 percent of all gay men in Costa Rica are honest and trustworthy, serious events have occurred in recent weeks which have motivated us to publish this warning." According to the *Tico Times*, a police spokesman estimated that 30 gay foreign men have been murdered in the last 15 years, and that the number of cases has increased since 2000. "Costa Rican men face the same risk, but often are more aware of their environment," said the police official. "Foreign men may be more adventurous and less careful." The main motive is robbery, according to the police. Victims are targeted in bars or parks known as "pick-up" spots. The assailant usually gains the trust of the victim over a few hours, days, or weeks.

Both Agua Buena and the Center for the Promotion of Human Rights in Central America recommend the following precautions:

• Avoid excessive consumption of alcohol or drugs when visiting nightspots.

- Avoid Parque Nacional and La Sabana park, which are very dangerous after dark.
- Use caution if someone approaches you or if you decide to invite
  someone to visit you. Meet their friends first and ask for home and
  work phone numbers. Make sure that numbers are valid before making further plans. If the person does not have a phone, don't go.

Gay and lesbian businesses are springing up throughout the Central
Valley. (See Chapter Six for gay and lesbian bars and discos in San José.)

You shouldn't have any trouble in other areas of the country. When
checking in to your hotel as a couple, you should both be at the desk so
they know you're staying together. Managers get nervous when they see
unknown people in their hotel. Many couples are going to Costa Rica for
their weddings. See gaymarriageworld.com.

For hotels, **Colours** in the western suburb of Rohrmosher remains the
city's most established exclusively gay/lesbian hotel. They have a similar
hotel in Florida, and their U.S.-based travel agency (colours.net) can make
reservations at Colours and throughout Costa Rica. **Hotel Kekoldi**
(kekoldi.com) is a midrange alternative in San José's historic Barrio Amon.
Or try the inexpensive **Casas Agua Buena** (2280-3548; aguabuena.org/
casabuena/index.html) in San Pedro, San José's university district.

Most gay and lesbian travelers head for the Pacific beach of Manuel
Antonio, where **Casa Blanca Hotel** (an exclusively gay and lesbian facility) is a favorite spot. La Playita, the tiny private beach just past the northern point of Manuel Antonio, has long been a nude gay beach, but it is now
patrolled by police because the new hotel Arenas del Mar wants to ensure a
more sedate atmosphere for its guests. It is not accessible at high tide. **Casitas LazDivas** (2656-0295; lazdivaz.com) provides a gay and lesbian oasis
on Playa Sámara in Guanacaste.

For up-to-date gay and lesbian information, go to gaytravelcostarica.
com and mujerymujer.com.

SPECIAL WAYS TO VISIT COSTA RICA

TRAVEL PLANNERS SPECIALIZING IN
COMMUNITY BASED ECOTOURISM

The following companies will help you with the sometimes-complicated
logistics of visiting rural community tourism destinations. They provide
bilingual naturalist guides, drivers, rental cars, airport pick-up and drop-off,
and will include more conventional ecotourism destinations as well.

ACTUAR
phone/fax:
2248-9470, 877-922-8827
actuarcostarica.com
info@actuarcostarica.com
Tours and connections to commu-
nity-based ecotourism. emphasizing
conservation and interactions with
local people.

ACTUAR CONSERVacations
877-922-8827
keytocostarica.com
beatrice@keytocostarica.com
Customized tours that include com-
munity-based destinations, planned
by the author of this book. Itiner-
aries are designed to fit your inter-
ests, budget and time frame.

Cultourica
2249-0687, 2249-1271
cultourica.com
cultourica@racsa.co.cr
Low-cost nature tours that visit co-
operatives and other community-
based tourism projects,

emphasizing community develop-
ment and interactions with local
people.

Selva Mar
2771-4582
exploringcostarica.com
selvamar@ice.co.cr
Trekking and birdwatching, espe-
cially in the Southern Zone.

Horizontes
San José, CR
2222-2022, fax: 2255-4513
horizontes.com
info@horizontes.com
Natural, cultural, and educational
tours to all locations; hiking tours.
Can arrange conventions, seminars.

Simbiosis Tours
2290-8646
turismoruralcr.com
cooprena@racsa.co.cr
Tours and connections to
community-based ecotourism.

LANGUAGE-LEARNING VACATIONS

Many people like the idea of learning Spanish on their Costa Rican vacation. The excellent language schools listed here offer a variety of experiences. Most schools arrange for students to live with Costa Rican families to immerse themselves in the language, but some have guesthouses where students can stay if they want more privacy. Most schools set up weekend sightseeing trips for participants. Intensive conversational methods are used for four to six hours a day in programs lasting from one week to several months. Students are placed according to ability. Programs range from $200 to $500 per week, $1000 to $2500 per month, including room and board. Most schools give academic credit.

Spanish schools provide an excellent opportunity to learn about Costa Rican culture and often place students in volunteer activities so that they can practice what they have learned.

Many schools have urban and rural campuses so you can combine language learning with a beach or mountain vacation. We offer the most salient features below.

CENTRAL VALLEY

Alajuela:

Instituto de Cultura y Lengua Costarricense
2458-8485, fax: 2458-8473
iclc.ws
info@iclc.ws
Includes afternoon classes in Central American issues, Costa Rican art, literature, and history, in addition to Latin dance, music, and cooking. Volunteer placements and programs for teens 14-17.

La Guácima de Alajuela and Playa Sámara:

Rancho de Español
phone/fax: 2438-0071, in the U.S.: 978-633-7500
ranchodeespanol.com
ranchesp@racsa.co.cr
One week at the beach during the four-week program. Special classes for children and teens. Spanish for Spanish teachers.

La Trinidad de Ciudad Colón:

El Marañon
2249-1271, fax: 2249-1761
cultourica.com
cultourica@racsa.co.cr
Combines 40 hours of Spanish with an inexpensive two-week tour to community-based ecotourism destinations.

Orosi:

Montaña Linda Youth Hostel and Spanish School
2533-3640, fax: 2533-1292
montanalinda.com
info@montanalinda.com
Very inexpensive classes; students choose direction and set the pace. Nice country town.

Santa Ana and San José:

Centro Lingüístico Conversa
2221-7649, in North America: 888-669-1664

conversa.net

info@conversa.net

Maximum four students per class. Six-acre hilltop campus in Santa Ana with pool, volleyball, basketball, and tennis courts, and plenty of hammocks. On-campus housing is in family suites or six-bedroom lodge. There is also a campus in San José. Special program for retirees includes field trips, cultural events, and fine dining. Summer program for high school students. Online courses also available.

BEACHES AND MOUNTAINS

Arenal, Dominical, and Turrialba:

Adventure Education Center

in North America: 800-237-2730

adventurespanishschool.com

main@adventurespanishschool.com

Midweek and weekend adventures include kayaking, river rafting, mountain biking, and snorkeling trips. Medical Spanish. Special programs for kids kindergarten to 13 years old. Includes surfing lessons for teens 14-17.

Heredia and Playa Sámara:

Intercultura Costa Rica

2260-8480, in Samara: 2656-0127, in North America: 866-978-6668

samaralanguageschool.com

info@interculturacostarica.com

Classes include Latin dance, music, and cooking; there are also cultural exchanges with local students.

Jacó:

Escuela del Mundo (School of the World)

2643-2462, in the U.S.: 404-935-4251

schooloftheworld.org

info@schooloftheworld.org

Combines Spanish study with classes in yoga, surfing, art, and digital photography. Excellent photos on their website. Nice lodging for students.

Manuel Antonio, Heredia, and San José:

Costa Rican Spanish Institute (COSI)

2234-1001, fax: 2253-2117

cosi.co.cr

office@cosi.co.cr

Offers a beach and rainforest program in Manuel Antonio, as well as a teen summer camp that takes place at a private high school in Heredia and includes homestays, tours, and volunteer opportunities.

Manuel Antonio:
Escuela de Idiomas D'Amore
phone/fax: 2777-0233 in North America: 818-434-7290
academiaadamore.com
info@academiadamore.com
Stunning views from classrooms, two-week minimum, homestays in Quepos. Weekly field trips focus on social and environmental issues.

Monteverde, San Joaquín de Flores de Heredia, and Playa Flamingo:
Centro Panamericano de Idiomas
2265-6306, 2265-7382, fax: 2265-6866 in the U.S.: 877-373-3116
cpi-edu.com
info@cpi-edu.com
Special programs in medical Spanish and Spanish in the social sciences. PADI certification is combined with Spanish at Playa Flamingo; Monteverde campus students can volunteer in the cloud forest or art center. Three-week summer camp for teens 14 to 17, and a soccer camp with homestays.

Nicoya and Playa Sámara:
Instituto Guanacasteco de Idiomas
phone/fax: 2686-6948
spanishcostarica.com
info@spanishcostarica.com
Never more than two to four students per class, and a new seven day teen summer program featuring tours to Manuel Antonio and Carrara National Parks.

Playa Grande, Arenal, and San José:
Kalexma Language Institute
2290-2624, 2290-7606, fax: 2231-0638
kalexma.com
instructor@kalexma.com
In addition to inexpensive classes, they offer a four-week language and travel option, with one week near San José, one week at Arenal volcano, and two weeks at Playa Grande in Guanacaste for a minimum of five people.

San Isidro de El General, Uvita de Osa, and Osa Peninsula:

SEPA

2770-1457, fax: 2771-5586

spanish-school-costarica.com

info@spanish-school-costarica.com

Volunteer placements; environmental education and Spanish for adults and kids.

Tamarindo:

WAYRA Institute

2653-0617, phone/fax: 2653-0359

spanish-wayra.co.cr

info@spanish-wayra.co.cr

Inexpensive. Housing with other students or with families; school is 150 meters from the beach, and offers a Spanish and surf program.

SAN JOSÉ

Comunicare

2281-0432, phone/fax: 2224-4473

comunicare-cr.com

info@comunicare-cr.com

In San Pedro, a ten-minute walk from the University of Costa Rica. Inexpensive courses for high school and college students, medical students, and tourists. Special three-week courses in Spanish and environmental studies, Central American studies, or women and society in Central America, with field trips during the third week. Discounts with International Student ID.

Forester Instituto Internacional

2225-3155, 2225-1649, 2225-0135, fax: 2225-9236, in the U.S.: 305-767-1663

fores.com

forester@racsa.co.cr

Special classes for children and teens, with excursions three days a week. Free Latin dance classes daily.

ICADS, Institute for Central American Development Studies

2225-0508, fax: 2234-1337

icads.org

info@icads.org

Four-week courses include studies in sustainable development, human rights, environmental issues, gender issues in Latin America, and indigenous and Afro-Caribbean culture in Costa Rica. Located in the quiet suburb of Curridabat on the east side of San José. Field trips to a women's cooperative, a medicinal plant farm, and an indigenous center. Volunteering in any of 40 placements.

ILISA, Instituto Latinoamericano de Idiomas
2280-0700, in North America: 800-454-7248
ilisa.com
Spanish for fun, or for your career. Lectures on national parks, Costa Rican history, society, and culture. Special programs for families, doctors, educators, therapists, and psychologists. Nannies available for small kids.

Intensa
2281-1818, fax: 2253-4337, in North America: 866-277-1352
intensa.com
info@intensa.com
Their Spanish and fine arts program includes trips to the theater, symphony, and art museum, plus a Tortuga Island tour.

IPEE, Instituto Profesional de Español para Extranjeros
2283-7731, fax: 2225-7860
ipee.com
pee@racsa.co.cr
Medical and business Spanish, Latin American literature, Spanish for Spanish teachers. Located in Curridabat.

Mesoamérica
2253-3195, fax: 2234-7682
mesoamericaonline.net
OurDirector@mesoamericaonline.net
Their $75 one-day Survival Spanish course includes tips on customs and travel. Inexpensive.

STUDY PROGRAMS
Spanish, architecture and planning, women's studies, Latin American culture, politics, economics, literature, music, dance, tropical biology, ecology, international relations, international business—you can study nearly any-

thing in Costa Rica. There are many options for university-level students who want to spend a semester or a year here, as well as shorter seminars for nonstudents. All programs require advance planning, so start thinking about it early. Also, since there are two decidedly different seasons, choose your months according to your preferred weather.

Many of the projects listed here, as well as some of the Spanish courses above, provide opportunities for volunteering. This is a great and inexpensive way to see the real Costa Rica.

Associated Colleges of the Midwest, Friends World College, University of California, University of Kansas, and **State University of New York** are among the many universities that send students to Costa Rica. Your college probably does, too, or can coordinate with an existing program. Check out **studyabroad.com** for a complete list of options with handy links to each program's web page.

Students in the Spanish program at the **University of Costa Rica** (2207-5634; spanishclasses.ucr.ac.cr) may attend lectures and cultural events and interact with native speakers on campus. Beginner, intermediate, and advanced levels are offered in one-month sessions.

The **University for Peace** (2205-9000; upeace.org, info@upeace.org), founded by the United Nations in 1980 and located on a beautiful tract of forested farmland in Villa Colón, southwest of San José, is the world's only truly international university. It offers master's degrees in international law and human rights; natural resources and sustainable development; media, conflict and peace; environmental security and peace; gender and peace-building; international law and the settlement of disputes: and international peace studies.

The **Monteverde Institute** (2645-5053; mvinstitute.org) offers unique courses in which architects and planners, biologists, ecologists, and those interested in public health can use the Monteverde forests and communities as laboratories for practical, hands-on learning experiences. Professors can collaborate with the institute to create courses, or individuals can sign up on their own. The institute also coordinates volunteer work in the zone.

Proyecto Campanario (2258-5778; campanario.org) runs rainforest conservation camps for teachers and families in the summers and a professional development course in Costa Rican Habitats and Culture for university students and teachers from its rainforest reserve on a beautiful cove in the Osa Peninsula. Campanario also accepts volunteers.

The **Organization for Tropical Studies** (2524-0607, in the U.S.: 919-684-5774; ots.duke.edu) is a consortium of universities and research institutions dedicated to education, investigation, and conservation in the tropics. They offer tropical ecology courses for all levels at their research stations in La Selva, Palo Verde, and Wilson Gardens, as well as undergraduate semester-abroad programs in tropical biology, and two-week tropical biology field camps for the general public.

The **Institute for Central American Development Studies** (2225-0508; icads.org, info@icads.org) was formed to educate first-worlders about Central America through hands-on experience in order to gain insight into current social and economic realities and their effect on women, the poor, and the environment. ICADS has a semester-abroad study program, including coursework and structured internship opportunities in Costa Rica and Nicaragua. One program is devoted solely to resource management and sustainable development. ICADS won the Iberoamerican award for Excellence in Education in 2006.

Costa Rica Rainforest Outward Bound (in the U.S.: 800-676-2018; crrobs.org, enrollment@crrobs.org) has students learn kayaking, rafting, surfing, and Spanish, living with local families, and spending two days alone in the wilderness. They offer week-long adventures for adults.

La Suerte and Ometepe Biological Field Stations (in the U.S.: 305-666-9932; lasuerte.org, info@lasuerte.org) offer undergraduate and graduate studies in primate ecology, ornithology, rainforest art, dance, medicinal plant ecology, and related subjects from their forest reserves in Costa Rica and Nicaragua.

Global Routes (in the U.S.: 413-585-8895; globalroutes.org, mail@globalroutes.org) is committed to strengthening global community by designing three- to five-week community-service/cross-cultural-exchange programs for high school and college students.

Artists and musicians will want to know about **Editus Academia de las Artes** (Avenida 9, Calle 31, three blocks east of Santa Teresita Church; 2253-7472; edituscr.com, academia@edituscr.com). Set in an old mansion in Barrio Escalante, this innovative art and music school was founded by the members of three-time Grammy award–winning instrumental trio, Editus. "With no barriers between the classic and the contemporary, our educational process is immersed in the creativity and improvisation that characterize modern art."

DENTAL VACATIONS

You'd love to go to Costa Rica but you've got too many dental bills? Why not get your dental work done here? The money you save could pay for your ticket. Costa Rican dentists are well-trained and professional, and charge a fraction of what you'd pay at home. For instance, a porcelain crown costs $350, as opposed to $900 in the U.S. Board-certified dentists and prices are listed at arrivacostarica.com.

MEDICAL VACATIONS

For many years Costa Rica has gained fame as a destination for **elective surgery** like face-lifts, liposuctions, and cosmetic dental procedures that are not covered by regular health insurance. Experienced doctors, low prices, and luxurious post-op recovery facilities offer a truly transformational experience. See **arrivacostarica.com** for listings of doctors, procedures and prices.

Now more and more foreigners are opting to do **non-elective surgery** in Costa Rica as well. Those who need hip and knee replacements, angioplasty, etc. and cannot afford medical insurance have found that they can be treated here for a fraction of what they would be charged in the U.S, and the savings can be put toward a tropical vacation as they recover.

San Jose's **Clinica Biblica** (hcbinternational.com) gives each of their international patients a personal health care assistant (HCA) who helps with immigration procedures, organizing medical appointments and consultations, handling all hospital paperwork, and coordinating phone and e-mail contact between patients and family members. The price also includes transportation to and from the airport, hotel and hospital rooms, and nursing care as the patient recovers. Clinica Biblica has been awarded accreditation stating that it meets or exceeds the most stringent international standards. **Clinica Catolica** in the northeastern suburb of Guadalupe, and **Hospital CIMA** in the western suburb of Santa Ana are in the process of qualifying for the same certification. Within these high standards, a knee replacement costs about $11,000 in Costa Rica as opposed to $45,000 in a U.S. hospital. Laser eye surgery costs $1800 compared to $5000 in the U.S. Similar procedures done in India might be a bit less expensive, but getting there will cost much more, making the Costa Rican procedure less expensive on the whole. The down side might be for some that it is more difficult to sue for malpractice here than in the U.S. The lack of malpractice insurance, lower wages paid to workers and the lower cost of equipment all go together to account for the lower costs.

SENIOR CARE

Those who need short- or long-term care or day care for seniors will want to know about **Finca Futuro Verde** (fincafuturoverde.com) in Rincon de Salas, near Grecia in the Central Valley. They have several rooms for seniors and are building one-bedroom garden apartments for assisted living.

NATURAL HEALTH VACATIONS

Costa Rica has many places to go for relaxation and healing. They are listed in the various geographical sections of the book. Below we list just a few of the more memorable ones:

Xandari Plantation Inn (xandari.com), known for its New Age architecture and its delightful garden spa, now has a sister hotel in Esterrilos Este on the Pacific Coast, the equally luxurious **Xandari Beach Resort. Pura Vida Spa** (puravidaspa.com) in the mountains above Alajuela brings yoga and growth workshops to Costa Rica and has weeklong wellness packages.

On the way to Arenal, **Hotel Villa Blanca** (villablanca-costarica) has its own **Serenity Spa. Finca Luna Nueva** (fincalunanuevalodge.com) is a great place to relax and heal with organic, biodynamic foods and a solar powered hot tub. It's in San Isidro de Peñas Blancas, also on the way to the volcano.

In the Northern Zone, **Tabacón Resort and Spa** (tabacon.com), at the base of Arenal volcano, offers thermal springs, massages, and mud packs in the middle of the famous hot spring gardens**. Arenal Paraíso** (arenalpariso. com) also has its own hot springs and spa. One of the most beautiful spas in the country is at the **Lost Iguana Resort** (lostiguanaresort.com), the only one of these with a view of the currently active side of the volcano. The elegant **El Tucano** (occidental-hoteles.com) near San Carlos has saunas, jacuzzis, and thermal and mud baths. **Sueño Azul Resort** (suenoazulresort. com) in Las Horquetas de Sarapiquí, with its yoga studio and spa, is the winter destination of the Omega Institute's Holistic Studies Program.

On the Atlantic, **El Encanto B & B** (elencantobedandbreakfast.com) has a quiet meditation room and an open-air yoga platform in the midst of well-tended tropical gardens. **La Diosa** (ladiosa.com), north of Cahuita, also encourages meditation and yoga. **Samasati Nature Center** (samasati. com) has twice-daily yoga classes in its large seminar room surrounded by jungle, a hot tub and spa services. Their week-long retreats combine yoga, massage, and trips to nearby beaches for swimming, snorkeling, and dolphin watching. South of Puerto Viejo, Hotel La Costa de Papito, offers its lovely, handcrafted **Pure Jungle Spa** (purejunglespa.com). In Guanacaste, **Nosara Wellness Service** (nosarawellness.com) offers yoga, Pilates, and physiotherapy as well as nutrition counseling in Playa Nosara. **Nosara Yoga Institute** (nosarayoga.com) trains teachers, provides yoga vacations, and gives classes in its spacious center.

On the Nicoya Peninsula, the **Ylang Ylang Beach Resort** (elbanano. com) offers yoga and natural food on the beach in Montezuma. The serene yoga room at the **Flor Blanca Resort** (florblanca.com) at the north end of

Playa Santa Teresa is watched over by hand-carved statues of deities from Indonesia.

The Southern Zone offers many opportunities to heal with diet and yoga. **The New Dawn Center** (thenewdawncenter.org), in the hills above San Isidro de El General, is devoted to teaching people how to grow and heal with plants. Their month-long courses include medicinal botany, naturopathy, massage therapy and holistic health care, permaculture design for ecological health gardens, agroforestry, and working with bamboo. They also offer a Spanish course. In the hills above Uvita, south of Dominical, **La Cascada Verde** (cascadaverde.org) is a communal retreat center focusing on organic permaculture farming, cleansing diets, and body-mind healing. **Durika** (durika.org) is a spiritual community in the mountains east of Buenos Aires, on the border of La Amistad International Park. They offer meditation, vegetarian food, excellent herbal teas, hydrotherapy, and other treatments. Part of your therapy can be working with them in their amazing high-altitude gardens.

Almost every lodge on the eastern Osa Peninsula has a yoga platform. The view from the open-air yoga studio at the **Luna Lodge** (lunalodge. com) in Carate is magnificent. **Chen Taiji International** (taichivacations. com) offers personalized tai chi vacation packages, retreats, and trainings in Pavones, south of Golfito. **Shooting Star Studio** (yogapavones.com) gives yoga and karate classes in Pavones.

GETTING MARRIED IN COSTA RICA

Although Costa Rica has been known as a honeymoon destination, more and more couples are coming here for their weddings. **Tropical Occasions** (in North America: 303-975-8092; tropicaloccasions.com) specializes in beach weddings, but can also help you tie the knot "in the rainforest, under a waterfall, or even on top of a volcano." Like healthcare, weddings can cost from 25 to 40 percent less in Costa Rica, not counting travel. The legal procedures take about a month to coordinate, and the rest of the plans can be made by e-mail. **Weddings Costa Rica** (in North America: 1-866-574-7213; weddingscostarica.net) was started by a U.S. guidebook author who fell in love with a Costa Rican and had trouble planning her own wedding. Now they help other couples.

FOUR

Once You Arrive:
Getting Around in Costa Rica

LOCAL TRANSPORTATION

FROM THE AIRPORT

After you have gone through immigration and customs and are leaving the San José airport with your luggage, you will come to a booth where airport taxi and van tickets are sold. A ticket to San José costs $20 per taxi; vans cost $24. You give your pre-paid ticket to a driver in one of the orange airport taxis which are waiting as you come out of the building. A normal tip is one or two dollars at the end of the ride—if he helps you with your luggage.

A bus (45 cents) goes into San José, but you can't take much baggage on it. A taxi to Alajuela from the airport should only cost $3-$7. If you have rented a car, vans will transport you to rental agency offices. Having the rental agency deliver the car to the airport involves a surcharge and is unnecessary because the offices are near the airport. Good B&Bs and hotels will arrange to have a rental car delivered to you the morning after you arrive in Costa Rica (we highly recommend this option).

TAXIS

Taxis are relatively inexpensive by American standards. In any taxi except the orange airport taxies, drivers are supposed to use computerized meters, called *marías*. As soon as you get in the cab they should press a button and a number should appear on the meter. Official rates in 2008 were ¢405 (80 cents) for the first kilometer and about 75 cents for each additional kilometer. A higher "delay fare" kicks in when taxis are forced to travel slower than 10 kilometers per hour, such as when caught in traffic jams, an all too frequent event throughout the Central Valley. Some *taxistas* charge more for bad road conditions.

Many travelers don't know that they can ask taxis to wait for them while they are at a tourist attraction, bank, restaurant or souvenir store. The official price for an hour of waiting is only about $5.

Outside towns and cities, taxis usually have a set rate they charge to different destinations. In the countryside, a taxi driver should be able to tell you how much he will charge before you get in the cab. It is not customary to tip taxi drivers here unless they have helped you with your luggage.

There are many honest taxi drivers and many dishonest ones. A few taxi drivers do not use their meters or claim that they are broken. Legally, they must have a letter from the Ministerio de Obras Públicas y Transporte certifying that their *maría* does not work. If your *taxista* doesn't put the *maría* on, write down the driver's ID number (which should be clearly displayed in the window) as well as the license plate number and call 2220-0102 to make a complaint. Keep your eye on the *maría* when you reach your destination. Some taxi drivers turn it off just before you get there and then charge you whatever they want.

In general, it's good to know your rights. Airport taxis are orange. All other legal taxis are red with a yellow triangle painted on the door. Do not accept rides in taxis that don't have this insignia, unless they have been recommended by a reliable source.

Most taxis are very well maintained. Taxi drivers cringe when passengers slam the doors shut because they feel it damages the car. One driver told us that he no longer stopped for foreign tourists because they usually slam doors. Ease the door closed, or let the driver do it for you.

Taxis can come in handy if you want to visit hard-to-get-to places but do not want the expense of renting a car, especially if there are several of you. For instance, a tour to Volcán Poás with a travel agency usually costs $40 per person. You can hire a taxi in Alajuela to take you to Poás for about $50-$60 per carload—including the time spent waiting for you at the top. Of course, with the price of gas rising unpredictably, all this information could change by the time you get to Costa Rica.

CARS FOR HIRE

As an alternative to a taxi, your hotel can probably recommend a bilingual driver you can hire to show you around. Sometimes these drivers have vans that can hold up to seven people. This usually costs $165 to $200 per day, plus the driver's expenses. Sometimes your hotel will find other guests who need the same service, and you can split the cost with them. The author of this book (keytocostarica.com) plans customized itineraries with knowledgeable and entertaining bilingual, naturalist guide/drivers for $250 per day, including vehicle, gas, and driver's expenses.

HITCHHIKING

Because bus service is widely available, most people prefer to take buses. Hitchhiking is rare. In the countryside, where bus service is infrequent or nonexistent, cars often stop to offer rides to people on foot. With crime on the rise, we do not recommend hitchhiking.

BUSES

Since most Costa Ricans don't have cars, buses go almost everywhere. Most buses that travel between San José and the provinces have well-padded seats and curtains on the windows to shade you from the sun. Tall people, however, tell us that the bus seats are too cramped for their comfort. Fares rarely run more than $10 to go anywhere in the country. Some provincial buses are a bit rickety, but you won't find pigs and chickens tied to the roof, and most buses are quite punctual. Costa Rica's bumpy, pot-holed roads do take a toll on buses, and buses sometimes break down. President Oscar Arias has already made a lot of improvements in the road situation. Buses from San José to the provinces are crowded on Friday and Saturday and the day preceding a holiday or three-day weekend. Likewise, it is difficult to get buses back to San José on Sunday, Monday, and the day following a holiday. This is especially true when trying to make connections to beach or mountain tourist destinations.

Many first-time visitors are reluctant to use the public bus system because they don't speak Spanish, are fearful of being robbed, or find it difficult to get to bus stops, etc. These problems are all addressed by **A Safe Passage** (cell phone: 8365-9678; costaricabustickets.com, rchoice@racsa.co.cr), founded by Californian John Koger. For $40/person, $75 for two, John will buy your bus tickets and pick you up at the airport, then take you to where you can safely board your bus. You must let him know at least a week in advance so that you get reserved seats at the front of the bus, close to the driver, for increased security. His **Home Base** program includes airport pick-up, first and last nights at an Alajuela hotel, and transportation to your bus or shuttle stop ($100-$160/person, depending on quality of hotel; $130-$200/double). This service can give you an extra day of vacation if your flight arrives early. The Safe Passage website contains a list of bus departure times to destinations all over the country.

Some buses don't have buzzers or bells to tell the driver when you want to get off. When the bus gets close to your stop, shout *"¡La parada!"* or whistle loudly. If you are not sure where you should get off, ask the driver to let you know when he reaches your stop—most drivers are very accommodating. If you are traveling cheaply by bus, it's a good idea to bring as little with you as possible and leave most of your luggage at your hotel. Big suitcases are very inconvenient for bus travel. We have traveled for up to two weeks with just what we could fit in a day pack. Always keep your baggage at your feet rather than putting it in the overhead racks.

The second part of this book gives detailed information on transportation, including locations of bus stops and numbers to call to check schedules. English is usually not spoken. The best way to get to a provincial bus stop in San José or Alajuela is to hail an inexpensive taxi and have them deliver you there.

The **ICT** (Tourism Institute) (underneath the Plaza de la Cultura, Calle 5, Avenidas Central/2; in North America: 866-COSTA RICA) keeps an updated, computerized list of bus stops and related information. Check bus schedules to provinces online at costaricabustickets.com/Destinations.htm.

For those of you who are shy about taking public buses, **Gray Line Tourist Bus** (2220-2126; graylinecostarica.com) runs daily air-conditioned buses to many destinations on the Pacific, the Northern Zone, and the Atlantic for $33 (if ordered from the U.S.) per person, with a 50 percent discount for kids. For $10 extra you can bring your surfboard along. **Interbus** ($30-$40; 2283-5573; interbusonline.com), has buses to even more destinations and is very reliable. Your hotel can make reservations for you once you are in the country if you ask a few days in advance.

PLANES

Because of Costa Rica's mountainous terrain, small aircraft are frequently used. A 35-minute flight can get you to Quepos and Manuel Antonio on the Pacific Coast, as opposed to a four-hour bus ride. **SANSA**, a government-subsidized airline, flies fairly inexpensively ($120-$200 roundtrip) to all corners of the country. **Nature Air** flights ($140-$220 roundtrip) cost a bit more than SANSA's but they're worth it for their increased reliability and convenience. Both airlines have additional airport and fuel surcharge fees.

Children over the age of 2 pay the adult fare with **SANSA**, while **Nature Air** gives a 25 percent discount for children ages 2 to 11. Nature Air has a maximum baggage allowance of 30 lbs. while SANSA's is 12 kilos (27 pounds) per passenger. Nature Air will safely store excess luggage for you.

SANSA (2290-4100; in North America: 877-767-2672; flysansa.com) flights leave from a small terminal just west of the Juan Santamaría Airport. SANSA is part of Grupo TACA, the alliance of Central American airlines, along with LACSA. It is best to make reservations a few weeks in advance in the dry season.

Nature Air (2299-6000; in North America: 800-235-9272; natureair. com, reservations@natureair.com) uses the Tobias Bolaños Airport in Pavas west of San Jose's La Sabana Park. You need to arrive at the Pavas airport 45 minutes before your departure.

Adobe Rentacar (adobecar.com) will let you pick up or drop off your car for free at any hotel in the San José area or in Manuel Antonio, Liberia, Tamarindo, or Flamingo if you are renting for three days or more. This way you can drive there and fly back, or vice versa.

Nature Air and SANSA fly daily to:
- Quepos (Manuel Antonio)
- Liberia (near Guanacaste beaches)
- Palmar Sur (near Uvita or the boats to Drake Bay)
- Drake Bay (on the Pacific side of the Osa Peninsula)
- Puerto Jiménez (on the Gulf side of the Osa Peninsula)
- Nosara, Sámara, and Punta Islita (on the southern Nicoya Peninsula)
- Tamarindo (central Guanacaste beaches)
- Tortuguero and Barra del Colorado (Northern Atlantic Coast)
- Limón (mid-Atlantic Coast)
- Golfito (gateway to Playas Zancudo and Pavones)

In addition, Nature Air flies to: La Fortuna (Arenal Volcano) and Bocas del Toro, Panama.

Sansa also flies to Playa Tambor (gateway to Playas Montezuma, Malpaís, and Santa Teresita), as well as various Central American destinations.

Alfa Romeo Aero Taxi (2735-5353, fax: 2735-5178; alfaromeoair.com) is one of several companies that has small planes available for charter.

DRIVING IN COSTA RICA

CAR RENTALS

A car rental costs around $50 per day, $300 per week in the high season, including insurance and mileage (four-wheel drives are about $65-$90/day, $390-$510/week). The insurance has a $800 deductible, which you can waive by paying $7 to $14 more. All major rental agencies have branches in Costa Rica, but you're more likely to get a special rate if you book a rental car in your country of origin. You can often get a discount of up to

STREET ADDRESS SYSTEM

As you can see from the Downtown San José map in Chapter Six, San José's streets are laid out in a very logical system. Odd-numbered streets (*calles*) are east of Calle Central, even-numbered streets are west. Odd-numbered *avenidas* are north of Avenida Central and even-numbered avenues are south. So if an address is on Calle 17, Avenidas 5/7, it is in the northeastern part of the city.

However, most Ticos completely ignore the street numbering system. *Calles* and *avenidas* appear in the phone book, and that's about it. The accepted way to give directions is from *puntos cardinales* or landmarks. If you call for a taxi, you have to give the name of a church or a *pulpería* (corner store) or a well-known business (like Pollos Kentucky). Then you state how many *metros* you are from there and in what direction. *Cien* (100) *metros* roughly corresponds to one city block. These are some examples of typical ways of giving directions: "*De la pulpería Los Amigos, cien metros al norte y cincuenta al oeste.*" ("From the Los Amigos grocery store, one block north and half a block west.") "*De la Iglesia La Soledad, doscientos al sur y trescientos al este.*" ("From the Soledad Church, two blocks south and three blocks east.")

30 percent in the off season. If you don't have an American Express, Visa, Diners Club, or MasterCard, you must leave a deposit of about $1000. Some agencies allow you to decline their insurance if you have a gold credit card; Visa's gold card is the most commonly accepted one. Find out what your credit card covers before you leave on vacation. If you are already here, reserve a car as far in advance as possible, especially in high season. Look under "*Alquiler de Automóviles*" in the phone book, or in the classifieds of the *Tico Times* for less expensive rentals.

To rent a car, you must be at least 21 years old, have a valid passport and driver's license, and a major credit card. You can rent a car at 18, but you must leave a double deposit. Some agencies charge more for people under 25 and won't rent to people over 75. Check websites for each company's rules. Valid foreign driver's licenses are good in Costa Rica for three months.

Car rental agencies will provide transport from the airport to their nearby offices. Avoid having a car wait for you at the airport—there is often a 12 percent surcharge for that. Better yet, take a taxi to your hotel and have your hotel arrange the delivery. Don't hassle with trying to navigate unfamiliar streets when you first arrive.

SAN JOSÉ & PROVINCIAL CAR RENTALS

Here are the websites of the car rental agencies in Costa Rica:

Alamo (2242-7733; alamocostarica.com)
Avis (2232-9922; avis.co.cr)
Dollar (2443-2950; dollarcostarica.com)
Economy (2299-2000; economyrentacar.com)
Hola Rent a Car (2520-0100; hola.net)
Mapache (2586-6364; mapache.com)
National (2242-7878; natcar.com)
Payless (2257-0026; paylesscarrental.com)
Poás Rentacar (2442-6178; carentals.com)
Thrifty (2257-3434; thrifty.com)
Toyota (2258-5797; toyotarent.com)

Some agencies have branch offices in the provinces. You could take a bus or plane and rent a car when you get there.

JACÓ AND HERRADURA
Alamo 2242-7733
Economy 2643-1719
National 2242-7878
Payless 2643-3224

LA FORTUNA (ARENAL VOLCANO)
Alamo 2242-7733
National 2242-7878
Poás 2470-8027

LIBERIA
Alamo 2242-7733
Dollar 2668-1061
Economy 2666-2816
Hola 2667-4040
National 2242-7878
Payless 2667-0511
Poás 2667-0214
Thrifty 2665-0787
Toyota 2668-1212

NOSARA
National 2242-7878
Toyota 2682-9041

PLAYA FLAMINGO
Economy 2654-4543

SÁMARA
Alamo 2242-7733
National 2242-7878

TAMARINDO
Alamo 2242-7733
Economy 2653-0752
Hola 2653-2000
National 2242-7878
Poás 2667-0214
Thrifty 2653-0829

QUEPOS AND MANUEL ANTONIO
Alamo 2242-7733
Economy 2777-5353
National 2242-7878
Payless 2777-0115

A high clearance is more important than four-wheel drive, especially in the dry season. Regular cars can take you most of the places you want to go in Costa Rica, but you'll feel less paranoid if your chassis isn't scraping on the edge of a sudden pothole. Some of the worst roads are the paved ones that have gone to potholes: They are more uneven and less predictable than a well-graded gravel road.

Note that all repairs must be approved first by the main office, or you will not be reimbursed. According to Jim Corven's "Consumer Almanac" column in the *Tico Times*,

> Stick shifts are the norm in most four-wheel-drive rentals; automatic four-wheel drive vehicles cost more and are sometimes hard to get. Coupled with the lethal potholes and winding roads, these cars must endure conditions unseen elsewhere. Reduce your chances of a breakdown by checking the car out thoroughly before heading out. Do not assume the agency did it for you. Check the oil, water, brake fluid, tire pressure, air conditioner, lights, belts, and hoses while still in San José. Make certain there is a spare tire and jack. Also report any small nicks or dents on the surface. If you have any concern whatsoever, contact the agency for service. You will have far less chance of getting their understanding after you've driven the car for a couple of days and develop problems.

He also points out that the insurance you pay covers damage to vehicles, but not your possessions within the vehicle. Make sure you return the car with a full tank of gas. The agency's rate may be four times as much as the gas would cost at a service station.

Renting a car makes exploring easier and is less time-consuming than taking the bus. However, if you get impatient driving roads riddled with potholes, washboards, or farm animals, or if crazy traffic makes you nervous, think twice about driving yourself. It is said that the more polite people are in person, the ruder they are behind the wheel. The impeccably courteous Costa Ricans are no exception. Passing on blind curves is common. Getting stuck behind an ancient truck overloaded with green bananas and climbing a two-lane highway at 5 mph is to be expected. Parking in the middle of the driving lane on a highway (often there is no shoulder) for repairs is the norm. Buses pull into traffic lanes without looking or signaling. Dividing lines and other road markings are ignored. And if you happen upon a pile of branches in your lane while feeling your way through the fog at night, *watch out*. Someone has broken down just ahead.

If you decide you want your own wheels, try to arrange to rent the car on the day you will be leaving San José for the provinces, because driving in San José is more hassle than it's worth. The car must be left in parking lots at all times to avoid theft. Driving in the city is like driving through a beehive, requiring a mix of finesse and aggressiveness. In San José and many other cities, most streets are one-way but are totally unmarked, so you have to guess if a street is one-way or not—and if it is, which way? Particularly tricky are streets that are two-way for a few blocks, then suddenly become one-way without any signs. Taxis or buses are much cheaper and easier for city travel.

If you do decide to rent a car, do not leave anything in it, even for a minute, unless it is in a well-guarded place. The parking lot at a grocery store is not safe unless you are paying someone to guard your car.

You should be aware that Costa Rica has strict traffic laws with high fines for a variety of infractions. Booklets with all the points are available in the car rental offices, but if you always wear your seatbelt, go the speed limit (90 kilometers per hour on multi-lane highways, 40 to 80 elsewhere), pay special attention to school zones (where the speed limit drops to 25 kph), and watch for occasional signs or numbers painted on the road surface, you will probably be okay.

Policemen usually station themselves in the shade at the side of the road and flag down drivers. Certain policemen stop tourists for "speeding," and tell them they must appear in court at an inconvenient time in an inconvenient place, then offer to let them "pay on the spot" to avoid ruining their vacation. If a cop demands payment, you should refuse, and demand that he issue you a ticket ("*Hágame el parte, por favor*"). Officers are legally required to show their *carné* (ID card) on request, so if you feel you are being harassed or unduly pressured, get the ID number or at least the license plate number and report the officer to 800-TRANSITO.

Here are some helpful vocabulary words:

despacio: slow

alto: stop

peligro: danger

ceda: yield

precaución: be careful

MAPS

Small yellow posts mark the distance in kilometers from San José on Costa Rica's highways, but these aren't enough to find your way around.

If you rent a car, you will be given a map.

The best map we have found is the one put out by Toucan maps ($11.95; mapcr.com). This incredibly detailed and accurate work of cartographic art shows national parks, kilometers between points and detailed maps of Monteverde, Arenal, Manuel Antonio, Puerto Viejo de Talamanca, Puerto Jimenez, the Central Valley, Alajuela, Heredia, Escazu, and downtown San José showing hotel locations. And it's WATERPROOF! The authors also run the highly informative website: costa-rica-guide.com

Even with a map, it's best to call a hotel at or near your destination and ask about current road conditions and travel times. A heavy afternoon rain can cause landslides, changing road conditions in a short time. Because of the unreliability of many roads, try to limit your driving to daylight hours. Hotels will also have current bus schedules.

Topographical maps can be purchased at **Librería Lehmann** (Calle 3, Avenidas Central/1), **Librería Universal** (Avenida Central, Calles Central/1), or the **Instituto Geográfico Nacional** (Avenida 22, Calles 9/11). Ask for *mapas cartográficos*. You'll be shown a little map of Costa Rica divided up into 20 by 30 kilometer sections. Indicate which sections you want. Maps show roads, trails, water sources including rapids, and contours at every 20 meters. They cost about $1.50 a section.

Most of Costa Rica has been mapped for Global Positioning System (GPS) devices. Car rental agencies will rent them for $5-$10 per day (and a refundable $350 deposit) with your car. Maps can be displayed on a touch screen, and the devices give voice commands so that drivers can keep their eyes on the road. They will work for most popular tourist destinations, but community-based destinations are probably not programmed in yet.

GAS

Gas costs about $4 per gallon, but is sold here by the liter, roughly equivalent to a quart. There are no self-service stations in Costa Rica.

ACCIDENTS

Costa Rica has one of the highest auto-accident mortality rates in the world, surpassed only by the United States. Thanks to longtime insurance agent Dave Garrett and the *Tico Times* for this updated information on what to do in case of an accident.

1. Do not move vehicles until you are authorized to do so by an official. This is very important. Let people honk their horns. Offer paper and pencils to witnesses to write their names and *cédula* numbers (legal identification). Take note of the make, model, and color of the other car involved, and get its license plate number.

2. Find out your location according to *puntos cardinales* or *señas,* i.e., *"300 metros al sur del antiguo higueron en San Pedro."* Call 911,

800-800-8000 ext.1 (National Insurance Institute) or 800-872-6748 for a traffic official if one doesn't immediately appear. If it appears that the other driver has been drinking, ask the officer to give him or her an *alcoholemia* test.

3. Do not remove badly injured people from the scene. Wait for the Red Cross ambulance (call 911 or 2233-7033). Find out which hospital they will be taken to. Make no statements on the cause of the accident except to the official or a representative of the National Insurance Institute (INS), whom you can summon by calling 800-800-8000. If an operator tells you that an inspector is unavailable, get the operator's name and number. These calls are taped and you can refer to them to show that you called in right after the accident. Later, call INS to find out how to proceed. If they give you a code number, keep track of it. The insurance inspector often gets there sooner than the police. Pay attention to what he says about how to proceed with your claim. Do not make any deals with other people involved in the accident. If the INS finds out that a deal has been made, it will not pay a claim.

4. A tow truck is likely to appear on the scene, even if you haven't called for one, as towing services routinely monitor the police radio. You may even have more than one to choose from. Make sure your car gets to one of the 270 body shops authorized by the INS. Do not allow a tow truck operator to take your vehicle to an unauthorized body shop, because they do not do the paperwork that the INS requires.

5. Make a sketch of the area and the positions of the vehicles before and after the accident. Make note of the principal characteristics of the other vehicles involved, as well as the damage to your car and others. Avoid further damage by staying with your car.

6. You should report the accident to the police, even if it is insignificant, in every case. If you don't report it and get witnesses' names, things can get changed around and you may be accused of doing terrible damage and then driving away.

7. You will be given a citation by the police, telling you when and where to appear at the traffic court. Make sure you understand what it says before the police official leaves. It usually gives you ten working days to appear. A copy of this report must be presented to the INS (Avenida 7, Calles 9/11; 2287-6000), along with your driver's license, insurance policy, police report, and information about injuries and witnesses.

Foreign insurance policies are not effective in court and only the INS can provide local service for defense or adjustment of claims. Insurance is included in car rental fees unless you have declined and are using a gold-card policy.

ROAD TROUBLE

If you have a rented car, call the rental agency first in all cases, and they will tell you what to do. You can also dial 911.

If you are driving your own car, by law you should have fluorescent triangles to place on the road in case of a breakdown or accident as a warning to other vehicles.

Do not abandon your car, if you can avoid it. If you don't speak Spanish well, have someone explain your location in Spanish when you make the phone call. For insurance help in case of a broken-down car, forgotten keys, or keys left in the car, call 800-800-8001.

SAFETY AND THEFT

THEFT

Take precautions to avoid theft. So far, San José is much safer than most other cities, except for theft. The whole downtown area of San José has become a mecca for pickpockets and chain-snatchers. Other places to watch out for are Limón, Quepos, and Playas del Coco. The zippered compartments of backpacks are excellent targets. It's best not to wear them downtown. Don't carry a lot of packages at once. Purses should be zippered and have short shoulder straps so that you can protect them with your upper arm. If you wear a waistpack, keep it under your shirt or jacket, or rest your hand on it when walking. Wallets and passports shouldn't be carried in your back pocket, and expensive watches, chains, and jewelry should not be worn. Unless you will need the original for banking, just carry a photocopy of your passport, specifically the pages with your photo and personal information and the Costa Rican entry stamp. Most hotels will keep your passport in their safety deposit box, and many now have safety boxes in each room. Before setting out for your destination downtown, check your route.

If, while on a bus or in a crowd, you feel yourself being jostled or pinched between several people at once, don't just be polite. Protect your purse or wallet and elbow your way out of the situation immediately. If you are driving downtown, keep your window rolled up high enough so that a thief can't reach in and grab your necklace, glasses, or watch. Don't leave tents or cars unguarded anywhere. Don't leave cameras or binoculars in sight of an open window, even a louvered one. A pole can be stuck in and they can be fished out. Beware of charming outdoor cafés and don't sit near the entrance at restaurants that are open on one side. If you are at one of these places, keep your belongings in your lap. Do not lay backpacks on the floor or hang them or purses over the back of your chair. While you are perusing

---

TOURISTS BEWARE!

Though San José is generally a safe city, it's not crime-free. Following are two scams to watch out for:

THE FLAT TIRE SCAM   Recently there have been more and more reports of tourists picking up rental cars and finding after a few minutes that they have a flat tire. They stop by the side of the road to repair the tire. What appear to be friendly passersby offer help and end up robbing them. If you get a flat tire, just keep going until you get to a gas station or a place where there are a lot of people. Work with a rental agency that will deliver the car to your hotel. Most hotels will set this up for you.

THE SLIMY GOO SCAM   Tourists are walking down the street and someone squirts their clothes with slimy goo. Helpful onlookers appear with tissues and before they know it, the tourists' purses and wallets are gone.

---

the menu, someone can walk by and snatch your stuff without your even noticing. If you follow these precautions, you probably won't have any trouble.

If you do have the misfortune of getting robbed, you might want to file a *denuncia* at the OIJ (Organismo de Investigación Judicial). There is one in most major towns and in San José at Avenidas 4/6, Calles 15/17 (2295-3643). It is unlikely that they will investigate your robbery, but the document they type up and give to you can be presented to your insurance company. Take a Spanish-speaker with you. There is also a 24-hour hotline (800-800-0645) for tourists who have been robbed.

EARTHQUAKES

These little surprises can make you question the very ground you walk on and remind you of the transience of being. The frequency of minor *temblores* (tremors) depends on the state of the tectonic plates Costa Rica sits on and can range from 40-plus times a month to only once or twice. Most of them register less than 4.5 on the Richter scale and are barely perceptible. Those that register 4.5 to 6 can rock you but cause little damage.

If you happen to be caught in a big *terremoto* (earthquake), here is the best advice we have heard lately: Stay calm. Turn off electric appliances and extinguish cigarettes. Move away from windows or other breakables, or places where something could fall on you. If you can't easily get outside, curl up in a fetal position beside a large object like a bed or a sofa. Disaster experts have noticed that when walls or ceilings fall, they usually leave a triangular space on all sides of large objects they fall on. Experiments showed that dummies which were placed in those triangular spaces were unharmed, where as dummies placed in doorways or under desks or tables were squashed. Don't use stairs or elevators during the quake. Afterward, use the stairs, not the elevator. Leave the building you're in through the closest exit, as soon as possible.

BOMBETAS

If you hear two very loud explosions in rapid succession, don't run for cover—that's just the Tico way of celebrating momentous occasions. Usually the fireworks are from the neighborhood church, which is celebrating a Saint's Day, or are to announce events at a *turno* (town fiesta). In the case of a *turno*, the *bombetas* often begin at dawn and are fired off at regular intervals during the day, usually ending around 9 or 10 p.m. Sounding all the sirens in town is another way of expressing joy, as when the Pope or Tico astronaut Franklin Chang Diaz arrived in San José.

EMBASSIES AND CONSULATES

Many consulates are only open in the mornings. Following is a list of phone numbers for embassies and consulates in San José:

British Embassy Centro Colón; 2258-2025, fax: 2233-9938, after-hours/emergencies: 2225-4049 (pager); britemb@racsa.co.cr

Canadian Embassy Sabana Sur; 2242-4400, after-hours/emergencies: 613-996-8885

Dutch Embassy Sabana Sur; 2296-1490, fax: 2296-2933; nethemb@racsa.co.cr

German Embassy Torre La Sabana, Sabana Norte; 2290-9091; info@san-jose.diplo.de

Japanese Embassy Sabana Sur; 2296-1650, 2232-1255; embjapon@racsa.co.cr

Nicaraguan Embassy Barrio California; 2222-2373, 2221-4156, fax: 2221-5481

Panamanian Embassy 2280-1570; panaembacr.racsa.co.cr

Swedish Consulate La Uruca; 2232-8549; erodriguez@ticolumbia.net

Swiss Embassy Centro Colón; 2233-0052, 2221-4829; vertretung@sjc.rep.admin.ch

United States Embassy Pavas; 2519-2000, after-hours/emergencies: 2220-3127

United States Consulate Pavas; 2519-2000 consularsanjose@state.gov

HEALTH CARE

According to a 2000 United Nations study, Costa Rica holds first place in Latin America for development of preventive and curative medicine. It is ranked ahead of the United States among the 40 best health systems in the world. Many Costa Rican doctors have been trained in Europe and the United States, and the University of Costa Rica Medical School is considered one of the best in Latin America. A full seven percent of visitors to Costa Rica come here specifically for medical or alternative treatments. See "Health Vacations" at the end of Chapter Three.

If you are involved in an accident, you will probably be taken to a hospital or clinic that is part of Costa Rica's nationalized health care system. You will probably be treated for free.

The following private hospitals also have emergency medical, x-ray, laboratory, and pharmacy services available to foreigners: **Clínica Bíblica** (Avenida 14, Calles Central/1; 2522-1000; clinicabiblica.com), **Clínica Católica** (Guadalupe; 2246-3000, 2283-6616; hospitallacatolica.com), **Clínica Santa Rita** (specializes in maternity care; Avenida 8, Calles 15/17; 2221-6433). **Hospital CIMA San José** (2208-1000; hospitalsanjose.net) located on the highway to the western Central Valley town of Santa Ana, is more like a five-star hotel than a hospital. Its "suites" have separate living rooms with TV and minibar. It enjoys an interhospital agreement with Baylor Medical University in Dallas that allows its doctors to go there for training. It has the latest CAT scan equipment as well as maternity, neonatal, trauma, and psychiatric units.

Many dentists are fluent in English. Services, such as crowns, fillings, and root canals, cost about half of what they would in the United States. See arrivacostarica.com.

TIPPING

A 10 percent service charge and a 13 percent tax are included in your restaurant bill, so it's not customary to tip unless you really feel like it. It is not customary to tip taxi drivers either. A nice thing about Costa Rica is that people aren't always standing around with their hands out—partly because of a tradition of equality and pride. We hope that these qualities survive the influx of massive tourism. You should tip airport porters about 500 *colones* (or $1) per bag. You would be surprised to know how little the staff at most hotels, including luxury hotels, earn (usually less than $200/month), so a little gratuity here and there for the maids who clean your room is certainly helpful. Some hotels leave envelopes in the rooms for this purpose. Guides should be tipped $5-$8 per person per day.

Many times when you park your car a man will appear, point to his eyes, and point to your car. That means he will watch your car for you, and it's worth it, for the 500 *colones* you will give him when you return (more at night or for long periods of time). Even though it might appear that he is hired by the restaurant, nightclub, or other facility he is in front of, he is probably only working for tips.

When you pay with a credit card at restaurants, the waiter will often leave the "tip" and "total" spaces blank, even though a 10 percent gratuity has already been included. *Beware:* Unless the "total" space is filled in by the customer, any amount could be written in later.

One place where tips are not appropriate is at community-based eco-tourism lodgings, where staff and owners are the same. You can make a donation to the community, which is always appreciated.

BUSINESS HOURS

Costa Ricans tend to start the day early. You'll find that stores are generally open from 8 or 9 a.m. until 6 or 7 p.m., six days a week (most businesses are closed Sunday). Core banking hours are 9 a.m. to 3 p.m.; government offices are open from 8 a.m. to 4 or 5 p.m.

THE METRIC SYSTEM

Whether you're getting gas, checking the thermometer, or looking at road signs, you'll notice the difference: Everything is metric. Costa Rica is on the metric system, which measures temperature in degrees Celsius, distances in meters, and most substances in liters, kilos, and grams.

To convert from Celsius to Fahrenheit, multiply times 9, divide by 5 and add 32. For example, 23°C equals [(23 x 9)/5] + 32, or (207/5) + 32, or 41.4 + 32, or about 73°F. If you don't have a pocket calculator along (but you probably should), just remember that 0°C is 32°F and that each Celsius degree is roughly two Fahrenheit degrees. Here are some other useful conversions:

- 1 mile = 1.6 kilometers. 1 kilometer = $3/5$ mile
- 1 foot = 0.3 meter. 1 meter = $3^1/3$ feet
- 1 pound *(libra)* = 0.45 kilo. 1 kilo = $2^1/5$ pounds
- 1 gallon = 3.8 liters. 1 liter = about $^1/4$ gallon, or about one quart
- 1 acre = .4 hectare. 1 hectare = 2.47 acres

TIME ZONE

All of Costa Rica is on Central Standard Time, which is six hours behind Greenwich Mean Time. During daylight saving time in the U.S. (early April to late October) Costa Rica is on Mountain Standard Time.

COMMUNICATIONS

While Costa Rica boasts more phones per capita than any other Latin American country, patience and perseverance are still key when dealing with the communications bureaucracies.

COUNTRY CODES

Throughout the text, Costa Rica phone numbers are listed without the country code, which is 506. Other country codes you may need are 505 for Nicaragua and 507 for Panama. To dial Costa Rica from North America, dial 011, then 506 and the number.

TELEPHONES

Most public phones now require that you use a "Servicio 197" telephone card. You can usually buy them for 500, 1000, or 3000 *colones* at a store located near the public phone. Ask for *tarjetas telefónicas*. You can also buy them at the airport when you arrive. They are handy to have in an emergency.

If you can't find a number in the directory, try dialing 113, the directory assistance line.

If your hotel room has a telephone, you can usually use it to call out; charges will be billed to you when you leave, unless you have made the calls on a 197 or 199 card (see below). Many hotels offer free local calls.

CELL PHONES

You can check messages on your home cell phone by dialing your number from a Costa Rican land line and punching in * and your password. AT&T phones do get coverage in Costa Rica, but cost about $2.29 per minute to call the U.S.

Many car rental agencies include cell phones in their rates and charge only for the minutes used.

Costa Rica Cellular Connection ($60 activation fee; in the U.S.: 800-372-3183) mails you a Costa Rica activated cell phone before you leave the U.S. It charges $.33 a minute for incoming and outgoing local calls and $.89 for outgoing international calls. **Celtrek** (celtrek.com) lets you buy a SIM card and $25 of airtime for $74.

If you have a laptop or a handheld internet device that has **skype**, you can talk for free to any other person anywhere who also has skype. Since most hotels in Costa Rica have high speed internet access in the rooms, your communication is greatly facilitated. The only problem is lugging around the laptop.

INTERNATIONAL CALLS

Calling cards with 800 numbers don't work in Costa Rica. Keep in mind that the calling cards you use at home have very expensive rates when calling from Costa Rica. You can purchase a *"Servicio 199"* calling card for $10 or $20 at the airport or local stores that will allow you to make international calls from any touch-tone phone at the normal rates. You key in the number on the card, dial your number, and the amount of your call is deducted from the value of the card. International call rates are cheaper evenings and weekends. The exact times are found in any telephone directory. You can also buy *"Servicio 197"* calling cards, which allow you to make calls within Costa Rica from private or public phones. You can call home also on these cheaper 197 cards and ask friends and family to call you back.

If you have access to a private phone, direct dialing is easy from Costa Rica. The telephone directory has a list of codes for various countries. To dial the U.S. or Canada direct, for example, dial 001 first, then the area code and number.

To call person-to-person or collect, dial 175 and an operator will then come on the line. For international information, dial 124.

If you don't have access to a phone in San José, go to **Radiográfica** (open daily, 7:30 a.m. to 9 p.m.; Calle 1, Avenida 5). Some internet cafés and youth hostels offer cheap international phone calls over the internet.

FAX AND E-MAIL SERVICES

If your hotel lists a fax or e-mail number, they will usually accept a fax or e-mail for you. Most hotels make a point of offering free e-mail access to guests. Internet cafés are found in tourist areas throughout the country.

MAIL

Mail letters from a post office. There are hardly any mailboxes on the streets, and they are seldom used. Provincial post offices are open weekdays 8 a.m. to 5:30 p.m., and Saturdays 8 a.m. to noon. Your hotel will mail postcards and letters for you.

Beware of having anything other than letters and magazines sent to you in Costa Rica. A high duty is charged on all items arriving by mail in an attempt to keep foreign merchandise from entering illegally. Receiving packages can mean two trips to the *Aduana* (customs office) in Zapote, a suburb of San José. The first trip is to unwrap and declare what you have received. The second one, that day or the following day, is to pay a customs charge on every item in the package before you can take it home. If the package contains food, medicine, or cosmetics, it must be examined by the Ministry of Health—a process that takes even longer. Usually anything that fits in a regular-sized or magazine-sized envelope will arrive duty-free.

There is a general delivery service (*Lista de Correos*). If you are planning to stay in Costa Rica for a while, you can rent a post office box (*apartado—Apdo.* for short), or have your mail sent to a friend's box, which is safer than having it sent to a street address. Many people are turning to private mail services like **Aerocasillas** (2208-4848; aeropost.com, servicesjo@aerocasillas.com), and **Mail Boxes Etc.** (2291-4761—Pavas; mbe.com). Courier services DHL (2210-3838), UPS (2290-2828) are both available in Costa Rica.

LAUNDRY

Many hotels have laundry services. Most cheaper hotels have large sinks (*pilas*) where you can wash your own clothes, or they can connect you with a person who will wash them for you. Beware of hotel laundry services that charge by the piece. We once spent over $10 on one load of laundry. Most provincial hotels will do your laundry for $5/load.

"TIQUISMOS"—
HAVING FUN WITH COSTA RICAN SPANISH

Ticos are amused and delighted when foreigners try to speak Spanish, especially when they include *tiquismos*, expressions that are peculiar to Costa Rican or Central American culture.

Not only the vocabulary, but the way you use words, is important. Spanish speakers use a lot of *muletillas* (fillers, literally "crutches") in their speech. They directly address the person with whom they are speaking more often than is done in English, and they do it in a way that English speakers might consider slightly offensive. It is common for women to be called *mamita*, *madre*, *mi hijita* (little mother, mother, my little daughter— all roughly corresponding to "honey"). Latins love to use salient physical characteristics as nicknames. Common ones are *gordo* (fatty), *flaco* (skinny), *macho* (Costa Rican for fair-skinned or fair-haired), *negro* (dark-skinned), *chino* (it doesn't matter if you're Asian or just have slightly slanting eyes, your name is Chino), *gato* (blue or green eyes). You need only be slightly *gordo* or *flaco* to merit those names. If you're really *gordo* or *flaco*, and people really like you, you get a special name like *repollito* (little cabbage) or *palito* (little stick). *Gordo* and *negro* are commonly used as terms of endearment, regardless of appearance. The feminine of all the above nicknames ends in -a instead of -o.

Younger Ticos and Ticas are usually called *maje* (pronounced "my") by their friends. This literally means "dummy," but figuratively is more like pal or buddy. It is used widely as a *muletilla*. *Majes* have various expressions of approval—such as the famous *pura vida* (great, terrific), *tuanis* (cool), and *buena nota* (awesome). *Mala nota* is ungroovy, *furris* is uncool, and *salado* means "too bad for you." Expressions of extreme approval are *qué bruto*, *qué bárbaro*, and disapproval, *qué horror*, or *fatal, maje*.

The above expressions are the slang of urban youth. However, all Ticos are aware of polite, courteous, and respectful forms of speech. They make their world more pleasant by using little expressions of appreciation. For example, if someone helps you in a store or on the street, you say, "*Muchas gracias, muy amable*" ("Thank you very much, you are very kind"), and they will say, "*Con mucho gusto*" ("With much pleasure").

It is customary in the morning to ask, "*¿Cómo amaneció?*" ("How did you wake up?") "*Muy bien, por dicha, ¿y usted?*" ("Very well, luckily, and you?") "*Muy bien, gracias a Dios.*" ("Very well, thank God.")

When talking about a future event or plan, Ticos will often include *si Dios quiere* ("if God wants" or "God willing"): "*Nos vemos el martes, si Dios quiere.*" ("We'll see each other Tuesday, God willing.")

If you are in the city and see someone on the other side of the street whom you know, you call, "*¡Adiós!*" In the countryside, when you pass someone on the road, it is customary to say *adiós* even if you don't know them. In these situations, *adiós* means hello. It is only used to mean goodbye when you're going away for good. Everyday good-byes are *hasta luego* (until then, until later), and the other person might add, "*Que Dios le acompañe.*" ("May God accompany you.")

Giving a coin to a beggar in the street often earns you a special blessing: He or she will say, "*Dios se lo pague.*" ("May God repay you.")

Although "now" and "in a little while" have very different meanings in English, here they can be expressed with the same word: *ahora*. Perhaps this is the linguistic root of the *mañana* attitude that so frustrates gringos. If

you want to express the idea of "right away," you can emphatically use the word *¡ya!* keeping in mind that *ya* can also be used to mean already, later, and soon. Eskimos have 26 different words for snow. Latin Americans have the same words for many different time concepts, perhaps because time is not of such vital importance to their existence. It's what foreigners love and hate about the tropics. Keep that in mind when dealing with the bureaucracy, or when deciding whether or not you have enough time to buy a cold drink when you've been told the bus is coming *ahorititica*.

Vos is a form of second-person-singular address used throughout Central America instead of *tú*. The verb form used with *vos* is made by changing the *r* on the end of an infinitive to *s* and accenting the last syllable. Thus with the verb *poder*, "*tú puedes*" becomes "*vos podés*," and with *sentirse*, "*tú te sientes*" becomes "*vos te sentís*." Much to the consternation of their Spanish and South American friends, more and more Ticos use the formal *usted* for everyone, probably because it's easier and safer.

Other common Spanish fillers are terms like *fíjate*, *imagínate*, and *vieras que*, for which there are no real equivalents in English. Roughly, they could be translated as "would you believe" or "just think!" These expressions are used to give emphasis to what the speaker is saying. For example: "*¡Fíjate vos que no me dejaron entrar!*" ("Would you believe it—they wouldn't let me in!") Or you might say, "*Imagínese cómo me dió pena verla así.*" ("Imagine how bad I felt to see her like that.")

Vieras is often used the same way we use "sure" in English: "*¡Vieras qué susto me dió!*" ("I sure was scared!" or, "You should have seen how it scared me!*")

Acharà is another particularly Tico expression and indicates regret at a loss: "*Fíjese que el perro comió mis begonias. Acharà mis florecitas.*" ("Would you believe it—the dog ate my begonias. My poor little flowers!")

When you come to someone's house, especially in the country, it is customary to stand on the ground near the porch and say "*¡Upe!*" as a way of letting them know you're there. When they ask you to come in, as you enter the house you say, "*Con permiso.*" ("With your permission.") If they offer you something to eat, it is polite to accept. Giving makes people happy; if you don't let them give to you, it hurts their feelings. People will ask you about your family, whether you're married, how many children you have. Most can't quite grasp the idea of people not being married or not having children. When you're sitting and talking and finally no one can think of anything else to say, you say, "*Pues, sí.*" ("Well, yes.")

Learn some of these expressions and practice them until you don't make any *metidas de pata* (literally, "putting your foot in it," or mistakes). Ticos will be glad to help you. If you do make a mistake, there is a word that is instant absolution: Just say, "*¿Diay?*" It means, "Well, what can you expect?" or "What can be done about it?" As you get to know the Ticos, you'll find that this little word comes in very handy.

FRUITS AND VEGETABLES

Costa Rica produces an amazing abundance of fruits and vegetables. To get an idea of their beauty and variety, go to any of the Saturday- or Sunday-morning neighborhood *ferias del agricultor,* where streets are closed to automobiles while farmers sell their fresh produce. Bring your own shopping bags. Many suburbs of San José also have weekend street markets—Escazú, Guadalupe, Tres Ríos, and Zapote, to name a few.

Here are some tips on how to identify and choose the best produce:

A ripe **papaya** will always be slightly soft, but still firm. A too-soft papaya should be avoided. To find the perfect papaya, shoppers will surreptitiously stick their thumbnail into the skin to see if it is thin enough to be easily pierced. That also lets them see if the color is of an intensity that indicates ripeness. It is customary for papaya vendors to cut a triangular piece out of the papaya to show you its color. Some people are fans of the rounder *amarilla* or yellow-orange papaya. Others will swear that only the more elongated, red-orange *cacho* papaya is worthy of the name. You don't have to buy a papaya just because the vendor cut a piece out of it for you—at least Ticos don't.

Mangos should be slightly soft but still very firm, and red and yellow in color, although it's okay for part of them to be green. Reject any that have mushy spots. By far the most delicious are the large *mangas*, given feminine gender because of their voluptuous size. The neatest way to eat *mangas* is to slice them close around the flat oval seed to get two meaty halves. With the skin side down, score each piece into one-inch divisions without cutting through the skin (use a butter knife for this part). Now gently turn each half inside out, and you will have a bunch of delicious bite-sized

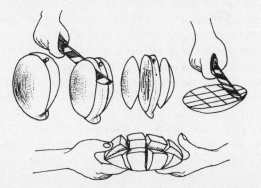

pieces offering themselves to you. Ticos also love to eat green mangos sliced and sprinkled with lemon and salt. (Some people get a rash or irritation around their lips from eating mangos. This can be avoided by cutting off the part of the fruit nearest the stem, as the irritation is caused by the sap.)

Ticos judge the ripeness of a **piña** (pineapple) by giving it a slap. A good *piña* should sound firm and compact. The yellow pineapple is best for eating. The white pineapple is more acidic and is used in cooking and to tenderize meats. It produces a hollow sound when thumped. A green color on the outside does not necessarily mean the fruit is unripe. You should be able to pluck a leaf easily from the top of a ripe *piña*.

Sandías (watermelons) are considered sweeter if they produce a firm rather than a hollow sound. The best watermelons come from the hot coastal zones. One of the nicest parts of driving to the Pacific Coast is stopping at a fruit stand in Esparza or Orotina for a delicious *sandía*.

Don't make the mistake of a friend of ours who, on a hot San José afternoon, came home with what he thought was a delicious, red, juicy watermelon. "And what a bargain!" he said as he thirstily cut into the **chiverre**, only to find a mass of whitish spaghetti-like pulp. *Chiverre* (spaghetti squash) looks just like a watermelon from the outside. You'll see it sold on the roadsides during Semana Santa. Its pulp is candied with *tapa dulce* to make special Easter treats.

Melón (cantaloupe) is judged for sweetness by its firm sound, but a fragrant smell is the best indication of a fully ripe *melón*.

Moras (blackberries) are used in *refrescos* and ice cream. You have to liquefy *moras* in a blender, strain, and add sugar and water to the sour juice.

Four types of **limones ácidos** (sour lemons) grow here. The seedless *verdelio* is rare. The *criollo* is small, juicy, and greener. The *bencino* is more the size of a North American lemon but is green and has much less juice than the criollo. The *limón mandarina* looks like a bumpy tangerine, and is very sour and juicy; it's good for making lemonade. The **limón dulce** (sweet lemon) has a mild, slightly sweet flavor, and is said to be an appetite stimulant and general cure-all.

Guayabas (guavas) are plentiful in Costa Rica from September through November. Their pink fruit is used for jam or guava paste.

Similar to the *guayaba*, **cas** is a little round fruit whose tart tropical flavor is popular in *refrescos* and sherbets. Try the *nieve de cas* at Pop's, a local ice cream chain.

Tamarindo is a tart and sweet *refresco* made from the seed pod of the tamarind tree. You will see the orange-sized balls of brown tamarindo seeds and pulp at the markets. The seeds are put in hot water so the sticky tamarindo dissolves. Then sugar and cold water are added. The resulting light-brown *refresco* is somewhat similar in flavor to apple juice. Add grated ginger and lemon juice for a fine alcohol-free cocktail.

Granadillas (passion fruit) are yellowish-red and slightly larger than an egg. They have a crisp but easily broken shell. Inside are little edible seeds surrounded by a delicious, delicately flavored fruit, which is first slurped and then chewed. **Maracuyá** is a larger, yellower cousin of the *granadilla*, too tart to slurp, but delicious in a *refresco*. Its taste has been described as a mix between pineapple and tangerine.

Marañón is an unusual fruit. Its seed, the cashew nut, grows on top of it in a thick, rubbery shell. Don't try to bite open the shell; it's very bitter. Cashews must be roasted before they can be eaten; they are poisonous when raw. The ripe fruit can be eaten or made into a *refresco* or fermented into wine. The dried fruit is like a cross between a prune and a fig and is sold in supermarkets. You can make a quick and elegant dessert with half a dried *marañón* topped with a dollop of cream cheese and a cashew.

When you travel to Limón, you'll see several highway stands near Siquirres selling large, green, bumpy **guanábanas**. Inside these football-sized fruits, you'll find a sensuous surprise. Some spoon out the fibrous white flesh and eat it as is, but most people prefer it in *refrescos*, *en leche*, or *en agua*. Its English name, significantly less melodious, is soursop.

Avocados are called **aguacates**. They are usually a little less buttery and flavorful than their North American counterparts. They are soft when ripe, but if bought green can be left inside a paper bag to ripen.

Zapotes look like big brown avocados, and their texture is avocado-like, but their pulp is bright red-orange and sweet. Some places make *zapote* ice cream.

Fresh **coco** (coconut meat) can be found at fruit stands downtown. **Pipas** or green coconuts are popular with Ticos on hot days at the beach. They are sold whole, with a straw stuck through a hole in the outer shell so that the coconut water can be drunk. The best way to get coconut meat out of its shell is to hack it open with a machete or a hammer, then heat the shells on the stove in a pan. This makes the meat shrink a little so it's easier to remove.

Pejibaye, a relative of the coconut, is one of Costa Rica's most unusual treats. *Pejibayes* grow in clusters on palm trees, like miniature coconuts.

Pejibayes

Mamón chino and carambola

The part that you eat corresponds to the fibrous husk, while the hard *pejibaye* seed, when cracked open, reveals a thin layer of bitter white meat around a hollow core. The bright orange or red *pejibayes* are delicious boiled in salted water, then peeled, halved, and pitted and eaten alone or with mayonnaise. You'll see them sold on San José streets year-round. Their flavor is difficult to describe. They are not sweet, but more a combination of chestnut and pumpkin with a thick, fibrous texture. You can buy cooked *pejibayes* in supermarket produce departments, or you can buy them peeled and canned to take home as souvenirs.

Palmito (palm heart) is another delicacy worth trying. It is sold raw at the *ferias* or tenderly pickled in jars or bags in the supermarkets. It is the succulent inner core of small palm trees. Even though whole trees must be cut so that you can savor *palmito*, the trees are cultivated as a crop, so are replaced.

As human nature would have it, the most highly prized fruits in Costa Rica are imported apples, grapes, and pears. They signify the advent of the Christmas season, and Ticos pay dearly for them. Highland Ticos grow a good, sweet-tart variety of apple. You also might enjoy the native **manzana de agua**, a dark-red, pear-shaped fruit that is light and refreshing.

Mamones are little green spheres, which you can break open with your fingers or teeth to expose a large seed covered with a layer of fruit that tastes like a peeled grape. Be careful when small children eat *mamones* or *mamones chinos*. Because of their size and shape they can get stuck in their throats.

Mamón chino is the *mamón*'s exotic cousin, sporting a red shell with soft spines growing all over it. It resembles a fat, round, red caterpillar and has a larger grapelike fruit inside its outrageous shell.

When you slice a yellow **carambola**, the pieces look like five-pointed stars. It makes a delicious *refresco*.

COMIDA TÍPICA (NATIVE FOOD)

Those who expect to find spicy food anywhere south of the border will be disappointed in Costa Rican cuisine. It is not spicy, but it is tasty. Except for being a little heavy-handed with the grease, Ticos have a wholesome, high-fiber diet, with rice and beans included in every menu. Lunch is the big meal of the day, and many businesses still give two hours off at lunchtime so that people can take the bus back to mama's for a substantial *casado*. People often content themselves with soup and toast in the evening. Those who stay in Costa Rica develop a certain affection for the noble bean, and a good *gallo pinto* is a real delight. Ticos who want to spice up their food usually have a jar of tiny pickled red and yellow chilies on the table. Be wary of these: They are pure fire!

Sodas are small restaurants where you can get inexpensive snacks and light meals. They line San José's streets and fill the Mercado Central. Following are some of the foods you'll run across at *sodas* countrywide.

arreglados—sandwiches, usually made of meat, on a tasty but greasy bun

arroz con pollo—rice with chicken and vegetables

cajeta de coco—delicious fudge made of coconut, *tapa dulce*, and orange peel

casado—a plate of rice, black beans, cabbage and tomato salad, meat or egg, and sometimes fried plantains

picadillo—a dish made with seasoned ground meat (usually beef), tomatoes, peppers and onions

ceviche—raw seabass cured in lemon juice with *culantro* (Chinese parsley) and onions—delicious

chicharrones—pork rinds fried crisp and dripping with grease, sometimes with wiry hairs still sticking out

chorreadas—corn pancakes, sometimes served with *natilla*

cono capuchino—an ice cream cone dipped in chocolate

dulce de leche—a thick syrup made of milk and sugar

elote asado—roasted corn on the cob

elote cocinado—boiled corn on the cob

empanadas—corn turnovers filled with beans, cheese, or potatoes and meat

gallo pinto—the national breakfast dish of rice and beans fried together

gallos—meat, beans, or cheese between two tortillas

guiso de maíz—fresh corn stew

horchata—a sweet drink made of roasted ground rice and cinnamon *masamorra*—corn pudding

melcochas—candies made from raw sugar

natilla—sour cream, often more of a liquid than North American sour cream

olla de carne—literally "pot of meat," but actually a meat soup featuring large pieces of *chayote* (a green, pear-shaped vegetable that grows on vines), *ayote* (a pumpkin-like squash), *elote*, *yuca*, *plátano*, and other vegetables

palomitas de maíz—"little doves," or popcorn

pan bon—a dark, sweet bread with batter designs on top—a Limón specialty

pan de maíz—a thick, sweet bread made with fresh corn

patacones—fried, mashed green plantains, served like french fries with meals on the Atlantic Coast

patí—flour-based *empanadas* filled with fruit or spicy meat, sold on the Atlantic Coast

picadillo—a side dish of sautéed vegetables, often containing meat

plátanos—plantains. They look like large bananas, but cannot be eaten raw. Sweet and delicious when fried or baked. Also sold in a form similar to potato chips. A Central American staple

queque seco—pound cake

refrescos—cold fruit drinks. Most *refrescos* are made with a lot of sugar. If you order a *refresco* that is not made in advance, like *papaya en agua, papaya en leche*, or *jugo de zanahoria* (carrot juice), you can ask for it *sin azúcar* (without sugar) and add your own to taste. Similarly, an *ensalada de frutas* (fruit salad) might come smothered in Jell-O and ice cream. You can ask for it *sin gelatina, sin helados*

sopa de mondongo—tripe soup

sopa negra—soup made from bean gravy, with hard-boiled egg and vegetables added

tacos—a bit of meat topped with cabbage salad in a tortilla

tamal asado—a sweet cornmeal cake

tamal de elote—sweet corn tamales, wrapped in cornhusks

tamales—cornmeal, usually stuffed with pork or chicken, wrapped in banana leaves and boiled—a Christmas tradition

tapa de dulce—native brown sugar, sold in a solid form that looks like an inverted flower pot. It's grated with a knife or boiled into a syrup from which is made *agua dulce*, a popular campesino drink

torta chilena—a many-layered pastry filled with *dulce de leche*

tortas—sandwiches on bread rolls

tortilla—may mean the Costa Rican thin, small, corn tortilla, but also another name for an omelette

tortilla de queso—a large, thick tortilla with cheese mixed into the dough

yuca—manioc, a thick tuber, another staple of the Central American diet. *Enyucados* are *empanadas* made from a yuca-based dough

SOUVENIRS

You can fill your entire list with inexpensive souvenirs that benefit local conservation and humanitarian efforts, making your gifts meaningful conversation items. **ANAI** (2224-3570) makes beautiful necklaces, earrings and belt buckles out of leatherback turtle shells that they find on the beach. The $5 to $15 you pay goes directly to supporting their turtle protection projects in the Gandoca–Manzanillo Wildlife Refuge on the Caribbean coast. The **Damas Voluntarias** (2228-0279) makes calendars and note cards featuring local artwork. Proceeds support needy children. The **Humanitarian Foundation** (2282-6358) sells journals and traditional bows and arrows and other crafts from the Cabécar indigenous community. The **Sarapiquí Conservation Learning Center** (2766-6482) offers a bilingual cookbook of Costa Rican dishes to support its after-school education programs.

Tiny *huacas*, copies of pre-Columbian jewelry representing frogs, lizards, turtles, and humanesque deities, are relatively inexpensive and make lovely necklaces, earrings, and tiepins. Authentic pre-Columbian artifacts cannot be taken out of the country, so don't believe anyone who tells you something is original. If it is original, the item has been stolen from an archaeological site.

David Norman's inexpensive Costa Rican **wildlife coloring books** are also good presents for kids. Intelligently written, they describe some of the animals you might encounter on a trip to Costa Rica. The drawings are so accurate that they can be used as guides to the animals. Look for the coloring books in gift shops or visit amerisol.com/costarica/shop/kids.html.

If you're staying for a while, avail yourself of the low prices and excellent work of local tailors and seamstresses. They make fine formal clothes, or can copy your favorite designs. The best way to find one is to ask well-dressed Ticos whom they would recommend.

You can buy freshly ground **coffee** or coffee beans at the Central Market, or at the airport in souvenir shops. It is usually ground fine for use in the *chorreador*, a filter bag that hangs from a wooden stand. Cafe Britt (800-462-7488; cafebritt.com) offers several gift packages featuring coffee, macadamia nuts, and chocolate-covered coffee beans, or an espresso-lover's kit including a grinder. Percolator grinds are available in supermarkets, where you'll find *Caferica*, a coffee liqueur, as well as dried bananas, coconut twirls, macadamia nuts, cashews, yummy Angel jams, fruit leathers, and pastes. *Tapa de dulce*, the native hard brown sugar, can be grated to add a rich flavor to baked goods or used on cereal and in coffee. We've heard of tourists who take home cases of **Salsa Lizano**, a tasty bottled sauce that Ticos love to sprinkle on their *gallo pinto*.

Souvenir shops all over the country carry souvenirs made from renewable resources by rural artisans. These include seed jewelry, carvings and boxes of plantation-grown wood, pencils made from coffee branches, and recycled paper notebooks and stationery.

The capital of Costa Rican **woodcraft** is Sarchí, about an hour northwest of San José (see the Central Valley chapter). Everything from salad bowls to rocking chairs to miniature ox carts (the rocking chairs fold, and the ox carts come apart for easy transport) can be purchased there. **Artesanía Napoleon** (2454-4118), across from Fábrica de Carretas Joaquín Chaverri, will take care of mailing your purchases home for you. The capital of Costa Rican **leathercrafts** is Moravia, a suburb of San José, where there are a couple of blocks filled with souvenir shops near the main square. **Artesanía la Rueda** (2235-8357), 100 meters south and 100 meters east of the Municipalidad in Moravia, will mail all your gifts for you.

If you are going to Monteverde, save some of your souvenir budget for **CASEM**, the women's crafts cooperative there, which specializes in embroidered and handpainted clothing depicting cloud-forest wildlife. You'll see it on the right as you enter Monteverde.

Wicker, raffia, and woven palm-leaf items should be spray varnished when you get home. Don't be tempted to buy tortoise-shell or alligator-skin goods—they are made from endangered animals that are internationally protected. Customs officials at your home-country airport will confiscate those items.

See the "Souvenirs" section in the San José chapter for more on where to shop in the capital.

FIVE

The Outdoors

Costa Rica is an outdoor adventurer's paradise. From volcanoes and cloud forests to pristine beaches, this tropical wonder boasts breathtaking beauty. You'll find every imaginable activity—from birdwatching to bungee jumping. This is definitely the place to come to take that walk on the "wild side."

NATIONAL PARKS, RESERVES, AND WILDLIFE REFUGES

Costa Rica's 30 national parks, ten biological reserves, and 66 wildlife refuges occupy approximately 16 percent of national territory and protect jewels of the country's rich but diminishing wilderness. The whole country is organized into ten mosaic-like "Conservation Areas." Each of these has as its nucleus one or more totally protected national parks or absolute reserves. These are buffered by forest reserves and "protected zones" where sustainable land use is supposed to take place, bringing protected areas to 27 percent of Costa Rica's territory.

In some areas surrounding the national parks there are private reserves. Visitors to these wild areas can stay at small private lodges and tour the privately held land, seeing flora and fauna similar to that in the national parks; their money helps preserve these important buffer zones.

Foreign visitors to the national parks pay $10 per person per day, children ages 6 to 12 pay $1.

All national parks, reserves, and refuges are indicated on the fold-out map at the back of this book, and many are described in our chapters on the various regions.

For specialized information on biodiversity in the protected areas, contact the Instituto Nacional de Biodiversidad (INBio, 2507-8100; inbio.ac.cr), located in Santo Domingo de Heredia, 15 minutes northwest of San José.

INBioparque (open daily, 8 a.m. to 6 p.m.; last admission, 4 p.m.; 2507-8107; inbioparque.org, inbioparque@inbio.ac.cr; entrance fee $23, children 3 to 12 $13, students with ID $17) provides a thorough introduction to Costa Rica's national parks for first-time visitors, and showcases the work of INBio and its parataxonomists, who are trying to identify all the plant, insect, and animal species in Costa Rica. Along the paved, wheelchair-accessible trails, you can see examples of several native ecosystems plus gardens of ornamental, medicinal, and aromatic plants and fruit trees, as well as exhibits of boa constrictors, turtles, iguanas, frogs, tarantulas, bees, ants, butterflies, fish, and orchids. You can see domestic farm animals and a sugar mill at "The Farm." Guided tours (adults $30, students $24, including lunch) last from two and a half to four hours, depending on visitors' interests. A delicious typical breakfast or lunch can be enjoyed in their attractive restaurant. Their souvenir shop is full of nature-based books, CDs, and gifts. Transportation from San José is also available as part of a package (two people minimum). It is located in Santo Domingo de Heredia, 400 meters north and 250 meters west of the Shell station.

HIKING

Although Costa Rica has been described as a Disneyland of ecological wonders, you must be aware that here you are dealing with Mother Nature in all her harsh reality. Every year several overconfident hikers get lost in Costa Rica's dense forests. For example, in recent years, hikers were lost in unseasonal fog and rain for 11 days on Barva Volcano on the west side of Braulio Carrillo National Park. Their goal was a simple day hike around the crater lake, but landslides blocking the trails threw them off course. Two hikers became lost and died in the mountains of Talamanca in 1999, and in 2000 a Canadian hiker ignored signs telling him to keep on the trail and ended up sliding into the crater of Volcán Rincón de La Vieja, where he was stranded for four days with only a water bottle and a camera. Luckily, the volcano was in an inactive phase, and he was rescued. In May 2006, even Carlos Manuel Rodriguez, Costa Rica's Minister of Energy and the Environment, got separated from his party and was lost for three days in Corcovado National Park. Part of the danger is caused by the fact that Costa Rica's famous parks are victims of the country's budget deficit, and trails are not maintained with the same rigor foreigners are used to. Tropical weather itself makes trail maintenance a full-time job.

The Red Cross gives the following recommendations for solo hikers:

- prepare for the worst
- tell someone where you're going and when you'll be back
- wear boots and layer your clothing
- carry a canteen, knife, flashlight with extra batteries, candy, dried fruit or granola bars, a compass, a map, a poncho or plastic in case you need to make a shelter, a first-aid kit, matches, a small piece of rubber and a candle (for lighting fires), and, if possible, a light sleeping bag
- pack everything in plastic bags
- don't touch anything without looking
- bring medications
- if you get lost, stay calm and work with other people in your group as a team

Always stay on the trail when hiking in mountainous areas. The hikers who have gotten lost for several days—and survived—have done so by drinking river water, eating *palmito* (the edible core of certain palm trees), and hunting wild animals. Rescuers recommend building a primitive shelter and tying a brightly colored cloth to it if you think anyone will come looking for you. If no one knows you are lost, following a river downstream is probably the best way to reach civilization.

CAMPING

Don't expect to find many well-organized campgrounds in Costa Rica. Most parks have camping facilities; most refuges and reserves don't. The main problems with camping are rain (it's better to come during the dry season if you plan to camp) and not being able to leave things in your tent unless there is someone around to watch it. Camping on public beaches is illegal unless it is in a designated area. With increasing crime in beach areas, camping is not recommended.

BEACHES

The Ecological Blue Flag program (Bandera Azul Ecológica) is an incentive for local communities to keep their beaches and rivers uncontaminated and clean. The 59 beaches that earned the coveted Blue Flag in 2007 scored at least 90 percent on a test that covers microbiological purity of ocean water, safety of drinking water, beach cleanliness, garbage disposal, environmental education, and security. Beaches that score 100 percent and receive an AA rating have signage indicating areas with dangerous currents and have lifeguards during the high season. The AAA rating is reserved for those beaches that meet all the above requirements, have zoning plans, are accessible to disabled people, and have public bathrooms and showers. Only one beach, Playa Blanca at Punta Leona, gained this distinction.

Thirty-three communities that depend on rivers for tourism also won the Blue Flag by passing tests on drinking water quality, waste disposal, signage, environmental education, availability of health care, water protection, and security. In order to teach children how to carry out the Blue Flag process, 206 educational centers were also given the award.

BEACH SAFETY

Each year, hundreds of ocean bathers suffer serious near-drownings or die due to their ignorance about rip currents, a phenomenon found on wave-swept beaches all over the world—including Costa Rica. Ironically, these currents can be fun if properly understood—yet they are responsible for 80 percent of ocean drownings, or four out of every five. Most of Costa Rica's beaches do not have lifeguards, so the information below is important.

A rip current is a surplus of water, put ashore by waves, that finds a channel to drain and reach equilibrium. All rip currents have three parts: the feeder current, the neck, and the head. The feeder current is made up of water moving parallel to the beach. You know you're in one when, after a few minutes, you notice that your friends on the beach have moved down 30 to 50 yards, yet you thought you were standing still.

At a depression in the ocean floor, the current turns out to sea. This can occur in knee- to waist-deep water, and is where the "neck" begins. The current in the neck is very swift, like a river. It can carry a swimmer out to sea at three to six miles per hour, faster than a strong swimmer's rate of two to four miles per hour, and can move a person 100 yards in just a moment. It's typical for an inexperienced swimmer to panic when caught in the neck, and it is here that most drownings occur.

What to do if you get caught in a rip current: If you're a weak swimmer, call for help as soon as you notice a current is moving you and making it difficult to get in toward land. Most drowning victims are caught in water just above waist level.

If you realize that you can't walk directly in, you should turn and walk sideways, leaping toward the beach with every wave, to let the water "push" you toward shore.

A crashing surf can throw you off balance, so it's dangerous to turn your back to it. Once off balance, a swimmer is unable to get traction on the ocean floor and can be dragged out five feet into deeper water with each swell. After a few swells you may be in over your head, and it becomes extremely important to float—by arching your back, head back, nose pointing in the air.

Floating conserves energy. The human body is buoyant, especially in saltwater. Everyone should learn to float because every minute you can salvage gives someone the opportunity to make a rescue.

Once you are no longer touching bottom and are in a rip, you should not fight against the current in an effort to get back to shore, for this is like "swimming up a river" and will sap your strength.

The rip current loses its strength just beyond the breakers, dissipating its energy and eventually delivering you to relatively calm waters. This area, known as the "head," may appear to have a mushroom shape when seen from the air, as debris picked up by the current is dispersed.

Here, the water is deep but calm. You can get back to shore by moving parallel to the beach in the direction of the bend of the current, and then heading toward shore at a 45-degree angle rather than straight in, to avoid getting caught in the feeder current again.

There are four types of rip currents: permanent, fixed, flash, and traveling.

Permanent rips occur at river mouths, estuaries, or by small streams, and can be quite wide. They also occur at finger jetties designed to prevent beach erosion, where the water's lateral drift is forced to turn seaward.

Fixed, flash, and traveling rips are caused by wind-generated waves.

Fixed currents, which appear only on long, sandy, surf-swept beaches, can move up or down the beach depending on shifts in the ocean floor, but they are generally stable, staying in one spot for several hours or even an entire day.

Flash, or *temporary*, *rips* are created when an increased volume of water is brought to shore from sudden wave build-ups. These currents can occur on a warm, sunny day, generated by distant storms whose waves do not lose their energy until they crash on a shore. The excess water build-up has no opportunity to drain and reach equilibrium while the unusually large and fast waves are coming in; a flash rip current therefore forms during a lull in wave action.

A *traveling rip current* is just what the name implies. You'll see it in front of you; then, five minutes later, it may have moved 15 yards up or down the beach. Traveling rips can move 30 yards in a minute. They occur on long, sandy beaches where there are no fixed depressions on the ocean floor.

How to spot a rip current: Some beaches, such as **Espadilla** at Manuel Antonio, **Playa Dominical**, **Jacó**, **Playa Grande** in Guanacaste, and **Playa Cocles** south of Puerto Viejo, are known to have rip currents and must *al-*

ways be approached with caution. The currents can be spotted by the trained eye by a brownish discoloration on the water's surface, caused by sand and debris; or there can be a flattening effect as the water rushes out to sea, making the surface appear deceptively smooth.

As a safety precaution, before you enter the ocean, throw a buoyant object like a coconut or a stick into the water and watch where the current carries it: This is the direction you will have to go before you can get back to shore. There is definitely one direction that is better than the other.

Rip currents aren't dangerous to people who understand them. The more you know about the ocean, the more fun it can be. Surfers use rip currents as an energy saver, since they provide "a free ride" out to sea just beyond the breakers. Good swimmers are encouraged to seek out rip currents under controlled conditions—and with experienced trainers. As long as you swim in the ocean, you might get caught in a rip current, so it's critical that you know how to get out of one. Following are some rip current rules of thumb:

- Weak swimmers should avoid surf-swept beaches.

- The safest beaches include Bahía Junquillal Wildlife Refuge, Playa Hermosa in northern Guanacaste, Playas del Coco, Sámara, Carrillo, Bahía Ballena/Tambor, any beach on the Golfo Dulce between Puerto Jimenez and Golfito, any beach in Ballena National Marine Park in Uvita de Osa, and the third beach at Manuel Antonio.

- Be sure to ask at your hotel where it is safe to swim, and observe other swimmers. At certain beaches, playing in knee-deep water is the only water play recommended.

- Never swim alone.

- Always be prepared to signal for help at the earliest sign of trouble.

- After a long period in the sun, rest in the shade before swimming to avoid hypertension.

FISHING

Deep-sea sportfishing for sailfish, marlin, tuna, wahoo, and more than a dozen other species is very big in Costa Rica. Most of it is catch-and-release. The most popular fishing areas are Guanacaste, Jacó, and Quepos on the Central Pacific, and Golfito and Drake Bay in the Southern Zone. Some claim that the world's best tarpon and snook fishing is in Barra del Colorado on the Atlantic. Tarpon can also be fished in Manzanillo (tarponville.com) on the southern Atlantic and in Caño Negro lagoon. Freshwater fishing for rainbow bass is good in Lake Arenal, Caño Negro lagoon, and Lago Hule in the Northern Zone. Trout can be fished in the Río Savegre, the Río

Chirripó Pacífico, in Copey de Dota, and Cerro de la Muerte in the mountainous Southern Zone. You can find out everything you need to know about fishing from **Costa Rica Outdoors** (costaricaoutdoors.com, info@costarica outdoors.com).

OUTDOOR ADVENTURE SPORTS

When it comes to adventure sports, it is good to stick to companies with a reputation for safety. It is not a good idea to go for the cheapest tour. Any adventure tour company worth its salt will be certified by the ICT, the Costa Rican Tourism Institute. Make sure the companies you travel with have met these standards. Whether or not a person is suitable for an activity is the outfitter's—not the client's—decision. This may seem obvious, but the economic pressure not to cancel trips is strong, and many outfitters fail to train their guides to enforce clear cancellation policies in the face of client pressure.

If your guide recommends that you do not do something, follow his or her orders.

The dry season (December 15 to April 15) is the best time to come for hiking, biking, and horseback riding because creeks are dry and rivers are low. Less rain makes for better diving, too. Rappelling and caving are best when the rocks are dry.

SURFING

Costa Rica has become famous for its great waves. The Pacific, with its long point breaks, river mouths, and beach breaks, keeps surfers busy all year. Guanacaste is best in the windy season from January through May; the Central Pacific is best August through October. If they want to get serious, surfers go to the Atlantic from December through March, where waves from deep water break over the shallow reef, creating the perfect imitation of Hawaiian surf.

Get the latest info at **crsurf.com**, with surf reports, beach descriptions and links to photographers, environmental groups and travel assistance for surfers. **World Wide Adventures** (800-796-9110; worldwideadventures.com) runs surfing trips to Costa Rica and can tell you which airlines charge extra for surfboards. *The Surfer's Guide to Costa Rica* is the original and still most detailed guide to surf destinations in Costa Rica, and can be found at **surfingtravel.com.**

The nearest surfing beach to San José is **Boca Barranca**, between Puntarenas and Puerto Caldera, known for long waves at high and low tide. The water can be very dirty. About a half-hour to the south are **Playa Jacó** and **Playa Hermosa** (not to be confused with Playa Hermosa in Guanacaste), where an international surfing contest is held each year. These beaches have a large expatriate and Tico surfing community that provides services like board repairs, wave reports, surfing tours, and cabinas with surfers' discounts. The whole area between Jacó and **Playa Dominical** to the south has many excellent surfing spots. Families might want to check out **Green Iguana Surf Camp** (greeniguanasurfcamp.com) in Dominical. It has an excellent, detailed "surf science" web page and teaches kids as young as 6. Students ages 18 and younger must be accompanied by an adult.

Playa Pavones, south of Golfito on the Golfo Dulce, is said to have a left "so long you can take a nap on it," but we have heard that it's been inconsistent lately. The waves at **Playa Zancudo**, just to the north, are better for beginners. Across the Golfo Dulce, **Playa Matapalo** near the tip of the Osa Peninsula attracts advanced surfers.

In central Guanacaste, **Tamarindo** is known for a smooth and slow wave that helps beginners get their bearings. For this reason it is often crowded. Beginners graduate from Tamarindo to **Playa Avellanas**, half an hour to the south. After that, they are ready to take on the rougher waves at **Playa Langosta** or **Playa Grande**, located on either side of Tamarindo. Avellanas also has areas for advanced surfers off of its reef. **Playa Negra**, south of Avellanas, is for experienced surfers, with a very fast wave at incoming high tide. Advanced surfers can benefit from hiring a guide who will take them to the secret spots. **Mop Adventures** (8833-7283; mopadventures.com, yeffreyr@hotmail.com) is run by Yeffrey Rojas, an International Surfing Association certified judge, so he is familiar with surfing in many countries.

Farther south, **Playas Nosara** and **Guiones** are known for great waves. **Corky Carol's Surf School** (surfschool.net) gives lessons in Nosara. **Playas Malpaís**, **Santa Teresa**, and **Coyote** on the west side of the Nicoya Peninsula are becoming known for their waves, and **Playa Cedros** on the east side of the Peninsula below Montezuma is good for beginners (see Central Pacific Zone chapter).

Farther north, **Playa Naranjo**, in Santa Rosa National Park, is known for **Witch's Rock**, where there are perfect tubular waves. The road to Playa Naranjo is very rough; rented SUVs get stuck there regularly. If you drive there, get the car with the highest clearance you can. Surfing outfitters run trips from Tamarindo and other beaches by sea to Witch's Rock. They *must* pay the $10/person park entrance fee even if arriving by sea. There is a campground right on the beach.

Puerto Viejo, south of Limón, is famous for "La Salsa Brava," a challenging ride responsible for many a broken surfboard. Take it right. If you take it left, you may crash. It is usually up January to April and only for advanced surfers. Playa Cocles farther south is easier.

There are board-rental shops in Puntarenas, Jacó, Manuel Antonio, Limón, Puerto Viejo, and Cahuita (around $20/day). Used boards cost $160-$260. Many car-rental agencies and hotels give discounts to surfers, especially May through November.

Kitesurfing is one of the fastest growing new sports. There is a kitesurfing instructor in Salinas Bay, Guanacaste, near the Nicaraguan border (suntoursandfun.com).

SCUBA DIVING

Costa Rica is blessed with coral formations on both the Pacific and Atlantic coasts. The reefs off Manzanillo in the Gandoca–Manzanillo Wildlife Refuge are the healthiest on the Caribbean, partly because the area is far from a major river mouth. Diving operations in Guanacaste, spearheaded by Hotel El Ocotal, have put floating moorings near dive sites so that anchors will not damage the coral.

Inexpensive diving excursions and courses are available through **Aquamor** (greencoast.com/aquamor.htm) in Manzanillo on the Talamanca coast. You'll find diving operations in Playa del Coco, Ocotal, Playa Hermosa, Brasilito, Flamingo, and Tamarindo. In the Central Pacific Zone, look for divemasters in Punta Leona, Playa Jacó, and Manuel Antonio. Drake Bay on the Osa Peninsula in the Southern Zone is a mecca for divers because of the clear waters found off Isla del Caño. Because its waters are protected, there are more fish. Many hotels offer diving there. Isla del Coco, 500 kilometers southwest of Costa Rica, is famous for excellent diving and lots of sharks; in 2005 a couple of divers disappeared there and were never found. **Undersea Hunter** (2228-6613, in North America: 800-203-2120; underseahunter.com) offers ten-day trips to the island.

KAYAKING AND CANOEING

Various companies and hotels along both coasts rent kayaks and offer sea kayaking trips. We mention them in the regional chapters. Kayaks are quite stable, and first-timers can feel safe and get a rush when exploring with a good guide. The gentle waters of the Golfo Dulce on the east side of the Osa Peninsula lend themselves to peaceful sea kayaking. See the Puerto Jimenez and Golfo Dulce sections of the Southern Zone chapter. **Southern Expeditions** (2787-0100; southernexpeditionscr.com) can lead you through the natural tunnels in **Ballena National Park** south of Dominical. The dolphins of the Caribbean know well the kayaks and guides of **Aquamor Adventures** (2759-9612; greencoast.com/aquamor.htm, aquamorl@racsa.co.

cr) based in the Gandoca–Manzanillo Wildlife Refuge south of Puerto Viejo de Talamanca. **Escondido Trex** (2735-5210; escondidotrex.com) specializes in sea kayaking on the Golfo Dulce side of the Osa Peninsula.

Vermont-based **Battenkill Canoe Ltd.** (in North America: 800-421-5268; battenkill.com) leads canoe tours to Yorkín in the Bribrí indigenous lands of Talamanca, and to rivers in the Northern Zone. See the Tortuguero section in the Atlantic Coast chapter for info on *cayucas*. **Canoe Costa Rica** (in the U.S.: 732-736-6586; canoecostarica.com) leads customized five- to ten-day trips all over Costa Rica.

WHITEWATER SPORTS

Rafters, canoers, and kayakers flock to Costa Rica for its exciting rivers. Rivers are rated Class I (still water) to Class VI (waterfalls). Most whitewater rafting tours are Class II (easy) to Class V (very advanced). Class II is the way to go if you want to relax and spot birds and other wildlife. Class III is good for family fun and thrills; Class III guides must have at least six months of training at a well-known guide school. Class IV rapids are long, very turbulent, and constricted, and require paying close attention to the instructions of an experienced guide. Make sure that rafts, life jackets, paddles and helmets are in excellent condition. River classification can change depending on water level.

In the Northern Zone, the Sarapiquí and Toro rivers offer both Class II and Class IV rapids. Guanacaste's Corobicí River is Class II. Near Manuel Antonio are the flowing Río Naranjo and the more complex Savegre. The Río General near San Isidro in the Southern Zone has Class III and IV rapids. Most rafters come to Costa Rica for the Pacuare (near Turrialba, about two hours east of San José), known for its scenic gorges, primary forest, wildlife, and Class III and IV rapids. Hopefully it will be made into a national park soon.

Wear closed-toed, lightweight shoes, such as old sneakers. Bring sunblock and a swimsuit. Leave your passport, money, and fragile equipment behind in a secure place because you *will* get wet.

The Río Pacuare is considered world-class by athletes and ranked one of the five best rafting rivers by the Discovery Channel. In addition to their one-day rafting trips, **Ríos Tropicales** (2233-6455, in the U.S.: 866-722-8273; riostropicales.com) offers four-day trips that include a whitewater paddle to its lodge on the Pacuare, with a short, complimentary canopy tour and hiking to jungle waterfalls. They also run sea kayaking trips to Curú on the Nicoya Peninsula, with camping on a deserted beach and paddles to nearby islands. Kayaking the quiet canals of Tortuguero is also on their menu.

Costa Rica Nature Adventures (2225-3939, in North America: 800-321-8410; toenjoynature.com) also has a jungle lodge on the Pacuare with a more complete canopy tour ($45). Their ten-day tour takes you to the Monteverde canopy tour, biking at the base of Arenal volcano, rafting on the Río Sarapiquí, kayaking in Tortuguero, and rafting on the Pacuare. In Turrialba, **Serendipity Adventures** (in North America: 877-507-1358; serendipityadventures.com) specializes in active adventures for families and other groups. **Tico's River Adventures** (2556-1231; ticoriver.com) offers whitewater rafting as well as kayak instruction. **Rio Loco's Tropical Tours** (2556-6035; whiteh2o.com) does rafting tours and gets you in touch with the local community in Turrialba.

In Manuel Antonio, **Iguana Tours** (2777-2052; iguanatours.com) and **Adventure Manuel Antonio** (2777-1084; adventuremanuelantonio.com) offer trips down the Savegre and Naranjo rivers as well as kayaking in the mangroves. In the Northern Zone, **Aventuras de Sarapiquí** (2766-6768; sarapiqui.com) rafts the Río Sarapiquí and has basic canoe instruction. **Aguas Bravas** (2292-2072; aguas-bravas.co.cr) rafts the Sarapiquí, Toro, and Peñas Blancas rivers, and runs mountain bike and horseback tours. You can usually book whitewater rafting tours through your hotel.

Do not be disappointed if your trip is cancelled due to too-high or too-low water levels. Six people have died in rafting accidents since 2000, and companies should err on the side of caution.

BIKING

Among Costa Ricans, mountain biking is second only to soccer. The Costa Rican Cycling Federation runs over 150 mountain bike races each year. The hills, heat, and humidity make biking in Costa Rica difficult for beginners; watch out for high winds in Guanacaste during the dry season. Most major roads in Costa Rica do not have bike paths, so it makes sense to go with an experienced guide who knows where the safe biking trails are. International biking superstars come each November to participate in the annual **Ruta de los Conquistadores Race** (2225-8186; adventurerace.com), which starts in Puntarenas, climbs Volcán Turrialba, and ends up on the Caribbean coast. You can take a tour along the same route at a more relaxed pace. **BiCosta Rica** (8380-3844, 4446-7585; bruncas.com/bicostarica.html) organizes mountain-bike tours lasting from one day to one week all over the country. **Coast to Coast Adventures** (2280-8054; ctocadventures.com) also offers hiking, biking, sea kayaking, and rafting tours. **Corcovado Expeditions** (8818-9962; corcovadoexpeditions.net) leads kayak and mountain bike tours in Drake Bay. **Lava Tours** (2281-2458, in North America: 888-

862-2424; lava-tours.com) offers grueling tours to Monteverde and Arenal. **Bike Arenal** (2479-9454, in North America: 866-465-4114; bikearenal.com) offers half-day to seven-day tours. **Costa Rica Sun Tours** (2296-7757; cr suntours.com) leads a three day combination of rafting and mountain biking in the Turrialba area, as well as guided 8- to 12-day excursions.

There are bike rental places in Puerto Viejo de Talamanca, La Fortuna, Sámara, Jacó, Puerto Jiménez, and many other destinations.

BUNGEE JUMPING

Bungee jumping has come to Costa Rica. Thrill-seekers jump from a 265-foot abandoned bridge near the Grecia exit on the highway to Puntarenas. **Tropical Bungee** (2248-2212, cell: 8398-8134; bungee.co.cr) offers this ultimate adrenaline rush as well as rock climbing and rappelling.

HOT AIR BALLOON RIDES AND ULTRALIGHTS

Floating in a hot air balloon will give you a bird's eye view of the Costa Rican countryside. **Serendipity Adventures** (2558-1000, in North America: 877-507-1358; serendipityadventures.com) is Costa Rica's only ballooning operator since 1991, and offers daybreak flights 20 miles east of Arenal Volcano. They specialize in custom adventures for families, couples, and groups of friends or co-workers.

The Flying Crocodile (2656-8048, cell: 8827-8858; flying-crocodile. com, flycroco@racsa.co.cr), specializing in ultralight flying trips, is run by a German pilot just north of Playa Sámara, who can also train you to become an ultralight pilot yourself. **Skyline of Costa Rica** (flyultralight.com, skyline@racsa.co.cr) operates out of Uvita, near Ballena National Marine Park, south of Dominical.

TREETOP EXPLORATIONS

Inspired by biologist Donald Perry's explorations of the rainforest canopy and his subsequent Rainforest Aerial Tram (Chapter Nine), there are now many opportunities for visitors (who don't suffer from vertigo) to ascend into the treetops, either to walk on hanging bridges at canopy level, sit on an observation platform, or to zoom from tree to tree using a cable-and-pulley system. Make sure that the company you go with has been certified by the ICT.

Bridges suspended at canopy level: Monteverde **Reserve**, the **SkyWalk** and **Selvatura** (also in Monteverde), **Arenal Hanging Bridges**, the **Rainmaker Reserve** north of Manuel Antonio, **Reserva Los Campesinos** inland from Manuel Antonio, the **Tirimbina Reserve** in the Northern Zone, and

Heliconias Rainforest Reserve in Bijagua de Upala north of Cañas all have bridge systems suspended in the canopy so that you can walk instead of zip.

Observation platforms: In the Osa, **Bosque del Cabo** (2735-5206; bosquedelcabo.com) has an observation platform you get to on a zipline, as does **El Remanso** (2735-5569; elremanso.com). In Dominical, **Hacienda Barú** (2787-0003; haciendabaru.com) has an observation platform near its Flight of the Toucan zipline canopy tour. In addition to its zipline, **Selva Bananito Lodge** (2253-8118; selvabananito.com), in Limón Province, teaches you how to climb into the canopy with a secure system of ropes, harnesses, and ascenders. **La Isla Botanical Gardens** (greencoast.com/garden) in Puerto Viejo de Talamanca also has an observation platform in a tree.

HORSEBACK RIDING

Most beach and mountain resorts rent horses, and we mention them throughout the book. Following are some places that are known for their love of horses. Many of them offer lodging as well. In Monteverde, **Sabine's Smiling Horses** (2645-6894; horseback-riding-tour.com) and **El Sol** (2645-5838; elsolnuestro.com) offer excellent horses and tours. In Montezuma, **Finca Los Caballos** (2642-0124; naturelodge.net) specializes in high-quality equine experiences. **Brisas del Nara** (2779-1235; horsebacktour.com) takes you to mountain waterfalls inland from Manuel Antonio, as does **Don Lulo's** (cataratasnauyaca.com), inland from Dominical, and **Rancho La Merced** (rancholamerced,com) in Uvita de Osa. For a beautiful down-home Costa Rican experience, rent a horse from **Poor Man's Paradise** (2771-9686; mypoormansparadise.com) to explore the beaches south of Drake Bay in the Osa Peninsula.

Make sure that the rented horses are not tired and do not have sores or swollen places. Give them plenty of opportunity to drink water during the

RECOMMENDED CANOPY TOURS

In February 2006, with the assistance of Horizontes Nature Tours, we sent two intrepid 16- and 18-year-old researchers off to experience 15 different canopy tours in Miramar, Monteverde, the Rincón de la Vieja area, Jacó, Parrita, Manuel Antonio, Río Pacuare, and Volcán Poás. Their three favorites were:

Skytrek (2645-5238; skytrek.com; minimum age/weight: 8 years/60 pounds) in Monteverde: "Recommended for people who want to go fast on long cables that are high in the air and still see beautiful forest. Handlebar pulley system enhances speed and safety but reduces visibility. Automatic braking is done by the guides. Very good view." Now the same company has another Skytrek in full view of the active side of Arenal Volcano. At Skytrek Monteverde, you have to hike with your harness on, but the Arenal Skytrek transports you up to the first platform in a state-of-the-art electric tram designed by the famous Austrian ski-lift maker, Doplmeyer.

The **Cañon Tour** (2665-3303; guachipelin.com) at Hacienda Guachipelin near Rincón de la Vieja: "With two Tarzan swings, one rappel, one rock climb, and nine average cables, a variety of adventure activities are combined into one two-hour tour in a beautiful canyon. Everything goes together to make a good overall experience. Recommended for people who want thrill and nature in one package."

Chiclet's Canopy Tour (jacowave.com; not suitable for ages 5 and under) in Playa Hermosa, near Playa Jacó: "Recommended for people looking for a canopy tour that is adventurous and exciting yet is educational and has very good views of Playa Hermosa and trees. Knowledgeable, friendly, and amusing guides."

For beginners, our researchers recommend the **Canopy Safari** (2777-0100; canopysafari.com; minimum age: 5) near Manuel Antonio because there is no braking and none of the nine cables are very fast. There are 21 platforms, one suspension bridge, two rappels and one Tarzan swing. Guides accompany smaller children. The five-hour tour is a 45-minute ride from Manuel Antonio. A meal is served at the beginning of the tour. "Enthusiastic and entertaining guides, nice forest."

Keep in mind that our researchers did not visit canopy tours in every area and that their main criteria for excellence was a combination of thrills and nature.

trip and don't leave them standing in the sun. If you feel horses or any other animals are being mistreated, you can report it to the Asociación Humanitaria para la Protección Animal de Costa Rica (2267-7158; animal sheltercostarica.com) in Los Angeles de San Rafael de Heredia.

Be sure to wear long pants when you ride, or you'll end up with sore, irritated skin on your legs, and check yourself for ticks afterwards.

SOCCER

Costa Ricans are very sports-minded. There isn't a district, town, or city where *fútbol* (soccer) isn't played. Much to the Ticos' delight, Costa Rica's national team made it into the World Cup in 2002 and in 2006. It's said that Costa Ricans learn to kick a ball before they learn to walk! There are teams all over the country in every imaginable category, including all ages and both sexes, although only men play on the major teams. If you want to experience the Ticos' love for this sport firsthand, attend a Sunday soccer match. Be aware that Ticos can get pretty crazy at these games. During the final games of the 1993 national championship at the Cartago stadium, a bad call was made. Fans cut through the chain-link fence and streamed onto the field in the middle of the game. A riot ensued. The referees fled, the National Guard was called to the scene, and the game was terminated. In the next week, the Cartago team went to the Supreme Court to demand retribution for this "violation of their human rights" (no joke). After tempers cooled, the teams had a private game with no spectators, and Heredia was declared the national champion. The whole episode gave Tico men something to discuss in the backs of buses for months.

TENNIS

Many upscale beach and mountain hotels, like El Ocotal, south of Playas del Coco, and Villa Serena in Playa Junquillal, have tennis courts. Both are in Guanacaste. Often courts are lighted at night because it's too hot to play during the day.

RUNNING

There are many marathons during the year, including the one sponsored each April by the **University for Peace**. The **Hash House Harriers** (costaricahhh.com), a worldwide organization devoted to running and beer-drinking, also meets here once a week.

SIX

Getting to Know San José

In 1821, after learning that Guatemala had declared its independence from Spain, Costa Rica began creating its own form of self-government. During this process, General Agustín de Iturbide, self-proclaimed emperor of Mexico, sent word urging immediate annexation to his empire. The citizens of the older cities of Heredia and Cartago were in favor of annexation, but the more liberal residents of Alajuela and San José saw de Iturbide's demand as imperialist and chose independence. A short civil war ensued; it was won in 1823 by the *independistas*, who moved the capital city from Cartago to San José.

Today San José is a noisy, bustling city—the economic, political, and cultural center of the country. If you have come to Costa Rica to get close to nature, you will probably want to get out of San José as fast as possible. Set in the middle of the Central Valley, surrounded by high mountains, it is battling the demons of its rapid growth: congested one-way streets filled with too many cars, buses, and taxis belching black diesel smoke into the mountain air; a lack of jobs for all the country people who have given up on working the land and are trying their luck in the city; increasing crime.

On the upside, San José still ranks as one of the safer cities in the Western Hemisphere and, although crime is increasing, has much less violent crime than most U.S. cities. Foreigners enjoy the city's springlike climate, the availability of high-quality cultural events like National Symphony concerts and international music, dance, theater, and film festivals. There are plenty of malls and services in the suburbs of Rohrmoser, Escazú, and Santa Ana to the west, and Moravia, Curridabat, and Trés Ríos to the east. Great places to dine are also plentiful in San José, as you'll see in this chapter. Modern supermarkets have largely taken the place of the Mercado Central, but Saturday morning farmers markets held in the streets of different neighborhoods still provide a folksy tone and a fair-like atmosphere. And city-dwellers are almost always friendly and polite, ready to take a moment off for a joke or to help you find where you're going.

Here are some tips for while you're in the city:

- When crossing streets in downtown San José, always look over your shoulder at the cars coming from behind you. In practice, the pedestrian does not have the right of way. Drivers love to whip around corners whether or not people are trying to cross.

- When a traffic light for oncoming cars changes from green to yellow or red, do not take it to mean that the cars will stop. Look at the cars, not the light. When you see that the cars have stopped, run quickly across. This habit is easily developed because another characteristic of San José is that traffic lights are hung so that pedestrians cannot see them. *Buena suerte.*

- Street numbers are attached to the sides of buildings near intersections. Not all corners have them, but keep looking and you're bound to find one somewhere.

- To ask directions, you don't have to use a lot of fancy Spanish. It is acceptable to say "*¿Para* [name of your destination]?" (like "*¿Para Heredia?*" or "*¿Para la Coca Cola?*") and the person you ask will point you in the general direction. We've found it's best to ask people who look like they drive, and it's best not to ask people standing in front of bars.

- If you're driving downtown, keep your window rolled up high enough so that a thief can't reach in and grab your purse, necklace, or watch. Better yet, don't even try to drive downtown unless you think of driving as a competitive sport.

For a description of the street address system, see Chapter Four.

A WALKING TOUR

The following tour can take several hours to a full day, depending on how involved you get.

We will start out at the **Correo Central** (2223-9766), or Central Post Office, on Calle 2 between Avenidas 1 and 3. The entrance is in the middle of the block. Stop by for an espresso, a latte, or a coffee milkshake at **Café del Correo** (open Monday through Saturday, 9 a.m. to 7 p.m.), a charming internet café specializing in fancy pastries and executive lunches. Philatelists will be interested in the **Stamp Museum** on the second floor that houses 1.5 million stamps from around the world

Walk two blocks west on Avenida 1 and you're at the **Mercado Central**, entering through the flower section. The market is a crowded, bustling maze of shops, restaurants, and produce stands covering the whole block between Avenidas Central/1 and Calles 6/8. Although there are quite a few more sedate places to buy souvenirs, at the Central Market you can get a glimpse of the lives of everyday Costa Ricans. Everything from hammocks to leather goods to fresh fish to mangoes is sold there. Of special interest are the stands where herbs are sold, labeled with their medicinal uses. It's easy to get quite disoriented in the market, but try to come out at the southeast entrance on Avenida Central and start walking east again. (If you don't like crowds, skip the market altogether.)

Avenida Central has been turned into a pedestrian mall throughout downtown. A block east of the market, looking left on Calle 4, you'll see one of San José's monuments to its democracy: a group of bronze *campesinos* stands humbly but solidly looking up at some unseen authority, waiting to be heard. The large building beside them is Costa Rica's **Banco Central**.

In two blocks, look to the left on Calle Central and you will see **La Casona**, a two-story wonderland of souvenirs. Half a block ahead on Avenida Central is **Librería Universal**, where you can buy anything from electronic appliances to art supplies, as well as books and stationery. It sells large-scale maps, which are helpful for hiking.

Look to your left at the intersection of Calle 1 and Avenida Central. Three blocks north is **Radiográfica** (open daily, 7:30 a.m. to 9 p.m.; 2287-0489), where you can make international phone calls, check your e-mail, or send and receive faxes.

You are still on Avenida Central. On the next block you'll see **Librería Lehmann**, another great bookstore. Next you'll come to the **Plaza de la Cultura** on Avenida Central, Calles 5/3. The eastern half of the plaza is full of children chasing pigeons and feeding them popcorn, and the center is often the stage for street comedians, concerts, and fairs. Since this is a prime tourist area, beware of pickpockets.

Cross the plaza to the famous **Teatro Nacional** (National Theater). In 1890, the world-renowned prima donna Adelina Patti appeared with a traveling opera company in Guatemala, but could not perform in Costa Rica because there was no appropriate theater. In response, newly rich coffee merchants financed the construction of a theater with a tax on every bag of exported coffee. Belgian architects were called in to design and supervise the building, and the metal structure was ordered from Belgian mills. Painters and decorators were brought from Italy, along with that country's famous marble. The Teatro Nacional was inaugurated in 1894 with Gounod's Faust and an opening-night cast that included singers from the Paris Opera. A source of cultural pride, the theater was made into a national monument in 1965. Extensive restoration work has renewed its beautiful ceiling paintings and sumptuous decor. The **Café del Teatro Nacional** (2221-1329 ext. 250), to the left as you enter the building, has changing art exhibits and specializes in hearty salads, sandwiches, and exotic coffee combinations and desserts. Take a moment to see the incredibly alive bust of Joaquin Gutierrez, one of Costa Rica's great modern writers, outside on the north side of the theater.

Down the grassy steps on Calle 5 is the information center of the **Instituto Costarricense de Turismo (ICT)**, or Tourism Institute, to the left (open Monday through Friday, 8 a.m. to 4 p.m.; 2222-1090; visitcostarica.com). There, too, is the entrance to the plaza's excellent underground exhibition rooms, which feature changing shows, as well as the famous pre-Columbian **Gold Museum** (open daily, 9:30 a.m. to 4:30 p.m.; 2243-4202; museodelbancocentral.org; admission $7, children under 11 free). This little gem features shimmering displays of over 2000 gold artifacts crafted by the Diquis master goldsmiths, who once inhabited the southwestern part of the country.

From the museum, head north (left) on Calle 5. **Parque Morazán**, with its domed **Music Temple** is one block ahead on your right. On the northwest corner of the park is the Aurola Holiday Inn, with mirrored panels reflecting San José's changing skies. On Avenida 7, directly behind the Holiday Inn, is **Galería Namú**, showcasing authentic indigenous crafts from Costa Rica and Panamá.

Three blocks north of the Music Temple is the entrance to **Parque Bolívar**, the location of San José's **zoo** (open daily, Monday through Friday 8 a.m. to 3:30, Saturday and Sunday 9 a.m. to 4:30 p.m.; 2256-0012; fundazoo.org; admission $1.50). Monkeys, crocodiles, and birds live there, as well as some felines. At the entrance to the zoo is an interactive exhibit for kids.

Northeast of the Music Temple is the green **Escuela Metálica**, a turn-of-the-20th-century school building built entirely of metal that was shipped from France. The story goes that the prefabricated school was destined for Puntarenas, Chile, but was mistakenly delivered to Puntarenas, Costa Rica. Next comes **Parque España**, which is filled with venerable and beautiful trees.

Continue to Avenida 7 and the tall National Insurance Institute (INS), which houses the largest collection of American pre-Columbian jade in the world in the **Jade Museum** on the first floor (open weekdays, 8:30 a.m. to

3:30 p.m.; 2287-6034; admission $2, children under 12 free). This museum rivals the National Museum in its extensive exhibits of pre-Columbian jade, gold, stonework, and ceramics. The Jade Museum should be high on your list of places to visit. A new building that will house the Jade Museum's complete collection is scheduled to be built across from the Plaza de la Democracia, so check its location before setting out.

Continuing east on Avenida 7, you will pass the **Casa Amarilla** with its wide stairways. It houses the country's Ministry of Foreign Relations. This building and the park in front of it were donated by Andrew Carnegie. The jagged concrete block displayed in front of the ministry is a chunk of the Berlin Wall. On the east side of the park is the former National Liquor Factory, founded by President Juan Rafael Mora in 1856. It has been converted into the **Centro Nacional de la Cultura**, an impressive museum and theater complex with delightful places for sitting, walking, or taking pictures. The **Museum of Contemporary Art and Design** (open Monday to Saturday, 10:30 a.m. to 5:30 p.m.; 2257-9370; madc.ac.cr; admission $2, kids free, free for all on Monday), inside, has exciting exhibits from all over the world.

Up a gentle hill on Avenida 7, you'll pass the Mexican Embassy on the left and arrive at the intersection of Avenida 7 and Calle 15. Turn right toward the **Biblioteca Nacional** (National Library).

The library faces the largest of San José's city parks, **Parque Nacional**. In the center of the park is the massive and beautiful **Monumento Nacional**, which depicts the spirits of the Central American nations driving out the despicable *filibustero* William Walker. The statue was made in the Rodin studios in France and shipped to Costa Rica.

Across the street from the park you will see a statue of **Juan Santamaría**, the national hero, holding aloft his torch. The elegant, white Moorish **Legislative Assembly** building he fronts houses the Costa Rican Congress.

Two blocks south of the Parque Nacional, on the Jimenez Oreamuno pedestrian walkway, is the **Museo Nacional** (open Tuesday through Saturday, 8:30 a.m. to 4:30 p.m., Sunday 9 a.m. to 4 p.m.; 2257-1433; museo costarica.go.cr; admission $4, students with ID $2, children under 12 free), housed in the former Bellavista Fortress. There are bullet holes in the turrets from the 1948 civil war. Inside are a lovely courtyard and large exhibits of indigenous gold, petroglyphs, ceramics, and incredibly intricate stonework. Well-done bilingual exhibits trace the history of Costa Rica, from prehistoric to modern times. Fittingly, the museum's last exhibit is "The Secret Garden," a screened **butterfly garden** with benches from which to enjoy a wide variety of the country's most beautiful species, including the large, iridescent blue morpho. On a sunny day, it's a real treat. Definitely worth a visit.

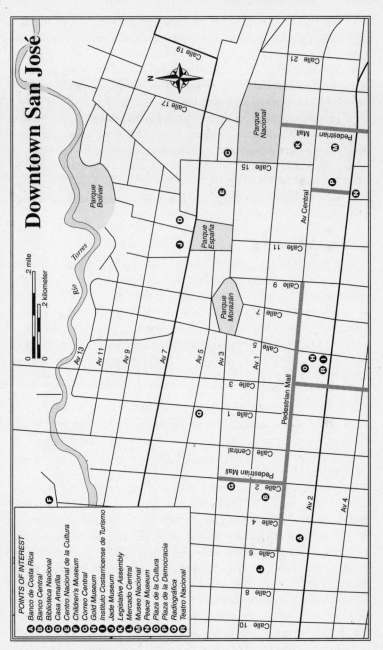

Downtown San José

POINTS OF INTEREST
A Banco de Costa Rica
B Banco Central
C Biblioteca Nacional
D Casa Amarilla
E Centro Nacional de la Cultura
F Children's Museum
G Correo Central
H Gold Museum
I Instituto Costarricense de Turismo
J Jade Museum
K Legislative Assembly
L Mercado Central
M Museo Nacional
N Peace Museum
O Plaza de la Cultura
P Plaza de la Democracia
Q Radiográfica
R Teatro Nacional

The museum overlooks the **Plaza de la Democracia**, built by the Arias administration to receive visiting presidents during the historic Hemispheric Summit in 1989. Here you will see a statue of former president Don Pepe Figueres, hero of the 1948 civil war, and the abolisher of the Army. His human stance and expression show that the citizens of this very small country know their leaders well.

Right off the plaza is the **Calle Nacional de la Artesania,** full of tented market stalls selling jewelry, clothing, hammocks, wood crafts, and more. It's one of the most pleasant places to buy souvenirs in the city.

On Avenida 2, Calle 13 is the **Peace Museum** (open daily, 8 a.m. to noon, 1:30 p.m. to 4:30 p.m.; 2223-4664; arias.or.cr), founded by current president and Nobel Laureate Oscar Arias. It documents regional peace accords from the 1980s and '90s, and explores peace issues.

CREATIVE ARTS

Costa Ricans are well known for their interest in culture and the arts. The Ministry of Culture stimulates activity by sponsoring theater, choral music, opera, dance, literature, poetry, art, sculpture, and film.

The **International Festival of the Arts**, held in March, features theater, dance, and music groups from all over the world. Tickets sell out early. Get more information at festivaldelasartescostarica.com, info@festivaldelasartes costarica.com, or by calling 2233-6441. The 2008 festival featured singers from the Peking Opera.

MUSIC

Costa Rica's **National Youth Symphony** was inaugurated in 1972 by ex-President Figueres' famous quote: "We need to concern ourselves not only with the standard of living but the quality of life as well. Why have tractors without violins?"

Many of the young musicians trained in the Youth Symphony have graduated to participate in the **National Symphony**, which performs in the **Teatro Nacional** (Avenida 2, Calle 3; 2221-9417; teatronacional.go.cr) on the **Plaza de la Cultura**. Internationally famous guest directors and soloists are often featured. Entrance fees are kept low so that people at all economic levels may enjoy the concerts. The least expensive seats are in the *galería* section, which is up three flights of stairs through an entrance on the back of the theater. The *butacas* are in the first tier of boxes above the *luneta* (orchestra) section. The *palcos* (box seats) are on the second tier. The symphony season starts in March and ends in December. Call or check the newspapers or the sign out front for current show times.

Teatro Melico Salazar (Avenida 2, Calle Central; 2233-5424, 2233-5387; teatromelico.gr.cr), across from the Parque Central, is not as grandiose as the Teatro Nacional, but often hosts performances by famous international musicians as well as the **National Youth Symphony** (2236-6669), the **National Lyric Company** (2222-8571), the **National Choir** (2236-6669), and the **National Dance Company** (2256-4838).

The world-renowned **International Music Festival**, presented each summer since 1990, has been compared to the Aspen and Salzburg music festivals. Tickets are sold through Credomatic (2295-9000).

Costa Rica has a number of gifted folk singers and musicians who regularly perform at some of the bars and theaters listed below. Look for posters around town or announcements in the *Tico Times* for concerts by some of the country's most creative contemporary performers: **Cantares** researches the history of Costa Rican music from all over the country, and writes songs with an ironic political twist; **Luis Angel Castro** sings *nueva trova* and calypso; Canto América adds to Afro-Caribbean rhythms with trumpets and flutes; **Malpais** combines heartfelt lyrics and a great Latin beat; **Solo Flamenco** calls up authentic Iberian music and dance, **Manuel Obregón** brings magic to the piano; and the very popular violin, guitar, and percussion group, **Editus**, which has won several Grammy awards, has a New Age yet distinctly Latin tilt to its sensitive compositions. All of these musicians have produced CDs that make great souvenirs, and most of them can be heard at the music festivals in Monteverde (see the Northern Zone chapter) and Playa Chiquita (see the Atlantic Coast chapter) or around San José. Highly recommended.

THEATER

Ticos are great actors. Even if you don't understand Spanish, it might be worth it to go to the theater to see the creativity that they bring to the stage. The English-speaking community also puts a lot of energy into its **Little Theater Group**, which presents musicals and comedies several times a year. Check the *Tico Times* for performance and audition information.

FILMS

North American movies dominate the film scene here; they're usually shown with Spanish subtitles. Check schedules in the *Tico Times* or *La Nación*. First-run movies are about $3 to $5.

The **Sala Garbo** (Avenida 2, Calle 28; 2222-1034) features excellent international films with Spanish subtitles. Next door, the **Teatro Laurence Olivier** offers films, plays, and concerts, as well as a gallery and coffee house. Take the Sabana–Cementerio bus and get off at the Pizza Hut on Paseo Colón. The two theaters are one block south. You can walk to them from downtown in 25 minutes.

The University of Costa Rica in San Pedro runs an excellent, cheap, international film series during the school year (March to December), Wednesday through Friday nights. The movies are shown in the auditorium of the Law School. Check current listings in the *Tico Times* or call **Cine Universitario** (2207-4717).

ART

The Ticos converted their former air terminal into the **Museum of Costa Rican Art** (open Tuesday through Friday, 9 a.m. to 5 p.m.; weekends, 10 a.m. to 4 p.m.; 2222-7155; musarco.go.cr; admission $5, students $3, free on Sunday). This tastefully done museum displays the work of the country's finest painters and sculptors, as well as international exhibits. Located in La Sabana at the end of Paseo Colón.

Following local tradition, the National Liquor Factory downtown has also been converted to **CENAC (Centro Nacional de la Cultura)**. Inside, the **Museum of Contemporary Art and Design** (open Monday to Saturday, 10:30 a.m. to 5:30 p.m.; 2257-9370; madc.ac.cr; admission $2, kids free, free for all on Monday), has exciting exhibits from all over the world.

Galería Namú (open Monday to Saturday, 9:30 a.m. to 6:30 p.m.; Avenida 7, Calles 5/7; 2256-3412; galerianamu.com) specializes in indigenous and women's art from around the country.

Check La Nación and the *Tico Times* for exhibits at the galleries downtown. **The Centro Cultural Costarricense-Norteamericano** (Barrio Dent) and the **Alianza Francesa** (Calle 5, Avenida 7) have monthly art exhibits. Their openings are a wonderful place to meet people and enjoy wine and *bocas*.

NIGHTLIFE

There's plenty to do after dark in San José. Besides dozens of theaters and cinemas, night owls can sample a wide variety of bars, discos, and all-night cafés.

The area bordered by Calle 4 on the west, Avenida 9 on the north, Calle 23 on the east, and Avenida 2 on the south is the heart of downtown nightlife. Of course, you should use common sense when walking around: keep your purse close to you; don't act drunk and out of control; and be extra-alert on deserted streets. Some of the nightspots listed here are in San Pedro, a ten-minute bus ride from downtown.

BARS

Most bars offer a traditional *boca*, or small plate of food, along with your drink. *Ceviche* (raw fish "cooked" in lime juice), fried fish, chicken wings, little steaks, and rice and beans are common *bocas*; they are usually free. You'll find a variety of local beers, and most are pretty good. We recommend Imperial, Pilsen, or the more expensive, locally brewed Heineken.

Cafe Expresivo (Avenida 9, Calles 29/31; 2224-1202) has live *trova, boleros,* an open mic, and dancing. Shows start at 8 p.m. It's across from **Editus Academia de las Artes**, where there are often concerts and art shows.

Chelles (open daily, 24 hours; Avenida Central, Calle 9; 221-1369) doesn't have much atmosphere, but if you're a people watcher, you'll enjoy hanging out here. Probably because it remains open all the time, Chelles has become a landmark. You'll see actors, musicians, and dancers from the National Theater there having a midnight snack. You'll see middle-aged Costa Rican men amusing each other with toothpick tricks. You'll be asked to buy wilted roses from intriguing old ladies and persistent young boys. There are free *bocas* with every drink. *Overpriced.*

El Cuartel de la Boca del Monte (open weekdays, noon to 2 p.m., 6 p.m. to 3 a.m.; weekends, 6 p.m. to 3 a.m.; Avenida 1, Calles 21/23; 2221-0327) is one of the most popular singles bars in San José. The *bocas* aren't free, but they're good, and the music is live. *Pricey.*

Jazz Café (open daily, 6 p.m. to 2 a.m.; make reservations at 2253-8933 after 2 p.m.; $5-$10 cover) is a restaurant/bar/art gallery on the main street of San Pedro, where you can hear Costa Rica's top live jazz bands, rhythm and blues, New Age, world beat, reggae, and Latin American music. The Café seats 200 and has shows five nights a week. Internationally famous jazz musicians play there at least twice a month. Now they have a branch near the CIMA hospital in the western suburb of Escazú.

La Nueva Esmeralda (Avenida 2, Calle 9; 2258-8643) is open 24 hours. Mariachi groups arrive between 8 p.m. and 10 p.m. You can hire trios or entire groups to serenade you and your date with gorgeous harmonies and romantic lyrics.

El Observatorio (across from the Cine Magaly on Calle 23; 2223-0725) has live music and films.

El Pueblo (2221-9434), in Barrio Tournón near the entrance to the Guápiles Highway, is a huge maze of Spanish Colonial–style alleyways and tiled roofs. You can spend hours wandering around there, getting lost and spending money. There is a small bar where you can hear authentic Argentinian tango, a sushi bar, a Bolivian *peña*, and three discotheques. **Lukas** (open daily, 11:30 a.m. to 2:30 a.m.; 2233-8145) is a popular place to go for a moderately priced late dinner or snack. El Pueblo is located north of downtown, across from Hotel Villa Tournón. Walk, taxi, or take a Calle Blancos bus.

TapaTapa (closed Monday; 2290-8526) serves authentic Spanish *tapas* and has Flamenco on Friday and Saturday nights. It's above the restaurant at Casa España in Sabana Norte.

DISCOTHEQUES

While partner dancing is a novelty in the United States, it has a long tradition and a set of rules down here. The more serious salsa discos and salons try to encourage a sense of style and frown upon T-shirts and sneakers. Women who go alone or in groups should expect and be prepared for relentless pickup attempts. Women do not usually invite men onto the floor.

At **Cafe 83 Sur** (open Tuesday through Saturday, 6 p.m. to 2:30 a.m.; Sunday, 6 p.m. to midnight; on the east side of town on Avenida 2, Calle 25; 2221-2369), live deejays spin hip-hop and rhythm and blues. The decor is Arabic/Indonesian. Reasonably priced food is served as well. Located 100 meters south of the Nicaraguan Embassy.

Club OH (Calle 2, Avenida 14/16; 2248-1500; clubohcr.com) is an upscale New York–style nightclub with good light shows on the dance floor, the sophisticated Marcande bar, and the comfortable orange-toned Moroccan Corner.

Cocoloco attracts an older crowd. The emphasis here is on dancing, despite the small floor. **Infinito** has three dance floors and attracts a younger crowd. Both are in the large nightlife complex, **El Pueblo** (2221-9434) on the north side of town. Security has been beefed up at El Pueblo and is better than at the larger discos across the street.

Luna Roja (Calle 1, Avenida 11; 2222-5944) has two levels to its dance floor and live music in Barrio Amón.

At **Salsa 54** (Calle 3, Avenidas 1/3; 2233-3814), it's worth the cover just to watch some of Costa Rica's best dancers strut their stuff on the raised stage. It's less expensive than El Pueblo.

GAY/LESBIAN NIGHTLIFE

For women, good salsa/merengue and a management that has supported many causes over the years make **La Avispa** (closed Monday; Calle 1, Avenidas 8/10; 2223-5343) the first stop on a nightlife tour of San José. Men are welcome there, too, especially on Tuesday. It features three dance floors, a snack bar, pool tables, a big-screen TV, and lots of local flavor. La Avispa attracts mostly locals and is known for being the country's first lesbian-owned bar.

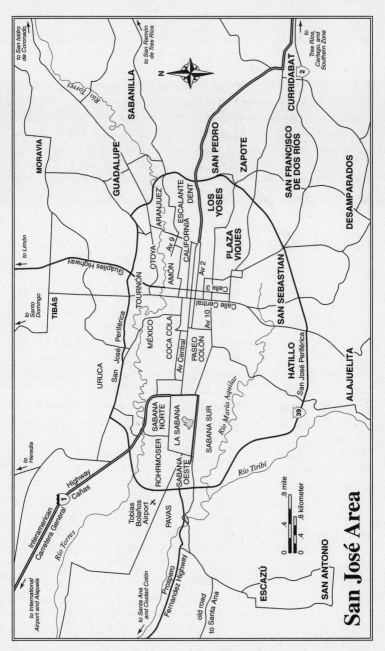

San José Area

Bochinche (Calle 11, Avenidas 8/10; 2221-0500) is upscale, trendy, and gay friendly.

For men, **Deja Vu** (Calle 2, Avenidas 14/16; 256-6332) is probably the hottest dance bar in Latin America, with pop, alternative, and techno music. It features a café, a quiet bar, a souvenir shop, and two large dance floors. On Saturday you'll usually find high-quality dancers and drag shows. Deja Vu attracts a younger, more upscale crowd than La Avispa. The management has invested thousands of dollars and many hours of work in support of gay and lesbian causes.

Al Despiste (open Tuesday through Saturday, 7 p.m. to 2 a.m.; Sunday, 6 p.m. to 10 p.m.; across from Mudanzas Mundiales in Zapote; 2234-5956) has *trova* on Wednesday, karaoke on Friday, and go-go dancers on Saturday.

Check current listings on gaycostarica.com.

RESTAURANTS

COFFEE SHOPS

Below are some of the best places we've found to eat a quick meal or have a cup of coffee. They are all rather pricey by Tico standards, but at any of them you can eat lunch for less than $5 and have coffee and a pastry for under $2.50. The traditional Tico way to serve coffee is in two separate pitchers, one filled with strong black coffee and the other with steaming hot milk. You can mix them to suit your taste. Many establishments have stopped this practice for economic reasons, but Giacomín (see below) has retained the tradition. Decaffeinated coffee is available only in those restaurants that serve Café Britt, Costa Rica's export-quality coffee. As an alternative to coffee, most places only offer black or chamomile tea, although many excellent herbal teas are manufactured here. Incidentally, the concept of smoking and nonsmoking areas in restaurants is just being introduced. If it matters to you, stick to vegetarian restaurants.

Azafrán (open daily, 9 a.m. to 7 p.m.; 2220-2008) makes delicious sandwiches, lasagna, cannelloni, and desserts. The food can be ordered to go, and they will deliver. Their torta Azafrán has to be one of the best cakes of all time. Located in Rohrmoser in the Plaza Mayor Mall and in Escazú in Plaza Atlantis.

Boston Bagel Café (open Monday through Saturday, 7 a.m. to 6:30 p.m.; 2291-1419) has the best bagels we've tasted here or in the U.S. They come in 12 flavors, and the café serves them with pastrami, four flavors of cream cheese, and other delicacies. Located on the road to Pavas across from La Artística. Recommended.

Bagelmen's (open weekdays, 7 a.m. to 9 p.m.; 2224-2432) offers a wide variety of bagel sandwiches and snacks. There's a branch on Avenida Central in Barrio La California east of downtown, one in Escazú in Plaza Florencia, and another in Curridabat across from the Indoor Club. They have wi-fi in all their branches and they deliver.

Café de Artistas (open Monday through Saturday, 8 a.m. to 6 p.m.; Sunday, 8 a.m. to 4 p.m.; 100 meters south of Plaza Rolex in Escazú; 2288-5082) provides fantastic breakfasts, gourmet lunches, and Sunday champagne brunch (sometimes with live music), all in a bohemian-café ambiance created by international art on the walls, antique furnishings, a book exchange, and a gift shop filled with ceramics and mosaics.

Café de la Posada (open Monday through Saturday, 7 a.m. to 7 p.m.; 2258-1027) is on the pedestrian walkway just south of the National Museum, offering daily main dishes, Argentine empanadas, homemade pastries and desserts, and quality coffee.

Café Milagro (Calle 7, Avenidas Central and 1; 2256-8183) made famous in Manuel Antonio, now has a branch inside **7th Street Books**, with comfy couches and tables for writing. They serve sandwiches, smoothies, pastries, and great coffee.

Giacomín (open Monday through Saturday, 8 a.m. to noon, 2 p.m. to 7 p.m.; 2234-2551) has an upstairs tea room; it's a nice place to enjoy coffee and Italian-style pastries or homemade bonbons. It is next to the Automercado in Los Yoses, with a branch in Escazú (open Monday through Saturday, 10 a.m. to 7 p.m.; 2228-1893) and in downtown San José (50 meters north of Fischel; 2221-5652).

Café Ruiseñor (open weekdays, 7 a.m. to 9 p.m.; weekends, 10 a.m. to 5:30 p.m.; 2225-2562) is a lovely place that serves delicious pastries and light meals made with pure, healthful ingredients. It has some outdoor tables. Located in Los Yoses, 150 meters east of Automercado—a 20-minute walk from downtown toward San Pedro.

INTERNET CAFÉS

Most hotels will offer you free or low-cost internet access. Here are two of the more interesting independent internet cafés:

CyberCafe Las Arcadas (open daily, 7 a.m. to 11 p.m.; 2233-3310) is a popular spot for tourists, who can people-watch at their indoor or outdoor tables in the Las Arcadas building in front of the National Theater while taking advantage of the book exchange and laundromat.

Cafe del Correo (2257-3670) is located at the Correo Central, Calle 2, Avenidas 1 and 3.

INEXPENSIVE EATERIES

The **Mercado Central** (Avenidas Central/1 and Calles 6/8) is filled with inexpensive places to eat—many of them, like the Marisquería Ribera, are recommended for good food. The only problem with the market is that the restaurants are usually so crowded you don't feel you can sit down and relax. Go in the late afternoon when things are winding down so you aren't competing with hundreds of hungry workers on their lunch hour.

La Gauchada (200 meters south of Canal 7; 2232-6916) in Sabana Oeste serves piping hot Argentinian empanadas with a variety of fillings, including vegetarian.

Don Wang (open daily, 8 a.m. to 10 p.m.; Calle 11, Avenidas 6/8; 2223-5925) has become famous for its dim sum but has an extensive Cantonese, Szechuan, and Pekinese menu as well. Three or four of their plump Chinese dumplings cost under $2.

Nuestra Tierra (Avenida 2, Calle 15; 2258-6500) is an all-night eatery specializing in *comida típica*. It's a good place to go if you are staying in the hostels on the east side of town.

Soda Tapia (2222-6734), facing the Sabana, is open 24/7 on Fridays and weekends. It has hearty breakfasts and huge fruit salads topped with ice cream and Jell-O. It's a good place to go if you are staying in the hostels on the west side of town.

VEGETARIAN RESTAURANTS

All of the restaurants listed here are inexpensive, offering prix-fixe lunches for under $3.

Shakti (open weekdays, 8 a.m. to 7 p.m.; Saturday, 10 a.m. to 5 p.m.; Calle 13, Avenida 8; 2222-4475) serves generous, inexpensive, high-quality vegetarian meals. Their *plato del día* has soup, salad, a main course, and a fruit drink for $3. Recommended.

Tin-Jo (open daily, 11:30 a.m. to 3 p.m., 5 p.m. to 10 p.m.; Calle 11, Avenidas 6/8; 2221-7605) certainly has the most interesting vegetarian menu in town, though it is not known as a vegetarian restaurant. Meat-free Chinese, Thai, and Indian dishes, as well as delicious sushi, are served in a quiet environment with classical music. Recommended.

Comida para Sentir (open weekdays, 10 a.m. to 6 p.m.; 2224-1163) is a small, organic, macrobiotic restaurant popular with students. It's located on the street just west of the San Pedro church near the train tracks. Recommended.

Vishnu (open Monday through Saturday, 7:30 a.m. to 9:30 p.m., Sunday, 9 a.m. to 7:30 p.m.; 2222-2549) gives inexpensive, generous servings. It's crowded at lunch—get there early. There are several locations: Avenida 1, Calles 1/3; Calle 1, Avenidas 4/6 next to the Banco Popular; Calle Central, Avenidas 6/8, across from the Cine Metropolitan; Avenida 3, Calles Central/1; in Zapote across from the Registro Civil, and in Rohrmoser at Plaza Mayor.

Most supermarkets have organic sections. Ask around about organic farmers markets.

MODERATE TO EXPENSIVE RESTAURANTS

San José has many excellent restaurants. In the following list you will find French, Italian, and Chinese places, but don't overlook those that specialize in Spanish, Korean, or Middle Eastern cuisines. See the Central Valley chapter for excellent restaurants less than an hour's drive from the city.

Moderate means that most entrées are under $8. Expensive indicates that entrées are $8 to $15. Wine can really increase the total price of a dinner, since wines in Costa Rica are imported and expensive. All restaurant bills include a 10 percent tip and a 13 percent tax. Tipping is not customary but is certainly appreciated, especially when the service is good.

Since getting around in San José is such a hassle, especially at dinnertime, we have arranged the following restaurants according to neighborhood:

DOWNTOWN/BARRIO AMÓN **Bakea** (open Tuesday through Saturday, noon to midnight; 2221-1051) is the place to go for French fusion–style food. It's housed in a restored Art Deco mansion in Barrio Amón at Calle 7, Avenida 11. Recommended. *Pricey*.

Café Mundo (open weekdays, 11 a.m. to 11 p.m.; Saturday, 5 p.m. to 11 p.m.; Avenida 9, Calle 15; 2222-6190), is a popular meeting place in a historic home offering "Costa Ricanized" international dishes. There are indoor and outdoor tables. They have their own parking lot. *Moderate*.

La Esquina de Buenos Aires (open daily, 11:30 a.m. to 3 p.m., 6 p.m. to 11 p.m.; 2223-1909) serves excellent Argentine food in a nostalgic 1940s atmosphere, close to the National Museum. The ample menu, featuring grilled meats, homemade pastas, and fine wines, is accompanied by great tango music. It is on the corner of Calle 11 and Avenida 4, behind the Iglesia de la Soledad. Recommended.

Tin-Jo (open daily, 11:30 a.m. to 3 p.m., 5 p.m. to 10 p.m.; Calle 11, Avenidas 6/8; 2221-7605) is a friendly, creative Asian restaurant that serves spicy Szechuan, Thai, Indian, and Indonesian dishes. The kitchen accommodates vegetarians. Recommended. *Moderate*.

LOS YOSES/BARRIO ESCALANTE   **Jurgen's Restaurant** (open weekdays, noon to 2:30 p.m., 6 p.m. to 10:30 p.m.; Saturday, 6 p.m. to 10:30 p.m.; call for reservations: 2283-2239) offers classy European cuisine and attentive service in an intimate atmosphere. It's in Hotel Boutique Jade, 300 meters north of Subaru in Barrio Dent. *Expensive.*

Il Ritorno (open Monday to Saturday, noon to 2:30 p.m. and 6 p.m. to 10:30 p.m.; 2225-0543), inside the Casa Italia, 2 blocks south of KFC Los Yoses, is famous for chef Tony D'Alaimo's sensuous Italian cuisine. Recommended. *Moderate.*

L'Île de France (open daily, 6 p.m. to 10 p.m.; 2283-5812) offers excellent traditional French cuisine and superb service. Even if you think you can't afford a full meal, stop in for a glass of wine and a delicious *crema de mariscos* and finish it off with a light, airy *parfait glace de maracuya*. But get there early—the place fills up with loyal patrons. Located in the relaxing garden court of the Hotel Le Bergerac, 50 meters south of the *"primera entrada Los Yoses."* Recommended. *Expensive.*

Restaurant and Pub Olio (Avenida 5, Calles 33/35, 200 meters north of Bagelman's; 2281-0541) is a hip tapas bar that also serves generous portions of Mediterranean main dishes. *Moderate.*

SAN PEDRO/CURRIDABAT   **Ichiban** (open Monday through Thursday, noon to 3 p.m., 6 p.m. to 10 p.m.; Friday through Sunday, noon to 11 p.m.; 2253-8012) has good sushi. Located in the Centro Comercial de la Calle Real in San Pedro. *Moderate.*

Marbella (open Tuesday through Saturday, 11 a.m. to 3 p.m., 6:30 p.m. to 10:30 p.m.; Sunday, noon to 5 p.m.; across from the Banco Popular; 2224-9452) is an elegant Spanish restaurant that serves a diverse assortment of tapas and *paella. Expensive.*

Ponte Vecchio (open Monday through Saturday, noon to 2:30 p.m., 6 p.m. to 10:30 p.m.; 200 meters west of San Pedro church, 25 meters north; 2283-1810) offers intimate, attentive service and good Italian food. *Expensive.*

Trio World Cuisine (in Centro Comercial Plaza Fresas in Curridabat; 2524-0380) has a lively international restaurant, a quiet area near the entrance for wine and conversation; and a second floor bar with *bocas* from around the world.

PASEO COLÓN/SABANA/PAVAS   **Casa Luisa** (open Tuesday through Sunday, noon to 3 p.m., 6 p.m. to 11 p.m.; 2296-1917) is a family-run restaurant with lovingly prepared Catalán cuisine. Make reservations for this popular restaurant, especially if you want the house specialty, *paella.* It's in Sabana Sur, 400 meters south of the Contraloría, and 40 meters east. *Moderate.*

Flor del Loto (open weekdays, 11 a.m. to 3 p.m., 6 p.m. to 11 p.m.; Saturday, 11 a.m. to 11 p.m.; 2232-4652) serves delicious Hunan and Szechuan Chinese specialties. Across from Colegio Los Angeles, Sabana Norte. *Moderate*.

Grano de Oro (open daily, 6 a.m. to 10 p.m.; Calle 30, Avenidas 2/4; 2255-3322) offers light, eclectic fusion cuisine like *crema de pejibaye,* goat cheese ravioli, and salmon *blini*. Newly remodeled in the opulent style of a 19th-century coffee baron's mansion, with stained glass panels and glowing gas lamps, vintage tile floors, and lavish flower arrangements, it is located within the Hotel Grano de Oro. *Pricey*.

Machu Picchu (open Monday through Saturday, 11 a.m. to 3 p.m., 6 p.m. to 10 p.m.; 2222-7384) features authentic Peruvian *ceviche*, pisco sours, and *anticuchos*. A good introduction to Peruvian seafood. Located on Calle 32, Avenida 1, 125 meters north of Paseo Colón, with another branch in San Pedro, 125 meters south of El Verdugo (2283-3679). *Moderate*.

La Cocina de Terra Nostra (open Tuesday through Sunday, 11:30 a.m. to 2 p.m., 6:30 p.m. to 10:30 p.m.; 2296-3528) serves Spanish and international cuisine in an elegant colonial atmosphere. Located in Casa España in Sabana Norte. *Expensive*.

Lubnan (open Tuesday through Saturday, 11 a.m. to 3 p.m., 6 p.m. to midnight; 2257-6071) serves authentic Lebanese fare, and has cushion seating in the back patio if you make reservations. Located on Paseo Colon, Calles 22/24. *Moderate*.

ESCAZÚ **Taj Mahal** (open Tuesday through Sunday, noon to 3 p.m., 6 p.m. to 11 p.m.; 2228-0980) offers East Indian cuisine, featuring tandoori and curry dishes and a delicious vegetarian menu. Located 800 meters west of Paco in Escazú. *Moderate*.

Le Monastere (open Monday through Saturday, 6 p.m. to 11 p.m.; 2289-4404) is a converted chapel. Waiters dressed as monks reverently take your orders while you gaze out over the shimmering lights of the Central Valley. The French cuisine is as good as the view. Downstairs, the less expensive, bohemian **La Cava** (open Tuesday through Saturday, 5 p.m. to 1 a.m.) offers grilled meats and live music. Take the old road to Santa Ana past Escazú and turn left just after the Multicentro Paco. Signs lead you up the mountain from there. Make reservations a few days in advance.

Sale e Pepe (open for lunch and dinner, closed Tuesday; 2289-5750) delivers the true taste of Italy in downtown Escazú behind Pop's. Recommended. *Moderate*.

Mirador Tiquicia (open Tuesday through Friday, 4 p.m. to 11 p.m.; Saturday, noon to 1 a.m.; Sunday, noon to 6 p.m.; 2289-5839) offers folkloric music and panoramic views from its rustic perch in the hills. *Moderate*.

LODGING

You will find lodgings scattered throughout metropolitan San José; see "San José Lodging by Neighborhood" on pages 146–47 for an overview of the city's neighborhoods. In addition to the accommodations below, you may want to check the listings in the following chapter, which covers the Central Valley area. The towns of Alajuela, Heredia, and Santa Ana are closer to the airport than San José and may be good places to stay on your way in and out of Costa Rica. For most lodging in San José in any price range, it's good to bring earplugs.

UPPER-RANGE HOTELS

For what you'd spend in a lackluster roadside motel in the States, you can get elegant accommodations in San José, with excellent service, attentive tour-planning information, and great restaurants. Double-occupancy room rates for these hotels range from $80 to $180; some offer luxurious, pricier suites as well. In our opinion, you can get all the luxury you need in this price range, and personalized service as well. All these hotels accept children. Amenities include private bathrooms with hot water showers, ceiling fans and, unless indicated, cable TV, phone, and internet access. If you come in the Green Season, most of them give discounts.

Le Bergerac (wi-fi; Calle 35, Avenidas Central/8; $100-$120, with refrigerators; $140-$160, including breakfast; children under 12 $10; 2234-7850, fax: 2225-9103; bergerachotel.com, info@bergerac.co.cr) is quiet and distinguished, with sunny, landscaped grounds. Several rooms have private gardens. The elegant French restaurant L'Île de France is in the garden courtyard. Recommended.

Hotel Bougainvillea (some bathtubs, pool, restaurant, bar, wi-fi; $110-$130; 2244-1414, in North America: 866-880-5441, fax: 2244-1313; hb.co.cr, info@hb.co.cr) is filled with Costa Rican and pre-Columbian art. Its quiet grounds have a pool, a conference room, a sauna, and tennis courts. Each room's private balcony overlooks the beautiful gardens or San José. The Bougainvillea name is associated with superb service and an excellent restaurant. Located 15 minutes from downtown in Santo Tomás de Santo Domingo de Heredia; microbuses provide a shuttle service between the hotel and San José. Recommended.

Britannia (bathtubs, a/c; $110-$140, children under 12 free; Calle 3, Avenidas 9/11; 2223-6667, in North America: 800-263-2618, fax: 2223-6411; hotelbritanniacostarica.com, info@hbritannia.com) is a remodeled mansion in Barrio Amón, with high ceilings, spacious rooms, and a reasonably priced restaurant in the cool, former wine cellar.

Don Carlos (spa, restaurant, bar, wi-fi; $90-$110, including breakfast; children under 12 free; Calle 9, Avenida 9, No. 779; 2221-6707, in North America: 866-675-9259, fax: 2258-1152; doncarloshotel.com, info@don carloshotel.com) is a well-run hotel in a pleasant historical neighborhood within walking distance of museums. It is filled with Costa Rican art and whimsical sculptures, has a sun deck, a gym, and a souvenir shop, and shows tour videos. Guests are greeted with a special Don Carlos cocktail. Family rooms (two double rooms separated by a bath) are available for $110-$120. Recommended.

Fleur de Lys (most with bathtubs, smoking allowed in all common areas; $100-$160; children under 12 free; Calle 13, Avenidas 2/6; 2223-1206, fax: 2221-6310; hotelfleurdelys.com, reservaciones@hotelfleurdelys.com) is a faithfully renovated mansion that has comfortable sitting areas on each floor as well as atriums. Rooms are graced by original works of art by Costa Rican painters and sculptors. There is also an excellent restaurant and pleasant porch-side bar. Near the National Museum.

Hotel 1492 ($80-$110, including breakfast; children under 5 free, children 5-12 $6; 2985 Avenida 1, 300 meters east of the Cine Magaly; 2256-5913, 2225-3752, fax: 2280-6206; hotel1492.com, contact-us@hotel1492.com) is a lovely small hotel in a Spanish-style house on a quiet residential street east of downtown. The walls are hung with gorgeous paintings of tropical flora, painted by the original owner of the house, artist Amalia Jiménez Volio. Rooms are quiet and well-appointed, and three different breakfast menus are served in the garden. Seniors might especially like this hotel because it is all on one level. Pets are also welcome. Recommended.

Grano de Oro (bathtubs, hot tubs, nonsmoking; $120-$320; Calle 30, Avenidas 2/4; 2255-3322, fax: 2221-2782; hotelgranodeoro.com, info@ hotelgranodeoro.com) has been expanded and remodeled to be a replica of a grand 19th century San José mansion with modern touches. It is located in a quiet neighborhood on the west side of town, yet close to restaurants, the National Art Museum, and shops. It has comfortable furnishings, deluxe baths, and one of the best restaurants in the city. The Vista de Oro Suite has a view of the Cordillera Central mountains and the Central Valley skyline.

Hotel Jade (pool, wi-fi; $130-$180, including breakfast; children ages 6-12 $12; 250 meters north of the Subaru dealership; 2224-2455, fax: 2224-2166; hotelboutiquejade.com, info@hotelboutiquejade.com) has recently remodeled spacious rooms in peaceful Barrio Dent, near San Pedro. A comfortable place for business travelers. It is home to the famous European gourmet restaurant, **Jurgen's.**

SAN JOSÉ LODGING BY NEIGHBORHOOD

DOWNTOWN   Downtown hotels are convenient for visiting museums but can be noisy. We define "downtown" as the area between Avenida 7 and Avenida 18, Calle 20 and Calle 17. The hostels are on the east side.

> *Upper-range*: Fleur de Lys; Hotel Santo Tomás
> *Mid-range*: Europa Centro; La Posada del Museo
> *Inexpensive*: Pensión de la Cuesta (B&B)
> *Hostels*: Casa Ridgeway; Green House Hostel; Pangea

BARRIOS AMÓN, OTOYA, AND ARANJUEZ   Most hotels in San José's historic northern neighborhoods are restored turn-of-the-20th-century homes with high ceilings and enclosed courtyards. Barrios Amón, Otoya, and Aranjuez are safe, quiet (except for the city's ubiquitous traffic noise), and close to downtown restaurants, shopping areas, and museums.

> *Upper-range*: Britannia; Don Carlos
> *Mid-range*: Taylor Inn; Aranjuez; Kap's Place

PASEO COLÓN   This area, on the Paseo (Avenida Central between Calle 14 and Calle 42) and the two or three blocks north and south of it, is convenient for travelers who are coming from or heading west on the Interamerican Highway—stay here and you can avoid crossing town. Many car rental agencies have their offices here. Several fine restaurants are also in this area.

> *Upper-range*: Grano de Oro; La Rosa del Paseo
> *Hostels*: Gaudy's Backpackers

EASTERN BARRIOS   Barrios Escalante, Dent, and Los Yoses are elegant embassy areas east of downtown toward San Pedro.

> *Upper-range*: Hotel Jade; Le Bergerac; Hotel 1492

María Alexandra (kitchen, a/c, cable TV, pool, bar; $100-$120, including breakfast; 2228-1507, fax: 2289-5192; mariaalexandra.com, apartotel@mariaalexandra.com) features one- to three-bedroom apartments that sleep up to five people. There are washing machines, a sauna, a gym, and **Embrujo Limeño** restaurant featuring Peruvian cuisine. Weekly and monthly rates are available. It is located in Escazú, west of San José.

Hotel Milvia ($80-$90, including breakfast; 2225-4543, fax: 2225-7801; hotelmilvia.com, hotelmilvia@racsa.co.cr) is filled with the colorful,

Mid-range: Apartotel Los Yoses; Ara Macao (B&B)

Hostels: Abril Hostal, Hostel Bekuo, Costa Rica Guesthouse,
Costa Rica Backpackers; Toruma

SAN PEDRO AND CURRIDABAT   This University area bus-
tles with students during the March–December academic year,
and is packed with good, inexpensive restaurants and nightspots.
Buses leave San Pedro frequently for the ten-minute ride downtown.

Upper-range: Hotel Milvia

Mid-range: Ave del Paraíso

Inexpensive: Maripaz (B&B)

SANTO DOMINGO   One of the area's best hotels is in the quiet
residential neighborhood of Santo Tomás de Santo Domingo:

Upper-range: Bougainvillea

PAVAS, ROHRMOSER, AND LA SABANA   The hotels in
sunny, upscale Pavas and Rohrmoser, or ringing the green La Sabana, are convenient to the park.

Upper-range: Colours (B&B)

Mid-range: Apartotel La Sabana; El Sesteo

ESCAZÚ   The road leading into town is lined with strip malls
and high-rises, but once you get into the village center and its
nearby hills, Escazú regains its traditional *campesino* feel. Many
B&Bs are here; walkers will enjoy their proximity to beautiful
country roads.

Upper-range: Casa de las Tías (B&B); Casa Laurin (B&B); María
Alexandra; Posada El Quijote (B&B)

Mid-range: Pine Tree Inn; Tapezco Inn

confrontational, and witty works of owner Florencia Urbina and other
members of the Bocaraca art movement. Exhibits in the elegantly restored
home near the University of Costa Rica change periodically. Rooms are
well appointed, following the principles of *feng shui*. Located in San Pedro,
100 meters north and 200 meters east of supermercado Munoz y Nanne.

La Rosa del Paseo (bathtubs, some jacuzzis, some a/c; $90-$140, including breakfast; children under 10 free; 2257-3213, 2257-3225, fax: 223-
2776; rosadelpaseo.com, info@rosadelpaseo.com) has quiet rooms around

a tropical courtyard in back of the restored home of one of San José's great coffee barons. There is a comfortable sitting room/bar with a good soundtrack. It is conveniently located on Paseo Colon between Calles 28 and 30, near many restaurants. Recommended.

Hotel Santo Tomás (some bathtubs, pool, nonsmoking; $80-$120; Avenida 7, Calles 3/5; 2255-0448, in North America: 877-446-0658, fax: 2222-3950; hotelsantotomas.com, info@hotelsantotomas.com) is in a beautifully remodeled old home with many nice touches. A solar-heated swimming pool and jacuzzi are set in an open courtyard beside the gym and **El Oasis,** their international restaurant/bar. The rooms are back off the street, a real boon in noisy downtown San José. Recommended.

BED AND BREAKFASTS

Bed and breakfasts can be found both in the city and the country. Even though there are many other hotels that include breakfast in their rates, the distinguishing characteristic of bed and breakfasts is that they are small and have a homelike atmosphere, usually with the owner in residence. All of the establishments listed below pride themselves on the personalized service they give to their guests in tour planning, car rentals, etc. Most will provide lunch and dinner on request and offer kitchen privileges and internet access. They range from basic to luxurious, with a wide variety of amenities, listed in each description. For pleasant B&Bs in San José and throughout Costa Rica, see costaricainnkeepers.com. To call Costa Rica, dial 011-506, then the number.

Ara Macao (private bath, hot water, table fans, cable TV, some refrigerators, internet; $50-$60, including breakfast; 2233-2742, fax: 2257-6228; aramacaoinn.com, aramacao@aramacaoinn.com) is very clean, with pleasant, sunny upstairs rooms, and a nice eating area. Near the National Museum in Barrio California, 50 meters south of the Pizza Hut.

Casa de las Tías (private bath, hot water, ceiling fans, nonsmoking, wifi; $80-$100, including breakfast; 2289-5517, fax: 2289-7353; hotels.co.cr/casatias.html, casatias@kitcom.net), an ample wood-paneled house, sits at the end of a quiet street in Escazú, near restaurants and transportation. Each comfy room is decorated with mementos of the owners' sojourns in Latin America as part of the foreign service. Recommended.

Casa Laurin B&B (use of kitchen, ceiling fans, cable TV, jacuzzi in Orchid Suite, wi-fi; shared bath, $50-$60; private bath, $70-$110, including breakfast; 2289-4198, fax: 2288-0380; casalaurin.com, casalaurin@gmail.com, lauring@racsa.co.cr) is located in Bello Horizonte de Escazú. Rooms are comfortable and spacious. Ginette Laurin, the attentive French-Canadian owner, creates a congenial atmosphere among guests and serves gourmet breakfasts near the lush gardens. Recommended.

Colours (private bath, hot water, fans, CD players, cable TV, jacuzzi, pool, mini gym, massage room, restaurant, bar; $70-$180, including breakfast; with kitchen, $180-$200; 150 meters west of Farmacia Rohrmoser; 2296-1880, fax: 2296-1597, in the U.S.: 877-517-4390; coloursoasis.com, info@coloursoasis.com) is a gay guesthouse in Rohrmoser. They welcome lesbian travelers as well as men. Special trips and social events are planned throughout the year that cater to visitors and the Tico community. Owned by a Florida travel agency, they can plan your whole vacation, booking gay-friendly hotels and travel agents for side trips.

Maripaz (shared or private bath, hot water, table fans on request, nonsmoking; $30-$50; 300 meters south and 100 to the east of the *antiguo higuerón*; phone/fax: 2253-8456, 8397-3435; bedandbreakfastcostarica.com, maripaz@racsa.co.cr) is located in a friendly Costa Rican home in San Pedro. Convenient for those visiting the University of Costa Rica or the area's many nongovernmental organizations.

Pensión de la Cuesta (shared bath, heated water, some table fans, shared kitchen, cable TV in living room, wi-fi; $30-$60 including breakfast; Avenida 1, Calles 11/15, 2256-7946, fax: 2255-2896; pensiondela cuesta.com, costaricahotel@gmail.com) has eight rooms (some rather dark) in an interesting old building—the rooms are filled with paintings and creative touches. The fun will be in hanging around with other guests in the light-filled living/dining room.

Posada El Quijote (private bath, hot water, ceiling fans, phone, cable TV, wi-fi; $100-$130; call for directions; 2289-8401, fax: 2289-8729; quijote.co.cr, quijote@quijote.co.cr) is a family home with great views of the Central Valley and a comfortable sitting room with a fireplace. The fruit tree-filled yard has sitting areas with tables and benches. Studio apartments are also available. In Bello Horizonte de Escazú.

MID-RANGE HOTELS

Hotel rates have gone down quite a bit in San José. A double room in most of these hotels ranges from $30 to $80, and they offer a wide variety of amenities. Some of these hotels are downtown; ask for a room off the street if you like quiet. Many places in the B&B section have similar rates, as do homestays (see below). Be sure to look there, too. All rates include taxes. Don't forget to ask for off-season discounts. If you want to call a hotel directly, dial 011 and Costa Rica's area code, 506.

Aranjuez (solar hot water, shared refrigerator, private bath, cable TV, wi-fi, café; shared bath $30-$40; private bath, $40-$50, including breakfast;

children under 8 free; Calle 19, Avenidas 11/13; 2256-1825, fax: 2223-3528, in North America: 877-898-8663; hotelaranjuez.com, info@hotelaranjuez.com) comprises several old-fashioned houses linked together in Barrio Aranjuez. There are sitting areas scattered throughout the hotel where people can gather and talk, and quiet gardens in the back. The Aranjuez is popular because of its low rates and the many services it offers so make reservations well in advance. A generous buffet breakfast is included in the rate.

Ave del Paraíso (heated water, cable TV, internet; $60-$90, including breakfast; children under 12 free; 350 meters north of the Fuente de la Hispanidad, San Pedro; phone/fax: 2225-8515; hotelavedelparaiso.com, info@hotelavedelparaiso.com), owned by a Polish-Tico family, is homey and quiet. A five-minute walk from San Pedro's many inexpensive restaurants and bars, this hotel borders the western side of the Universidad de Costa Rica's campus.

Europa Centro (cable TV, internet, a/c, some bathtubs, pool, restaurant, bar; $70-$80, including breakfast; children under 12 free; Calle Central, Avenidas 3/5; 2222-1222, fax: 2221-3979; hoteleuropacr.com, info@hoteleuropacr.com) is a distinctive European-style hotel on a busy, crowded, downtown street. Ask for an inside room.

Kap's Place (shared bath and private bath, hot water, ceiling fans, cable TV, phone, kitchen privileges, wi-fi; $30-$110, including breakfast; 2221-1169, fax: 2256-4850; kapsplace.com, info@kapsplace.com) is in quiet Barrio Aranjuez. Comfortable rooms are off a common living/dining area, and there are hammocks in a covered patio. More rooms are across the street. Located at 1142 Calle 19, between Avenidas 11 and 13.

La Posada del Museo (private bath, hot water, cable TV, free parking, wi-fi; $70-$100, including breakfast; children under 10 free; apartments also for rent; 2258-1027, fax: 257-9414; hotelposadadelmuseo.com, info@hotelposadadelmuseo.com) is a restored home built in 1928 with decorative ceramic tile floors and an inner second-floor balcony that gives a spacious, airy feel to the main entrance. Rooms are simple with many old-fashioned touches that add to the charm. Next door, the friendly, helpful Argentine owners have a popular café and art gallery that serves daily specials, a host of homemade pastries and desserts, and cappuccino. The hotel's location, kittycorner from the entrance to the National Museum (Calle 17, Avenida 2) on the relatively peaceful Jimenez Oreamuno pedestrian walkway, is a major reason for staying there. Recommended.

The Pine Tree Inn (private bath, hot water, ceiling fans, cable TV, phones, pool, pet friendly; $70-$80, including breakfast; 2289-7405, fax:

2228-2180; hotelpinetree.com, pinetree@racsa.co.cr) has a very helpful staff and is within walking distance of many of Escazú's best restaurants. It is located in the exclusive Barrio Trejos Montealegre in Escazú, 200 meters north and 100 meters west of Rostipollo.

Apartotel La Sabana (a/c, cable TV, phone, pool, wi-fi; $60-$70; apartments, $80-$120, including breakfast; 2220-2422, in North America: 877-722-2621 fax: 2231-7386; apartotel-lasabana.com, info@apartotel-la sabana.com) is a sunny complex on a quiet street near La Sabana, with clean, carpeted rooms, a laundromat, and a sauna. Their family-sized apartment sleeps up to five people.

El Sesteo (private bath, ceiling fans, cable TV, pool, jacuzzi, laundromat, conference room, wi-fi for fee; $50-$60, including breakfast; with kitchen, $60-$100, including breakfast; 200 meters south of La Sabana McDonald's; 2296-1805, in North America: 877-623-3198 fax: 2296-1865; sesteo.com, sesteo@racsa.co.cr). The rooms and apartments surround the unheated pool, the hot tub, and the lush garden. It's a great place to stay with kids, and there is a nice view of the hills from the buffet-breakfast area.

Tapezco Inn (private bath, hot water, table fans, cable TV, sauna and splash pool, phone, wi-fi; $40-$50, including breakfast; just south of the Escazú church; 2228-1084, fax: 2289-7026; tapezco-inn.co.cr, info@ tapezco-inn.co.cr) is in downtown Escazú.

Taylor Inn (private bath, hot water, phone, cable TV, ceiling fan, nonsmoking, shared kitchen, internet; $60-$70 including breakfast; children under 10 free; 2257-4333; taylorinn.com, info@taylorinn.com) is a graceful home built in 1908. Located on quiet Avenida 13 between Calles 3 and 3 bis, it is convenient to the restaurants of Barrio Amón and close to buses going to the Caribbean and Sarapiquí. Recommended.

Costa Rica Tennis Club and Hotel (a/c, cable TV, pool, restaurants, bar; $40-$60, including breakfast; 2232-1228, fax: 2232-3867, in North America: 888-790-5264; costaricatennisclub.com, prensa@costaricatennis club.com) comes complete with nine lighted outdoor and three indoor tennis courts, a gym, a sauna, three pools, a bowling alley, playgrounds, and two restaurants. Located on the south side of La Sabana. A good value.

Apartotel Los Yoses (ceiling fans or a/c, cable TV, kitchens, pool, wi-fi in some suites; $70-$140; 2225-0033, 2225-0044, in North America: 888-790-5264, fax: 2225-5595; apartotel.com, losyoses@apartotel.com) is very clean. Their larger apartments can accommodate big families or groups, and they have a babysitting service. In Los Yoses, on the main thoroughfare 100 meters west of the Fuente de la Hispanidad.

HOSTELS

Hostelling has undergone a transformation. Now those who want to experience San José on the cheap can find swimming pools, hammocks, and inhouse restaurants with international menus in pleasant neighborhoods with good security. Meeting people from all over the world is still part of the fun. Both dormitory-style and private rooms are available. Most of them will arrange for airport pick-up. Taxis to bus stations from these places cost $2-$3 at most. Hostels book up fast, so make reservations in advance.

Abril Hostal (shared bath, heated water, shared kitchen, large lockers, wi-fi, garage; dorms $12/person, including breakfast; 2234-1310, fax: 2233-6397; abrilhostal.com) is located in a pleasant older house near the National Parks headquarters. It's clean and well run, with a 10 p.m. curfew. There's a large back yard and a sunporch with a nice view of the city. It's on the corner of Avenida 10, Calle 25. Tell taxi drivers it's "*tres cientos metros al este de la casa Matute Gómez.*"

Hostel Bekuo (shared or private bath, hot water, wi-fi, cable TV, kitchen; $30-$40 including breakfast; dorms, $12/person; 2234-1091; hostelbekuo.com, info@hostelbekuo.com) is clean and spacious with a large communal kitchen, a homey living room, pool table, darts, a garden with hammocks and a barbecue. It's 325 meters west of Spoon in upscale Los Yoses. Recommended.

Costa Rica Backpackers (shared bath, heated water, pool, lockers, kitchen and laundry facilities, wi-fi; dorms, $12/person; private rooms, $20-$40; 2221-6191, fax: 2223-2406; costaricabackpackers.com, costarica backpackers@gmail.com) has lawn chairs and hammocks surround a swimming pool in a walled rooftop garden, banks of computers that offer internet access 24/7, and a restaurant serves anything from nachos to Thai green curry. The rooms downstairs are small and crowded together, and the walls are thin. The hostel is located in a nice neighborhood, 100 meters east of the Supreme Court building, on Avenida 6 between Calles 19 and 23, just three blocks from the National Museum. Airport pick-up available.

Costa Rica Guesthouse (private and shared baths, hot water, free parking; $30-$40; 2223-7034; costaricabackpackers.com) across the street, has large rooms with king beds. Guests can use the pool, internet and restaurant at CR Backpackers, but can retreat to a quieter atmosphere. Recommended.

Casa Ridgway (hot water, no smoking, shared bath, cable TV, free parking; shared and private rooms, $10-$12/person, including breakfast; children under 4 free, children 5 to 12 half-price; Avenida 6 bis, Calle 15; 2255-6399, 2233-6168; amigosparalapaz.org, casaridgway@yahoo.es) helps to support the Quaker Peace Center next door. It has a convivial atmosphere, kitchen and laundry privileges, and dormitory-style bunks in some rooms. Make reservations in advance—it is often full. Guest have access to the Center's library on peace and human rights.

Gaudy's Backpackers (hot showers, wi-fi, laundry service; dorms, shared bath, $10/person; private room, shared bath or private bath, $15-$30; Avenida 5 between Calles 36/38, north of Paseo Colón; phone/fax: 2248-0086, 2258-2937; backpacker.co.cr, gaudys@backpacker.co.cr) has courtyards with plants and hammocks and shared kitchen facilities.

Green House Hostel (heated water, wi-fi, kitchen, TV room, guarded parking; dorm, $14/person; private bath, $20-$40, including breakfast; 2258-9084, 2258-0102, fax: 2258-9193; greenhousehostel.altervista.org, greenhousehostel@infowebco.net) does not have the amenities of some of the fancier hostels, but it makes up for it with the helpfulness of its friendly Tica owners. Most rooms look onto large central space with sitting areas and games. Located near the sports complex at Plaza Viquez, it is convenient to the MUSOC bus station. The nearby Restaurante Meylin, open 24 hours a day, has good, cheap food, and you can watch nattily dressed *mariachis* hang around, waiting for gigs. The Green House is a bit of a roundabout to get to, on Calle 11 between Avenidas 16 and 18. Don't confuse taxi drivers by calling it "La Casa Verde" because there is a hotel by that name in Barrio Amón. Tell taxi drivers *"Del restaurante Meylin, cincuenta al norte."*

Pangea (hot water, cooking facilities, lockers, solar heated pool and jacuzzi, wi-fi; dorm, $10/person; private room with shared bath or private bath, $20-$30; 2221-1992, 2256-6674; pangea.hostel.com,) is on Avenida 7 between Calles 3 bis and 3. There are lots of high-speed computers, and the glassed-in top-floor bar/restaurant has a great view of Poás and Barva volcanoes to the north. The pool is on the first floor. Despite the psychedelic jungle motifs painted on every inch of wall space, security is tight—guests receive plastic ID bracelets that are changed every day. Rooms are clean and set back from the street, mattresses are good. Enthusiastic, hardworking Tico twin brothers own the Pangea, the Toruma, and a sister hostel in La Fortuna. Airport pickup is $6 to $14, depending on the number of people.

Toruma (hot water, nonsmoking, wi-fi, communal kitchen, pool, guarded parking; dorms $10/person; shared bath, $20-$30; private bath, $30-$50; Avenida Central, Calles 29/31/33; 2234-8186, 2224-4085; hosteltoruma.com, hosteltoruma@yahoo.com) is owned by the Pangea. This lovely remodeled mansion on the east side of town has a pool, gardens, hammocks, and an open-air bar/restaurant. Private rooms have terraces.

HOMESTAYS

This is a good way to get to know the local people and to practice your Spanish. To find a compatible family, call the language schools, look for signs at the University of Costa Rica, or use one of the contacts below. Be prepared for a lot of hospitality. If noise bothers you, check first to see if your family leaves the TV or radio on all the time. Amenities run the gamut and depend on the household you choose.

Bell's Home Hospitality (shared or private bath; $30-$50; 2225-4752, fax: 2224-5884; homestay.thebells.org, homestay@racsa.co.cr) matches you with a compatible Costa Rican family. Breakfast is included in the rates; dinner is $7 extra. Owners Vernon and Marcela Bell are excellent hosts and very generous with helpful information. Recommended.

Sra. Soledad Zamora (phone/fax in Spanish: 2224-7937) specializes in connecting longer-term renters with inexpensive rooms (Spanish speaking only). Inexpensive rates include breakfast, dinner, and laundry service.

MISCELLANEOUS INFORMATION

SOUVENIRS

Moderately priced souvenirs can be found at the **Mercado Central** (Avenidas Central/1, Calles 6/8), **La Casona** (Calle Central, Avenidas Central/1), and at the **Calle Nacional de la Artesania** off the Plaza de la Democracia. One of the most charming, complete, and inexpensive souvenir shops, called **Annemarie's** (Calle 9, Avenida 9), is in the converted home of one of Costa Rica's ex-presidents, now the Hotel Don Carlos. You can see indigenous crafts at **Galería Namú** (Avenida 7, Calle 5).

If you have a little more money to spend, check out the innovative woodwork of two North Americans, **Barry Biesanz** and **Jay Morrison**. Biesanz specializes in exquisitely crafted bowls and boxes priced from $15 to $1500. He also makes a lot of unique items that might be perfect for someone on your gift list: Scrabble tile holders and counters, kendo swords, guitar pegs, wooden musical spoons, drumsticks, shadow boxes, credit card cases, and free-standing or wall-hung earring frames, boxes, and displays. Here you can also find authentic, high-quality indigenous masks and textiles made with natural dyes by Brunca artisans in the Southern Zone. You can tour Barry's workshop and showroom, and stop for a *refresco* overlooking his wife Sarah's herb garden and pond in Escazú. Call 2289-4337 for directions (biesanz.com). Morrison's creative hardwood furniture is displayed at his showroom, **Tierra Extraña** (2282-6697), in Piedades de Santa Ana. Faced with the dilemma of using precious hardwoods in danger of extinction for their work, both Biesanz and Morrison have reforested farms with the varieties they use, and Barry sells hardwood saplings at his showroom.

Because the airlines want you to be at the airport two or three hours before your return flight, the well-run, attractive souvenir shops near the airport boarding gates are a good place to stock up on Costa Rica's excellent export coffee, Café Britt. Britt also sells all manner of inexpensive goodies to bring home. Chocolate-covered bits of pineapple, guava, passion fruit, macadamia nuts, and coffee beans can be sampled before purchase, as can CafeRica, the Costa Rican answer to Kahlúa.

BOOKS, NEWSPAPERS, AND MAGAZINES

English-language newspapers and magazines, including the *New York Times*, *Wall Street Journal*, *Miami Herald*, *Time*, and *Newsweek*, are sold throughout the metropolitan area.

The **Mark Twain Library** (open daily, 8 a.m. to 8 p.m.; Saturday, 8 a.m. to 5 p.m.; 2207-7575) of the **Centro Cultural Costarricense-Norteamericano** in Barrio Dent has the latest newspapers, books, audiobooks, and a special room for watching CNN. They also have computers for internet access. Francophiles can visit the **Alianza Francesa** (open weekdays, 8:45 a.m. to 11:45 a.m., 3 p.m. to 7 p.m.; 2222-2283) on the corner of Calle 5 and Avenida 7, behind the Hotel Aurola Holiday Inn in San José.

The best source of local news in English, the *Tico Times* (2258-1558, fax: 2233-6378; ticotimes.net, info@ticotimes.net; $1) is published Friday and available at the above places and at many hotels. Winner of the Interamerican Press Association award for distinguished service to the community, as well as other prestigious awards, the *Tico Times* offers a well-researched synthesis of weekly events in Costa Rica and Central America. It is without comparison in its coverage of local environmental and political issues and gives an excellent rundown of cultural activities. See their online edition for up-to-the-minute news and facts.

With a convenient central location, **7th Street Books** (Calle 7, Avenidas 1/Central; 2256-8251), boasts many shelves of contemporary English-language fiction and an excellent selection of books on tropical ecology and travel. They also buy and sell used books. **Café Milagro** serves sandwiches, smoothies and its famous coffee in a comfortable lounge inside the bookstore.

Mora Books (open 11 a.m. to 6:30 p.m.; in the Omni Building, Avenida 1, Calles 3/5; 2255-4136) offers a wide selection of used books, CDs,

DVDs, comics, and magazines. They will buy or trade English and German books.

The **Librería Internacional** (300 meters west of Taco Bell in Barrio Dent; 2253-9553; libreriainternacional.com) is a large trilingual (Spanish, German, English) bookstore with special selections of travel books, esoterica, art, and children's books, as well as a good fiction collection. It has branches in Rohrmoser (200 meters east of Plaza Mayor; 2290-3331), in the Multiplaza in Escazú (2201-8320), in Plaza Cemaco (100 meters north of the Rotonda de los Garantías Sociales; 2280-8065), and on Avenida Central (75 meters west of the Plaza de la Cultura; 2257-2563).

MEETING PLACES

The **Friends' Peace Center** (open weekdays, 10 a.m. to noon, 1:30 p.m. to 6 p.m.; Calle 15, Avenida 6 bis; phone/fax: 2233-6168; friends@racsa. co.cr) in San José is a training center for conflict resolution, and addresses issues involving human rights, community development, and ecology. It provides meeting space, activity coordination, a library, and educational programs, and hosts a weekly Quaker meeting. The staff of the center is made up of both Central and North Americans, most of them volunteers.

A variety of clubs meet regularly in San José and the Central Valley, including the Women's Club, Bridge Club, Newcomer's Club, Republicans Abroad, Democrats Abroad, American Legion, La Leche League, Rotary, Canada Club, Coffee Pickin' Square Dancers, AA, OA, Ultimate Frisbee Club, and the Women's International League for Peace and Freedom. Current hours and numbers are often listed in the *Tico Times*.

MUSEUMS

Most of the downtown museums are mentioned in our walking tour at the beginning of this chapter or in the Creative Arts section. The Children's Museum is mentioned in the "Notes for Traveling with Children" section in Chapter Three. A living museum is the **Pueblo Antiguo** (closed Monday and Tuesday; 2242-9200), a theme park of Costa Rican history and cultural traditions at the Parque Nacional de Diversiones in La Uruca, two kilometers west of the Hospital México. The park re-creates the city at the turn of the 20th century, as well as a rural town and a coastal village. Professional actors take you into the past in the *Vivencias Costarricenses* tour (weekends from 10 a.m.), in which they trace the roots of Costa Rican traditions and democracy in an entertaining one-hour presentation. Friday and Saturday nights from 6:30 to 9 p.m. you can enjoy a typical dinner and folkloric show, **Noches Costarricenses**, with a historical view of Costa Rican dance and music. Wheelchairs and baby strollers are available at the entrance. Kids will enjoy the amusement park on the same property. Proceeds from Pueblo Antiguo fund the local children's hospital.

LIVING CULTURE IN THE HILLS

The town of San Antonio, in the hills above Escazú, is full of tradition. At **El Encanto de la Piedra Blanca** in San Antonio, you can see how sugarcane juice is pressed and boiled to make *tapa de dulce*, try on the gigantic papier maché masks that local dancers wear for fiestas, and enjoy a delicious local lunch while learning about the valiant efforts of CODECE to protect their water sources and prevent overdevelopment. ACTUAR (2248-9470; actuarcostarica.com, info@actuarcostarica.com) can set up a half-day tour, or combine a San Jose city tour with a trip to San Antonio. At their **Noches Magicas,** a colorful folkloric dance troupe will receive your group in a traditional adobe home, where you will enjoy a variety of time-honored native recipes. You'll learn about Latin rhythms and dance, then be treated to a moonlit serenade. This makes a great *fiesta* for your first or last night in town.

ORCHIDS AND INSECTS

Orchid lovers should plan to visit during March when the **National Orchid Show** (2223-6517) is held. Butterfly enthusiasts will enjoy the **Insect Museum** (open Monday through Friday, 1 p.m. to 4:45 p.m.; 2207-5318; insectos.ucr.ac.cr; admission $1.50) run by the University of Costa Rica's Facultad de Agronomía. It is located on the University of Costa Rica campus in San Pedro, in the basement of the Artes Musicales building.

LA SABANA

San José converted its former international airport into a metropolitan park with sports facilities. The National Gymnasium is on the southeast corner of the former airfield, the National Stadium on the northwest corner. The Air Terminal Building has become the National Art Museum. With jogging and walking paths; tennis, volleyball, and basketball courts; and soccer and baseball fields, La Sabana is a favorite recreation area on weekends and a training ground for runners and joggers during lunch hours (showers are provided). There's a hill for kite flying and lots of trees for shady relaxation. People fly-cast in the lake. During the International Arts Festival each March, La Sabana is full of artists, artisans, and performers.

Canopy Urbano (2215-2544; admission $20) gives city dwellers the experience of a zip line tour, with ten platforms and a rappel. The longest cable takes you 600 feet across the park's lake and through the spray from its fountain at up to 20 kilometers per hour. Kids 5 to 12 ride with a guide. To get to the zipline, take the Sabana–Cementerio bus, and get off at La Sabana. Take the path behind the Art Museum past the swimming pool to the start of Canopy Urbano. *Warning:* La Sabana can be dangerous at night.

SEVEN

Central Valley and Surroundings

Costa Rica's Central Valley, or Meseta Central, is a large, fertile plateau surrounded by high mountains. Seventy percent of the country's population lives in this region, which centers around the towns of Alajuela, Heredia, and Cartago, as well as the city of San José. As you leave the more densely populated areas and drive toward the valley's western edge at San Ramón, or wind down through spectacular scenery to its eastern edge at Turrialba, you'll see large fields of sugarcane and corn.

Exploring the highlands leading to the volcanoes Poás, Barva, and Irazú, you will see hills full of coffee bushes, flower plantations, and dairy farms. People enjoy the varying climates of the Central Valley, ranging from year-round summer in the lower western towns of Alajuela, Santa Ana, and Villa Colón, to year-round spring at higher elevations.

Pleasant accommodations have sprung up all over the Central Valley. Since the Juan Santamaría International Airport is much closer to Alajuela and Heredia than to San José, it's possible to stay in or near these towns, avoiding the noise and pollution of the capital city.

ALAJUELA AREA

Although only 20 kilometers from San José, Alajuela is 200 meters lower and considerably warmer. It is full of shady parks. Sundays, the park fills with families, ice cream vendors, street entertainers, and kiosks selling balloons. The **Juan Santamaría Museum** (open Tuesday through Sunday, 10 a.m. to 5:30 p.m.; 2441-4775), housed in the former jail one block north of Parque Central, features relics of the 1856 rout of William Walker, as well as an orchid garden and art gallery.

Catch big league soccer games at the **Stadium** at the northeast corner of town. Check ldacr.org for schedules.

Ojo de Agua (open daily 6 a.m. to 4 p.m.; admission $5, including parking and lockers; kids under 6 free; 2441-0655) has an Olympic-sized swimming pool, a waterfall pool where you can sit and let the water massage your shoulders or get a workout swimming against the current, a round pool for kids who are learning how to swim, and a shallow pool for toddlers. There's a beach-like area for making sand castles. The pools are fed by a prolific spring, so the water is changed twelve times a day, eliminating the need for chemicals. There is a lake with kayaks and small boats. There are basketball courts and soccer fields. As many as 9000 people per weekend visit this popular spot. It is less crowded during the week. There are buses from San José, Alajuela and Heredia. To get there by car from Alajuela, turn right at the Firestone turnoff on the highway to San José and drive south about four kilometers. Ojo de Agua will be on your left.

The park-like **Butterfly Farm** (open daily, guided tours at 8:30 a.m., 11 a.m., 1 p.m., and 3 p.m.; 2438-0400, fax: 2438-0300; butterflyfarm.co.cr, info@butterflyfarm.co.cr) is devoted to raising live butterflies for exhibit in Europe. On the entertaining Butterfly Tour (two hours; $15; students $10; children 5 to 12 $7, children under 5 free; $25, including transport to and from San José; $15 for children), you learn about the relationships between the beautiful winged insects, their host plants, and their predators. The farm's owners have made it possible for all visitors to observe a butterfly emerging from its chrysalis by presenting an informative video during each tour. Visitors on the morning tour may even see butterflies emerging and taking off on their maiden flight. You can stay as long as you want to photograph the butterflies. The Butterfly Farm is located southwest of the airport in La Guácima de Alajuela on the left, just beyond Los Reyes Country Club.

The **Zoo Ave Wildlife Conservation Park** (open daily, 9 a.m. to 5 p.m.; 2433-8989; zooave.org, info@zooave.org; adults $15; students $13; children under 10 $2), 15 minutes west of Alajuela, houses the world's most comprehensive exhibit of Costa Rican wildlife, while also breeding and releasing more native species than any other zoo in Latin America. All the animals at Zoo Ave were former pets, or injured or confiscated wildlife. They are now healthy and living in a beautiful jungle environment, and are released to the wild whenever possible. If you missed seeing monkeys, wild felines, toucans, or crocodiles on your trip, you can catch plenty of them here. Birders visit Zoo Ave to familiarize themselves with the calls of the birds they want to see. Highly recommended. See their website for **volunteer** opportunities. To get there, drive five minutes west of the airport

NO NEED TO GO TO SAN JOSÉ

You no longer need to go into San José to catch a bus to the provinces. Most of the direct buses to major tourist destinations like Guanacaste, Volcán Arenal, Manuel Antonio, and Monteverde pass through Alajuela on their way west, about 25 minutes after they leave San José. Most of them go to a bus stop called *parada la Radial*, right next to the Centro de Servicio la Radial, and 200 meters north of the big Mas x Menos grocery store near the airport. The Soda Nandayure, which sells snacks at the bus stop, has a list of the buses that pass each day. There are usually plenty of seats on the morning buses from Sunday through Thursday, but it's safer to go to the San José terminals if you're leaving on a Friday or Saturday, or during holidays.

A Safe Passage (8365-9678; costaricabustickets.com, rchoice@racsa.co.cr) will buy your bus tickets ($40/person, $75/two people) for you in San José, pick you up at the airport, and take you to their own special bus stop. If you need to go to the bank or market on the way, they'll take you. If your flight arrives early and you need to rest before your bus, take advantage of their Waiting Room or Home Base option. They will get you a room where you can recuperate from your flight for a few hours, then deliver you to your bus, or arrange for an inexpensive first- and last-night's stay in Alajuela. There is also a no-frills "tickets only" option for $15/person, $25/two people. Their **Costa Rica Van Go** provides transport to anywhere in the country using biodiesel-fueled vans. They encourage passengers to bring their favorite traveling music and provide headphones. They stop at local sodas and mingle with the locals. They donate seedlings and school uniforms for every transfer they provide. Their website has a list of bus departure times. This is a great service, well worth the price.

and take the exit just after the large Zoo Ave sign. Cross a small bridge after the exit, and continue 2.5 kilometers east. You'll see the entrance on your left. A taxi from downtown Alajuela costs about $3.

The **Botanical Orchid Garden** (open 8:30 a.m. to 4:30 p.m., closed Monday; adults $12, kids $6; 2487-8095; orchidgardencr.com) teaches you about the life cycle of orchids and how to grow them. There are trails and peaceful water gardens. To get there, turn left west of the airport on the road to Jacó, then left again at La Fiesta de Maíz. It will be on your right in about 800 meters.

Doka Coffee Tour (2449-5152; dokaestate.com, info@dokaestate.com) takes you through the Vargas family's farm and coffee-processing plant on the road to Poás volcano to see how they create their prize-winning, organically fertilized, shade-grown coffee. Tours are almost hourly, Monday through Saturday ($16). You can sample their Three Generations brand brew and have breakfast or lunch on the tour.

RESTAURANTS   **Delicias del Maiz** (2433-7206) in Barrio San José, a $3 cab ride from downtown, is great for homemade traditional Costa Rican dishes. **Mi Choza** (open Monday through Saturday, 7 a.m. to 3 p.m.; 2442-7179), north of the Cathedral, is recommended by locals for cheap and good *comida típica* for breakfast or lunch. **Soda El Banco**, across from the Banco Popular, also has good, cheap *Tico* food (open Monday through Saturday, 7 a.m. to 4 p.m.). There are always inexpensive places to eat at the Mercado Central, one block west of Parque Central.

At **Cuginis** (open 4 to 10 p.m.; 2440-6893) a former Philadelphian recreates his Sicilian grandma's recipes (including, of course, Philly Cheese Steak) in a second floor brick-walled dining room above the bar. It's unpretentious yet atmospheric, a nice place to be. It's two blocks east of the Cathedral on Avenida Central, Calle 5.

Alcielo Bar and Grill (open 7 p.m. to midnight; 8354-4631) is a lively nighttime meeting place, 250 meters south of the La Agonía Church on the east side of town.

Como en Casa (open 11:30 a.m. to 10 p.m.; closed Mondays; 2440-4300) serves up Argentine/Tico fusion one block east of the Tropicana gas station (Avenida 10, Calle 5) on the south side of town.

Mirador del Valle (open Monday to Thursday, 4 p.m. to 11 p.m., Friday to Sunday noon to midnight; 2441-9347), six kilometers north of town in Sabanilla, specializes in grilled meats, has fantastic valley views and offers music on weekends.

LODGING   There are a variety of accommodations in or near Alajuela. This is a convenient place to stay your first or last night in Costa Rica, much closer to the airport (about a $3-$7 cab ride to any of the hotels shown on the map) than San José. Downtown Alajuela has an abundance of cheap, friendly hotels in the $10-$30 range, most of which are in converted older homes. If you are not on a budget, stay in one of the beautiful hotels that dot the hillsides around Alajuela. The owners of most of these hotels will arrange for airport pickup and can have rental cars delivered to you at the hotel.

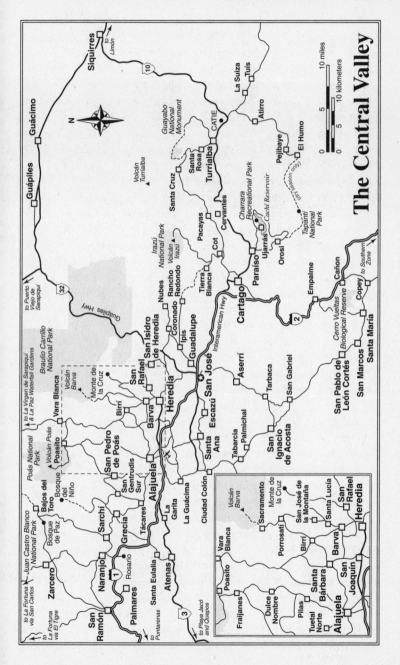

Budget Hotels: **Hotel Coconut House** (private bath, hot water; $20-$30, including breakfast; 2441-1249, fax: 2442-7158; coconuthouse.info, hotel@coconuthouse.info) is located in a quiet neighborhood. It's clean, has a cooking area for guests, and the friendly German owners will help you make travel arrangements. It's in Alajuela's Barrio La Trinidad, 400 meters west, 100 meters south, and 50 meters west of La Jarra Garibaldi. Recommended.

Hotel Los Volcanes (shared or private bath, hot water, cable TV, internet, outdoor patio/kitchen; $40-$60, including breakfast; 2441-0525, fax: 2440-8006; hotellosvolcanes.com, losvolcanes@racsa.co.cr), across from the Juan Santamaría Museum, has the polished tile floors of a fine old house. Ask for the quieter rooms behind the garden. Their special package includes airport pickup and transportation to or from Montezuma (see Chapter Eleven) for $45 to $70 per person, depending on the type of room you have.

Hotel Mi Tierra (shared or private bath, heated water, pool, cable TV, wi-fi, shared kitchen; $30-$40, including breakfast and airport pickup; 2441-1974, fax: 2441-4022; hotelmitierra.net, info@hotelmitierra.net) is welcoming and relaxed. It's centrally located on Avenida 2 between Calles 3 and 5, 250 meters east of Parque Juan Santamaría in downtown Alajuela. Rooms are clean and cozy, and the small pool is nice. Rooms in the back are quieter. The owner, Roberto, is an expert kayaking guide. Recommended.

Hotel Pacandé (shared or private bath, hot water, kitchen facilities, wi-fi; $20-$50, including breakfast; 2443-8481; Avenida 5, Calles 2/4; hotel pacande.com) has clean, attractive rooms and a small, quiet garden breakfast area in back. Room 8, upstairs, overlooks the garden. It's two blocks north and half a block west of Parque Central. Recommended.

Vida Tropical (shared bath, heated water, fans, communal kitchen; $30-$50, including breakfast; children under 12 free; 8840-6964, 877-661-1863, phone/fax: 2443-9576; vidatropical.com, ranchos@racsa.co.cr) is a friendly guesthouse in a quiet residential neighborhood. It's one block east and three blocks north of the Alajuela Hospital.

Villa Bonita B&B (private bath, hot water, ceiling fans, cable TV, wi-fi, free parking; $50-$60, including breakfast; children under 10 free; 2441-0239, cell: 8370-0921; hotelvillabonita.com, reservations@hotelvillabonita.com) has big airy rooms, a spacious garden sitting area and provides a hearty, gourmet breakfast. It's located near the southeast entrance to town on Avenida 8, between Calles 7 and 9. Taxi directions: *"Del Servicentro La Tropicana, 300 metros al este, 100 al norte, y 50 al oeste."* Recommended.

Hillside Hotels: In the villages surrounding Alajuela there are several more hotels, with more tropical settings than those in downtown Alajuela.

Pura Vida Hotel (private bath, hot water, refrigerator; $90-$140, including breakfast; 2430-2929, fax: 2430-2630; puravidahotel.com, info@ puravidahotel.com), a friendly B&B with bungalows in a hillside garden in Tuetal, northwest of town. Two bungalows have two bedrooms. Owners Berni and Nhi are welcoming hosts; Nhi makes delicious dinners for guests, using her Chinese grandmother's recipes, having fun with local fruit (homemade pineapple ginger sorbet), and decorating everything with flowers. Light, late-night meals are available for late arrivals (with prior reser-

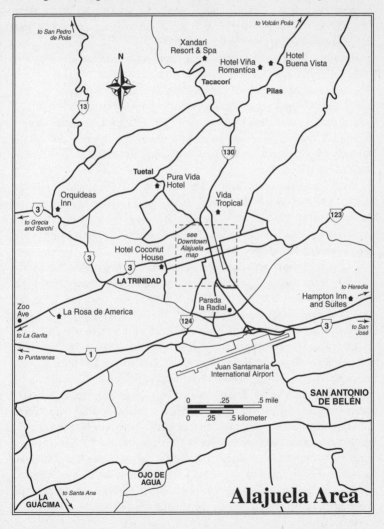

vations), as well as "breakfast to go" for early departures. Their website has a wealth of information. Airport pick-up included. Recommended.

Orquideas Inn (private bath, hot water, ceiling fans, a/c, pool, satellite TV, bar/restaurant, spa, wi-fi; $80-$180, including breakfast; children under 4 free, children 5 to 12 $5; 2433-7128, phone/fax: 2433-9740; orquideas inn.com) is on the road to San Pedro de Poás, about three kilometers northwest of Alajuela (ten minutes from the airport) at the turnoff to the old road to Grecia. The grounds are lush, with tall trees and vines. Their domes have kitchens, sunken baths, and small skylights for looking up at the stars. Guests gather in the Marilyn Monroe Bar to eat roast pig and sing around the player piano.

La Rosa de America (private bath, hot water, ceiling fan, cable TV, internet, pool; $70-$80, including breakfast; children under 5 free, children 5 to 11 $8; phone/fax: 2433-2741; larosadeamerica.com) is a great place to land when you first get off the plane. Rooms are set around a beautifully tended gardens that attract lots of birds. The owners, a Canadian family, help orient you and make sure you have a smooth trip. It's near Zoo Ave in Alajuela's Barrio San José, "*de La Mandarina, cien metros al sur y cien al este.*" Recommended.

Villa Pacandé (private bath, hot water, wi-fi; $40-$60, including breakfast; 2441-6795; villapacande.com) has a veranda with hammocks and sunny gardens in the hills above Alajuela. If coming from the airport, take a taxi to Hotel Pacandé on Avenida 5 in downtown Alajuela, and they will send a taxi to take you to Villas Pacandé. Recommended.

Xandari Resort and Spa (hot water, natural ventilation, lap pools, heated jacuzzi, open-air gym; $200-$350, including breakfast; children under 3 free; 2443-2020, fax: 2442-4847, in North America: 866-363-3212; xan dari.com, info@xandari.com) is a dream of a place. Created by a California architect and his artist wife, the stone terraces of the spacious villas overlook Alajuela. They will pack you a picnic lunch to take on the trails leading through their plantation to five waterfalls. Xandari's spa is unique: Each massage room is a small thatched-roof building with one wall open to the gardens and valley views. The two-person hot tubs are sheltered by the cozy room, yet give a wonderful feeling of being in nature. Xandari is located in the suburb of Tacacori, about ten minutes north of Alajuela. Recommended.

Hotel Buena Vista (private bath, hot water, phone, TV, pool, restaurant; $80-$140; 2442-8595, fax: 2442-8701, in the U.S.: 800-506-2304; hotelbuenavistacr.com, bvista@racsa.co.cr) offers comfortable, carpeted rooms with balconies and a spectacular view of rippling coffee fields and the Central Valley below. It's in the small town of Pilas, five kilometers north of Alajuela.

Hotel Viña Romantica (private bath, hot water, cable TV; $80-$90, including breakfast; 2430-7621; vinaromantica.com, reserve@vinaromantica. com) is a comfortable boutique hotel with a gourmet Euro/Asian restaurant. They offer a "hello and goodbye" package that includes airport pickup and drop-off, a welcome cocktail, one massage, and a five-course farewell dinner. It's 25 meters south of Hotel Buena Vista.

Siempreverde B&B (private bath, hot water; $60-$70, including a hearty breakfast; 2449-5562, fax: 2239-0450; siempreverdebandb.com, info@siempreverdebandb.com) is on the Vargas family's extensive coffee farm. Rooms have views of the plantations, and tree-lined paths lead you to even more incredible vistas. It is located ten kilometers north of the Alajuela courthouse; turn left at the San Isidro high school on the way to the Poás volcano.

GETTING THERE: *By Air:* The Juan Santamaría International Airport (SJO) is in Alajuela.

Large Hotels Near the Airport: On the General Cañas highway to the airport, about 20 minutes from San José, there are several major hotels.

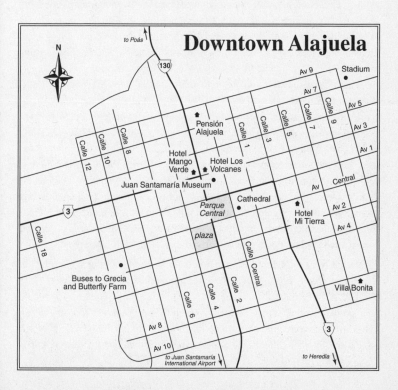

Downtown Alajuela

The Hampton Inn and Suites (private bath, hot water, a/c, cable TV, pool, free airport shuttle; $120-$160, including breakfast; extra bed, $8; 2436-0000, fax: 2442-2781, in North America: 800-426-7866; hamptonhotel. co.cr, hamptonsuites@grupomarta.com), despite being two minutes from the airport and on a major highway, seems quiet inside. They encourage their guests to "think green" by providing recycling bins in each room and composting restaurant waste to fertilize the hotel's gardens. Recommended.

Doubletree Cariari (cable TV, a/c, wi-fi, business center; $100-$160; two-bedroom suites, $440-$1000; 2239-0022, fax: 2239-2803, in North America: 800-336-3542; doubletree1.hilton.com) offers a fitness center, pools, a casino, bars with live music, restaurants, a 600-person convention center, and children's activities.

Another large-scale resort and convention center is the 232-room **Ramada Plaza Herradura** (cable TV, pool, spa, business center, wi-fi; $170-$210; suites, $290-$940; including breakfast; children under 12 free; 2209-9800; ramadaherradura.com, reservaciones@ramadaherradura.com) has a state-of-the-art conference center with two ballrooms and a golf course. There are mountain views from the back of the hotel, and a wonderland of swimming pools: one is fed by a waterfall, another has four jacuzzis in it, another laps serenely on a sand-like beach, inviting you to swim up to the bar. The Herradura is also on the highway to the airport roughly 20 minutes from San José and has frequent bus service into town for guests.

The **Marriott Hotel and Resort** ($250-$340, including breakfast; 2298-0000, in North America: 800-228-9290 fax: 2298-0011; marriott. com) in San Antonio de Belén, just south of the airport, is built in the style of a colonial coffee hacienda. The stone arches, wrought-iron balconies, tiled roofs and mosaic staircases, the spacious courtyard, carved furniture and tapestries, and the small chapel are a welcome relief from the boring or pretentious architecture of most large hotels. The Marriott has four restaurants, 15 conference rooms, a convention center, pools, gym, sauna, jacuzzi, tennis courts, golf-practicing course, an amphitheater, and a heliport. A taxi from the airport takes 5 to 15 minutes. The Marriott also has its less-expensive Courtyard Hotel on the Prospero Fernandez Highway. Recommended.

SANTA ANA LODGING   These hotels are located south of the airport, in the sunny, warm outlying area of Santa Ana, popular with expatriates.

The **Alta Hotel** (private bath, hot water, fan, a/c, phone, wi-fi, cable TV, pool, jacuzzi, sauna, gym; $190-$460; penthouse, $950; including breakfast; children under 12 free; 2282-4160, fax: 2282-4162, in North America: 888-388-2582; thealtahotel.com, info@thealtahotel.com) is a special place to stay because of its innovative yet harmonious architecture, blending Moorish arches, wooden balconies, and tiled roofs with clean, contemporary spaces to create an elegant mix of old and new. The hall leading down to the restaurant is reminiscent of a street in Barcelona's old Gothic Quarter. Local art graces the walls. The hotel's **La Luz Restaurant** is known for fine gourmet dining. Their all-day Sunday brunch features Costa Rican *nouvelle cuisine*. With a pristine, cobalt-blue tiled elliptical pool, state-of-the-art gym, outdoor hot tub, and views of the Santa Ana Valley, the Alta is an experience to be savored. Recommended.

Albergue El Marañón (shared or private bath, solar hot water; $60-$70, including breakfast; two-bedroom apartment, $80-$90; 2249-1271, fax: 2249-1761; cultourica.com, cultourica@racsa.co.cr) is a pleasant B&B and language school for individuals or groups. Their tour company, Cultourica, takes guests to community-based ecotourism projects. There is a shady garden with hammocks strung beneath the fruit trees and a great view. Their wellness center offers massage, yoga, and dance classes in a natural surrounding. El Marañón is located next to the church in Barrio La Trinidad, on a back road between Piedades and Ciudad Colón. It's about 20 minutes from the airport. Their **Restaurant El Aguacate** features traditional ingredients and spices in creative combinations, like peppers stuffed with goat cheese, tilapia with coconut and tamarind sauce, chicken in mango sauce, and lots of avocado dishes. Recommended.

Casa Alegre Hotel (private bath, hot water, wi-fi, TV, pool; $60-$90, including breakfast; 2235-5485; hotelcasaelegre.com, reservations@hotel casaalegre.com) has pleasant rooms, well-tended gardens, and a pool within walking distance of Santa Ana's restaurants, pottery shops, and the colorful farmers' market on Sunday mornings.

Corteza Amarilla Art Lodge and Spa (private bath, hot water, cable TV, phones, wi-fi; $160-$220; children under 12 free; 2203-7503, fax: 2282-6641; cortezamarillalodge.com, reservations@cortezaamarillalodge. com) combines luxurious accommodations with vintage architectural elements salvaged from historic San José mansions that were being demolished. Rescued stained glass, wooden staircases, carved moldings, and graceful windows now have places of honor throughout the lodge. The indoor/outdoor **restaurant**'s walls are a mélange of invited artistic statements by local painters and guests. It is frequented by well-to-do suburbanites who appreciate its sophisticated international menu and the unique atmosphere. The rooms are nothing short of opulent. The spa offers daily yoga classes and a hot tub. Recommended.

Text continued on page 172.

INNOVATIVE COMMUNITIES

The mountains to the south of San José have not been opened to tourism like those to the north. This is a good place to get a sense of rural Costa Rica. **Nacientes Palmichal** (private bath, heated water, restaurant, meeting room; $50-$60, including breakfast; 2248-4328, phone/fax: 2418-4360; nacientespalmichal.com, san joserural@racsa.co.cr, or info@actuarcostarica.com) is a cloud forest reserve and lodge about an hour south of the airport, owned by ADESSARU, a grassroots organization dedicated to the conservation of the many rivers and streams that spring from these mountains and give life to the valley below. Surrounded by greenery and flowers, the chalet-style lodge is about four kilometers uphill from the village of Palmichal de Acosta. Tables and benches in secluded nooks along the trails behind the lodge are perfect for writing, conversing or contemplating the rushing river. Rooms have bunk beds or a queen bed and a bunk bed. The community's reserve (4000 to 4650 feet above sea level) protects one of the few remaining cloud forests in this area. The shady trail along the Tabarcia river above the lodge is frequented by many species of beautiful butterflies.

Palmichal and the neighboring town of Tabarcia are models of how tourism can help to support small conservation-minded businesses. Through the lodge, you can visit family farms that have incorporated many sustainable practices:

- At **La Finca de Don Manuel,** experience a traditional shade-grown coffee farm and learn how to make tortillas.
- At **Finca los Vindas** see how a family roasts their own coffee and converts the coffee berry into organic fertilizer
- At **ASOPROAAA** learn how a local cooperative produces prize-winning coffee in a sustainable manner
- At **Paraiso de la Bendicón,** observe how a family uses pig manure in biodigestors. The odorless methane gas from the biodigestors is piped into the house and supplies all the family's cooking needs. They also raise cattle in a way that cuts down on soil erosion.
- Visit a bamboo workshop

With **Familias Emprendedoras** in Tabarcia, you can

• push sugar cane through a water-powered press and drink the cane juice. This is the traditional first step in making either *tapa de dulce,* the delicious hard brown sugar, or *guaro,* the local fire water

• see many species of precious hardwood trees and hike to a waterfall

• visit a goat farm and sample their creamy, delicious strawberry yogurt

• eat bread cooked in a traditional adobe oven

• visit an organic vegetable farm

• pick a wide variety of fresh tropical fruit next to a beautiful river.

In nearby **Quitirrisi,** you can

• see how indigenous families make baskets from the fibers of the colorful *estococa* plant

• learn about and buy indigenous herbal preparations

A visit to any four of these projects can be included in a day tour arranged by Nacientes Palmichal ($30-40, including lunch and snack).

This area can be a **gateway to the Southern Zone**. The road that leads east through the Los Santos region is well-paved and the countryside is beautiful. In two hours you can be in El Empalme on the Interamerican Highway south of Cartago, saving you the hassle of driving through San José with its traffic jams. For more about Los Santos, see the Southern Zone chapter.

GETTING THERE: By Car: Take route 27, the Prospero Fernandez highway to Ciudad Colón. After you drive though Ciudad Colón, you'll be on the road to Santiago de Puriscal. Continue uphill for about 11 kilometers of winding, paved roads. Look for a Café Palmichal sign on your left before the road descends into Puriscal. Turn left and go 5 kilometers to Tabarcia. Turn left at the Church and go another 4 kilometers to the village of Palmichal. Nacientes Palmichal Lodge is another four kilometers uphill from the Palmichal Church. The last 2 or 3 kilometers are unpaved.

By Bus: Take the Contrasuli bus to Palmichal from the Puriscal bus terminal on Avenida 1, Calles 20/22 (2249-2706). That will take you to Palmichal. Call ahead to arrange for a ride to the lodge from there (about $4).

WEST OF ALAJUELA

The following towns offer country lodgings within an hour of the airport. Don't try to find these places by yourself after dark (5:30 p.m.) when you are fresh off the plane. Also see sections on Grecia and Heredia for more hotels within half an hour of the airport.

ATENAS

Fifteen minutes west of La Garita de Alajuela on a winding road is the sunny coffee- growing town of Atenas. On the right, just before you reach the town, **Las Molas** displays a large variety of excellent souvenirs at reasonable prices in an elegant setting. It's a great place to take a break (nice bathrooms!) on your way back from the coast.

At the entrance to town is the impressive **Monumento al Boyero**, commemorating the struggle of oxen and their drivers as they brought coffee and sugarcane down to the Pacific port of Puntarenas for export. As many as 800 oxcarts per day would rumble through Atenas in the 1800s on the trip to the Pacific, and the sturdy oxcart was often both ambulance and hearse in surrounding villages. The iron monument was inaugurated in 2003 with a visit from 400 teams of oxen from all over the country. Due to Costa Rica's rough terrain, the oxcart is still the vehicle of choice in many farm areas, and oxcart parades take place yearly in San José and San Antonio de Escazú.

The **Gourmet Store** (open Monday through Saturday, 9:30 a.m. to 7 p.m.; 2391-7480), on the east side of the Atenas plaza, offers everything from European cheeses to Asian curry paste to Swiss chocolate.

Mirador el Cafetal (open weekdays, 6 a.m. to 6 p.m.; 2446-7361), four winding kilometers west of Atenas, is a charming place to stop for gourmet coffees, fruit daiquiris, *comida típica*, warming soups, or artistic souvenirs and crafts while enjoying views of the lush forested hills.

Off the main road, in Santa Eulalia de Atenas, is the comfortable **El Cafetal Inn** (private bath, hot water, ceiling fans, pool; no smoking inside; $70-$90, including breakfast; bungalow with kitchenette and private terrace, $110-$120; 2446-5785, fax: 2446-4850; cafetal.com, cafetal@ cafetal.com); its owners, an English-speaking Colombian-Salvadoran couple, are helpful and warm hosts. All rooms have expansive views of the Central Valley. Guests can walk to a nearby river, or pick coffee from October through February. If you are coming from the airport on the Interamerican Highway, take the Grecia exit. After less than a mile, take the first left, which will take you underneath a bridge on the Interamerican. Follow the winding road for three miles. El Cafetal will be on the right. If you are arriving late, it's best to take a taxi there ($25).

In nearby Rosario de Naranjo, **Vista del Valle Plantation Inn** (private bath, hot water, ceiling fans, some kitchens, pool, jacuzzi; $120-$200; villa $180-200; including breakfast; phone/faxes: 2451-1165, 2450-0800, 2450-0900; vistadelvalle.com, frontdesk@vistadelvalle.com), one of the most beautiful B&Bs we've seen. It sits on a coffee and citrus farm, on the edge of a forested 500-foot-deep gorge that is a protected nature reserve. For this reason you might not want to stay there with small children. A little road leads to the river below and a 300-foot waterfall. Private cottages are furnished in a simple, elegant Japanese style and surrounded by lovingly tended gardens. Some overlook the reserve, as does the poolside dining area. Most have outdoor showers and private sun-bathing patios. Suites in the main building have balconies and views. The turnoff is just after the Rafael Iglesias bridge, going west on the Interamerican Highway. From there, it's five kilometers on a gravel road. Signs mark the way. Recommended.

GRECIA

The Grecia area offers many possibilities for day trips, by itself or including La Garita and Volcán Poás. Grecia was voted the cleanest town in Latin America, and its citizens take pride in maintaining that reputation. From its airy red metal church with delicate wooden filigree altars to the well-kept homes of its farmers, it still exudes the goodness and simplicity that many other parts of the Central Valley have lost.

Grecia is home to the **Academia Centroamerica de Español** (2444-6161; acce.co.cr). **Restaurant Casa de Miguel** (open Wednesday through Monday, 11 a.m. to 9 p.m.; 2494-6767), 120 meters behind the church, offers elegance at reasonable prices. **Soda El Oasis** (open daily, 11 a.m. to 10 p.m.; 494-6303), on the southwest corner of Parque Central, is a clean and pleasant family-style restaurant with attentive service, reasonable prices, and an ample menu. **Coopevictoria** (2494-1866; coopevictoria.com), the local sugar cane and coffee cooperative, will take you on a tour of its installations.

In the village of Poró, five minutes east of Grecia, is the **World of Snakes** (open daily, 8 a.m. to 4 p.m.; 2494-3700; theworldofsnakes.com; admission $11, children under 15 $6), in which snakes from all over the planet are exhibited in outdoor concrete habitats. The young Austrian owners give a fascinating hour-long guided tour. They also breed endangered species for release into the wild.

In the sunny village of Rincón de Salas, 20 minutes west of the airport, is **Posada Mimosa** (private bath, solar-heated water with back-up, ceiling fans, pool, wi-fi; $90-$110, including breakfast; cabins that sleep two to four, $100-$140; 2494-5868, phone/fax: 2494-2295; mimosa.co.cr, mimosa@

mimosa.co.cr), owned by Tessa Borner, author of the no-nonsense guide, *Potholes to Paradise: Living in Costa Rica—What You Need to Know*, and her husband Martin, who does fascinating research on organic agriculture with his Tico neighbors. The grounds have beautiful tropical gardens and fruit trees, with 65 species of birds. Almost half of the farm, descending to a stream below, is protected primary forest. Comfortably furnished rooms in the main house open onto a shady corridor. There are beautiful views of the Central Valley from here.

GETTING THERE: *By Bus*: An hourly bus goes to Grecia from the Coca Cola in San José.

By Car: Head west on the Interamerican Highway past the airport and turn right at the well-marked Grecia intersection. To get to Posada Mimosa, go two kilometers toward Grecia, then turn right and go three kilometers to the first crossroads at the village of Rincón de Salas. Turn right again, and go two blocks to Posada Mimosa. Their yellow signs will guide you.

SARCHÍ

The small town of Sarchí is the home of Costa Rica's traditional brightly painted ox carts. You can watch artisans creating beautiful wooden bowls, plates, furniture, and walking sticks decorated with animals and birds. There is a 45-foot, two-ton oxcart in the center of town. With the influx of tour buses full of souvenir-hungry tourists, the main road through Sarchí has become pretty tacky. Although you can buy the same items in souvenir stores throughout the country, if you have a lot of wooden crafts on your gift list it is nice to go right to the source. At the entrance to town, **Chaverri Oxcart Factory** (2454-4411) sells only Costa Rican-made crafts. You can watch the oxcart painters at work. Next door, **Las Carretas** (2454-1633) offers traditional food. The most inexpensive place to buy crafts is at the cooperative, **Coopearsa**, on the right at the west end of town. **Restaurant La Finca** at Coopearsa has a river view.

GETTING THERE: *By Bus*: Take the hourly Grecia bus from the Coca Cola in San José. In Grecia, connect with the Alajuela–Sarchí bus. You can catch the latter bus in Alajuela, but it takes a long, roundabout route to Grecia.

By Car: To get to Sarchí, take the Grecia exit off the Puntarenas Highway, 30 minutes west of San José. When you get to Grecia, turn left behind the church, left again (circling the church), then right for three blocks. The road going diagonally to your left is the road to Sarchí.

BOSQUE DE PAZ   Serving as a biological corridor between Poás and Juan Castro Blanco National Parks, **Bosque de Paz** is a pristine forest sanctuary owned by a Costa Rican family, about an hour due north of

Sarchí near the town of Bajos del Toro. Well-maintained and -marked trails through the 3000-acre reserve range from a mild one-kilometer loop to a six-kilometer half-day trek to waterfalls. Quetzals nest here between December and February, orchids bloom most exuberantly in April, and monkeys can be spotted all year. Your hike will most likely be accompanied by the flutelike song of the *jilguero* (black-faced solitaire). Iridescent purple hummingbirds flit around their feeders.

Bosque de Paz Lodge (private bath, hot water; $100-$140/person, double occupancy, including meals and entrance to the reserve, by reservation only; 2234-6676, fax: 2225-0203; bosquedepaz.com, info@bosquedepaz. com) has comfortable, spacious rooms with balconies whose simple design blends with their beautiful natural surroundings. Genuine Costa Rican country food is served in the restaurant.

GETTING THERE: From Sarchí, take the first road to the right after Chaverri's Oxcart Factory, then the first left, then wind around and around until you get to Bajos del Toro. The entrance to Bosque de Paz is located to the left on the road that connects Bajos del Toro with Zarcero. It is less complicated to get there from Zarcero: Take the road beside the Zarcero church for 15 kilometers (about 25 minutes, paved except for the last 300 meters) to Bosque de Paz. The drive has stunning views of the ancient oak forests of Juan Castro Blanco National Park. If you are continuing from here into the Northern Zone (west to Volcán Arenal or east to Sarapiquí), drive through Bajos del Toro and down to Río Cuarto in the San Carlos plains. The road is well-paved the whole way down.

VOLCÁN POÁS NATIONAL PARK

Poás is one of the few active volcanoes on the continent that is accessible by a good road. The 37-kilometer trip from San José is marked by beautiful scenery, with lookouts over the Central Valley. The famous Café Britt is served at **Cafe Botos** in the park's visitors center, along with sandwiches, pizza, and a variety of delicious pastries. The visitors center shows videos about the volcano and its history.

The main crater of Poás is one and a half kilometers wide and 300 meters deep. There is a hot, sulfurous lake at the bottom. Active fumaroles are visible from the lookout point above the crater. A 20-minute uphill hike takes you to another lookout over jewel-like Botos Lake, which fills an ancient crater.

The volcano spewed a 4000-meter column of water and mud in 1910, sending ash as far as Puntarenas. Lava flow increased also in 1953. In May 1989, Poás shot ash a mile into the air. After a dormant period between 1994 and 2006, Poás staged a series of eruptions between March 24 and

View with sombrilla del pobre.

30, 2006, and was closed to the public for a few days. The eruptions of mud, water, and rocks were only 50 meters high.

Scientists believe that Poás has a relatively open passage from its magma chamber to its huge crater, so it lets off steam more easily than other volcanoes and doesn't build up the pressure that causes large eruptions. Nevertheless, it is under close observation. The Seismological Network of the University of Costa Rica has a geochemical weather station at Poás. It detected seismic tremors three days before the March 2006 eruptions.

Volcán Poás National Park (usually open daily, 8 a.m. to 3:30 p.m.; 2460-1412, 2460-0055; admission $10, students with ID and children $1) protects the headwaters of several rivers, which feed the Río Tárcoles to the southwest and the Río Sarapiquí to the north. While the active crater is full of subtle, moonscape colors, the rest of Poás is intensely green, with a great variety of wildflowers, bromeliads, ferns, mosses, and lichen. One of the most interesting plants there is the *sombrilla del pobre* (poor man's umbrella), which has thick, fuzzy leaves up to two meters in width, designed to trap airborne algae. Hummingbirds are among the 26 species of birds most easily seen along the road or on the trails. Don't miss the 20-minute hike along *Sendero de la Escalonia* that connects the upper parking lot to the picnic area farther along the main road. It's a green mossy tunnel through a shaggy cloud forest. Birders will want to visit the section called *El Canto de las Aves*.

The average temperature on misty Poás is 50 degrees F, dropping as low as 22 and climbing as high as 70, so it is important to dress in layers. It can be very windy. Bring rain gear. If you arrive too late in the day, clouds will be covering the crater, so the earlier you go the better. When it's clear, you can see Poás on the horizon to the northwest of San José. If you can't see it, it's probably too late to go. You can ask at the admission booth whether the crater is visible or not. If you are driving, be sure to get gas before you go up because there are few gas stations along the way. There is one in Poasito.

The 14-cable **Las Colinas del Poás Canopy Tour** (two-hour tours daily at 9 a.m., 11 a.m., and 2 p.m.; 2430-4113, fax: 2443-5896; colinasdelpoas.com; admission $50, students $45) is in Fraijanes, on the way to the volcano in a beautiful forest with good views of Barva volcano. According to our researchers, the last cable is the longest and most exciting. Call for reservations and weather conditions. Their restaurant serves trout, and you can fish for trout in their ponds.

LODGING AND RESTAURANTS NEAR POÁS   The road to Poás is lined with strawberry plantations and restaurants. Be sure to stop at **Chubascos** (open Wednesday through Monday, 11:30 a.m. to 5:30 p.m.; 2482-2069), one of the nicest places we know for native Costa Rican food. It is set in a hillside garden with covered outdoor tables. If it's windy, brightly colored tablecloths lend a welcoming touch to the indoor dining area. Native *olla de carne* (beef and vegetable soup) and *sopa de ayote* (pumpkin soup) are delicious and warming. The freshly handmade *tortilla aliñada con olores* is served with beans, sour cream, and salsa. Yummy *refrescos* are made from local strawberries and blackberries. It's about 16 kilometers (20 minutes) above Alajuela. Recommended.

Jaulares (open Monday through Thursday, 10 a.m. to 10:30 p.m.; Friday and Saturday, 10 a.m. to 2 a.m.; Sunday, 10 a.m. to 6 p.m.; 2482-2155; jaulares.com) is a large, rustic bar/restaurant at the intersection of the road from Alajuela with the road from San Pedro de Poás on the way to Poás National Park. It's a happening place after 9 on Friday and Saturday nights, when city musicians come to play *trova, boleros*, world music, jazz, *salsa,* and rock. They have rustic cabins in the back with small fireplaces (private bath, heated water; $20-$30).

At Poasito, there's a six-kilometer road going east to Vara Blanca, along the Continental Divide on the pass between Poás and Barva volcanoes. **Villa Calas** (private bath, heated water, restaurant, some kitchens; $40-$80; 2482-2222; villacalas.com, villacalas@gmail.com) is a series of cute, two-story A-frame bungalows with fireplaces, located on the left as you leave Poasito on the road to Vara Blanca.

Half a kilometer west of the junction with the Heredia-Sarapiquí road, at Vara Blanca (16 kilometers from Poás), is the turnoff for **Poás Volcano Lodge** (hot water, internet; shared bath, $70; private bath, $100; suites, $120-$150; children under 5 $10; children 5 to 12 $15; breakfast included; 2482-2194, fax: 2482-2513; poasvolcanolodge.com, info@poasvolcano lodge.com), an imposing English manor house 6175 feet above sea level, with cozy rooms and a sunken fireplace in the living room to take the chill out of the air. About one kilometer off the road on a lush dairy farm, this bed and breakfast is especially suited for hikers and birders who like to roam the countryside. There are trails through the forested sector of the farm. The manager can connect you with neighbors who run horse tours through the mountains. To get there by bus, take the Río Frio–Sarapiquí bus from the Terminal Caribe and get off in Vara Blanca (see below).

There is a gas station in Vara Blanca. Next door, **Restaurant Vara Blanca** is known for generous servings of local food and friendly service.

LA PAZ WATERFALL GARDENS   Just about ten minutes (6 kilometers) north of Vara Blanca, **La Paz Waterfall Gardens** (open 8 a.m. to 5 p.m.; 2225-0643, 2482-2720; waterfallgardens.com; admission $32, children 3 to 12 $20) are really worth seeing. Sturdy, non-slip steel bridges and stairways have been built right next to a series of rushing waterfalls, higher tiers of the famous La Paz waterfall that can be seen a few kilometers down the road. To walk next to such power and feel safe is rare, but when you add the incredibly exuberant cloud forest vegetation around the misty waterfalls, and the ozone in the air, this is a truly exhilarating experience. Along the paved trails, you will encounter a serpentarium, an orchid garden, an open air frog exhibit, a trout lake for fishing, an aviary, a lagoon pool, and a jacuzzi. If that weren't enough, there is a huge butterfly observatory and a hummingbird garden where large charts help you identify the jewel-like iridescent creatures flitting around their birdfeeders, seemingly oblivious to visitors. The hike can take as long as you like, but you should allow at least an hour and a half. The trail goes downhill, and a mini-bus picks you up at the end and brings you back to the entrance where you can enjoy a *comida típica* buffet ($11).

There is nothing ordinary about the **Peace Lodge** (private bath, hot water, jacuzzi, cable TV; $240-$380; villa, $420-$460; including breakfast and access to La Paz Waterfall Gardens; 2486-2720; waterfallgardens.com, peacelodgereservations@waterfallgardens.com). The private stone terrace or balcony of each room has a hot tub with jacuzzi, from which you can gaze out over the billowing forest during the day, or stargaze at night. The focal point of the huge garden/bathrooms is a stone waterfall shower and another hot tub. The bedrooms have king or queen-sized beds, a gas fireplace, cable TV and a sound system. The two-story Monarch Villa, their honeymoon suite, has a kitchenette and a fireplace in the bathroom and the sleeping loft. Recommended.

TOURS   Many companies, including the Peace Lodge, will arrange tours that include the Waterfall Gardens as well as Poás volcano and the Doka coffee plantation, or canopy tours and river rafting, or Arenal Volcano and Tabacón hot springs.

GETTING THERE: By Bus: A bus to Volcán Poás leaves daily at 8 a.m. from the Tuasa station across from Parque de la Merced in San José (Avenida 2, Calles 12/14; 2442-6900). It stops at the Tuasa terminal near the Alajuela central market around 8:30 a.m. Get there early to reserve yourself a seat. The bus from San José arrives at the volcano around 11 a.m. and returns at 2 p.m. Many tour companies offer day trips to Poás for between $30 and $60 per person, but a taxi from Alajuela to Poás costs about $60 per taxiload (including waiting and return trip) and a taxi from San José costs about $75. Ask at your hotel for reliable *taxistas*.

To go to La Paz Waterfall Gardens, take the 6:30 a.m. Río Frío bus (2222-0610) from the Caribe station, Calle Central, Avenida 13 in San José.

By Car: Take the Alajuela turnoff from the General Cañas (Interamerican) Highway. It goes past Alajuela's Central Park. Stay on the same road until you get to Fraijanes Lake and Chubascos. There you will connect with the road from San Pedro de Poás, which leads to the volcano. If you are near Heredia, take the Barva–Birrí road to Vara Blanca and turn left for 6 kilometers, then right at Poasito.

If you are in Grecia, take the back road to Alajuela through Tácares, turn left at Hotel Las Orquídeas to get to San Pedro de Poás, and continue on to the volcano. You can make a nice circular route, entering through Alajuela, and returning through Vara Blanca and Heredia, with a detour at the waterfall gardens, six kilometers north of Vara Blanca.

If you start out early, you can get to Volcán Arenal by way of Poás and the waterfalls. Continue north of the waterfalls to San Miguel, where you take a very sharp left to go west to La Fortuna by way of Aguas Zarcas and Muelle. You can get from the waterfalls to the volcano in about three hours. To visit Sarapiquí, continue north from San Miguel to La Virgen de Sarapiquí, about an hour north of the waterfalls. See the Northern Zone chapter.

EAST OF ALAJUELA

HEREDIA AND SURROUNDING TOWNS

Just east of Alajuela, Heredia has retained a friendly, small-town atmosphere. Its colonial 1796 church has a pretty facade and a peaceful garden. Here, too, is the Universidad Nacional, which has a substantial student population.

The verdant hills above Heredia are home to many artists and craftspeople. On the **Art Tour** (2359-5571; costaricaarttour.com; $95, including lunch), you visit the studios of painters like Rodolfo Stanley, or the incredible gallery of stained-glass artist Sylvia Laks. Each visit allows a direct exchange with the artist, with translation if necessary. It's a great way to experience both the beauty of the Heredia hills and get to know some fascinating people. The varied Art Tour itineraries visit five different artists all over the Central Valley each day, including ceramicists, sculptors, and printmakers.

In the **Mercado Florense** (300 meters south and 50 meters west of the church) there's an inexpensive place to have a good seafood lunch. **Vishnu Mango Verde** (open Monday to Saturday, 8 a.m. to 7 p.m.; Sunday, 9 a.m. to 6 p.m.; 2237-2526) is a vegetarian restaurant downtown on Calle 7, Calle

Central/1. Servings are generous and inexpensive. **Fresas** (open daily, 8 a.m. to 11 p.m.; 2265-6844), half a block north, has a great lunch menu, and is known for smoothies and ice cream treats. **Oky Delishop** (open 11 a.m. to 8 p.m.; closed Sunday; 2253-6633), 500 meters north of the university, is an elegant German delicatessen with good pastries, coffee, and chocolates.

Located about 750 meters north of Colegio Santa Cecilia in Heredia, **Apartotel Vargas** (private bath, hot water, fans, TV, kitchens, internet, parking; $80-$90; 2237-8526, fax: 2260-4698; apartotelvargas.com, apartotelvargas@yahoo.com) offers clean, fully equipped apartments.

The stucco highrise **Hotel Valladolid** (private bath, hot water, a/c, phone, cable TV, kitchen, internet; $90-$100, including breakfast; Calle 7/Avenida 7; 2260-2905, fax: 2260-2912; hotelvalladolid.net, contactenos@ hotelvalladolid.net) hosts dignitaries visiting the Universidad Nacional. From the top-floor jacuzzi, sauna, and solarium there are 360-degree views of the Central Valley, and at sunset, the Pacific Ocean is a bright sliver on the horizon.

Hotel Hojarascas (private baths, heated water, cable TV, fans, wi-fi, phone; $70-$80, including breakfast; apartment, $100; 2261-3649, fax: 2263-3407) has been recommended for cleanliness and excellent attention from its friendly Tico owners. It's in the block between the Central Market and the Los Angeles Church on Avenida 8, Calles 4/6.

GETTING THERE: *By Bus*: Buses to Heredia leave every five to ten minutes from Calle 1, Avenidas 7/9 in San José, 5:20 a.m. to midnight (through Tibás), and from Avenida 2, Calle 12 every five minutes (through La Uruca).

By Car: From downtown San José, you should have a good map and ask for detailed instructions. From the General Cañas Highway there are good signs from the turnoff near the airport.

BARVA DE HEREDIA   The town of Barva, two kilometers north of Heredia, is one of the oldest settlements in the country. Its historic church and the houses near it have been restored.

The **Museo de Cultura Popular** (open Sundays, 10 a.m. to 5 p.m.; 2260-1619; ilam.org/cr.museoculturapopular, mcp@una.ac.cr) in Santa Lucía de Barva, just outside of Barva, is a colonial-era dwelling that has been carefully restored to show what Central Valley life was like at the end of the 19th century. The seven stages of *bahareque*, or reinforced adobe construction, are demonstrated, and the cool house is proof that this is a practical technique in hot climates. Adobe construction without reinforcement has been illegal in Costa Rica since 1910, when an earthquake toppled many adobe houses, killing the people inside. The museum's fruit tree–shaded *solar* (yard) is decked with traditional children's playground equipment: a plank seesaw, rope-and-stick swings, and homemade stilts. A *soda* serves economical and delicious *comida típica*, and a little crafts shop sells inexpensive children's toys. By car, follow the signs that start on the road to Barva from Heredia. Otherwise, take the bus 25 meters north of the Heredia high school gymnasium.

The **Ark Herb Farm** (open by appointment only; 2239-2211, 8846-2694, fax: 2269-8166; arkherbfarm.com, info@arkherbfarm.com; admission $12, lunch $13) in Santa Barbara de Heredia, grows fresh culinary herbs. Its extensive botanical garden has over 400 varieties of medicinal plants from around the world. Owner "Tommy" says that the huge medicinal plant garden is "a hobby that got out of control." During the one-and-a-half-hour tour, you smell and taste herbs, and learn about their healing properties. After tea and crackers, you may browse the gift shop of natural products, seeds, teas, and handmade crafts from the Boruca indigenous community. Call or see the website for directions.

Maker of Costa Rica's excellent export-quality coffee, **Café Britt** (open daily; high season tours at 11 a.m., 3 p.m., rest of the year 11 a.m. only; 2277-1600, fax: 2277-1699; cafebritt.com, info@cafebritt.com, enlace@cafebritt.com; $20; $37 including transportation, children ages 6 to 11 $16/$33; by reservation only) has an educational tour of its operations, including a lively show about coffee's vital role in forging Costa Rican democracy, featuring professional performers and multimedia entertainment. Their **Teatro Dionisio Echeverría** also features weekly concerts by some of Costa Rica's finest musicians, as well as innovative plays and cinema. After the tour, visit **Café Don Próspero**, where local delicacies are used to create dishes like macadamia chicken, accompanied by an extensive fruit and salad bar, and finished off by gourmet coffee and pastries. To get to Café Britt, continue uphill from McDonald's in Heredia, turn left at the first stop sign and right after the 500 meters, then follow the Coffeetour signs on the road to Barva.

On the Barva–Santa Barbara road, Spanish chef Vincent Aguilar prepares Valencian specialties at **La Lluna de Valencia** (open Thursday, 7 p.m. to 10 p.m.; Friday and Saturday, noon to 10 p.m.; Sunday, noon to 5 p.m.; phone/fax: 2269-6665). His restaurant has become a gathering place for the international NGO crowd., who come there for authentic *paella* accompanied by pitchers of *sangría*. The restaurant is located 50 meters from Pulpería La Máquina in San Pedro de Barva.

La Rosa Blanca (private bath, hot water, spring-fed, chemical-free pool, internet, cable TV, spa, trails, nonsmoking; $340-$400; villas, $340-$530; including breakfast; children 3 to 12 half-price; 2269-9392, fax:

2269-9555; finca-rblanca.co.cr, info@fincarosablanca.com) is near Santa Barbara de Heredia. Each room has a theme, and the architecture and hand-crafted furnishings are full of fantasy and delightful, creative touches. The honeymoon suite features a tower room with a 360-degree view and a bath-room painted like a rainforest, with the water for the bathtub bubbling out of a rocky waterfall. Enjoy massage, wraps, or body scrubs in their **El Targua Spa**. Gourmet dinners are available for guests only. Guests are encouraged to participate in the picking, processing and roasting of Finca Blanca coffee. La Rosa Blanca has received the highest possible score of all hotels participat-ing in the Certification for Sustainable Tourism of the ICT. Recommended.

SAN RAFAEL AND MONTE DE LA CRUZ   The mountains above Heredia are full of evergreen forests and pastureland. It's exhilaratingly chilly year-round, and a bright, sunny day can turn into a rainy one in min-utes, especially after noon. From these mountains you can see the sun glinting off the Gulf of Nicoya in the west. A hike to **Monte de la Cruz Recreation Area** (open daily, 8 a.m. to 4 p.m.; admission 75 cents) gives you an incredible panorama of the entire Central Valley and beyond. Take a picnic lunch, an umbrella, and a sweater. This large, well-maintained park has a basketball court, plenty of playground equipment, a soccer field, cov-ered picnic tables, and trails permeated with the smell of evergreens. Many Ticos go there on Sunday. The road from San Rafael de Heredia forks at the entrance to Monte de la Cruz. If you take the left fork, in about one kilometer you will arrive at the **Hotel Chalet Tirol** (hot water, bathtubs, electric heating; $100-$110; children under 12 free; 2267-6222, fax: 2267-6373; tirolcr.com, tirolcr@racsa.co.cr). At 1800 meters (5900 feet), the ho-tel is surrounded by a private cloud forest reserve that borders Braulio Carrillo National Park. The older rooms are charming two-story, vine-covered cabins with hand painted Tyrolean designs, and the newer, larger rooms are in a more modern building, warmed by fireplaces. Their Salzburg Café Concert features international musicians. The hotel's private reserve is a great place for a hike, and you can warm up with hot chocolate and pastries on the second floor of the Chalet's restaurant.

Añoranzas (open Tuesday through Thursday, noon to 10 p.m.; Friday and Saturday, noon to midnight; Sunday, noon to 6 p.m.; 2267-7406), down a road on your left from the main road four kilometers above San Rafael, features *Tico* memorabilia, and good *comida típica* .

For nightlife in this area, 600 meters to the left from Añoranzas is the classy Lebanese **Baalbeck Bar and Grill** (2267-6683), with authentic Ara-bian food, a great view of the Central Valley, belly dancing on Friday nights and live music on Saturdays. Cheery fireplaces add to the warmth. They also rent cabins.

GETTING THERE: By Bus: Buses for this area leave from one block south of the Mercado in Heredia. For Monte de la Cruz and Chalet Tirol, take the San Rafael "Monte de la Cruz" bus, which leaves hourly during the week and every half-hour after 8 a.m. on Sunday. The terminus is at a fork in the road, one kilometer from Chalet Tirol (left) or from Monte de la Cruz (right). The bus goes all the way to Monte de la Cruz on weekends.

By Car: Monte de la Cruz and Chalet Tirol are about 35 minutes from San José by car. Take the San Isidro exit to the left about 14 kilometers down the Guápiles Highway right after the Restaurant Las Orquídeas. When you reach San Isidro, turn right uphill in front of the church and go two kilometers to Concepción (ignore any previous Concepción signs). Continue a few minutes more to San Rafael, and again turn right uphill at the church, to reach the road that goes through Los Angeles to Monte de la Cruz. If you are staying in Alajuela, ask for directions from your hotel.

VOLCÁN BARVA

On the western edge of Braulio Carrillo National Park is **Barva Volcano** (open Tuesday to Sunday; 2256-2611; admission $10). This ancient volcano, on whose slopes Heredia and its neighboring villages roost, offers a good heavy-duty hike through pastureland and, near the top, cloud forest. You usually must walk about four kilometers from where the road gets too bad for most vehicles, and then it's an hour's hike from the park entrance to the 2900-meter-high **Laguna Barva**, a forest-rimmed green lake in the old crater. The vegetation is vibrant and full of birds. The other, smaller **Laguna Copey** is a more difficult hour-long hike from the turnoff for Laguna Barva. The Copey trail crosses the divide from the Pacific side to the very moist, muddy Atlantic side. This trail is lined with flowering bushes and huge, primordial *sombrilla del pobre* plants, making it a pretty walk. Try to go early in the day so you can see the views from the trail to Copey. Allow five to six hours at the park if you wish to hike it all. Since there are 2000-year-old trees in the cloud forest surrounding the old crater, scientists surmise that the volcano has been dormant for at least that long. However, vulcanologists have been noticing some volcanic activity in the pass between Barva and Volcán Irazú, and speculate that Barva will act up again soon.

Quetzals are sometimes visible here. Also heard on Volcán Barva is the black-faced solitaire, which has been compared to the nightingale for the sweetness and delicacy of its song.

Note: Hikers have gotten lost in this area. The lucky ones are discovered by search parties or follow a stream down to the Atlantic plains. Be sure to take food, water, warm clothes, a flashlight, raingear, plus camera and binoculars. Do not stray from the trail. The forest is too dense and the terrain too hilly for you to navigate on your own. The best strategy is to sign in at the ranger station and tell them which trails you will use. If you get lost, stay put, rig a brightly colored shelter, and drink water from the cups formed in bromeliads.

Cabañas de Montaña Tamarak (private bath, hot water, kitchen; $50-$80; 8396-4847, 2228-4041; tamarak.ve.vg, volcan.barva@gmail.com) are charming, two-story wooden chalets with decks, and cozy cabins with fireplaces set in a forest about 600 meters beyond Restaurante Sacramento..

Restaurante La Campesina, three and a half kilometers above Paso Llano, serves tasty, wholesome country food at outdoor tables overlooking the valley, as does **Restaurante Sacramento.**

El Ranchito (open Tuesday through Sunday, 11 a.m. to 9 p.m.; 2266-1081) in Paso Llano serves *Tico* favorites grilled on a wood stove. A bit farther down the road, rustic **Chago's** is popular on weekends for good *bocas*.

GETTING THERE: By Bus: To climb Volcán Barva, you should catch the 6:20 a.m. San José de la Montaña–Paso Llano bus from the south side of the Mercado Nuevo in Heredia. (Later buses leave at 11 a.m. and 3:55 p.m. Check schedules at 2237-5007.) At Paso Llano (Porrosatí), you'll see signs for the park entrance 8 kilometers uphill to the left. It's a steep uphill walk. The crater lake is 2.6 kilometers beyond the entrance. Be sure to make it back for the 5 p.m. Paso Llano bus to Heredia. A taxi from Heredia to the park entrance costs $30-$40.

By Car: Follow the road north of Heredia through Barva. Take the right fork north of Barva to lovely San José de la Montaña, with its peaceful church and charming country houses. Continue five kilometers beyond it and turn right at the signs for Braulio Carrillo. In a few hundred meters you'll arrive at Paso Llano. Turn left. Four-wheel drive is necessary.

CARTAGO AND VOLCÁN IRAZÚ

Though **Cartago** was the birthplace of Costa Rican culture and the capital for 300 years, many of its historic buildings were destroyed in the earthquakes of 1823 and 1910. The 1910 quake prevented the completion of a cathedral in the center of town. The ruins of that church, **Las Ruinas,** have been made into a pleasant garden.

On August 2 every year, thousands of Costa Ricans walk from all over the country to Cartago in honor of La Negrita, the Virgin of Los Angeles, who appeared to a peasant girl in 1635. She has become Costa Rica's patron saint, and her shrine is surrounded by offerings from grateful pilgrims whom she has miraculously cured. Tiny metal arms, legs, hearts, and other charms decorate the walls inside **La Basílica de Nuestra Señora de Los**

Angeles, an imposing structure on the east side of town. Pilgrims collect water from a spring in back of the church, then go down to the basilica's basement to touch the rock where the virgin repeatedly appeared. **La Iglesia de Maria Auxiliadora** on the west side of town is known for the delicate wooden filigree that decorates its vaulted ceiling. The church and its gardens are more peaceful than the Basilica.

The **Mercado Central**, one block north of the west side of Las Ruinas, overflows with local produce Friday to Sunday mornings. Inside are lots of *sodas* where you can have an inexpensive lunch. **Aki Café** (open weekdays, 9 a.m. to 7 p.m.; 2591-0668) is owned by prize-winning barista Enrique Morales, famous for his artistically prepared cappuccino. It's three blocks south of Las Ruinas on Avenida 7, Calle 1. **Tukasa Café** (open Monday to Saturday, 11 a.m. to 8:30 p.m.; Sunday, 2 p.m. to 8:30 p.m.; 2552-1006) with its cool covered terrace is a popular place to go for crepes and other light meals. It's on Calle 5, Avenidas 9/11, across from the Seguro Social. The ritzy **Viene Qua** (open daily, 11:30 a.m. to 10 p.m.; 2591-6086) serves excellent Italian food. It's four blocks south of the María Auxiliadora Church.

Soluciones de Comida Fresquita (open Monday to Saturday, 8 a.m. to 6 p.m.; Sunday, 8 a.m. to noon; 2552-8996) has a great salad bar and fresh fruit sundaes. It's 100 meters east and 25 meters north of the Tribunales de Justicia on the east side. **Restaurant and Bar La Puerta del Sol** (open daily, 8 a.m. to 10 p.m.; 2551-0615) in a historic building on the north side of the Basilica, is the traditional place to go for a hearty lunch or dinner, with live music on Saturdays.

Casa Mora Factory Lodge (shared or private bath, hot water, wi-fi; $50-$80, including breakfast; phone/fax: 2552-8223, 2552-8234; casa moracr.com, morawalthen@casamoracr.com), located 75 meters north of the Basilica, was created to lodge the executives who visit the factories in Cartago's Free Trade Zone. Thus the name, which does not transmit in English what the owners were trying to convey: The rooms are well-appointed, comfortable, and elegant, with polished wood furnishings. Some have balconies and fireplaces.

The best bet for budget travelers is **San Francisco Hostel and Lodge** (private bath, heated water, kitchens; $15-$40; 2551-4804) located 25 meters northwest of the Mercado Central.

GETTING THERE: *By Bus*: Buses to Cartago leave often from Avenida 2, Calles 3/5 (2537-2320) in San José. It's a 40-minute trip.

By Car: Just follow Avenida Central east of San José through the suburbs of San Pedro and Curridabat. That will put you onto the Autopista Florencio del Castillo

(50 cent toll), part of the Interamerican Highway, which leads to Cartago. Be sure to follow signs into Cartago to avoid continuing south on the Interamerican.

PARQUE NACIONAL VOLCÁN IRAZÚ **Volcán Irazú** (open daily, 8:30 a.m. to 3:30 p.m.; 2256-2611; admission $10) is 32 kilometers north of Cartago. On a clear morning, the trip up its slope is full of breathtaking views of farmland, native oak forests, and the Central Valley below. The craters are bleak and majestic. On March 19, 1963, the day John F. Kennedy arrived in Costa Rica on a presidential visit, Irazú erupted, showering black ash over the Central Valley for the next two years. People carried umbrellas to keep the ash out of their hair, roofs caved in from the weight of piled-up ash, and everything was black. Since then the volcano has been dormant, but there were a few tremors in 1991. Gases and steam are emitted from fumaroles near the sulfurous green lake in the crater. It is said that you can see both the Atlantic and the Pacific from Irazú's chilly 3432-meter (11,260-foot) summit. This is true on occasion, but often the Atlantic side is obscured by clouds. You can get plenty of exercise there, hiking along the rim of the crater from the *mirador.* Irazú is at high altitude, so you might experience fatigue and lightheadedness.

If you want to try to catch the view of both oceans, you must go early. Bring warm clothes and rain gear. There are clean restrooms at the top and a restaurant and souvenir shop offering soup, *tamales*, and gourmet coffees. Rain ponchos are available for rent.

On the way to or from the volcano in the town of Cot, be sure and stop at **Restaurant 1910** (open daily, 11 a.m. to 9 p.m.; phone/fax: 2536-6063). Their plentiful and varied Sunday buffet includes delicious salads and excellent Costa Rican and international entrées (about $14, including dessert). You can eat indoors or out. Be sure to look at the historical photographs on the walls—1910 was the year of the earthquake that destroyed Cartago. Recommended.

Nochebuena Volcano Museum (open daily, 8:30 a.m. to 4:30 p.m.; 2530-8013; nochebuena.org; admission $4, kids $2), five kilometers before the entrance to Irazú National Park, shows a 20-minute video about Costa Rica's position in the volcanic Ring of Fire, and footage of Irazú's 1963-65 eruptions. In addition to interactive displays about the world's volcanoes and volcanoes on other planets, they present the social history of Irazú, with a model *campesino* house and a video about *campesino* life on the mountain. Their restaurant serves breakfast all day as well as reasonably priced main dishes and tempting homemade sweets. They have nature trails past huge old oaks and bubbling springs. If you want to spend the night, they rent a cabin with kitchen and fireplace for $50.

GETTING THERE: By Bus: Buses to Irazú (2530-1064; $4.50 round trip) leave daily at 8 a.m. from Avenida 2, across from the Gran Hotel Costa Rica in San José. You can also catch this bus in Cartago at 8:40. The bus leaves Irazú at noon, arriving in San José at 2 p.m.

By Car: Take the Interamerican Highway east from San Jose, and veer left at the Taras Intersection, two kilometers before the entrance to Cartago. Go straight, then take the first left. The road signs after that are pretty good. Stay on the main road, veering left at the large statue of Christ. A taxi from San José should cost $50-$60 for one to four people. A taxi from Cartago costs about $30.

OROSI VALLEY

In just a few hours you can visit an amazing variety of sites on a trip to the Orosi Valley, south of Cartago. The trip can be as quick as an hour or as long as a couple of days. The following is a description of a circular 60-kilometer route from Cartago.

After passing through the town of Cartago, continue six kilometers east and, you will pass the turnoff on the right for **Lankester Gardens** (open daily, 8:30 a.m. to 4:30 p.m.; 2552-3247; jardinbotanicolankester.org; admission $5, children under 6 free), which display the hundreds of varieties of the orchids and bromeliads for which Costa Rica is famous. The wheelchair-accessible labyrinthine gardens are run by the biology department of the University of Costa Rica. Orchids are abloom all year, but the best show is between February and May. They also have a butterfly garden.

Next you'll come to the town of Paraíso, which is about seven kilometers from Cartago. Drive through town until you see the park, where you turn right. Continue straight down this street, which becomes a narrow country road. Before descending into the valley, you will come to **Sanchiri Lodge** (private bath, hot water, phone; $60-$70, including breakfast; children under 7 free; 2574-5454, fax: 2574-8586; sanchiri.com, sanchiri@racsa.co.cr), a row of individual wooden cabins on a hillside and a new building with 12 rooms, all with a balcony and great view. A wooded glen has hiking trails. The family that runs the lodge has been on the land for five generations. There is a restaurant (open daily, 7 a.m. to 9 p.m.) with reasonably priced *comida típica.* They have a butterfly garden and a biodigestor.

Continue on to the **Mirador de Orosi** (closed Monday), a well-tended public park and picnic ground with another great view. It's easy to miss the entrance on the right after Paraíso, but the place is definitely worth a stop. An intimidating flight of steps goes uphill at the entrance, but you can take a path to the left, circle around by the *mirador,* and end up at the top without losing your breath.

Once you get to the floor of the valley, you will soon arrive at the town of **Orosi**. It has a colonial **church** whose beautiful wooden altar and shrines were carved with a special grace. This is one of the few churches in Costa Rica that has survived enough earthquakes to preserve its original atmosphere. A small museum of colonial religious history, **Museo Franciscano** (open Tuesday to Friday, 1 p.m. to 5 p.m.; Saturday and Sunday, 9 a.m. to 5 p.m.; 2533-3852; admission $1) is next door.

There are two thermal swimming pools/recreation areas in town: **Balneario Termal Orosi** (open daily, 7:30 a.m. to 4 p.m.; admission $1.25), southwest of town, and **Los Patios** (open Tuesday to Sunday, 8 a.m. to 4 p.m.; 2533-3009; admission $2), two and a half kilometers beyond Orosi. The pools are lukewarm, reputed to be medicinal, and full of kids and their families. Both have picnic areas and restaurants, and Balneario Termal Orosi has a basketball court and soccer fields. This is a worthwhile stop if you have young children. Weekdays are more tranquil here.

Montaña Linda (shared bath, heated water, shared kitchen; dorms, $7.50/person; private room, $10/person; camping, $4/person in their tent, $3/person in your own tent; kitchen for guests, $1; meals, $4-$7; 2533-3640, fax: 2533-1292; montanalinda.com, info@montanalinda.com) is a friendly youth hostel and **language school** with an emphasis on conversation. There are many inexpensive options for class length and lodging. One option: five days of classes including two meals a day and homestay for $230 per week. Opportunities to play soccer, learn salsa dancing and exchange English/Spanish conversation are offered each week. Their **Dragonfly Guesthouse** (private bath, fans, hot water; $30-$40), offers more privacy than the hostel and has a nice view. Guests can use the kitchen and laundry facilities. Montaña Linda runs the **Orosi Travel Information and Art Center (OTIAC)** which offers a variety of services from car rentals to tours, and has a café with fresh juices and a salad bar. To get to the hostel, ask to be let off the Orosi bus at Super Anita Numero Dos, the local supermarket, then walk back half a block to Bar La Primavera. Turn left at the bar and go two and a half blocks. To get to OTIAC, get off at the Super Anita, walk forward half a block, turn right at the corner and OTIAC will be at the end of the block. The Dragonfly is one block east of OTIAC.

The motel-like **Hotel Reventazón** (private bath, hot water, fans, TV, free local calls, restaurant, wi-fi; $50-$60, including breakfast; phone/fax: 2533-3838; hotelreventazon.com, info@hotelreventazon.com) is clean and loaded with amenities. The second-floor rooms look up to hills covered with a patchwork of coffee and bananas. The *cabinas* are 200 meters past the plaza and 25 meters to the right.

The attractive **Orosi Lodge** (private bath, hot water, ceiling fan, TV, internet; $50-$70; chalet with kitchen, $80-$100, maximum five guests; children under 12 free; phone/fax: 2533-3578; orosilodge.com, info@orosi lodge.com) has verandas with stunning views of the Irazú and Turrialba volcanoes. Its charming and airy **Art Café** serves good home-cooked meals and is decorated with local art work.

Tetey Lodge (private bath, hot water, phone, cable TV, ceiling fan, internet; $40-$60; with kitchen, $50-$70; 2533-1335, fax: 2533-1122; teteylodge.com, info@teteylodge.com) has well-appointed rooms around a plant-filled garden. It's on the right, 800 meters south of the church.

TAPANTÍ NATIONAL PARK   A few kilometers after Orosi take a right and drive ten kilometers over gravel roads (about 30 minutes) to **Tapantí National Park** (2200-0900; admission $10). Tapantí protects the rivers that supply San José with water and electricity. It's a great place for birdwatching (black-faced solitaires, hawks, guans, to name a few). There are three trails, one a short trek to the Río Grande, another to a swimming hole (beware of the current!), and another a two-kilometer circuit.

Tapantí has been incorporated into Costa Rica's twenty-sixth national park, which bears the unwieldy name of Tapantí–Macizo de la Muerte. By connecting tiny Tapantí to the 52,000-hectare Río Macho forest reserve, the new park extends to Chirripó National Park, which then connects to Parque International La Amistad, making a total of 75,696 protected hectares. This is an important step toward the goal of forming a Mesoamerican biological corridor so that species can migrate between Mexico and South America without interruption.

The nearby **Kiri Mountain Lodge** (private bath, heated water; $40-$50, including breakfast; 2533-2272, fax: 2533-1289; kirilodge.net, info@kirilodge.net) has trout ponds, picnic huts, and a restaurant that will cook your catch. The family-run lodge has its own reserve. Since hiking and birdwatching in Tapantí are best early in the morning, it's a convenient place to spend the night. If you are traveling without a car, it's a pleasant (albeit long) nine-kilometer hike from Orosi, or you can hire a jeep-taxi in Orosi ($10 one way).

Intrepid birders with four-wheel drive can take the dirt road past Kiri Lodge and drive about an hour to **El Copal Reserve** (2248-9470; actuarcostarica.com) another great birding site. Just walking and birding along the scenic but terrible road to El Copal could be very rewarding, and Beto Chavez of El Copal is a great birding guide. Make reservations in advance. If you're experienced with four-wheel drive, this road is a shortcut to the Turrialba area (see Turrialba section).

Heading back toward Orosi, one kilometer from the Río Macho, the road to Tapantí passes the entrance to **Monte Sky Mountain Retreat** (by reservation only; no electricity, shared bath, cold water; $50-$60, with meals, including tour; 2231-3536, phone/fax: 2228-0010; intnet.co.cr/montesky, monte sky@intnet.co.cr), a private reserve whose Costa Rican owner considers it a spiritual retreat. The reserve stretches over 536 mountainous hectares; 80 percent is primary forest. Trails lead to waterfalls and mountain peaks. You can have lunch in the rustic farmhouse, located about half a kilometer uphill from the parking lot. There are also camping platforms ($10) in the forest. Taxis from Orosi will charge $5-$6 each way to Monte Sky. Four-wheel drive is recommended.

Back on the main circuit, as soon as you cross the Río Grande de Orosi on a narrow suspension bridge, you will see a driveway to the left for the **Hotel and Restaurant Río Palomo** (private bath, heated water, some with kitchen, pools; $30-$40; 3533-3128, phone/fax: 2551-2919; palomalodge@hotmail.com), which has a huge, tour group–size restaurant (open daily, 8:30 a.m. to 5 p.m.), and has traditionally been the place for a fresh-fish lunch.

CACHÍ LAKE   As you circle Cachí Lake, you'll see the entrance to **La Casona del Cafetal** (open daily, 11 a.m. to 6 p.m.; 2577-1414) on the left. This open-air restaurant has a creative menu featuring trout, crêpes, and a wide range of coffee specialties made with coffee grown on the farm. They have a breakfast buffet on Sunday morning ($15), after which you can take a refreshing stroll on lakeside trails.

Several kilometers later, continuing around the Cachí reservoir, you'll see the **Casa del Soñador** on your right. This whimsical, sculpture-filled house built by the late sculptor Macedonio Quesada is also worth a stop. His sons, Hermes and Miguel, fashion melancholy *campesino* and religious figures out of gnarled coffee roots. Some are for sale at moderate prices.

Just down the road is the workshop of **Denis Sojo**, whose sculptures, big and small, are made from wood he has salvaged from the rivers or otherwise found. Each one has a story and a message. Definitely worth seeing.

Soon after is the **Cachí Dam** and the left-hand turnoff for **Ujarrás**, home to the ruins of Costa Rica's oldest church, **Nuestra Señora de la Limpía**. There is a procession from Paraíso to the ruins each year on the Sunday closest to April 16.

GETTING THERE: By Bus: Take the Cartago bus from San José (Avenida 2, across from the National Theater), which leaves every 10-20 minutes for the 40-minute trip. Ask to be let off at Las Ruinas and walk to the Orosi bus stop 100 meters east and 25 meters south of the southwest corner of the ruins (leaves every half hour; 45 minutes to Orosi). The Orosi bus passes Mirador Sanchiri and goes through Orosi (but get off at the central park in Orosi if you want to hire a taxi for Tapantí).

TURRIALBA AREA

Whitewater and still-water rafting, kayaking, canoeing, canyoning, hiking, biking, horseback riding, canopy tours, birding—there is hardly any adventure or naturalist sport that cannot be done in **Turrialba**. It is also the site of Costa Rica's most developed archaeological site, **Guayabo National Monument**. Definitely off the beaten track, Turrialba has a life of its own beyond tourism, and its residents are open and friendly to visitors. The area offers many possibilities for an interesting day or weekend trip. The famous one-day whitewater rafting trips on the Pacuare river usually pick you up at your San José hotel, bus you to Turrialba, take you rafting, and bus you back to San Jose. But if you stay in Turrialba and go rafting with a local company like **Rio Loco's Tropical Tours** (2556-6035, 8841-8026; whiteh2o.com, riolocos@whiteh2o.com) or **Tico's River Adventures** (2556-1231, fax: 2557-6100; ticoriver.com, info@ticoriver.com) you can get a feel for the culture, and spend more time on the river. Rio Locos also offers horseback, canyoning, photo safari, mountain biking and bar hopping tours. Ticos River is connected to a river kayaking school.

Aventuras Naturales (2225-3939, fax: 2253-6934, in North America: 800-321-8410; toenjoynature.com, toenjoy@toenjoynature.com) and **Ríos Tropicales** (2233-6455, in North America: 866-722-8273; riostropicales. com) both have lodges on the river that you can paddle to, making your rafting adventure a two- or three-day experience. Both companies require a minimum age of 12 for this trip and their canopy tours. Paddling to the **Pacuare Jungle Lodge** (owned by Aventuras Naturales) involves Class II rapids. The second day goes through a canyon with Class III and IV rapids ($340-$420 for two days, including meals, lodging, and transportation from San José). You can paddle in and leave by jeep or be driven both ways. The lovely individual bungalows are nestled in the rainforest; the cuisine is "jungle gourmet" by candlelight (there's no electricity). Our researchers recommend their canopy tour for people who want to see remote and untouched primary forest up-close in an adventurous setting, and who don't plan on doing a canopy tour in another location. The scenery is beautiful and the last three cables are very good. The **Ríos Tropicales Lodge** has water-generated electricity and a shorter, complimentary canopy tour.

Don't be disappointed if your river-rafting company calls off your trip because it has been raining. Sometimes *cabezas de agua* can develop when water becomes dammed behind fallen trees upriver and then releases with life-threatening power. Low water levels can be dangerous as well. Prudent companies will call off their trips when they see a potential for these conditions.

Some of the rapids in the mighty Reventazón that made Turrialba famous have disappeared under Costa Rica's newest and largest hydroelectric dam, **Lake Angostura**, which flooded the valley southeast of town in May 2000. Before the valley was flooded, ICE, the national electricity institute, conducted an exhaustive archaeological study of the dam area, unearthing 42 distinct pre-Columbian sites. You can learn about regional archaeology at the **Omar Salazar Obando Regional Museum** (open Monday to Friday, 9 a.m. to noon, 1 p.m. to 4 p.m.; 2556-7707; museoturrialba@sa.ucr. ac.cr), located at the University of Costa Rica's Turrialba campus east of town.

Turrialba is the home of **CATIE (Centro Agronómico Tropical de Investigación y Enseñanza)**. Established in the 1940s, it is one of the five major tropical research and education centers in the world. Tour its fascinating **Botanical Gardens** (open weekdays 7 a.m. to 3 p.m.; 2556-2700; catie.ac.cr; admission $15). The tour lets you taste, smell and touch a wide variety of tropical fruits, medicinal herbs and ornamentals. Over the past 30 years, CATIE has been a major force in helping rural farmers in remote places, from Bolivia to Nicaragua, find added value and market niches for their goods, like organic coffee, chocolate, and bananas, which you can also see and taste on the tour. Birders will enjoy spending time in the forests and along the Río Turrialba at the back of the gardens. By car, drive toward La Suiza and Siquirres, four kilometers to the east from Turrialba. A taxi charges about $2, and La Suiza buses leave hourly from the main terminal in Turrialba.

Located on CATIE grounds, the **Adventure Education Center** (2556-4609, in North America: 800-237-2730; adventurespanishschool.com) is one of Costa Rica's most dynamic language schools. With campuses in Turrialba, Dominical, and La Fortuna, near Arenal volcano, the school offers a serious language program in regular, medical, and business Spanish plus many opportunities for adventure and cultural exchange for the whole family.

Spanish by the River (phone/fax: 2556-7380; spanishbythesea.com, info@spanishbythesea.com) is a language school located five kilometers from the center of Turrialba, in the middle of a coffee field with a beautiful view of Volcán Turrialba. They serve delicious breakfasts on their wide balcony and have inexpensive accommodations at the school (shared room,

$10; private, $15). They can also arrange lodging with local families. In addition to medical Spanish and business Spanish, they give a six-hour Spanish Survival course for travelers. Children's and volunteer programs are also offered.

El Copal (shared bath, cold water; $50-$60 per person, including meals; 2248-9470; actuarcostarica.com) is a 190-hectare rainforest reserve in El Humo de Pejibaye, south of Turrialba. The quiet reserve is great for birding, and native food is excellent in their spacious, light filled dining room. Their **El Copal for Birdwatchers** tour starts out in Tapantí National Park near Orosi, then takes a scenic back road about one hour to El Copal for a delicious lunch and more birding. An early start the next morning will take you to another trail within the reserve, where eagle-eyed local guides will help you spot the rare species that are found there. After a hearty *campesino* breakfast, more birding on the trails or from your hammock on the lodge's ample verandah ($80/person for groups of eight or more, $160/person for groups of two to four; including expert birding guide, entrance fees to El Copal and Tapanti, lodging and three meals). They also offer tours of the community and local sugar mills.

Parque Viborana (open daily, 9 a.m. to 5 p.m.; 2538-1510; viborana@racsa.co.cr; guided one- to two-hour tours $7-$15), a 20-minute drive from downtown Turrialba in the village of Pavones, is one of the country's model wildlife rehabilitation and education centers. Owner Minor Camacho worked in the venom extraction laboratories of the University of Costa Rica for over two decades before moving back to this area; he knows as much as anyone in the country about snakes. He is a man with a mission: to teach people about snake behavior so that they can avoid being bitten and thus avoid killing snakes. For instance, we learned that snakes are likely to be out the day after several days of heavy rains because they want to dry out in the sun (see snake section in Chapter Two). Exhibits here include well-designed terrariums for Costa Rica's most dangerous serpents and a large walk-in cage for nonvenomous boa constrictors. Don Minor has planted his small farm with flowers and trees that attract birds, and many species that had disappeared from the sugarcane-monopolized landscape are beginning to come back to his land. Recommended.

RESTAURANTS **La Feria** (2556-0336) across from the gas station at the entrance to town, is a reasonably priced family-style restaurant with good food and service. **La Castellana** (open 24 hours) 25 meters east of Hotel Wagelia, is a great place to go to get some cheese and freshly baked bread for your hikes. There's a **farmer's market** along the railroad tracks in Turrialba on Friday and Saturday.

Café Toscana (open 9 a.m. to 10 p.m.; Sundays, noon to 10 p.m.; 2556-1222) offers salads, sandwiches, pastries, specialty coffees, and wi-fi. There's live music on weekends. It's above the popular **Charlie's Bar** in the Centro Comercial Rojas Cortes in the center of town.

Don Porfi's (closed Wednesday; 2556-9797) above Santa Rosa is also a favorite with locals for seafood. **Rancho de José** (open 11 a.m. to 10 p.m. Thursday through Sunday; 2538-8020) in El Carmen, on the way to Santa Cruz, is popular for grilled meats and stuffed potatoes. **Rancho de Sapito** (open daily, 6:30 a.m. to 7 p.m.; 2534-1818) in Capellades, 12 kilometers west of Santa Cruz, is on a vast dairy ranch on the slopes of Turrialba volcano. There you can sample home-made cheeses or eat trout fresh from the ponds in their charming gardens.

The charming and folkloric **Turrialtico** (open daily, 7 a.m. to 10 p.m.) is high on a hill about eight kilometers east of town. The spacious open-air dining room has a magnificent view of the valley. Native food is the specialty. Above the restaurant are comfortable rooms (private bath, fans, heated water, trails, orchid nursery; $50-$70, including breakfast; 2538-1111, fax: 2538-1575; turrialtico.com, info@turrialtico.com) with the same great view. Enjoy their orchid collection, which blooms in March and April.

LODGING   The **Hotel Wagelia** (private bath, hot water, phone, a/c or fans, cable TV, refrigerator; $60-$70, including breakfast and welcome cocktail; 2556-1566, fax: 2556-1596; hotelwagelia.com,), at the entrance to Turrialba, 150 meters west of the central park downtown, has clean, small rooms and a restaurant that offers an elegant menu with reasonable prices.

The best budget place to stay is the **Hotel Interamericano** (shared or private bath, hot water, TV, internet; $20-$40; 2556-0142, fax: 2556-7790; hotelinteramericano.com, hotelint@racsa.co.cr). It's well run, with caring, helpful, socially responsible management. It is centrally located, has guarded parking, and a place to hang your wet equipment and store gear. The rooms are painted cheerful colors and comfortable rockers enhance the sitting area. Recommended.

The nicest place to stay in this area is **Guayabo Lodge** (private bath, solar hot water; $90-$100, including breakfast; children 12 and under free; 2538-8400, phone/fax: 538-8492; guayabolodge.com, reservaciones@ guayabolodge.com). Perched on the slopes of Turrialba volcano, only half an hour from the center of town, it is the perfect starting place for peaceful birding walks, trips to the village of Aquiares, with its charming hand-painted church, or mountain biking to Guayabo. The hotel is designed with European grace by the Dutch owner, with a sunny dining area, and cozy sitting area with sofas and a tiled fireplace. The rooms are decorated with elegant fabrics and have mountain and valley views that delight the eye. A spacious area on the first floor has become a **gourmet cooking school.** Breakfasts include delicious European baked goods, and other meals are available on request. Recommended.

Volcán Turrialba Lodge (private bath, hot water, wood stove, bar; $70/person, including all meals; 2273-4335, fax: 2273-0703, cell: 8383-6084; volcanturrialbalodge.com, info@volcanturrialbalodge.com) is near the top of the Turrialba volcano. Access is only via four-wheel drive. The volcano has been spewing out gases recently, so visitors are only allowed to be at the crater for a maximum of 20 minutes.

Located on a curve in the Reventazón river, **Hotel Casa Turire** (private bath, balcony, cable TV, phone, pool; $140-$200; two-level master suite with jacuzzi, $340-$390; children under 8 $20; 2531-1111, fax: 2531-1075; hotelcasaturire.com, info@hotelcasaturire.com) is a unique Art Deco–style hotel. The elegant lodge overlooks Lake Angostura, the new dam in the flooded valley south of town. Here you'll find a pool, kayaks, and a fancy international restaurant. The very well-appointed rooms are reached by a wide staircase leading up from a spacious covered courtyard. Comfortable sitting and game rooms complete the amenities. It is 15 minutes southeast of Turrialba.

Catering to birders, naturalists, and photographers, **Rancho Naturalista** (private and shared baths, hot water, internet access; $175/person, including meals, horses, and guided birding tours; 2433-8278, fax: 2433-4925, in North America: 888-246-8513; costaricagateway.com, crgateway@racsa.co.cr) sits high in the hills above Tuís, east of Turrialba. There are nature trails through their private virgin rainforest reserve, the habitat of four species of toucans, the snow-capped hummingbird, and many other bird and butterfly species. The comfortable lodge overlooks the wide valley, and there are three separate cottages, one with two bedrooms. The restaurant's creative cookery is a special attraction.

GETTING THERE: By Bus: Buses leave San José hourly for Turrialba from Calle 13, Avenidas 6/8 (2222-4464; $1.25). The trip takes an hour and a half. Be sure to get a Directo bus.

By Car: The traditional route is through Cartago and Paraíso, then winding through sugarcane fields into Turrialba, about one and a half hours total from San José. There is also a delightful, paved back road that starts slightly south of the town of Cot on the slopes of Volcán Irazú, skirts Volcán Turrialba, and passes through the towns of Pacayas and Santa Cruz before arriving in Turrialba itself. This route takes less than two hours from San José.

GUAYABO NATIONAL MONUMENT

Guayabo National Monument (restaurant; open daily, 8 a.m. to 3:30 p.m.; 2559-1220; admission $6, children under 6 free; camping, $2), on the slopes of Volcán Turrialba, is considered the most significant archaeological site in Costa Rica. It offers a glimpse into the harmony between people and nature that existed in pre-Columbian times. Birds abound in the ruins, which are set in premontane rainforest and dotted with the guava trees that give the town its name. *Oropéndolas* (related to North American orioles) hang their sacklike nests from tree branches. Water sings its song in ancient aqueducts.

Archaeologists have excavated only the central part of a 10,000-inhabitant city that existed from 1000 B.C. to about A.D. 1400. The exposed area is composed of circular mounds, which were the floors of large buildings raised to keep them dry; paved sidewalks, some of whose stones are decorated with petroglyphs; a large stone carved with stylistic representations of two Indian gods: the jaguar, god of the forest, and the crocodile, god of the river; a system of covered and uncovered aqueducts that still functions well; and the oldest bridge in Costa Rica, a flat rock, now broken in several places, which crosses one of the aqueducts. Several roads radiate from the center of the town. Spot excavations verify that some of them extend at least eight kilometers. It is thought that Guayabo was an important conduit between the Aztec and Maya peoples of the north and the Incas of the south.

There are many mysteries about the civilization that inhabited Guayabo. No one knows why the people left (just before the *conquistadores* discovered Costa Rica), nor why Spanish explorers never found or never kept records of finding the site. Yet the peace and beauty that reign in Guayabo echo a wise and gentle people.

From the *mirador*, you can see green grassy mounds and stone sidewalks nestled within the rainforest. Hawks and vultures swoop and sail in front of the striking four-layered backdrop of mountains. Across the road from the site, behind the campground, a steep trail leads down to the

Oropéndolas

fast-flowing Guayabo River, where you can sit bathing your feet and looking for birds. You can also walk up the road past coffee and sugarcane fields for views of the green Guayabo valley.

Park personnel orient visitors when they arrive, then give them a pamphlet to do a self-guided tour. Bring rain gear.

GETTING THERE: By Bus: Direct Turrialba–Guayabo buses leave at 9 a.m. and 3 p.m., returning at 12:30 and 4 p.m. (Transtusa, 2556-0073). A taxi costs $15-$20 each way.

By Car: From Turrialba, follow the signs off the main highway through downtown, crossing the river on the old steel bridge. Stay on the main road until you see the sign indicating a left to the Park. It's a 19-kilometer trip and takes about 30 minutes, all on paved roads.

From San José you can choose to take the above-described back road from San José to Turrialba, via Pacayas and Santa Cruz. There's a shortcut to Guayabo National Monument. Watch for a steep left turn a few kilometers after the village of Santa Cruz. Drive approximately six kilometers on this road, then take a right. From here it's only four kilometers to Guayabo.

EIGHT

The Atlantic Coast

A trip to the Atlantic coast in Limón Province offers a chance to enjoy this area's wild beauty and the distinct culture that characterizes it. Much of the region is a jungle-covered lowland, skirted by a coastline of beautiful white- and black-sand beaches where turtles come to nest and monkeys and sloths hang out in the trees. The tall Talamanca mountains force migrating birds from North America to fly over the narrow strip of land to the south of Puerto Limón. The Nature Conservancy has named the Talamanca area a birding hot spot, with as many as three million raptors (hawks, kites, falcons, eagles, vultures) touching down during their spring and fall migrations. The birds' presence indicates a healthy ecosystem. You can visit and participate in many fascinating projects combining bird-friendly agriculture, conservation, community development, and ecotourism when you choose this region, and you can get in plenty of swimming, snorkeling, surfing, and fishing, too.

People who want to avoid touristy atmospheres will enjoy the slow-moving rhythm of life in Cahuita, Puerto Viejo and Manzanillo, south of Limón.

Tortuguero, several hours by boat north of Limón, is unique in Costa Rica because of its jungle-lined canals and the famous green turtle nesting season from July to October, but you can also observe the less numerous leatherback turtles nesting all up and down the coast from mid-February to mid-June.

Barra del Colorado, near the Nicaraguan border, has become famous as a sportfishing destination, but it also has a turtle beach and lovely canals, and is one of the largest wildlife refuges in the country.

Limón is the least populated province in Costa Rica and is unique in its mix of ethnic groups. Afro-Caribbean peoples migrated to the Atlantic coast in the 19th century to fish, work on the railroad, and farm *cacao* and coconut, and they now comprise roughly a third of the province's population. A variety of English dialects are spoken here, including an elegant Jamaican English and a patois called *mekatelyu*. "What happen" (pronounced "whoppen") is the common greeting. Instead of saying "*adiós*" when they pass each other, people say "all right" or "okay." For a fascinating history of the region, read Paula Palmer's *What Happen* (now in its fifth edition), in which elders of the black community tell their life stories (see "Recommended Reading" in Chapter Thirteen).

A relatively large population of indigenous Bribris and Cabécars inhabits the rainforests of Talamanca. They try to maintain their traditional lifestyle in harmony with nature. Limón also has many Chinese residents whose relatives immigrated in the 19th and early 20th centuries.

PUERTO LIMÓN

The people of Puerto Limón, Costa Rica's Atlantic port, are making great strides in improving the appearance of their town for the 400,000 tourists that arrive each year on cruise ships between October and April. Near the cruise ship landing, **Parque Vargas** is pleasant with its towering palm trees. The street going west from the park has been made into a pedestrian boulevard with restaurants and souvenir shops. On the east side of the park, you can take a refreshing walk along the sea wall.

The **National Band of Limón** (2758-5123) performs on the boulevard in front of the Edificio Cristal on Tuesdays at 4:30 p.m.

The **Festival of Black Culture** (*Festival de las Flores de la Diáspora*) is celebrated during August, culminating in Black Culture Day, August 31. Most events are held in the **Black Star Line Cultural Center**, which was built in 1911 as a shipping office by Marcus Garvey (founder of the United Negro Improvement Association, one of the largest African-American organizations in history). The Center is still managed by the Limón chapter of the UNIA.

Real Adventures (realadventures.com/listings/1035483_Black-Culture-Tour-in-Costa Rica) runs a seven-day tour to Talamanca and Limón, featuring participation in the Black Culture Day Parade, and time at a beach resort and in the rainforest. Limón's biggest celebration is **Carnaval**, held in October near *El Día de las Culturas*, the Costa Rican version of Columbus Day. Brightly costumed *Limonenses* parade to the rhythm of drums, tambourines, maracas, and whistles. The *comparsa* groups practice their dance steps all year in preparation for the festival, which has been held

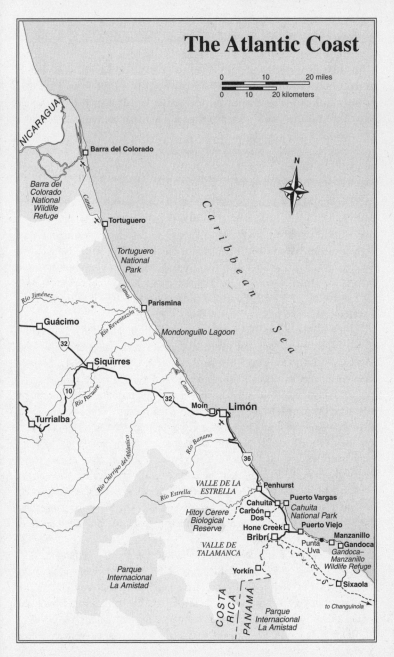

The Atlantic Coast

0   10   20 miles

0   10   20 kilometers

N

NICARAGUA

Barra del Colorado

Barra del
Colorado
National
Wildlife
Refuge

Canal

Tortuguero

Tortuguero
National
Park

Caribbean

Río Jiménez

Canal

Parismina

Guácimo

32

Río Reventazón

Mondonguillo Lagoon

Sea

Siquirres

10

Río Pacuare

32

Moín

Limón

Turrialba

Río Chirripó del Atlántico

Canal

Río Banano

36

Río Estrella

VALLE DE LA
ESTRELLA

Penhurst

Hitoy Cerere
Biological
Reserve

Cahuita

Carbón
Dos

Puerto Vargas

Cahuita
National Park

Hone Creek

Bribrí

Puerto Viejo

Manzanillo

Gandoca

VALLE DE
TALAMANCA

Punta
Uva

Gandoca–
Manzanillo
Wildlife
Refuge

Parque
Internacional
La Amistad

Yorkín

Sixaola

COSTA RICA

PANAMÁ

Parque
Internacional
La Amistad

to Changuinola

since 1949. You're part of the parade, too, drawn in by the irresistible Afro-Caribbean beat. The ten-day festival includes concerts, fireworks, and local food. Make sure you reserve a hotel room in advance.

Isla Uvita, a small island off the coast of Puerto Limón, is purported to be the place where Christopher Columbus landed on September 18, 1502, on his fourth and final trip to the new world. A half hour hike takes you around the island. A new dock is being built to make landing easier amidst the coral reefs surrounding it.

Stevedores load containers of bananas and pineapples onto huge freighters at **Moín,** a few kilometers to the north. Moín is where independent boatmen dock for trips up the canals to Tortuguero.

RESTAURANTS AND LODGING   At **Restaurant Brisas del Caribe** (open daily, 11 a.m. to 10 p.m.; 2758-0138) you can sample Caribbean cuisine at outdoor tables overlooking Parque Vargas. **Restaurant and Bar Placeres** (open 11 a.m. to 1 a.m., closed Sundays; 2795-3335) is more expensive, but has ocean views. Across from the northeast corner of the *mercado* is the **Hotel Acón** (private bath, hot water, a/c, TV, phone; $30-$40; 2758-1010, fax: 2758-2924), with a restaurant and a big disco on the second floor. Ask for a room off the street.

If you can get a room facing the sea, you will find the **Park Hotel** (private bath, wall fans, a/c, hot water, restaurant, some balconies, cable TV, phone; $70-$90; kids under 8 free; 2798-0555, fax: 2758-4364; irlixie@ racsa.co.cr) very pleasant. It's located a block north of Parque Vargas.

You might prefer to stay at one of the comfortable hotels north of Limón on the road to Moín, a short ride from downtown. From the *mercado*, drive straight north until you reach a T intersection, then turn right and follow the road that winds along the coast through Playa Bonita to Moín, finally intersecting with the main highway back to San José. Buses leave frequently from the Radio Casino bus stop, a block north of the *mercado*.

The first hotel along this road is the **Hotel Oasys del Caribe** (private bath, unheated water, fans, some a/c, pool, cable TV; $30-$40; phone/fax: 2795-0024; moyso@racsa.co.cr), which has cute, clean, individual *cabinas* and an open-air restaurant.

Hotel Maribú Caribe's (private bath, hot water, a/c, pool, phone; $70-$90, including breakfast; 2795-4010, fax: 2795-3541; maribu@racsa.co.cr) white, circular, thatch-roofed cabinas are perched on the only cliff in the area, and the complex resembles a tribal fort. The cabinas and pool are spotless, the restaurant is overpriced but good, the view is terrific.

Reina's Bar and Restaurant (2795-0789) has a great view of Playa Bonita, beach access, and live music on Fridays.

White-faced monkeys (mono cariblanco) are one of four types of monkeys that make Costa Rica's forests their home.

Right: Of the 136 species of snakes in Costa Rica, 18, including the eyelash viper, are lethal.

Below: The poisonous dart frog spends its entire life high above the rainforest floor.

Left: The three-toed sloth's upside-down position is ideal for scooping hanging leaves into its mouth.

Right: Mosses, ferns, lichens, and other epiphytes grasp tree branches and absorb their nutrients from leaf matter and water dripping off the canopy.

Below: Caymans live in creeks, ponds, mangrove swamps, and beach lowlands.

Right: Elephant beetle.

Below: Leaf-cutter ant.

Right: The Catarata La Fortuna is so powerful that swimming is not possible beneath it.

Above: Day breaks through the morning clouds along one of Costa Rica's many beautiful beaches.

Below: Its remote location, tremendous rainfall, and variety of unique habitats make Corcovado National Park an ecological treasure.

Left: The exuberant red, yellow, or orange bursts of the heliconia flower are a common rainforest sight.

Below: Costa Rica is an outdoor adventurer's paradise—definitely the place to take a walk on the "wild side."

Above: Verdant farmland blankets the agriculturally rich area around Lake Arenal in the Northern Zone.

Below: Fiery-billed aracaris, which make their homes in old woodpecker holes, sometimes gather berries from the ground.

Three species of herons, the tiger heron among them, inhabit the lowlands of Costa Rica.

GETTING THERE: By Bus: In San José, the buses for Limón (2221-2596; $4) leave hourly from the Terminal Caribe at the north end of Calle Central. Buy tickets in advance for a weekend or holiday trip. To get to the area north of Limón, on the road to Moín, take the Moín or Villa del Mar bus near Radio Casino in Limón.

By Car: Driving to the Atlantic coast is fairly easy and enjoyable, unless you get behind a long line of trucks heading for the port. It takes about two and a half hours from San José. The first part of the drive is through the mountains of Braulio Carrillo National Park. It's hard to believe that when it's raining cats and dogs in San José, it can be clear and hot on the other side of those mountains. It's true, though, especially in September and October, usually the heaviest months of the Pacific rainy season. The reverse is true as well. Limón can be very wet during the rest of the country's dry season. Try to go early in the day to avoid fog and rain. And if it has been raining a lot, ask around about landslides in Braulio Carrillo before you set out. The second half of the drive is through the Atlantic lowlands, past towns with names like Cairo, Boston, and Liverpool. There are plenty of open-air restaurants to stop at along the way.

By Air: Nature Air (natureair.com) offers daily flights to Limón.

TORTUGUERO NATIONAL PARK

Tortuguero National Park protects a unique series of natural inland waterways throughout rainforests that are home to freshwater turtles, river otters, crocodiles, sloths, howler, spider, and white-faced capuchin monkeys, toucans, *oropéndolas*; parrots; morpho butterflies; and many other species. In addition, it is known as one of the world's richest fishing grounds for tarpon and snook. Manatees also inhabit the canals. Some scientists claim that manatees are distant relatives of the elephant. These shy creatures and a related species, the dugong, are said to have given rise to the legend of the mermaid. When frightened, they can stay underwater for as much as half an hour, but usually they stop grazing on aquatic plants and seaweed

Green sea turtle

long enough to surface every 10 to 15 minutes. That is when they become vulnerable to the propellers of the dozens of motor boats that ply the canals. For more information, see savethemanatee.com.

Tortuguero is the largest nesting area in the Western Hemisphere for the green sea turtle. These turtles return to Tortuguero every two to four years to mate offshore and dig their nests. Although their feeding grounds can be as far away as Florida and Venezuela, none of the thousands of green turtles tagged in Tortuguero has ever been found to nest at any other beach. Green turtle nesting season is from June to November, with peak nesting season in late August or early September. Their flipper marks look like tractor treads, showing up as wide black lines on the beach at night.

Tortuguero has been famous for its turtles (as a source of meat, shells, and eggs) since the 1600s, when the Spanish set up cacao plantations on the Atlantic coast. Turtles were valued as a meat source on early ships because they would stay alive if they were kept out of the sun and sprinkled with water. Turtle soup became a delicacy in England around the end of the 1800s. Large-scale turtle export from Tortuguero started in 1912, and by the 1950s, the green turtle faced extinction.

Long-term biological research on the green turtle, started by the **Caribbean Conservation Corp.** (CCC; 2297-5510, in North America: 800-678-7853; cccturtle.org, ccc@cccturtle.org) in 1954, has helped greatly in understanding and preserving this species. Dr. Archie Carr, the founder of CCC, wrote an entertaining and informative book, *The Windward Road* (see the CCC website), about his wanderings in search of the green turtles' nesting ground, which finally led him to Tortuguero. Thanks to international interest in Carr's work, Tortuguero was declared a national park in 1970 by the Costa Rican government. Today Tortuguero is the premier center for turtle monitoring in the world.

Tortuguero also hosts a globally important nesting population of the critically endangered leatherback turtle *(Dermocheys coriacea)*. Leatherbacks arrive earlier in the year (March to June) and in much fewer numbers than the greens. Typically fewer than 1000 nests are laid each season. Unlike the green turtles, leatherbacks do not always return to the same beach to lay their eggs, so turtle protection groups up and down the coast are cooperating to monitor them. The leatherback population on the Pacific coast has diminished 90 percent in the last decade, mainly due to fishing practices that trap and kill turtles along with whatever fish the boats are trying to catch. Turtles are somewhat safer on the Atlantic coast because shallower water makes fishing more difficult.

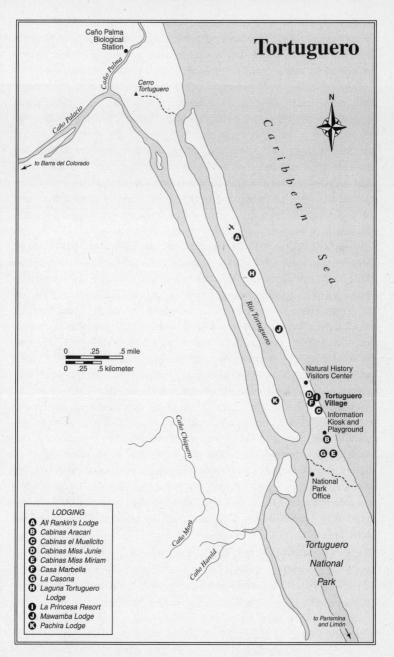

Tortuguero

Caño Palma
Biological
Station

Caño Palma

Cerro
Tortuguero

Caño Palacio

to Barra del Colorado

Caribbean Sea

Río Tortuguero

0   .25   .5 mile

0   .25   .5 kilometer

Caño Chiquero

Caño Mora

Caño Harold

Natural History
Visitors Center

Tortuguero
Village

Information
Kiosk and
Playground

National
Park
Office

Tortuguero

National

Park

to Parismina
and Limón

LODGING
Ⓐ All Rankin's Lodge
Ⓑ Cabinas Aracari
Ⓒ Cabinas el Muellcito
Ⓓ Cabinas Miss Junie
Ⓔ Cabinas Miss Miriam
Ⓕ Casa Marbella
Ⓖ La Casona
Ⓗ Laguna Tortuguero
   Lodge
Ⓘ La Princesa Resort
Ⓙ Mawamba Lodge
Ⓚ Pachira Lodge

When we were in Tortuguero one March, we saw two huge *baulas* (leatherback females) laboriously digging holes in the soft brown sand by the light of the full moon. Witnessing this age-old ritual left us with a deep respect for the primordial instincts of all creatures, including humans.

The turtles lay about 100 eggs in each clutch, and return to nest several times each season. The eggs incubate for approximately 60 days, then the baby turtles bite through the rubbery shells and clamber out of the nest, heading straight for the ocean, which they try to reach before dawn. Once they hit the water, their instinctive navigational powers direct them to the open sea. Research has shown that turtle hatchlings are attracted to the light reflected off the sea. (In an experiment a few years ago, researchers blocked their view of the sea and set up a light source in another direction; the turtles headed toward it. That is why it is not good to have lighted hotels near turtle beaches.)

The CCC's biological field station and **Natural History and Visitors Center** are at the north end of Tortuguero village. In addition to beautiful photographs and interpretive material on the area's wildlife, the center features a life-size model of a mother turtle laying her eggs, and a nest full of hatchlings. They show an excellent video about sea turtles and the work of the CCC over the last 50 years. Visitor center staff is available to answer questions and tell you about volunteer opportunities with the CCC. The center also sells T-shirts, books, laminated field guides to the flora and fauna of the region, and other wildlife gifts. You can adopt a turtle in Tortuguero or through cccturtle.org. Proceeds help fund the CCC's conservation programs. The visitors center is open from 10 a.m. to noon and 2 p.m. to 5:30 p.m. Monday through Saturday, and 2 p.m. to 5 p.m. Sunday. Admission to this excellent small museum is about $1.

In the information kiosk near the playground at the center of Tortuguero village, there is a fascinating exhibit on the cultural history of the area, illustrated by Deirdre Hyde. To learn more about the human inhabitants of Tortuguero, where they came from, and how they made their living for so many years before tourism discovered the area, read *Turtle Bogue* by Harry LeFever.

LOCALLY GUIDED TURTLE WALKS Recognizing that no conservation effort can succeed without full support from the community, the CCC, in partnership with the National Parks Service, has helped to train local people as turtle guides. Young men and women have learned a new way to make their living from the town's unique natural resource. During the Leatherback nesting season (March to June) and the green turtle nesting season (July to November), access to the beach is prohibited between 6 p.m. and 6 a.m. to assure that no one disturbs the female turtles when they come ashore to lay their eggs. Visitors who want the opportunity to observe this fascinating natural phenomenon must participate in an organized tour with a registered guide. The guides are familiar with the stages of the nesting process; they only let people approach once the mother turtle is so fully absorbed in laying her eggs that the observers' presence will not disturb her.

The turtle walks are undertaken in two shifts, at 8 p.m. and at 10 p.m. Each guide is limited to ten visitor permits, so the guides line up early to buy permits for night tours. Arrangements must be made with a guide during the day so that the guide can get a permit for that night's tours. Before the tours, specially trained "turtle spotters" patrol the beach looking for nesting females. Your tour group will be assigned to one of five designated waiting areas. Once a turtle is spotted in your area, the spotter radios your guide. Then your group walks on a trail above the beach, and enters the beach close to where the turtle is located.

This system eases the negative effects of groups of tourists walking along the beach and disturbing the turtles as they come ashore. Tourists are invited to make a $4 donation to the Turtle Spotter Program. All donations help directly with turtle conservation in Tortuguero.

Guided turtle walks cost $10-$15. Park admission costs $10/day (2710-2929). Most package-deal hotels do not include the turtle tours in their rates, but will arrange for you to hook up with a guide. Flashlights, cameras, and video equipment are not allowed on the beach during turtle tours. Dark clothing is also requested to reduce your visibility to the mother turtles on the beach.

TOURING BY BOAT   One way to enjoy the exuberant vegetation and abundant wildlife of Tortuguero's canals is to rent a *cayuca*, or dugout canoe (about $5/hour, three hours for $15/person with a guide, see tortuguerovillage.com). *Cayucas* are quite stable and easy to paddle. Paddle around for awhile to see if your dugout is the right size for you and make sure it is of solid, one-piece construction and not caulked together. Check also that it has a plastic bailer. **Miss Junie** at the north end of town rents nice fiberglass canoes ($10 for the morning) and the **Paraiso Tropical Souvenir** shop rents bicycle canoes for $9/hour.

You have to pay $10 admission to the park at the administration office (2710-2929), just south of the village, before you set off in a *cayuca*. The main waterway of the park is inland from the canal that comes from Moín. Paddle south. You will see smaller waterways branching off that you can explore. If you go out without a guide, ask where the currents are most gentle. The current in the Río Tortuguero can be quite strong.

To make your boat trip more comfortable, bring the following:

Thick-soled athletic shoes	Lightweight long-sleeved
Socks	and short-sleeved shirts
Insect repellent	Towels
Sunblock	Lunch in waterproof bags
Broad-rimmed hat	Drinking water
or visored cap	Swiss Army knife
Umbrella for sun or rain	Flashlight
Lightweight plastic poncho	
or picnic cloth for rain	

Most lodges use electric motors to reduce noise that disturbs the quiet beauty of the jungle streams and four-stroke engines to reduce pollution. Make sure you tour the canals in quiet boats. Daryl Loth of **Tortuguero Wildlife Tours** ($15/person for three hours; tortuguero_s.tripod.com), enjoys giving educational tours of the area, emphasizing not only wildlife observation but insight into the community. You'll find him at Casa Marbella across from the Jungle Shop. Tortuguerovillage.com has direct links to some of Tortuguero's most experienced guides.

FISHING **Elvin Gutierrez** (2709-8071; tortuguerosportsfish.tripod.com, jungle@racsa.co.cr) has decades of experience in providing fishing trips. Kids 12 and under fish for free. **Modesto Watson** (phone/fax: 2226-0986; tortuguerocanals.com, info@tortuguerocanals.com) also has years of experience in fishing trips and is a great wildlife guide.

CAMPING   Camping is allowed in the park, but remember that Tortuguero has one of the highest annual rainfalls in the world: more than 200 inches a year. *Terciopelo* (fer-de-lance) snakes are not uncommon on land, especially at night. There is a swampy nature trail on the narrow piece of land between the large canal and the sea.

Note: If you want to go swimming, Tortuguero is not the ideal place. The beach offers very little shade, has rough, dangerous surf, and is frequented by sharks.

LODGING AND RESTAURANTS   Many people splurge on a tour to Tortuguero because the logistics seem difficult. But it is quick, easy, and cheaper to fly there on SANSA or Nature Air and stay in one of the hotels in the village. Compare 20 minutes by air with the trip by bus, taxi, and boat from San José through Limón and Moín (six hours travel time). If you want to return via the canals, it is easier to arrange boat transportation *from* Tortuguero than *to* it. The boat trip up the canals from Moín takes about three to five hours, depending on the condition of the canals, and is noisy and boring for some. It is worthwhile if you have a good guide.

Note: There is no bank in Tortuguero, and many local hotels and guides do not take credit cards or traveler's checks, so be sure and change money before you get there. Some shops and restaurants will take credit cards if you make a purchase, but they don't have the cash flow to handle money changing. There are public phones in Tortuguero that you can use with a 197 or 199 phone card.

There are several inexpensive hotels in the village. **Cabinas Miss Miriam** (private bath, heated water, fans; $20-$30; 2709-8002, 2709-8107; tortuguerovillage.com), on the north side of the soccer field offers clean and secure lodging. The second floor rooms are breezy and have an ocean view. Her restaurant serves delicious Caribbean dishes.

On the south side of the soccer field, beyond the information kiosk and the playground, is **Cabinas Aracari** (private bath, heated water, wall fans; $15-$20; 2709-8006; tortuguerovillage.com), also in the southwest side of the soccer field are nice, clean cabinas surrounded by a garden with native fruit trees: mango, avocado, water apple, and cashew.

La Princesa Resort (private bath, heated water, $30-$40, including breakfast; 2709-8131; tortuguerovillage.com) is a large two-story Caribbean-style hotel south of the soccer field, Their restaurant, open 6 a.m. to 9 p.m. serves Caribbean dishes.

Restaurante y Cabinas el Muellecito (private bath, heated water, fans, $10-$20; 2709-8104; tortuguerovillage.com) near the southwest corner of the soccer field, offers lodging, meals, and a canoe or turtle tour for $40.

Budda Café (open daily, 11 a.m. to 9 p.m.; 2709-8084) 25 meters north of the main dock, serves crepes, pasta and lasagna. Their deck overlooks the river.

Casa Marbella (private bath, hot water, fans; $30-$40, including breakfast; 2709-8011, 8833-0827; casamarbella.tripod.com, safari@racsa.co.cr) has nicely designed, comfortable rooms with great breakfasts and a communal kitchen for guests, in the heart of Tortuguero right on the water across from the Catholic church. Some rooms have river views. It is owned by nature guide Daryl Loth and his family.

At the northern end of the village are **Cabinas Miss Junie** (private bath, hot water, ceiling fans; $30-$40, including breakfast; 2709-8102; iguanaverdetours.com, turtle@racsa.co.cr). Each room has its own pastel color theme, with walls and bed linens that blend harmoniously. The tiled bathrooms are impressive. Miss Junie gained fame over the years as the cook at the CCC, and now has her own **restaurant**. If you want to sample her cuisine, you must let her know in advance so that she can give your meal the preparation it deserves. The hotel arranges transportation from San Jose and nature tours.

When the CCC puts radio transmitters on the turtles, it gives each turtle a catchy name and includes the villagers in the events around the turtle's release. A few years back, one of the turtles was named in honor of Miss Junie. Unfortunately, the reptilian "Miss Junie" swam up to Nicaragua and wound up in someone's stew pot. After the researchers found out what had happened and recovered the transmitter, the CCC put out press releases to draw attention to the plight of green turtles in the Caribbean. The real Miss Junie and her kin were phoned for weeks by people expressing their sympathy for poor Miss Junie, who had been captured and eaten in Nicaragua's Miskito Cays. The transmitter was attached to another turtle, Miss Junie 2, who luckily did not suffer the same fate as her predecessor, at least during the life of the transmitter.

All Rankin's Lodge (private bath, heated water, fans; $50/person, including meals; 2758-4160, 2815-5175, 2709-8101; greencoast.com/all rankin, allrankinstours@hotmail.com), about one and a half miles north of Tortuguero village near the airstrip, has simple, rustic but comfy cabins and serves generous meals in its dining room on the lagoon. The setting is extremely tranquil, except for when the planes arrive in the morning. Durham Rankin and his wife Tomasa Gonzalez were among the first families to settle the area that became Tortuguero village back in the late 1940s. They fished and farmed and brought up their brood of seven when Tortuguero was an unknown outpost. The whole family worked with Dr. Archie Carr and the CCC on the sea turtle research and monitoring that eventually led to the creation of the national park. Willis Rankin runs the lodge, he and brother Danny run transport from Moín to Tortuguero ($65 roundtrip) and tour services ($125 for a two-day tour during turtle season), and are both excellent naturalist guides along with brothers Alonso and Eddy.

La Casona (open daily, 9 a.m. to 9 p.m.; 2709-8092) is an excellent restaurant on the north side of the soccer field. They cook delicate fish, chicken *à l'orange*, and vegetarian dishes, as well as specialties like banana pancakes for breakfast. They also rent four rooms, surrounded by tropical gardens.

There are several souvenir shops in the village. **El Paraíso Tropical**, an unmistakable purple building that you can see from the water, has many things that you'd find in souvenir shops in San José, and not many locally made articles. The **Jungle Shop**, a few houses to the south, has better-quality, more interesting, locally made items, as well as cold drinks.

The **Internet Café** is just south of El Paraiso Tropical.

LARGE HOTELS   All of these lodges offer two- and three-day packages that include food, lodging, tours of the canals via motorboat, and ascent of Cerro (Mount) Tortuguero (though park fees are not included). Most tours include bus and boat transportation between San José and Tortuguero, and all offer an air transport upgrade.

Mawamba Lodge (private bath, hot water, ceiling fans, restaurant, game room, nature trails, hammocks, pool; 2293-8181, fax: 2239-7657; grupomawamba.com, info@grupomawamba.com) has pleasant cabinas and a large, airy dining room that serves very good food. Because it's just one kilometer north of Tortuguero village on the ocean side of the canal, you can walk to the village or the ocean. There is a large, fanciful pool with a waterfall, near a bar where tropical drinks are served. With its air-conditioned conference room and resident multilingual biologist, it's a good setting for seminars or small conventions. Their one- to four-night tours run from $260-$600; children 5 to 12 half-price. They also have river kayaking trips (not suitable for children under 12).

Next door, **Laguna Tortuguero Lodge** (private bath, hot water, ceiling fans, open-air restaurant, swimming pool with jacuzzi; 2709-8082, fax: 2709-8081; lagunatortuguero.com, info@lagunatortuguero.com) is owned by the brother of the owner of Mawamba, a noted Costa Rican poet and author. They have a huge shell-shaped gift shop/conference room/internet café and their pool has an island where you can spot red-eyed frogs. On their 15-acre site, there are trails, a botanical garden, and an open butterfly garden. Their one- to three-night packages run from $210 to $360; children 5-11 half-price.

Pachira Lodge (private bath, hot water, ceiling fans, pool; $100/person, including breakfast and lunch; 2256-7080, 2223-1682, fax: 2223-1119; pachiralodge.com, info@pachiralodge.com), located on the canal to Barra, across from the village, and situated on 34 acres, is decorated in a traditional Caribbean style, with many attractive touches. A one- to two-night package costs $200-$450/person double occupancy, depending on the type of transportation used.

GETTING THERE: Because there are no roads to Tortuguero, getting there cheaply can be complicated. That's why most people go there in a packaged tour that includes meals and transportation by bus and boat or plane from San Jose. The new website, tortuguerovillage.com is the most complete source of up-to-date information about independent travel to Tortuguero. Because transportation options change frequently, it's best to communicate with them when planning your trip.

By Boat: One of the most pleasant and enlightening ways to get to Tortuguero is aboard the **Riverboat Francesca**. Modesto and Fran Watson offer tours in their canopied boat (two days/one night from San José, including lodging and meals, an early-morning tour of the national park, and a canal tour; $170-$200; three days also offered; phone/fax: 2226-0986; tortuguerocanals.com, info@tortuguerocanals.com). Modesto has an eagle eye for animals and pointed out caimans, toucans, an osprey, jacanas, basilisk lizards, monkeys, sloths, a pair of scarlet macaws (a rare sight on the Atlantic coast), a roseate spoonbill, freshwater turtles, and lots of water birds on our trip up the canals. They also use a quiet, fuel-saving four-stroke motor. Recommended.

Many independent operators offer transport out of Moín. Competition can be fierce and some of these have been known to mislead visitors who have pre-arranged travel agreements with other operators in order to steal their business. Some reliable and safe operators offering tours and transport are **Tropical Wind** (Sebastian Torres and Alexis Soto; 2798-6059, 2758-4297), **Willis Rankin** (2758-4160, 8815-5175), and **Danny Rankin** (2386-3972). All are particularly adept at spotting wildlife along the way. They charge $65 roundtrip, and depart from Moín at 10 a.m. Take the 6 or 7 a.m. Limón bus from the Caribe terminal (2221-2596) in San José (buy your ticket a day early in high season), then a $5 taxi from Limón in order to get to the JAPDEVA (hap-DAY-vah) dock on time.

The boats to Tortuguero stop more often to see wildlife than the returning boats, so going up takes around four hours and coming back around three hours. Returning boats leave Tortuguero around 10 a.m., getting you to Moín around 1 p.m.

If you haven't made arrangements with one of the boats above, you can just arrive at the JAPDEVA dock. The boat owners in Moín have formed a cooperative and there is a loose rotation organized to give all the captains a chance to take people to Tortuguero. You will have to negotiate a price, and there is bargaining power in groups, so try to pair up with someone before arriving at the docks. Make sure your boat has lifejackets. Prices should run about $50-$70/person, or $200 per boat roundtrip.

By Public Bus or Rental Car and Boat through Cariari: This can be the cheapest way to get to Tortuguero. Since details change often, follow the detailed directions at tortuguerovillage.com.

By Air: Nature Air ($70 one way; 2299-6000, in North America: 800-235-9272; natureair.com, reservations@natureair.com) flies to Tortuguero every morning at 6:15 a.m. SANSA ($70 one way; 2290-4100; flysansa.com, info@fly sansa.com) leaves for Tortuguero daily at 6 a.m. If you are visiting Tortuguero on your own, this might be a quick and easy way to travel at least one way. SANSA provides boat transportation to the village, two miles south of the airstrip ($5/person). For boat transport to the Tortuguero airstrip, call Victor Barrantes at the SANSA office (2709-8055) in Tortuguero the day before you will need a ride. Victor, a bilingual local guide, can be found at the airport upon arrival of both SANSA and Nature Air flights.

PARISMINA

Parismina is a small fishing village about halfway between Limón and Tortuguero.

MONDONGUILLO LAGOON   About half an hour by boat south of Parismina is Mondonguillo Lagoon, where the Pacuare River runs into the sea. The area is protected by the private **Pacuare Matina Forestry Reserve**. The beach is one of the most frequented leatherback nesting beaches in the Caribbean. Two projects are based here to protect the leatherbacks and other nesting turtles.

Ecology Project International (2222-5864, in the U.S.: 406-721-8784; ecologyproject.org) has a nine day package that includes whitewater rafting on the Pacuare, a visit to Selva Bananito Reserve, and four days of turtle monitoring in the Pacuare Reserve.

On the south side of the lagoon is the Costa Rican–owned **Estacion Tortugas** (estacionlastortugas.org), which monitors the beach south of the lagoon from March to September. **Ecoteach** (in North America: 800-626-8992; ecoteach.com) brings groups to this station each year.

BARRA DEL COLORADO

Barra del Colorado, at the northeast end of Costa Rica, is a sleepy, rainy, car-free town occupying opposite banks near the mouth of the Río Colorado. The west bank of the river has the village, the east bank has the expensive lodges. There is excellent fishing in the river, nearby canals, and the Caribbean Sea. All of the hotels here specialize in fishing.

Tarpon season is from January to June and September to December. Snook run from October to January and also in May. The rainy season on the Atlantic Coast is unpredictable, so bring a good windbreaker and sweatshirt. The lodges usually provide rain gear. The beach in Barra is too rough for swimming, snorkeling, or scuba diving, but it is a nesting ground for sea turtles from July through September.

The **Barra del Colorado National Wildlife Refuge** (admission $10; 2710-2929), at 92,000 hectares, is the second largest in Costa Rica. If you fly to Barra, you'll see its importance. Everywhere between the Central Mountains and the Atlantic Coast, the land looks like an animal whose pelt has been shaved in large patches. Bright green spots littered with fallen trees finally give way to the beauty of the rich coat of billowing, dark green treetops extending north into Nicaragua. It is a great relief to see that this one expanse of virgin forest has been saved. SINAC (National Conservation Areas System) operates on a shoestring budget, with too few poorly equipped guards to patrol this huge area and to keep its monkeys, sloths, jaguars, and birds safe from hunters and loggers.

Because Barra is traditionally known as a fishing area, it is less crowded with naturalists than nearby Tortuguero, but its lagoons and streams offer just as many opportunities to commune with nature, often in a less regimented way, at least at this point. Researchers estimate that the reserve has 700 different kinds of orchids.

LODGING **Tarponland Lodge** (private bath, heated water, ceiling fans, a/c; $25/person, including meals; 2710-2141, cell: 8818-9921), right on the airstrip, is the only Tico-owned place in Barra. The basic rooms are not bad, and they have a funky swimming pool. Fishing trips cost $295 per person. Owner Guillermo Cunningham Aguilar also does natural history trips to beautiful Caño Nueve.

The **Río Colorado Fishing Lodge** (private bath, hot water, ceiling fans, a/c, recreation room; $450-$610/person, including meals and a day of fishing; non-fishing rate, $120-$170/person; $2095 for six days and five nights, including three days of fishing, transportation, and licenses; 2232-8610, fax: 2231-5987, in North America: 800-243-9777; riocoloradolodge.com, tarpon@riocoloradolodge.com) was one of the original lodges that gave Barra del Colorado its name as a world-class fishing destination. The lodge is a survivor from the days before Costa Rica got fancy, when fishing places at the beach were simple and shabby but had a certain charm. As do most other lodges in Barra, it has a bar with a free happy hour, cable TV, and a ten-person hot tub with jacuzzi. The fishing fleet is outfitted with sonar fish finders, radios, and skilled guides.

The best Barra accommodations are at the **Silver King Lodge** (private bath, hot water, ceiling fans, a/c, pool, wi-fi; call for current package rates; phone/fax: 2711-0708, in the U.S.: 800-847-3474; silverkinglodge.net, hal@silverkinglodge. net). Each spacious room has two huge orthopedic mattresses, real closets, and a large bathroom with plenty of hot water. Rates include food, beverages, flights to and from lodge, guides, boats, and laundry service—a real boon in Barra's wet weather. The gourmet food is excellent and plentiful, and the staff is friendly.

The most memorable part of our stay there was the green-lighted hot tub with jacuzzi, followed by a very good massage—the perfect end to a cool, misty day of buzzing around Barra in speedboats. They also have a swimming pool with a waterfall. Their fishing fleet is as well-equipped as the rest of their operation. One of their guides took us on a heavenly jungle float at his farm.

A few minutes more down the waterway is the homey **Casamar** (private bath, hot water, ceiling fans, free bar, free laundry, VCR room; $585; four- to seven-day packages, $2500 to $4525; phone/fax: 2710-0136, in North America: 800-543-0282; casamarlodge.com, info@casamarlodge. com), with well-designed, comfortable duplex cabinas. Mango trees shade the grounds; howler monkeys provide the sound effects. For non-anglers, there are guided nature walks in the reserve.

GETTING THERE: Most of the lodges in this area have tour packages that include transportation from San José.

By Air: SANSA has daily flights to Barra (6 a.m.; $155 each way; 2290-4100; flysansa.com). Nature Air also flies daily at 6:15 a.m. ($160 round trip; 2299-6000; natureair.com).

The people of Barra del Colorado go in and out by way of Puerto Lindo and Cariari. Check for current schedules at tortuguerovillage.com. Don't go to Barra without reservations.

TALAMANCA REGION

When we first went to Talamanca in 1975, there was no road. We took a two-hour train ride from Limón to Penshurst on the Río Estrella, where we were met by a man in a dugout canoe who ferried us across the river to a rickety bus. Then it was another hour on a dirt road to Cahuita, a small village where horses grazed on the grassy paths between houses. That has all changed now that there are roads. Cahuita's grassy paths have become dusty streets, and the people of Talamanca find themselves thrust uneasily into the 21st century. During the 1980s and '90s, it seemed that independent farming and fishing were giving way to a tourism-based economy. But Talamancans have seen that tourism is a fickle industry: If you sell the farm to build cabins, and then bad weather or a negative news report cause tourism to dry up, you are left with nothing. So, although tourism is thriving in this area, Talamanca is also the center of intense collaboration between local farmers and conservation organizations to grow and market organic cacao, bananas, and medicinal plants. The Bribri and Cabecar indigenous people are an integral part of this effort, and are slowly opening up to tourism in a way that is harmonious with their values.

Naturalists and birders love this area because 88 percent of the land in Talamanca is protected: the pristine beaches of Cahuita National Park and Gandoca–Manzanillo Wildlife Refuge, the rainforests that the Bribri and Cabecar tribes have preserved for centuries, and the wild mountains of La Amistad International Park, covering the central part of southern Costa Rica and stretching into Panamá. Together, they form the **Talamanca-Caribe Biological Corridor**. To find out more about this experiment in conservation, sustainable agriculture, community development, and eco-tourism, contact the Biological Corridor office (2756-8136, 2756-8033; corredortalamanca.org, corrbiol@racsa.co.cr).

The beaches are uncrowded, and the weather, from February to April and in September and October especially, can be beautiful. Because of community efforts, five beaches in the area have been awarded the prestigious Bandera Azul Ecológica for cleanliness. They are Playas Puerto Vargas and Negra and Blanca in Cahuita and Playas Cocles, Chiquita, and Punta Uva south of Puerto Viejo.

At the Pacific beaches, the local culture takes second place to a tourist milieu created by highland Ticos and foreigners of all nationalities. Talamanca, however, is still terra incognita for most Ticos, so local culture remains intact. Life on the Atlantic coast is definitely laidback. Because of this, it is a great place to relax. There are a few places that offer air conditioning and hot water, but service everywhere is generally very slow. When going to a restaurant, bring along some snacks to eat while you're waiting, or dance with your waiter or waitress.

Single women should know that they could become targets for hopeful gringa-chasers, who see them as possible trust funds or at least a good time for a weekend. Most of these guys are gentlemanly enough to accept a flat "no." Also, if you look slightly bohemian you might be offered coke or crack, both of which are taking their toll on the local youth. Be aware that there are lots of narco-police on duty. Many tourists have gotten into trouble for their naivete. It is not a good idea to walk alone at night in solitary areas.

CAHUITA AND CAHUITA NATIONAL PARK

The town of **Cahuita** is a 45-minute drive or a one-hour bus ride down the coast from Limón. The Playa Blanca entrance to Cahuita National Park is two blocks south of the bus stop. The first 400 meters of this beach can be dangerous to swim in. The currents can be very strong and unpredictable. Green and red flags are placed along the beach to indicate which areas are safe for swimming. The waves are gentler near the point. When we were last there, the sea was as placid as a bathtub and many bathers were enjoying the water. Cahuita celebrates its *carnaval* the last ten days in November.

Cahuita National Park (open daily, 8 a.m. to 4 p.m.; 2755-0302) is the primary reason that Cahuita has become the tourist destination it is. The park was established to protect the coral reef that extends 500 meters out from Cahuita Point. This underwater garden is home to 123 species of tropical fish, as well as crabs, lobsters, shrimp, sea anemones, sponges, black and red sea urchins, and sea cucumbers. Try not to touch the coral while you explore its nooks and crannies.

Dissatisfied with the way the park was being administered in the early 1990s, the citizens of Cahuita decided to administer the park in conjunction with the government. Your donation at the Playa Blanca park entrance goes toward upkeep and security, the school, and other community projects. Cahuitans are proud of the way they have managed the park. The usual $10 park entrance fee is required at the Puerto Vargas entrance to the south.

To reach the reef, take a shady, scenic hike down the nature trail that starts from the Playa Blanca entrance to the national park. It runs between the beach and the jungle, and is a good place to see wildlife. Tanagers, iguanas, sloths, and white-faced and howler monkeys are common along the trails. The freshwater rivers and estuaries are good places to spot caimans and herons. It's four kilometers by trail from the park entrance to the point and another three kilometers to the Puerto Vargas area of the park, where the campgrounds are. We don't recommend camping in the park.

Cahuita Tours (2755-0000, fax: 2755-0082; cahuitatours.com, cahuita tours@yahoo.com) can take you to the reef. (If it has been raining and the water is cloudy, it's not worth going out.) They can also take you to Bocas del Toro, Tortuguero, Hitoy Cerere Biological Reserve, or the local indigenous reserves. They also rent snorkeling equipment and binoculars; lead scuba and sportfishing expeditions; connect you with Western Union; and rent bikes. They're on Cahuita's main street, half a block from the Guardia Rural.

North of Cahuita is long, beautiful **Black Beach** (Playa Negra). The water laps the grassy shore at high tide; low tide is the right time to swim or walk along the beach. Surfers like this black-sand beach, but currents can be strong, so be careful. At the entrance to Black Beach are the police station, post office, and surf and boogie board rentals.

RESTAURANTS   **Roberto's** (open Wednesday through Monday, 7 a.m. to 10 p.m.), on the main street at the entrance to town, is a good place for fresh fish. **Soda Tranquilo** (8844-7463) nearby, has reasonably priced Tico/Caribbean fare. **Restaurant and Bar Sambal** (open 5 p.m. to 2 a.m.; closed Tuesday; 8833-8553) on the road to Playa Negra across from the

MAG office, serves Thai/Tico fusion. **La Fé** (open daily, 7 a.m. to 10 p.m.; 8875-2054) is known for tasty coconut seafood. A few blocks down the main street, across from the Salón Comunal, the welcoming, candle-lit **ChaChaCha Restaurant** (dinner only; closed Monday; 8394-4153) features seafood, tenderloin, and Tex-Mex cooked with French-Canadian *savoir faire*. Try their Black Magic Woman dessert, made with chocolate chip ice cream, coffee liqueur, and cinnamon. One block to the right from the Guardia Rural, **Miss Edith** (open Monday through Saturday, 11 a.m. to 10 p.m.; Sunday, 1 p.m. to 9 p.m.; 2755-0248) cooks up a storm, ladling out tasty, down-home Caribbean food—jerk chicken, spicy curry, fish soup with coconut milk. In response to the requests of her customers, she now includes vegetarian fare in her menu, as well as native medicinal teas such as bay rum, *guanabana* leaves, *sorosi*, and lemongrass—good for what ails you.

At the beginning of Black Beach, **Café Bluspirit** (open by reservation only; 2755-0122), on the beach, is owned by a Cahuitan who specializes in Caribbean barbecue, lobster, and fish in pineapple sauce; his Italian wife specializes in pasta and exotic salads. They serve fresh piña coladas in a hollowed-out pineapple shell with a straw.

Sobre la Olas (open daily, noon to 10 p.m.; closed Tuesday; 2755-0109), also on the beach, has been recommended for great Italian seafood, but only when the Italian owner/chef is in the kitchen.

The road that intersects 100 meters later will take you to the main highway. At the intersection is the Swiss-owned **El Cactus** (open Tuesday through Sunday, 6 p.m. to 10 p.m.; 2755-0276), which specializes in pizza, pastas, and barbecue, has been recommended by many visitors. They will deliver to any hotel in the area.

At the next corner, one and a half kilometers from the bus stop, are **Chao's Paradise** (open daily, 2 p.m. to 10 p.m.; 2755-0421), famous for soup and Caribbean cuisine, and the **Reggae Bar**. Here a road will take you inland to several European-owned places: **Restaurant and Cabinas Brigitte** (private bath, heated water, fans; $30-$60, including breakfast; 2755-0053, fax: 2755-0450; brigittecahuita.com, brigittecahuita@hotmail.com) has cute little rooms and an internet café (open all day for breakfast and snacks). Bike rentals and laundry service are also available. Brigitte offers beach, mountain, and moonlight horseback rides, suitable for all, including children.

La Casa Creole (open Monday through Saturday, noon to 3 p.m., 6 p.m. to 9 p.m.; 2755-0104), part of the Magellan Inn, serves delicious French Creole and seafood dishes for dinner by candlelight.

LODGING   Many of the cabinas in town are mom-and-pop establishments. While not the most deluxe accommodations, they are clean, with friendly owners. Staying at one of these places is a good way to give direct support to a community trying to raise its standard of living while maintaining its cultural values. The first few places are right at the entrance to the national park.

National Park Hotel (private bath, hot water, ceiling fans; $40-$50; with a/c, satellite TV, kitchen, $50-$60; beachfront room, $80-$90; three-room suite, $140-$150; 8382-0139, fax: 2755-0244; cahuitanationalpark hotel.com, cgongaware@hotmail.com) is at the park entrance next to one of the most popular eateries in town, the **National Park Restaurant** (open daily, 11 a.m. to 9:30 p.m.). These nice rooms have the best views in town.

The **Sol y Mar Restaurant**, across the road, offers hearty breakfasts and local specialties, and also has spacious, clean cabinas (private bath, heated water, table fans; $30-$40; 2755-0237; cabsolymar@hotmail.com). The upstairs rooms have balconies with views. Recommended. They are

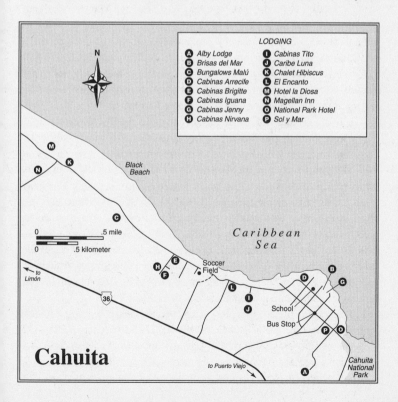

LODGING

- **A** Alby Lodge
- **B** Brisas del Mar
- **C** Bungalows Malú
- **D** Cabinas Arrecife
- **E** Cabinas Brigitte
- **F** Cabinas Iguana
- **G** Cabinas Jenny
- **H** Cabinas Nirvana
- **I** Cabinas Tito
- **J** Caribe Luna
- **K** Chalet Hibiscus
- **L** El Encanto
- **M** Hotel la Diosa
- **N** Magellan Inn
- **O** National Park Hotel
- **P** Sol y Mar

Black Beach

Caribbean Sea

0   .5 mile
0   .5 kilometer

Soccer Field

to Limón

36

School

Bus Stop

Cahuita

to Puerto Viejo

Cahuita National Park

owned by the family of Walter "Mr. Gavitt" Ferguson, Cahuita's famous calypso composer, whose songs often contain humorous commentary on the issues of the day. If you run into Mr. Gavitt at the restaurant, you might be able to buy one of his CDs.

The road to the left of the Sol y Mar is cluttered with cabinas of all kinds. But if you bear left, you will come to the Austrian-owned **Alby Lodge** (private bath, heated water, mosquito nets, table fans; $50-$60; phone/fax: 2755-0031; albylodge.com, alby_lodge@racsa.co.cr), individual thatch-roofed A-frames with hammocks on the porches in a peaceful, parklike setting. There are lots of nice details here that will make your stay more comfortable, like mosquito coils and broom and dustpan provided in each room, as well as communal kitchens. Bring a flashlight. Recommended.

Two blocks northwest of the little town park is a fun-loving French-Canadian place called **Cabinas Jenny** (private bath, heated water, ceiling fans, mosquito nets; $30-$40; 2755-0256; jennys@racsa.co.cr). Overlooking the sea, this breezy two-story building has hammocks and internet access.

One block north, also near the sea, is **Brisas del Mar** (private bath, heated water, wall fans; $20-$30; 2755-0011). The clean, simple rooms are in the backyard of an older local couple, with hammocks on the porches.

Cabinas Arrecife (private bath, heated water, wall fans; $30-$40; 2755-0081), around the corner from Miss Edith's, are shady and quiet. There's a small *soda*. The owner claims you can fish for snapper off the reef in front. Bikes and snorkels are available for rent.

There are cabinas and restaurants up and down the Black Beach road. If you stay at the lodgings that are farther along the road, you should either enjoy walking, rent a bike, or have a car. Remember that it's not advised to walk along this road at night. As you leave Cahuita and walk north on the Black Beach road, the first sign is for **Cabinas Tito** (private bath, heated water, table fans, some kitchens; $20-$30; 2755-0286). These are very clean little houses with porches run by friendly owners. The road can be muddy; check before driving in. Behind Tito's, the **Caribe Luna** (private bath, heated water, wall fan, some kitchens; $30-$50; house that sleeps five to eight, $130-$200; 2775-0131; caribeluna.com, caribeluna1@disimob. com) has new cabins that can be combined to sleep up to eight people comfortably in three bedrooms. Kitchens can be included.

El Encanto (private bath, hot water, ceiling fans, TV, pool; $70-$80, including breakfast; with kitchen, $90-$100; 2755-0113, fax: 2755-0432; elencantobedandbreakfast.com, info@elencantobedandbreakfast.com) is a comfortable bed and breakfast run by a friendly French-Canadian couple. Lovingly tended gardens, a quiet meditation room, an open-air yoga platform, and delicious breakfasts add to the charm of this enchanting place. They also rent a house that sleeps six to nine people ($190-$210).

Inland from Chao's Paradise is **Cabinas Iguana**. There are natural wood rooms (shared bath, heated water, mosquito nets, pool; $20-$40; private bath, bungalows $40-$70; with kitchen, $80-$100; 2755-0005, fax: 2755-0054; cabinas-iguana.com, iguanas@racsa.co.cr) with porches and two houses. A clean swimming pool with jacuzzi is in a secluded setting at the back of the property. The helpful Swiss owner rents bicycles and runs a multilingual book exchange in the office; he will pick you up at the bus stop.

Cabinas Nirvana (private bath, heated water, fans, mosquito nets, some kitchens, pool; $30-$40; four-person apartment, $60-$70; 2755-0110; nirvana99@racsa.co.cr), on the right at the end of the road, is a nice place for families, with kitchens, hammocks on the porch, and a pool.

Bungalows Malú (heated water, ceiling fans, refrigerators, a/c, pool, restaurant; $60-$70; phone/fax: 2755-0114; bungalowsmalu@gmail.com) are artistically designed cabinas that incorporate driftwood and stone into the furniture and have porches with overhangs and benches. The owner is an Italian artist whose paintings also decorate the rooms.

From here on, the establishments are farther apart.

The **Chalet Hibiscus** (private bath, hot water, wall fans, game room, volleyball court, pool; $40-$60; 2755-0021, fax: 2755-0015; hotels.co.cr/hibiscus.html, hibiscus@ice.co.cr) offers one- and two-bedroom bungalows, some with ocean views, and chalets that sleep six to ten ($100-$140).

An elegant option at the end of the road is the **Magellan Inn** (private bath, hot water, ceiling fans, some with a/c, restaurant, bar, pool, wi-fi; $80-$120, including breakfast; children under 10 free; phone/fax: 2755-0035; magellaninn.com, hotelmagellaninn@yahoo.com). The carpeted rooms are quiet, the Canadian hosts are attentive, and the garden setting is serene.

Hotel la Diosa (private bath, hot water, fans, pool, wi-fi; $70-$80; with a/c and jacuzzi, $80-$120; breakfast included; children over 6 half price; 2755-0055, in North America: 877-623-3198, fax: 2755-0321; hotelladiosa.net, reservation@hotelladiosa.net) is devoted to meditation and yoga. In the meditation room, you can listen to tapes by Osho and Eckhart Tolle. Located on a shady cove, it has easy beach access. It's just beyond the Magellan Inn, accessible via the first entrance road to Cahuita.

GETTING THERE: By Bus: Direct buses leave San José's Caribe terminal (Transportes MEPE, 2257-8129) for Cahuita at 6 a.m., 10 a.m., 12 p.m., 2 p.m. and 4 p.m. The ride takes three to four hours. Buses return to San José at 7, 8, 9:30 and 11:30 a.m., and 4:30 p.m. Buy tickets at the Sixaola ticket booth.

Text continued on page 225.

THE TALAMANCA ECOTOURISM NETWORK

Talamanca is unique in that it offers several community-based ecotourism options that can all be booked through ACTUAR, 2248-9470, actuarcostarica.com, info@actuarcostarica.com.

RURAL SLICE OF LIFE   A spacious, attractive inn with a great view, **Casa Calatéas** (private bath, screened windows, unheated water; $95, including all meals, lodging, and tours for two days and one night; lodging alone, $15-$30/person; 8361-1715, 2248-9470; casacalateas@yahoo.com) is located in Carbon Dos, in the hills above Cahuita. Carbon Dos is a pristine rural community where you can relax and get to know the people. You can visit Don Ramon's *cacao* farm and hike in their 60-hectare rainforest reserve. Doña Josefa prepares delicious meals for guests and will teach groups to make the sublime blend of coconut milk and seafood known as *rondón*. This is a great place to get a taste of rural life in a community that cares about nature. It's located 7 kilometers south of Cahuita and 4 kilometers uphill from the Comadre bus stop. Four-wheel drive required.

TROPICAL GARDENS AND PEACEFUL RIVER   **El Yüe** (private bath, screens, fan, heated water; $30-$40/person, including breakfast; 2756-8089, 2248-9470) was started by 13 women in 1995. They now have an organic banana and medicinal plant farm. Their attractive cabins are set in gardens of tropical flowers, great for photographers. The paths on the farm are flat and easy to navigate, leading to a tranquil bend in the river with a small, sandy beach. Sloths, iguanas, toucans, and frogs are easily observed there. It's located about two kilometers above the entrance to Samasati, in Hone Creek.

YORKÍN RIVER ADVENTURE   One of the most exciting adventures in the area is the trip in a motorized dugout canoe to the village of **Yorkín**. The trip up the Yorkín River, which borders Panama, goes against the current, and the boatmen strain every muscle in their bodies to maneuver the boat away from rocks with strong poles, using their life-long knowledge of the river. When we arrived at the village, a refreshing dip in the river readied us for a delicious lunch at the **Casa de las Mujeres**, featuring freshly harvested *palmito* and fiddle-head ferns served on a banana leaf.

In Bribrí mythology, the *cacao* tree was made from the sister of their creator, Sibu. The women showed us a fresh *cacao* pod, and let us suck the fruit around the seeds. They showed us how the seeds are dried and fermented, then toasted and ground to make the bitter hot chocolate favored by the Bribrí. Their organic banana and palm heart plantations are also cultivated in harmony with the forests that cover half of their territory.

After the presentation, Bernarda Morales, head of the Stibrawpa Women's Group, asked us about ourselves and what we thought of their project. One member of our group said that visiting Yorkín and seeing the conservation efforts there gave her hope for the future of the planet. The Stibrawpa Women's Group has built a new lodge (shared baths, unheated water), where the sound of the rushing river calms the mind. There is also covered space for camping. If you stay overnight, there will be time to visit a waterfall or hot springs. For this trip, just bring a small backpack, bathing suit, change of clothes, flashlight, and two plastic bags—one to put your backpack in while you are in the dugout, and one for your wet bathing suit. (One-day trip $124, including roundtrip transportation from your hotel to the river; $70, without transportation; two-day tour, $145; 8375-3372, 2248-9470).

Aventuras Naturales Yorkin (private and shared baths, overnight tour $70, not including transportation to and from the river; 2200-5211, 2290-8646; turismoruralcr.com) also offers tours to Yorkin. Their lodge has three bedrooms downstairs and a platform upstairs with mosquito net tents and sleeping mats.

BIRDS   Talamanca is one of the best places in the world to observe hawks, ospreys, eagles, and kites during their February-to-May and September-to-November migrations. It's easier to see the birds in the fall, when up to 300,000 migrating birds have been counted in one day, 3 million in a season. Researchers study migrant songbirds there, too. For volunteer opportunities, visit talamancaraptors.org.

Wa Ka Koneke Iro Soum (shared bath, cold water; half-day tour $20-$30/person; $50-$60/person including full-day tour, lodging, and meals; 8884-2671, 2248-9470) is a lodge for bird lovers. It takes about two hours to hike to the lodge and tower at a leisurely pace; you'll learn about the rainforest from expert guides Sebastian Hernandez and Lucas Angel (Spanish) and Alex Paez (English). At the beginning, you'll pass the home of Juanita Sanchez, dedicated preserver of Bribrí legends and lore. You can purchase her illustrated book, *Mi Libro de Historias Bribris.*

The spacious dining area of the Wa Ka Koneke (Earth Protectors) lodge is at canopy level, with a couple of hammocks to relax in. The six guest rooms are upstairs and the bathrooms with unheated showers are downstairs. Sebastian's wife and mother serve well-seasoned native food. The 30-foot birding tower is located at 700 feet above sea level, a ten-minute walk uphill from the lodge, with an almost 360-degree view of the Carbón range to the north, Puerto Viejo to the southwest, and the forested mountains of Panama's La Amistad International Park to the east.

There is a 75-foot waterfall another 45-minute walk beyond the tower, down a steep path with slippery rocks. A friend spotted a *jaguarundi* at the waterfall when we were there. Take a flashlight, sunscreen, insect repellent, hat, and lightweight windbreaker. You can also take half-day and full-day guided hikes in the reserve without staying at the lodge. *Note:* Only authorized guides are allowed to lead tours within the Keköldi Reserve.

TURTLES   The Blue Flag beach at **Gandoca** (leatherback nesting tour $28; $91 including transportation; 2248-9470; actuarcostarica.com), on the southern end of the Gandoca–Manzanillo Wildlife Refuge, is the nesting ground for four kinds of sea turtles. The leatherback season is between February 15 and June 15. Dedicated volunteers help protect the turtles, patrolling the beach at night and moving nests if they might be disturbed. Contact ANAI (2750-0020; anaicr.org, anaicr@racsa.co.cr) if you would like to be part of this effort. ANAI also accepts volunteers on its experimental farm in Gandoca. You either go on an evening tour of Gandoca, getting back to your hotel in Puerto Viejo around 12:30 a.m., or stay over with a local family.

From the bus terminal (2758-1572) 100 meters north of the *mercado* in Limón, buses leave for Cahuita (90 cents) hourly, starting at 6 a.m.

If you are staying at one of the hotels on Black Beach, you can get off at the first or second entrance to Cahuita and walk from there (not recommended at night). The first two entrances take you several hundred meters to the Black Beach road, and the last leads in half a kilometer to the center of town.

There are daily buses from Cahuita to Puerto Viejo and Manzanillo. Check with locals for schedules.

Interbus (2283-5573; interbusonline.com) has air-conditioned buses that leave San José daily for Puerto Viejo ($35; children half-price). They will drop you off at your hotel in Cahuita.

By Car: From Limón it's pretty much a straight shot down the coast. Turn south at the first intersection as you arrive in Limón; there's a Texaco plant at the intersection. It's an hour from there to Cahuita. Cahuita is about half a kilometer off the main highway; the first two marked entrances take you to the Black Beach area and the last takes you to the center of town.

AROUND CAHUITA   Ten kilometers north of Cahuita is the bird-filled **Estrella River delta**, with narrow waterways similar to those near Tortuguero. This area is a flyway for migratory birds and a haven for waterfowl like herons, kingfishers, *jacanas*, and *gallinules*. You can relax with a three-hour birding tour ($30, including breakfast), gliding silently through the canals by canoe. Luis and Judy Arroyo, proprietors of a comfortable bed and breakfast here, have worked hard to protect what is now a private wildlife sanctuary encompassing the delta. **Aviarios del Caribe Lodge** (private bath, hot water, table fans, bar, large souvenir shop; $90-$120, including breakfast; 2750-0775, fax: 2750-0725; slothrescue.org, slothsanctuary@gmail.com) has large rooms downstairs and a screened-in library/dining room upstairs. Their **Sloth Rescue Center** has become the main facility in the country that takes care of injured sloths and educates schoolchildren and visitors about the plight of these loveable creatures. You can meet resident sloths that are used to being with people. Volunteers welcome. Recommended.

Selva Bananito Lodge and Preserve (private bath, solar hot water, natural ventilation; $130-$150/person, including meals; 2253-8118, fax: 2280-0820; selvabananito.com, reservas@selvabananito.com), originally a farm owned by a German family, is now a wilderness preserve at the foot of the Talamanca mountains offering excellent birding and canopy explorations with rope and harness. There is no electricity, but each of the spacious, nicely designed cabins is provided with flashlights and gas lamps. The rooms have wide verandas with hammocks for stargazing at night. Candles grace the flower-adorned tables in the dining room to provide a warm and cheery atmosphere for people to exchange ideas while enjoying meals. Three-day, two-night packages are offered for $430-$450/person, including roundtrip transportation from San José.

GETTING THERE: The entrance to Selva Bananito is located 27 kilometers north of Cahuita and 20 kilometers south of Limón. You must have a four-wheel drive vehicle to get to Selva Bananito yourself. If you have a regular car, you can leave it at the village of Bananito, a few kilometers inland from the main road, and they will come and pick you up. The hour-long trip from the highway involves fording several rivers and can be confusing. They will send you a map before you set out.

Hitoy Cerere Biological Reserve (reservations: 2758-3170, 2754-2133; admission $6; food and lodging possible with prior reservation) is definitely off the beaten track. For hardy explorers, there are beautiful views, clear streams, waterfalls, and lots of birds to see, including some lowland species that are hard to find elsewhere due to deforestation. The nine-kilometer Espavel trail has the best primary-growth forest. You have to take a Valle de la Estrella bus from Limón to get to Hitoy Cerere. The bus winds its way into the banana plantations. Get off at Finca 12, the end of the line. Jeep-taxis there will take you ten kilometers farther and leave you at the entrance. They will return to pick you up at an agreed-upon time and can take you back to Cahuita if you want. Try to arrange a ride with park personnel for the cheapest rates. Samasati Nature Retreat (below) arranges tours to Hitoy Cerere. You will need four-wheel drive for the last 14 kilometers if you drive yourself.

Samasati (private bath; $120-$140/person, double or triple occupancy, including meals; 2756-8015, in the U.S.: 800-563-9643; samasati.com, samasati@samasati.com) is a private 250-acre rainforest reserve in the hills between Cahuita and Puerto Viejo. You can swing in a hammock on the porch and gaze out over acres of forest to the blue Caribbean. Rooms in the guesthouse (shared bath; $90-$100/person, including meals) do not have the views, but are cozy. Everyone shares the view and the congenial atmosphere at the open-air restaurant where delicious vegetarian meals are served buffet-style. An energetic movement meditation to music gets your energy flowing in the morning, and yoga classes, bodywork and hot tub will soothe you after a day on the nature trails. They also three rent three private and unique houses by the month, all with jungle and sea views. Samasati is located ten kilometers south of Cahuita, then 800 meters inland on a gravel road, then uphill about ten minutes (four-wheel drive needed—they will meet you below if you don't have a car). Take the Sixaola bus from the Caribe station at the north end of Calle Central in San José (2257-8129) and ask to be let off at the Samasati sign in Hone Creek.

PUERTO VIEJO

Puerto Viejo is 19 kilometers south of Cahuita on paved roads. A boom in tourism has taken place in the last few years and a plethora of restaurants and discos have opened in town; new hotels have sprung up along the road south to Manzanillo. Fortunately, the development is low-density, leaving most of the forest standing. The pristine beaches are some of the most beautiful in the country. Puerto Viejo can also be a base for excursion into the Bribri and Cabécar indigenous territories.

Puerto Viejo on the web: Almost all our favorite places in this area have websites on **greencoast.com**, which promotes "responsible and organic tourism." You can also get a lot of information and see many locations from the air at **puertoviejosatellite.com**.

Culture: The Puerto Viejo area is home to at least three different cultures: the English-speaking black farmers who grew cacao and coconut until a blight in the early 1980s ruined the cacao harvest; the indigenous people of the Bribri and Cabécar tribes who live in the foothills; and the Spanish-speaking immigrants who came to the area in search of land. Because the Talamanca region was so isolated from the rest of Costa Rica until recently, many of its cultural traditions are still alive.

Check with Miss Perlina to find out when she is going to bake journey cakes; then get there on time because a line forms and locals and keyed-in tourists snap them up quick.

Local ladies make bread with coconut milk, which is good with their homemade guava jam. You can buy ginger biscuits, pineapple rolls, plantain tarts, *patí* and *pan bon* from other bakers, just ask any resident. Doña Guillermina cooks family-style in her home in Playa Negra.

Services: To learn more about the area, plan to stop by the office of the **Talamancan Ecotourism and Conservation Association** (ATEC) (phone/fax: 2750-0191; greencoast.com/atec.htm, atecmail@racsa.co.cr), across from Soda Tamara in "downtown" Puerto Viejo. ATEC is the local communications center, with a public phone, fax machine, and internet access. They sell phone cards for the public phones in front of the office. They also have a spring water dispenser where you can fill your water bottles. It's usually open Monday through Saturday, 8 a.m. to 9 p.m., and Sunday, 10 a.m. to 6 p.m. There are several other internet cafés on the main street.

The **Girasol** will do your laundry. The **Banco de Costa Rica** is on the right as you enter town. Hotel Los Almendros will also change traveler's checks.

There is a **medical clinic and doctor** at the Hone Creek *cruce,* five kilometers from Puerto Viejo.

Taxi drivers hang out at the bus stop, and your hotel can always call a taxi for you.

Along the stretch of beach before you get to town is the entrance to the **Tropical Botanical Garden** (open Friday to Monday, 10 a.m. to 4 p.m.; 2750-0046; $5; $10 with guided tour; greencoast.com/garden.htm, crgarden@mac.com), where black pepper, tropical fruits, and spectacular flowering plants are grown. Colorful frogs live among the bromeliads. You can sample fruits and spices from all over the world, or take a walk on a rainforest loop trail. Wear sturdy shoes for the two-and-a-half-hour tour. To get there, walk or drive 500 meters inland from the sign on the beach road, then bear to your right, following the signs.

Canopy tours: **Terraventuras** ($40-$50; 2750-0750; terraventuras@hotmail.com) has an 18-platform canopy tour in Hone Creek, just north of Puerto Viejo. Some cables span forested gorges from over 100 feet in the air.

Water sports: The area outside the reef in Puerto Viejo has become famous in surfing lore as **La Salsa Brava**. Experienced surfers wear helmets to protect themselves from the sharp coral reef that produces the eight-foot wave. La Salsa Brava is definitely not for neophytes. If you're not a surfer, you can watch the action from some of the beachside restaurants in town. **Cariblanco Surf School** is run by certified instructor and former surf champ Topo Hernandez, who works with all levels and all ages. Cesar Campos makes surfboards and fixes broken ones at his workshop next to the Hotel Puerto Viejo, the main surfer hangout.

During the high season, surfers on their way out often sell their boards to new arrivals. This avoids the tremendous hassle of taking surfboards on the plane or bus. Some surfers hire a taxi or truck to haul their gear from Limón ($30-$40). This is cheaper than renting a car in San José, and most of the good waves are an easy walk from Puerto Viejo.

In March, September, and October the sea is calmer and better for snorkeling and swimming. But weather patterns are becoming less predictable with global warming. You can get a five-day forecast at wunderground.com. As in most good surfing areas, riptides are common; ask about conditions before swimming. If caught in a riptide, don't try to swim against it—swim parallel to the beach and the tide will eventually bring you back in. (See "Beach Safety" in Chapter Five.)

Sea kayaking and snorkeling rentals are available from **Reef Runner Divers** (2750-0480), **Aventuras Bravas** (8849-7600, 2750-2000), or **Juppy and Tino Adventure Tours** (2750-0621).

Bicycles: Other activities you can do on your own in the area include walking the beach trail between Puerto Viejo and Manzanillo, or renting a bike to pedal the flat, coastal road between these two towns. Being on a bicycle, even if you have rented a car, seems like the best method of locomotion in the area. A bike can provide just enough breeze to keep you cool. There are many bike rental places in town ($5 for a full day).

Note for bicyclists: Always lock your bike to a post or a tree. If your bike is stolen, the rental company will charge you about $80. If your bike has a problem, the rental companies will come and pick you up, or other bike rental companies along the road might be able to help you. Be sure to be back by dark—bikes don't have headlights. Beware of slippery gravel at the side of the road. Ride in single file. Stop before going onto the narrow bridges while trucks or cars pass.

Note for drivers: If you are driving, do so slowly: the bridges are unmarked and you can be on them before you know it. Also, locals ride without reflectors, becoming another hazard at night.

You can **rent motor scooters** at several places in town.

Insects: Whether you will be bothered by mosquitoes depends on the climatic conditions and the location and design of your hotel. Most hotels have screened windows or mosquito nets. Check when you make reservations. If there are mosquitoes, they will only bother you at night. Worse than mosquitoes are no-see-ums in the sand, which bite your ankles around dusk. And watch out for mean biting ants in the grass. Bring a good insect repellent (see Chapter Three).

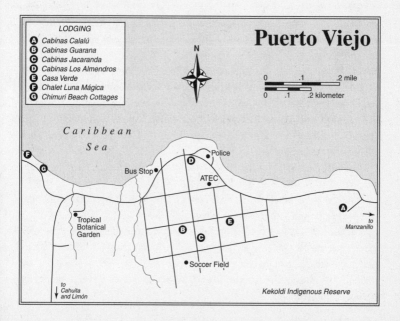

LODGING
- Ⓐ Cabinas Calalú
- Ⓑ Cabinas Guarana
- Ⓒ Cabinas Jacaranda
- Ⓓ Cabinas Los Almendros
- Ⓔ Casa Verde
- Ⓕ Chalet Luna Mágica
- Ⓖ Chimuri Beach Cottages

Puerto Viejo

N

0   .1   .2 mile
0   .1   .2 kilometer

Caribbean Sea

• Police
Bus Stop •
ATEC

• Tropical Botanical Garden

• Soccer Field

Ⓐ
→ to Manzanillo

to Cahuita and Limón

Kekoldi Indigenous Reserve

Water: Have bottled water in your hotel to brush your teeth with and drink at night. Many hotels supply drinking water for guests. Make sure the bottle is filled before you settle in.

Art: Across the street from Cabinas Guarana, **Galería Luluberlú** (open 10 a.m. to 9 p.m.; 2750-0394) showcases the intricate, beautiful work of prolific French mosaic artist, Luluberlú. She also exhibits high-quality indigenous art and crafts. Recommended.

RESTAURANTS If you want a taste of the culture, stop by **Miss Sam's** (2750-0108) front porch restaurant, two blocks inland from the main street. Her fluffy rice and beans are served with a delicious cabbage *curtido* at rock-bottom prices. Recommended.

Soda Isma (open daily, 8 a.m. to 9 p.m.; 750-0579) on the main street serves rice and beans, whole fish in Caribbean sauce, and *rondon*, a flavorful fish stew made with coconut milk (order in advance). **Jammin' Jerk and Juice Joint** (open Monday to Wednesday, 8 a.m. to 8 p.m.; Thursday to Sunday, 9 a.m. to 9 p.m.; 8826-4332), located across the street from the new Catholic Church, cooks their jerk chicken and fish in a Jamaican-style smoker. Vegetarians will enjoy their salads with homemade dressings, Middle Eastern vegetable dips, and many other meatless dishes. They also serve a wide variety of freshly made fruit and vegetable juices, and fresh fruit smoothies and sorbets.

Peace and Love (open daily, 6:30 a.m. to 6:30 p.m.; 2750-0293), near the bus stop, serves homemade breads, pastas and pastries. **Bread and Chocolate** (2750-0723) serves waffles, egg and cheese sandwiches with homefried potatoes, and French-pressed coffee, but their real claim to fame are their delectable chocolate truffles. The **PanPay Bakery** (2750-0081) is also popular for breakfast, serving *tortilla espanola* and making baguette sandwiches to go. They show movies at night. **Stanford's Restaurant and Disco El Caribe** (open daily, 7 p.m. to midnight; 2750-0608) has always been the place to go for fresh Caribbean seafood. Their disco jumps most nights.

Sushito, across from the Hotel Guarana, and the **Lotus Garden,** at the far side of town, are both good for sushi.

Our favorite place to eat in Puerto Viejo is **El Loco Natural** (open Thursday through Tuesday from 6 p.m.; 2750-0263). If you are tired of *comida típica* and have a hankering for something truly exotic, try their artistically presented Guayanese fusion of East Indian and Caribbean flavors, accompanied by tropical coconut concoctions. With *bossa nova* on the sound system and live music after 8:30 p.m., this is a very happening scene. Recommended.

It is just south of **Restaurant Elena Brown** (open daily, 11:30 a.m. to 10:30 p.m.; 8841-4223) known for fajitas, seafood, and chicken curry. Farther south is **Patagonia,** the pricey Argentine steakhouse.

Travelers craving Italian cuisine will have no problem satisfying their taste buds in Puerto Viejo. **Amimodo** (open Friday through Wednesday, noon to 10 p.m.; 2750-0257), just south of town, offers authentic pastas and Italian-style seafood like lobster ravioli, gracefully served in their lovely open-air restaurant. **Ristorante Café Viejo** (2750-0817), on the main street, has tasty Italian food. See next section for more Italian. There is a **farmer's market** behind the cultural center on Saturday mornings.

LODGING   If you make a left at Pulpería Violeta instead of veering right to Puerto Viejo, you'll drive along an intensely black beach. After about 300 meters you'll come to the following beach establishments, which we recommend for their simplicity, tranquility, reasonable rates, and proximity to the sea. **Chimuri Beach Cottages** (private bath, heated water, kitchens, fans, mosquito nets, wi-fi; $40-$60, minimum two-night stay; $240-$330/week; phone/fax: 2750-0119; greencoast.com/chimuribeach.htm, chimuri@ice.co.cr) are simple, campesino houses with porches and hammocks. Ask about their jungle cabins on the edge of the Kekoldi Reserve.

Just down the road is **Chalet Luna Mágica,** (hot water, ceiling fans, mosquito nets, water filter, washer/dryer, cable TV, phone, wi-fi; $140-$150/two people; $800/week; $2500/month; 2750-0212, in North America: 888-877-1698; magicmooncr.com, info@magicmooncr.com), a three-bedroom beach house that sleeps up to six and a one-bedroom beach bungalow surrounded by gardens ($80/day, $500/week, $1500/month).

The next cabinas are in Puerto Viejo proper. There are many others, but these are our favorites in town. See the next section for beach cabins south of Puerto Viejo.

The Italian-owned **Cabinas Guarana** (private bath, heated water, ceiling fans, wi-fi; $30-$60; 2750-0244; hotelguarana.com, guarana@hotel guarana.com), across from Luluberlu, have light, pleasantly decorated rooms with hammocks around a garden courtyard, and a treehouse for admiring the sunset. The dense garden gives a sense of privacy to each room. There is a shared kitchen for guests. Recommended.

The locally owned **Cabinas Los Almendros** (private bath, heated water; $60-$70; with refrigerator, a/c, TV, $70-$80; children under 5 free; 2750-0246, fax: 2750-0728; flchwg@racsa.co.cr) are well run and have a money-changing service.

Nicely furnished and decorated, the **Cabinas Jacaranda** (shared or private bath, heated or cold water, kitchen use, table fans, mosquito nets; $30-

$50; phone/fax: 2750-0069; cabinasjacaranda.net, veragarden@yahoo.ca) have bright mosaic walkways and a garden gazebo.

One of our favorite places in town is the Swiss/Tica-owned **Casa Verde** (heated water, ceiling fans, mosquito nets, pool; with shared bath, $30-$60; with private bath, refrigerator, cable TV, $50-$80; 2750-0015, fax: 2750-0047; cabinascasaverde.com, info@casaverde.com), famous for its very clean and nicely decorated rooms. There is a massage *rancho*, or you can venture behind the cabins to see the poisonous-frog collection. Laundry service, secure parking, money exchange, and a coffee shop are among the many services offered at the Casa Verde. Recommended.

As you leave town, set back from the road on the right, is **Cabinas Calalú** (private bath, hot water, ceiling fans, pool, mosquito nets, some with kitchens; $30-$50, including breakfast; 2750-0042; bungalowscalalu.com). The thatch-roofed cabins are surrounded by trees. Guests can eat breakfast overlooking the **butterfly garden** (open daily, 8 a.m. to 4 p.m.; $5 for non-guests) or at the pool.

GETTING THERE: By Bus: MEPE (Caribe terminal, at the north end of Calle Central; 2257-8129, 2758-1572) runs buses daily between San José and Puerto Viejo (at 6 a.m. and every two hours until 4 p.m.; $7). The ride is about four hours. Buy tickets at the Sixaola booth.

A bus leaves Puerto Viejo for Manzanillo at 7:30 a.m., 11:30 a.m. and 4 p.m.

From the Talamanca bus stop in Limón (100 meters north of the *mercado*, 2758-1572), a bus leaves for Puerto Viejo hourly starting at 5 a.m. ($2). You can also take the Limón–Manzanillo bus (6 a.m., 10 a.m., 2:30 p.m.; $2.85), which passes through Puerto Viejo and follows the coastal road south of Puerto Viejo through Cocles and Punta Uva. Get there early to buy a ticket. You can check these schedules at thebusschedule.com.

Interbus (2283-5573; interbusonline.com) has air-conditioned buses that leave San José daily for Puerto Viejo ($39). They will drop you off at your hotel. They will also take you to Puerto Viejo from Siquirres, La Fortuna, and Sarapiquí.

By Car: From San José, the trip to Puerto Viejo takes three and a half to four hours, depending on the number of trucks on the highway to Limón. From Limón, it is about an hour to an hour and a half to Puerto Viejo. When you reach Hone Creek there is a *cruce*, where the road curves to the right toward Bribrí and the Panama border, and the road straight ahead continues six kilometers to Puerto Viejo.

Note: Cars and buses are often stopped by the Guardia Rural and checked for Panamanian contraband as they leave Talamanca, so be sure to carry your passport and have all immigration documents in order.

By Air: Nature Air (natureair.com) has flights to Limón. Vans from the Limón airport to Puerto Viejo cost $10/person.

BEACHES SOUTH OF PUERTO VIEJO

Lovely hotels and *cabinas* are scattered all along the 15-kilometer road be-tween Puerto Viejo and Manzanillo. Most of them are within the Gandoca–Manzanillo Wildlife Refuge. We list them in appearance north to south. Most of them are clustered around **Punta Cocles** (four kilometers from Puerto Viejo), **Playa Chiquita** (five kilometers from Puerto Viejo), and **Punta Uva** (seven kilometers from Puerto Viejo). Punta Uva is gorgeous and has the best swimming. All of these shady beaches, especially Playa Cocles, have strong currents; pay attention to signs on the beach directing you to the most secure areas (November through February are the most dangerous months). There is a lifeguard at Cocles. All three have won the coveted Bandera Azul Ecológica award for cleanliness of water and sand. These are the kind of places to stay if you're looking for tranquility and less contact with town (and disco) life than you would get in Puerto Viejo. Since there are *pulperías* and restaurants dotting the coast, you won't have to return to Puerto Viejo for meals. Four buses a day travel this road.

The Playa Chiquita Lodge hosts the **Music Festival of the South Caribbean Coast**, several weekends of concerts by Costa Rica's most lively jazz, calypso, salsa, and reggae musicians. There's also poetry, cinema, dance, and theater presentations, and workshops on mask-making, Afro-Caribbean dance, and Latin percussion. Definitely worth catching if you're in the area in March and April. For more information, call Wanda Paterson (2750-0062; playachiquitalodge.com, info@playachiquitalodge. com).

Celia's Hair Braiding in Punta Cocles will give you beaded braids, cornrows, or dreadlocks. **Echo Books**, (open Friday to Tuesday, 11 a.m. to 6 p.m.; 8841-1565), located down a path 25 meters before Cabinas el Tesoro in Playa Cocles, offers a great selection of new and used books as well as handcrafted chocolates.

RESTAURANTS **Qué Rico Papito!** (open 2 p.m. to 10 p.m.; closed Sun-day; 2750-0704), the new restaurant and bar at Hotel La Costa De Papito with a delightfully tropical atmosphere, serves some of its delicious, creative cui-sine in a biodegradable manner, like *ceviche* inside hollowed out peppers or oranges. The menu ranges from Thai curry to Peruvian *causa*. Recommended.

There is an organic **farmer's market** (every Saturday at 10 a.m. at the corner of Shawandha Lodge) that features homemade cheeses and baked goods. **Danny's Pirriplí Market** in Playa Cocles carries everything from freshly baked bread to caviar. The best restaurant in the area is **La Pecora Nera** (2750-0490), where the enthusiastic owner and chef, Ilario Giannoni, rhapsodizes about what he can make for you, how he will do it, and which wine you should choose. You can watch his every move through a window that looks into the kitchen, easily visible from all the tables. Pricey. Now he has built a less expensive *trattoria* in front of the Pecora Nera called the **Gatta Ci Cova** (2750-0730) serving pizza, pasta, and lasagna.

The Café Rio Negro at the bridge before the plaza near in Cocles has wi-fi, as does **Miss Holly's Deli Café** (open 8 a.m. to 3 p.m.; closed Tuesday), at the Aguas Claras, halfway to Punta Uva, known for gourmet coffee and Key lime pie.

Selvin's, at Punta Uva, is the place to go for authentic Caribbean cooking (including fresh lobster) in a relaxed, friendly atmosphere.

LODGING   The Italian-owned **Escape Caribeño** (private bath, heated water, ceiling fans, refrigerators, some a/c, TV, mosquito nets, wi-fi; $60-$80; phone/fax: 2750-0103; escapecaribeno.com, escapec@racsa.co.cr) has tidy bungalows with porches and hammocks set in a garden across the road from the beach, and beach cabins designed to catch the sea breezes. All manner of beautiful birds flock to the bird feeders outside their welcoming breakfast *rancho*, and they have beautiful aquariums of native fresh water and salt water tropical fish. Recommended.

Rocking J's (shared or private bath, solar hot water, phone/fax: 2750-0657; rockingjs.com, jj@rockingjs.com), right on the beach, seems to be the place to stay for young people, with your choice of dorms, wall-to-wall rows of tents, or hammocks all under $7/person, or $20-$60 for private rooms and suites. Rocking J's has taken Caribbean mosaics to the mind-blowing max, with every square inch of the huge tent-lounge-bar-tree-house-internet café-communal kitchen complex covered with someone's love affair with broken tiles. A concierge is there to plan tours and transportation for J's guests.

The beachfront **Apartments Agapi** (private bath, hot water, fans, mosquito nets, hammocks, kitchens, wi-fi; rooms, $40-$100; apartments, $70-$120; 2750-0446, fax: 2750-0418; agapisite.com, hotelagapl@hotmail.com), 800 meters south of town, are a good value. Some rooms have balconies with a nice view of the water.

Italian-owned **Cariblue** (private bath, heated water, ceiling fans, mosquito nets, game room, pool, jacuzzi, wi-fi; $110-$130, including breakfast; with kitchen and room for seven, $250-$260; 2750-0035, fax: 2750-0057; cariblue.com, cariblue@racsa.co.cr), is set back from the road in a tranquil, park-like setting. The individual wooden bungalows sleep up to six, and are private and polished, with nice touches like hammocks on the porches and creative mosaics in the bathrooms. They have a great restaurant featuring Italian specialties and seafood. Recommended.

Azania Bungalows (private bath, heated water, restaurant/bar, pool; $80-$100, including breakfast; children under 10 $7; 2750-0540, fax: 2750-0371; azania-costarica.com, info@azania-costarica.com) are two-story, thatched-roof bungalows set in a jungly garden. The high roof, cross ventilation, and screened windows keep them cool and fresh inside, and there are many nice decorative touches, including softly lit sauna style bathrooms, and hammocks on the private decks. Their restaurant features Argentinean cuisine, combined with local flavors. Their free-form pool has a beach-like shore.

La Costa de Papito (private bath, hot water, ceiling fans, internet, bar, restaurant; $60-$90; kids free; 2750-0080; lacostadepapito.com, info@la costadepapito.com), set in a five-acre garden, offers individual wood bungalows with good mattresses. Their spacious porches with hammocks, surrounded by lush greenery, and their open-air bar/restaurant, **Qué Rico Papito**, make this a true tropical paradise. Bike, snorkel, and surf equipment rentals are available. Their **Pure Jungle Spa** (2750-0536; purejunglespa.com) is housed in a beautifully hand-crafted building. Local and international massage therapists give facials, massages, and foot treatments with freshly made pineapple, papaya, coconut, and cocoa butter concoctions. They sell natural beauty products and Bribrí chocolate bars. Recommended.

Villas del Caribe (private bath, hot water, fans, some a/c, some kitchens, restaurant; $90-$120, including breakfast; 2233-2200, 2750-0202, fax: 2750-0203; villasdelcaribe.com) are spacious and beautifully decorated beachfront rooms with terraces, hammocks and ocean views.

Aguas Claras (private bath, hot water, ceiling fans, kitchens; $70-$220/day; $350-$1100/week; 2750-0131, fax: 2750-0368; aguasclaras-cr.com, aguasclaras@racsa.co.cr) has cute gingerbread cottages of different sizes in a parklike garden. These are some of the most charming accommodations at the beach, with open-air kitchens and living rooms built in a colorful Caribbean style. Good for families or groups. The path to the beach is through an arbor of ancient trees; a shallow tide pool forms there at low tide. Recommended.

Six kilometers south of Puerto Viejo is the German/Tica-owned **Playa Chiquita Lodge** (private bath, solar hot water, ceiling fans, wi-fi; $60-$70, including breakfast; children under 8 free; 2750-0062, 2750-0408; play-achiquitalodge.com, info@playachiquitalodge.com), which organizes the yearly Music Festival of the South Caribbean Coast. The connected cabins are nicely designed and are shaded by exuberant vegetation. The seemingly secluded beach, down a path from the rooms, has three tide pools where kids can enjoy themselves at low tide.

Across the road, the elegant, tranquil **Shawandha Lodge** (private bath, heated water, fans, pool; $100-$130, including breakfast; 2750-0018, fax: 2750-0037; shawandhalodge.com, info@shawandhalodge.com) comprises several tasteful thatch-roofed A-frames set in the forest. Each large, half-moon bathroom is adorned with a different fanciful tile mosaic. A 200-meter path leads directly to Playa Chiquita. Their spacious, open-air restaurant features French-tropical cuisine.

At the intersection, **CJ Marketplace** is a well-stocked grocery store, next to a **laundry**. Just north is **La Casa del Pan** (open Wednesday through Monday, 8 a.m. to 9 p.m.; 8879-1548), a cute little open-air place for breakfast through dinner, with lots of homemade baked goods. Just south is **Vida Sana**, with ice cream and natural treats. **Itaitá Villas**, near Punta Uva (private bath, hot water, fans, internet; $50-$60; with kitchen, $60-$100; including breakfast; children under 8 free; 2750-0414, 2229-0950, 2750-2029; costaricaitaitavillas.com, reservations@costaricaitaita villas.com), are two-room cabins with porches and Caribbean-style gingerbread details.

About one kilometer farther down the road on the left is **Selvin's Restaurant** (closed Monday and Tuesday during peak season; open weekends only during the low season; 2750-0664) one of the best in the area, specializing in Caribbean in fish and lobster dinners. They serve the local dish of rice and beans on weekends. Selvin's is a short walk from the most beautiful part of the beach at Punta Uva. Recommended.

Casa Viva (private bath, hot water, fans, $50-$60; one- and two-bedroom houses, $90-$130/day, $560-$800/week; 2750-0089; puntauva.net, puntauva@racsa.co.cr) is right on the best part of Punta Uva beach. These lovely, handcrafted, two-bedroom houses have wide verandahs strung with hammocks, fully equipped kitchens, and are placed well apart from each other amidst beautiful tropical gardens. Recommended.

Almonds and Corals Lodge (private bath, hot water, mosquito netting, jacuzzi, meeting room; $200-$350/person, including two meals; children under 5 free; 2271-3000, fax: 2759-9056; almondsandcorals.com, info@almondsandcorals.com) is right in the middle of the Gandoca–Manzanillo Wildlife Refuge (see below), Their 24 bungalows reside under giant trees throughout the mostly intact jungle. Their open air restaurant and bar (with pool table) is situated along the boardwalk that connects the bungalows and the beach. The entrance is a few hundred yards south of Punta Uva.

MANZANILLO

Seven kilometers beyond Punta Uva is the small fishing village of Manzanillo. The **Gandoca–Manzanillo Wildlife Refuge** protects a 9-kilometer beach where four species of turtles lay their eggs, including the giant *baula* (leather-back). The turtles' main nesting season is February 15 through June 15.

Just offshore and within easy snorkeling distance, the varied corals of the **Manzanillo reef** look like brains, stars, lettuce, cacti, flowers, and cups. Their tunnels, channels, nooks, and crannies are home to sponges, lobsters, eels, sea stars, and amazing tropical fish. The many beaches of the area are lined with coconut palms. Monkeys, sloths, parrots, butterflies, frogs, and wild felines like jaguars live in the lush forest of the refuge.

In the southern part of the refuge, the Gandoca River estuary is a nursery for tarpon; manatees, crocodiles, and caimans are also seen there. Dolphins, as well as pygmy, sperm, and pilot whales, are often present offshore.

Get information about the refuge and pay the $6 admission fee at the turquoise-and-white gingerbread-style MINAE headquarters. Always go with a guide when you explore the jungle here.

At the entrance to Manzanillo, on the left, you'll see the bright green office of **Guías MANT** (2759-9064), part of the Talamanca Ecotourism Network. They will arrange dolphin watching, medicinal-herb walks, and bird- or insect-watching trips on foot or horseback, depending on your interests.

Aquamor (2759-9012; greencoast.com/aquamor.htm, aquamor1@racsa.co.cr) rents kayaks and snorkeling equipment, and offers inexpensive kayak tours, scuba diving, and PADI certification. The owners, siblings Greg, Katrina, and Shawn Larkin, are the founders of the **Costa Cetacea Institute**

Puerto Viejo–Manzanillo Road

0   1   2 miles
0' 1   2 kilometers

Puerto Viejo
Cabinas el Tesoro

Punta Cocles

Playa Chiquita   Punta Uva

Punta Manzanillo

Manzanillo

Gandoca–
Manzanillo
Wildlife
Refuge

LODGING

- Ⓐ Aguas Claras
- Ⓑ Almendros y Corales Lodge Tent Camp
- Ⓒ Apartments Agapi
- Ⓓ Azania Bungalows
- Ⓔ Cabinas Something Different
- Ⓕ Cariblue
- Ⓖ Casa Viva
- Ⓗ Congo-Bongo
- Ⓘ Dolphin Lodge/Coral Reef Lodge
- Ⓙ Escape Caribeño
- Ⓚ Itaitá Villas
- Ⓛ La Costa de Papito
- Ⓜ Playa Chiquita Lodge
- Ⓝ Rocking J's
- Ⓞ Selvin's Cabinas
- Ⓟ Shawandha Lodge
- Ⓠ Villas del Caribe

N

LEGEND
------- Unpaved road
········ Trail

which works with MINAE to protect dolphins. They are trying to get the refuge extended to include the newly mapped reef and dolphin area offshore. Their love and respect for dolphins is reflected in their dolphin tour: these wonderful creatures are not chased, but allowed to approach boats out of their own curiosity. Aquamor has also set up buoys in shallow water that you can tie your kayak to so that you can explore the reefs as long as you want. They welcome committed **volunteers**, especially those experienced with boats.

Locals gather in **Maxi's Bar** to play dominos, and tourists flock there for the Caribbean cuisine in the breezy second-floor restaurant (2759-9086). There is a row of clean, hotel-like cabins (private bath, heated water; $30-$40) next to the restaurant.

The Dutch-owned **Congo-Bongo** (private bath, hot water, screens, kitchens; $70-$80/day; $450/week; $1350/month; 2759-9016; congo-bongo.com, info@congo-bongo.com) has five well-made, widely separated houses in the jungle, 200 meters from the beach. Relaxed and quiet, they make for a real rainforest experience. You'll see the entrance on the left, about a kilometer before you get to Manzanillo.

Cabinas Something Different (private bath, hot water, fans, a/c, refrigerator, direct TV; $30-$50; 2759-9014), are a good value and very neat and clean.

The **Talamanca Dolphin Foundation** (2759-9115, 2759-0612; dolphin link.org, info@dolphinlink.org) works to further dolphin research and sustainable community development in Manzanillo. They have two comfortable houses on a small, shady beach 200 meters beyond the end of the road. The four-bedroom **Dolphin Lodge** sleeps eight and the three-bedroom **Coral Reef Lodge** sleeps four ($1200-$1400/week; bozemancottage.com). It is rare to find such nicely situated beach houses.

Between Manzanillo and Gandoca, on lovely Monkey Point, **Punta Mona** (solar heat and electricity; wi-fi; $40, including meals, kayaks and snorkeling equipment; puntamona.org, puntamonainfo@gmail.com) is a 100-acre organic farm and educational retreat dedicated to setting an example of sustainable living through permaculture. They host school and retreat groups (up to 40 people) for a day or several weeks, so visitors can get the experience of living a "simple unplugged life" ($400/month for room and board). It's accessible by a 1.5-hour hike five kilometers south of Manzanillo (ask at Aquamor or Maxi's for someone to walk you in; $20/person), or by arranging for a boat to take you there in 15 minutes. You can meet their captain, Bako, at Maxi's ($15/person).

GETTING THERE: By Bus: Buses leave Limón at 6 a.m., 10:30 a.m. 3 p.m. and 5 p.m., passing through Puerto Viejo at 7:30 a.m., noon and 3:30 p.m. to continue on to Manzanillo (check exact times at thebusschedule.com). They can drop you off at your hotel of choice. Buses leave Manzanillo for Puerto Viejo and continue to Limón at 5 a.m., 8:15 a.m., 12:45 p.m. and 5p.m., and will pick you up if you wait on the road outside your hotel.

By Car: If driving, pay special attention to the bridges along the road. Some are on curves, some are in great need of repair, all are narrow.

NINE

The Northern Zone

Costa Rica's Northern Zone extends from the Atlantic plains in the east to the San Juan River on the Nicaraguan border in the north, and to Lake Arenal and the Tilarán mountain range and Monteverde in the west. More and more visitors include a visit to the Northern Zone's towering rainforests and the spectacular Arenal volcano in their itinerary.

SARAPIQUÍ

The quickest way to get to Sarapiquí is through Braulio Carrillo National Park. Founded in 1978, it represented a compromise between ecology and development. Environmentalists were concerned that the opening of a highway between San José and Guápiles would result in the ecological disasters that accompanied the opening of other roads in Costa Rica: indiscriminate colonization and deforestation. The government agreed to make 80,000 acres of virgin forest surrounding the highway into a national park. The Guápiles Highway, opened in 1987, is an education in itself for all the motorists who pass through it on their way to Sarapiquí or the Atlantic coast— mountains of untouched rainforest as far as the eye can see. And just 50 years ago, most of Costa Rica looked like that!

On your way to Puerto Viejo de Sarapiquí, as you descend from Braulio Carrillo, you'll see a sign on your right for the **Rain Forest Aerial Tram** (open daily from 6:30 a.m. to 3:30 p.m.; $55; half price for children and students with ID; 2257-5961, fax: 2257-6053, in the U.S.: 866-759-8726; rfat.com, info.cr@rfat.com; make reservations two days in advance. Children under 5 are not allowed on tram). Six-person gondolas, hanging from a 1.3-kilometer cable, glide silently through the forest at heights ranging from three feet off the ground to mid-canopy to 120 feet. The ride lasts 80 minutes. This sedate guided tour is an informative and easy introduction for those short on time or endurance and who don't need the thrills of the ziplines and hanging bridges. The Aerial Tram has attractive cabins (private bath, hot water; $110/person, children $90/person, including meals and tram ride) to stay in. They also make special arrangements for disabled access.

Rancho Roberto (open daily, 7 a.m. to 10 p.m.), at the turnoff to Sarapiquí, is a nice place to stop for a meal. Their ample menu includes delicious grilled tilapia and good *bocas*.

LAS HORQUETAS Back when people were first learning of the destruction of rainforests worldwide but didn't know what to do about it, Amos Bien, an ecologist and former manager of La Selva, had a brilliant idea. He decided that the best way to convince people not to cut down rainforests was to demonstrate that it was economically viable to conserve them through tourism and sound land management. The result of Amos Bien's efforts is the now-famous Rara Avis, a 1500-acre forest reserve near the small village of Las Horquetas. Through its excellent tours, visitors get a short course in how the rainforest works, why it is being cut down, and how it can be restored—without feeling that they have been in school.

Various accommodations are available at **Rara Avis** (2764-1111, fax: 2764-1114; rara-avis.com, raraavis@racsa.co.cr), Costa Rica's original rainforest lodge. The comfortable, eight-room **Waterfall Lodge** and the more secluded **River Edge Cabin** (private bath, hot water; $70-$90/person, double occupancy) are both close to a gorgeous three-tiered waterfall. The River Edge Cabin is especially designed for birdwatchers. Their *casitas* (shared bath, cold water; $50/person, double occupancy) are more rustic but still comfortable. Prices include three hearty meals, guided tours, and transportation from Las Horquetas. Discounts for children, (ages 4 to 12 half price), students, hostel card-holders, and researchers are available.

Because transportation to Rara Avis is difficult, you need to make reservations. Transport is by a tractor-pulled *chapulín* or horse. (Don't attempt this adventure if you have a bad back.) The trip takes three hours.

GETTING THERE: By Bus: Take the 7 a.m. Río Frío bus from the Terminal Caribe in San José. A car from Rara Avis will meet you at the bus.

By Car: Las Horquetas can be approached from San José, Arenal volcano, or Limón. See details at rara-avis.com.

Just outside the town of Horquetas is the 50-room **Sueño Azul Resort** (private bath, hot water, ceiling fans, a/c, pool, hot tub; $90-$120; children 11 and under free; 2764-1000, fax: 2764-1049; www.suenoazulresort.com, info@suenoazulresort.com) winter headquarters for the Omega Institute's Holistic Studies program. Located on a 1200-acre ranch and forest reserve with lakes and lush gardens, this peaceful place has a yoga studio and spa offering a variety of healing treatments. There is also a 1600-square-foot, air-conditioned conference center. Each room has a private terrace overlooking a lake, and there are nice decorative touches reflecting the Costa Rican and Nicaraguan heritage of the owners. The food is well-prepared and always includes a vegetarian entrée.

Three kilometers by horse, jeep, or on foot from the lodge is a veritable wonderland of nature activities. Among them are a **zipline** that's good for beginners, **tubing** on the river, multiple waterfall pools, a huge spring-fed swimming pool, and a beautiful **butterfly garden**. You can experience all this in a one-day tour from San José ($79, including transportation and lunch, half price for children under 11). Sueño Azul is a bit difficult to find on your own, and involves driving across two hanging bridges. The lodge provides transport. If you have your own car, ask for directions in Las Horquetas. Recommended.

PUERTO VIEJO DE SARAPIQUÍ   Puerto Viejo de Sarapiquí is the major town in the region, and was Costa Rica's main port in colonial times. Boats embarked from here to cruise down the wide Río Sarapiquí, north to the Río San Juan, which forms Costa Rica's border with Nicaragua, and from there to the Atlantic. During the 1980s, the years of Contra activity in northern Costa Rica, the area was closed to tourists. During the late 1980s, this zone was the scene of large-scale deforestation. Primary forest gave way to orange, banana, and pineapple plantations. At first, the *almendro* tree (or almond tree, a primary food source for the endangered great green macaw, or *lapa verde* in Spanish) was left standing in the fields because its wood was too hard to cut. But as logging technology progressed during the 1990s, the *almendros* began to fall, and the *lapa verde* began to disappear.

The large rainforest reserves that made Sarapiquí famous, Rara Avis, Selva Verde, La Selva and Tirimbina, became islands in a sea of monoculture agribusiness. The area's population increased by 300 percent in 20 years, as people came to work on the plantations. Seeing the many houses along the road, you might wonder where the famous jungles are. They are there, behind the houses, and the people in those small unattractive houses are the key to the area's future.

Now some of the areas most famous reserves are teaming up with local landowners and community organizations to form the San Juan-La Salva Biological Corridor (see Innovative Communities box). Hopefully, due to

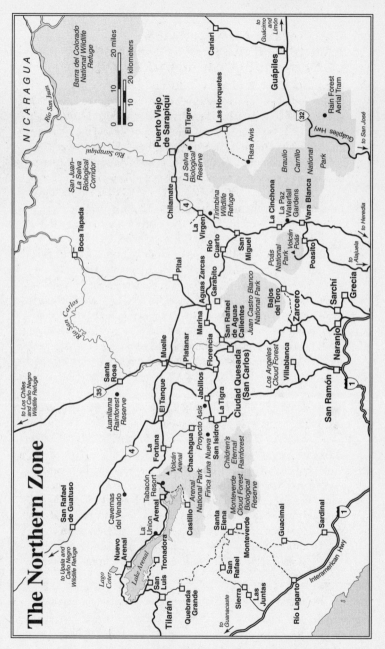

The Northern Zone

INNOVATIVE COMMUNITIES:
A BIRDING CIRCUIT IN THE SAN JUAN-
LA SELVA BIOLOGICAL CORRIDOR

The **Costa Rican Bird Route** (costaricanbirdroute.com) consists of 12 birding sites, pairing established rainforest reserves and newly created ones. The **Rainforest Biodiversity Group** with funding from the U.S. Fish and Wildlife Service and the Neotropical Migratory Bird Act (NMBCA), has been able to protect 3178 acres of habitat with the bird route, in addition to the thousands of acres now protected by the La Selva-San Juan biological corridor. The region has 520 species of birds. You can do the route from any one of the following lodges. The first four are located near Puerto Viejo de Sarapiquí. The last two are in the more remote Boca Tapada area near the Nicaraguan border:

El Gavilan Lodge Río Sarapiquí (private bath, hot water, fans, hot tub, restaurant; $70-$90; children 3 to 10 half price; 2234-9507, 2766-6743, fax: 2253-6556; gavilanlodge.com, gavilan@racsa.co.cr), one kilometer southeast of Puerto Viejo, has cozy rooms next to the Sarapiquí River, a hot tub, and a 60-hectare rainforest reserve.

La Selva Biological Station (shared or private bath; $85/person, including meals and half-day tour; children 5 to 12 $34; 2524-0607, in the U.S.: 919-684-5774, fax: 2524-0608; ots.ac.cr, edu.travel@ots.ac.cr).

Selva Verde Lodge (private bath, hot water, ceiling fans, pool; $60-$90/person, including meals; children under 5 free; children 6 to 11 $30-$40; 2766-6800, in the U.S.: 800-451-7111; selva verde.com, info@selvaverde.com) in Chilamate, a five-minute drive west of Puerto Viejo, is a complex of covered walkways leading through beautiful gardens to a riverside dining room, an airy lounging area, and a conference room. Its comfortable cabins are raised on pillars to jungle level. There are also bungalows across the road near the botanical garden, nestled at the forest's edge.

Tirimbina Lodge (private bath, hot water, air-conditioning, wi-fi, restaurant; $60-$70; tirimbina.org, info@tirimbina.org) is

habitat protection by this coalition of ecotourism businesses, local landowners, government and NGOs, the endangered great green macaw will survive, the almendro trees will flourish, and they will bring economic growth and well-being to the inhabitants of this area.

surrounded by gardens and offers easy access to the Tirimbina Rainforest Center (see below). Those who want closer contact with nature can stay at the **Tirimbina Field Station** (shared bath, heated water, kitchen facilities; $40/person, including meals), which provides bunk bed accommodations accessed via a 50-minute hike from the main offices, in the southeastern corner of the reserve; also accessible by car on a gravel road.

Laguna del Lagarto Lodge (private bath, screened windows, fans; $60-$70; 2289-8163, fax: 2289-5295; lagarto-lodge-costa-rica.com, info@lagarto-lodge-costa-rica.com) offers 1250 acres of virgin rainforest with over 10 kilometers of trails that you can explore on your own or with a naturalist. Canoes for use on the lagoon are free for guests; horses are available. It's near Boca Tapada.

The locally owned **Pedacito del Cielo** (private bath; $70-$80; 8308-9595; pedacitodecielo.net, info@pedacitodelcielo.net) has pretty wooden cabins with balconies overlooking the San Carlos river in Boca Tapada. To get to Boca Tapada from Sarapiquí, drive south of La Virgen to San Miguel. Take a sharp right and drive about half an hour to Aguas Zarcas. Once there, drive north about 20 minutes to Pital, where the pavement ends. Boca Tapada is 35 kilometers (an hour and a half) on gravel roads north of Pital.

There are other locally owned reserves on the bird route: **Bosque Tropical del Toro, Finca Paniagua** and **Lomas de Sardinal** are all northeast of Puerto Viejo by boat or 4WD. **Finca Pangola** is accessed by boat on the Río Cuarto, between Sarapiquí and Pital. **Quebrada Grande Reserve**, managed by the Women's Association with guiding provided by the Environmental Youth Group, is near Pital. **Maquenque Eco-Lodge** is just north of Boca Tapada. **Albergue El Socorro**, in the hills of Sarapiquí, offers the highest elevation of all the sites. Lodging at these sites is less developed than at the hotels mentioned above, but possible. Find out which birds frequent each site and get directions and contact info at costaricanbirdroute.com.

Adventure Activities: **Pozo Azul** (2761-1360, toll free: 877-810-6903; pozoazul.com, info@pozoazul.com) offers a one-day tour that combines horseback riding to their nine-cable canopy tour, lunch and class II and III whitewater rafting ($107; minimum age 9). Or take a half-day horseback and canopy tour ($70; minimum age 6). Stay at their **Magsaysay Jungle Lodge** (shared bath, solar hot water; $40-$60 per person, including meals), accessible by Jeep, next to the Peje river, or their **Cuculmeca Tent Camp** (shared bath; $40-$50 per person, including meals), near the Sarapiquí River. Aventuras del Sarapiquí (2766-6768; sarapiqui.com, info@sara-piqui.com) leads rafting, kayaking, hiking, and mountain biking tours throughout the Northern Zone, as does Aguas Bravas (2292-2072; aguas-bravas.co.cr, info@aguas-bravas.co.cr).

In La Virgen, the family-run **Jardín de Serpientes** (adults $6; children $5; 2761-1059) has over 50 local and exotic snake species, including a non-venomous 15-foot Burmese python. It is 400 meters south of the Centro Neotrópico.

Intercultural Activities: Originally founded by Selva Verde Lodge, the **Sarapiquí Conservation Learning Center** (2766-6482; learningcenter-costarica.org) works to link local communities and conservation through education and ecotourism. You can interact with local people through their Latin dance classes, cooking classes, and reforestation expeditions. Your kids can meet local kids through the center's after-school program.

Reserves: The 1516-hectare **La Selva** research station and biological reserve is owned by the Organization for Tropical Studies (OTS). Over 350 different bird species have been observed there in a single day by the Audubon Society Birdathon. Research and education are the reserve's top priorities. One of the many courses offered at La Selva is not for biologists but for the world's decision makers: government and business leaders who need to balance economic development with the use, management, and conservation of nature.

Roam La Selva's 57 kilometers of well-kept trails through primary and secondary forest, and its arboretum. La Selva rents bicycles and kayaks to guests. For guided walks (full-day $36, half-day $28), call the station at least a day ahead for reservations (2524-0607; edu.travel@ots.ac.cr). Some of the trails are wheelchair accessible.

La Selva is about five kilometers east of Puerto Viejo. From that turnoff it is about two kilometers to the main administration building. Take the San José–Río Frío bus from the Caribe station (Via Guapiles) and walk in from the main road.

Selva Verde's primary rainforest forest reserve is accessed by a bridge across the river. Early-morning birdwalks are offered for guests, and three- to four-hour walks with naturalist guides can be arranged.

TIRIMBINA RAINFOREST CENTER   The **Tirimbina Rainforest Center** (open daily, 7 a.m. to 5 p.m.; 2761-1579, fax: 2761-1576; tirimbina.org, info@tirimbina.org) is one of the most beautiful rainforests we've seen. The University of Wisconsin and the Milwaukee Museum have taken pains to make access to the reserve as unobtrusive as possible. A long hanging bridge over the wild Sarapiquí River separates the reserve from the 21st century, and from there on it's just you and nature on seven well-maintained trails, one of which goes to a waterfall. A bridge in the heart of the reserve lets you walk beside the forest canopy. Admission for a self-guided tour is $15 (kids under 6 free, 6 to 14, $8, students, $10) and is good for three days. A guided tour costs about $5 more per person. In addition to birding tours, there are night tours for viewing amphibians and bats. Multiday educational programs are offered to student groups; they also have volunteer and internship opportunities. Accommodations are available through the Tirimbina Lodge or the Field Station (see above). Tirimbina is in La Virgen de Sarapiquí, half an hour southwest of Puerto Viejo. Recommended.

PUERTO VIEJO LODGING AND RESTAURANTS   The town of Puerto Viejo has several hotels. **Mi Lindo Sarapiquí** (private bath, heated water, ceiling fans; $20-$30; 2766-6281, fax: 2766-6074; lindo@sarapiquirain forest.com) is next to the soccer field. It is a newer building with bright, sunny rooms upstairs and good food and service in the restaurant below.

El Bambú (private bath, hot water, ceiling fans, air conditioning, cable TV, phones, pool, security boxes, guarded parking, internet; $60-$90; children under 12 free; 2766-6005, fax: 2766-6132; elbambu.com, info@el bambu.com) is comfortable and airy, with good mattresses. Downstairs you'll find a bar and restaurant built around a stand of giant bamboo.

Andrea Cristina Bed & Breakfast (private bath, heated water, table fans, small kiddy pool; $30-$50, including breakfast; children under 5 free; phone/fax: 2766-6265; andreacristina.com, alex6265@hotmail.com) is owned by one of Sarapiquí's foremost environmental activists, Alex Martinez, who is also a naturalist guide. The grounds are shady and quiet; its quaint A-frame and cottage rooms have a European flavor, with outdoor tables and hammocks. Special rates for families.

Ara Ambigua (private bath, heated water, ceiling fans; $50-$70, including breakfast; children under 12 free; 2766-7101, fax: 2766-6401; hotel araambigua.com, info@hotelaraambigua.com) is a good inexpensive place for families. It's back from the main road so it's quiet, and has a pool, volleyball court, a small lake for fishing, and plenty of green areas and trails. Their restaurant, **La Casona**, is open 11 a.m. to 10 p.m. daily. To get there, go to the cemetery of Barrio La Guaria, west of Puerto Viejo, and go north 400 meters.

La Quinta de Sarapiquí Country Inn (private bath, hot water, ceiling fans, pool; $70-$150; 2761-1300, 2761-1052, fax: 2761-1395; laquintasara piqui.com, info@laquintasarapiqui.com), on the Río Sardinal, one kilometer off the main Puerto Viejo-La Virgen road, has lush gardens that attract a variety of birds. Guests can visit their butterfly garden, or fish in their tilapia pond for free. Their restaurant serves delicious, country-style food with fresh vegetables from their organic garden.

Centro Neotrópico Sarapiquís (private bath, ceiling fans, phones, wi-fi; $90-$110; children half-price; 2761-1004, fax: 2761-1415; sarapiquis. org, sarapiquis@ice.co.cr) is a beautiful ecolodge on the banks of the Río Sarapiquí, patterned on a 15th-century pre-Columbian village. The restaurant terrace overlooks the river and the Tirimbina rainforest reserve. A digital telescope brings guests closer to the stars. Their environmental education center and their use of solar energy and natural wastewater treatment make this a truly ecologically sound project.

During construction, workers discovered **pre-Columbian tombs** that you can now see next to a petroglyph garden at the entrance to Centro Neotrópico. Their state-of-the-art **museum** focuses on rainforest ecology and indigenous and pre-hispanic history ($12; $26, including lunch).

Rancho Leona (shared baths, hot water, ceiling fans, wi-fi, restaurant; $30-$40; 2761-1019, 2761-0048; rancholeona.com, info@rancholeona.com) is a boon for budget-adventure travelers. The clean rooms have beautiful stained-glass windows made by the owner herself. She arranges rafting and kayaking tours on the Sarapiquí. There's a sweat lodge in the garden.

See more lodgings in Innovative Communities box.

GETTING THERE: *By Bus*: Buses to Puerto Viejo de Sarapiquí (Río Frío; 2222-0610) leave from the Caribe terminal in San José. The 6:30 a.m., 1 p.m., and 5:30 p.m. buses travel the scenic route above Heredia. The trip takes a little over three hours. Hourly buses take the Guápiles Highway through Braulio Carrillo and turn north to Las Horquetas, La Selva, and Puerto Viejo, where they end. The latter route takes only an hour and a half. You will have to change buses or get a taxi to go to Chilamate or La Virgen if you go through Guápiles. Buy tickets at the Río Frío ticket booth.

Interbus (2283-5573; interbusonline.com) has private bus routes to Sarapiquí and all over Costa Rica.

By Car: A scenic route above Heredia winds around the northeast side of Poás Volcano to the northern plain and passes through La Virgen, Chilamate, and Puerto Viejo before reaching La Selva. (Don't go this way if you tend to get carsick.) It is one of the most beautiful rides you can take, passing by the amazing La Paz Waterfall Gardens, with vistas of the forests of Braulio Carrillo to the east. This route takes two and a half hours from Heredia, all on paved road. To combine this trip with a visit to Poás, go straight instead of turning right at the gas station in Vara Blanca, travel about six kilometers to Poasito, and follow signs to the national park. You should be at Poás in about 20 minutes. Recommended.

A quicker, less winding route is along the Braulio Carrillo Highway from San José. Turn left at Rancho Roberto's after you descend out of Braulio Carrillo National Park. The road to Puerto Viejo from the turnoff is smooth, wide, and virtually straight, taking you through cow pastures and oil palm plantations and passing Las Horquetas, the entrance to Rara Avis and Sueño Azul on its way to La Selva and Puerto Viejo.

You can get from Volcán Arenal to Puerto Viejo in under two hours, avoiding San Carlos, if you turn left at El Tanque, 8 kilometers out of Fortuna, then take the turnoff to Muelle (Route 4), following signs to Aguas Zarcas and turning right at each turn. At Aguas Zarcas, 23 kilometers west of San Carlos, turn left to San Miguel, and left again to La Virgen, Chilamate, and Puerto Viejo, all on paved roads.

ON THE WAY TO VOLCAN ARENAL

There are three ways to get to Volcán Arenal from the Central Valley. One is through Naranjo and Zarcero. Another is through San Ramón. Another is to visit Poás volcano, La Paz Waterfall Gardens, and Sarapiquí, returning to San Miguel to go to Aguas Zarcas and La Fortuna. There are interesting things to do on each route to break up your trip.

ZARCERO

Zarcero is one of the most charming Costa Rican towns, perched on the hills that divide the Central Valley from the San Carlos plain. At 1700 meters above sea level, its climate is fresh and invigorating. Its ruddy-cheeked inhabitants are famous for their peach preserves and homemade white cheese.

Hotel Don Beto (heated water, internet; shared bath, $20-$30; private bath, $30-$40; phone/fax: 2463-3137; hoteldonbeto.com) offers waterfall rappelling on the Río Toro and horseback riding and hiking in nearby Juan Castro Blanco Natural Park and El Chayote Reserve.

But Zarcero's real claim to fame is the fancifully sculpted **topiary garden** in front of its picturesque little church: bushes shaped into gigantic green rabbits, a bullfight, a couple dancing, a monkey riding a bicycle, ox carts, and elephants. The topiary garden has been lovingly pruned by Don Evangelista Blanco, who says that God has been telling him what to sculpt for the last 40 years. You can buy postcards at the park that help fund this unique effort. Just before you reach Zarcero coming from San José, there is a group of restaurants and stands selling cheese, candied fruit, and flowers. If you want to stop for something to eat, the restaurants here are better than those in Zarcero itself. **Doña Chila's** is open 24 hours. **Rancho Típico Zarcereño** is nice, too.

GETTING THERE: *By Bus*: Buses leave every half hour from San José for San Carlos from the Atlántico Norte station (2255-4300) on Calle 12, Avenida 9, passing through Zarcero an hour and a half later. It's easy to catch a bus back to San José, or on to Volcán Arenal.

By Car: Zarcero is an hour and a half from San José. Take the Naranjo–Ciudad Quesada exit off the Interamerican Highway to Puntarenas and drive about an hour north. There are so many supply trucks going to La Fortuna now that this route can be slow.

SAN CARLOS

Ciudad Quesada is a bustling commercial center in the San Carlos plain of central Alajuela Province, one of Costa Rica's most agriculturally productive zones. The countryside is a vibrant green with pastoral, rolling hills. Ten minutes to the east, in San Rafael de Aguas Calientes, are two ways to visit the local hot springs.

Termales del Bosque (2460-4740, fax: 2460-1356; termalesdel bosque.com, termales@racsa.co.cr; admission $10; children 2 to 11 $5) is a great place for the travel-weary to stop on their way to La Fortuna. After a short hike through this 100-hectare forest reserve, you arrive at a series of thermal pools of different temperatures next to a rushing stream. There is a stone sauna cantilevered over the river, a place to change with showers and lockers, a little building for massage and mud treatments, and a rustic bar. Everything has been left as natural as possible, so you bathe under the canopy of the trees. Don't spend more than 15 minutes in the warm baths before immersing yourself in the river to cool off. Up near the road is a **restaurant** and clean, comfortable rooms (private bath, ceiling fans; $70-$80, including breakfast and access to trails and hot springs; children 4 to 11 $7). It's seven kilometers east of San Carlos in San Rafael de Aguas Calientes on the road to Aguas Zarcas.

On the other side of the Río San Rafael, set back from the road in forest shade, sits **Hotel Occidental Tucano** (private bath, hot water, some bathtubs, air conditioning, cable TV, phones; $110-$120; children under 12 free; 2460-6000, fax: 2460-1692; occidentalhoteles.com). Its elegant European-style spa, graced with marble fountains, offers massage, hydrotherapy, and mud treatments. The natural warm mineralized waters of the area are channeled into a swimming pool. It has jacuzzis, a sauna, a gym, a beauty salon, a gift shop, and a conference center.

If you are worried about the dangers of Tabacón Hot Springs at the foot of Volcán Arenal, this is a very safe alternative. You can visit Hotel Occidental Tucano's hot springs for the day for about $8.

GETTING THERE: *By Bus:* San José–San Carlos (Ciudad Quesada) buses leave almost every hour, 5 a.m. through 7:30 p.m., from the Atlántico Norte station on Calle 12, Avenida 9. It's a three-hour trip. Try to get a Directo bus—it makes fewer stops. Take any of the buses from the fancy new Ciudad Quesada terminal (Río Frío, Puerto Viejo, San Miguel, Pital, Venecia, or Aguas Zarcas) to get to the places above.

By Car: Take the Naranjo exit, about an hour down the General Cañas Highway from San José, and continue north through Zarcero to San Carlos (Ciudad Quesada). Signs will direct you to the Aguas Zarcas road just north of the cathedral. San Rafael de Aguas Calientes is about ten minutes away. To stop here on your way from Sarapiquí to La Fortuna, just follow signs from San Miguel to Aguas Zarcas, going straight through town until you get to El Tucano and Termales del Bosque.

JUAN CASTRO BLANCO NATIONAL PARK

Parque Nacional Juan Castro Blanco is a relatively new national park. You can access this beautiful, thickly forested area through the small town of Garabito, a few kilometers south of Aguas Zarcas. The dynamic youth group, Alianza Garabito, is building trails and a ranger station at the Garabito entrance to the park. There are inexpensive accommodations in the homes of local families (Elena Cubilla Mora; 2474-0964; mecm84@yahoo.com or through Yeudi Herrera of **Vacaciones con Familias Campesinas**; 2479-7062; costaricaruraltours.com, yeudi@costaricarural tours.com). Volunteers can stay and work on the trails for about $15/ day including meals.

CAÑO NEGRO AREA

Eight kilometers northwest of Ciudad Quesada, in the town of Florencia, you can get on Route 35 north. This well-paved road was built by the US Army Corps of Engineers during the contra war in Nicaragua in the 1980s. Ten kilometers north of Florencia you'll come to Muelle de San Carlos. The landscape is monoculture pineapple fields from Muelle all the way up to Los Chiles, near the Nicaraguan border.

The 60-acre **Juanilama Rainforest Reserve** (2248-9470; actuarcostarica.com) is an oasis in this area. Hike about half an hour in the reserve to **La Leona waterfall**, where you can go for a refreshing swim. Get to know the villagers in Juanilama, ride horses to the river, fish for your dinner in Don Felix's lagoon, or get a cooking lesson from Doña Giselle. Various villagers have built comfortable rooms for guests ($50 per person including meals and reserve tour). You could use Juanilama as a base for visiting Caño Negro.

Caño Negro Wildlife Refuge comprises the Río Frío and Caño Negro Lake, which grows and shrinks seasonally. The wetland refuge was created to protect the diverse aquatic birds that live and breed there including the northern jacana, which builds its nest on lily pads; the endangered jabiru; black, long-necked, and sharp-billed anhingas; and roseate spoonbills, the only pink birds in Costa Rica. Caño Negro is home to the country's largest colony of olivaceous or neotropical cormorants, glossy black birds that fish in groups then dry out their wings in the sun. Birding is best between January and April. Sloths, iguanas, and three types of monkey inhabit the trees on the shores of the Río Frío; you will probably see caimans and turtles, and maybe even the gar fish, a prehistoric relic with a caiman-like snout and a hard exoskeleton. Fishermen are enthusiastic about the lake because of the tarpon, snook, rainbow bass, *machaca*, and drum that abound there. Park rules prohibit fishing from May through July.

The village of **Caño Negro** is within the refuge, right on the western side of the lake. It still has not been impacted by tourism, because most of the tours that say they are going to "Caño Negro" actually go to the bustling border town of Los Chiles, 19 kilometers northeast of the village, where a fleet of canopied tourist boats takes people to the eastern edge of the refuge, but not inside it, so they won't have to pay the park entrance fee ($6).

The **Caño Negro Natural Lodge** (private bath, hot water, ceiling fan, air conditioning, TV, pool, jacuzzi; $90-$110; children 3 to 11 $10; including breakfast; 2471-1426, fax: 2471-1100; canonegrolodge.com, info@ canonegrolodge.com) is an Italian-owned lodge offering fishing and birding tours. Their airy, attractive restaurant has an international menu for both meat lovers and vegetarians.

Hotel de Campo (private bath, hot water, ceiling fans, air conditioning, pool, jacuzzi, restaurant; $80-$90, including breakfast; 2471-1012, fax 2471-1490; info@hoteldecampo.com, hoteldecampo.com) has spacious rooms, two per bungalow, on grounds shaded by tropical fruit trees. They specialize in fishing and photography trips to Caño Negro.

Beside the main dock, the **Salón El Danubio Azul** is a popular restaurant/bar serving good fresh fish. **Soda La Palmera** is good for breakfast and lunch.

GETTING THERE: *By Car*: Take the Los Chiles road—Route 35 north from Muelle. Seven kilometers before you get to Los Chiles, at El Jobo, a National

Park sign indicates the road to Caño Negro on the left. It's 19 kilometers (1 hour) on rough gravel road from there. To take the tour, go straight at El Jobo and continue 7 kilometers into Los Chiles, where canopied boats leave from the main dock.

SAN RAMÓN

Another way of getting to Volcán Arenal from the Central Valley is through the agricultural town of **San Ramón de Alajuela**. This medium-sized, non-touristy town is home to **Don Pedro's Cigars** (2447-0093), a learn-how-to-roll-your-own Cuban-and-Tico-owned cigar store. The *feria del agricultor* (farmer's market) on Saturdays is huge and worth going to. The clean, well-organized **Mercado Central**, half a block north of the plaza, sells fruits, vegetables, and meat on the first floor and has several inexpensive places to eat on the second floor, including a macrobiotic store. **La Colina Centro** (open daily, 7 a.m. to 10 p.m.; 2445-7348) is a friendly, inexpensive cafeteria, located 50 meters west of Pop's at the plaza. The town's saint's day, August 31, is celebrated with religious processions.

The **José Figueres Ferrer Historic and Cultural Center** (open Monday to Saturday, 10 a.m. to 7 p.m.; 2447-2178; centrojosefigueres.org, cceh jff@ice.co.cr), 25 meters east of the plaza, has exhibits about the 1948 civil war and hosts concerts and theater productions.

Balneario Las Musas (2445-0059) in Alfaro, four kilometers west of town, has a waterfall, a pool with water slide and trails. The ex-pat hangout **Solo Bueno** (2447-7467; solobuenosanramon.com) one block past the first traffic light and gas station as you enter San Ramón, has an internet café, new and used books, and an art gallery.

Hotel La Posada (private bath, hot water, refrigerator, TV, CD player, internet; $50-$80, including breakfast; 2445-7359, fax: 2447-2021) has pleasant rocking chairs on its front porch from which to observe life in this Costa Rican town. This well-appointed and comfortable hotel is located 400 meters north of the back of the church.

GETTING THERE: San Ramón is about one hour west of San José on the main road between San José and Puntarenas. Buses leave every half hour from the Puntarenas terminal (Calle 16, Avenidas 10/12; 2222-0064).

Villablanca Cloud Forest Hotel and Spa (private bath, hot water, phones; $180-$210; two-room bungalows with jacuzzi, private garden terrace, $220-230; all rates include breakfast; children under 6 free; 2461-0301, fax: 2461-0302; villablanca-costarica.com, information@villa blancacostarica.com), next to the **Los Angeles Cloud Forest Reserve**, consists of 35 charming and comfortable private *casitas*, each with its own fireplace, terrace, and stained-glass window. Some have great views across

INNOVATIVE COMMUNITIES: PERMACULTURE NEAR ARENAL

Finca Luna Nueva is owned by Steve Farrell, a visionary with decades of experience in organic farming and permaculture in Costa Rica. The farm and gardens provide an example of how self-sufficient organic communities can work, and the farm involves the local community as much as possible. The huge ethnobotanical garden, designed by the famous horticulturist and author Rafael Ocampo, brings together plants from all over the world. At the organic farm, foraging pigs do the plowing, then carefully prepared organic biodynamic compost is applied. Crops, flowers, herbs and trees are planted together in a way that creates synergy between them, avoiding the pitfalls of the monoculture model that has dominated agriculture in recent history. EARTH University in Guápiles sends its students to Finca Luna Nueva to see what permaculture is all about, and classes in sustainable living are offered at the farm. Sample a stir-fry or a salad at Luna Nueva, and you will experience the taste sensations that can only come from an incredible variety of freshly picked organic ingredients. There is a wheelchair accessible path through their rainforest reserve. Transportation to the volcano can be arranged for about $20.

a lush patchwork of dairy farms. These hills and valleys stay green even in the dry season. Each *casita* takes a maximum of three people. The welcoming, plant-filled central lodge houses Villablanca's excellent **restaurant**, featuring healthfully prepared Costa Rican *nouvelle cuisine* served by their attentive staff. There is a lounge with a comfy sitting area, pool table, TV, and games upstairs.

Villablanca's experienced naturalists lead day or night tours ($25-$30) of the lodge's well-maintained cloud forest trails, or you can tour via **zip-line**. From February to June, **quetzals** can be observed at a farm on Azahar Peak in La Paz de San Ramón (five-hour tour, $55). Villablanca also offers a **cultural tour** of nearby San Ramón, as well as trips to Volcán Arenal and Sarchí. Villablanca rates high on the Certification of Sustainable Tourism and is a member of Green Hotels of Costa Rica. The quiet, well-appointed **Serenity Spa** near the lodge offers expert facials and massages. Recommended.

The highlight of Villablanca is the **Mariana Chapel**, whose vaulted ceiling is covered with beautiful hand-painted tiles. The tiles depict religious figures, *campesinos,* and folklore figures, as well as tropical flora and

Finca Luna Nueva welcomes **volunteers** who are fluent in Spanish and can commit to a minimum of three months.

Finca Luna Nueva Lodge (private bath, hot water, fans, some a/c, wi-fi; $80-$120, including breakfast; children under 6 free; 2468-4006, 2468-0352; fincalunanuevalodge.com, info@ fincalunanuevalodge.com) has very comfortable rooms with wide verandahs above its spacious open air dining room and meeting space, as well as three-person cabins and two-bedroom cabins that sleep six. A separate building has air-conditioning for those who require it. All rooms are furnished with rich natural fabrics in harmonious tones. Guests can cool off in a natural fresh-water pool and or relax in a solar-heated hot tub with Jacuzzi. Recommended.

GETTING THERE: Finca Luna Nueva is off the San Ramón-La Fortuna road, route 142, in San Isidro de Peñas Blancas, between La Tigra and Chachagua. From San José or Alajuela, take the Interamerican Highway to San Ramón, turn right into town, and follow the road to La Fortuna for about an hour north of San Ramón. You'll arrive at the single lane suspension bridge over the Río Peñas Blancas. After the bridge, watch for a church and cemetery on the left. Turn left onto a gravel road about 150 meters past the cemetery and drive 2.3 kilometers west, always bearing right at intersections. Soon you'll see the gates of Finca Luna Nueva. You'll need four-wheel drive for the last couple of kilometers.

fauna, interspersed with the words of the rosary. The large windows of the chapel look out on greenery. This would be a great place for a wedding. The chapel was the fiftieth wedding anniversary gift from former First Lady Doña Estrella Zeledón to her husband, former Costa Rican President (1978–82) and founder of the University for Peace, Don Rodrigo Carazo, who owned the original lodge.

GETTING THERE: From the main highway's entrance to San Ramón, follow the main street through town, where good signs for Villablanca will direct you to the La Tigra road (200 meters west of the hospital). Villablanca is 30 minutes from San Ramón, all on a paved road. A taxi to Villablanca from San Ramón costs about $10. As you leave San Ramón, a winding road branches off to the right from the La Tigra road and takes you to Zarcero.

VOLCÁN ARENAL

Volcán Arenal is the quintessential volcano. Its perfectly conical shape emerges from Alajuela's gentle green hills. From time to time, loud explosions are heard, a gray, brown, orange, or blue mushroom cloud of gases and steam billows out of the top, and you can watch the ejected boulders as they bounce down the slopes. Although the volcano is capable of inspiring intense fright and awe in visitors, inhabitants of nearby La Fortuna de San Carlos and the hotels at the volcano's base seem to live with relative peace of mind.

Arenal was dormant until the late 1960s, and the only people who suspected that it was a volcano were those who had scaled it and found a crater and steam vents at the top. But few listened to them, until a series of earthquakes began shaking the area late in the evening of July 28, 1968. The following morning, Arenal blew, sending out shock waves that were recorded as far away as Boulder, Colorado. All damage occurred roughly five kilometers west of the volcano, where people were knocked down by shock waves, poisoned by volcanic gases, and struck by falling rocks. Lava flows eradicated the town of Pueblo Nuevo, and by the end, 78 people had died. Three new craters formed during the explosion.

Arenal is most impressive at night—in the dark, incandescent material cascades down the slopes, especially on the western side. In the daytime, you only see steam and hear the volcano's terrible roar. There are explosions every few hours during Arenal's active phases. Very often the volcano is shrouded in clouds and it's hard to see anything—even if it's active. Sometimes it appears and disappears several times a day. If you see the volcano, take your pictures right away.

Note: Although the volcano is not dangerous at a distance, it is very perilous to climb. One tourist was killed and another burned in July 1988 when they hiked too near the crater, foolishly trusting Arenal's placid appearance between explosions. The volcano is not safe to scale even partway. There are steam vents and abysses, and lava sometimes descends quite far down the side. *Do not climb this volcano.* Even observation areas can be deadly. On August 23, 2000, a tour guide and a tourist were fatally burned when a sudden pyroclastic avalanche of hot gases, rocks, and mud opened up on Arenal's northeast slope above Los Lagos. This was the strongest eruption since 1968. The guide and his tourists were in an area previously regarded as safe when the avalanche traveled toward them at 80 kilometers per hour. Just stay completely off the volcano and you'll be fine. For updates on current volcanic activity, see http://volcanism.word press.com/2008/06/10/arenal-recent-activity.

ATTRACTIONS   Between La Fortuna and Lake Arenal, there are a few spots worth checking out.

The **Catarata La Fortuna** is a beautiful waterfall five and a half kilometers from the town of La Fortuna. If you have the time, it's a nice walk.

There are two ways to get there. At the back of the church you'll see a sign pointing south to the La Fortuna–San Ramón road. Go one kilometer toward San Ramón and turn right up a country lane. The entrance to the waterfall is four kilometers from there, negotiable in a regular car. Or you can stay at Cerro Chato Lodge, Arenal Oasis, or La Catarata (see below) and walk or ride horseback two or three kilometers. There is a parking lot and information office at the entrance (open daily, 8 a.m. to 4 p.m.; admission $6). If you want to walk down to the bottom of the falls, keep to the right on the ravine trail. The trail has steps built into it at the steepest parts, and there are guardrails. The force of the waterfall is such that swimming is not possible. There is a place to swim if you take a trail to the left near the bottom of the falls. Don't try this hike if you have high blood pressure, asthma, or diabetes. The hike is an exhilarating workout—it took us about 45 minutes to descend and huff and puff back up again.

Dedicated hikers will enjoy the steep two-and-a-half-hour climb to **Cerro Chato's** blue-green crater lake. Cerro Chato is a dormant volcano southeast of Arenal.

There are several choices for enjoying the **thermal waters** that spring out of the volcano. However, you should be aware that the famous Tabacón area was the site of a 1975 hot avalanche deposit (the ongoing source of heat for the thermal waters) and vulcanologists consider the location hazardous and at risk for future hot avalanches. In fact, during stronger-than-usual explosions on May 5, 1998, and October 25, 1999, lava flowed to within 500 meters of Tabacón. Four hundred tourists and employees were evacuated, but business was back to normal within 48 hours. Another blast on September 5, 2003, sent lava to the north/northeast. With that in mind, you can die happy at Tabacón Resort (open daily, 10 a.m. to 10 p.m.; 877-277-8292, 2519-1900; tabacon.com; unlimited day pass, $60/person; children ages 6 to 11 $20; children under 5 free). Here a stream is channeled into a veritable thermal wonderland: twelve pools of varying temperatures and depths; one waterslide; benches tucked under waterfalls; jacuzzis and individual tubs. There is a great restaurant (open daily, noon to 10 p.m.) with a creative and varied menu including vegetarian dishes and a great volcano view. The place seems a bit hectic out front, especially when you see all the tour buses parked there (all cars and buses must park facing out toward the road for quick evacuation), but there is plenty of room once you get onto the lushly landscaped grounds to find your own little stream and a steaming hot waterfall to massage your shoulders. There are several cold pools and showers to cool off in. The management recommends that you alternate hot with cold water every 15 minutes to avoid high or low blood pressure. Two paramedics are employed by the resort.

We loved the mud wrap experience at Tabacón's **Iskandria Spa**. Your massage therapist rubs your body with a thin layer of warm, gritty volcanic mud. You are then wrapped in a large sheet of plastic and covered by a hot towel. Your therapist might burn incense as you relax into the warmth, feeling the mud drawing toxins out of you as it dries. After half an hour you are unwrapped, given a towel, and led down a path to a private, warm stream that flows into a swimming hole, where you skinny-dip to swim off the mud. Bliss! Prices range from $105-180 for various treatments including manicures, mud wraps, facials, and massage to $150 for The Grand Temazcal (a sweat lodge ritual). shiatsu, reiki, aromatherapy and yoga are also offered.

Across the street you'll find where the locals go, the budget thermal springs **Las Fuentes** (open 10 a.m. to 9 p.m.; 460-2020; admission $12-$15; children 4 to 11 $5-$10), with the same water but in a creek that's terraced into sandy-bottomed pools. Catarata la Amistad gives a pretty good shoulder massage. There are picnic areas with grills, a *soda*, and changing rooms with showers on the nicely landscaped grounds.

Ecotermales La Fortuna (2479-8484; adults $24; children 10 and under $16; meals extra) is a peaceful alternative to Tabacón, in a safer location. There are hot pools and waterfalls, a good restaurant, a bar serving delicious tropical fruit smoothies, and attractive dressing rooms and lockers. It's great to go there after a day of hiking. Make reservations through your hotel, because Ecotermales limits visitors to 100 at each of three daily times: 10 a.m., 1 p.m., and 5 p.m. The entrance is across from Baldi Termae on the road to the volcano.

Baldi Termae ($20-$30; 2479-9651; baldihotsprings.com, baldihot springs@hotmail.com) is also an extensive series of hot pools of different temperatures and a giant jacuzzi, but they play Muzak and put too much emphasis on their four bars.

To get to the hot springs from La Fortuna (if you don't have a car), take the 8 a.m. bus to Tilarán. The driver will let you off at any of the hot springs or parks. A taxi costs about $5.

Three kilometers beyond the springs, as the road curves around the volcano, you'll come to a turnoff on the left to **Arenal National Park** (open daily, 8 a.m. to 4 p.m.). The guard station is two kilometers down a bumpy dirt road. If you pay the entrance fee ($10/person), you can visit their four-kilometer "Los Tucanes" trail, which leads through the area devastated by the 1968 eruption. Visits can only be made with an experienced, certified guide and in groups no greater than ten people at a time. In our opinion, you don't gain anything by being on the volcano. It is more interesting to observe from a distance. A taxi from La Fortuna to the park costs about $12.

Arenal Hanging Bridges (open daily, 7:30 a.m. to 4:30 p.m.; 2290-0469, fax: 2290-0259; hangingbridges.com, info@hangingbridges.com; admission $22; students $12; children under 12 free; with guided natural history walk 8 a.m. to 2 p.m., $34; students $24) is a series of six well-constructed bridges spanning lush forest ravines. The bridges allow for sweeping views of the dramatic terrain as well as close-ups of sensuous tropical leaves as they sprout and howler monkeys moving through the trees. If you want to learn about the variety of life forms that crowd into every square foot of tropical nature, take this hike with an experienced guide (two to two and a half hours, depending on how many questions you ask). When we were there one May, it was drizzling all day, but that just seemed to enhance the rainforest experience. The circle of trails that connects the bridges has only one steep climb and is suitable for people of all ages. This is rainforest viewing at its best, very much like the Skywalk in Monteverde. Their **Restaurant Los Puentes** (open daily, 8 a.m. to 6 p.m.) has a view of the lake and volcano. The entrance to Arenal Hanging Bridges is a few kilometers down a paved road to the right immediately after you cross Arenal Dam.

Costa Rica Sky Adventures (adults $66, students $52, kids 8 to 13 $40. Tram only: adults $55, students $44, kids 6 to 10 $28, under 5 free; tours at 7:30, 9, 10:30 and 11:30 a.m., 2 and 3 p.m.; prices including transportation from your hotel; 2479-9944; skytram.net, reservations@arenal reserve.com) has an aerial tram designed and built by the famous Austrian ski-lift company, Doppelmayr. The silent electric funiculars glide slowly over a kilometer-long route to a platform that is so close to Arenal Volcano you can hear the sound of ejected rocks as you watch them tumble down the mountain. At the platform, guides harness participants and give them instructions for the Arenal version of the **SkyTrek zipline canopy tour**. Participants can try two practice zips before embarking on cables that range from 100 feet to half a mile in length, at times as much as 650 feet in the air. As on the Monteverde SkyTrek, guides apply the brakes, so participants don't have to worry about how to control their landings. Unlike the Monteverde version, there is no walking between cables. A photographer goes with each group (maximum 12 participants). Those that don't want to zip can take a 30 to 45-minute guided hike near the platform or visit the orchid and butterfly gardens near the entrance. Take a lightweight jacket—it can be chilly up there. The Skytram and Skytrek are in El Castillo, on the west side of the volcano. Recommended.

Pure Trek Canyoning (2479-1313, 2479-1315, fax: 2479-1314, toll free: 866-569-5723; puretrekcostarica.com) takes you rappelling down four waterfalls and a rock face in its four-hour tours ($90, including lunch and round trip transportation from your Arenal-area hotel; minimum age 6). Designed by experienced rock climbers, this tour has high safety standards and three guides on duty for each rappeller.

Butterflies, frogs snakes, tarantulas: **Hotel Arenal Oasis** (2479-9526) on the Z 13 (Zeta Trece) road, has frog ponds, a butterfly garden, and enclosed exhibits of snakes, tarantulas and other denizens of the rainforest. They do day tours and night tours.

The **Butterfly Conservatory** (adults $15, kids $7.50; open daily, 8 a.m. to 5 p.m.; 8306-7390; arenalbutterfly.com) in the village of El Castillo, has four large atria that represent the four ecosystems in the Arenal area and show how butterflies, frogs, insects and plants are reproduced for reintroduction to deforested lands. Sloths and monkeys can often be seen on a walk around Quebrada Mariposa, which runs through the property. They also have well-appointed rooms, **Villas Volcán,** near the owner's house with great lava views (private bath, hot water; $90-$100, double; $120-130 for two-bedroom house; villasvolcan.com).

Safari River Float and Don Pedro's Farm (reserved through Sunset Tours: 2479-9800, in the U.S.: 866-417-7352, fax: 2479-9415; sunset tourcr.com, sales@sunsettourcr.com) offers relaxation, wildlife viewing, and the chance to meet a Costa Rican farming family. A bus takes you 20 minutes east of La Fortuna to the beautiful green Río Peñas Blancas, where you float silently in inflatable rafts, keeping an eye out for sloths, howler monkeys, and birds. After an hour and a half of gentle floating, you stop and climb up a trail carved into the riverbank to Don Pedro's finca for a snack. The trip can be taken in the morning or the afternoon, although our guides told us that wildlife are more visible in the afternoon. Be sure to take a camera and binoculars.

Advertised as the "rapid transit system," the horseback ride to Monteverde was very big business in La Fortuna, but has largely been discontinued because it was too hard on the horses. The real rapid transit system is the **bus–boat–bus** which boats you across Lake Arenal to the Río Chiquito, where a four-wheel-drive minivan transports you on gravel roads to Monteverde. That trip takes about three hours ($25). Otherwise, you have to drive around the north side of Lake Arenal to Tilarán (2 hours) and then take the Tilarán–Santa Elena road for another two hours to Monteverde. You can also drive past Tilarán to Cañas on the Interamerican Highway and drive south to the Lagarta road to Monteverde, about a four-hour drive from Arenal.

Desafío's Community, Culture and Conservation tour (2479-9464; desafiocostarica.com, info@desafiocostarica.com) takes you to the AMURECI women's arts and crafts workshop, the Proyecto Asis Animal Rescue Center, where you can help feed animals who are in the process of being rehabilitated for release into their original environment, and to **Finca Luna Nueva** (see page 254-55) where you'll learn the amazing properties of medicinal plants and have a fresh, organic lunch. You can also combine **volunteering** at Proyecto Asis with river rafting or canyoning through Desafío.

There are many other canopy and adventure tours in the area.

Note: Because there are so many hotels in La Fortuna, the competition is fierce. Cheap hotels often send people to meet the buses and convince tourists to go one way or the other. Don't be swayed by these people. They also will try to sell you tours, but never accept a tour from someone who doesn't have an office and a business permit in case something goes wrong and you need somewhere to go to complain. Once you are at your hotel, the staff will take care of reserving tours for you.

There are a number of internet cafés in La Fortuna. **Destiny Tours** (open daily, 7 a.m. to 9 p.m.; 2479-9850), across from Sunset Tours, does digital photo processing.

Expediciones Fortuna (open daily, 7 a.m. to 10 p.m.), on the east side of the plaza, and **Pura Vida Tours** (open daily, 7 a.m. to 10 p.m.), on the south side, also offer high speed internet, tours, and shuttles.

LA FORTUNA RESTAURANTS   **La Nena**, 100 meters east and set back about 20 meters from the main road, serves generous helpings of good, inexpensive food. Their lunch costs less than $3. **Pizzaria La Parada**, across from the bus stop at Parque Central, is popular with locals and tourists and is open 24 hours a day. They offer $3 *casados* and $4 pizzas. **La Choza de Laurel**, on the main road west of the church, offers an international menu with lobster and *lomito* in a friendly atmosphere with brightly colored oil-cloth tablecloths. Service is excellent and meals are served with style. It has a sister restaurant on the west side of Las Brasitas. **Las Brasitas**, 250 meters west of the park, has Mexican food and a volcano view. **Rancho La Cascada**, a large thatch-roofed restaurant across from the plaza, caters to many tour groups. **Soda Familiar Tobogan**, just west of town on the left, has a huge waterslide. **Hotel Pizzería and Spaghettería Vagabondo**, one and a half kilometers beyond La Fortuna on the left, just after Cabinas Rossi, serves genuine Italian food. For a flavorful, well-prepared meal on your way to or from the hot springs or the volcano, visit the large, thatch-roofed **La Pradera** (open daily, 11 a.m. to 11 p.m.; 2479-9167), three kilometers west of La Fortuna.

LA FORTUNA LODGING   We don't recommend staying in La Fortuna unless you are really on a budget. There are so many buses around the pretty central square that the air and noise pollution are quite unpleasant. Below, we mention a few places that are off the main street and offer some green areas. Since La Fortuna is on the east side of the volcano and the lava flow is currently on the southwest side (this could change, see arenal.net), the money you save on lodging could be used up in taxi fares to the active side (about $20 one way). See below for lodging west of La Fortuna, nearer Arenal.

Budget Hotels (under $30): **Cabinas Las Palmas** (private bath, heated water; $15-$20; 2479-9379) has been recommended by happy budget travelers for its cleanliness and organized, helpful staff. It's on a side street behind the MegaSuper supermarket, 100 meters south and 50 meters west of the back of the La Fortuna Church.

Gringo Pete's and **Gringo Pete's Too** (under $3-$4/person in dorms; $6/person with private bath; $5/person with shared bath, kitchen facilities, barbecue; 2479-8521; gringopetes2003@yahoo.com) is one of the best deals in La Fortuna. It's clean, well-run and offers inexpensive tours and shuttles. Both hostels are painted bright purple. Gringo Pete's is one block down the second street on the left as you enter town from the east. There's a nice garden area in the back. Gringo Pete's Too is 100 meters south of the back of the church and 50 meters west, some rooms have views of the inactive side of the volcano.

Cabinas Mayol (private bath, hot water, cable TV, pool; $20-$40; 2479-9110) has a pool for adults and one for kids, good water pressure in the showers, good mattresses, and nice gardens, with the sound of the Río Burió in the background.

Arenal Backpackers' Resort (hot water, air conditioning, pool, internet; six-person dorm, $10/person; room with private bath, cable TV, $25/person; 2479-7000, 2479-7118; arenalbackpackersresort.com, arenal hostel@yahoo.com), on the right just west of town, is a sister hostel to the well-run Pangea in San José. Amenities include a beautiful pool, quality mattresses, free internet, kitchen access, lockers, and a good view of the east side of the volcano. Recommended for budget travelers.

Mid-range Hotels ($30-$90): These are some of the nicest accommodations in La Fortuna, listed from east to west. All have good mattresses, new furnishings, and views of the inactive side of the volcano.

Cabinas La Rivera (private bath, heated water, ceiling fan, air conditioning, communal kitchen, pool; $40-$50; 2479-9048, fax: 2479-8220; cabinaslarivera.com, info@cabinaslarivera.com) is located at the end of a quiet street and has peaceful gardens that attract brightly colored euphonies and tanagers, as well as hummingbirds and toucans. Sixty species of birds have been sighted amidst the orchids, heliconias, and fruit trees. From the Banco Nacional at the eastern entrance to town, go right 100 meters, right again 400 meters, and left 50 meters.

Three more of our favorite budget places are down a dirt road to the north of Catarata La Fortuna, one and a half kilometers west of La Fortuna. Located at the base of the volcano, all have the advantage of being at a slightly higher altitude than La Fortuna and are thus cooler. They are also off the main road enough to avoid sounds of grinding gears that are audible from almost all of the previously mentioned hotels. All provide easy walking access to the Catarata La Fortuna.

Arenal Oasis (private bath, hot water, bathtubs, wi-fi; $60-$70, including breakfast; 2479-9526, fax: 2479-8472; arenaloasis.com, info@arenal oasis.com), on the right, 800 meters down the "Zeta Trece" road, has five comfortable cabinas near its regenerated rainforest reserve, an attractive open air restaurant for guests, and a series of exhibits about rainforest butterflies, frogs, snakes and insects. The owner, José, is fascinated with these denizens of the rainforest and has consulted many biologists in the design of his exhibits. He has created four pond environments that attract different types of frogs. You can see the poison dart frogs during the day, and nocturnal species on the night tour. The frogs are free to come and go, but the

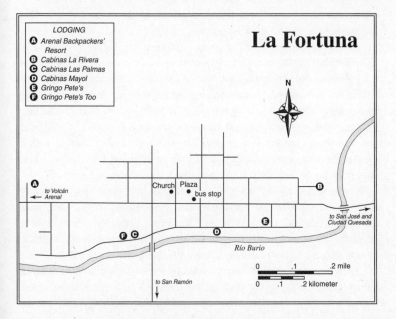

LODGING

Ⓐ Arenal Backpackers' Resort
Ⓑ Cabinas La Rivera
Ⓒ Cabinas Las Palmas
Ⓓ Cabinas Mayol
Ⓔ Gringo Pete's
Ⓕ Gringo Pete's Too

La Fortuna

N

Ⓐ

to Volcán Arenal ←

Church Plaza bus stop

Ⓑ

to San José and Ciudad Quesada →

Ⓔ

Ⓕ Ⓒ   Ⓓ

Río Burio

0   .1   .2 mile
0   .1   .2 kilometer

to San Ramón ↓

snake and tarantula exhibits are enclosed. There is a birding tour at 5 a.m. Recommended.

Cerro Chato Lodge (hot water, ceiling fans, internet, shared or private bath; $40-$50, breakfast included; 2479-9494, fax: 2479-9404; cerro chato.com, reservations@cerrochato.com) has tidy grounds and offers a two-night tour for families or groups that includes transportation to and from San José, visits to Grecia, Sarchí, Zarcero, and Tabacón, horseback riding to La Fortuna falls, a night tour of the volcano and lake, meals, and lodging ($250/person). There is also a flat, grassy camping area ($3/person) with clean bathrooms and hot showers. Owner Miguel Zamora is involved in many ecological community development projects in this area. He provides transportation from your hotel in San José, Alajuela, or Liberia (minimum four people).

La Catarata Eco Lodge (private bath, hot water, restaurant, pool; $50-$60; children 6 to 12 $6; including breakfast; 2479-9522, fax: 2479-9168; cataratalodge.com, info@cataratalodge.com) is a lodge run by a cooperative of *campesinos*. Their rooms are quiet and comfortable and the down-home breakfast included in their rates will last you all day. This hotel also has a frog pond and butterfly garden.

To get to the above places, go one and a half kilometers west of La Fortuna. Take a dirt road on the left at the large blue supermarket. After passing Arenal Oasis and Cerro Chato, bear left to get to La Catarata. You might need four-wheel drive in the rainy season.

Hotels on the North Side of Arenal: You can see Arenal Volcano from miles around, but the lava flow changes course as it encounters obstacles at the volcano's rim. From January 1996 to February 2005, the lava flow was visible on the north and northwest sides of the volcano, so hotels began to spring up on the north side. When we were there in March 2008, the lava flow had been on the southwest side for a year (see below). These days, if people want to see the lava at night but aren't staying in a place with a view of the southwest side, they drive past the National Park and stand on the bridge on the way to El Castillo to watch the volcano at night.

The best way to find out which hotels have lava views is to go to arenal.net/hotel and click on "show only lava view hotels." Why does it matter? During the day, the lava is only visible as a trail of smoke rushing down the mountain. At night, even though the lava may be only an intermittent stream, it glows red-hot, a beautiful sight to see.

There are several small hotels owned by the siblings of a dairy farming family that grew up in the shadow of Arenal. All have great views of the northern side and spacious, well-appointed rooms. **Campo Verde** (private bath, hot water, some with jacuzzi, fans, TV; $60-$80, including breakfast; 2479-1080, fax: 2479-1081; hotelcampoverde.com, info@hotelcampoverde. com) and **Hotel Don Carlos del Arenal** ($60-$70; 2479-1923; hotel campoverde.com) are almost across the street from each other. **Erupciones Inn** (private bath, hot water, cable TV, fans; $50-$60; with a/c and jacuzzi, $70-$110; breakfast included; 8833-0038, phone/fax: 2479-1400; erup cionesinn.com, info@erupcionesinn.com) has cute, homey cabins located away from the road. The friendly local owners serve fresh milk and eggs for breakfast from their dairy farm. Horse rentals are available. It's about ten kilometers west of La Fortuna, close enough to the volcano to hear its rumblings.

Volcano Lodge (private bath, hot water, ceiling fans, a/c, spa, restaurant, pools; $90-$110, including breakfast; children under 3 free; 2479-1717, fax: 2479-1716, in the U.S.: 866-208-9818; volcanolodge.com, info@ volcanolodge.com; or in the U.S. and Canada: sales@volcanolodge.com) features comfortable rooms with volcano views and an outdoor, warm-water jacuzzi. Their **Restaurant Arenal** is decorated with lush tropical murals and built around a giant fish tank. It features Costa Rican cuisine with a modern flair.

Arenal Paraíso Resort and Spa (private bath, hot water, ceiling fans, a/c, refrigerator, pools, jacuzzi, phones, cable TV; $80-$90; with glassed-in balcony, $120-$130; suites, $340-$350; including breakfast; free for children under 6; 2479-5333, fax: 2479-5343; arenalparaiso.com, info@arenal paraiso.com) has trim wooden cottages with porches. Their spa offers a variety of treatments from mud masks to reflexology. **Arenal Paraíso Steakhouse** is on the property. Arenal Paraíso has pools fed by thermal waters. They also have a 12-platform canopy tour.

Montaña de Fuego Resort and Spa (private bath, hot water, fans, air conditioning, cable TV, spa, phones; $120-$240, including breakfast; children 5 to 9 $19; children under 4 free; 2479-1220, fax: 2479-1455; mon tanadefuego.com, info@montanadefuego.com) has 40 cabinas with glass-enclosed porches and its own exclusive restaurant, **Acuarelas**. It boasts a spa with a jacuzzi, a swimming pool, and ten massage rooms with jungle views. A conference room and another restaurant complete their extensive installations. Both Arenal Paraíso and Montaña de Fuego have forest reserves and offer tours on horseback.

Another two kilometers toward Lake Arenal is **Tabacón Lodge** (air conditioning, cable TV, pools, jacuzzi, spa and fitness room, internet access: $10 a day; $270-$470, two night minimum stay; children under 5 free; children ages 6 to 11 $43; breakfast and access to Tabacón resort included; 2519-1900, fax: 2519-1940, in the U.S.: 877-277-8291; tabacon. com, sales@tabacon.com), a luxury hotel across from the famous hot springs. Hot water is piped into the tubs, showers, and swimming pools from the springs. Many of the 73 rooms and nine suites have terraces with a close-up view of the volcano. The price includes unlimited access to Tabacón hot springs and a fantastic breakfast buffet.

Hotels on the South and West Sides of Arenal· As of this writing, there are only seven hotels that have lava views on the south and west sides of the volcano. Since the five near El Castillo are 20 minutes to half an hour away down bumpy gravel roads, you will want a car with a high clearance in this area. The entrance to the SkyTram and SkyTrek is also on the road to El Castillo. Again, check arenal.net/hotel for updated information.

Arenal Volcano Observatory (hot water; with volcano views, $130-$160; without views, $90-$100; budget rooms with shared bath and common sitting room with fireplace, volcano view from porch, $60-$80; including breakfast; children under 6 free; children 7 to 11 pay half-price for meals; 2290-7011, 2479-1070, fax: 2290-8427; arenalobservatorylodge. com, info@arenalobservatory.com) is on a hill opposite the south side of the volcano. Most rooms have excellent lava views. Five rooms and one nature trail are wheelchair-accessible. There is also the **White Hawk Villa**, with fantastic views and a kitchen (sleeps eight; $425). This site was chosen by Smithsonian volcanologists who wanted a safe vantage point from which to study the volcano's activity. There is a small museum with a seismograph monitoring current action. The climate at the lodge is cool and fresh, and there are tours and self-guided hikes to a nearby waterfall and to Cerro Chato, a dormant volcano. The lodge has an attractive spring-fed pool and three five-person jacuzzis nestled below the cabins. If you cannot afford to stay, $2 will get you a day's access to the trails and a seat on the restaurant's well-appointed viewing deck. Birding is great there. Though the road to the entrance is bumpy, the steep road up to the lodge from the entrance is paved.

Hotel Linda Vista del Norte (private bath, hot water, fans, pool; $70-$80, including breakfast; suites with air conditioning and bathtubs, $110-$120; honeymoon suite, $150-$160; 2479-1551, fax 2479-1552; in the U.S.: 866-546-4239; hotellindavista.com, info@hotellindavista.com), is a family-owned restaurant and hotel with a fantastic view of the volcano, lake, and nighttime lava. Some of the rooms don't face the volcano, so request one that does; the restaurant terrace provides great views for all. To get there, take the turnoff to the right before you get to the Observatory entrance and continue several kilometers west.

Hummingbird Nest Bed and Breakfast (private bath, heated water, ceiling fans, refrigerators, kitchen facilities; $70-$80, including breakfast; 8835-8711; hummingbirdnestbb.com, nidocolibri@hotmail.com) has fantastic views of the volcano and lake from its two rooms and outdoor hot tub. A long, steep cement path leads you through lush gardens up to the house. It's located on the right on the road that climbs into the village of El Castillo.

Cabinas El Castillo (private bath, hot water; $50-$60, breakfast $3, children under 10 stay free; 2479-1949, cell: 8371-1264; arenal.net/cabinas-el-castillo.htm, cabinascastillo@arenal.net), are on a hill west of Linda Vista. There's a restaurant, and great volcano views. To get there, turn left on the main street of El Castillo and drive uphill through the town until you see the entrance on the right.

Arenal Vista Lodge (private bath, hot water, restaurant, pool; $80-90, including breakfast; children under 12 pay for meals only; 2220-0163; arenalvistalodge.com, arenalvi@racsa.co.cr), 2 kilometers beyond El Castillo, is surprisingly conventional for being in such a remote location.

Lake Arenal is dammed at its southeastern tip, 20 kilometers west of La Fortuna. Just north of the dam is the road to Arenal Hanging Bridges.

Lost Iguana Resort (private bath, hot water, fans, restaurant, bar, pool, air-conditioning, satellite TV; $250-$300; suites, $460-$540; breakfast included; 2479-1555, 2479-1557 fax: 2479-1556; lostiguanaresort.com, taraca@mac.com) perched on a hill off the road to the Hanging Bridges, is the last word in jungle elegance. The leather rocking chairs on each private terrace face the active side of the volcano, and the spacious rooms are uniquely decorated with handcarved iguanas, turtles, and snakes. The suites have outdoor jacuzzis on their porches and open-air, lava-rock showers. Lighted, brick-paved paths unite the rooms with the restaurant and the two-tiered pool with swim-up bar. There is a yoga platform, and nature trails. But the crowning glory of the Lost Iguana is its spacious new **spa,** with gorgeous carvings from Asia, delightful aromas and two massage rooms situated over a stream, so that the sound of the rushing water is all you hear. They also have an irresistible boutique full of unique clothing and jewelry. Recommended.

Arenal Lodge (private bath, hot water, cable TV, butterfly garden, pool; without view, $80-$100; with view, $150-$160; suites and chalets with kitchens, $130-$180; with private terrace, kitchen, hot tub, $200; breakfast included, as well as use of mountain bikes; in the U.S.: 888-790-5264, 2290-4232, fax: 2290-5125; arenallodge.com, info@arenallodge.com), with its entrance about a kilometer beyond the dam, is a comfortable place, high on a hill two and a half kilometers above the main road. There is a lovely view of the active side of Volcán Arenal from the dining room, most guest rooms, and the chalets even higher on a hill. A library with leather chairs and a fireplace, three outdoor jacuzzis, a video game room, a gym, a playground, and a pool table contribute to the clubby atmosphere; fishing trips on the lake are a specialty.

There is a large wooden **house** for rent in San Gregado, near Arenal Hanging Bridges, with a great view of the active side of the volcano and a rushing stream nearby (8370-4038, 8399-4967; rolandomoca@yahoo.com).

GETTING THERE: *By Bus:* From San José, buses (2255-4318; $4) leave the Atlántico Norte terminal for La Fortuna every day at 6:15 a.m., 8:30 a.m., and 11:30 a.m., returning at 12:30 p.m. and 2:30 p.m.

If you are coming from Manuel Antonio, you can catch a Quepos bus to Puntarenas, and from there a bus to San Ramón on the Interamerican highway. Buses leave San Ramón for La Fortuna at 5:30 a.m., 9 a.m. and noon. Buses leave La Fortuna for San Ramón at 5:30 a.m., 9 a.m., 1 p.m. and 4 p.m.

Gray Line buses (2220-2126; graylinecostarica.com) and **Interbus** (2283-5573; interbusonline.com) will take you to La Fortuna from San José, Monteverde, and most Pacific or Atlantic beaches for $35-$45. Reservations can be made by your hotel.

Bus-Boat-Bus: Your hotel can arrange a bus-boat-bus trip to Monteverde ($25/person). The trip takes three hours.

By Car: A direct road connects La Fortuna with San Ramón de Alajuela. From San José, follow the Interamerican Highway west and turn north at San Ramón, 55 minutes west of San José. Follow the signs for Villablanca through town, then north along the lovely La Tigra road. This road borders a reserve that protects a beautiful rainforest southeast of Monteverde and conserves the water supply for the town of San Ramón. It ends right in La Fortuna. Alternate routes are: through Naranjo, Zarcero, and Ciudad Quesada; through Heredia, Varablanca, San Miguel, and Aguas Zarcas; or from Monteverde or Guanacaste by way of Tilarán and Lake Arenal. All of them are beautiful drives. La Fortuna is about three and a half hours from San José.

Car Rentals: **Alamo** (479-9090) and **National** (2242-7878; natcar.com) have offices in La Fortuna.

By Air: **Nature Air** (2299-6000; natureair.com) flies from San José to La Fortuna in 25 minutes.

LAKE ARENAL

Lake Arenal is a large reservoir at the foot of the volcano. The original Laguna Arenal was the source of a river whose waters flowed east to the Atlantic. Dams built for a hydroelectric energy plant enlarged the lake and

INNOVATIVE COMMUNITIES:
LIVING OFF THE GRID NEAR EL CASTILLO

Rancho Margot (private bath, hot water, refrigerator, wi-fi; $130 double; shared bath, hot water, $40 single, $60 double; all rates include breakfast; 2479-7259, cell: 8302-7318, fax: 2479-7260; ranchomargot.org, info@ranchomargot.org) is in a valley beyond El Castillo on the west side of the volcano. The ranch produces its own energy, using a hydroelectric generator in the river and a series of methane biodigestors to heat its hot tub and provide gas for cooking. They invite guests to milk the cows, make cheese, yogurt and marmalades, tend the chickens, horses, and pigs, learn about composting and organic gardening, or make furniture, all the while practicing Spanish with the ranch's 63 employees.

Guests can hike half an hour uphill from the farm to watch the volcano, or hike deep into the rainforest, fish in the farm's rivers, swim in the freshwater pool (with wet bar) or join a class at the yoga center. The individual **bungalows**, on a rise looking out to the Children's Eternal Rainforest, are attractively designed with wide wooden verandas, rocking chairs and hammocks.

The **bunkhouse** (shared baths, hot water; $40 single; $60 double; including breakfast) is clean, comfortable and tidy. **Volunteers** who can stay for at least two weeks can receive free room and board for working six full days a week.

A **day pass** to Rancho Margot ($35) includes a guided tour of the facilities, a yoga class, lunch, and roundtrip transportation on the bus (see below). Other tours include hiking or horseback riding to a waterfall, waterfall rappelling, horseback riding and kayaking on Lake Arenal.

Rancho Margot's Chilean-born owner wants it to be a **model of organic self-sufficiency** for the whole region. Besides employing over 60 people, he provides a brightly painted old bus that transports workers, schoolchildren and tourists back and forth between El Castillo and La Fortuna. You can take advantage of this service (free of charge at present) to make the bumpy hour-long trip, which can be grueling. The Rancho Margot bus leaves the west side of the plaza in La Fortuna for El Castillo at 7 a.m., noon and 5:45 p.m., returning at 6 a.m. and 11 a.m. To get there by car, just keep bumping along the road, about three kilometers past the entrance to the village of El Castillo.

diverted the waters. Now they flow from the northwest side of the reservoir to irrigate Costa Rica's dry northern Pacific coast.

Many people enjoy boating and fishing on the lake, which also offers the best windsurfing conditions in the country. The lodges on the west side specialize in windsurfing and rent equipment.

Even though crocodiles are not native to Lake Arenal, local residents swear they have seen them in the lake. The presence of these large, dangerous reptiles has not been documented on film, but it is probably best not to swim in the lake until more is known.

Lake Arenal's eastern and northern banks are flanked by a road. The road is a great way to connect Volcán Arenal, Sarapiquí, and Tortuguero with Monteverde and the beaches and parks of Guanacaste. Be sure to call ahead and check on its condition before setting out.

Sixteen kilometers west of the dam, in La Unión de Arenal, **Toad Hall** (open daily, 8 a.m. to 6 p.m.; 2692-8020; toadhall-gallery.com, info@toad hall-gallery.com) is a nontraditional general store with a fabulous selection of local and national handicrafts (Cecilia Figueres' fanciful ceramics, hand-sewn dolls made by a local *campesina*, indigenous masks, and spears, to name a few). There is a used book nook and a delightful restaurant with outside tables overlooking the lake and a healthy menu featuring organic vegetables, fruit drinks and smoothies, espresso, and herbal teas. Recommended.

NUEVO ARENAL   Nuevo Arenal was founded by ex-inhabitants of the old Arenal when that town was submerged by the lake in the 1970s. It is cool and breezy there.

Two kilometers before Nuevo Arenal is **Villa Decary** (private bath, hot water, ceiling fans, hiking trails; $110-120; with kitchen, $140-150; one-bedroom bungalows with kitchen and a great view of the lake, $160-170, including breakfast; phone/fax: 2694-4330, cell phone: 8383-3012; villade-cary.com, info@villadecary.com), with large, clean, comfortably furnished rooms whose balconies overlook the lake below. Within moments of our arrival we saw seven species of small, jewel-like birds. About a hundred meters from the hotel a troop of howler monkeys sojourned by the lake, oblivious to our presence. Rates include delicious breakfasts with home-made preserves. No credit cards.

On the right as you enter Nuevo Arenal, **Tom's Pan** (open daily, 8 a.m. to 4 p.m.; 2694-4547) is a great German bakery and café featuring pretzels, blueberry cheesecake, baguettes, and croissants. Hearty wiener schnitzel, goulash, sauerbraten, and delicious sandwiches loaded with fresh veggies

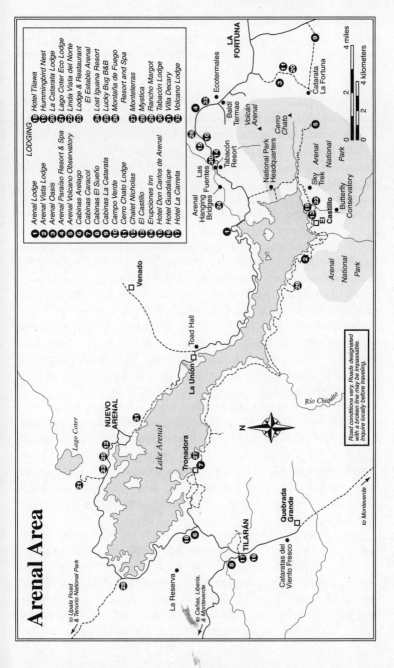

Arenal Area

LODGING

1. Arenal Lodge
2. Arenal Vista Lodge
3. Arenal Oasis
4. Arenal Paraíso Resort & Spa
5. Arenal Volcano Observatory
6. Cabinas Arelago
7. Cabinas Caracol
8. Cabinas El Sueño
9. Cabinas La Catarata
10. Campo Verde
11. Cerro Chato Lodge
12. Chalet Nicholas
13. El Castillo
14. Erupciones Inn
15. Hotel Don Carlos de Arenal
16. Hotel Guadalupe
17. Hotel La Carreta
18. Hotel Tilawa
19. Hummingbird Nest
20. La Catarata Lodge
21. Lago Coter Eco Lodge
22. Linda Vista del Norte
23. Lodge & Restaurant El Establo Arenal
24. Lost Iguana Resort
25. Lucky Bug B&B
26. Montaña de Fuego Resort and Spa
27. Monteterras
28. Mystica
29. Rancho Margot
30. Tabacón Lodge
31. Villa Decary
32. Volcano Lodge

Road conditions vary. Roads designated with a broken line may be impassable. Inquire locally before traveling.

complete the menu. They rent a homey cabin (private bath, heated water; $40-$50, including breakfast) with huge windows in their garden. Next door, Ellen's souvenir shop features crafts from the different indigenous tribes of Costa Rica. Recommended.

Chalet Nicholas (private bath, hot water, table fans, wireless; $70-$90; breakfast included; nonsmokers only; phone/fax: 2694-4041; www.chalet nicholas.com, ChaletNicholasBandB@gmail.com) is a small B&B run by a friendly North American couple in their home. They will accompany guests on hikes through a large rainforest reserve bordering their own reforested farm or down to the lake. On a clear day, you can see a distant view of the active side of Volcán Arenal from every room. Visitors should like dogs because the owners have several Great Danes. No credit cards.

El Caballo Negro (open daily, 8 a.m. to 8 p.m.; 2694-4515) on the right, three kilometers west of Nuevo Arenal, is an open-air restaurant in a garden setting featuring hearty European and vegetarian home cooking using organic ingredients. Next door is an excellent gift shop featuring ceramics and handmade furniture and lamps. Recommended.

The **Lucky Bug B&B** (private bath, hot water; $80-$90, including breakfast), has delightful rooms in a garden set back from the road. A different theme—frogs, butterflies, turtles, flowers—is highlighted in the handcrafted tiles, wrought-iron furniture, and artwork in each room. Two rooms have balconies overlooking their private lake where you can go kayaking or canoeing. This is one of the most delightful B&Bs we have seen. Recommended.

Lodge and Restaurant El Establo Arenal (private bath, heated water, fans; $30-$40; 2694-4434, 2694-4412; thestablearenal.com, info@the stablearenal.com) has nice clean rooms and a restaurant with food cooked on a wood fire. They have over 40 horses and give horseback tours of their private reserve for all skill levels. Owner Gordo takes you up to a ridge where you can see heart-shaped Lago Coter on one side and Lago Arenal on the other. Guests can hike all over their farm, help with milking, or talk to their crazy parrot.

Lago Coter Eco Lodge (private bath, hot water, ceiling fans, restaurant; children under 6 free; 2289-6060, fax: 2288-0123, in the U.S.: 866-211-0956; ecolodgecostarica.com, info@ticoresorts.com) has individual cabins with lake and volcano views from their private balconies ($105) and comfortable hotel rooms ($70-$80). They offer two-day, one-night packages including meals, horseback riding, and kayaking for $160-$180 per person. In addition to an eight-platform canopy tour ($55), water sports and volcano trips are offered. Access to the lodge's site on a small mountain lake is via a three-kilometer gravel road in good condition.

GETTING THERE: *By Bus:* All of the lake lodgings and Nuevo Arenal are served by the Tilarán–Ciudad Quesada bus, which leaves Ciudad Quesada at 6:30 a.m. and 3 p.m. and passes through La Fortuna around 8 a.m. and 5 p.m. It returns from Tilarán at 7 a.m. and 12:30 p.m. You can ask to be let off anywhere along this route. More frequent buses from Tilarán to Nuevo Arenal stop at all the hotels in the northwestern section of the lake. From Nuevo Arenal you can get a taxi to places east of town.

By Car: From La Fortuna, drive around the volcano, then bear right to skirt the lake's northern shore. The full distance from La Fortuna to the town of Arenal is 47 kilometers. It takes an hour to an hour and a half to drive, given the curves and possible bad road conditions.

The northwestern shore of Lake Arenal has become a mecca for windsurfers and kitesurfers, providing the most stellar conditions for this sport that you will find in Central America. **Tico Wind Surf Center** (2692-2002; ticowind.com) has a lot of windsurfing information on their website.

The rooms at **Mystica** (private bath, hot water; $90-$100, including breakfast; phone: 2692-1001, fax: 2692-2097; mysticalodge.com, mystica@racsa.co.cr) are comfortable and have delightful artistic touches. The flowering vine-covered porches have distant views of the volcano across the lake. They offer yoga retreats. Their restaurant features Italian home cooking, including homemade pasta, fresh salads, and excellent pizza, enlivened by fresh tomatoes and herbs grown in their garden.

The largest hotel on the western shore is the sports-oriented **Hotel Tilawa** (private bath, hot water, ceiling fans, pool, tennis court, work-study internships; $60-$120; apartments with lake view and fireplaces, $100-$130; children under 5 stay free; 2695-5050, fax: 2695-5766; hotel-tilawa.com, crfun@hotel-tilawa.com). Their **Windsurf Center** on the banks of the lake, a kilometer away, offers both guests and walk-ins windsurf equipment rental. They also rent kiteboards and provide a safe place to learn this exciting sport. Their spacious restaurant is adorned with unique frescos patterned on the Palace of Knossos in Greece, and has a terrific view of the lake. They rent kayaks, and offer on-site massage as well as their own microbrewery, the **Tilawa Brew Pub**.

Cabinas Arelago (private bath, heated water; $20-$30; 2695-8573, 8384-6927; arelago@hotmail.com), on a farm owned by a Swiss family, has inexpensive bungalows with glassed-in porches and distant volcano views. They make their own bread and delicious fruit preserves and will cook for guests.

SAN LUIS AND TRONADORA   Soon you will see signs for Tilarán to the right and **Tronadora** to the left. The western Arenal Lake area was under threat by developers a few years ago, but they seem to be giving up because of enforcement of environmental regulations. The local environmental non-profit, **Fuentes Verdes**, has worked in a low-key manner to prod municipal and other authorities to step up inspections, improve garbage management, and protect the lake from sedimentation and other pollution.

If you are on your way to Monteverde or Guanacaste, turn right to go into Tilarán. But you might want to stay at one of the cozy B&Bs in the San Luis/Tronadora area.

Cabinas Caracol (private bath, hot water, pool, kitchens, wi-fi; 2693-1036; cabinascaracolcr.com, reservations@cabinascaracolcr.com) has four cabins with kitchenettes on its beautiful five-acre grounds. It's located roughly a kilometer past San Luis on the road to Tronadora.

Monte Terras (shared bath, hot water in B&B; $50-60, including breakfast; in cabinas: private bath, kitchen, hot water, $50-60; 2693-1203, fax: 2693-1075; monteterras.com), is located on a point of land with a lovely view of the lake and Arenal volcano. The Dutch owners give massage and reiki treatments, rent bikes, and have a high-powered telescope for volcano viewing.

GETTING THERE: Buses leave every two hours from the Tilarán bus station for Tronadora. Local taxi drivers can be hired to take you around the area or to the volcano. By car, Tronadora is a few kilometers to the left at Cinco Esquinas, where the road around Lake Arenal meets the road to Tilarán.

TILARÁN

Fifteen minutes beyond the lake is the clean, pleasant mountain town of Tilarán. Leaving Tilarán through Quebrada Grande on the road to Monteverde, you can see three sources of non-fossil-fuel energy: the large white windmills that catch the wind off Lake Arenal to the northeast, the three fumaroles at the Miravalles geothermal plant to the north, and the candy-striped surge tank of the Arenal hydroelectric plant. The Costa Rican government is committed to finding alternative sources of energy by the year 2020. On a clear day you can also see four volcanoes from this site: Tenorio, Miravalles, Rincón de la Vieja, and Orosi.

Each year since 1992, Tilarán has hosted the biggest bike race in the country, the **Vuelta al Arenal** (2695-5297). In 2008 there were 3000 participants. The 137-kilometer race circles Lake Arenal in two days.

Cataratas del Viento Fresco ($10; guided horseback tour, $40; open daily, 7:30 a.m. to 5 p.m.; 2661-8193, 2294-6544; vientofresco.net), 11

INNOVATIVE COMMUNITIES—
IF YOU PLANT IT, THEY WILL COME!

Roberta Ward Smiley offers two- and four-hour guided tours of the tropical rain forest at **La Reserva** (8856-2977; la-reserva.org) in the Tilaran Mountains overlooking Lake Arenal.

Roberta founded the La Reserva Forest Foundation, dedicated to reversing the widespread conversion of tropical forest to farmland. She calls the work "oxygen farming" because forests produce oxygen and absorb CO_2, thus helping to curb global warming. The critical importance of La Reserva lies not only in its reversal of deforestation but also in its ability to create a hospitable environment for species forced out by over 80 years of farming and cattle ranching and 20 years of real estate development in the western Arenal area. La Reserva's natural regeneration with native species has proven sound: their reserve now teems with more and larger families of Mantled Howler Monkeys, sloths and other forest mammals, dozens of species of reptiles and amphibians and over 150 species of tropical birds.

LRFF is now concentrating on creating forest corridors through pastureland to connect isolated forest islands in adjoining areas, and always welcomes **volunteers** for tree planting, seed and seedling collection, computer help, fundraising strategies, inspecting farms, etc.

kilometers from Tilarán on the road to Quebrada Grande, has five beautiful waterfalls, horses, hiking trails, picnic areas and a restaurant. This would be a nice place to take a break from the Arenal-Monteverde trip.

Taquería Las Leñitas (open weekdays, 11 a.m. to 9 p.m.; Saturday, 2 to 9 p.m.; Sunday, 5 to 9 p.m.; 2695-8949), 75 meters north of the cathedral, is popular with locals and ex-pats for Mexican food. Next door, **Cybercafe Tilarán** (open Monday through Saturday, 7 a.m. to 9 p.m.; Sunday, noon to 8 p.m.; 2695-9010) offers inexpensive internet access. Go to **La Tejona**, on a windy hill north of town, for good grilled meats and sunset views.

At **Hotel La Carreta** (private bath, hot water, cable TV, ceiling fans, wi-fi; $50-$70, including breakfast; 2695-6593, fax: 2695-9145; lacarreta cr.com, lacarretacr@gmail.com. No credit cards). Each room is decorated with a hand-painted mural from one of the nearby ecosystems. Their veranda faces the back of the Tilarán Church. It is the perfect place for travelers to enjoy a homemade breakfast or lunch made with fresh ingredients.

Cabinas El Sueño (private bath, heated water, cable TV; $20-$30; 2695-5347), half a block from the northwest corner of the park, has a nice interior garden fountain and sitting area. **Hotel Guadalupe** (private bath, hot water, fans, cable TV, restaurant, gym; $20-$30; 2695-5943), one block south of the cathedral, is very clean with a nice atmosphere. Both of the above hotels have guarded parking.

GETTING THERE: *By Bus:* It's a four-and-a-half-hour trip to Tilarán from San José (Avenida 3, Calle 20 on the north side of the Coca-Cola station; 7:30 a.m., 9:30 a.m., 12:45 p.m., 3:30 p.m., 6:30 p.m.; 2256-0105, 2695-5611; $6). If you are traveling to Tilarán from Monteverde, catch the 7 a.m. bus (a two-hour trip on bumpy but passable roads). You can continue on to La Fortuna by connecting in Tilarán to the 12:30 p.m. San Carlos bus. The bus from San Carlos to Tilarán passes through La Fortuna around 8 a.m., arriving in Tilarán around 11 a.m. You can continue to Monteverde on the 12:30 p.m. Tilarán-Santa Elena bus.

By Car: From the Interamerican Highway, turn into Cañas and continue 22 kilometers up into the mountains on a good paved road.

From Monteverde: Passable gravel roads connect Tilarán with Monteverde. In the rainy season, ask first about the best route and current road conditions. A high-clearance vehicle is necessary.

From La Fortuna: It's a pleasant two-hour drive, longer with stops at the attractions along the shores of Lake Arenal. The road conditions were quite good in March 2008.

MONTEVERDE

The road from the Interamerican Highway to Monteverde is graded but unpaved. Monteverde residents, in an attempt to protect the simple, friendly lifestyle that has made their community such a special place, have fought against paving the road, believing that easier access would ruin the peaceful ambiance of the area. Despite the bad roads, Monteverde receives over 200,000 visitors a year.

After the slow hour and a half of bumping uphill from the Interamerican highway, you will be surprised to feel smooth pavement in the thriving towns of Santa Elena, and Cerro Plano. They are burgeoning with hotels, restaurants, spas, and support services for the tourism businesses in the area. Keep going around a few more curves and you'll arrive at the heart of the Quaker community, where houses are hidden in the forest and there are still no streetlights. Seven kilometers beyond is the famous Monteverde Cloud Forest Reserve.

A group of Alabama Quakers who felt that Costa Rica's disarmament policy was in line with their pacifist tradition started dairy farming in Monteverde in the early 1950s. Visiting biologists found the cloud forest above their community rich in flora and fauna, and the Quakers, along with the Tropical Science Center, had the foresight to make it a reserve.

Despite the amount of concrete, glass, and electric light that have miraculously made their way up the bumpy road, Monteverde still retains its creative, innovative spirit, exemplified by the three new performance theaters in the area—the lotus-shaped amphitheater near Stella's Bakery, the auditorium at the Bat Jungle, and the lovely Galerón Cultural Center in Cerro Plano.

Monteverde is not a place you can visit in one day. You need a day for travel and recovery each way, plus at least two days to visit all the nearby attractions.

What to bring: Rain gear, long-sleeved shirts and long pants (preferably made of material that dries quickly) and good socks. Most hotels rent rubber boots. Be sure to dress in layers for the trip up and down. You forget when you are in cool, windy Monteverde how swelteringly hot you'll be by the time you get to the Interamerican Highway.

Arranging tours: CETAM, the Chamber of Tourism (2645-6565, fax: 2645-6464; monteverdecr.com), will help you with reservations for tours and hotels. They can address security and medical problems, and more. Their office is in an attractive wooden building in downtown Santa Elena on the corner one block to the right of the bus stop.

Guides: The Monteverde Guides Association is made up of experienced naturalists who can greatly increase what you see and what you learn in the rainforest. You can see the range of their expertise at cloudforest alive.org/tour/guide_bios.htm.

Helpful websites: monteverdeinfo.com, monteverdetours.com. Research biologists have placed cameras to monitor wildlife activity in the Monteverde Reserve. See live QuetzalCams and HummingbirdCams at cloud forestalive.org.

VOLCANO VIEWING FROM MONTEVERDE   Although many people make a circuit from Volcán Arenal to Monteverde, it is not widely known that you can see the volcano from the hills north of Monteverde—clouds on the rainy Atlantic slope often obscure the view. But when it is clear, the view of the volcano behind the forested slopes of the Children's Eternal Rainforest is awe inspiring. We know of four ways to access this lovely sight: by hiking to the observation tower of the Santa Elena Reserve or the San Gerardo station in the Bosque Eterno, or by walking or driving (four-wheel drive is necessary) to Mirador San Gerardo or the Hotel Vista Verde. The latter two are about a 45-minute drive from Monteverde. More information below.

SANTA ELENA FOREST RESERVE   The 765-acre **Santa Elena Forest Reserve** (open daily, 7 a.m. to 4 p.m.; *soda*, crafts shop; phone/fax: 2645-5390; reservasantaelena.org, rbnctpse@racsa.co.cr; admission $12, students $6), located six kilometers northeast of Santa Elena, has 12 kilometers of trails, with one leading to an 11-meter observation tower that overlooks the forest canopy; on clear days, you have a view of Arenal Lake and Volcano. Guided tours ($15 plus admission) start at 7:30 and 11:30 a.m. daily. You can rent boots and ponchos there. Owned and maintained by the Santa Elena High School, this reserve is an inspiring, community-run effort that helps fund courses in environmental education, biology, language, and tourism. It is usually less crowded than the Monteverde Preserve. Volunteer opportunities are available. Daily shuttles leave the Camino Verde Information Center (2645-5296) on the main street in Santa Elena for the reserve at 6:30, 8 and 10 a.m. and at noon and 3 p.m., returning at 11 a.m., 1 p.m. and 4 p.m.

MIRADOR SAN GERARDO   On the way to the Santa Elena Forest Reserve, a fork to the left leads three kilometers to the private 100-hectare reserve at **Mirador Lodge Private Reserve** (2645-5354, fax: 2645-5087; miradorlodge.com, info@miradorlodge.com), famous for its spectacular views of Arenal Lake and Volcano during the dry season and its cloud forest trails. They have nice new cabins with volcano views (hot water, fireplaces, $90; children under 6 free; children 6 to 11 $25; including breakfast). Meals in the restaurant are moderately priced. Four-wheel drive required. The shuttle to the Santa Elena Reserve can leave you three kilometers from the Mirador.

THE CHILDREN'S ETERNAL RAINFOREST   Children from all over the world have been inspired by the efforts of a group of Swedish fourth-graders who organized the first Children's Rainforest campaign in 1987, in response to a presentation at their school by a biologist who talked about growing deforestation in the Monteverde area. Since then, schoolchildren and adults from 44 countries have raised money to buy more than 56,000 acres of rainforest on the Atlantic slope to the east of the Monteverde Cloud Forest reserve. This land, now the largest private reserve in Costa Rica, is called the **Children's Eternal Rainforest** (*Bosque Eterno de los Niños*, or BEN) in honor of the children of the world who have helped protect this special place. So far, 707 species of birds, reptiles, and mammals have been identified in the BEN, representing over half of all species found in Costa Rica.

Two rustic stations in the forest offer lodging for groups of students or tourists. The **San Gerardo Station** (private bath, cold water), at 4000 feet

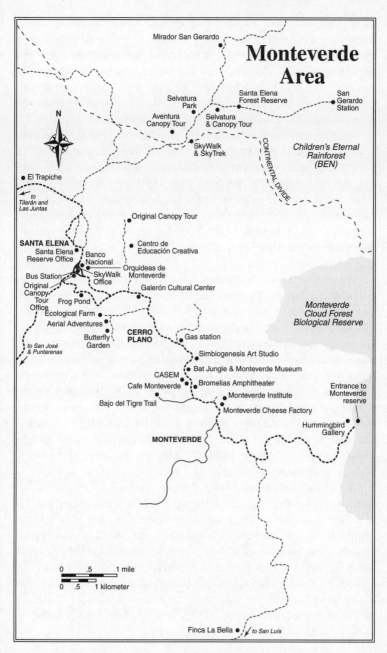

Monteverde Area

Mirador San Gerardo

Selvatura Park

Santa Elena Forest Reserve

San Gerardo Station

Aventura Canopy Tour

Selvatura & Canopy Tour

SkyWalk & SkyTrek

Children's Eternal Rainforest (BEN)

CONTINENTAL DIVIDE

El Trapiche

to Tilarán and Las Juntas

Original Canopy Tour

SANTA ELENA

Santa Elena Reserve Office

Banco Nacional

Centro de Educación Creativa

Bus Station

SkyWalk Office

Orquideas de Monteverde

Original Canopy Tour Office

Galerón Cultural Center

Frog Pond

Ecological Farm

Aerial Adventures

CERRO PLANO

Gas station

Monteverde Cloud Forest Biological Reserve

Butterfly Garden

to San José & Puntarenas

Simbiogenesis Art Studio

Bat Jungle & Monteverde Museum

CASEM

Cafe Monteverde

Bromelias Amphitheater

Monteverde Institute

Bajo del Tigre Trail

Monteverde Cheese Factory

Entrance to Monteverde reserve

Hummingbird Gallery

MONTEVERDE

0   .5   1 mile

0   .5   1 kilometer

Finca La Bella   *to San Luís*

above sea level, offers a breathtaking view of Arenal Volcano and Lake Arenal. It can be reached in an hour's downhill (3.5 kilometers) hike from the Santa Elena Forest Reserve. The station has comfortable bunk beds and sleeps four to a room. The trails, and the chances of seeing the volcano, are best in the dry season. Recommended for those who enjoy hiking. Birders will enjoy San Gerardo from April to June when the melodious songs and courtship displays of the Bare-necked Umbrella Bird are at their peak.

The **Poco Sol Station** (dorms with shared bath), 2350 feet above sea level and accessible from La Tigra, south of La Fortuna, is near a waterfall, hot mudpots, and a mountain lake, with excellent hiking and wildlife observation opportunities. To get there, drive 13.5 kilometers from the BEN office, across from the police station in La Tigra between San Ramón and La Fortuna (four-wheel drive only). Contact Poco Sol (2468-8382; mv@acmcr.org) or San Gerardo (2645-5003, fax: 2645-5104; acmcr@acmcr.org) for reservations ($47/person; students and volunteers $30/person; all rates include meals).

The only section of the Children's Rainforest currently open to walk-in visitors is the **Bajo del Tigre Trail** (open Monday through Saturday, 8 a.m. to 5 p.m.; Sunday, 9 a.m. to 4 p.m.; admission $8, students with ID $5; children under 12 free). The entrance is down a side road on the right about 100 meters past Stella's Bakery and CASEM as you enter Monteverde—watch for the sign. Our favorite is the Murciélago trail, which goes along the canyon's edge. Bajo del Tigre has a **Visitors Center**, with a spectacular view of the Gulf of Nicoya. Next door is the one-room **Children's Nature Center** (open daily, 8 a.m. to 5 p.m.), painted inside to look like a rainforest. Here you'll find magnifying glasses, fossils, puzzles, interactive games, and examples of different animal tracks. The BEN offers a guided **twilight tour** from 5:30 to 7:30 p.m. ($20; $22 including roundtrip transportation. Make reservations at 2645-5923).

The **Monteverde Conservation League** (2645-5003, fax: 2645-5104; acmcr.org, acmcr@acmcr.org) administers BEN. Besides ongoing projects in environmental education, reforestation, protection, and biological research, the League, through its Forests on Farms and Continuous Forest programs, has planted over 700,000 trees as windbreaks and to protect streams as well as to link patches of Pacific and Atlantic slope forests. The Monteverde Conservation League has been a real pioneer in the promotion of biological corridors that will ensure the continued existence of habitats for migratory birds and butterflies. Donations for the League's important work are welcome.

MONTEVERDE CLOUD FOREST BIOLOGICAL RESERVE   At Monteverde Cloud Forest (field station open daily, 7 a.m. to 4 p.m.; cct.or.cr, admission $15, children 6 to 12 and students with ID $7.50, children under 6 free), you can walk along the well-maintained trails with a map available at the field station. Guided tours start at 7:30 a.m., noon, and 1:30 p.m.; ($15 plus entrance fee, nine-person maximum). There are also private tours for two to four people, $90 plus entrance fee). Birding hikes leave Stella's Bakery at 6 a.m. (minimum two, maximum six people, $50 per person, six hours) and hike up to the reserve. Night hikes in the reserve begin daily at 7:15 p.m. ($15 plus entrance fee, $17 including round trip transport). Call 2645-5122 or e-mail recepcion-mtv@cct.or.cr to arrange any of the above tours, or have your hotel arrange them. These guided hikes, are given by naturalists with years of experience in the cloud forest, so you'll be shown wonders that your eyes alone would probably never catch.

In addition to the beautiful fauna and flora, other highlights of a hike in the reserve are a cascading waterfall, a *mirador* with stunning views of the area, and a 328-foot-long suspension bridge spanning the forest canopy.

Quetzals feed on the tiny, avocado-like fruits of *aguacatillo* trees. They are most visible in the early morning from January through June, especially during the mating season from February to May, but we talked to happy tourists who had seen them in November and December, too.

Behind the ticket office, **La Foresta Restaurant** is open 7 a.m. to 4 p.m. Comfortable bunk beds are offered at **La Casona** (private or shared bath, hot water; $40-$50 per person, including meals and entrance fee), the seven-room lodge above the restaurant. The famous **Hummingbird Gallery** is on the left at the entrance to the reserve.

If you like to live in nature, you'll enjoy hiking to the rustic shelters, **Eladio's** and **El Aleman**, within the Monteverde reserve. The lodges have bunk beds with foam padding and gas stoves. The largest lodge, Eladio's, sleeps 20 people and is 13 kilometers (five hours) from the entrance. El Aleman sleeps 12 people and is 8 kilometers (three hours) from the entrance. Hikers must bring food, bedding, flashlights, and candles. You can hire a guide for $20. Contact the reserve for more information.

GETTING THERE: The reserve is a lovely one-hour uphill walk from "downtown" Monteverde; farther from most hotels. Only El Bosque, La Colina, Fonda Vela, Mariposa, Trapp Family Lodge, and of course, La Casona, are hiking distance from the entrance. A bus ($1) leaves Santa Elena daily at 6:15 a.m., 7:20 a.m., 9:20 a.m. 11:30 a.m., 1:20 p.m. and 3 p.m. and picks up passengers all the way through Cerro Plano and Monteverde to the reserve, where it arrives half an hour later. Taxis to the reserve cost $5 from Monteverde.

Text continued on page 284.

ZIPLINES AND RAINFOREST WALKWAYS

It seems like many people think that Monteverde is the only place you can do the famous canopy tour. Although zipline tours started in Monteverde, the industry, which is a pretty low-impact way to earn money while preserving forests, has made its way into the farthest corners of the land. There are now four major zipline tours in Monteverde, and several hanging bridge walkways for the less adventurous.

For the **Original Canopy Tour** and most canopy tours, you are strapped into a harness, then you take a short hike through gorgeous forest and climb up to the first platform. Your harness is then attached to a pulley system on a steel cable, and you jump off the platform and zoom among the treetops to another platform. There you climb a tower to another platform and zoom off again. After a few more zooms you rappel down the last tree. Our seven-year-old was afraid to cross the first time, so a guide went across with her; the next crossings she did by herself. The kids loved this trip but our older male researchers found the harnesses uncomfortable. They recommend this trip for the beautiful cloud forest, not for the adrenaline rush. The Canopy Tour office is in Santa Elena across from Super La Esperanza. They provide transportation to the Cloud Forest Lodge, where the tour takes place (canopytour.com; info@canopytour.com; $45; student and child discounts; minimum age 5 years, maximum weight 245 pounds).

The **SkyTrek** (tours every two hours from 7:30 a.m., last tour at 2 p.m.; adults $44, students $35, kids $31; 2645-5238; sky trek.com) is a much longer and higher cable ride. You have to be at least eight years old or weigh between 60 and 240 pounds. It is more thrilling than the Original Canopy Tour, with cables up to 770 meters long. Our 18-year-old researchers gave this canopy tour one of their highest ratings: "For people who want to go fast on long cables that are high in the air while still in a beautiful forest." There is some hiking involved and some very high cables (over 100 meters from the ground), and it can be windy at the highest point. Their handlebar pulley system enhances speed and safety but reduces what you can see from the air. Braking is done by the guides. The Skytrek office is in "downtown" Santa Elena next to the bus stop, but the reserve itself, which protects 563 acres of forest, is on the road to San Gerardo, a bumpy 20-minute ride from Santa Elena. The SkyTrek near Arenal Volcano is does not involve hiking and starts with a ride in an electric tram (see Arenal section).

The **SkyWalk** (open 7:30 a.m. to 4 p.m.; 2645-5238; sky trek.com, faq@skytrek.com; admission $17, children $7) is for those who aren't quite up to a zipline. It is a two-and-a-half-kilometer walk through a series of easy, well-maintained trails that lead to six narrow bridges with cyclone fencing on the sides, suspended as much as 120 feet above the ground, surrounded by gorgeous forest. As with any wildlife tour, you should go early in the morning if you want to see animals. Guided walks are offered three times a day for an extra $10. The hike takes about an hour and a half at a leisurely pace. SkyWalk and SkyTrek are on the same property and provide transportation for $1 from their offices, $2 from your hotel.

Selvatura (2645-5929; selvatura.com) claims to out-zip the SkyTrek with 18 platforms and two miles of cable (tours at 8:30 a.m., 11 a.m., 1 p.m. and 2:30 p.m., adults $40, students $30, kids $25 including transportation) and an eight-bridge forest walkway that's good for birding ($20-$35). Located down the same bumpy road as the SkyTrek, Selvatura also has butterfly and hummingbird gardens, a reptile exhibit, and the Jewels of the Rainforest—one million arthropods, including incredible silver- and gold-colored beetles. Their La Casona Restaurant serves international cuisine. Their office is across from the church on Santa Elena's main street.

Aventura Canopy and Bridges (tours at 8 a.m., 11 a.m. and 2:30 p.m.; adults $40, students and kids $30, including round trip transportation; 2645-6959, 2645-6388; cienporcientoaventura.com, reservations@cienporcientoaventura.com) has 16 cables, a rappel and a tarzan swing, and eight suspended bridges.

RESERVA SENDERO TRANQUILO **Reserva Sendero Tranquilo** (2645-5010) is the uncrowded 200-acre private reserve of the Lowther family. Visitors must go with one of their excellent bilingual guides (reservations required; $20/person, including entrance fee). Visitors are usually pleased with the amount of wildlife they see in the leisurely three- to four-hour hike.

FROGS, BUTTERFLIES, BUGS, ORCHIDS, AND BATS Beautiful, strange frogs used to live in the cloud forest. The golden toad, once endemic to the Monteverde area, was remarkable for its color and the poison glands behind its ears, but it has not been observed since 1989 and is feared to be extinct. Biologists believe that global warming has caused a general drying trend in the cloud forest, depriving the frogs of the gentle mists that were vital to their existence. The best place to see frogs now is the **Frog Pond** (open daily, 9 a.m. to 8:30 p.m.; 2645-6320, fax: 2645-6318; ranario. com, info@ranario.com; admission $9, students $7), a fascinating 45-minute guided tour of Costa Rica's most beautiful frogs and toads. The project is dedicated to studying amphibians and preventing their extinction. It's open at night so you can see the many frogs that are more active after dark. The entrance fee can be used twice on the same day. They also have a **butterfly exhibit** with over 40 species, open 9 a.m. to 4 p.m. It's south of downtown Santa Elena just before Hotel Poco a Poco. Recommended.

The Monteverde Butterfly Garden (open daily, 9:30 a.m. to 4 p.m.; admission $9, students $7, children $3; monteverdebutterflygarden.com, mariposamonteverde@yahoo.com; 2645-5512) is a biodiversity center dedicated to teaching the world about insects, featuring four butterfly gardens representing different habitats. They have exhibits on live insects, a leaf-cutter ant nest under glass, a medicinal plant trail, and a Bug Theater. Guides give a fascinating explanation of the habits of each species, with ample botanical information. There are volunteering opportunities. To get there, follow the small butterfly-shaped signs that start across from the Hotel Heliconia in Cerro Plano. Take the dirt road to the right 600 meters, turn left, then go another 300 meters.

Selvatura Park (open daily, 7 a.m. to 4 p.m.; 2645-5929; selvatura.com, info@selvatura.com), located 9 kilometers from Santa Elena near the entrance of the Santa Elena Reserve, houses the Jewels of the Rainforest exhibit ($10 for an hour's tour), a vast collection of moths, butterflies, beetles, and other insects. The iridescent creatures are displayed in geometric patterns, or arranged on velvet to highlight their jewel-like colors. There you can learn about insect camouflage, mimicry, parasitism, prey–predator relationships, and other tropical biology topics. They also have butterfly and hummingbird gardens, a reptile and amphibian exhibit, canopy tour ziplines, a series of hanging bridges and a restaurant. Transportation included for packages over $10.

Orquídeas de Monteverde (open daily, 8 a.m. to 5 p.m.; 2645-5308; admission $7, students $5, children under 8 free) exhibits more than 430 species of orchids. Visitors are presented with magnifying glasses so they can observe Platystele Jungermannioids, the world's smallest flower. At least 40 orchid species will be in bloom at any given time in the garden, located in Santa Elena one block toward Monteverde from Banco Nacional.

The Bat Jungle (open daily, 9:30 a.m. to 7:30 p.m.; 2645-6566; paseodestella.googlepages.com, paseodestella@gmail.com; admission $10, children $8) created by Dr. Richard Laval, one of the world's leading bat biologists, is a fascinating view into how the rainforest works. Expert guides lead you through many innovative exhibits demonstrating phenomena like the acuteness of a bat's hearing, and the way their bones are related to our bones. Then you enter a dark area where 70 live bats of eight species fly free on the other side of a glassed in enclosure that resembles the cloud forest at night. The bats have been accustomed to a reversed light schedule, so they are active in the daytime. The guided tour can last one to two hours and includes a video presentation. It is located on a hill across from Hotel El Bosque in Monteverde. Recommended.

EDUCATION, ART, AND MUSIC IN MONTEVERDE The **Monteverde Institute** (2645-5053; mvinstitute.org, info@mvinstitute.org) offers courses in tropical biology and conservation, sustainable design (landscape architecture, resource management, community design, and planning), public health, Spanish, and Costa Rican culture. These courses are linked to ongoing research and community programs.

The **Festival Sol y Música de Monteverde**, held on weekends in March and April, is a wonderful chance to hear some of Costa Rica's best musicians. Concerts range from New Age, jazz, and Afro-Caribbean to folk groups. Don't miss it. Bring warm clothing.

Be sure to find out what's happening at the **Galerón Cultural Center** in Cerro Plano. Among its presentations are the 40-person Ballet Mexicano, international choral groups, film festivals, and many other cultural events. It offers daily yoga classes and an art gallery. The cultural center is next to Flor de Vida vegetarian restaurant.

The Centro Panamericano de Idiomas' language school (2265-6306, in the U.S.: 877-373-3116; cpi-edu.com, info@cpi-edu.com) is located on the road into Monteverde, just before the gas station. Staying with local families is part of the program, and volunteer work can be arranged in

Monteverde or at their Heredia or Flamingo beach campuses. They have a summer camp program for 14- to 17-year-olds, and an intensive two-week "survival" course.

Simbiogénesis Art Studio (open daily, 9 a.m. to 6 p.m.; 2645-5567) is nestled in the forest down a road to your left as you enter Monteverde. Using only wood from fallen trees, local sculptor Marco Tulio Brenes elaborates on the work already done by insects and fungi; his pieces follow the natural form and beauty of the wood. You can see him and several other up-and-coming Costa Rican artists at work in the three-story studio.

Above the Bat Jungle in Paseo de Stella, **Meg's Terrace Gallery** (open 10 a.m. to 8 p.m.; 2645-5419) showcases an extensive selection of handmade jewelry, tasteful t-shirts, ceramic and wood pieces, stained glass, watercolors, and more, plus special bat-related items for the bat aficionado. Next door, Susana Salas's **handmade chocolates** are also works of art, on display at her great terrace café, **Caburé.** Recommended.

For arts and crafts, be sure to stop by **CASEM**, a cooperative of local women who make beautiful embroidered and handpainted clothing and souvenirs portraying quetzals, golden toads, and other cloud-forest flora and fauna. It's located on the right as you enter Monteverde.

Patricia Maynard's **Hummingbird Gallery** (open daily, 7 a.m. to 5 p.m.; 2645-5030), near the entrance to Monteverde Reserve, exhibits Michael and Patricia Fogden's photographs from around the world. The Fogdens spend months at a time with sloths, frogs, snakes, insects, and birds, trying to get just the right shot. You'll never see better wildlife photographs. The framed photographs are not for sale, but slides and postcards are. The gallery sells beautiful Guatemalan textiles, locally made batiks, woodcrafts, ceramics, jewelry, CDs, posters, books, T-shirts, and paintings.

Chunches (open Monday through Saturday, 8 a.m. to 6 p.m.; 2645-5147), in the village of Santa Elena, could be the best-stocked **bookstore** in rural Costa Rica, with a great selection of literature in Spanish and English for children and adults, naturalist books, art, international newspapers and magazines, educational games, office supplies, and very useful topographical maps. It's also a **laundromat** ($5/load, washed and dried) and serves espresso, bagels, and fresh-squeezed orange juice.

The **Centro de Educación Creativa** (2645-5161, fax: 2645-5480; cloudforestschool.org, info@cloudforest.org) is a bilingual K–12 school whose main focus is environmental education. Children maintain organic gardens, a recycling center, compost bins, a native tree nursery and a trail system, and study in the rainforest itself. With more than half the students on scholarship, the school welcomes volunteers and stateside collaborators.

CHEESE, COFFEE, SUGAR   The famous **Monteverde Cheese Factory** (open Monday to Saturday, 7:30 a.m. to 4 p.m.; Sunday, 7 a.m. to noon) sells cheddar, jack, gouda, and other cheeses. You can also buy ice cream, fresh milk, and *cajeta* (delicious milk fudge) there. An observation room off the store allows you to watch the workers as they go about making cheese in the factory's huge vats.

The **Monteverde Coffee Tour** (2645-5006) starts at the coffee roaster at **Café Monteverde**, next to CASEM. From there you travel to the San Luis Valley while learning about the history of the area. In San Luis you tour **Finca La Bella**, where 24 families cultivate coffee. Here you will learn about the role of agriculture in Monteverde's development, and how Fair Trade coffee benefits local farmers. You'll see the whole coffee process from bush to cup. The tour ends with coffee tasting. The tour is given daily at 8 a.m. and 1 p.m.

El Trapiche tour: The Santamaría family of Cañitas takes you on a two-hour tour of their coffee and sugarcane farm, including a demo on how juice is extracted from the cane and boiled to make brown sugar ($30, students $25, children 6 to 12 $10; 2645-5834; eltrapichetour.com).

HORSES   **Sabine's Smiling Horses** ($15/hour; 2645-6894; horseback-riding-tour.com) do sunset and moonlight tours, and tours to waterfalls. Sabine carefully selects horses for children to ride, and kids will enjoy her farm, with ponies, ducks, rabbits, and guinea pigs. Horse lovers can volunteer at the farm. Sabine has a nice vacation house for rent.

INTERNET ACCESS   Many hotels offer internet access for guests, and more are converting to wi-fi every day. The **Tree House Hotel and Restaurant**, built around a huge tree on Santa Elena's main street, has computers for rent, as does **Tranquilo Communications** (open daily, 10 a.m. to 8 p.m.; 2645-6782), 100 meters before the supermarket at the entrance to town.

HOTELS AND RESTAURANTS

The Monteverde area is made up of several small communities. Santa Elena, the bustling commercial and transportation center of the area, is the first town you come to on the road from the Interamerican Highway. Most of the budget accommodations are here, but some nice, quiet hotels are as well, like the Poco a Poco and the Arco Iris. North of Santa Elena, Mirador San Gerardo is famous for views of the active side of Arenal volcano. South of Santa Elena on the four-kilometer road to Monteverde is the community of Cerro Plano, where most of the hotels are located. There are only seven hotels in the community of Monteverde itself, including the rooms at the reserve. There are accommodations in each area for all budgets. At the lowest end, campers can pitch their tents at La Colina Lodge (lacolina lodge.com) and use their facilities for $6. If you're tempted to do this, be aware that temperatures are low and wind and precipitation are high most of the year. Note: Christmas and Easter are booked months in advance.

LA LINDORA   Before you get to Santa Elena, near La Lindora, in a climate that is lower and thus somewhat drier and sunnier than Monteverde's, is **El Sol** (private bath, hot water, bathtubs, kitchens, pool, sauna, horses; $70-$100; 2645-5838, 2645-6645, fax: 2645-5042; elsolnuestro.com, info@elsolnuestro.com). It is the project of Elizabeth, an artist and healer from Germany, and her husband and chef Ignacio from Spain, memorable hosts. Their two cabins are built of local teak with great attention to detail and wonderful views of the hills from their private porches. The larger one sleeps five. Guests can come for the day to enjoy their wood-heated sauna, a swim in their lovely pool, an energy bodywork session, and a hike, or take a more adventurous trip to a waterfall.

La Pradera ($30-$40; 2645-5740; lapraderamonteverde.com) and **Valle de Campanas** ($50-$120; 2645-5631; vallecampanas.com) are locally owned bungalows with kitchens, private baths, and hot water, set in tranquil gardens with a nice view of the Gulf. To get there, turn left just after the toll booth on the way into Santa Elena. Turn left again at the cemetery and drive about 600 meters. You will see the signs on your left. The nearby **Finca La Lindora** (2645-5656) does horseback tours to waterfalls and swimming holes and rents cabins.

SANTA ELENA   Many of the *pensiones* here will cook for you and make you box lunches, or you can eat at **Morpho's Cafe** (open daily, 9 a.m. to 9:30 p.m.; 2645-5607), upstairs across from the supermarket, where freshly squeezed fruit and vegetable juices and gourmet coffees complement an extensive menu. They are known for their gringo-style hamburgers with all the fixings. They sometimes show sports events and movies. If you just want a snack, stop at **Chunches** around the corner from the bus stop. **El Marquéz** (open Monday through Saturday, noon to 10 p.m.; 2645-5918) next to the bank serves fresh seafood, *bueno y barato*.

You can change money or cash traveler's checks (bring your passport) or use the ATM at the Banco Nacional, around the corner from the bus stop.

Three hundred meters uphill from the bus stop are two sets of cabins owned by brothers. Spiffy **Cabinas Don Taco** (private bath, heated water; $40-$50, including breakfast; 2645-5263, fax: 645-5985; cabinasdon-taco.com) has views of the Gulf of Nicoya from both the breakfast room and the new individual cabins. Don Taco originated the "rapid-transit" system from Monteverde to La Fortuna (see "Getting There," below). **Cabinas Mar-Inn** (heated water; shared or private bath; $20-$30, including breakfast; 2645-5279; cabmarinn@racsa.co.cr) are clean rooms behind the family's house.

Monteverde Rustic Lodge (private bath, hot water; $50-$60, including breakfast; 2645-6256, fax: 2645-9961; monteverderusticlodge.com, info@monteverderusticlodge.com) has pretty rooms with large windows near the Santa Elena soccer field.

Pensión El Tucán (heated water; shared or private bath; $15-$20; 2645-5017, fax: 645-5017), down the street from Chunches, has small, pleasant rooms above a very clean *soda* featuring delicious fruit smoothies and native food.

Up a side street to the left, on a grassy hillside, is **Arco Iris Eco-Lodge** (private bath, hot water; $70-$120; honeymoon cabin, $180; bunk beds, $30-$50; 2645-5067, fax: 2645-5022; arcoirislodge.com, arcoiris@racsa.co.cr), a circle of private cabins set in beautifully landscaped grounds. You can birdwatch right on the property from nature trails near a small creek. Internet access and international phone and fax service are also offered, as well as same-day laundry service. Guests were raving about their German breakfast buffet. Recommended.

On the same side street, **Pensión Colibrí** (heated water, private baths; $25-$30; 2645-5682), run by an accommodating local family, is inexpensive and serves great breakfasts.

Just before you get to Santa Elena, going left after the toll booth, is a growing neighborhood with several hotels. **Tina's Casitas** (shared bath, $10-$15; private bath, hot water, $20-$40; house, $40-$50; 2645-5641, fax: 2645-5130; tinascasitas.de, tinascasitas@gmail.com) are rooms around a stone patio with an open-air communal kitchen. Tina is involved in a tree-planting project to reforest the Pacific slope. There is a view of the Gulf of Nicoya on clear days and of the Monteverde mountains.

Hotel Claro de Luna (private bath, hot water; $60-$80, including breakfast; children under 7 free; children 8 to 12 half-price; 2645-5269; clarodelunahotel.com, reservations@clarodelunahotel.com), down the street, has charming chalet-style architecture and a very attractive breakfast area with a distant view of the Gulf.

Farther along on this street are **Cabinas Sol y Luna** (hot water, internet, private bath; $30-$40; 2645-5629; cabinassolyluna.com, info@cabinassolyluna.com), with clean, spacious rooms.

SAN GERARDO AND CAÑITAS   One and a half kilometers above Santa Elena, on the way to the Skywalk and Santa Elena Forest Reserve,

Sunset Hotel (private bath, hot water; $30-$40, including breakfast; children under 12 $7; children under 4 free; 2645-5048, fax 2645-5698; monteverde info.com/hotel; sunsethotel@monteverdeinfo.com) is nicely landscaped and has fantastic views of the Gulf of Nicoya. There are birdwatching trails on their 35-acre reserve. The beautiful, glassed-in restaurant serves moderately priced dinners to non-guests (who must make reservations). Some readers really enjoyed their stay here.

About six kilometers farther down this beautiful but bumpy road, beyond the SkyWalk and Selvatura, is the turnoff to **Hotel Vista Verde** (private bath, hot water, restaurant; $80-$120, including breakfast; children 4 to 9 $7; toll free: 877-623-3198, 380-1517, fax: 2645-6178; info-monte verde.com, booking@info-monteverde.com), with an incredible view of Arenal Lake and Volcano from each room (if the weather is clear) and a nearby waterfall with swimming hole on their private reserve. You should have four-wheel drive to get to these two places and to the nice new cabins at Mirador San Gerardo.

In Cañitas, on the road to Tilarán, **Miramontes** (private bath, hot water; $60-$90, including breakfast; 2645-5152, fax: 2645-5297; swisshotelmira montes.com, miramont@racsa.co.cr) has a fine restaurant (open 1 p.m. to 8:30 p.m.) serving Swiss, French, Italian, and Costa Rican specialties and homemade strudel. Their wood-paneled rooms are comfortable and reasonably priced. Their orchid garden has over 350 species.

CERRO PLANO   Along the winding road between Santa Elena and Monteverde are most of the area's hotels. Taxi service from this area to the Monteverde reserve costs about $6, or you can take the bus. Many of the following hotels are accessible for disabled people.

Cloud Forest Lodge (private bath, hot water, patios, restaurant, bar; internet, $80-$90; 2645-5058, toll-free: 877-623-3198, fax: 2645-5168; cloud forestlodge.com, info@cloudforestlodge.com) is about a kilometer off the road, nestled in a hilly forest. Its reserve is where the Original Canopy Tour takes place. There is plenty of good hiking right around the lodge. Look for the turnoff on the left, almost one kilometer outside Santa Elena on the road to Monteverde. The lodge has a stunning view of the Gulf of Nicoya and beautiful old-growth forest.

El Sapo Dorado (private bath, hot water; internet, $120-$150; 2645-5010, fax: 2645-5180; sapodorado.com; reservations@sapodorado.com) with large, comfortable rooms featuring either sunset-view terraces or fireplaces, is one of the area's finest hotels. Their Fountain Suites have a separate bedroom for families. A five-kilometer self-guided nature trail behind the hotel circles through a private cloud forest reserve. Their gourmet restaurant, open to the public, serves generous helpings of fantastic food and sinful desserts in an elegant setting, with excellent service. The carefully prepared cuisine is low in fat, sugar, and salt, and covers all tastes, from steak to vegetarian dishes to pizza for the kids.

Along the main road as you approach the community of Cerro Plano are two delightful restaurants. **Johnny's Pizzería** (open daily, 11:30 a.m. to 9:30 p.m.; 2645-5066) offers a salad bar and crispy, wood stove-baked pizzas, with some ingredients coming from the backyard vegetable garden.

The **Flor de Vida** (open daily, 7 a.m. to 9 p.m.; 2645-6328), set back from the Galerón Cultural Center, serves good, healthy vegetarian food in a nice atmosphere.

In "downtown" Cerro Plano, **Moon Shiva** (open daily, 11 a.m. to 10 p.m.; 2645-6270) is a happening place, with good food, live music on weekends, and movies twice a week.

The **Dulce Marzo** bakery next door offers an excellent Sunday brunch.

On the street that leads to the Monteverde Butterfly Garden, **Restaurant Sofía** (open daily, 11:30 a.m. to 9:30 p.m.; 2645-7017) is livening up the Monteverde cuisine scene with *nuevo Latino* recipes like sweet-and-sour fig-roasted pork loin and plantain-crusted sea bass. The relaxed yet tasteful ambience is enhanced by peaceful music. Their bar serves creative cocktails like mango-ginger *mojitos*.

Across the street, **Heladería Sabores** (open daily, 11 a.m. to 8 p.m.; 2645-6174) serves 15 flavors of locally made ice cream.

Down the same street, the **Restaurant De Lucía** (open daily, 6:30 a.m. to 9 p.m.; 2645-5337) serves breakfast made only with locally produced ingredients and light lunches; dinner specialties are steak and fish filets, which are displayed raw so you can see how fresh they are—you pick the one you want. Their delicious hors d'oeuvres feature freshly made tortillas, salsa, and guacamole.

De Lucia Inn (private bath, hot water; $80-$90; 2645-5976, fax: 2645-5537; costa-rica-monteverde.com, delucia@racsa.co.cr) has comfortable rooms across the street from the restaurant, within easy walking distance of the Monteverde Butterfly Garden, Aerial Adventures, and the Ecological Farm.

Next door, **Nidia Lodge** (private bath, hot water, some bathtubs, internet, meeting room, jacuzzi; $70-$110, including breakfast; 2645-5236, fax/phone: 2645-6082; nidialodge.com, nidialodge@racsa.co.cr) is owned by local naturalist guide Eduardo Venegas and his family. The quiet, comfortable wooden rooms have garden views, and the restaurant (open 6 a.m. to 10 p.m.) serves seafood and *comida típica*. Eduardo can take you anywhere you want to go.

Back on the main road, in about 100 meters, you'll find a road to the right, which leads to **Manakin Lodge** (shared or private bath, heated water; $40-$70, including breakfast; phone/fax: 2645-5080, fax: 2645-5517; manakinlodge.com, manakin@racsa.co.cr). It offers clean rooms and private cabins, some with kitchens. We have heard good reports about the filling breakfasts served there.

The beautifully landscaped **Hotel de Montaña Monteverde** (private bath, hot water; $70-$140, including breakfast; 2645-5046, fax: 2645-5320; monteverdemountainhotel.com, info@monteverdemountainhotel.com) has a sauna and jacuzzi overlooking the Gulf of Nicoya, a restaurant, some homey wooden cabins with forest views, other rooms with Gulf views (deluxe rooms have two-person bathtubs), and a private reserve with nature trails.

On the left is the entrance to **Cabañas Los Pinos** (private bath, hot water, kitchens; one bedroom, $60-$80; three bedrooms, $120; 2645-5252, fax: 2645-5005; lospinos.net, info@lospinos.net), offering cabins in a peaceful setting—a good value. The kitchens and separate bedrooms make them great for families. Recommended.

The **Belmar** (private bath, hot water; $80-$110; 2645-5201, fax: 645-5135; hotelbelmar.net) has beautiful views, comfortable rooms, and a good restaurant. Its entrance is uphill from the gas station on the left.

At this point, you still have not arrived in the community of Monteverde, and when you do you might not realize it because Monteverde is not what we usually think of as a town. Most houses are back in the woods where you don't see them, and are connected by footpaths. Please pay attention to gates, fences, and posted signs.

MONTEVERDE   On the right as you enter Monteverde, the recently remodeled **El Bosque Lodge** (private bath, hot water, cable TV, refrigerator; $50-$60; 2645-5158, 2645-5221, fax: 2645-5129; monteverdeinfo.com/hotel, info@bosquelodge.com) has clean, comfortable rooms set in a quiet garden back from the road. The entrance is on the right, just after **Restaurant Tramonti** (2645-6120), specializing in pizza, pasta, and salads with authentic Italian flavor.

Across the street is one of Monteverde's newest and best attractions: the hacienda-style **Paseo de Stella**, with the **Bat Jungle** (see above), **Meg's Terrace Gallery** and **Caburé** (open 8 a.m. to 8 p.m., closed Sunday; 2645-5020) owned and managed by Argentine chef Susana Salas. You can dine inside or out on the spacious terrace. Susana's cooking seeks out authentic flavors from around the world like Argentine *empanadas,* Mexican *mole,* or Indonesian *satay,* using only fresh natural ingredients. The tropical fruit drinks are not to be missed—even the lemonade has a unique flavor. And leave room for dessert, like the *bocanegra*: chocolate *soufflé* with walnuts and blackberry sauce, and Susana's handcrafted chocolates. Recommended.

After the entrance to El Bosque is a food **market**. Next door are **Alquímia Art Gallery** (2645-5847; alquimiaartes.com) selling paintings, prints and crafts by local artists, **Café Monteverde** (open daily, 8 a.m. to 6 p.m.; 2645-5901) where the coffee tour starts, and **CASEM,** the crafts cooperative.

Across the street is **Stella's** (open daily, 6 a.m. to 6 p.m.; 2645-5560), a spacious bakery/coffee shop serving treats such as apple pie, brownies, and strudel. Fresh, organic produce from the greenhouses out back appears in their salads, and you can construct your own sandwich.

You'll see the **Monteverde Cheese Factory** up ahead, marked by a sign with a big silver cow's head between two mountains. To the left is the **Monteverde Institute**. The road turns right and crosses a bridge, then turns right again, then goes left at La Colina, leading to the Monteverde Reserve in about two uphill kilometers.

La Colina Lodge (hot water; shared bath, $30-$50; private bath, $40-$60; breakfast included; 2645-5009, phone/fax: 2645-5580; lacolinalodge. com, info@lacolina.com) is the remodeled Flor-Mar, one of the first lodges in Monteverde, now more open, yet welcoming, with comfortable rooms upstairs, some with balconies. Camping is $6/person.

Hotel Fonda Vela (private bath, hot water, TV, phone; $120-$160; children 3 to 8 years $6; 2645-5125, fax: 2645-5119; fondavela.com, reservations@fondavela.com), a few hundred meters up the hill toward the reserve, has lovely large rooms, some with views and balconies, a **restaurant** with a large, dramatic design and huge windows, and a cozier dining room with a fireplace.

Mariposa Bed and Breakfast (private bath, hot water; $40-$50, including breakfast; 2645-5013; vmfamilia@costarricense.com), across the road from the Fonda Vela is comfy and locally-owned; a good value for its close proximity to the Monteverde reserve. They also rent a nice 3-bedroom house with a kitchen and a balcony at canopy level.

The Trapp Family Lodge (private bath, hot water, phone; $90-$100, children ages 3 to 11 $7; 2645-5858, fax: 2645-5990; trappfam.com, trappfam@racsa.co.cr) is only a 15-minute hike from the reserve. Its spacious wooden rooms with balconies have views of the treetops. Its Mountain Suites (TV; $110-$120) have spectacular views of the reserve. It's probably best to have a car to stay here.

See Monteverde Cloud Forest Biological Reserve section above for information on staying at **La Casona** at the reserve.

SAN LUIS   Only 20 minutes by horseback, car or taxi from all the attractions in the Monteverde area, the **University of Georgia** (formerly known as San Luis Ecolodge; 2645-8049, fax: 2645-8050; uga.edu/costarica, este banv@uga.edu) offers lodging at its farm and biological reserve in the scenic San Luis Valley. Facilities include a dining hall, internet, and **ethnobotanic gardens**. Guided hikes, workshops, lectures and slide presentations are included in the rates. Reforestation, birdwatching, and fiestas with the San Luis community are some of the activities you can get involved with here. Two types of lodging are offered: nicely appointed family rooms with private bath that sleep 5 ($60-$80/person), and a row of more secluded rooms ($90-$100/person) about a kilometer from the main lodge, with balconies at canopy level and the sound of a rushing stream in the background. All rates include meals and activities. Children 7 to 13 pay $30-$40; children 4 to 6 $10-$20; children 3 and under free. Recommended.

Finca La Bella is a 49-hectare community farm in the San Luis Valley. The pristine views and the tranquil country lanes on the farm remind me of the Monteverde of 30 years ago. Visitors can stay from a couple of days to a couple of months with welcoming local families, milking goats, picking, drying and roasting organic coffee (December and January), learning how organic sugarcane is processed and helping in the schools or on the farm. You can also tour the area for a day (Arrange through the UGA, above). To set up a homestay, contact Oldemar Salazar (2645-8046; $15-$20/person including meals). With a minimum of ten people, Alvaro Vega will show you how brown sugar is processed at his hilltop *trapiche* with a view of the Gulf. Recommended.

GETTING THERE: *By Public Bus*: Direct buses leave the Terminal Atlántico Norte in San José (Calle 12, Avenida 7 and 9; 2222-3854; $5) every day at 6:30 a.m. and 2:30 p.m., leaving Santa Elena for the return trip at these same hours. Buy tickets in advance. The bus does not go beyond Santa Elena, so if you are staying in Cerro Plano, Canitas, or Monteverde, make arrangements to be picked up or take a taxi. Beware of theft on this bus, especially on the way up. Make sure your large luggage gets safely into the luggage compartment underneath the bus and keep valuables with you at all times. We have heard many stories of someone who poses as a bus employee, and tells vulnerable-looking tourists that they may not keep their backpacks with them, but must store them in another place. Later their backpacks are gone. This said, we have ridden this bus many, many times and have never had any problems. The warning is to keep you alert, not to discourage you from taking this most economical way of reaching Monteverde. This bus is full of interesting people, and often the five-hour trip passes very quickly if you get into a good conversation. The last time we took this bus it broke down and we chose to pay for a taxi to San José instead of waiting for it to be fixed.

Note: Seats on the Monteverde–San José bus are reserved. You should purchase tickets in advance at the Santa Elena bus station (open weekdays, 5:45 a.m. to 11:30 a.m., and 1:30 p.m. to 5 p.m.; weekends until 3 p.m.).

A daily bus from Puntarenas to Santa Elena leaves Puntarenas (bus stop on the oceanfront, one block from the San José–Puntarenas terminal) at 2:15 p.m., turns off the Interamerican Highway at Río Lagarto around 3:30 p.m., and arrives in Santa Elena around 5:30 p.m. If you are coming from the north, any San José–bound bus will let you off at Lagarto, where Monteverde-bound buses pass around 3:30 p.m. and 5:30 p.m. If you are coming from Manuel Antonio, take the 10:30 a.m. Quepos–Puntarenas bus to connect with the Puntarenas–Santa Elena bus. The bus returns from Santa Elena to Puntarenas at 6 a.m.

By Private Bus or Taxi: As you can tell from the above description, getting to Monteverde on public buses can be done, but if you're not sure of your Spanish or have a limited time frame, you are not going to want to get involved in the intricacies of busmanship. You might want to consider spending $35-$40/person to take one of the private bus or taxi services to Monteverde. Most of them have family or group rates: **Interbus** (2283-5573; interbusonline.com), **Transport Costa Rica Monteverde** (2645-6768, 2290-7307; transportcostarica.net), or **Grayline** (2220-2126; graylinecostarica.com). Many hotels offer special transportation deals, too.

By Taxi, Boat, and Minivan: Your Arenal area hotel will arrange for you to be taxied to Lake Arenal where a 25-minute boat ride will get you to the Río Chiquito. A minivan waits for the boat and takes you about two hours up to your hotel in Monteverde (and vice versa). This is the fastest way to get to or from Volcán Arenal ($25/person). There is a rest stop at a café in El Dos de Tilarán. The whole trip takes three to three and a half hours.

By Car: Most people turn off the Interamerican Highway at Sardinal, about a half-hour north of the Puntarenas turnoff. It has been paved until Guacimal, so it's the current route of choice. Go uphill from Sardinal for one and a half to two hours.

If you are going directly to San Luís and don't want to stop in Monteverde, turn right at the covered bus stop about 12 kilometers before you reach Monteverde, and descend into the San Luis Valley.

If you have four-wheel drive, you can travel by car from Tilarán to Monteverde by way of Quebrada Grande, San Rafael, Cabeceras, and Santa Elena. During the rainy season, the Tilarán–Santa Elena bus can make it through when cars can't. The trip takes two hours. Check with your hotel on the best route to take before setting out.

TEN

Guanacaste Province

Guanacaste was a separate province of Spain's Central American empire until 1787, when it was given to Nicaragua. In 1812, Spain made Guanacaste part of Costa Rica so Costa Rica would be large enough to be represented in the colonial government, which ruled from Guatemala. After independence, both Costa Rica and Nicaragua claimed Guanacaste. Guanacastecos were divided, too. Liberians, whose founders were Nicaraguan cattle farmers, wanted to join Nicaragua. Nicoyans were in favor of joining Costa Rica. Nicoya won in a vote, and an 1858 treaty declared Guanacaste part of Costa Rica. Costa Ricans celebrate annexation of Guanacaste on July 25.

Guanacaste's long period of autonomy, sizeable indigenous population, and geographic isolation from the Meseta Central have contributed to make it a unique province in Costa Rica. Many "Costa Rican" traditions originated here. The people, dark-skinned descendants of the Chorotega Indians, are possibly closer to their cultural and historical roots than are other Costa Ricans, and there is a special *campesino* richness in their friendly manner.

During the last century, most of Guanacaste was converted into pastureland for beef production. The deforestation of the region altered its climate and ecosystems, causing occasional droughts. But over the last thirty years, due to the evolution of conservation consciousness in Costa Rica, many landowners are allowing trees to regenerate naturally. The landscape is not as dry as it was. Brahma bulls lounge under the graceful, spreading shade trees that gave the province its name. The brilliant yellow blossoms of the *corteza amarilla* dot the plains in February, and in March the light red blossoms of the *carao* (carob tree) brighten the landscape.

We enjoy Guanacaste more in the rainy season, when its trees still have their leaves, and a pale green tints the savannahs. It is clean and lush then, like the rest of Costa Rica. It doesn't usually rain a lot in Guanacaste until September or October, and often there is just an hour of rain late in the day.

When you stop for *refrescos*, be sure to try some typical Guanacastecan grain-based beverages: *horchata* (rice), *resbaladera* (barley), and *pinolillo* (roasted corn) are all sweet, milky drinks. *Tamarindo* is made from the sticky fruit found in the pod of the tamarind tree. If you're prone to iron deficiency, buy a bottle of *miel de carao*, the iron-rich syrup made from the *carao* tree's pods. It doesn't taste too good, but it's very effective.

LAS JUNTAS DE ABANGARES

Las Juntas de Abangares, the old gold-mining capital, is a historic part of Costa Rica that is just beginning to open up to tourism. From 1884 to 1931, its mines attracted workers and gold seekers from all over the world. Now it is a quiet town in the foothills of the Tilaran range, a nice place to get a sense of rural Costa Rican life. Also, unlike most of Guanacaste, it is mountainous, with a cool climate.

The **Eco Museo** (closed Monday; 2662-0150; admission $2) has trails through tropical dry forest to the top of an old gold mine built into the beautiful Río Abangares. The old mine structure bears a striking resemblance to a Mayan ruin rising out of the forest. To get there, turn right at the **Monumento a los Mineros** in front of the historic **Caballo Blanco Cantina** in Las Juntas, which has a good collection of turn-of-the-20th-century artifacts, and marks the road to Monteverde. Go four kilometers to a fork in the road, where there is a sign. The entrance is three3 kilometers to the right. It is a nice, shady walk from town. Taxis (about $3.50) and horses can also be hired in Las Juntas.

One of the biggest saint's day celebrations in Guanacaste is the day of San Jorge, the patron saint of Abangares, on April 23. People from 15 surrounding communities bring statues of saints from their churches to participate in a procession led by the Archbishop in Las Juntas.

LODGING **Pueblo Antiguo Lodge** (private bath, hot water, pools, restaurant; $60-$70, including breakfast; 2662-0033, 888-437-6251, fax: 2662-0549; puebloantiguo.com, reserve@puebloantiguo.com), located four kilometers north of Las Juntas on the road to Monteverde, has a lovely thermal pool with jacuzzi looking out over the rainforest, a spring-fed swimming pool, and a Turkish bath with steam from its hot springs. Rooms are clean, comfortable, and quiet. They will take you on a "miner for a day" tour of the old mining tunnels and teach you about gold panning. This is truly an off-the beaten-track destination.

Agrolodge (2225-3752; cr-hotels.com) to the left down a rough road beyond the Ecomuseo, has private trails that take you to the old Abangares Gold Mine, where you can witness gold extraction as it was done decades ago, and participate in the process yourself. San Jose's Hotel 1492 provides a one-day tour.

GETTING THERE: By Car: Las Juntas is about three hours (145 kilometers) from San José. The turnoff is clearly marked on the Interamerican Highway. Las Juntas is only an hour from Puntarenas and 30 minutes from Cañas, so you could make it your base for exploring this area. If you are coming from Monteverde, it is better to use the Lagartaos exit. Even though there is a road between Monteverde and Las Juntas, it is not as well-maintained as the Lagartaos road. The bus makes it, but it can be hard for cars. Check with your hotel for current road updates.

By Bus: Buses from San Jose leave daily at 8:40 a.m., 10:30 a.m. and 3 p.m. from Calle 12, Avenidas 7/9. A bus leaves Santa Elena de Monteverde every morning at 5:30 a.m. for Puntarenas via Las Juntas, arriving in Las Juntas at 7:15 and at the Interamerican Highway at 7:30. There you can hail a bus going north to Liberia or to the Nicaraguan border, hail one going south to San José, or stay on the bus and get to Puntarenas at 8:30 a.m. The return bus leaves from Puntarenas at 1 p.m., arriving in Las Juntas around 3 p.m. and in Monteverde at 5 p.m. From Guanacaste, get off the Interamerican Highway at the Las Juntas turnoff (named "La Irma" after a restaurant there) and take a taxi ($3) into town, or flag down the Puntarenas–Monteverde bus at La Irma and take it to the Eco Museo or Pueblo Antiguo.

CAÑAS AND RÍO COROBICÍ

Cañas is a busy, hot town where you might stay en route to somewhere else. If you're en route to Guanacaste, it is more pleasant to stay in Las Juntas (see above) or Miramar (see Chapter 11). Fifty meters from the Interamerican Highway (turn in at the Hotel El Corral), the **Nuevo Hotel Cañas** (private bath, hot water, ceiling fans, a/c, cable TV, phone, internet, hot tub; $50-$60; 2669-1294, fax: 2669-6055) has light-filled rooms around a swimming pool.

Two and a half kilometers north is **Capazurí** (private bath, heated water, ceiling fans, a/c, pool; $50-$60, including breakfast; children 5 to 10 $10; phone/fax: 2669-6280, fax: 2669-6080; capazuri@racsa.co.cr), whose name means "deer" in the indigenous Chibcha language. Rooms are simple; despite some highway noise, it has a nice family atmosphere. Camping is permitted in the groves near the main house ($9/person, including breakfast).

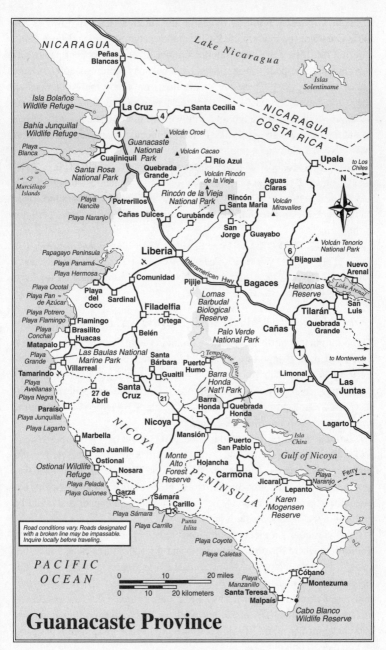

Road conditions vary. Roads designated with a broken line may be impassable. Inquire locally before traveling.

PACIFIC OCEAN

Guanacaste Province

Four kilometers north of Cañas on the Interamerican Highway is **Safaris Corobicí** (phone/fax: 2669-6191; nicoya.com, greggdean@msn.com), offering raft trips down the smooth Corobicí River. Two-hour trips are $37 per person, three-hour trips are $45, and a half-day tour costs $60 (children under 14 half-price). These are scenic floats on which the guide does all the work, and are good for breaking up the monotony of a long trip. As with any wildlife observation tour, you will see more if you go early or late in the day. Bring a swimsuit, hat, camera, binoculars, and sunscreen. Trips run between 7 a.m. and 4 p.m.

Right on the Corobicí River **Rincón Corobicí** (2669-1234, fax: 2669-0303) is a cool, pleasant place to stop. Its Swiss-owned restaurant specializes in beef and seafood, and there is a souvenir shop, a playground, clean baths, a small campground, and a trail along the riverside. They also offer rafting trips.

GETTING THERE: Buses leave San José seven times a day between 8:30 a.m. and 6:15 p.m. to Cañas ($3; Calle 14, Avenidas 1/3; 2222-3006; three and a half hours). By car, Cañas is about three hours from San José, right off the Interamerican Highway.

BIJAGUA DE UPALA AND TENORIO NATIONAL PARK

Three kilometers north of the Río Corobicí crossing on the right, Route 6 heads to Upala. **Bijagua de Upala**, 34 kilometers north on this road, is on a flyway between Palo Verde and Caño Negro, so it is good for birding. It's the gateway to Tenorio National Park. At 1700 feet above sea level, the climate is cool and refreshing. On the road north of Bijagua, you can see the Solentiname Islands in Lake Nicaragua.

Tenorio National Park (admission $10, 2200-0135) is famous for the **Río Celeste waterfall**, an hour's hike from El Pilón, the park ranger station. Two rivers come together inside the park. When they meet, their waters blend to form an amazing turquoise blue color. It's a lovely sight, but the color is caused by naturally-occurring sulphur and copper that could be harmful to swimmers, so don't jump in.

You can hike, on nicely maintained trails, beyond the waterfall to **Los Teñideros**, where the clear rivers meet and the water turns blue, and to hot springs you can bathe in. Allow three to four hours to walk to the hot springs and back. Bring your own water and rain gear. There are restaurants on the road to the park. The eastern park entrance, La Paz, is accessible from San Rafael Guatuszo, but we have heard that the trail is muddy and not as nice as at the El Pilón entrance. Signage is good within the park, so you can go on your own.

GETTING THERE: Six kilometers north of Bijagua, turn right and follow signs 6 kilometers to San Miguel. Turn right again and drive 6.5 kilometers to the El Pilón park entrance, all on bumpy gravel roads.

Finca Agroecologica (admission $6, open 8 a.m. to 4 p.m., closed Monday; 2466-8069) has a butterfly farm with blue morphos, a shady orchid garden with Venus fly-traps, and an easy-to-walk guided nature trail. To get there, turn right after the Banco Nacional and take the right fork after the school. You will see the entrance on your right.

LODGING **Sueño Celeste** (private bath, hot water; $60-$70, including breakfast; 2466-8221, cell: 8370-5469; sueno-celeste.com, sueno_celeste@racsa.co.cr) is a small B & B in a peaceful setting with a great view. The Belgian owners serve memorable breakfasts. They love to show visitors around the town, and can take you to a farm where they make delicious strawberry goat-milk yogurt, or to visit a women-run bakery, local artisans and organic gardens. The entrance to Sueño Celeste is three3 kilometers south of Bijagua, at the cell phone tower.

Heliconias Rainforest and Lodge (private bath, hot water, restaurant; $40-$80, including breakfast; 2466-8483; www.heliconiaslodge.com, info@heliconiaslodge.com) has a row of simple rooms, and some spacious new wooden bungalows with jacuzzis bordering the forest. I saw three large white-faced monkeys outside my room when I stayed there. You can take an easy one-hour hike through their rainforest reserve on well-kept trails connected by three suspended bridges. Birders flock there to see the ornate hawk eagle. Cristian, their excellent bilingual guide, will take you to Tenorio National Park, about one-and-a-half hours away. A soon-to-be-completed road will cut the travel time to the park considerably. You can also ride horses from Heliconias to the park entrance (two hours on horseback, return by jeep). To get to Heliconias, turn right after the Banco Nacional and take the left fork after the school. It is about 4 kilometers from Route 6 on gravel roads. 4WD Four-wheel drive recommended.

La Carolina Lodge (shared or private baths, hot water, no fans, screened windows; $60-$80 per person, including meals, discount for children 5 to 14; 4380-1656, in US: 843-330-4178; lacarolinalodge.com, info@lacarolinalodge.com) is set in an old hacienda. The heart of the lodge is the open kitchen with a large, old-fashioned wood stove, where a couple of welcoming Costa Rican *señoras* pat out tortillas and serve *café recién chorreado*. The graceful trees are full of orchids and birds. Horses are free for guests to use. There is a large, stone-lined hot tub next to a swimming hole in the river that runs beside the lodge. A deck lends itself to yoga or fishing. At night the entire lodge is filled with candles, and rocking chairs are gathered in front of the stone fireplace. The rooms in the main lodge have shared baths off a cozy reading room and the honeymoon suite is in a separate bungalow with a view of the rushing river. A house up the hill has three double beds, good for families. Although U.S.-owned, La Carolina's staff give you the feeling that they are welcoming you into their own home. To get there, take the turnoff to Tenorio National Park, 6 kilometers north of Bijagua, and drive 6 kilometers to San Miguel. Turn left instead of following signs to the Park and drive one kilometer to the La Carolina entrance. It's about 7.5 kilometers from Tenorio National Park. Recommended.

Posada La Amistad (shared bath, heated water; $30-$40 per person, including meals; 8356-0285) is a pleasant rustic lodge next to the home of Doña Socorro Ramírez and surrounded by her well-tended gardens. She has a wood-fired oven and makes pizza for guests. Follow signs one kilometer beyond the park entrance. Recommended for budget travelers with cars or bikes.

RESTAURANTS Fish for your lunch at **Tilapias El Angel** (open daily 9 a.m. to 6 p.m.; 2466-8393), known by locals for their delicious family recipes. Run by the women's association AMAYA, the **Casita de Maíz** (2466-8281) is located in a cute wooden building on the left near the police checkpoint. They serve pork tamales, sweet corn tamales called *yoles*, and yummy freshly prepared *chorreadas*, corn pancakes. **Soda Los Mangos** (open daily 7 a.m. to 9 p.m.; 2466-8604) at the main bus stop, serves good native food.

Bar and Restaurant Río Celeste (8365-3415) and **Doors Tenorio** (8306-6878) both offer meals on the way to the national park and inexpensive lodging as well.

GETTING THERE: By Car: Bijagua is about three hours from Arenal and three hours from Monteverde, about 90 minutes from Liberia, and three hours from Playa Nosara.

A gravel road goes from Mystica Lodge, on the western tip of Lake Arenal, through Tierras Morenas and ends about 17 kilometers south of Bijagua. The road is kept in good condition, because it is used by the state-run electricity company to service the windmills in the hills on the western side of the lake. This route can save you some time if you're traveling between Arenal volcano and Tenorio.

By Bus: Upala buses leave San José at 10:15 a.m., and 3 p.m. (five hours, $6, 2221-3318; Calle 12, Avenidas 3/5). Ask to be let off at Bijagua and get a taxi to your hotel lodge. To get to Bijagua from Liberia, take a bus to Cañas and catch an Upala bus to Bijagua.

The best way to get to Arenal from Bijagua is to catch a bus north to Upala (a half-hour trip) and take an Upala–San Carlos bus two hours south to El Tanque. Once in El Tanque, you can take a bus or taxi about ten minutes west to La Fortuna. There is a bus from Upala directly to La Fortuna daily at 7:30 a.m.

PALO VERDE NATIONAL PARK

In addition to being a resting spot for 60 migratory and 200 native birds, such as the black-bellied whistling chick and the blue-winged teal, **Palo Verde** (admission $10) has 15 different types of habitat for mammals, amphibians, and reptiles, many of which can be observed relatively easily. During the dry season, animals stay near the few permanent springs in the area, one of which is only 100 meters from the park's administration building and campsite. There you can see peccaries, armadillos, jaguarundis, coatis, deer, and monkeys. The best observation spot for birds is in the swamp across from the OTS headquarters. The best months to go are January, February, and March. It is very hot and dry during these months. Palo Verde's **Isla de Pájaros**, in the Río Tempisque, is an important nesting ground for many showy waterbirds, including the roseate spoonbill, glossy ibis, anhinga, and several species of egrets and storks.

Palo Verde is on the east side of the mouth of the **Tempisque**, Guanacaste's major river. Stretching along the banks of the river is a plain that floods during the rainy season and dries to a brown crisp in the dry season. Away from the river rise bluffs dotted with limestone cliff outcrops. The park administration at the base of the bluffs; a couple of trails begin there and go up to lookout points.

Palo Verde became known as an important bird refuge when it was still a large cattle ranch. When it was granted park status, the cattle were removed. Over the years, vegetation formerly grazed by the cattle started to grow up and overrun the wetlands. The cattle were recognized to have become a natural part of the ecosystem and were reinstated selectively. This practice, along with other techniques, has resulted in the restoration of Palo Verde's wetlands. Cattle are also an important element in reducing fire hazards, since they eat vegetation that makes the park prone to fires. Being able to graze their cattle in the park helps local *campesinos*, who in turn do fire prevention work.

The **Organization for Tropical Studies** has a research station one kilometer before the park administration. Each room has a bunk bed and a reading lamp (though lamps attract insects at night). Food is plentiful and good. Arrangements must be made as far in advance as possible through OTS in San José ($60-$70/person, including food, orientation, and guided walk; children 5 to 12 $34; half-day visits $16; 2524-0607; threepaths.co.cr, edu.travel@ots.ac.cr). OTS can arrange transportation by taxi from Bagaces to their station.

Camping ($4, make reservations at 2671-1290) is allowed in the park. Even though there are restrooms, showers and potable water, bring water, a flashlight, and insect repellent for camping. You don't need to bring your own water if you are staying at the OTS.

GETTING THERE: Turn left at the gas station in Bagaces, north of Cañas. The park administration is 28 kilometers (one hour) from there. Signs mark the way. A taxi from Bagaces costs about $25. There is a small building at the entrance to the park, and some housing for personnel beyond it, but don't get off there because it's about eight more hot, dry kilometers to the administration building.

Tempisque Eco Adventures (2687-1212, phone/fax: 2687-1110; teacr.comecoaventuras@racsa.co.cr) takes you on a covered boat tour near Palo Verde. They also have a canopy tour and a restaurant. They are located four kilometers north of the Puente La Amistad over the Río Tempisque.

LOMAS BARBUDAL BIOLOGICAL RESERVE Just north of Palo Verde, **Lomas Barbudal Biological Reserve** (admission $6) has the most diverse tropical dry forest in this area as well as birds, monkeys, waterfalls you can hike to, and rivers with pools you can swim in shaded by graceful trees. Be careful here if you are sensitive to bees and wasps. There is a campground and picnic area near the river with bathrooms and potable water. Visitors can also stay at the ranger station ($20-$30, including meals; 2695-5180, 388-3753; Spanish only).

Lomas Barbudal is the site of a long-term project studying the social behavior of wild white-faced capuchin monkeys. You can read about this research in *Manipulative Monkeys, The Capuchins of Lomas Barbudal,* by Drs. Susan Perry and Joe Manson, who have spent two decades observing the language and traditions of four generations of these intelligent and fascinating primates. Find out more at the reserve's small museum, where capuchin political and social life is recorded. There you can get a self-guided nature tour brochure, written from a monkey's perspective. If you do meet the monkeys, keep your distance, do not feed them or give them access to your backpacks, and treat them with respect. Hard working research assistants are often needed for the monkey project, under the auspices of UCLA's Anthropology Department (12-month commitment required, see pin.primate.wisc.edu/jobs/listings). Volunteers who can only stay a week or two can do trail maintenance, biological inventory, and other needed tasks with the park rangers.

GETTING THERE: To get to Lomas Barbudal, drive to the town of Pijije, about 15 kilometers north of Bagaces on the Interamerican Highway. Turn left on the gravel road in Pijije and follow it 6 kilometers to the reserve. A taxi from Bagaces costs about $10.

LIBERIA

Liberia, the historic capital of Guanacaste's beef industry, is now its tourism hub. Most major U.S. airlines have flights to Liberia's Daniel Oduber Quirós International Airport, making it a good option for those who want to avoid the winding mountainous roads between San José and Guanacaste or Arenal.

Many of the old houses in town are made of adobe, the traditional building material of this hot, dry area, and have orange tile roofs, which help keep the temperature cool inside. You'll notice that some of the corner houses have a door on each side of the corner. This is known as the *puerta del sol*. The door on the east side lets in the morning sun, while the door on the south side lets in the afternoon sun. Liberia is bright and hot, so bring a hat or use your umbrella.

Tourists can make international phone calls at ICE (open weekdays, 7:30 a.m. to 5 p.m.; Saturday, 8 a.m. to noon), 50 meters south of the Banco Nacional on the right.

RESTAURANTS **Las Tinajas**, on the main square, has pleasant outdoor tables where you can drink beer and munch *bocas* on hot Liberian afternoons. **Los Comales**, 100 meters north of the park, serves *comida típica*.

Restaurante Romanesca Jauja (2666-1111) two blocks toward town from the highway on the main boulevard, serves gooey Italian food in a pleasant, open-air ambiance. Seventy-five meters south of Bancredito, **El Café Liberia** (open Tuesday to Saturday, 8 a.m. to 12:30 a.m., Mondays, 8 a.m. to 8 p.m., closed Sunday; 2665-1660) serves wine, French cheeses, sandwiches, and homemade tarts and *gateaux,* and runs a book exchange in air-conditioned comfort. **Pizza Pronto** (2666-2098) near the Posada Del Tope, has a wood-fired brick oven and a pleasant garden atmosphere.

Spaghetteria, Pizzeria, Caffe La Toscana (open Sunday to Thursday, noon to 11 p.m.; Friday and Saturday, noon to midnight; 2665-0653, 8837-7340), in Plaza Santa Rosa, one block west of the main intersection, is a so-

---

LIBERIA RENT-A-CAR AGENCIES

Alamo Rent A Car (2242-7733), Dollar (2668-1061), Economy (2666-7560, Hola (2667-4040), National Car Rental (2242-7878), Payless (2667-0511), Thrifty (2665-0787), and Toyota (2668-1212) have car rental agencies in Liberia and provide transportation to and from their offices for customers. Make advance reservations in the dry season.

phisticated northern Italian *trattoria*. Each of their 33 pizzas is named for a different town or region in Italy, and features ingredients from that area. Imported cheeses and prosciutto, homemade pasta, and Italian wines give the entire menu an authentic taste.

Not to be missed is **Café Europa** (2668-1081), a German bakery and café on the left, two kilometers past the airport, near two large souvenir stores.

LODGING   There are gas stations on each corner where the main road to Liberia intersects the Interamerican Highway. (They are the surest places to get fuel on holidays.) At this intersection are **Hotel Boyeros** (private bath, hot water, a/c, phone, pools, conference center, restaurant open 24 hours; $50-$80; children under 10 free; 2666-0722, 2666-0809, fax: 2666-2529; hotelboyeros.com, hboyeros@racsa.co.cr) and **Hotel El Bramadero** (cold water, cable TV, pool; with fans, a/c; $30-$60; 2666-0371, fax: 2666-0203; hotelelbramadero.com, info@hotelelbramadero.com), which has quieter rooms in the back away from the pool. Restaurant Bar El Bramadero serves Tico-style meats and seafood. **Best Western Hotel El Sitio** (private bath, hot water, a/c, pool, cable TV, gym, restaurant, wi-fi; $80-$100, including breakfast and airport pickup; children under 12 free; 2666-1211, in North America 800-780-7234, fax: 2666-2059; bestwestern.com) has huge concrete walls around its spacious, shady grounds, making for a peaceful environment despite its proximity to the highway.

Best Western Las Espuelas (private bath, hot water, a/c, TV, pool, hot tub, restaurant/bar, conference center, casino; $80-$90; 2666-0144; bestwestern.co.cr) is well-run and often has rooms when El Sitio doesn't. It's shady grounds are about two kilometers south of Liberia on the Interamerican highway.

El Punto (private bath, hot water, a/c; $80-$100, including breakfast; 2665-2986, 8877-3949, fax: 2666-2313; hotelelpunto.com, info@hotelelpunto.com) is a unique place to stay. Located in a colorfully remodeled school on the highway near supermarkets and restaurants, El Punto is known for the hospitality of its Tica owner, and for delicious breakfasts. It can be a little noisy, so ask for a room near the back.

The **Hotel La Siesta** (private bath, cold water, a/c, TV, pool, restaurant; $50-$60; 2666-3505, fax: 2666-2532; lasiestaliberia@hotmail.com) is clean and quiet.

The quiet neighborhood south of the central church has good options for budget travelers in converted historical homes. All offer guarded parking.

Hotel Liberia (shared and private baths, cold water, fans; $10-$30; dorms $6; phone/fax: 2666-0161;) has quiet rooms in the back, a souvenir shop, and a bar/restaurant, as well as internet access. It is half a block south of the church.

Hotel La Casona (some fans, some a/c, TV, guarded parking; $20-$30; 2666-2971) is half a block south of the southwest corner of Parque Central.

Hotel La Guaria (private bath, heated water, TV, some a/c, pool; $40-$50; 2666-0000), two blocks east of Parque Central, has bright, modern rooms, as does its sister hotel, **La Primavera** (private bath, cold water, fans, some a/c; $4-$50; 2666-0464) facing the park.

Note: During the dry season, you need to make reservations for all Liberia hotels.

GETTING THERE: By Bus: Buses leave the San José Pulmitán station at Calle 24, Avenidas 5/7 ten times a day (2222-1650; $2.75). Buses connect Liberia with Puntarenas, Bagaces, Canas, La Cruz, Santa Cruz, Nicoya and the Nicaraguan border. Schedules are clearly marked at the municipal bus station, five blocks north and two blocks east of the main entrance to Liberia. Pirate taxi drivers have been known to tell tourists that the posted bus schedules are wrong: always check with the bus companies.

Note: Buses from Liberia to San José may be stopped for passport checks, so bring at least a copy of your passport with your entry date stamp and make sure your visa is in order.

By Car: Take the Interamerican highway north from San José. You can take a circular route through Liberia, Santa Cruz, and Nicoya, the gateways to the Guanacaste beaches, and come back on the Tempisque bridge. Roads are paved along that circular route, making it a two-hour trip by car from Liberia to the bridge.

Liberia

Stadium

Quebrada Panteón

Av 11

Av 9

Calle 12 · Calle 14 · Calle 10 · Calle 8 · Av 7 · Calle 6 · Calle 4 · Av 5 · Calle 2 · Av 3 · Calle Central · Calle 1 · Calle 3 · Calle 5 · Calle 7 · Calle 9 · Calle 11 · Calle 13

Bus Station to beaches · Market

Bus Station to San José

Correo

to Rincón de la Vieja

Av 1

O Parque Central

Church

F

E H

Av Central

Río Liberia

N

Av 2

Av 4

Interamerican Highway

to Airport **21**

C

G Av 6

A **B**

to Cañas, Arenal, & San José

D

Av 8

Av 10

0 .... .2 mile
0 .... .2 kilometer

LODGING
A El Punto
B Hotel Boyeros
C Hotel El Bramadero
D Hotel El Sitio
E Hotel La Cosana
F Hotel La Guaria
G Hotel La Siesta
H Hotel Liberia
I La Primavera

By Air: SANSA flies to Liberia from San José every day ($210 roundtrip; 2290-4100, in North America: 877-767-2672, fax: 2290-3543, fax: 2255-2176; flysansa.com, reservations@flysansa.com). Nature Air flies daily to Liberia four times a day with some flights by way of Tamarindo ($230 roundtrip; 2299-6000, in North America: 800-235-9272; natureair.com, reservations@natureair.com).

You can fly into Costa Rica via the **Daniel Oduber Quirós International Airport** just west of Liberia. We have heard of people getting "open-jaw" flights that arrive in San José and depart from Liberia, or vice versa.

NORTH OF LIBERIA

GUANACASTE CONSERVATION AREA

The Guanacaste Conservation Area north of Liberia has been declared a UNESCO World Heritage site. It not only protects one of the last well-preserved stands of tropical dry forest in Central America, but also ensures migratory habitat from the Pacific coast to 6000 feet above sea level for an estimated 230,000 species of animals, birds, and insects: 65 percent of Costa Rica's biodiversity. It includes cloud forests at the top of Orosi and Cacao volcanoes, as well as the rainforests on their Atlantic slopes and 43,000 hectares of marine habitat.

Northern Guanacaste's parks benefited from the debt-for-nature swaps of the late 1980s and early 1990s and now form one of the best-endowed conservation areas in the country, and one of the most consolidated conservation areas in Latin America. Communities here have over a decade of experience in forming a model for non-destructive human use of biodiversity. Several of the ecotourism lodges mentioned in the following pages were, and still are, large haciendas involved in cattle ranching. But now these large holdings are incorporated into the conservation area as buffer zones for the national parks, and are actively preserving their forests, reforesting with native species, practicing organic agriculture, and welcoming visitors to their canopy tours, hot springs, and nature trails.

RINCÓN DE LA VIEJA NATIONAL PARK

Rincón de la Vieja (admission $10; open daily 8 a.m. to 4 p.m.; 2695-5598) is one of Costa Rica's richest and most varied parks. The centerpiece is a broad massif formed by the Rincón de la Vieja and Santa María volcanoes, with nine craters that melded about a million years ago. Its flanks are pocked by mudpots and fumaroles, which help the volcano vent its heat. The crater that is currently active cups a steaming lake, and periodically erupts, sending hot mud and volcanic ash into the sky and down the rivers to the north of the volcano. Its most active episode in recent history was between 1966 and 1970, but in 1995 and 1998 eruptions caused its *campesino* neighbors to flee their volcano-side homes. The damage has always occurred on the northern slopes of the volcano because the southern rim of the crater is higher than the northern rim. All lodging and park attractions are on the south and west sides.

The park is a watershed for 32 rivers, many of which empty into the Tempisque. Three hundred species of birds have been identified there, as well as deer, collared peccaries, coatis, pacas, agoutis, raccoons, jaguars, two-toed sloths, and three species of monkeys. When we were there, we easily observed toucans, manakins, and crested jays.

There are two entrances to the national park: **Rincón–Las Pailas** ($10), above the village of Curubandé, and **Rincón–Santa María** ($10), five kilometers beyond the village of San Jorge, which is 25 kilometers northeast of Liberia on a dirt road. The Las Pailas entrance offers the more spectacular thermal sites, while Santa María has trails through a forest that is unusually moist for Guanacaste, due to its Atlantic exposure, and offers easier access to the hot springs.

RINCÓN–LAS PAILAS   Las Pailas (The Cauldrons) is a 124-acre wonderland of pits of boiling water; vapor geysers that stain the rocks around them red, green, and yellow because of the iron, copper, and sulfur in the steam; minivolcanoes that emerge spontaneously, last a few days or weeks, then dry out, leaving a conical pile of mud; fumaroles, which are deep holes that emit billows of sulfurous vapor; and seven bubbling pots of gray mud called the Sala de Belleza (Beauty Salon). Face masks made from this smooth glop are supposed to have rejuvenating and refreshing powers, but the Park Service no longer allows you to reach in and pull out a stick covered with the mud because too many beauty-seekers have been scalded. Albergue Rincón de La Vieja or Hacienda Guachipelín, on the way to Rincón, Buenavista Lodge, and Hotel Borínquen, north of the park, have access to

Collared peccary

warm volcanic mud that you can rub all over your body, let dry in the sun, and wash off for smooth, soft skin.

Note: In Las Pailas, the dry, crusty earth around the mudpots is brittle and thin in some places; unsafe areas are clearly marked. Be sure to stay away from any area that has warning signs and fences, and don't believe anyone who tells you about "shortcuts" off the marked trails. Sulfur fumes can cause bad headaches for some.

The Río Blanco forms a lovely **swimming hole** that's reachable by following a path to the left, about 100 meters beyond the ranger station. At the ranger station you can get a map that shows you how to get to **Catarata La Cangreja** (5.1 kilometers), a 75-foot waterfall with a gorgeous blue-green pool at its base, and **Cataratas Escondidas** (4.3 kilometers). You can see two of the waterfalls from the rim of a canyon, and can reach a third by walking along a creek.

Note: Signs along streams and pools in the park state that the water is drinkable (*agua potable*), but that refers to the concentration of minerals in the water and not to the absence of bacteria. We have heard of people getting severe intestinal upsets from these streams.

The park is great for hiking. The trails are not too steep and are dry most of the year. Unlike the slippery, muddy cloud forests and rainforests, Rincón is a transitional area between dry forest and cloud forest. The trails get a bit muddy only at higher altitudes, right before the forest gives way to rocky, windblown volcanic terrain.

If you want to hike to the volcano's craters, and Von Seebach peak, 7.3 kilometers from the ranger station, start out by 10 a.m. in order to be back by nightfall. If you'd like to go at a more relaxed pace, it's best to camp overnight. March and April are the best months for this, but it is always wise to bring rain gear, warm clothes, several changes of clothing wrapped in plastic, good hiking boots, a waterproof tent, and a compass.

Note: It's a good idea to hire a guide from a local hotel or tour company if you are going to the craters because the paths are not clearly marked in the rocky terrain near the top, and thick mists come up frequently. If you go without a guide, the Park Service recommends that you turn back when you emerge from the forest to the barren crater area if you see that the crater is obscured by clouds. In the dry season, the dried lava flows at the top can be extremely windy. It is tempting to walk closer to the edge than you should. But note that the crater's edge is made of gravel and ash, which can give way in a miniature landslide, taking you with it, toward the lake of boiling acid, 200 meters down. You can contact guides through the park administration, 2695-5598; acg@acguanacaste.ac.cr.

LODGING   Lodges are listed according to their distance from the Park, from closest to farthest:

Rincón de la Vieja Lodge (private bath, hot water, pool, internet; $80-$100, including breakfast; 2200-0238, fax: 2666-2441; rincondelaviejalodge.net, rincondelaviejolodge@gmail.com) is located two kilometers from the Las Pailas entrance to the park. They offer half- to full-day hiking and horseback-riding expeditions. Their 17-platform **canopy tour** is in tropical dry forest.

Several kilometers before you get to the park, **Hacienda Guachipelín** (private bath, solar hot water, fans, pool, wi-fi; $80-$90; children under 4 free; including breakfast; 2665-3303, fax: 2665-2178, cell phone: 8384-2049; guachipelin.com, info@guachipelin.com), several kilometers before the park entrance, has grown from a working cattle ranch to a comfortable lodge. The gracious reception area was built inside an old barn with many authentic touches. The charming, airy new rooms have alcoves with lovely decorative tile work and candles at each entryway, and there are cool, breezy sitting areas between each building, set around well-manicured gardens. The huge, well-designed bar and restaurant serves good native food. Recommended.

Gauchipelín has become one of the major adventure centers in the area because of the wide variety of experiences you can have there. You can purchase any of the following tours separately, or, with their one-day **Adventure Pass** (9:30 a.m. to 4:30 p.m., including lunch; adults $80, students ages 11 to 17 $75, children ages 4 to 10 $70; 2665-3303) you can ride horses to the Río Negro for tubing or to the lodge's mud pots and hot springs, hike in the national park, or take the lodge's excellent **Cañon Canopy Tour** (minimum age 6; adults $50, students $40, children $30), which includes rock climbing, rappels, ziplines, hanging bridges, and a Tarzan swing. Recommended for those who want thrills and nature.

Casa Aroma de Campo (private bath, hot water, fans; $60-$70, including breakfast; children under 10 $10; two night minimum; 2236-8100, fax: 2665-00111; aromadecampo.com, info@aromadecampo.com) is a small, cozy B&B where you can relax in hammocks or rockers on the wide veranda. Breakfasts are bountiful, and other meals are served family-style, featuring the owner's specialty: Thai cuisine. It's two kilometers past the village of Curubande and 300 meters to the left.

El Sol Verde Lodge and Campground (tents $20; rooms with private bath $40; 2665-5357, 8357-4593; elsolverde.com, info@elsolverde.com) owned by a friendly Dutch couple, offers platform tents with air mattresses as well as rooms, and a chance to be part of village life in Curubandé. You might see howler monkeys at one of two rivers near the lodge. To get there, drive to Curubandé and turn right at the El Sol Verde signs. With advance notice, the owners will pick you up at the Liberia bus stop ($10) or airport ($15).

Located 3 kilometers from the Interamerican Highway, **Cañon de la Vieja** (private bath, hot water, fans, a/c, pool, restaurant; $60-$70; 2665-5912, fax: 2665-5928; canyonlodgegete.com, canyonlodge@gmail.com) has a nice pool with a waterfall and spacious cabins. They specialize in two-person rafting trips down the narrow Colorado River next to the lodge and also offer **rock-climbing, rapelling** and their own version of a zipline **canopy tour**. It's on the right, three kilometers toward the park from the Interamerican Highway.

Rancho Curubandé (hot water, shared bath, fans, $30-$40; private bath, a/c, $50-$60; with kitchens, $90-$100; including breakfast; 2665-0375, fax: 2665-6331; rancho-curubande.com, info@rancho-curubande.com) has economical attached rooms and two-bedroom villas. Located 600 meters from the Interamerican highway on the road to the National Park, they offer horseback riding and have a river you can swim in.

GETTING THERE: By Bus: No public buses run all the way to the Rincón–Las Pailas entrance, but a bus leaves Liberia for Curubandé daily at 6:45 a.m., 12:15 and 4:15 p.m. To go all the way to the park, take a Jeep taxi from Liberia ($25 one way).

By Car: Go 4.5 kilometers north of Liberia on the Interamerican Highway to the turnoff for Curubandé. You'll see signs directing you to the Las Pailas entrance of the park. It's 600 meters to Rancho Curubande, three kilometers to Canon de la Vieja, 12 kilometers to Curubandé and El Sol Verde, two more kilometers to Aroma de Campo, another kilometer to Hacienda Guachipelin; another three to Rincon de la Vieja Lodge, and two more to the National Park entrance. It's a fairly good gravel road, interesting because it was cut through deposits of white and pinkish pumice. Just beyond Curubandé you have to pay $1.50/person to enter the part of the road maintained by Hacienda Guachipelín. It takes about 45 minutes to drive from the Interamerican Highway to the park entrance.

RINCÓN–SANTA MARÍA   This entrance to the park has a park administration center and a small historical exhibit, with campsites nearby. Fifteen kilometers of trails are explorable on your own, but you should not walk to Las Pailas without a guide, since it's easy to get lost.

Three kilometers from the Santa María entrance are **Los Azufrales**, hot sulfur springs at a perfect bathtub temperature, right next to a cold stream to splash in (don't let the sulfurous water get in your eyes, and don't stay in longer than five minutes before alternating with the cold water). These springs can also be accessed by a four-kilometer trail from Rincón de la Vieja Lodge.

In San Jorge, three kilometers toward Liberia from the park entrance, you can stay at the inexpensive **Rinconcito Lodge** (private bath, heated water, restaurant/bar; $40-$50; 2666-2764, fax: 2666-9178; rinconcitolodge.com).

GETTING THERE: No buses run to San Jorge or the Rincón–Santa María entrance (25 kilometers east of Liberia). The road is passable only with four-wheel drive. From Liberia, take the Barrio La Victoria road.

BUENA VISTA LODGE   Thirteen kilometers north of Liberia on the Interamerican Highway, you come to the turn off to Cañas Dulces. Beyond that, **Buena Vista Lodge and Adventure Center** (private bath, hot water, restaurants/bars, internet; $60-$100, breakfast included; 2690-1414, fax: 2661-8158; buenavistalodgecr.com, info@buenavistalodgecr.com) offers lodging in a series of either stone faced, log, or wood cabins, each with different views. Buena Vista has a thrilling 1300-foot-long waterslide in the forest, ending in a swimming tank (minimum age 7). At the **Buena Vista Spa**, two miles from the main lodge, there are three thermal pools of differing temperatures to soak in, and a Turkish bath where the steam comes from naturally boiling water. The steam opens your pores to enhance the effect of the warm mud that you then apply to your skin. You relax in the sunshine until the mud dries, then you wash it off and feel like new. You can hike there, ride on spirited horses, or take a very bumpy ride in a large cart with padded seats attached to a tractor. It's downhill going and uphill coming back. If you do visit the spa, you're going to be too relaxed to hike two dusty miles up again. Better to take the bumpy tractor ride. Their "mega" tour (adults $80, children $60) includes the canopy, the waterslide, a visit to the spa, and lunch.

Buena Vista's one-hour, ten-cable **canopy tour** (2690-1414; $35; minimum age 5) is in secondary forest that is quite dry in the high season. They also have a series of 17 **hanging bridges** for bird and wildlife watchers in their 1000-acre forest reserve. They offer a guided night hike on the bridges to see nocturnal animals and insects. You can learn a lot about snakes in their **serpentarium**, or see crocodiles in their lagoon. Most of the food served in their restaurants is raised right there.

Hotel Borínquen Mountain Resort and Spa (private bath, hot water, a/c, fans, refrigerator, satellite TV, pool; $240-$420, including breakfast and use of spa; 2690-1900, fax: 2690-1903; borinquenhotel.com, info@borinquenresort.com) has large, well-appointed individual and duplex bungalows, a fancy restaurant, and little golf carts to take you up and down its nicely paved roads. They offer a spa and mud treatments.

GETTING THERE: Drive north from Liberia about 15 minutes until you see signs for Cañas Dulces. Turn right and follow the road 18 kilometers to the entrances to the hotels. Borínquen is to the left before the Buena Vista gate. The road is bumpy in some places but you can make it in a regular car.

SANTA ROSA NATIONAL PARK

While most of Costa Rica's parks aim to preserve virgin forest, **Santa Rosa National Park** ($10; 2679-9692, fax: 2666-5020; acguanacaste.ac.cr) not only protects the little remaining tropical dry forest, but promotes its regeneration. This park encompasses almost every ecosystem that exists in Guanacaste. Part of the park was a large tract of pastureland, overgrazed and biologically bankrupt, where biologists have applied research findings about how forests propagate themselves. You will see, from the lush greenery as you drive in, that these methods have worked very well.

Seeds for forest regeneration are primarily carried by the wind and by mammals and birds who eat seeds and then defecate in treeless pastures. Poles stuck into barren pastures encourage this kind of seed dispersal. By burning fire lanes to control the spread of wildfires, the scientists are allowing the dry forest to renew itself.

The latest addition to the park, by the way, includes the location of the clandestine airstrip that figured in the Iran-Contra fiasco. The North American owner of this land won a legal dispute with the Costa Rican government over the expropriation that made it part of the park, and was paid $22 million for the property. This part of the park is closed.

The three times that Costa Rica has been attacked by military, the invaders were defeated at the **Hacienda Santa Rosa's Casona** (big house) which is now a museum (open 8 a.m. to 4 p.m.). Near the museum is a trail you can follow for a short natural-history jaunt.

There is **camping** (minimal fee) in a central area of Santa Rosa, with water, toilets, showers, and nice big shade trees. The ranger will tell you which parts of the park are especially rich in wildlife at the moment.

A 12-kilometer trail will take you to **Playa Naranjo**, a long stretch of white sand that you can usually have all to yourself. Near the ranger station, right off the beach, there is a camping area, an outhouse, and a water well for washing, but not for drinking. Off Playa Naranjo is **Witch's Rock**, famous with surfers the world over for creating the perfect wave. Surfers must pay the $10 park entrance fee to go to Witch's Rock, even if they arrive by boat.

The six-kilometer **Carbonal** trail takes you through dry forest, rock formations, and mangroves. It starts 300 meters before the ranger station at Playa Naranjo.

If you don't want to go all the way down to the beach, the trail to **Mirador Valle Naranjo**, where you can get a panoramic view of the coast, starts from six kilometers down the road to Playa Naranjo. It takes about 20 minutes to hike the one and a half kilometers to the lookout point from the entrance to the Mirador Trail.

The road to Playa Naranjo is probably a creek in the rainy season, and is only open to vehicles from December 15 to April 1. We have heard that this road has been greatly improved, but call the park before driving it because when it is in bad condition the typical four-wheel-drive rent-a-cars routinely get stuck near the beach. The rangers have to call a tow truck from Liberia to get them out, which costs the tourists a lot of money. **Bahía Junquillal Wildlife Refuge**, accessible by the Cuajiniquil entrance, about five minutes north of the main entrance to Santa Rosa on the Interamerican Highway, is a lovely place to camp and much easier to drive to, though it's not as wild (see below). The walk to Playa Naranjo takes three hours, and you must start early because of the heat.

Santa Rosa is home to a wide variety of easily observed animals, including three types of monkeys: loud howler monkeys, agile spider monkeys, and white-throated capuchin monkeys. You'll also see vultures, falcons, and the *urraca*, a blue-and-white jay, which has a feather on top of its head that looks like a curled ribbon. Twenty-two species of bats inhabit the park. Pelicans, gulls, herons, and sandpipers are the most common birds on the beach, while cicadas buzz from tree branches.

There are collared and white-lipped peccaries whose reputation for ferocity is undeserved, according to a Santa Rosa biologist we talked to. White-tailed deer wander in the savannah, coatimundis prowl around the forests, and caimans live in the estuaries of Playa Naranjo. As in most areas of the Pacific coast, iguanas are everywhere.

Olive ridley turtles nest in the park from July to November at **Playa Nancite**, the next beach north from Playa Naranjo. Their *arribadas* (ar-

Olive ridley turtle

rivals by sea) take place on moonless nights, with the largest (thousands at a time) arrival in October and November. After an approximately 45-day incubation period, the baby turtles hatch and crawl into the sea. About five percent survive all the hazards of turtle "childhood" to become adults.

Playa Nancite is covered with turtle eggshell fragments and a few shells and skeletons of unfortunate mother turtles who didn't make it. You can't stay at Nancite overnight without a permit from the ecotourism office at Santa Rosa (2666-5051 ext. 219)—it serves mainly as a biological research station. Only 25 people are allowed on the beach at one time. To see olive ridley more easily, go to Ostional Wildlife Refuge (see pages 336–37).

GETTING THERE: By Bus: Buses that go to La Cruz and Peñas Blancas on the Nicaragua border pass the entrance to Santa Rosa. Check thebusschedule.com for current schedules. You have to buy tickets in advance. Because of the tremendous heat, it's better to take a San José–Liberia bus, stay overnight in Liberia, then take a La Cruz (not Santa Cruz) bus from Liberia at 5:30 a.m. (check the bus schedule the night before). Ask to be let off at the "*entrada a Santa Rosa*." You must walk or hitchhike about seven kilometers to the Casona and camping area before you start the 12-kilometer hike to Playa Naranjo.

By Car: Santa Rosa is only 20 minutes north of Liberia on the Interamerican Highway, to the left. The entrance to the Murciélago Sector, through Cuajiniquil, is about five minutes (ten kilometers) beyond Santa Rosa, also to the left.

BAHÍA JUNQUILLAL WILDLIFE REFUGE AREA

North of Santa Rosa, the beautiful **Bahía Junquillal Wildlife Refuge** (2679-9692; admission $6), near the picturesque inlet of **Cuajiniquil**, north of Santa Rosa, protects a calm bay that is good for swimming and snorkeling, a tropical dry forest, and a mangrove swamp. Three species of turtles lay eggs there, and whales visit in December. A lovely campground has showers and toilets ($2/person). This is one of our favorite camping and swimming spots, but beware of the jellyfish. Bring your own water and toilet paper. Camping is first-come, first-served. This beach has the Blue Flag.

Playa El Hachal is another lovely beach known for its multicolored stones. It's five kilometers beyond the Murciélago Ranger Station, south of Cuajiniquil, and only open in the dry season. You can get information through the Santa Rosa contact numbers.

West of Cuajiniquil on the Santa Elena peninsula are peaceful **Bahía Santa Elena** and **Bahía Playa Blanca**, accessible by car only in the dry season. There is a camping and picnic area with baths and potable water at the Murciélago ranger station, nine kilometers west of Cuajiniquil. Confirm that there is space at 2679-9692. From the campground you can hike 600 meters to a swimming hole, Poza del General. It's easy to spot monkeys, birds, and iguanas in this area.

GETTING THERE: By Bus: Buses to Cuajiniquil leave Liberia daily at 5:45 a.m. and 3:30 p.m., returning at 7 a.m. and 4:30 p.m. There is also a 12:30 p.m. bus from La Cruz (see below), which returns at 6 a.m. It takes about an hour to walk to the Bahía Junquillal campground from Cuajiniquil.

By Car: If you're going by car, keep on the Interamerican Highway for ten kilometers beyond the Santa Rosa turnoff, then turn left on the nicely paved road to Cuajiniquil (seven kilometers). Playa Junquillal campground is four kilometers to the north of Cuajiniquil on a good gravel road. The Murciélago campground is seven kilometers southwest of Cuajiniquil, Playa El Hachal is five kilometers to the southwest. Bahía Santa Elena is 12 more kilometers southwest on a difficult road, and Playa Blanca is another six kilometers beyond that. These last three trips can only be done in the dry season with a four-wheel-drive vehicle.

GUANACASTE NATIONAL PARK

Guanacaste National Park (2661-8150) was created in 1989 to protect the migratory paths of animals that live in Santa Rosa, so it extends from the Interamerican Highway east to the Orosi and Cacao volcanoes. Many species of moths procreate in the high mountains during the dry season, then fly down to spend the rainy season at a lower, warmer altitude. The *zahino*, a wild pig, retreats from the volcanoes to the dry forest in January to search for seeds of the *encino* (evergreen oak) tree. Scientists studying the wildlife in Santa Rosa have found that in order to protect these and other animals, the environments so necessary to their existence must also be protected. The whole Guanacaste Conservation Area now protects 220,000 hectares of land.

Although Costa Rica has about .001 percent of the world's landmass, it has 5 percent of the world's biodiversity. For instance, an estimated 3800 species of moths live in Santa Rosa alone. Studying all of them would take years. However, under the auspices of **INBio** (see Chapter Five) local park employees are being trained in biological inventory techniques by some of the best scientists in the world. By all reports, the program is a tremendous success due to the sharp powers of observation of the *campesinos*, their familiarity with the region and its wildlife, and their motivation to learn a new career that was not open to them until a few years ago (45 percent of the conservation area's employees are women). People from parks all over the country are being trained in the same techniques. All specimens will be turned over to InBio in Santo Domingo de Heredia, which hopes to identify every plant and animal species in Costa Rica.

Guanacaste National Park is not set up for tourism, but you can get close to Volcán Cacao by visiting **Curubanda Lodge** (private bath, hot and heated water, jacuzzi, restaurant, internet; $60-$70, including breakfast; phone/fax: 2691-8177; curubanda.com, reservaciones@curubanda.com). Their nine-hour hike to Volcán Cacao's Pedregal Peak affords views of Lake Nicaragua and the Papagayo coast. They also offer a two-hour loop by horseback through primary forest to a beautiful waterfall and swimming hole. The lodge is on a working cattle farm where you can help milk the cows. The special cabin with the jacuzzi has a nice balcony for sunset viewing. Rooms have chandeliers full of candles. The countryside is a gorgeous combination of forest patches and dairy land reminiscent of Monteverde. It's part of the Rincón/Cacao Biological Corridor. To get there from the Interamerican Highway, take the turnoff on the right to Potrerillos, about 15 minutes north of the turnoff for Rincón de la Vieja. In about ten minutes you'll come to the village of Quebrada Grande, also known as Garcia Flamenco, where you turn left. In 20 minutes you'll be at Finca Nueva Zelandia, where the lodge is.

LA CRUZ AND BAHÍA SALINAS

The region around La Cruz, near the Nicaraguan border, is still off the beaten track for tourists. There are spectacular views from the breezy west side of town.

Isla Bolaños, a small island in Bahía Salinas west of La Cruz, is part of Santa Rosa National Park. It is the only place in Costa Rica where frigate birds and American oyster catchers nest. Several hundred nesting pairs of frigate birds inhabit the cliffs on the southwestern side of the island; 500 to 600 pairs of brown pelicans nest on the northern side from December to July.

On Bahía Salinas, the **Blue Dream Hotel and Kite Surfing Center** (private bath, hot water, jacuzzi, spa, yoga terrace, restaurant, watersports/rentals; $30-$40, or shared room/bath for $15 per person; 2676-1042, 8826-5221; bluedreamhotel.com, bertoldi@racsa.co.cr) caters to the windsurfing crowd. It has an Italian restaurant and a spa. In addition to watersport equipment rentals, it offers 4WD adventures.

In the town of La Cruz, **Soda Santa María** (679-9347) is good for *comida típica*.

Cabinas Santa Rita (shared bath, small rooms, $10; private bath, cold water, fans, $12-$20; with air conditioning, $20-$30; 2679-9062, phone/fax: 2679-9329) has well-kept, spacious rooms across from the Tribunales de Justicia. You can leave your car there if you want to take side trips by bus to Nicaragua. Good value. Recommended for budget travelers.

Right on the edge of the cliff, with a stunning view of Bahía Salinas, is **Amalia's Inn** (shared or private bath, hot or heated water, satellite TV, pool; no children under 14; $30-$40; phone/fax: 2679-9618), originally built as a gallery for the paintings of American artist Lester Bounds. His widow, Doña Amalia, is a charming hostess. The rooms are eclectic; all have their own sitting areas. There is also a restaurant to the left of the hotel.

There are a couple of nice hotels like **Ecoplaya** (ecoplaya.com) down on the beach, but the wind-sports enthusiasts claim that this is one of the ten windiest places on the planet; the wind is so strong, especially in the dry season, that it's unpleasant to be on the beach. The hotels have glassed-in pool areas where you can relax out of the breeze. We don't recommend this area for those who are not into windsurfing or kitesurfing.

GETTING THERE: By Bus: Check thebusschedulemonteverdeinfo.com for current bus schedules to La Cruz. You can get a bus or taxi from La Cruz to the Nicaraguan border.

By Car: La Cruz is a straight shot up the Interamerican Highway from Liberia.

BEACHES NEAR LIBERIA

Guanacaste Province has some of the most beautiful beaches in Costa Rica. Part of Guanacaste's popularity is due to the fact that it has only 65 days of rainfall a year, compared to seven months or more of afternoon rains in other parts of the country. But given that fact, rapid development of new hotels, condos, luxury homes and gated communities at Playas Panama, Hermosa, Coco, Ocotal, Pez Vela, Grande, Tamarindo and Langosta, puts water resources in peril. Most buildings have their own septic systems. But the sheer density of development creates the need for public wastewater treatment facilities, none of which exist in this area as yet. You can read more about the problems this has caused in the Ecology Chapter.

While there are many residents of these areas working very hard to create and implement zoning plans and waste disposal and treatment plants, this part of Guanacaste is in the grips of a struggle that may take years to resolve. Even though there are responsible businesses in this area, their efforts at sustainability count for little if the community as a whole cannot learn to meet the challenges posed by big money, government corruption and inefficiency, and real estate speculation. Since this edition of *The New Key to Costa Rica* focuses on examples of innovative, sustainable communities, we cannot publicize tourism attractions in this area until basic improvements are made that will guarantee the water supply for all residents, prevent environmental pollution, and limit development. None of the beaches mentioned above are listed here. It would be wonderful if somehow this area could turn itself around and set an example for the rest of the country, which sooner or later will have to confront the same problems.

SANTA CRUZ

Santa Cruz is the home of much of Costa Rica's folklore. The music department of the University of Costa Rica has a special branch there, devoted to researching and celebrating traditional songs, dances, and instruments.

Just a 15-minute drive from Santa Cruz, through the beautiful hill country that is the heartland of the Nicoya Peninsula, are the villages of **Guaitil** and **San Vicente**, where local artisans have revived the art of Chorotega-style pottery making. With little use of a wheel, they recreate every known original design from native clay and natural paints and colors. Pieces range in price from $2 to $50. The pottery is displayed at the local shop and in front of homes.

At **Casa del Sol** (open Monday through Saturday, 9 a.m. to 4 p.m.; 2248-9470, 6681-1015; actuarcostarica.com, info@actuarcostarica.com), on the road to Guaitil, local women use solar ovens and water heaters. They go all over the country teaching other women how to build solar ovens. Food that is slow-cooked in a solar oven doesn't stick or burn, retains more flavor and nutrients, and leaves the cook free to do other things, as well as saving energy, and eliminating the use of firewood. Call ahead for reservations for a solar lunch and workshop ($18).

Santa Barbara buses leave Santa Cruz for Guaitil every two hours; to drive there, head towards Nicoya and take the left after you cross a bridge leaving Santa Cruz. Recommended.

Coopetortillas (open daily, 3 a.m. to 6:30 p.m.; 2680-0688), 250 meters south of the church, is our favorite place to eat in Santa Cruz. It has grown from a tortilla factory to a popular restaurant featuring typical Guanacaste food. We don't know if you get emotional about huge hand-patted tortillas made from freshly ground corn, but they are well worth the $2 charged for a hearty breakfast of *gallo pinto* with eggs and *café con leche*. The place looks unattractive from the outside, but the primal smell of wood smoke will lead you inside, where *señoras* in lovely pink aprons take you back into the kitchen area to show you the pots on the huge cement wood-stove so that you can pick what you want to eat. This restaurant is a cultural experience in itself. Recommended.

There is an open-air **farmer's market** at Plaza los Mangos on Saturday mornings and under the trees on the block behind the church on Monday mornings. Another block south is the **hospital**, which offers 24-hour emergency care.

LODGING   Hotels in Santa Cruz are not that exciting. Try to plan your time so you can get to the beach before nightfall (5:30 p.m.). **Hotel Diriá** (private bath, hot water, a/c, table fans, cable TV, phone; $40-$50; 2680-0080, fax: 2680-0442; hoteldiria@hotmail.com), at the entrance to Santa Cruz near the highway, is the fanciest option in town, a large hotel whose rooms enclose gardens and pools.

Close competition comes from **Hotel la Calle de Alcalá** (private bath, hot water, a/c, phones, cable TV, pool, restaurant; $40-$50; suite with jacuzzi, $80-$90; 2680-0000, fax: 2680-1633; hotelalcala@hotmail.com), one block east of the Tralapa bus stop in Santa Cruz.

Hotel La Pampa (private bath, cold water, cable TV, fans or a/c; $40-$50; 2680-0586) is clean and attractive, 50 meters west of the southwest corner of Plaza Lopez.

Cabinas Permont (private bath, cold water, ceiling fan or air conditioning; $20-$30; 2680-0425) is a very clean establishment by the highway on the southeast side of town. Look carefully for the sign; it's on the left as you leave Santa Cruz for Nicoya.

GETTING THERE: By Bus: Nine direct buses leave daily from the Alfaro terminal between 7 a.m. and 6 p.m. (2222-2666; half a block west of the Coca Cola; $5; four-hour trip) Buses leave hourly from Liberia and Nicoya for Santa Cruz.

By Car: Santa Cruz is about four hours from San José, crossing the Tempisque river on the Puente La Amistad. The bridge is about 25 kilometers west of the Limonal turnoff on the Interamerican Highway.

Guaitil is 12 kilometers east of Santa Cruz and 19 kilometers northwest of Nicoya. The road is paved between Santa Cruz and Guaitil, unpaved between Guaitil and Nicoya.

BEACHES NEAR SANTA CRUZ

This area gives more of a sense of Costa Rican rural life than the more populous beaches farther north. The hotels are just as nice—quieter and often more reasonably priced than in nearby Tamarindo, and not that much harder to get to.

PLAYA JUNQUILLAL

This wide, almost deserted Blue Flag beach can have high surf and strong rip currents, but when we were there, the waves were calm and the sense of tranquility was pervasive, compared to Tamarindo. Horseback riding, surfing, kayaking on the estuary, and dolphin tours are available. At the southern and northern ends are tide pools big enough to snorkel in. Leatherback turtles lay their eggs at Junquillal from October to March, with greater activity from November to January. **Paradise Riding** (phone/fax: 2658-8162; paradiseriding.com) offers horseback rides in the hills or on the beach.

The Canadian-owned **Iguanazul** (private bath, hot water, ceiling fans, some a/c, pool, spa, wi-fi; $60-$90; with a/c, $90-$130; including breakfast; 2658-8124, fax: 2658-8235; iguanazul.com, info@hoteliguanazul.com) is one kilometer north of Playa Junquillal on a cliff overlooking the ocean. You can rent surfing equipment, kayaks, and horses here, there is an entertainment room and volleyball net. This isolated 24-room hotel and its gourmet restaurant could be rented as a whole for a retreat. They also have houses and condos for rent. To get there, turn right at the arched Iguanazul entrance and go one kilometer toward the beach.

Next door, **Camping Los Malinches** ($5/person; phone/fax: 2683-0264) has a lovely view from its shady campsites, and clean bathrooms and showers. Although you have to hike for a kilometer to get to the campsite from the road, once you are there it's a short walk to the great restaurant at Iguanazul. In front of Los Malinches and Iguanazul the beach is mostly rocky tidepools, but sandy Playa Blanca is just 200 meters north.

Just before arriving in Junquillal, you'll pass the lovely hilltop **Guacamaya Lodge** (private bath, hot water, ceiling fans, a/c, internet, pool; $60-$70; with kitchens, $70-$100; 2658-8431, fax: 2658-8164; guacamaya lodge.com, alibern@racsa.co.cr), which has attractive screened rooms around the pool, studio apartments with ocean views, and a restaurant with international gourmet cuisine. They also rent a two-bedroom house for $110-$150 a night.

In Junquillal proper, the German-owned **Hotel Hibiscus** (private bath, heated water, ceiling fans; $40-$60, including breakfast; phone/fax: 2658-8437; adventure-costarica.com/hibiscus, hibiscus@adventure-costarica.com) has well-designed and -decorated bungalows. Their restaurant serves seafood and French and German cuisine. Across the street, with gardens leading to the beach, is **La Puesta del Sol** (2658-8442), an attractive Italian restaurant serving handmade pasta and gelato. We've heard that their pricey, authentic Italian cuisine is worth a trip to Junquillal.

Our favorite place in Junquillal is **Land Ho At Hotel Villa Serena** (private bath, hot water, ceiling fans, some a/c, tennis court, gym, pool; $130-$150; 2658-8430, fax: 2658-9020; land-ho.com, serenaho@racsa.co.cr), run by the owners of the famous Cape Cod restaurant, Land Ho. The hotel's restaurant looks out over the tranquil beach and serves delicious food.

Costa Rican art and sculpture grace the walls. The rooms are quiet and comfortable. A poolside spa offers European facials, mud and seaweed wraps, and massage.

GETTING THERE: By Bus: A Tralapa bus (Calle 20, Avenidas 3/5; 2221-7202; $4.50) leaves San José at 2 p.m. and makes a connection in Santa Cruz for Junquillal. It returns at 5 a.m. The trip takes five and a half hours. Or take any San José–Santa Cruz bus and get a taxi to Junquillal ($30-$40).

By Car:. If you are coming from the Amistad Bridge and Nicoya, turn left after you cross a small metal bridge as you leave Santa Cruz. Follow the road 18 kilometers to 27 de Abril. After you pass another metal bridge, turn left. After 200 meters turn right. Follow that road into Paraíso. Turn left after the soccer field and continue about 4 kilometers to Junquillal.

If you are coming from Liberia, turn right just before the metal bridge at the entrance to Santa Cruz and follow above directions. The road from Santa Cruz to 27 de Abril is paved with potholes; the other roads are not. You'll feel a lot better if you have a sturdy car with high clearance on these bumpy roads.

By Air: SANSA (2233-0397; flysansa.com) and Nature Air (2299-6000; natureair.com) fly to Tamarindo. A taxi from Tamarindo to Junquillal costs about $30-$40 and takes about 45 minutes.

PLAYAS NEGRA AND AVELLANAS

Just north of Playa Junquillal, Playas Negra and Avellanas have been a secret destination for surfers for many years. After surfers graduate from the slower waves at Tamarindo, they are ready for the waves at Avellanas. Only advanced surfers should take on the very fast wave at incoming high tide at Playa Negra, 5 kilometers south of Avellanas. The beaches themselves are quite pretty, with lovely shade trees all along the coast.

On the beach, **Hotel Playa Negra** (private bath, hot water, ceiling fans, restaurant, pool, internet; $90-$100; 2652-9134, fax: 2652-9053; playanegra.com, hotelplaynegra@ice.co.cr) has well-designed circular bungalows, a circular swimming pool, and a breezy circular restaurant on the beach.

Cafe Playa Negra Bed & Breakfast & Bistro (private bath, fans, internet, some a/c, screened windows; $40-$60, including breakfast; phone/fax: 2652-9351; playanegracafe.com, info@playanegracafe.com), a five-minute walk to the beach, is a nice little hotel with six cozy, sunlit rooms decorated with artwork. The café specializes in Peruvian food but also prepares huge sandwiches for hungry surfers.

Lola's (open Tuesday through Sunday, 11 a.m. to 3 p.m.; 2658-8097) on Playa Avellanas is an alfresco restaurant and bar that features organic chicken and responsibly harvested seafood. Pizza, salads, *ceviche*, and fruit smoothies round out their menu. Lola's is named after a 750-pound pig that enjoys bathing at the beach.

The Italian-owned **Cabinas El León** (private bath, hot water, fan, restaurant; $30-$40; 2652-9318; cabinaselleon.com) is known for its thin-crust pizza and other authentic Italian dishes.

GETTING THERE: By Bus: No public transportation goes all the way to Playas Negra and Avellanas. See the Junquillal bus directions and get off in Paraíso, where you can hitch, hire a taxi, or walk the rest of the way (4.5 kilometers) to Playa Negra. It takes half an hour to walk from Playa Negra to Avellanas at low tide.

By Car: For Playa Negra, drive to Paraíso as described in the "Getting There" section for Junquillal. In Paraíso, turn right (instead of left for Junquillal) and drive along the gravel road. In 15 minutes you will be at Playa Negra. Playa Avellanas is 10 minutes north on the coastal road. It's best to have four-wheel drive in the rainy season, and a high clearance at any time of year.

FROM PARAÍSO TO OSTIONAL

This area is largely undeveloped and has a peaceful feel, with glimpses of the sea now and then. About 20 minutes south of Paraíso is the little fishing village of Playa Lagarto, then Playa Manzanillo. Another ten minutes and you're in Marbella, famous for surfing. Next comes the fishing village of San Juanillo, where the deserted coves are protected by a rock reef and snorkeling is good. In another half hour you are in Ostional. Four-wheel drive is best on this road because there are some small streams to ford, and some larger rivers to ford if you want to continue on to Nosara. There are two hotels of note on this road.

Al Mare (private bath, unheated water, fans, a/c, TV, pool; $60-$80, including breakfast; children under 12 free; 8350-8871, 2293-3456; 1-costaricalink.com, tatotime@interfree.it), on a slight rise above Playa Manzanillo with a beautiful view of the bay, has six individual cabins with rooftop terraces. When we were there, a troop of howler monkeys relaxed in the trees next to the cabins. The Italian family that runs the place made quite a name for itself with its Restaurante La Campanna in Dominical, but now it has moved to this more isolated spot, where it still serves its famous handmade raviolis, bakes its own bread, and grows its own organic veggies. The sea is calm here, good for families, and it's very quiet, except for the howler monkeys. To get there, follow the brightly painted Al Mare signs south of Playa Lagarto.

The Swiss-owned **Luna Azul** (private bath, solar hot water, fans, a/c, refrigerators, pool, jacuzzi, spa, language courses, restaurant; $110-$180, including breakfast; 8821-0075; hotellunaazul.com, info@hotellunaazul.com) is a stylish boutique hotel famous for its gourmet cuisine. The well-designed, multilevel alfresco restaurant looks out onto an infinity pool framed by forest, with the sea in the distance; the seven rooms and villas reveal the same attention to comfort, color, and detail. The restaurant's beef and chicken fondue features six different sauces, and their proximity to the sea means the octopus *carpaccio* is totally fresh. Their changing menu features fish-based soups, intriguing salads, and pasta. During the high season, they have international theme dinners. Diners from nearby Nosara are willing to ford a couple of rivers to get to the Luna Azul, which is located in Ostional.

NICOYA

While Liberia is the transportation and commercial capital of Guanacaste, Nicoya is the cultural capital. Its church (open daily, 8 a.m. to noon, 2 p.m. to 6 p.m.), dedicated to San Blas, was built in 1644 and is an adobe monument to the austere faith of the Spanish colonists. Next to it is a lovely, shady square abloom with flowers.

Café Daniela, an open, airy restaurant on the main thoroughfare one block from the park, has freshly baked goods, pizzas, and ice-cold *refrescos,* plus a full Tico menu, including a vegetarian *casado* and carrot juice. **El Presidente**, 25 meters east of the plaza, serves generous portions of tasty fried fish and Chinese food.

LODGING   The nicest place to stay in this area is the **Cabinas Río Tempisque** (private bath, hot water, fans, a/c, refrigerator, cable TV, phones, pool, restaurant; $50-$60; 2686-6650, fax: 2686-4650), with spacious, peaceful, well-kept grounds and clean modern rooms. It's on the highway to Santa Cruz, one kilometer west of the entrance to Nicoya.

Hotel Curime (private bath, hot water, pool, ceiling or table fans, TV, a/c, refrigerators; $40-$50; 2685-5238, fax: 2685-5530), south of town on the road to Playas Sámara and Nosara, has a recreation complex, including a large pool, tennis, volleyball and basketball courts, a playground, and a restaurant.

GETTING THERE: By Bus: Buses to Nicoya leave San José from Tracopa Alfaro (Calle 14, Avenida 5; 2222-2666; $5) 7 times a day. You must buy tickets in advance.

By Car: Take the Interamerican Highway and look for signs for the Tempisque (La Amistad) bridge right after the turnoff for Las Juntas, at Limonal. The bridge is about 25 kilometers to the west. Cross the bridge and follow the signs to Nicoya.

Coming from Liberia, it's about 20 minutes from Santa Cruz to Nicoya on the paved road and an hour on the scenic old road that passes through Santa Bárbara and Guaitil. Buses run hourly between Santa Cruz and Nicoya.

MONTE ALTO FOREST RESERVE   Monte Alto is a community-owned rainforest reserve near the town of **Hojancha**, a cool, coffee-growing region in the hills southeast of Nicoya. In response to increasing water shortages, the community banded together in 1992 to buy 290 hectares of land, which they have left untouched. It has regenerated into beautiful rainforest that will insure the survival of the Río Nosara and thus the community itself. Visitors can hike within the reserve and stay at the lovely wooden **lodge** (shared or private bath, cold water; $30-$40/person, including meals; kids under 12 free; 2659-9347, 248-9470; montealtohojancha.com, info@ actuarcostarica.com) the community has built. You can bring your own picnic, or call in advance and they will cook for you. A small visitors center displays old farm implements and has pictures of the animal and bird species in the area. The 500-meter Orchid Garden Trail has 67 varieties of orchids (best between December and February) and trogons frequent the reserve from February to May. There is an attractive open air meeting room, a barbecue, and a cabin for families. During their annual April celebration, they run the old *trapiche* to show how sugar is made. They have a couple of short loop trails, and a steep two-kilometer climb to a *mirador* where you can see both sides of the Nicoya Peninsula.

Hojancha is one of the only regions in Guanacaste that is high enough to grow coffee. At the **Coopepilangosta Coffee Tour** you'll learn about the history of this rural cooperative, and see how coffee is dried and then roasted. After tasting a freshly made cup of coffee, take a look at their souvenir store. Tours start at 9 a.m. and 1 p.m. and cost $25. The season is in November and December. Arrange through Monte Alto.

GETTING THERE: By Bus: A bus leaves San José (2222-2666; Calle 14, Avenida 5) for Hojancha at 2:30 p.m. daily, returning at 7:30 a.m. There is also bus service from Nicoya.

By Car: The 14 kilometers from Nicoya to Mansion, and then Hojancha are scenic and the road is nicely paved. The six kilometers from Hojancha to the reserve are best done with four-wheel drive, especially in the rainy season. There are four small streams to cross. Be sure to arrive before sundown so people can easily direct you to the reserve. Everyone in the community knows where it is.

NOSARA, SÁMARA, AND CARRILLO

NOSARA

Playas de Nosara, one of the only ecotouristic beaches in Guanacaste, is an international community with many North American and European resi-

Frigates

dents who have set aside thousands of acres of their land as a wildlife reserve and park. The Nosara Civic Association governs the community and
so far has been successful in keeping out large developers. You won't find
many hotels right on the beach here because the residents respect and obey
Costa Rican laws concerning development within the Maritime Zone, unlike many other more touristy beaches in the country. Nosara is about half
an hour from the Ostional Wildlife Refuge (see pages 336–37), which protects an important olive ridley turtle nesting ground. Because of these reserve areas, Nosara is generally much greener than the rest of Guanacaste.
No hunting has been allowed there for decades, so birds and wildlife are
plentiful. It is common to see coatimundis, armadillos, howler monkeys, and
even the jaguarundi, a cat that looks black from a distance but actually has
a gray diamond pattern on its fur. Parrots, toucans, cuckoos, trogons, and
pelicans are easily observed. Humpback and gray whales can be seen offshore during the winter months. The beaches have community-maintained
shelters for picnicking, but the beaches can be shadeless in the morning.

Note: Bring a flashlight for walking around at night.

Playa Pelada is a small, S-shaped beach. Its volcanic outcrops house
tidal pools and a blowhole that sends up a surprising shower and spray during high tide. There are coral reefs and tidepools on **Playa Guiones** that
are good for snorkeling and safe for children at low tide. Surfing is best at
Guiones and at the mouth of the Nosara River.

Kayaking on the Río Nosara and through the mangroves in a boat with
a quiet electric motor is offered by **Toni's River Tours** (2682-0610; tonis-
rivertours.com, info@tonis-rivertours.com). Sea kayaking is available
through **Iguana Expeditions** (iguanaexpeditins.com). Sunset horseback
rides on the beach or to a local waterfall are through **Boca Nosara Tours**
(2682-0280; bocanosaratours.com, info@bocanosaratours.com). There are a
lot of surfing teachers (both male and female) in town. Ask at your hotel.

Nosara Wellness Services (2682-0360, fax: 2682-0084; nosarawell ness.com, jane@nosarawellness.com) provides individualized health plans, including yoga and bodywork performed by a Swiss therapist.

Nosara Yoga Institute (2682-0071, fax: 2682-0595, in North America: 866-439-4704; nosarayoga.com, info@nosarayoga.com) is dedicated to professional training for teachers and practitioners in the fields of yoga and bodywork. Don Stapleton, who heads the program, is the author of *Self-Awakening Yoga: The Expansion of Consciousness Through the Body's Own Wisdom*. Their large yoga studio is on the left as you enter Nosara. Yoga classes are open to the public.

Next to the Café de Paris (info@cafedeparis.net) is a **bank** (don't wait to cash your traveler's checks in Nosara because the lines are long), a **pharmacy**, a **laundromat**, a **tourist information center**, a massage and bodywork center, an ice cream store, a surfing photographer, and several souvenir stores and boutiques.

National (2242-7878; natcar.com) has a car rental agency in Nosara, and other agencies will charge about $35 to deliver a car to Nosara. Alternatively, you can rent electric golf carts at **Coconut Harry's Surf Shop** or ATVs from **Gunther's Quad Rentals** or the **Nosara Surf Shop**. You can rent **bikes** in Nosara village. If you're thinking of using open-air transport during the dry season, be aware that any vehicle kicks up a lot of dust on the roads and you don't want to be caught in a dust cloud. There is a local taxi service—ask your hotel to call one for you.

In Nosara village, there is a **health clinic** on the far side of the airstrip. The police station is next to the post office in Nosara village. There are no gas stations, but you can buy gas at local stores. You should fill up before you get to Nosara.

First we describe the lodgings and restaurants closest to Playa Guiones, then we move northward to those close to Playa Pelada and inland, to the village of Nosara. (This is the order in which you will find them if you drive in from Nicoya.) You'll find a good map of the area at nosara.com, and there is a lot of good info about travel and **house rentals** at nosara-travel.com. Many hotels will take Visa cards.

LODGING AND RESTAURANTS   Near the southern end of Playa Guiones, **La Dolce Vita** (open daily 11 a.m. to 11 p.m.; 2682-0107) is worth the hike (or drive) from where you are staying. They serve gourmet Italian pizza, pasta, and seafood.

The Bocas de Nosara area has several friendly places near the beach. The first is **Café de Paris** (2682-0087, fax: 2682-0089; cafedeparis.net, info@cafedeparis.net), which bakes French bread and croissants for its poolside restaurant (open daily, 7 a.m. to 11 p.m.) and has an internet café.

Their rooms (private bath, hot water, ceiling fans, a/c, pool, wi-fi; $420 weekly; with kitchen and hammocks, $560-$900 weekly; three-bedroom villas with ocean views, $1400/week) offer a variety of configurations for families and groups.

Down the street is **Harmony Hotel** (private bath, hot water, ceiling fans, a/c, refrigerators, pool, wi-fi, healing center, book shop; $160-$180; private one-bedroom bungalows, $230-$270; with two bedrooms, $340-$400; 2682-4114, fax: 2682-4113; harmonynosara.com, inquiries@harmonynosara.com). The rooms around the pool have a private sun deck in back. Their restaurant (open 7 to 10:30 a.m., noon to 3:30 p.m., and 6 to 9 p.m.; call for reservations) serves organic seafood, fruits, and veggies. The smaller garden *rancho* serves vegetarian *tapas*, freshly squeezed juices, and herbal teas. No bottled or canned drinks are served. The hotel is run in harmony with nature as much as possible, with many eco-friendly practices built into its infrastructure. Recommended.

Harbor Reef Lodge (private bath, hot water, ceiling fans, a/c, pool, wi-fi, TV; $110-$230; villas, $180-$260; houses, $190-$350, weekly rentals available; 2682-0059, fax: 2682-0060; harborreef.com, reservations@harborreef.net) offers well-designed guest rooms with many amenities, some with private porches. Meals are served in the tastefully decorated restaurant. There is a supermarket next door.

Back on the main road, **Giardino Tropicale** is an open-air Italian restaurant surrounded by tropical gardens. Their pizza and focaccia is baked in a wood-fired oven. **Hotel Giardino Tropicale** (private bath, solar hot water, a/c, refrigerator, lap pool, wi-fi; $80-$110; apartment that sleeps five, $140; 2682-4000, fax: 2682-0353; giardinotropicale.com, info@giardinotropicale.com) is friendly and comfortable with a very clean lap pool, and a kiddie pool. All rooms have balconies or porches with hammocks and rocking chairs. Owners Marcel and Miriam are very helpful and knowledgeable about the turtle tours in Ostional. Recommended.

From Giardino, follow signs to **Casa Romántica** (private bath, hot water, ceiling fans, pool, wi-fi; $80-$90; with refrigerator and a/c, $90-$100; two-room suites, $90-$120; breakfast included; phone/fax: 2682-0272; casa-romantica.net, info@casa-romantica.net). This small Swiss-owned hotel is where the international community goes when they want a special meal by candlelight. Delightful salads, filling Swiss, Italian, and seafood specialties, delicious desserts, and fine wines make up the menu.

The nearby **Villa Canadiense** (private bath, hot water, fans, a/c, pool, kitchens; $100-$250, weekly and monthly rentals available; 2682-0350; villacanadiense.com, reservations@villacanadiense.com) consists of one-bedroom apartments, simply furnished and secure, that sleep four; the gardens and pool are quiet. They give substantial green-season discounts.

The main road winds around a bit after the Giardino Tropicale, then you come to **Rancho Congo** (private bath, hot water, ceiling fans; $40-$50, including breakfast; phone/fax: 2682-0078; rcongo@infoweb.co.cr) on the left, a pleasant B&B owned by Monika Theil. The porch is strewn with hammocks and the gardens are beautifully tended.

The **Gilded Iguana** (2682-0259; gildediguana.com, pattydoe@gildediguana.com) is a bar/restaurant famous for its Black Panther cocktail, named after the local jaguarundi. It also rents rooms ($40-$70) and two-room suites (private bath, hot water, fans, refrigerators; $60-$100) 200 meters from the beach, and offers a pool, sportfishing, sea kayaking, and horse rentals.

Lodge Vista del Mar (private bath, hot water, fans, a/c, pool, wi-fi; $40-$60, including breakfast; two-bedroom apartments with kitchens, $90-$100; 2682-0633, fax: 2682-0611; lodgevistadelmar.com, g_ottley@yahoo.com) has a unique setting high in the hills, with a great view over the forest, down to Playas Pelada and Guiones. Birds and monkeys visit the trees surrounding the lodge, which borders the private Amigos de Nosara Reserve. The hospitable owner is a triathlete who coaches the local swimming team. Guests can work out in the 25-meter lap pool. Rooms are simple and comfortable. Short- and long-term rentals available. Recommended.

At the summit of a rocky hill, with a terrific view of the meandering Nosara River and the beaches north of Nosara, is **Lagarta Lodge** (private bath, hot water, restaurant/bar, ceiling fans, pool, internet access; children under 12 free; $60-$100, including entrance to reserve; 2682-0035, fax: 2682-0135; lagarta.com, lagarta@racsa.co.cr). This secluded, peaceful private reserve descends to the river with six different nature trails to explore. There are shady places to sit and take in the view. Their Sunday barbecue and seafood fondue are legendary. Make reservations. Look for signs at the foot of the hill as you leave Nosara. This place is great for birders but a little too quiet for children. Recommended.

If you turn left at the road just before you get to the Lagarta Lodge turnoff, you'll be on your way to Playa Pelada. Spanish-owned **Refugio del Sol** (private bath, hot water, fans; $40-$50; with kitchen, $50-$60; phone/fax: 2682-0287, cell: 8825-9365; refugiodelsol.com, info@ refugiodelsol.com) has rooms with hammocks around a garden patio and is only a five-minute walk from the beach. The **restaurant** serves breakfast and dinner and is famous for its *paella*. It's about 150 meters from the turnoff.

NOSARA VILLAGE   The village of Nosara is about three to four kilometers inland from the beaches. There are a couple of food markets in town, and disco dancing on Saturday nights at the **Tropicana**. **Rancho Tico** (open Monday through Saturday, 11 a.m. to 10 p.m.; Sunday, 4 p.m. to 10 p.m.; 2682-0006) is on the left on the way to Nosara village. Tables are set among nicely polished tree trunks that hold up the roof. Their inexpensive chicken tacos feature a generous quantity of succulent chunks of marinated meat with tortillas—really delicious. They also know how to prepare whole fried fish. Recommended.

GETTING THERE: By Bus: A direct bus from San José leaves the Alfaro terminal (Calle 14, Avenida 5; 2222-2666; $8) at 6 a.m. daily, returning at 12:30 p.m. Buy tickets a day in advance. **Interbus** (2283-5573; interbusonline.com) will also take you to Nosara from almost anywhere in Costa Rica. From Nicoya, buses leave for Nosara at 5 a.m., 10 a.m., noon and 3 p.m.. Check schedules at 2685-5352. The trip from Nicoya to Nosara takes about two hours by bus.

By Car: From Nicoya, follow the road southwest toward Sámara and Nosara. After about 30 kilometers, you will come to a Y intersection. Veer right and continue another 27 kilometers (about an hour) on a gravel road to Nosara. You can make it in a regular car, but four-wheel drive in the rainy seasons helpful if you are staying in the hills. You can also take the coastal road that connects to the first road about halfway between Samara and Nosara. The only thing that slowed us down was a herd of cattle that surrounded us, but that is what gives Guanacaste its charm. Be sure to ask about road conditions before setting out. When it has been raining, there are sometimes streams to ford. If you encounter this situation, wait until local drivers come by and follow them, instead of attempting to cross by yourself. The San José–Nosara trip takes about five hours by way of the Tempisque bridge.

You can also reach Nosara in the dry season from the northern coast, entering just north of the town of Santa Cruz, and going to 27 de Abril and Paraíso. You have to ford about three rivers when you come this way. The San José–Nosara trip takes four to five hours by way of the Tempisque bridge.

By Air: SANSA flies to Nosara (2290-4100, in North America: 877-767-2672; flysansa.com) daily. Nature Air also has daily flights (2299-6000, in North America: 800-235-9272; natureair.com). Ask your hotel to arrange transportation from the airport. If you fly into Oduber International Airport in Liberia, you'll be two and a half hours from Nosara by car.

PLAYA SÁMARA

Playa Sámara is a large half-moon bay with shallow, gentle waters. It's popular with swimmers and windsurfers, and is a favorite weekend destination for Costa Ricans during the dry season. The five-kilometer beach is protected from riptides and sharks by a barrier reef. In contrast to Nosara, there are a lot of hotels and restaurants right on the beach, because Samara existed as a beach town before the enactment of the 1975 Maritime Law. There you'll see a lot of coconut palms, but little jungle. Even though it is not as green as Nosara, Sámara has an exemplary community water committee that works closely with local institutions to keep development in check.

There are a lot of things to do in Sámara. You can watch dolphins, ride horses, snorkel or learn to sea kayak with **Tio Tigre Tours**; fish with **Delicial** or **Sámara Sportfishing**; learn Spanish at **Intercultura Language School**; or zip through the treetops with **Wing Nuts Canopy Tour**. You can explore all these options at samarabeach.com. **Samara Travel Center** (open daily 8 a.m. to 10 p.m.) on the left as you enter town, has a nice internet café, rents bikes and scooters. **C & C Surf School** (2656-0628) rents surfboards, boogie boards, and kayaks and does kayak and snorkeling trips to nearby Isla Chora ($25). They specialize in teaching kids and first-time surfers on Sámara's gentle waves. They also rent inexpensive rooms and houses.

Hotel and Restaurant Flying Crocodile (2656-8048, 8827-8858, fax: 2656-8049; flying-crocodile.com, flycroco@web.de), run by a German pilot with an excellent safety record, takes people flying in ultralights in the dry season. His family also has very nice cabins (private bath, hot water, fans, internet, pool; $40-$100; six-person apartment, $170; children under 12 free) near Bahía Montereyna, a mostly deserted beach, with open-air cooking facilities for guests, and a Euro/Costa Rican/Caribbean restaurant. To get there, turn north at the large gas station on the coastal road about 25 minutes north of Sámara.

Because it is easily accessible (only 40 minutes from Nicoya on a good paved road), **Playa Sámara** is crowded with hotels and vacation homes. Make reservations if you want to visit on a weekend between December and April. Substantial discounts are available in the green season.

Sámara's international community provides appetizing dining possibilities: **El Lagarto** (2656-0750) serves up tasty barbecue on the beach and of-

Coatimundi

ten has dance parties at night. **Al Manglar** (2656-0096) offers fresh, home-made Italian food and pizza. Both are one block west of the main road.

Casa de Coco (open 10 a.m. to 10 p.m.; 2656-0665), in a shady garden behind Samara Travel Services, offers generous servings of salads, sandwiches and fruit smoothies.

Restaurant Esmeralda, down the third entrance on the road to Carillo, offers good local food at reasonable prices.

LODGING **Entre Dos Aguas** (private bath, hot water, ceiling fans, pool, internet; $50-$60, including breakfast; phone/fax: 2656-0998; hoteldos aguas.com, info@hoteldosaguas.com) is a unique bed and breakfast on the right as you enter Sámara, before you get to the Cangrejal road. They make creative use of rocks and shells in the spacious bathrooms, and also rent bikes.

Hotel Belvedere (private bath, hot water, table fans, a/c, refrigerator, pools; $50-$80, including breakfast; with kitchen, $80-$100; 2656-0213; belvederesamara.net, hotelbelvedere@hotmail.com) has small neat rooms, two apartments, and an outdoor jacuzzi. It's just off the road from Nicoya, at the first left-hand turn (toward Puerto Carrillo).

Rising three stories on the hill that backs the town, the imposing **El Mirador de Sámara** (private bath, hot water, fans, kitchens, TV, pool; $110-$130; children 3 to 11 $11; 2656-0044, fax: 2656-0046; miradordesamara. com, mdsamara@racsa.co.cr) has large, comfortable apartments and views of the coast from the restaurant. Their sky rooms ($90-$110) include a continental breakfast.

Casa del Mar (hot water, ceiling fans, pool, jacuzzi, bar; with shared bath, $30-$40; with private bath and a/c, $70-$90; children 5 and under free; breakfast included; 2656-0264, fax: 2656-0129; casadelmarsamara.net, reservations@casadelmarsamara.net), down the street from the Super Sámara, is a tranquil and clean establishment.

Samara Tree House Inn (private bath, hot water, fan, kitchen, TV, phone, wi-fi, pool, guarded parking; $130-$140, including breakfast; 2656-0733; samaratreehouse.com, samaratree@yahoo.com) makes excellent use of a small beachfront lot by raising five apartments on varnished tree trunks so they receive ocean breezes and have lovely views. The shady spot underneath the apartments lends itself to hammocks, tables and a barbecue. There is another poolside apartment, and a house next door that sleeps six ($130-$140). Only two guests are allowed in each trim, one-bedroom apartment, and no children under 12 are allowed in the small, handicapped-accessible pool and Jacuzzi. Down the street is **Casa Valeria** (private bath, hot water, kitchen for guests, TV; $40-$60; 2656-0511), with rooms near the street and nice little bungalows right on the beach.

Villas Kalimba (private bath, hot water, fan, a/c, TV, phone, pool, guarded parking, wi-fi; $140-$160; kids under 6 $7; 2656-0929; villaskalimba.com, villaskalimba@hotmail.com), across the street, are charming two-bedroom villas with porches and hammocks set around a pool that's fed by a bubbling waterfall. Kids were having fun there when we visited. They also rent two houses that sleep five or six ($150-$190).

Heading toward Playa Carrillo, beachfront accommodations are accessible both from the beach (keep your eyes open for signs) and the parallel road that passes by the Belvedere and Mirador de Sámara.

Casitas LazDívaz Bed and Breakfast (private bath, hot water, ceiling fans; $80-$90, including breakfast; 2656-0295, fax: 2656-0296; lazdivaz.com, lazdivaz@hotmail.com) offers three cabinas, one with a full kitchen, designed by one of the owners, a German architect. She and her partner (from the U.S.) serve generous breakfasts in their beachfront rancho and provide shady hammocks. They fly the rainbow flag. To get there, turn left on the Carrillo road at the entrance to Sámara, turn right at the road adjacent to the parking lot of the Hotel Las Brisas, turn left at the beach, and you'll see the cabins in about 50 meters.

GETTING THERE: By Bus: A direct bus from the Tracopa/Alfaro terminal in San José serves Sámara daily at 12:30 p.m. and 6:15 p.m., returning at 4:30 a.m. and 8:45 a.m., except on Sundays when it returns at 1 p.m. (Avenida 5, Calles 14/16; 2222-2666; buy tickets one day in advance or see costaricabustickets.com). It's a five-hour trip. Traroj buses (2685-5352) leave the Nicoya bus station for Sámara almost hourly and continue down to Playa Carillo. Private Interbus and Grayline companies will also take you there.

By Car: The trip from Nicoya is approximately 40 kilometers and takes 45 minutes on paved roads. The road from Nosara is unpaved. We drove it in a four-wheel drive in the rainy season with no problem; it took 45 minutes to reach the Sámara road. Sámara is 4.5 hours from San José by car and an hour and a half from Liberia.

By Air: See "By Air" in Playa Carrillo below for more information.

PLAYA CARRILLO   Playa Carrillo, just a 15-minute drive east of Sámara, is a beautiful white-sand beach with waters kept calm by a reef outside a small semi-circular bay. Majestic palms at the beach's edge provide shade for campers and day-trippers. Unlike Sámara, where hotels and restaurants line the beach, Carrillo beach is business free. The town of Carrillo is uphill at the eastern end of the beach. The western end is best for swimming and snorkeling. Carrillo is an ecological Blue Flag beach.

Popo's Adventures (2656-0086; fireworks@racsa.co.cr) offers rubber-duckie trips through the estuaries of the Río Ora and sea kayaking to Isla Chora. He'll tell you where the secret surfing spots are. He also rents cozy "treehouses" and cabinas in his family's compound ($60-$70, including breakfast; two-night minimum; vrbo.com/48060).

Dining at **Pizzeria El Tucan** (2656-0305) is like being in Italy. When we were there, it was crowded with Italians who all seemed to know each other. The food had that authentic Italian flavor. It's down a side street, across from El Rancho Bar.

Club Carrillo (private bath, hot water, a/c, refrigerator, internet, pool, restaurant/bar; $70-$90; with kitchen, $70-$90; including breakfast; children under 6 free; 2656-0316, 2656-2012; www.clubcarrillo.com, info@carrilloclub.com), up a hill before the entrance to town, has rooms with an excellent view of the beach from their wide porches, and high-tech European showers with five sprayers.

In rows descending the hilly southern rim of the bay are the comfortable units of sportfishing hotel **Guanamar** (private bath, hot water, fans, a/c, TV, phones, pool, bar, restaurant, casino; $130-$170; suites that sleep five, $250-$260; breakfast included; children under 12 free; 2656-0054, fax: 2656-00011). Many rooms as well as the restaurant/bar complex have stunning ocean views.

Two kilometers inland from Puerto Carrillo, and one and a half kilometers from Camaronal, the next beach south of Carrillo, is **El Sueño Tropical** (private bath, heated water, ceiling fans, pools; $80-$110; two-bedroom apartments with kitchens, $120-$160; 2656-0151, in North America: 877-456-4338; elsuenotropical.com, info@elsuenotropical.com). This small hotel, with a renowned restaurant/bar featuring Italian, Japanese, and American favorites, is on a hilltop, with 3 acres of tropical gardens, next to an appealing pool. They give guests free rides to the beach.

GETTING THERE: By Bus: The 12:30 p.m. San José–Sámara bus (six hours) continues to Carrillo. Call 2222-2666 to check schedules. Buy tickets a day in advance. The private, air-conditioned buses of **Interbus** (2283-5573; interbusonline.com) and **Grayline Bus** (2220-2126; graylinecostarica.com) also take you to Carrillo from San José, Arenal, Manuel Antonio, and Monteverde.

By Car: From the Nicoya–Sámara road, turn left immediately before arriving in Sámara, at the Belvedere hotel. It's 15 minutes and about five kilometers from there to Carrillo, all on paved roads.

By Air: A SANSA flight (2290-4400; flysansa.com) goes to Playa Carrillo, stopping in Punta Islita on the way. Nature Air flies to Playa Carrillo (2299-6000, in North America: 800-235-9272; natureair.com) daily.

Text continued on page 338.

ADVENTURE REPORT: TURTLE WATCHING AT OSTIONAL WILDLIFE REFUGE

The sunset from Lagarta Lodge was magnificent—delicately colored clouds billowed over the misty mangroves and beaches that stretch for miles north of Nosara. We could see at sunset that the Nosara and Montaña rivers were swollen from previous rains. Playa Ostional lay across those rivers. In the dry season it's easy to ford the rivers with four-wheel drive, but in November there was a risk that even the sturdiest SUV could become a boat.

Around 9 p.m. we got the word that the rivers were down and we could go. We drove in the darkness down the narrow winding road from the lodge, and then north from Nosara. When we got to the first river, a man with a strong flashlight met us. We parked and he guided us across the river on a hanging bridge. We all loaded into a cattle truck for a breezy drive down country roads to another river, which we forded in the truck, reaching the village of Ostional in about 20 minutes.

The refuge office was alive with young people from the village. They took our $6 entrance fee and introduced us to our guide José, an intelligent and very well-informed high school senior.

Just five days before, there had been a huge *arribada*, with an estimated one MILLION olive ridley sea turtles (lepidochelys olivacea) arriving over several days. Their name comes form their olive-colored shell, which measures about 30 inches long. Turtles nest at Ostional year-round, but the *arribadas* are more predictable from July through December. The turtles generally land at night, but during an *arribada* they start arriving around 2 p.m. and keep coming until 7 the next morning.

Even though the *arribada* had past, we saw five turtles at different stages in their nesting process. They dug holes about 20 inches deep on the beach and deposited about 100 eggs each. They then covered their nests and camouflaged the spot by spreading sand over it with their flippers.

The first *arribada* occurred at Ostional in 1959 and has happened regularly since then, usually occurring during the last quarter of the moon. As scientists studied the turtles, they found that eggs laid by the first wave of turtles were often excavated by turtles that arrive later, or by the strong surf at high tide. If excavated eggs are left to rot on the beach, they can contaminate healthy eggs as well.

Turtle eggs are thought to have aphrodisiac properties, and are a favorite *boca* at Costa Rican bars. The scientific studies mentioned above served as the basis for Ostional to become one of the only communities in the world where turtle eggs are harvested and sold in a sustainable way. Since 1987, the Integral Development Association of Ostional (ADIO) governs the harvesting and marketing of the eggs, and hires a biologist to monitor the health of the turtle population. Each of ADIO's 240 members is allowed to collect eggs for 10 to 15 hours during the first 36 hours of each arribada. After that, it is their responsibility to protect the nests.

When the turtles hatch, 40 to 55 days after the eggs are laid, women and children from the community follow the baby turtles as they clamber toward the sea at dawn, protecting them from dogs and birds. Tourists can accompany them.

Seventy percent of the income from the sale of turtle eggs is distributed among ADIO's working members. The other 30 percent goes to beach protection and patrol, scientific research, scholarships, and support of the community's schools, health center, sports teams, churches, and environmental education and social welfare programs.

During our tour, it started raining again and we were pretty wet by the time it was over. We got back in the truck and rode to the river we had easily forded a few hours before. It was too high to cross, even for the monster cattle truck. But by then the skies had cleared. The few remaining clouds had been given silver linings by the rising moon.

In the moonlight on a country road, we entered a true Costa Rican moment, where there is nothing else to do but be where you are. We all got to know each other a little better as nature's timetable took over and we waited for the river to go down.

VISITING OSTIONAL   Olive ridleys seem to be much more stable and plentiful than the critically endangered leatherbacks at Playa Grande, where numbers have dwindled from 1340 in 1990 to 57 in 2006 (find out more at leatherback.org), compared with 500,000 to a million per month at Ostional. Your hotel will radio Ostional at night to learn if there is any turtle activity. If there is, the turtle tours are set into motion.

PUNTA ISLITA   Eight kilometers south of Carrillo, **Punta Islita** (private bath, hot water, fans, a/c, satellite TV; rooms and suites, $300-$560; villas with private pools, $670-$730; breakfast included; children under 12 free; 2290-4259, fax: 2232-2183, in North America: 866-446-4053; hotelpuntaislita.com, info@hotelpuntaislita.com) is a remote luxury resort (gym and spa, conference room, pool, mountain bikes, kayaks, horseback riding, and sport fishing). They have a canopy tour and nature walks in their large tropical dry-forest reserve combed by trails. Punta Islita has a Blue Flag.

GETTING THERE: By Air: Punta Islita is most easily accessible by air. SANSA flies there daily on its way to Sámara and Nosara (flysansa.com). Nature Air's (natureair.com) daily flight to Tambor continues to Punta Islita.

By Car: If you decide to drive to Punta Islita, take a four-wheel-drive vehicle and consult with the management about the best route. Don't expect to make it to Punta Islita from Carrillo in the rainy season. In the dry season you can drive all the way from Carrillo to Playas Santa Teresita and Malpais, near Cabo Blanco, if you have four-wheel drive and go at low tide. (See Central Pacific Zone chapter.)

BARRA HONDA NATIONAL PARK

El Cerro Barra Honda is part of a flat-topped ridge that juts up out of the dry cattle-grazing land of the Nicoya Peninsula. People used to call the ridge a volcano because it's covered with large white limestone rocks piled around deep holes that look like craters. In the 1960s and '70s speleologists discovered that the holes were entrances to an intricate series of caves, some as deep as 240 meters. The caves are so spectacular that the area was made into a national park in 1974.

When the region was under the sea millions of years ago, marine animals deposited calcium carbonate that hardened and became limestone. Later, when the land was pushed up out of the ocean, rainfall combined with carbon dioxide and dissolved the limestone to hollow out the caves. In a process similar to how icicles form, dripping water carrying calcium carbonate formed stalactites and stalagmites that resemble curtains, pipe organs, fried eggs, and pearls.

In the **Nicoa cave**, speleologists discovered human skeletons that were quite old—a stalagmite was growing on one skull. It is assumed that indigenous people used this cave as a *cenote* (chamber for religious rituals), since some artifacts were found near the skeletons. Fortunately, the deep vertical drops at the entrances have discouraged all but the best-equipped spelunkers from entering, so the caves have suffered almost no vandalism.

The 260-foot-deep **Terciopelo cavern** is the only one open to the general public. Two local guides must accompany you—whether you visit alone or with a group. The $10 park entrance is included in the $45 fee per descent. All equipment is included. To get there, first walk one hour to the cave entrance; then, assisted by your guides and the equipment (harness, ropes, helmets), enter by way of a 50-foot aluminum ladder. Visitors who suffer from vertigo, claustrophobia, or hypertension are not allowed to go down and you had better like bats. You must wear pants and good shoes with closed toes, and bring your own drinking water, sunblock and flashlight. Children under 12 are not allowed in the caves. Tours last three to four hours.

Arrange your descent in advance by visiting the park headquarters the day before or by calling the ranger station (2659-1551; actbarrahonda@ sinac.go.cr) or let ACTUAR arrange a tour for you (2248-9470; info@actuarcostarica.com). Many beach hotels arrange tours to Barra Honda. The caves are usually closed in the rainy season.

Even if you can't get down into the caves, a visit to Barra Honda is rewarding. You can explore the flat top of the ridge on trails where birds screech, iguanas stand motionless, and howler and white-faced monkeys fill the trees. The 1400-feet-above-sea-level lookout point, reached by following the seven-kilometer **Sendero Los Laureles** trail, affords wide views of the peninsula and the Gulf of Nicoya. You can take a six-kilometer hike (guide required) to a waterfall decorated with lacy calcium carbonate formations, and individual-sized bathing pools formed by the build-up of calcareous deposits in the waterfall's gently sloping path.

In the dry season it's very hot, so wear a wide-brimmed hat and bring a canteen. An unprepared European couple died several years ago from dehydration and heat exhaustion during their hike through the park.

LODGING   The park offers inexpensive and simple meals and lodging (private bath, cold water; $6/person) in dormitory-style rooms that accommodate up to six. Let them know in advance if you want them to cook for you.

GETTING THERE: By Bus: You can catch a bus at 11:30 a.m. and 4 p.m. from Nicoya to the village of Santa Ana (an hour-and-a-half trip) and walk one kilometer to Barra Honda National Park. A taxi from Nicoya to the park costs about $10.

By Car: Barra Honda is a half-hour from Nicoya by car. Take the main road east and make a left when you see signs for Barra Honda village. Follow signs to the park. You can also come from the east via the Tempisque bridge and turn right at the Barra Honda turnoff. The dirt road to the park gets narrower and bumpier, but national park signs clearly mark the way.

ELEVEN

The Central Pacific Zone

Puntarenas Province extends along the Pacific Coast from Guanacaste to the Panamanian border. The Central Pacific Zone roughly corresponds to the northern part of the province, from the town of Puntarenas and the Montes de Oro area just northeast of it, to the Nicoya Peninsula and the islands in the Gulf, to Quepos and Manuel Antonio National Park, about halfway down Costa Rica's Pacific Coast. Like Guanacaste, the Central Pacific is famous for its beaches—from the rocky coves of Montezuma on the Nicoya Peninsula to the half-moon jewels of Manuel Antonio.

The climate of the Central Pacific is not as dry as that of Guanacaste, however. You'll feel the heat and the heaviness of the moist, tropical air, so be prepared to slow down and let your body adjust to the change. Bring sunblock, insect repellent, and an umbrella to use in the sun or in case of sudden showers.

Note: Sanitary conditions are generally good on the Pacific Coast, but if you don't want to take chances, bottled water is readily available. Don't swim in estuaries or rivers; most of them are polluted. However, the heavy surf and currents of the Pacific keep the beaches free of contamination. (Be sure to read the section on how to handle rip currents in Chapter Five.)

PUNTARENAS

The town of Puntarenas was Costa Rica's main port for most of the 1800s. The treacherous terrain between San José and the Atlantic Coast made an eastern port impossible until the railway was completed in 1890. So oxcarts laden with coffee rumbled down to Puntarenas, from which the precious beans were shipped to Chile, to be re-exported to Europe. In 1843, English

Captain William Le Lacheur landed in Puntarenas on the way back from a business failure in Seattle, Washington. Worried about the danger of sailing with an empty ship, he traveled five days by mule to San José, hoping to find some cargo for ballast. It turned out that coffee had been over-produced that year, and growers were desperate for new markets. Even though he was a stranger and had no money to give them, the growers entrusted him with a weighty shipment. He came back two years later with the payment, and a thriving trade with England was established.

Traditionally the vacation spot for Ticos from the Central Valley, the port city of Puntarenas now receives thousands of cruise ship passengers during their September-to-May season. A tourist information and communications center, a crafts market, a restaurant, and an amphitheater are housed in airy well-designed buildings across from the huge dock on the ocean side of downtown. The **Puntarenas Marine Park** (open Tuesday through Sunday, 9 a.m. to 5 p.m.; 2661-5272; parquemarino.org; admission $4, students $2, seniors over 65 free) is an indoor aquarium showcasing the sea creatures of the Pacific Coast and the Gulf of Nicoya. The 21 large aquariums are full of hermaphroditic fish, yellow seahorses, coral, and anemones. There is also a crocodile pond. The marine park is 200 meters east of the cruise dock near the bus station.

The town is only four blocks wide for most of its length because it is built on a narrow spit. Fishing boats and ferries dock on the estuary side; a beach runs along the Gulf of Nicoya side. The Ministry of Health warns against bathing in the estuary. The beaches on the gulf side of town are safe for bathing.

Sunset in Puntarenas is a community event; locals gather on the beach at the Paseo de los Turistas to picnic, dance, and enjoy the view, and people sit on their front porches to catch the evening breezes and greet passersby. Puntarenas has a ten-day *carnaval* (2661-4439; puntarenas.com/carnavales) in February, with costumed dancers, horse parades, fireworks, beach volleyball, karaoke contests, theater performances, and street dances every night.

The main reason ecotourists go to Puntarenas is to catch a ferry boat to Playa Naranjo or to Paquera en route to the Nicoya Peninsula, or to make bus connections from Guanacaste and Monteverde to Manuel Antonio.

Calypso Tours takes you around the gulf in the luxurious Manta Raya, a speedy yacht with on-deck jacuzzi pools and trampolines, live music, and a spacious air-conditioned cabin with a bar ($100-$110, including transportation to and from San José; wheelchairs can be accommodated but the bathrooms are not wheelchair accessible; 2256-2727, in North America:

800-877-1969; calypsocruises.com, info@calypsocruises.com). The crew offers fresh tropical fruit snacks, and serves *ceviche* and a gourmet lunch on Tortuga Island, where you can swim and snorkel. Calypso also offers a cruise to their private nature reserve at Punta Coral on the Nicoya Peninsula. They arrange transport from San José, Quepos and Jacó.

La Yunta (open noon to midnight; 2661-3216), in a charming older building with a wide veranda overlooking the sea, serves good traditional *Tico* food, specializing in seafood and steak. It's 100 meters west of Hotel Tioga.

Matobe's (2661-3498), an Italian pasta and pizza restaurant about 50 meters east of the Hotel Tioga, has been recommended by readers.

The open, airy restaurant at **Hotel Las Brisas** serves Greek and Mexican cuisine. Their Greek-style sea bass is excellent. Recommended.

LODGING The **Gran Hotel Chorotega** (cold water, ceiling fan, shared or private bath, some cable TV and a/c; $30-$40; 2661-0998), a three-story building diagonally across from the Banco Nacional, is the best of the low-cost options in the crowded, funky downtown area of Puntarenas. It's clean and well-run, with secure parking, a refrigerator for guests, and laundry service. Try to get an inside room. It's a couple of blocks from the municipal market and passenger ferry dock—convenient for the early-morning passenger boat to the Montezuma area.

The beachfront hotels have more pleasant surroundings. **Hotel Tioga** (private bath, hot water, gym, casino, internet, a/c, TV, phone, pool; $70-$150, including breakfast; 2661-0271, fax: 2661-0127; hoteltioga.com, costarica@hoteltioga.com) is comfortable and well-maintained, with a cafeteria. They give large off-season discounts.

The other places are at the western end of the Paseo de los Turistas, a few blocks from the dock for the car ferries. **Hotel Las Brisas** (private bath, heated water, cable TV, phones, a/c, pool, airport transport, wi-fi; $90-$100, including breakfast; suites, $200 2661-4040, fax: 2661-2120; lasbrisashotelcr.com, hotellasbrisascostarica@ice.co.cr), has and elegant fountain-fed pool and two hot tubs, a spacious and airy Greek restaurant and an upstairs bar, all supported by classic Greek columns. Many rooms have balconies with views of the sunset over the Gulf. **Hotel Alamar** (private bath, hot water, pool, jacuzzi, cable TV, internet; $110-$150; 2661-4343, fax: 2661-2726; alamarcr.com, info@alamarcr.com), next door, has rooms with fully equipped kitchens and plantation-style decor.

GETTING THERE: By Bus: San José-Puntarenas buses (Calle 16, Avenidas 10/12; 2222-8231; $3) leave at 4 a.m., then every 40 minutes between 6 a.m. and 7 p.m. Get there early on weekends and holidays. *Directo* buses take two and a

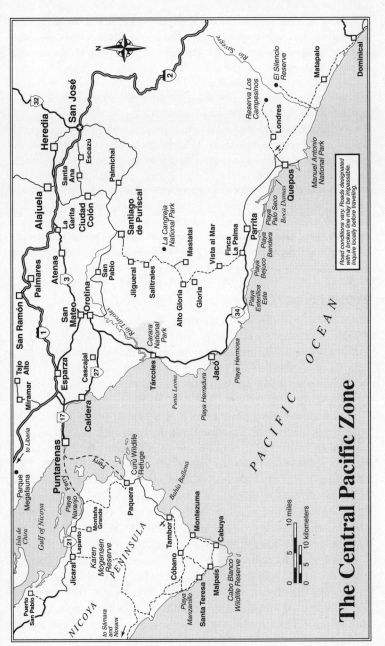

The Central Pacific Zone

Road conditions vary. Roads designated with a broken line may be impassable. Inquire locally before traveling.

half hours. In Puntarenas, the bus stop is at Calle 2 and Paseo de los Turistas. Return buses begin departing at 4:15 a.m. Buses leave the Monteverde Cheese Factory for Puntarenas daily at 5:30 a.m. (by way of Las Juntas de Abangares) and 6 a.m. (via Lagarto).

By Train: The **Tico Train Tour** (2233-3300; ticotraintour.com; $12 round trip, four hours each way) runs on weekends to the port of Caldera. From there a bus ($3) shuttles you 18 kilometers to Puntarenas.

By Car: On the map, it looks like the Interamerican Highway is the most direct route to Puntarenas, but the last 31 kilometers between San Ramon and Esparza can take 45 minutes to an hour if there are a lot of trucks. The best route is the Atenas–Orotina road, accessed by the Atenas turnoff on the Interamerican Highway about 15 minutes west of the airport. Big freight trucks are not allowed on this road because it is so curvy. For this reason, the Atenas route can be a faster way to get to the Pacific (if you don't mind winding roads). Follow signs to Jacó. When you get to the Jacó turnoff just past the town of Orotina, ignore it and go straight to Caldera. The turnoff to Puntarenas is about 30 minutes from the Jacó turnoff, 18 kilometers north of Caldera.

MONTES DE ORO

If you'd like to get the flavor of small, non-touristy Costa Rican towns and villages, take a canopy tour, or go horseback riding, hiking, and/or birding, you'll love the **Montes de Oro** area, just northeast of Puntarenas. The hills above the small town of Miramar have cloud forests similar to those in Monteverde, where quetzals are visible, especially from February through April.

Finca Daniel (finca-daniel.com) is an adventure option in Tajo Alto, only 35 minutes from the Interamerican Highway above Miramar. They offer two **canopy tours**: the 11-platform tour ($45, including lunch; two hours) features ziplines up to 2100 feet long offering incredible views of the Gulf of Nicoya; the 25-platform tour ($89, including lunch; five hours; minimum age 12), reached on horseback, crosses 11 waterfalls and can include plunges into waterfall pools, swimming in narrow canyon passageways, and rappelling. Bring your towel and swimsuit! They also have a large spring-fed pool, a climbing wall, and a bungee trampoline.

Hotel Vista del Golfo (private bath, hot water, cable TV, pool, exercise room, restaurant; $60-$140, including breakfast; 2639-8303, fax: 2639-8130; finca-daniel.com, info@vistagolfo.com), located five kilometers above the town of Miramar, has a beautiful view and offers clean, comfortable rooms at Finca Daniel. Day visitors receive lunch, and can use the pool, trails, climbing wall, and bungee trampoline for $17.

Nearby, **Finca el Mirador** (private bath, hot water, some kitchens, pool; $60-$70; phone/fax: 2639-8774; finca-mirador.com, heckmann@racsa.co.cr) is a lovely place to stay. With great views, airy, comfortable rooms, and a friendly, attentive hostess, this is a great base for exploring this beautiful region. At the end of the day, you can relax in a hammock and watch the sun set over the Gulf of Nicoya. Finca Mirador is located in Tajo Alto, seven kilometers above Miramar, on Calle Pavones. Recommended.

La Mancuerda (2661-5006 or arrange through Finca el Mirador), 18 kilometers above Tajo Alto, is a private cloud forest reserve just before the entrance to Juan Castro Blanco National Park. This forest has the same misty, mossy enchantment as Monteverde, and owner Don Chicho knows where the quetzals nest between February and April. His family rents cabins for up to eight people in their garden. The charming, rustic dining area behind the family's home is open on one side to gardens, a great place for watching hummingbirds while you eat.

Quetzals are also visible at the private cloud forest reserve at **Cabinas las Orquideas** (private bath, heated water, TV; $20-$30; 2661-8245) in the village of Zapotal. They offer a well-maintained one-kilometer trail, and a more adventurous 9-kilometer trail through primary forest for hikers or horseback riders. Their restaurant serves tasty local food, using organic ingredients and fresh white cheese made just down the street. The cabins are clean, spacious, and very reasonably priced.

GETTING THERE: By Bus: Buses to Miramar leave from the San Carlos bus station (2248-0045) in San José at 7 a.m., 12:30 p.m., 4:15, and 5:40 (8 a.m. on Sunday only); the trip takes about three and a half hours. Buses leave almost every half-hour from Puntarenas to Miramar. The bus stop is between the cruise ship dock and the marine park on the ocean side of Puntarenas. Try to get a *directo* bus. An alternative with more options is to take one of the hourly Liberia buses from the Pulmitan station in San José (Calle 24, Avenidas 5/7; 2266-0458; $3) and ask to be let off at Cuatro Cruces, the name of the turnoff for Miramar, about five minutes past the turnoff for Puntarenas on the Interamerican Highway. **Restaurant Cuatro Cruces** (open daily, 6 a.m. to 10 p.m.), right on the highway, is a clean, well-run, affordable place to stop for a meal before going up the hill. A taxi from Cuatro Cruces to Tajo Alto costs about $10. If you want to make Monteverde your next stop, the San José–Monteverde bus stops just before the restaurant between 4:30 and 4:45 p.m.

By Car: The turnoff for Miramar is only five minutes north of the turnoff to Puntarenas on the Interamerican Highway. From there it's a 10-minute drive to the town of Miramar, where there are grocery stores and a bank. It's another 20 minutes uphill on a paved but pot-holed road to Tajo Alto. After Tajo Alto, four-wheel drive is recommended. Ask locals for directions to La Mancuerda from there.

PARQUE MEGAFAUNA

Seventeen kilometers north of the Miramar turnoff on the Interamerican highway, **Parque Megafauna** (open daily 8 a.m. to 5 p.m.; adults $9; kids 4 to 14 $4; 2638-8193, 2638-8229; monteverde.net/fauna) is an outdoor exhibit of life-sized statues of 18 prehistoric animals and eight animals that are in danger of extinction today. All profits go to supporting environmental education and habitat restoration through reforestation. Their **restaurant** features Monteverde cheese and delicious Monteverde ice cream.

NICOYA PENINSULA

The southeastern edge of Guanacaste's Nicoya Peninsula is part of Puntarenas Province. This is because ferries have traditionally connected the eastern side of the Gulf of Nicoya with the mainland through the port of Puntarenas. Except for flying to the Tambor airstrip, the fastest way to get to the Nicoya Peninsula from San José is by boat, although it's still a time-consuming adventure. Tourism in the area has centered around Playa Naranjo, where one of the car ferries from Puntarenas docks; Bahía Ballena, located midway down the coast; the beaches of Montezuma to the south; the Cabo Blanco Absolute Biological Reserve at the very tip of the peninsula; and the beaches of Malpaís and Santa Teresa. A terrific website for maps and information about this area is **nicoyapeninsula.com**. The less touristy northern coast of the peninsula gives access to the wilder Karen Mogensen Reserve, the mangroves around Puerto San Pablo, and the Isla de Chira.

THE PENINSULAR BIOLOGICAL CORRIDOR AND THE KAREN MOGENSEN RESERVE

Apart from being one of Costa Rica's fastest growing tourism destination, the Nicoya Peninsula has one of the most developed biological corridors in the country. ASEPALECO, the ecological association named after the peninsula's three main towns, Paquera, Lepanto, and Cóbano, has a model recycling and landfill program in Lepanto, on the peninsula's northern coast. Just to show off how pretty a landfill can be, the community built their Sol Naciente Cultural Center there. ASEPALECO has trained an active volunteer fire department, and has made great progress toward a biological corridor extending from Cabo Blanco Reserve to Barra Honda National Park, 55 miles to the north. Their enthusiastic work has put an end to the droughts, forest fires, and illegal logging that used to plague the area.

Central to the Peninsular Biological Corridor is the **Karen Mogensen Reserve**, which offers opportunities for wilderness adventure that are rare in this region. Doña Karen and her husband, Nils Olof Wessberg, came to Nicoya in the 1950s. They were instrumental in the 1963 founding of Costa Rica's first biological reserve, Cabo Blanco, at the end of the Nicoya Peninsula. For information on staying at the reserve, see the Adventure Report on pages 348–48.

GETTING THERE: By Car and Boat: A ferry boat (2661-1069, 2661-3834; $1.40/adult, 75 cents/child, $10/car) leaves Puntarenas four times daily, with exact schedules varying according to the season. To reach the dock, drive right through downtown Puntarenas on the same street you came in on until you see a little sign directing you to turn right. The dock is near the northwestern end of town. Make sure you take the Naranjo ferry, not the Paquera/Tambor one. Snacks are sold on board.

Note: If you have a car, be sure to get in line at least an hour before the ferry leaves from either end because only a limited number of cars can fit. It is especially crowded on weekends and during the dry season. Allow two hours for the trip, including boarding and disembarking time. Actual sailing time is about 75 minutes. Only drivers are allowed to board the ferry in their cars. Passengers must walk on. A bus to Lepanto and Jicaral meets the ferry. There are numerous car-watchers at the ferry landing whom you can pay to watch your car while you buy tickets or have lunch.

By Car from Guanacaste: Take the road to Playa Naranjo from Nicoya and stop at the ASEPALECO office in Jicaral (in the office of the Ministerio de Agricultura) to meet your guides.

ISLA DE CHIRA   The **Isla de Chira** is a large island in the Gulf of Nicoya. The story of the community and the way they took conservation into their own hands with bravery and determination is inspiring. Traditionally, both men and women here made their living fishing from small boats, but due to long line fishing in other parts of the Gulf, the fish started disappearing. The women of Chira started raising *pianguas*, a small native shellfish. Then they built La Amistad Lodge, with spacious rooms and a restaurant decorated with colorful murals of island life. They learned how to build fiberglass boats and started giving tours of the island and the nearby mangroves. Inspired by the women's efforts, local fishermen got together to protect the reef outside the island, a natural nursery for marine life. Only traditional fishing in tiny boats is allowed near the reef, and already local fish stocks are returning.

To take their tour or stay overnight on the island, you are met in Puerto San Pablo, located in the mangrove swamps northwest of Jicaral, by one of the fisherwomen of Isla de Chira. She will take you in a covered boat to see the aquatic birds and caimans that inhabit the mangroves. Once you get to the reef, she might buy some huge, freshly harvested shrimp, which will be

ADVENTURE REPORT:
CERRO ESCONDIDO LODGE

The car ferry ride across the Gulf of Nicoya to Playa Naranjo was a "trip," with salsa blaring on the upper deck, seagulls screaming overhead, and pelicans skimming the water's surface as the ferry glided by the verdant islands of the Gulf. From Playa Naranjo, it was a short drive west to Jicaral, where we stopped at ASEPA-LECO's office in the MAG, across from the *Colegio Tecnico*. After a warm greeting, they stored our luggage and took us to the village of Montaña Grande, where we saddled up on small, gentle horses for the ride up to the Karen Mogensen Reserve. As we rode into the reserve, we watched the landscape change from dry pastures to a leafy green paradise; bushes with yellow flowers arched over the trail. In about an hour we could see the islands of the Gulf, then we descended into the hidden valley at the top of the mountain and saw the red roofs of Cerro Escondido Lodge below.

Luis Mena, biologist extraordinaire and one of the principal movers behind ASEPALECO, told us that when he was growing up, he had heard about the farm in this hidden valley, but that it seemed "as far off as Africa." In the early 1990s, he visited the elderly *campesino* couple that had homesteaded on the farm for 50 years. They were getting old and wanted to sell. Luis saw that several rivers that supply drinking water to the whole peninsula were born on the farm. Before she died, Doña Karen Mogensen heard about the farm and offered to bequeath money to ASEPA-LECO to buy it.

The old farmhouse is still there. The wood stove is made of rocks and ashes, and the kitchen is just as it was in the old days. Now there are attractive wooden cabins near the farmhouse, each with two bunk beds and a private bath. Doña Mary cooks when guests are there, and polishes the old stove with ashes each time she prepares a meal, adding to the stove's burnished glow. The

added to the delicious fish stew you'll have for lunch. Transport to their cheerful, open-air dining room and lodge is by bike or truck. If you stay overnight, you can hike up to the *mirador* near the lodge, visit a women's craft cooperative, learn traditional fishing techniques, or play soccer with the islanders.

meals were delicious, served in the charming open-air dining room abloom with flowering vines.

In the morning, Don Arnulfo led us on a 90-minute hike down into the gorge. The steep trail had cement steps built into it all the way down. Someone had worked hard to make the trail safe and secure. When we reached the Río Blanco, we walked upstream over some slippery rocks until we could see the jewel of the Karen Mogensen Reserve: **Catarata Velo de Novia**, or **Bridal Veil Falls**, an incredible 60-foot waterfall that spreads out over a curved cliff like a lacy bridal veil. Below the falls, there is a pristine swimming hole with the most amazing pale-green crystalline water, a testament to ASEPALECO's work in assuring the water supply for the surrounding area.

On the hike out to the village of San Ramón, we met the two *campesino* brothers who had carefully laid cement blocks into the trail from the cabins. You could tell that this was a labor of love for them, and that they were totally involved in ASEPALECO's vision for the health of their community.

The best way to experience Cerro Escondido is with a guided tour. The one-night tour ($70-$80 including meals) starts in San Ramon with lunch at the rancho of the *hermanos Rojas*, the brothers who created the trail. From there it is only 20 minutes on foot to the Velo de Novia. After a refreshing swim at the waterfall pools, you hike 75 minutes up to the lodge (private bath, cold water). The next day is spent hiking in the primary forest, before descending again to San Ramon. The two-night tour ($160-$170 including meals) begins with a horseback ride (dry season only) from Montana Grande to the lodge, and includes tree-planting. The next day is for birdwatching and visiting the falls. Set up your visit through ACTUAR (2248-9470, in North America: 877-9-ACTUAR; actuarcostarica.com, info@actuarcostarica.com) or call ASEPALECO at 2650-0607. Recommended.

You can also reach Isla de Chira on the public boat that leaves the village of Costa de Pajaros, north of Puntarenas, daily around 2:30 p.m. Tours to Isla de Chira from there include a first-class shrimp lunch cooked by the Association of Active and Progressive Women of Costa de Pajaros. Set up a tour from either Puerto San Pablo or Costa de Pajaros through ACTUAR

(2248-9470, in North America: 877-9-ACTUAR; actuarcostarica.com, info@ actuarcostarica.com). Recommended.

PAQUERA AND CURÚ WILDLIFE REFUGE

Paquera is one hour from Playa Naranjo by car (on a gravel road), or an hour and 15 minutes from Puntarenas on either of two car ferries: the Naviera Tambor or Ferry Peninsular. You can also get there on the lancha, a smaller boat that carries people only. The ferry landing is a 15-minute drive east from Paquera itself, a small town that has gas stations, food and clothing stores, a bank, and pharmacies. The commercial center for the beach towns and farming communities on the lower Nicoya Peninsula, Paquera is not where you'd want to spend your vacation, but it's convenient for visiting Curú or if you need to spend a night near the ferry docks.

Twenty minutes down a rough road north of Paquera, in a lush horseshoe valley downhill from the road, is **Hotel Bahía Luminosa** (private bath, hot water, pool, wall fans or a/c; $60-$80; two-bedroom house, $110-$120; 2641-0386, in the U.S.: 530-842-1339; bahialuminosa.com, info@ bahialuminosa.com), with both hilltop and poolside *cabinas*.

In Paquera, **Cabinas Ginana** (private bath, heated water, fans, a/c; $30-$40; children under 12 free; 2641-0119, fax: 2641-0419) are clean and inexpensive.

Located on a private farm seven kilometers south of Paquera is the **Curú Wildlife Refuge** (open 7 a.m. to 3 p.m.; 2641-0100, 2641-0590; curu wildliferefuge.com, info@curuwildliferefuge.com; admission $10). A recent study rated Curú as the ecologically richest reserve on the Nicoya Peninsula due to its diversity of habitats, including beach, mangroves, rainforest, and a lagoon, which is the only one left on the peninsula. The farm has banana plantations that are specifically for wildlife, so it's not difficult to see howler and white-faced monkeys, coatimundis, iguanas, and more than 150 species of birds from the 11 different hiking trails. The beach is home to thousands of phantom crabs, one of which stole my watch while I was enjoying the warm, gentle waters of the picturesque, cup-shaped bay. Luckily, we spotted the watchband at the bottom of the nearest crab hole and we fished it out with a stick. Snorkeling is supposed to be good there, but we didn't stay long enough to find out because no-see-ums and other nasty biting bugs were making mincemeat of us.

Curú is better as a day trip, although there are rustic, candlelit accommodations only 50 meters from the beach. There are many opportunities here for volunteers ($20/day, including meals) and researchers. The bus from Paquera passes the entrance, which is easy to miss—if you're coming from the north it's on the left next to a house on stilts, seven kilometers south of Paquera.

About half an hour south of Paquera, **Tango Mar** (2683-0001, fax: 2683-0003; tangomar.com information@tangomar.com) is a unique resort on a beautiful stretch of beach south of Bahía Ballena. It has a variety of accommodations (all with hot water, ceiling fans a/c, cable TV, phones; $200-$280 two- to five-bedroom villas, $460-$1200; children under 6 free): some on the beach, some with views, some with private jacuzzis. All rates include a lavish breakfast. Tango Mar boasts a massage and yoga studio, a seaside golf course, and offers sportfishing, sailing, surfing, scuba diving, tennis courts, two spring-fed swimming pools, horseback riding, mountain biking, and beach volleyball. They'll arrange to have you picked up in Paquera, or you can fly from San José to the airstrip at Bahía Tambor. By car, Tango Mar is about an hour south of Paquera; follow the signs south of Tambor. Reservations are required.

GETTING THERE: See "Getting There" in Montezuma section, below.

MONTEZUMA

Enchanted visitors have spread the word about Montezuma's lovely rocky coves and waterfalls and its bohemian atmosphere. Because of the rocky coastline, it is not ideal for swimming, but the many tidepools lend themselves to a refreshing dip.

Montezuma was for many years known as a campers' free haven, but now things have changed. The only public campground (often full) is at the northern end of the first beach: **Rincón de los Monos** ($3; 2642-0048).

The first few rocky bays to the north of the village have very strong currents, especially during high tide. **Playa Grande**, about 30 minutes north by foot, is calm and shallow, the best and safest place for bathing, especially at low tide. At the far end of Playa Grande is a picturesque waterfall where you can sit and watch pelicans dive. Several locals offer horseback trips here. Ask your hotel owner which guides they recommend.

The **Waterfall Canopy Tour** (2642-0808, 8823-6111; montezumatravel adventures.com) in the hills above Montezuma offers three tours a day.

There is a series of gorgeous waterfalls about 30 minutes out of town with pools that are nice for swimming. People like to cliff-dive here, but it's dangerous, so be very careful. Several people have slipped and fallen to their deaths in recent years. To get there, walk along the road to Cabo Blanco until you get to Restaurant La Cascada (about 10 minutes). At the bridge, scramble upstream over the rocks for half an hour to an hour. You should be surefooted to attempt this hike. We used to recommend that people wear shoes that could get wet, but we've heard reports of many a twisted ankle on this slippery, rocky stream bed, so good hiking boots would be the best choice.

Cocozuma Traveler (2642-0911; cocozumacr.com) offers horseback riding tours, snorkeling tours to Isla Tortuga in the Gulf, and sportfishing. They'll also take you across the Gulf in speedboats to Playa Jacó.

Cóbano, seven kilometers inland from Montezuma, has the only bank, post office, clinic, pharmacy, and car rental agency in the area. There are a couple of internet cafes. The Banco Nacional is almost always crowded, so try to get money changed before you get to the peninsula. Bring *colones* in small denominations to pay for buses and restaurants. **Soda La Cobanena** (open daily 6:30 a.m. to 7:30 p.m., 8864-8058), on the right at the entrance to Cóbano, is a great place to go for an early breakfast. Recommended.

RESTAURANTS   Montezuma has some excellent dining choices. You might almost miss **Playa de los Artistas** (open for lunch and dinner; closed Sundays and May to October; 2642-0920), on the beach across from Hotel Los Mangos, and if you enter the gate and see the rickety tables set in the sand, you might not think it's much, but taste the stuffed eggplant or the homemade breads and organic salads and you'll know you are in a very special place.

El Sano Banano (2642-0638; open 7 a.m. to 9:30 p.m.), in the center of town, has excellent vegetarian and vegan food and a varied menu, which includes Caribbean curry, pasta, Mexican dishes, and seafood specialties like tropical shrimp with pineapple. It's open for breakfast, lunch, and dinner as well as internet use. They show movies at night. On the north side of the village, the European-owned **Cocolores** (open 11 a.m. to 11 p.m.; 2642-0348) specializes in seafood curry and pasta but also makes tasty sandwiches and salads. Across the street, **Café Finis Terrae** makes homemade ice cream, muffins, and chocolates. The nearby **Bakery Café** (open 6 a.m. to 10 p.m.; 2642-0458) serves delicious breakfasts and baked treats.

LODGING   In the dry season, Montezuma books up; call for reservations. As in most beach towns, hotels here offer significant discounts in the "green season" (May through November). "Downtown" Montezuma can be very noisy at night due to the mighty sound systems at the two bars. A helpful service for booking any hotel, house, or activity in this area is **Cabo Blanco Enterprises** (in the U.S.: 805-773-9700; caboblancoent.com, caboent@yahoo.com). For beach house rentals, see playamontezuma.net and for detailed maps and updated ferry and bus schedules, see nicoya peninsula.com.

You'll see a couple of places as you drive toward Montezuma from Cóbano. The turnoff for **The Nature Lodge Finca Los Caballos** (private bath, hot water, fans, pool; $80-$160; phone/fax: 2642-0124; naturelodge.net, naturelc@racsa.co.cr) is about halfway between Cóbano and Montezuma. Rooms are tastefully designed and comfortable. Some have private decks or terraces. The suites have an ocean view The breezy open-air restaurant has an international menu with a Latin flair. Organic produce is used as much as possible. Excellent horseback trips, plus guided nature and bird walks are offered, as well as a quieter and more relaxing atmosphere than in downtown Montezuma.

In the hills almost two kilometers above the town, **Horizontes de Montezuma** is a tranquil place to learn Spanish. It is also a lovely B&B (private bath, hot water, pool; $50-$80; 2642-0534; horizontes-montezuma.com, collina@racsa.co.cr). Rooms with balconies and hammocks offer ocean and jungle views, and a central atrium with skylight keeps interior spaces bright. The German owner gives a week long Spanish survival course as well as longer courses.

As you enter town, to the right is **El Jardín** (private bath, heated water, ceiling fans, a/c, refrigerator, pool; $70-$100; phone/fax: 2642-0074; hoteleljardin.com, jardin@racsa.co.cr). These spacious rooms have wide, tiled balconies and porches with hammocks. The houses up the hill sleep four and provide views ($100-$120). Across the street is **Hotel La Aurora** (private bath, hot water, a/c, fans, cable TV, communal kitchen; $30-$70; phone/fax: 2642-0051; playamontezuma.net/aurora.htm, aurorapacific@hot mail.com), with a hammock-strewn balcony upstairs, where it's easy to meet fellow travelers.

Hotel El Tajalín (private bath, heated water, ceiling fans; $50-$60; with a/c, $60-$90; 2642-0061, fax: 2642-0527; tajalin.com, tajalin@racsa. co.cr) overlooks the park and has ocean views from its third-floor café.

Next door is **Hotel Montezuma Pacific** (private bath, heated water, shared refrigerator; with fans or a/c; $30-$50; 2642-0204), which has a nice upstairs porch.

The main street of Montezuma has become a brightly painted block of souvenir stands, trendy beach boutiques, travel agencies, an ice cream shop, internet cafés, and a laundry. In the midst of all this is **El Sano Banano Village Hotel**, which has comfortable rooms (private bath, heated water, a/c, cable TV; $80-$90, including breakfast; 2642-0638; elsano banano.com) above and behind the El Sano Banano restaurant. If you stay there, you can hang out at the pool and beach of its sister hotel, the Ylang

Ylang. The **Ylang Ylang Beach Resort**, in a gorgeous setting, consists of peaceful "jungalows" and comfortable suites (private bath, hot water, small refrigerator, fans, wi-fi; $140-$270, includes breakfast and dinner; 2642-0636, fax: 2642-0068; ylangylangresort.com, reservations@ylangylang. com) set in a forested preserve on the second beach to the north (a 10-minute walk from downtown). A truck will transport you and your luggage from El Sano Banano to the Ylang Ylang. Because of the walk, these cabins are not the best for little children, but older kids are welcome. Be sure to get there by 4 p.m. so you can check in and do your first beach walk before dark. There is a lovely swimming pool with a waterfall that massages your shoulders, daily yoga classes ($10) and lush gardens full of flowers and monkeys. Their **Ylang Ylang Restaurant** serves candlelit dinners made of the freshest ingredients, and their **VuJadé Bar** completes the natural romantic atmosphere. Both El Sano Banano and Ylang Ylang donate a dollar a day per guest to ASEPALECO's conservation efforts. Recommended.

Luz de Mono (2642-0090, fax: 2642-0010, in North America: 877-623-3198; luzdemono.com) is a large restaurant and bar with artistic bas-relief murals of monkeys doing all sorts of naughty things. They feature barbecue and an array of tropical cocktails. They host a house music party and reggae party each week, as well as a yearly gathering, *Chunches de Mar,* where artists make original works from driftwood and other found objects. In back are rooms (private bath, solar hot water, fans, screened windows; $70-$120). Cabins with kitchens run from $110-$220. The high-end cabins have panoramic views and jacuzzis on their sun decks.

At this end of town you'll also find **Librería Topsy**, where you can rent books, trade or sell used books, and buy souvenirs. They have a good selection of local and international newspapers.

South of downtown, along the coastal road (the one that leads all the way to Cabo Blanco), are several more good places to stay. The farthest are only a five- to ten-minute walk from downtown, and all are accessible by car:

Hotel Los Mangos (pool, jacuzzi, restaurant; 2642-0076, fax: 2642-0259; hotellosmangos.com, homangos@racsa.co.cr) has comfortable precious-wood bungalows (private bath, hot water, ceiling fans, some refrigerators; $80-$110) dotting a hillside orchard, and other rooms with shared or private bath ($40-$90). Yoga classes are offered daily.

Down the street is **Hotel Lucy** (shared or private bath, cold water, table fans; $20-$30; 2642-0273). In 1993, just as we were about to leave town, some friends informed us that the municipality had a bulldozer on its way to destroy Lucy's. Like many other establishments at Montezuma, Lucy's is built within 50 meters of the high-tide line, a zone the Costa Rican government has wisely established as an inviolable public area. But destroying Lucy's would be a case of selective enforcement. Since the owner of Lucy's is a feisty guy without connections to politicians, his hotel was targeted. We went to Lucy's that morning and saw half of the town staked out in front of the hotel in defiance of the approaching bulldozer. Along with the dozer came several rural guards and the mayor of Cóbano. The crowd successfully intimidated the officials; Lucy's still stands, and has been recently renovated.

The friendly **Hotel Amor de Mar** (heated water, table fans; with shared bath, $60-$70; with private bath, $80-$110; ages 3 to 11, $5; phone/fax: 2642-0262; amordemar.com, info@amordemar.com) has spacious grounds, its own private tidepool, and hammocks overlooking a stream that flows into the ocean. Upstairs rooms are quieter. They also rent two houses, **Casa Luna** and **Casa Sol**, (kitchens, hot water; $190-$210) for up to six people. It's located a few hundred meters south of Lucy's, across the street from the waterfall trailhead.

GETTING THERE: By Bus and Boat: Transportes Rodriguez (2642-0740, 2642-0219) leaves the Coca Cola bus terminal in San Jose daily for Montezuma at 7:30 a.m. and 2:30 p.m. The $10 fare includes a bus to Puntarenas, the car ferry to Paquera (see below) and a bus from Paquera to Montezuma, Malpais and Santa Teresa. The trip takes about five hours.

If you are already in Puntarenas, take the large, comfortable car ferry (see below) or the smaller *lancha Don Bernardino* (passenger ferry, 2641-0515) to Paquera, which leaves Puntarenas 11:30 a.m. and 4 p.m. Several public buses wait for the *lancha* at Paquera. Be sure to take the bus marked Montezuma ($3.50), which makes the trip through beautiful country, in about an hour and a half. Buses leave Montezuma for Paquera about every two hours between 5:30 a.m. and 4 p.m.. Check schedules at nicoyapeninsula.com. The last Paquera-Montezuma bus leaves at 6:15 p.m. A taxi from Paquera to Montezuma costs about $40 per carload. It's faster than the bus.

By Car and Boat: Car ferries (2641-0515, 2220-2034) leave Puntarenas every about every two hours between 5 a.m. and 10:30 p.m. from the dock near the far end of town. To get to the ferry landing, drive through Puntarenas on the same street you come in on, until a sign directs you to turn right. If in doubt, ask. Find current schedules at nicoyapeninsula.com.

You have to leave your car and go inside the terminal to buy your tickets. Be sure you are in the line for cars if you want a car ticket, for passengers if you want a passenger ticket. On Barceló's Naviera Tambor (2661-2084) you can opt for a first-class seat in the air-conditioned (freezing) snack bar and TV lounge. Otherwise, you ride on rather uncomfortable benches on top of the boat. The older, funkier Ferry Peninsular (2641-0515) doesn't offer a first-class option.

Check schedules at nicoyapeninsula.com. Cars start boarding about 50 minutes before departure time, so drivers should get there an hour early at either end. Only drivers can drive onto the ferries—passengers must walk on. The trip takes an hour and a quarter, with another 15 minutes to disembark. The landing is a 15-minute drive from Paquera. After that, the roads are paved until you get to Cóbano, where you make a left for the final seven kilometers (15 minutes) downhill to Montezuma. The trip from Paquera takes about an hour. The nearest gas station to Montezuma is in Cóbano.

By Private Shuttle: Montezuma Expeditions (2642-0919, fax: 2642-0482; montezumaexpeditions.com) will pick you up at the airport, let you stay at Hotel Los Volcanes in Alajuela, and transport you to Montezuma. They will also take you from Montezuma to Hotel Los Volcanes and deliver you to the airport in the morning. Daily shuttles leave Montezuma at 10:30 a.m. for Monteverde, Arenal and San José ($35-$50/person). They also have a daily shuttle to Playas Samara and Tamarindo. This shuttle will drop you off in Jicaral, to go to ASEPALECO's Cerro Escondido Lodge.

Travel notes: If you want to get from Guanacaste to the Nicoya Peninsula in the rainy season, you have to go through Playa Naranjo. The roads coming into Playa Naranjo from Guanacaste are paved, so even if it looks longer on the map, it's quicker to go from Sámara or Nosara to Montezuma by way of Playa Naranjo rather than dealing with the river crossings at the Río Ora and the Río Bongo between Malpaís and Playa Carrillo, which are impossible in the rainy season. Staying in Playa Naranjo is convenient if you are coming from Guanacaste en route to Montezuma. The 27-kilometer stretch between Playa Naranjo and Paquera is unpaved. It takes three hours to get from Playa Naranjo to Montezuma or Malpaís in the rainy season. In the dry season you can take a short cut from Malpaís to Carmona on the way to the town of Nicoya. Ask at your hotel for exact directions.

By Air: The nearest airstrip to Montezuma is in Tambor, about an hour from Montezuma by car ($30-$40 in a taxi). Ask the airline or your hotel in Montezuma to help coordinate transportation in advance. SANSA flies to Tambor from San José (2290-4100, in North America: 877-767-2672, fax: 2290-3543; flysansa.com; $70-$80 one way) five times daily. Nature Air flies to Tambor twice daily (2299-6000, in North America: 800-235-9272; natureair.com; call for pricing). The flights last 30 minutes.

CABUYA AND CABO BLANCO WILDLIFE RESERVE

A road continues south from Montezuma through Cabuya and on to Cabo Blanco Wildlife Reserve. Cabo Blanco was the first national reserve in Costa Rica—its founding in 1963 was the initial step in the development of the country's extensive national park system. Preserved with the encouragement of Swedish biologist Nils Olof Wessberg and his wife Karen Mogensen, who were concerned about the encroaching deforestation that was threatening the area's rich and varied wildlife, it is an "absolute reserve," which means most of the area is accessible only to scientific researchers.

Stop at the "Area Turistica" building to get an entrance permit (open Wednesday through Sunday, 8 a.m. to 4 p.m.; 2642-0093; $10). You can take a fairly strenuous two-hour hike up the **Sendero Sueco** and down to Playa Cabo Blanco (bring food and plenty of water). You'll see lots of howler monkeys. (Don't stand directly underneath them—they like to pee on sightseers.) There are pelican colonies on the point, which has beautiful pinkish coral sand. Another trail is the semicircular **Sendero Danés**, which takes about an hour to complete. Bring insect repellent and boots in the rainy season.

LODGING   For assistance in booking hotels or renting houses in this area, see caboblancoent.com or playamontezuma.net.

Near the town of Cabuya, two kilometers before the reserve entrance, is an island that holds an indigenous cemetery. You can walk to the island at low tide (wear water walkers because of the rocky sea floor). Snorkeling is good there during the dry season, and reef-protected areas and tide pools make for safe swimming.

The nicest place to stay in Cabuya is **El Celaje** (private bath, heated water, ceiling fans, pool; $70-$90, including breakfast; 2642-0374; celaje. com, celaje@racsa.co.cr), two kilometers from the entrance to Cabo Blanco. It is right on the beach and features Belgian cuisine, Belgian beer and Belgian chocolate.

El Ancla de Oro (private bath, cold water, fans; $20-$40; 2642-0369; caboblancopark.com/ancla, elancladeoro@racsa.co.cr) offers inexpensive rooms and "jungalows" and rents snorkeling equipment.

GETTING THERE: By Bus: A minibus leaves Montezuma for Cabo Blanco daily at 8 a.m., 10 a.m., 2 p.m., 4:30 p.m. and 7 p.m., returning to Montezuma at 7 a.m., 9 a.m., 1 p.m., 4 p.m., and 6:30 p.m.

By Car: A taxi from Montezuma to Cabo Blanco costs about $7. Driving there takes about 45 minutes.

Howler monkey

MALPAÍS AND SANTA TERESA

The long white beaches at Malpaís and Santa Teresa are renowned among surfers. Swells are especially high at Santa Teresa, but nonsurfers will enjoy the tidepools and shell-strewn beach. Locals tell us that the area in front of Hotel Tropico Latino is the best for playing in the waves. The best snorkeling is at **Playa Las Suecas** down a path to the right after the small fishing port at the southern end of Malpaís.

A lively community of Brazilians, Israelis, French Canadians, Czechs, Belgians, Swiss, Italians, gringos, and Ticos makes for good food and lots of internet cafés. Both foreigners and locals participate in beach clean-ups, recycling, and environmental education. This is one of the trendiest beaches in the country, with several gorgeous yoga retreats with spas, and many luxury villas.

Santa Teresa is developing at a rapid pace, and the roads are being improved, but four-wheel drive is still needed. ATVs, bikes, and SUVs are available for rent. This area, like most popular beach destinations, has had its share of problems with crime, and has joined with Montezuma to request more police. Make sure that you know and follow the security measures that your hotel has in place. Camping on the beach is not recommended.

First we'll talk about lodging to the south in Malpaís. Santa Teresa is to the north. See nicoyapeninsula.com for maps and information.

MALPAÍS The road from Cóbano intersects with the coastal road at **Frank's Place** (restaurant, pool; 2640-0096, fax: 2640-0071; frank5@racsa.co.cr), just 200 meters from a good surfing spot. Over the years, Frank has studied what surfers need and provides good, clean, cheap rooms (shared or private bath, some a/c, cold water, some kitchens; $50-90, including breakfast) and a wide range of other possibilities, including a house (hot water, a/c, cable TV, refrigerator; $60-$70). His corner kiosk also has internet, phone and fax access, and a Sansa reservation center.

Two hundred meters to the left, **The Place** (private bath, heated water, mosquito nets, restaurant/bar; rooms with a/c, $70-$120; bungalows, $120-$150, including breakfast; children under 10 free; 2640-0001, fax: 2640-0234; theplacemalpais.com, info@theplacemalpais.com) has well-designed cabins. The charming Swiss owner has used a variety of colors and styles to create light, airy rooms with louvered wooden doors opening onto private patios, about 200 meters from the beach. There is also a villa ($230-$300) that sleeps five. Recommended.

Apartotel Oasis (private bath, hot water, ceiling fans, kitchen, pool, snack bar; cottages, $70-$80; rooms with a/c, $70-$100; phone/fax: 2640-0259; nicoyapeninsula.com/malpais/oasis, oasismalpais@racsa.co.cr) has comfortable two-room bungalows with kitchens and views of the ocean 200 meters away.

Next on the left, you'll see the North American–owned **Malpaís Surf Camp** (pool, gym, cable TV, billiards, horses, bikes, restaurant; 2640-0031, fax: 2640-0061; malpaissurfcamp.com, surfcamp@racsa.co.cr), which also offers a variety of options. If you've brought a tent, camping is $8-$10/person. Their breezy ocean-view *ranchos* (shared bath, cold water; $60-$70 for up to four) have gravel floors and are open on all sides, with bamboo curtains for privacy. There are swings and hammocks and a big wooden trunk to store things in. There are also smaller rooms with shared bath ($40-$50) and spacious, elegant pool-side cabinas (private bath, hot water, ceiling fans, screened windows, some kitchens; $110-$160). Individual surfers can share a *rancho* with other surfers for $15-$20. They offer many services, from surfing instruction and board rental to laundry and babysitting. They welcome families—children under 10 stay for free, and offer a $70-$80/person a day package which includes meals, and use of a surfboard.

About one kilometer farther south down a side road to the beach, **Restaurante Piedra del Mar** (2640-0069) serves freshly caught fish and lobster, Tico style. This inexpensive *soda* is popular with locals at sunset.

Back on the main road, **Moana Lodge** (private bath, hot water, fan, a/c, pool, jacuzzi, wi-fi; $90-$150, including breakfast; 2640-0230, fax: 2640-0623; moanalodge.com, info@moanalodge.com) was founded by a Belgian from the Congo who decorated with African sculpture. The new Irish/Tica owners have preserved the African theme and transformed the lodge into a romantic getaway. Guests gather in the evenings to cook at the newly built barbecue.

About 400 meters south, on the right, **La Bella Napoli** (closed Monday; 2640-0224) is worth a trip to Malpaís. We enjoyed delicious smoked fish made in Montezuma, lasagna prepared with homemade pasta and basil from the garden, and fantastic *bruschetta,* beautifully served. The meal was topped off with homemade lemon liqueur. Recommended.

Beija Flor Resort (private bath, hot water, a/c, wi-fi, pool, spa, restaurant; $80-$150; villa with kitchen, $200-$210; 2640-1007, fax; 2640-1006, beijaflorresort.com, info@beijaflorresort.com) has spacious rooms and bungalows in a garden setting. The bungalows and villa have back patios with hammocks and showers open to the sky. Their spa offers reiki, acupuncture, watsu, and reflexology as well as massage, and detoxifying clay and seaweed wraps. There are daily yoga classes on the open-air yoga deck. They host yoga retreats. The restaurant offers a light menu featuring fresh fish and local produce.

Less than a kilometer south, **Soda Restaurante Ambiente Marino** (2640-0261) specializes in *ceviche*, fresh fish filets and *comida típica* at the Cabuya turnoff. (Cabuya is only accessible by this road between December and May).

SANTA TERESA   If you turn north at the intersection of the Cóbano road and the coastal road (at Frank's Place), you head toward Santa Teresa.

At **Horizon Yoga Hotel** (private bath, hot water, a/c, kitchens, pools; cabins, $90-$210; one- and two-bedroom villas, $100-$230; 2640-0524; horizon-yogahotel.com) most of the cabins and villas have lovely ocean views. The most expansive view is from the yoga deck, where classes are offered three times a day. Their **vegetarian teahouse** features organic teas and freshly squeezed fruit juices. Their spa offers reiki, reflexology, shiatsu, and massage. The entrance is 100 meters north of Super Ronny and 50 meters uphill. Four-wheel drive required.

The **Trópico Latino** (private bath, hot water, ceiling fans, air conditioning, pool, internet; $100-$160; one child under 12 free; 2640-0062, fax: 2640-0117; hoteltropicolatino.com, troplat@racsa.co.cr) is a beautiful retreat, with spacious, well-ventilated rooms. Only the front cabinas have an ocean view. They offer horseback riding, fishing trips, and surfboard rentals. Their **Playa Boa Restaurant** is a good place to go for freshly caught seafood and fusion cuisine on the beach. They also rent a house in Malpaís that sleeps up to 10 ($700-$800/day). Their spa offers a variety of treatments including wraps, facials, massage, and yoga.

Luz de Vida Resort (private bath, heated water, ceiling fans, a/c, refrigerators, restaurant, pool; $100-$120; 640-0320, fax: 640-0319; luzdevida resort.net, reservations@luzdevidaresort.net) is the dream of seven friends from Israel who moved here with their families and collaborated on every aspect of the project's design. The bungalows are scattered among tall trees near the beach. They sometimes host dance parties at their poolside restaurant/bar.

Casa Zen (private and shared baths, hot water; dorms, $12; private rooms, $20-$50; apartment with kitchen, $50-$60; 2640-0523; zencostarica.com) has been recommended by younger travelers as "a must" for its "super chill" owner from Kansas City, its cheap and good Thai restaurant, surf board rentals, movie nights and "beautiful artwork throughout." To get there, turn left at the Costa Supermarket.

Wave Trotter Surf Hostel (shared bath, hot water, fans, communal kitchen; $10/person; 2640-0805; wavetrotterhostel.com, info@wavetrotter hostel.com), 200 meters south of the soccer field, has a spacious communal kitchen with an espresso machine, a comfy sitting area with a good sound system, and stylish shared baths, all in keeping with the good taste of its Italian hosts. Located near one of the most consistent surf breaks in the country, the owners give surfing lessons, sell used and new surfboards, and do board repair.

Jungle Juice Bar, 200 meters after the soccer field, serves organic juices, smoothies, veggie burgers, and burritos. Uphill at that corner, the **Funky Monkey Lodge** (private bath, heated water, fans, pool; rooms, $60-$100; bungalows with kitchens or apartments with kitchen access, $90-$180; 2640-0272, fax: 2640-0317; funky-monkey-lodge.com, office@ funky-monkey-lodge.com) rents well-designed bungalows that sleep four to eight. They rent surfboards and have surfboard storage racks in the rooms. Their restaurant serves fresh fish sushi.

Two hundred meters farther, on the ocean side of the road, look for the friendly **Cabinas Zeneida's** (shared and private bath, cold water, table fans; $30-$50; 2640-0118). The comfortable rooms are kept very clean. There is one family-size *cabina* and a camping area ($6/person). There's a basketball court for days when the waves aren't good.

Milarepa (private bath, hot water, ceiling fans, pool; $200-$240, including breakfast; phone/fax: 2640-0023, 2640-0663; milarepahotel.com, milarepahotel@mac.com) is worth the bumpy drive. Bungalows decorated with a relaxed grace feature antique Indonesian canopy beds that are draped with filmy mosquito nets, giving them a medieval air. Folding wooden doors lead to beach-front stone terraces. Bamboo curtains roll down to block the sun and wind if needed. The outside is invited in, yet you are sheltered in a lovely way. Even the bathrooms are open to the sky, with lush tropical gardens inside. Tide pools in front are safe for kids at low tide. Milarepa's **Restaurante Soma** features cuisine from the south of France, with meals served at a leisurely pace and topped off by excellent coffee and homemade desserts.

The masterpiece of Santa Teresa hotels is **Florblanca Resort** (private bath, hot water, ceiling fans, a/c, phones, internet access in rooms, pool; $400-$770, no children under 12 allowed; 2640-0232, fax: 2640-0226; florblanca.com, info@florblanca.com) at the north end of the beach. An artistic eye for space, form, and color shapes every aspect of Florblanca, from the open-air bathroom/gardens with driftwood towel racks, to the molded Santa Fe–style plasterwork and *vigas* in the rooms, to the yoga studio with statues of Balinese deities in each corner, inspiring reverence. The one- and two-bedroom villas are open to the air and gardens, but can be closed off in case of rain. Two swimming pools joined by a waterfall are off the **Nectar Restaurant**, where fusion cuisine includes vegetarian selections, and a pastry chef is in residence. Also in residence is a naturalist guide, who can take you to a nearby nature reserve. Their **Spa Bambu** has four private treatment rooms suspended over a reflective pool. A fitness center, music room, art studio and complimentary bikes, surfboards, and snorkeling equipment complete the amenities. For a truly special beach vacation or honeymoon, this would be one of our top choices. You can also rent all ten villas for a retreat, workshop, or wedding. Recommended.

GETTING THERE: By Bus: Buses leave the Coca Cola in San José for Montezuma, Malpaís and Santa Teresa daily at 7:30 a.m. and 2:30 p.m.

If you are already in the area, buses leave Cóbano five times daily to Malpaís and Santa Teresa (2642-0219; $2). Scheduling is unreliable in the rainy season.

By Car: Before driving your own car, check with the hotels about road conditions. It takes half an hour to drive the eight kilometers from Cóbano to Malpaís. You can drive from the southern end of Malpaís to Cabuya and Cabo Blanco in the dry season only.

NORTH OF SANTA TERESA

The beaches to the north of Santa Teresa are best accessed from the road going west to Río Negro and Manzanillo from Cóbano. It is possible to drive along the coast all the way to Playa Carrillo (see Guanacaste chapter) in about four hours, but you have to ford several rivers. In the rainy season this route is impassable, so it's best to go back to Paquera and Playa Naranjo, then on paved roads to Nicoya and then to Sámara, Carillo, and Nosara. If you do decide to explore this route in the dry season, wait at the river crossings to see where the locals cross. The shallowest way is not always evident.

Ylang Ylang Lodge (private bath, hot water, fans, wi-fi, pool; $160-$180; 8369-2616, lodgeylangylang.com, info@lodgeylangylang.com; closed in October), not to be confused with Ylang Ylang Beach Resort in Montezuma, is a group of simple but tastefully designed and comfortable wooden A-frame cabins on a hill with a distant view of the Pacific. The French owner has created giant driftwood mobiles that hang from the thatched roof of the main lodge. A good swimming beach is a five-minute car ride or a 20-minute hike through a teak plantation. Their gourmet restaurant features fresh, natural ingredients. It's near Playa Manzanillo, about 12 kilometers (45 minutes) west of Cóbano.

Tucked eight kilometers northwest of San Francisco de Coyote, in Playa San Miguel, the **Flying Scorpion** (private bath, hot water, fans; $40-$50, including breakfast; 2655-8080; vbro.com/101715) is a little hotel and restaurant that deserves mention mainly because it has the best homemade ice cream we have had anywhere. They make their own pasta, too, from the owner's Italian grandmother's recipes.

CARARA NATIONAL PARK AND ENVIRONS

Located near Orotina, **Carara National Park** (open daily, 7 a.m. to 4 p.m.; 2200-5023, 8383-9953; admission $10) is one of the closest wildlife observation spots to San José. The 5242-hectare park is in a transitional area between the dry climate of Guanacaste and the humid climate of the southern coast. It has wildlife common to both regions, including scarlet macaws, toucans, trogons, waterfowl, monkeys, crocodiles, armadillos, sloths, and peccaries. Birders stand on the bridge over the Río Tárcoles about 5 p.m. to witness the scarlet macaws' nightly migration from the Carara forest to the mangroves at the mouth of the river. You can see crocodiles measuring up to 12 feet long from this bridge as well. The name "Carara" is derived from the Huetar Indian word for crocodile. It is more secure to park your car in guarded parking at local restaurants and ask them to indicate the best vantage points for crocodile viewing. The new visitor center at Carara has ample parking, an information desk where you can hook up with a guided tour ($15), a cafeteria, and gift stores. It is the starting point of the well-maintained trail system, including one accessible for wheelchairs. It's better to leave personal belongings at your hotel rather than in your rental car when you stop here.

Birders are usually delighted with the amount of species they see on the **Mangrove Birding Tour** (2637-0472, for English: 2433-8278; costarica gate way.com) a boat trip on the Tárcoles river than can be set up by your hotel.

The 90-minute **Waterfalls Canopy Tour** (2643-3322; waterfalls canopy.com; adults $58, kids $28; minimum age/weight 8 years/65 pounds, maximum 260 pounds) has seven cables, the longest of which is 400 meters. It starts with a steep uphill nature hike in premontane rainforest. The enthusiastic, entertaining guides make it educational and fun. The tour has a treehouse, a suspended bridge and a Tarzan swing, and ends with a 90-foot rappel; they use a handlebar pulley system with braking.

If you would like a more sedate adventure, take the **Rainforest Aerial Tram** (2257-5961, in North America: 866-759-8726; rainforesttram.com; $55, kids half-price), 2 kilometers northeast of Jacó. Nine-person gondolas glide silently on an electric cable while a naturalist guide tells you about the flora and fauna of the 225-acre reserve. The tour includes a heliconia garden, a medicinal plants garden and a snake exhibit in the middle of the forest.

The town of Turrubares, about a third of the way between Orotina (near the Jacó turnoff on the Atenas highway) and Puriscal, is becoming famous because of **Turu Ba Ri** (turubari.com), a huge project started by the Saborío family, former owners of one of Costa Rica's major grocery chains. It starts out with a state-of-the-art electric funicular on which tourists make their entrance from a dizzying height of 265 feet into the *finca* on the floor of a river valley. The more adventurous can enter the park by horseback or on a **"Superman" zipline**, where participants are strapped into a harness face-down, and shoot through the air as if they were flying. They offer normal ziplines as well. The wheelchair-accessible park boasts a huge butterfly garden and exhibits of bromeliads, orchids, and bamboo. The forested area has paved trails and bridges over streams, completely eliminating the mud found in less civilized rainforests. There is even a countryside farm and restaurant where Ticos and Ticas clad in bright typical costumes serve a native buffet. Admission is $90-$100, including roundtrip transportation from San José and Jacó and lunch ($60-$70 if you get there yourself; discount for kids).

LODGING   The riverside complex at **Villa Lapas** (private bath, hot water, ceiling fans, a/c, phones; $110-$130, including meals, snacks, and drinks; children, $60; 2637-0232, fax: 2637-0227; villalapas.com) is composed of beautifully cared-for gardens, an open-air restaurant, a pool, and a 120-person conference center. The hotel protects a natural reserve that follows the Río Tarcolitos, bordering Carara National Park to the south, and is known for great birding. Over 225 species have been seen on the grounds and in the reserve. Their **Skyway** ($40) is a system of trails and hanging bridges similar to the famous Monteverde SkyWalk. The 2.5-kilometer trail has a downward slope and is safe for children. They also have a **canopy tour** ($50). Next to the hotel is **Santa Lucia,** a re-created Costa Rican village with a lovely little chapel whose back wall is open to the surrounding gardens. In front of the church is a lily pond, a gazebo and, as in most villages, there is a *cantina* with cow hides draped over the barstools. The other colonial style buildings house three different souvenir stores, specializing in wood, ceramics and clothes. Villa Lapas is easy to find: the sign is on the left as you head toward Jacó from the north, and it's 600 meters from the highway turnoff.

Hotel Carara (private bath, heated water, fans, some a/c, TV, pool, restaurant; $70-$80, including breakfast; 2637-0178; hotelcarara.com, hotelcarara@hotelcarara.com) in the town of Tárcoles, has second floor rooms with balconies overlooking the beach, which is not swimmable. It also has a three-bedroom apartment on the third-floor with a kitchen, terrace and jacuzzi.

If you would like to get off the beaten track but need your creature comforts too, treat yourself to a relaxing long weekend or wellness retreat at **Ama Tierra** (private bath, hot water, bathtub with jacuzzi, refrigerator, phone, wi-fi, cable TV, pool, restaurant; $150-$180, including breakfast; children over 12, $20; 2419-0110, fax: 2419-0094, in North America: 866-659-3805; amatierra.com, info@amatierra.com), a quiet mountain retreat that offers a three-day wellness and adventure package for $595/person. The junior suites are very well appointed, with comfy sitting rooms and a cable TV with a DVD player. The restaurant menu features organic foods, served on their terrace overlooking hilly farms and forests. They are located about 35 minutes east of Orotina on the road to Puriscal, two minutes after San Pablo de Turrubares, on the left, not far from TuruBaRi.

GETTING THERE: By Bus: To reach Carara by bus, take a Jacó or Quepos bus from the Coca Cola station in San José, or from Puntarenas. The entrance to Carara is on the coastal highway.

By Car: Carara is a two-hour drive from San José on a winding road through beautiful countryside. Take the Atenas turnoff on the Interamerican Highway. The road is in fairly good repair through the mountains and offers some magnificent views. Near Orotina, you can buy watermelon, mangos, and sugar cane juice. After Orotina, the road becomes a four-lane highway for a few miles. Be careful when a median forms at underpasses because you can easily get in the wrong lane if you're not alert. After the turnoff for Jacó (again, pay attention—it's easy to miss it and find yourself en route to Caldera/Puntarenas), the road becomes a two-lane highway again, with sea views on one side and green rice fields on the other. You'll soon pass the entrance to Carara National Park on your left. You can continue on to Quepos (an hour south of Carara), Dominical, and points farther south on the same road.

If you feel more comfortable with less-winding roads, skip the Atenas route and take the Interamerican Highway from San José west to Puntarenas, then drive south to Jacó. The trade-off is that there is a lot more truck traffic on the Interamerican.

CENTRAL PACIFIC BEACHES

PUNTA LEONA   This unique development is striving to combine environmental conservation with intense tourist development. Surrounded by 750 acres of primary rainforest, the hotel has allowed Universidad Nacional researchers to build artificial nests for scarlet macaws. Researchers estimate that about 450 macaws live in the Carara–Punta Leona area. The nests at Punta Leona are protected from poachers to help this endangered bird population expand. Free guided nature walks are offered daily. Punta

Leona's beautiful Playa Blanca has been awarded the Blue Flag for cleanliness and safety.

You must drive through two guarded gates and several kilometers of rainforest and bamboo to reach **Selva Mar** (private bath, hot water, ceiling fans and a/c, phone, cable TV, refrigerator, wi-fi; $100-$150, children under 12 free; 2231-3131, fax: 2232-0791; hotelpuntaleona.com, info@hotel puntaleona.com), Punta Leona's jungle hotel. Selva Mar's restaurant is surrounded by forest, and monkeys often visit for breakfast. The three-story condo complex **Leona Mar** (suites with kitchens; $150-$310) is on a cliff above Playa Blanca. There are also one- and two-bedroom apartments and chalets without views ($170-$360). Guests have access to the two white-sand beaches, by far the cleanest and most beautiful in this area. The resort offers a butterfly farm, a playground, several pools, playing fields, mini-golf, tennis, basketball and volleyball courts, aerobics and Latin dance classes, several restaurants, a discotheque, a spa and electric carts to ferry you around from one point to another. You can rent an electric golf cart for $55/day. For families with children of various ages and interests, Punta Leona could make everyone happy. Watch for the turnoff to Punta Leona on the right, a few kilometers south of Tárcoles.

NORTH OF JACÓ Built in a charming French Colonial style and perched on a hilltop 1000 feet above the Pacific with magnificent views, **Villa Caletas** (private bath, hot water, a/c, ceiling fans, cable TV, phone; in main building, $170-$220; in more private villas, $200-$260; suites with private jacuzzis or swimming pools, $300-$490; 2637-0505, fax: 2637-0303; hotelvillacaletas. com) is real elegance. Its two restaurants specialize in excellent French and international cuisine. The 150-person Greek amphitheater has been the scene of many sunset weddings. Each luxury suite has its own crystal-clear swimming pool in a lush private garden (three-night honeymoon packages run $960-$1650, including breakfast, welcome cocktails, and a champagne dinner; their spa packages include mud wraps, aromatherapy, and massage). The entrance is between Punta Leona and Playa Herradura, then it's about three kilometers up on a paved but precipitous road.

PLAYA JACÓ Playa Jacó has undergone a development boom, and many of its funky surfer hotels have been torn down to build condos. Now the grey hulks of high-rises under construction loom over the town. The density of development here has reached a point where it overtaxes the existing infrastructure. Money has just been approved for the construction of Jacó's first sewage treatment plant. Until it is in place, we will not include information about Jacó.

SOUTH OF JACÓ **Club del Mar** is on a quiet cove a few kilometers south of Playa Jacó (private bath, hot water, fan, a/c, kitchen, pool, cable TV, wi-fi; $180-$400; penthouse, $360-$390; phone/fax: 643-3194, in the U.S.: 866-978-5669; clubdelmarcostarica.com, hotelclubdelmar@racsa.co.cr). The one- and two-bedroom condominiums that sleep up to six are spacious, very comfortable, tastefully decorated, and have private balconies or terraces. There is a good restaurant, and their own **Serenity Spa**. This is the most peaceful place to relax in the area, and swimming is safer here than in Playa Hermosa. Recommended.

PLAYA HERMOSA   Surfers use Playa Hermosa as a base for trips to nearby beaches like **Boca Barranca** (a very long left), **Playas Tivives** and **Valor** (rights and lefts), **Escondida** (accessible by boat from Herradura), and **Playas Esterillos Este**, **Esterillos Oeste**, **Bejuco**, and **Boca Damas**, which are all on the way to Quepos. **Playa Hermosa** itself is the site of an annual surfing contest. Many hotels give surfers discounts from May to December, and there are several surfing teachers in town.

Surfers like Playa Hermosa for its consistent, strong break. There are southern swells between April and December, with the biggest waves in June and July. All the lodgings here are right on the beach. This is not a good beach for children because of the wild waves.

Chiclet's Tree Tour (2643-1880; jacowave.com; $60) was one of our young researcher's favorites. The longest of its 11 cables is 350 meters. It got high marks for being adventurous yet educational, with great views of Playa Hermosa and beautiful trees. Guides are knowledgeable, friendly, and amusing. A photographer takes pictures throughout the tour, which starts at 7 and 9 a.m., and 1 and 3:30 p.m. and lasts one-and-a-half to two hours.

Jungle Surf Café (2643-1495) has great atmosphere and service and outstanding food. The menu changes daily with the fresh seafood available. They rent basic rooms ($15/person, including breakfast).

Fuego del Sol (private bath, hot water, ceiling fans, a/c, satellite TV, pool, spa, internet; $100-$120; with kitchens, $140-$210; children ages 6 to 11, $7; breakfast included; 2289-6060, in North America: 800-850-4532, fax: 2288-0123; fuegodelsolhotel.com, info@fuegodelsol.com) has well-designed rooms with balconies and fanciful decorations on the walls. It's right on the ocean and the gardens are lovely.

Casa Pura Vida (private bath, heated water, fans, a/c, cable TV, kitchen, pool; $70-$80; 2643-7039; casapuravida.com, info@casapuravida.com) is an elegant Mediterranean-style house in the heart of Playa Hermosa that rents fully equipped apartments. The house can be rented as a whole and sleeps 18 ($2600/week).

Cabinas Rancho Grande (shared or private rooms, private bath, heated water, fans, a/c option, shared kitchen, cable TV; $10-$20/person; 2643-7023; cabinasranchogrande.com) offers surfing packages that are matched to your skill level and include morning yoga lessons. It's on the right, after the soccer field and the school.

Las Olas (private bath, heated water, ceiling fans, pool; $50-$100; 2643-7021; lasolashotel.com, lasolascr@hotmail.com) is a friendly, gringo-run surfers' hostel with some rooms in the main house, a row of thatched A-frames with refrigerators and a popular beachside restaurant. Waves are good right in front of the hotel. They rent surfboards and have a shady seaside hammock area. **Wavehunters** (888-899-8823; wavehunters.com) puts together five- to seven-day surfing trips based at Las Olas, including transport from San José for $600-$1000/person.

Next door, **Hotel Surfside** (private bath, cold water, kitchen, a/c; $40-$50; 2643-7085; surfsideparadise@hotmail.com) has nicely designed rooms and rents a house that sleeps four to five.

The **Backyard Hotel** (private bath, hot water, fans, a/c, cable TV, pool; $150-$160; suites for five, $200-$220; 2643-7011; backyardhotel.com, reservations@backyardhotel.com) has wide porches overlooking the surf. Their restaurant and bar features barbecued chicken and steak, burgers, pizza, and a very festive atmosphere, including frequent live music.

GETTING THERE: Playa Hermosa is 10 minutes south of Jacó.

ESTERILLOS OESTE AND ESTE   Esterillos is a wide, uncrowded beach 22 kilometers south of Jacó. Because it is such a long beach, it is divided into three parts. You cannot drive between the three, but must go along the highway from one to the other. Just 30 minutes south of Carara and 45 minutes north of Manuel Antonio, this area would be a great base for trips to both with plenty of tranquility in between. You can still see locals riding horses on the beach or go for a ride yourself. Surf instructors will come to your hotel. As on all long stretches of beach, riptides can be a problem, so use caution when swimming. Locals tell us it is safer at high tide.

Esterillos Oeste is more built up than its sister beach, and is slated to become the site of a large gated community.

Hotel La Sirena (private bath, cold water, fan, a/c, cable TV, some kitchens, pool, restaurant; $50-$90, children under 12 free; 2778-8020, fax: 2778-8021; sirenacr.com) is a vestige of the way Costa Rica used to be. This funky, Tico-owned hotel is not fancy, but it is right on a stony part of the beach where a giant tide pool forms at low tide, great paddling for adults or kids. On the rocky point beyond the tidepool is a large statue of a kneeling mermaid staring out to sea. She was built many years ago by the late owner of the hotel. Room #13, on the second floor, has a nice view from its wraparound balcony and two bedrooms. Hammocks are strung from the shade trees in front of the *comida tica* restaurant. To get there, turn right at the Super Sol Market once you reach the village of Esterillos Oeste. Recommended.

Esterillos Este, 5 kilometers farther along the Costanera highway, is home to some peaceful retreats.

Xandari by the Pacific (private bath, hot water, fans, a/c, mini-bar; $240-$420, including breakfast; children under 3, free; 2778-7070, fax: 2778-7878, in North America: 866-363-3212; xandari.com, xanpac@xandari. com) brings new-age architecture and tropical chic, created by the famed Xandari Inn in the hills of Alajuela, to its sister hotel at the beach. Here, the colors have intensified into bright hues that match the flowers in the villas' private gardens and terraces. Their spa features massage and yoga, the palm-roofed dining pavilion features fresh fish and organic produce grown onsite, and their bar makes a mean *mojito*. Recommended.

Encantada Beach Cottages (private bath, heated water, fans, a/c; $30-$100, including breakfast; 2778-7048; encantadacostarica.com; encantada costarica@yahoo.com) are spacious two-story cabinas around a pool with hammocks by the beach, a good option for budget travelers in this area.

Pelican Beachfront Hotel (private bath, hot water, ceiling fans, wi-fi, pool, restaurant; $60-$110, including breakfast; children 2-11, $5; 2778-8105, fax: 2778-7220; pelicanbeachfronthotel.com, info@pelicanbeach fronthotel.com) is a good place to go when you really need a break. There are hammocks under shady *ranchos* for relaxing or listening to the waves, and a balcony for sunset-watching. The upper rooms, 4 to 8, are the most popular among this hotel's loyal clientele. Recommended.

Flor de Esterillos (private bath, hot water, ceiling fans, kitchenettes, pool, restaurant; $60-$100; $360-$510/weekly; 2778-8045; pages.video tron.com/taus, fleurdesterillos@racsa.co.cr) is a cluster of spacious cabins, some of which sleep up to six, surrounded by flowering bushes. Their **Restaurante Tulú** (open 8 a.m. to 8 p.m.) is a great place to have a relaxed lunch.

Arena de Fuego (open daily 10 a.m. to 10 p.m.; 2778-7278), near the end of the beach, features pizza, pasta, beef and fish—and occasionally, sushi.

GETTING THERE: By Bus: The San José–Quepos or Puntarenas–Quepos buses will drop you off at the entrance to either Esterillos Oeste or Este, and then you must walk about a kilometer to the beach. For schedules, see Quepos "Getting There" below.

By Car: The beach is one kilometer off the coastal highway. The turnoffs are clearly marked.

PARRITA AND PLAYA PALO SECO   In the hills above Parrita, **Sky Mountain Canopy Tour** (2770-8325, 8830-1699; canopycostarica.com) · has a six-cable zipline, the longest of which is a whopping 700 meters. This tour is mainly for the thrills and the panoramic views since none of the cables go through forest. The tour can include a hike to some waterfalls in the Creando Naturaleza Reserve.

Just south of the town of Parrita, five kilometers off the Costanera, **Playa Palo Seco** is home to **El Beso del Viento** (private bath, heated water, fans, some kitchens, pool, cable TV, some a/c; 2779-9674, fax: 2779-9675; besodelviento.com, info@belsodelviento.com). Two types of lodging are available; double rooms ($90-$100, including breakfast), and four-person suites which have spacious, tiled kitchens and good cross-ventilation ($140-$150). There is a lovely pool, and a French restaurant. Children are welcome.

GETTING THERE: By Bus: Take the San José-Quepos or Puntarenas-Quepos bus (see below in the "Quepos" section), and get off at Parrita. Take a taxi from Parrita to Playa Palo Seco (about $4).

By Car: Follow signs five kilometers down a pretty good gravel road from Parrita. Palo Seco is about a half-hour drive from Esterillos Este.

LA CANGREJA NATIONAL PARK

The mountains between the Central Valley and the Pacific are a new frontier for tourism. Because of their rugged terrain, they have been skirted by the roads leading to the Pacific. La Cangreja National Park, one of Costa Rica's newest national parks, protects the last virgin rainforest of the remote mountainous area between Santiago de Puriscal and the coast. Sloths, monkeys, boa constrictors, poison-dart frogs, coyotes, anteaters, blue morpho butterflies, scarlet macaws, toucans, motmots, and many other species live in La Cangreja National Park (2416-6359; lacangreja.com), a largely undiscovered region.

The hospitable agricultural village of **Mastatal**, at the entrance to La Cangreja, is a great place to get a glimpse of *campesino* life.

Rancho Mastatal (leave a message at 8301-2939; ranchomastatal.com, info@ranchomastatal.com) is a learning center and lodge that practices and promotes responsible living in the tropics. They will help you get to know the community, and you can hike their 7 kilometers of trails to rivers and waterfalls. They have composting toilets and use natural building techniques, methane biodigestors, solar arrays and solar cookers in their community. They also host many high school and college educational programs. You can choose to stay in rooms, tents, or hammocks (shared bath, solar hot water; $40-$80 including meals). Rates include wholesome, delicious vegetarian meals prepared with locally grown ingredients. A handcrafted house that sleeps six rents for $175/night, and home stays with local families can be arranged. **Volunteers** are welcomed (minimum commitment of one week).

GETTING THERE: By Bus: From downtown San José, take one of the frequent buses to Puriscal (Avenida 1, Calle 20/22). One bus a day leaves from near the church in Puriscal around 3 p.m. and gets to Mastatal around 6 p.m.

By Car: Four kilometers northwest of Parrita on the Pacific Coast, you'll see signs for Puriscal and La Gloria. This mostly gravel road takes you up into the mountains for an hour and a half to a right turn with a bus stop and a La Cangreja sign. Mastatal and the national park are about 5 kilometers to the right. You can also get there following signs from Puriscal to La Gloria and Parrita (about 90 minutes on unpaved winding roads).

QUEPOS AND MANUEL ANTONIO

Before you get to the inspiring vistas of Manuel Antonio, you pass through the bustling former United Fruit banana port of **Quepos**, where lodging is generally less expensive than the low-cost alternatives near the beach. It's about another three miles to the reason why you're here: Manuel Antonio National Park.

When you first glimpse the sea from the hills above Manuel Antonio, the word "paradise" might cross your mind. Then you'll go a little farther and see what happens when mortals fight to get the best view of paradise. These hills have become one of Costa Rica's most elegant tourist destinations. Several huge projects have been stopped in their tracks by local activism, but the region is under pressure. Blessedly saved from development within its boundaries, **Manuel Antonio National Park** is the area's crowning glory. The park is one of the few remaining habitats of the *mono tití* (squirrel monkey). Only 1500 *mono titís* remain in the area, down from an estimated 200,000 in 1983. **Kids Saving the Rainforest** is collaborating with the Electricity Institute to convert the electric lines in the area to shock-free ones, thus eliminating one of the main causes of death of these tiny monkeys.They are also planting fruit trees in order create biological corridors to restore the habitat of the *mono tití* and strengthen its gene pool.

To find out more about this area, see visitingmanuelantonio.com.

MANUEL ANTONIO NATIONAL PARK   In addition to the *mono tití,* howler and white-face monkeys, two-toed sloths, coatimundis, and raccoons frequent the beaches, which are shaded by leafy trees. Manuel Antonio includes one of the best beaches on Costa Rica's Pacific coast for swimming and snorkeling, as well as trails where you can hike for at least a full day.

The wedge-shaped piece of land that is now Cathedral Point was once an island. A neck of land connects it to the beach. This rare phenomenon is known as a *tombolo:* a deposit of sand that builds up over thousands of years and finally connects an island to the mainland. North-flowing currents pushed water and sand through the opening between the island and the beach, and then flowed on to Punta Quepos, farther north, which forced the water back. The sand-bridge was formed after about 100,000 years of this action. Grass and shrubs gained a foothold on it, followed by the present-day trees that keep the formation from returning to the sea. The Manuel Antonio *tombolo* is one of the most perfect in the world.

The indigenous people who lived in Manuel Antonio 1000 years ago observed that while female green turtles were laying their eggs in the sand at high tide, the male turtles were waiting for them in the water. They fashioned balsawood models of female turtles to attract the males into an area surrounded by rocks. The males would stay with the decoy females and be trapped by the rocks when the tide went out. These pre-Columbian turtle traps are still visible on either end of Manuel Antonio Beach at low tide.

A trail takes you through the jungle to the top of Cathedral Point, where you can look down the vertical cliffs to the blue ocean 300 feet below. You start from **Playa Espadilla Sur** (the second beach) and take a circular route, about an hour from start to finish. At low tide, you can also begin or end on **Playa Manuel Antonio**, the third beach. The trail is very steep in some parts and muddy and slippery in the rainy season, so don't go alone. Sandals with good treads and straps that attach them firmly to your feet are probably the most appropriate footwear. In the rainy season you will want to wear hiking boots or rubber boots with long socks.

Snorkeling is a rewarding adventure at Manuel Antonio. In the dry season, when the water is clear, you'll see iridescent, peacock-colored fish, conservative pin-striped fish, and outrageous yellow fish with diaphanous capes, all going in and out between the coral rocks—especially at **Playa Escondida**, a half-hour walk beyond Playa Manuel Antonio. Fins and a mask are all you need. If you burn easily, watch out—you'll lose track of time staring at the fish while the sun is reddening your back. It's best to wear a T-shirt in addition to waterproof sunblock. Ask for the hour of low tide at your hotel or as you enter the park. Playa Escondida can only be accessed at low tide. At high tide snorkeling is good at the turtle traps at the third beach.

Entrance information: The entrance to the park is a 200-meter walk south of the end of the Quepos–Manuel Antonio road, and is clearly indicated (2777-4122; open Tuesday through Sunday, 7 a.m. to 4 p.m.; $10). A bridge is being built across the stream at the entrance, but as of this writing, so you still have to wade across. Be sure to take food and water with you into the park because it is a hassle to go in and out. If you do wish to leave the park for lunch, the ranger will stamp your hand so you can re-enter without paying again.

Camping is not allowed within the park.

Note: Do not leave your belongings unattended on the beach. If anyone offers to guide you through remote areas of the park, they should have an official ID card, or be in a park service uniform. Guides at the entrance offer two-hour tours ($20). Perhaps more of a risk than *ladrones* are the white-faced monkeys on the beach. They have become very bold about stealing food and will grab your backpack and carry it up into a tree if you don't keep an eye on them. When they are through investigating your bags, they will unceremoniously drop them—not good for cameras or binoculars. Don't feed the monkeys anywhere in this area.

If you long to visit this still-beautiful area, try to go in the off-season (May through November). As we've stated elsewhere, you'll still have most of the day to play, you can relax with a book in your hammock if it rains, there are substantial discounts on lodging in most hotels, and you'll be able to enjoy Manuel Antonio in its more pristine, uncrowded state.

QUEPOS AREA AND MANUEL ANTONIO ACTIVITIES **Iguana Tours** (2777-2052; iguanatours.com, web@iguanatours.com) offers sea kayaking through the mangroves and whitewater-rafting tours down the Río Savegre as well as horseback, dolphin watching and natural history tours. **Amigos del Rio** (2777-0082; amigosdelrio.net) and **Ríos Tropicales** (2233-6455; riostropicales.com) also offer rafting and kayaking trips. **Planet Dolphin** (2777-2137; planetdolphin.com) offers several dolphin-watching and snorkeling cruises on either their *Tom Cat*, a 60-foot catamaran, or the *Spanish Dancer*, a 37-footer. **Samantha's Paradise Tours** (2774-0258; samanthatours.com) offers trips aboard the *Paradise* in the morning and at sunset to see dolphins, whales, and turtles. Both include snorkeling gear and refreshments.

The **Canopy Safari** (2777-0100; canopysafari.com; $65, including transportation and breakfast or lunch; minimum age 5) in Paso Real, about

45 minutes from Manuel Antonio, is one of the best canopy tours in the country for small children or those who want to be able to enjoy their surroundings as they zip. The braking system is not left up to the visitor but is handled remotely by the guides, so the cables are slower. In addition to the nine cables, the longest of which is 200 meters, there are two rappels and a Tarzan swing. The guides are enthusiastic and entertaining and the forest is very beautiful.

For the more adventurous, the **Tití Canopy Tour** (2777-3031; titi canopytours.com; $55; minimum age: 4), in the forest reserve of Hotel Rancho Casa Grande near the airport, has faster cables, ranging up to 430 meters in length, and offer both day and night tours. The guides are knowledgeable about the forest, and snacks (or dinner) are provided at the end of the three-hour tour.

Butterfly Botanical Gardens (open daily, 9 a.m. to 3 p.m., tours run at specific times; 2777-1043; butterflygardens.co.cr) across from Sí Como No hotel, is a 30-acre reserve bordering the national park. A short hike takes you to a beautifully designed 400-square meter atrium where you can see many butterfly species, including the heavenly blue morpho. It's best to go on a sunny day because the butterflies are more active. The tour is also a great botany lesson as you learn the relationship between plants and butterfly life cycle. At night, the atrium's amphitheater is the setting for an audiovisual presentation where animals' sounds are paired with their images so that you can recognize a toucan, for instance, before you see it. You can take the night tour in combination with a great dinner at Sí Como No. They also have a reptile exhibit and frog ponds.

Rainmaker is a private 1500-acre reserve protecting part of the Quepoa biological corridor used by migrating birds and animals. It also protects the streams that supply some of Manuel Antonio's water. In a well-run tour, visitors learn about rainforest botany on a guided hike along one of these streams to several magnificent waterfalls, ending at a swimming hole. A circular canopy walk along suspension bridges gives beautiful views of the forest, ocean, and waterfalls. Other tours include an amphibian/reptile night tour and an early morning birding tour ($60-$90; 2777-3565; rain makercostarica.org). They welcome volunteers.

In **Londres**, 13 kilometers inland from Quepos, **Brisas del Nara** (2779-1235, fax: 2779-1049; horsebacktour.com, brisasnara@racsa.co.cr) offers horseback tours to nearby waterfalls ($65, including transportation, breakfast, and lunch; $50 half day). They have special horses for kids.

Villa Vanilla (2779-1155; rainforestspices.com, vanilla@racsa.co.cr), in Villa Nueva, near Londres, is a working organic biodynamic farm. On

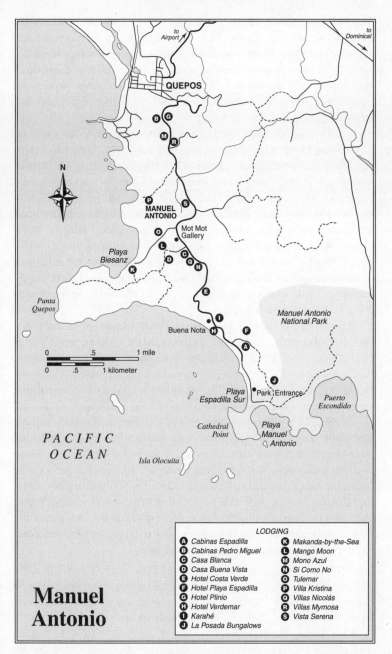

to Airport

to Dominical

QUEPOS

N

**MANUEL
ANTONIO**

Mot Mot
Gallery

*Playa
Biesanz*

*Punta
Quepos*

Buena Nota

*Manuel Antonio
National Park*

| 0 | .5 | 1 mile |
| 0 | .5 | 1 kilometer |

*Playa
Espadilla Sur*

Park Entrance

*Puerto
Escondido*

*PACIFIC
OCEAN*

*Cathedral
Point*

*Playa
Manuel
Antonio*

Isla Olocuita

LODGING

A *Cabinas Espadilla*
B *Cabinas Pedro Miguel*
C *Casa Blanca*
D *Casa Buena Vista*
E *Hotel Costa Verde*
F *Hotel Playa Espadilla*
G *Hotel Plinio*
H *Hotel Verdemar*
I *Karahé*
J *La Posada Bungalows*

K *Makanda-by-the-Sea*
L *Mango Moon*
M *Mono Azul*
N *Si Como No*
O *Tulemar*
P *Villa Kristina*
Q *Villas Nicolás*
R *Villas Mymosa*
S *Vista Serena*

Manuel
Antonio

their **Spice and Garden Tour**, you learn about permaculture, worm culture, composting, and spice drying. They produce their own natural pesticides. The tour highlights where food comes from and the importance of wholesome food for nutritional benefits. They sell their certified biodynamic vanilla beans and extract, as well as green, black, and white pepper, allspice, chocolate, cinnamon and essential oils. They rent both a one- and three-bedroom cabins with kitchens ($40-$50).

Run by an agricultural cooperative that has been together since the early 1970s, **El Silencio** (private bath, heated water; $30-50/person, including meals; 2290-8646, fax: 2290-8667; turismoruralcr.com, cooprena@ racsa.co.cr) about an hour inland from Manuel Antonio, also protects the watershed. They are a rescue and release point for green and scarlet macaws and many other injured or confiscated animals. They have a good restaurant, clean cabins, nature trails, orchid propagation projects, and a butterfly garden, and will guide you to waterfall pools in the jungle. Volunteers are needed to help with the animals. To get there, turn left at kilometer 22 of the Quepos-Dominical road, and continue another six very bumpy kilometers to the village of El Silencio. A bus to El Silencio leaves Quepos at 4 p.m. every day but Sunday.

Beyond the entrance to El Silencio, **Rafiki** (private bath, hot water, pool with waterslide; $270-$340, including meals; children under 4 free; 2777-2250, 2777-5327; rafikisafari.com, rafikisafari@gmail.com) is a unique wilderness adventure site for hiking, horseback riding, fishing, whitewater rafting, kayaking, and birding. The South African owners have recreated a safari tent camp on wooden platforms that make as little impact on the area as possible. Huge safari tents sleep four in very comfortable beds, and the spacious bathrooms are made from rocks from the nearby river. Rocking chairs and fresh flowers make these simple structures very inviting. There is a honeymoon suite ($400-$470) in the forest. The menu at the open-air restaurant adds to the safari elegance: chicken souvlaki with tzatziki sauce, grilled tarragon tuna, pork with tropical fruit salsa. Rafiki arranges horseback rides to Reserva Los Campesinos, over the hill on the other side of the river (see above). They have two- to three-day packages for $550-$650/person, including meals, rafting, and horseback riding.

SOUVENIRS **Regalame** (pronounced ray-GA-la-may: a very Costa Rican way of saying "give me"), in the small shopping center next to the Si Como No in Manuel Antonio, features original work from Costa Rican artists and craftsmen. They also offer **internet access**.

Kids Saving the Rainforest (2777-2592, fax: 2777-1954; kidssaving therainforest.org, janine@kidssavingtherainforest.org) was started by Janine Licare-Andrews and her friend when they were 9 years old. At first they sold their artwork to raise money to protect local land from deforestation. Their project has now grown to include reforestation with native species, building monkey bridges, an environmental summer camp, an Adopt a Tree program for travelers who wish to offset their carbon usage and a new Wildlife Sanctuary located at the Blue Banyan Hotel (see below). They host Saturday activities for kids 7 to 17. Their store, located online and in the Hotel Mono Azul, still features donated works from local artists. All proceeds go to support KSTR. They welcome volunteers.

La Buena Nota (open 8 a.m. to 5 p.m.; 2777-1002) is a well-stocked beachwear and gift shop that sells the *Tico Times* and the *New York Times*. It's on the Manuel Antonio road, close to the beach between Karahé Hotel and Cabinas Piscis. The **Mot Mot Gallery** sells arts and crafts in Quepos.

LANGUAGE SCHOOLS **La Academia de Español D'Amore** (phone/fax: 2777-0233, in North America: 818 434-7290; academiadamore.com, info@ academiadamore.com) offers a Spanish immersion course in a pleasant building overlooking the sea on the road to Manuel Antonio. Students are housed at the beach or with local families in not-so-elegant Quepos. If you have the discipline to study in such a heady tropical environment, this school might be a great learning vacation. **COSI** (2234-1001; cosi.co.cr) also has its beach campus here. They have a summer camp for teens and teach all ages.

DIVING **Costa Rica Adventure Divers** (2231-5806, in North America: 866-553-7073; costaricadiving.com) offers diving tours and PADI certification as well as resort and open-water courses. PADI-certified **Manuel Antonio Scuba Divers** (2777-3483, in North America: 866-884-4436; manuelantonio divers.com), next to the Hotel Malinche in downtown Quepos, provides similar services.

Manuel Antonio

SPORTFISHING   There are over a dozen sportfishing companies that will take you out. El Gran Escape and the Dos Locos (see page 380) will cook your catch.

IMPORTANT NUMBERS   *Hospital*: 2777-0922; *Red Cross*: 2777-0116; *Police*: 911; *Taxi*: 2777-1695, 2777-1068, 2777-0425, 2777-1207, 2777-0734.

BANKING   There are three ATMs and four banks in Quepos and one in Manuel Antonio (Banco Promerica; open Monday through Saturday, 10 a.m. to 2 p.m.; Sunday, 9 a.m. to noon; 2777-5101) in the shopping center next to Hotel Divisamar. Bring your passport. You can usually exchange money at your hotel for a slightly lower rate.

CAR AND SCOOTER RENTALS   You really do not need a car once you are in Manuel Antonio because buses are frequent and taxis are cheap ($4-$10 to go anywhere in the area). But if you want to fly here and rent a car to drive down the coast, **Adobe** (2777-4242). **Alamo** (2777-3344; alamo-costarica.com), **Economy** (2777-5353), **National** (2242-7878), and **Payless** (2777-0115) have offices in Quepos. It costs about $35 extra to drop the car off in San José. **Fast Eddie's** (2777-4127) rents scooters and motorcycles in Quepos.

SPAS AND YOGA   Among the massages and bodywraps offered at **Spa Uno** (2777-2607; spauno.com), to the right at Villas del Parque, are Skin Illumination Treatments, a Sea Slimming Ritual, a Four Hands Warm Stone Massage, and a Warm Mango Butter Hand Wrap. **Raindrop Spa** (2777-2880, in North America: 800-346-9724; raindropspa.com), set in a Japanese garden, also offers massage and body treatments, in a quiet, elegant atmosphere. There are rental homes nearby in case you want to make a weekend out of it.

LODGING, RESTAURANTS, AND NIGHTLIFE

QUEPOS LODGING   You might like staying in Quepos if you like bars and nightlife. If we were going to Manuel Antonio, we would not stay in Quepos, and if you want to save money, you might as well go to another area entirely. Although there are many hotels in Quepos, we list just a few of the cheap and good ones below. Some hotels are putting in security boxes for valuables; be sure and use one if you can. *Note:* The beach at Quepos is polluted. Do not swim there.

On the northwest corner of the soccer field, near the post office, **Cabinas Doña Alicia** (private or shared bath, cold water, ceiling fans; $10-$20; 2777-3279) are recommended for their cleanliness and the friendly owners.

Some of the cabinas have three rooms, handy for families. They are on a quiet street with guarded parking.

The Widemouth Frog (hot water, fans; dorm rooms, $10/person; shared bath, $20-$30/double; private bath, refrigerator, $30-$40/double; add $10 for a/c, all rates include breakfast; 2777-2798; widemouthfrog.org, info@ widemouthfrog.org) is the backpacker's paradise in Quepos. Its clean, spacious rooms are set around a large swimming pool with tropical gardens, beach umbrellas, and hammocks. There is a large kitchen area for guests, wi-fi, a pool table, a TV room, a DVD library, surfboard, boogie board, and snorkel rentals, and laundry service. It's located 125 meters inland from the bus station, past the Banco de Costa Rica. Recommended for budget travelers.

The German-owned **Hotel Villa Romántica** (private bath, hot water, ceiling fans, a/c, cable TV, wi-fi; $90-$120, including breakfast; children 6 and under, free; 2777-0037, fax: 2777-0604; villaromantica.com, info@villa romantica.com), tucked in on the right as you leave town, has a pool and shady sitting area.

QUEPOS RESTAURANTS AND NIGHTLIFE   Our favorite seafood place is **Jiuberth's** (pronounced "Hubert's"; 2777-1292), located on the road to the airport. This is a real mom-and-pop place, with brightly colored oilcloth tablecloths, and decorations all over the walls and ceiling—full-size dried fish, wonderful wood carvings of saints, iguanas, and toucans, and beautiful paintings by Jiuberth's wife Isabel. Jiuberth runs a sportfishing operation and will prepare your catch for you.

At the entrance to town, **El Patio Restaurant** (open all day; 2777-4982; cafemilagro.com) is famous for its breakfasts and is now becoming famous for its Latin-fusion cuisine, made with fresh, local ingredients; you'll find dishes such as red snapper in banana leaf and mango salad.

Next door, **Café Milagro** (2777-1707; cafemilagro.com) roasts and distributes organic Tarrazú coffee, the best that Costa Rica has to offer. You can't always find decaf in Costa Rica, but they have it. They have a branch in Manuel Antonio across from the Barba Roja.

El Gran Escape (2777-0395; elgranescape.com; open Wednesday through Monday, 8 a.m. to 10:30 p.m.), one block south, is popular with sportfishers for seafood and burgers. They also serve a hearty breakfast and desserts.

Around the corner is **Tropical Sushi** (open daily 4:30 p.m. to 11 p.m.; 2777-1710) with all-you-can-eat sushi from 5 to 7 p.m.

The market at the bus terminal is a good place to grab a quick bite to eat and to stock up on fruits and vegetables. Half a block toward the ocean,

ADVENTURE REPORT:
RESERVA LOS CAMPESINOS

After a four-hour trip to the coast, we arrived in Quepos, near Manuel Antonio National Park. Our destination was not the beautiful but over-visited beach, but an isolated community an hour and a half inland. In Londres, about 30 minutes from Quepos, we changed from our bus to a four-wheel-drive taxi to negotiate the 45-minute trip to the village of Quebrada Arroyo and **Reserva Los Campesinos** (private bath, heated water; $36/person, including meals and tours). After a delicious dinner in their open-air restaurant, we retired to our spacious cabins overlooking a forested gorge.

In the morning, Don Miguel, president of the Vanilla Producers Association, talked about the history of the village and showed us beautiful crafts that villagers had made out of the vanilla pods. Now they are raising organic vanilla and supplementing their farm earnings with income from their cabins and tours.

Miguel and his friend Misael led us up through the Los Campesinos reserve, stopping often to tell us the uses of different flowers, trees, and plants. Almost everything is used for food or medicine—and Miguel and Misael even showed us which plants they used to make into toys when they were kids. The wide, round leaves of one tree make terrific pinwheels. Miguel deftly shaved off part of the stiff hairs on "monkey's comb" pods with his machete, making monkey faces on the pods to give to the kids.

Halfway up the trail, at the edge of a deep gorge, is an *andarivel*, a sturdy metal box suspended from a cable. Four people

Dos Locos features Mexican food and a lively open-air atmosphere with live music Wednesday and Saturday. Try their Guaro Sour, a creative new use of the local firewater. **Escalofrio** (open Tuesday through Sunday from 2:30 p.m.; 2777-0833), next door, is known for its brick-oven pizza and freshly made Italian ice cream.

MANUEL ANTONIO HILLS LODGING AND RESTAURANTS   Near Manuel Antonio, the most beautiful places to stay are in the hills between Quepos and the park. There you'll find small, elegant hotels owned by tropics-lovers of many nationalities.

Make reservations six months in advance for Christmas or Easter, and several months in advance during the rest of the tourist season (December through April). Most of these places offer a discount during the off-season.

can fit inside the contraption, which zips maybe 75 feet across to the other side of the gorge, controlled by ropes and pulleys that Miguel and Misael handle. It was a quick and exciting ride, and saved us having to hike down into the gorge and up again.

Not long after that, we reached the covered lookout at the top of the ridge, from where you can see the coast south of Manuel Antonio. I asked Miguel if he had ever imagined that all the things he learned working beside his father in the countryside would someday be so fascinating to foreign tourists. "I never imagined it," he said. "Never." What an incredible way of preserving culture!

Misael told me that with farming as precarious economically as it is, his eight children would have had to move to the city to look for work, where they might have fallen in with the wrong people and developed bad habits. With the village ecotourism project, the family can stay together and make a living in the country.

Pineapple grown in the village awaited us when we came down, and then we were off across a narrow 380-foot suspended bridge that offers a view of the village's spectacular waterfall. At the other end of the bridge is a large waterfall-fed swimming hole, refreshingly cool after our long walk. We were in paradise! Our lunch featured heart of palm, which we had seen freshly harvested that morning. Reluctantly, we left Reserva Los Campesinos, and made our way back over the steep, muddy roads to our little bus.

To visit Reserva Los Campesinos, contact ACTUAR (248-9470; www.actuarcostarica.com, info@actuarcostarica.com), or see@ keytocostarica.com.

Make sure that rooms you reserve are back from the road. If you're trying to save money, keep in mind that this area as a whole is not for budget travelers. Those who can afford $70-$150 per day will find some of the most beautiful accommodations in the country, but if you're looking for budget beachfront places, go south to Dominical or the Golfito area or east to the Caribbean coast.

House rentals: If you have more time to spend, you might want to rent a house by the week or month. For example: Fully equipped houses and apartments with breathtaking ocean views rent for about $200-$600 per week or $700-$2000 per month during the high season, and half that in the low season. Contact **villacostarica.com,** for assistance with rentals, and details like babysitters, chefs, or in-home spa services. **Geminis del Pacifico** (in the U.S.: 773-472-7127; http://itsmycasa.com) and **Villa La Macha** (villalamacha.com) offer luxury villas in Manuel Antonio.

We will mention facilities in order of their appearance on the road between Quepos and Manuel Antonio.

The family-run **Cabinas Pedro Miguel** (private bath, cold water, ceiling fans, a/c, cable TV, pool; phone/fax: 2777-0035; cabinaspedromiguel. com, reservations@cabinaspedromiguel.com) have two types of lodging: a two-story construction ($50-$90), and large rooms with kitchens and a wall-sized screened window overlooking jungle with the sound of a rushing stream in the background.

Across the road, the European-owned **Hotel Plinio** (private bath, hot water, ceiling fans, pool; breakfast included in high season; 2777-0055, fax: 2777-0558; hotelplinio.com, info@hotelplinio.com) has single-story jungle-view rooms ($50-$80; with a/c, $60-$90), and suites of either two ($70-$110) or three levels ($80-$130), featuring raised king-size beds from which you can enjoy a coastal view. There is also an A-frame house (with kitchenette) in the jungle with an ocean view. The hotel is surrounded by lush foliage, and has a 70-acre forest reserve with a nature trail that leads up the mountain to a 15-meter observation tower. The hotel's **restaurant** (open daily for breakfast, lunch, and dinner), offers Italian cuisine, and their tiki bar at the pool serves lighter fare.

Next on the left, the **Bamboo Jam** (2777-3369) is famous for live music and tropical/French fusion.

Next on the right, the **Mono Azul** (private bath, heated water, ceiling fans, some with air conditioning, some cable TV, internet, three pools; $70-$170; 2777-2572, in North America: 800-381-3578, fax: 2777-1954; mono azul.com) has reasonably priced rooms and villas in all different sizes and configurations, some with kitchens. Some have patios and jungle views. Their **restaurant** (open daily, 7 a.m. to 10 p.m.) delivers delicious pizza, burgers, fish, Mexican and Tico specialties, salad, and homemade cake anywhere in the area. This is the home of Kids Saving the Rainforest, where you can buy the work of local artists. KSTR now has a wildlife sanctuary at the Mono Azul's new sister hotel, the **Blue Banyan Inn**, (private bath, hot water, fans, a/c, refrigerators, internet, pool, restaurant; $70-$120, including breakfast; 2777-2572, 8308-6071; bluebanyaninn.com, info@blue banyaninn.com) eight miles east of Quepos. The Blue Banyan's grounds offer rainforest trails, organic gardens and mountain views.

Back on the road to Manuel Antonio, a small road leads to the left to **Villas Mymosa** (private bath, hot water, ceiling fans, a/c, cable TV, kitchens, pool, wi-fi; $80-$180, including breakfast; 2777-1254, fax: 2777-2454; villasmymosa.com, info@villasmymosa.com), spacious, clean one-

and two-bedroom condos with balconies that sleep up to six, around a large pool. There are no railings on the stairs, so these might not be good for toddlers. **Mymositos Restaurant** (8386-2112) next door is open daily for breakfast, lunch, and dinner.

Back on the main road, a turnoff to the right leads to **Villa Kristina** (private bath, hot water, a/c, kitchen, cable TV; $50-$200, $270-$1150/week; phone/fax: 2777-2134; villakristina.com, villa_kristina@hotmail. com), secluded, one- and two-bedroom apartments that sleep two to six. They have ocean views, balconies with hammocks, and quiet gardens, 400 meters from Playa La Macha. You need four-wheel drive to get there.

Mirador Mi Lugar (2777-5120), down the next road to the right, is famous for its great view and creative cocktails. They have live music on weekends.

Vista Serena (dorms $10-$15/person; private bath, heated water, fans, kitchen, internet; $50-$100; 2777-5162; vistaserena.com) is the most inexpensive place to stay that has an ocean view. They have dorm rooms and houses with terraces and hammocks. On the same property, **Internet El Chante** (open 9 a.m. to 10 p.m., Sundays 4 to 10 p.m.; 2777-9224) has wi-fi, webcams and Skype so you can make inexpensive international calls.

Kapi Kapi (open daily 4 p.m. to 10 p.m.; 2777-5049) is the trendy new place to go for dining in tropical elegance. Pricey but worth it. It's uphill and around a few curves, on the left before the Tulemar.

Next on the right is the gated entrance to **Tulemar** (private bath, hot water, ceiling fans, a/c, TV with VCR, hairdryer, kitchen, pool; $210-$320 for up to four, including breakfast; children 10 and under, free; 2777-0580, 2777-1325, fax: 2777-1579; tulemar.com), luxurious octagonal one-bedroom houses with skylights, and stunning ocean views, which accommodate four people; there are also four villas ($900-$8800/weekly). A small private beach 800 meters below the bungalows has kayaks and snorkeling equipment for guests. Their poolside restaurant, **Tulecafe**, features international and multiethnic cuisine. Their three-night honeymoon package ($1000-$1500) includes champagne and flowers on arrival, massages, and dinner for two.

Right after the Tulemar, the **Salsipuedes Cantina** (opens daily at 4 p.m., closed Tuesday; 2777-5019) serves *tapas* and has a great view.

At the top of the hill is the **Barba Roja** (2777-0331; open daily, 4 to 10 p.m.), a favorite with visitors because of its gringo-style lunches and dinners, such as steak, burgers, nachos, and BLTs, and its sinful desserts—try the macadamia pie à la mode.

On the next corner, the **Casa Blanca** (private bath, hot water, ceiling fans, cable TV, a/c, pool; rooms, $90-$100; apartments with kitchens,

$110-$150; two-bedroom suites, $150-$220; phone/fax: 2777-0253; hotel casablanca.com, cblanca@racsa.co.cr) is an intimate and private gay resort catering to gay men, lesbians, and their open-minded relatives and friends. Be sure to ask for the rooms or apartments with ocean views—they are spectacular.

Down the steep road at Casa Blanca that takes you to Biesanz Beach, **Mango Moon** (private bath, hot water, ceiling fans, a/c, cable TV, pool; $130-$240, no children under 12; 2777-5323, fax: 2777-5128; mango moon.net, stay@mangomoon.net) has luscious views of Biesanz Cove from its balconies. All rooms are decorated with tropical charm; there are some two-bedroom suites ($230-$410). A private path takes you down to the beach in 10 minutes.

Further down this road on the left is **Casa Buena Vista** (private bath, hot water, some kitchens; $50-$60, including breakfast; 2777-1002, fax: 2777-1946; casabuenavista.net, casabuenavista1@hotmail.com), a converted home with terraces looking out into the jungle. Adjoining rooms 1 and 2 have a lovely view of Manuel Antonio. Not to be confused with the posh Buena Vista Villas at the Tulemar, this is a good value for the view and proximity to Biesanz Beach.

One kilometer from the main road is **Makanda-by-the-Sea** (private bath, hot water, ceiling fans, a/c, cable TV, kitchen, pool; $290-$470, including breakfast delivered to your room; 2777-0442, in North America: 800-MAKANDA, fax: 2777-1032; makanda.com, info@makanda.com), secluded villas with wide balconies and a sunset ocean view set in a 12-acre nature reserve. It's much closer to Biesanz Beach than hotels nearer the road. Several rooms can be connected to sleep up to eight ($1050-$1400). No children under 16 allowed. Honeymoon packages available. Makanda's **Sunspot Grill** (open 11 a.m. to 10 p.m.; 2777-0442) is *the* place to go for a romantic lunch or dinner. Lobster with saffron-garlic dipping sauce, wasabi tuna, and pork tenderloin with chipotle marinade are among the ever-changing dinner offerings. Recommended.

Returning to the main road, just over the hill on the right is the **Restaurant Agua Azul** (closed Wednesdays; 2777-5280), a favorite with visiting families for its laid-back, friendly atmosphere, terrific view, and tasty food.

The comfortable and well-designed **Villas Nicolás** (private bath, hot water, ceiling fans, a/c, pool; $100-$170; with kitchen, $140-$360; no children under 6 allowed; 2777-0481, fax: 2777-0451; villasnicolas.com, sales@villasnicolas.com), are condos with private terraces. The floor plans of the various-sized villas give an open, airy feel. Most have beautiful ocean views. The larger ones sleep four and two smaller ones can be combined to sleep five. A trail from the hotel leads to the beach.

Si Como No Resort and Spa (private bath, hot water, ceiling fans, a/c, kitchenette or wet bar, phones, pool, jacuzzi, spa, restaurant/bar; $220-$360, including breakfast; children under 6 free; 2777-0777, fax: 2777-1093, in North America: 800-282-0488; sicomono.com, information@sico mono.com) is a wonderland of gardens, waterfalls, and cascading pools. Our kids loved the waterslide; there is a quieter pool for people over 18 as well. The **Rico Tico**, a swim-up bar and grill, serves Tico and Tex-Mex food and icy fruit smoothies. The air-conditioned restaurant, **Claro Que Sí**, features authentic Caribbean seafood. They even have a 46-seat movie theater under the lobby, free for guests. **Tico Net** is their internet café, located in the Regalame Gift Shop, and they have their own **Serenity Spa**. They welcome gay and straight people alike. Their two- and five-night honeymoon packages cost $1100-1800; wedding packages are also available. This luxury resort is a showcase of eco-friendly alternative technologies for saving energy and water (double-paned windows and insulated ceilings, low-voltage lighting, solar-heated jacuzzi, self-cleaning pool, graywater recycling system, etc.). Recommended.

The romantic Italian restaurant **El Gato Negro**, is known for its excellent homemade pasta and seafood dishes. Try their *carpaccio*, raw fish marinated in lemon juice and spices. Make reservations. Expensive.

Hotel Costa Verde (private bath, hot water, ceiling fans, some a/c, some kitchens, some cable TV, pools, restaurants; $110-$190; penthouse or bungalows, $170-$250; 2777-0584, in North America: 866-854-7958, fax: 2777-0560; costaverde.com, reservations@costaverde.com) offers spacious rooms with balconies, and a variety of amenities to suit differing needs. The Studio Plus rooms and the Penthouse have panoramic ocean views. There is a separate building and pool for adults only, and others where children are welcome. Ask for rooms off the road. They have nature trails through 30 acres of rainforest, two restaurants, and an internet café.

BEACH AREA LODGING AND RESTAURANTS   The following hotels have easy access to **Playa Espadilla**, a long beach known for surfing and dangerous rip currents. Access to the national park is from the south end of Espadilla. Some of Manuel Antonio's least expensive rooms are in this area, although several comfortable, luxurious hotels are here, too.

Karahé (private bath, solar hot water, fans, a/c, some kitchens; $120-$150, including breakfast; 2777-0170, fax: 2777-1075, in North America: 877-623-3198; karahe.com, information@karahe.com) offers three types of rooms: the villas have magnificent views, but you must walk up more than a hundred steps to get to them; the newer "deluxe" rooms near the road have terraces; the junior suites also have terraces, are across the road, near the pool and 200 meters from the beach. The solar showers are hottest in the afternoon.

Next on the right is **Buena Nota**, a well-stocked newsstand and beach shop. High-quality souvenirs and beachwear plus lots of tourism information make this a worthwhile stop.

Hotel Verdemar (private bath, hot water, ceiling fans, a/c, pool; $70-$110; with kitchens, $80-$140; 2777-1805, fax: 2777-1311, in North America: 877-872-0459; verdemar.com, verdemar@racsa.co.cr) has pleasantly decorated rooms with a pool and a raised wooden walkway to the beach.

Restaurant Mar y Sombra (2777-0510) is the traditional place to eat on Playa Espadilla. It's about 500 meters before the entrance to the national park; you'll see it from the main road. Seafood, including delicious calamari and tropical *batidos*, are featured on their menu. They have a big disco dance on Saturday nights.

Across from the beach, the popular and affordable **Restaurant Marlin** (2777-1134) serves Tex-Mex, seafood, soups, and salads, on an airy upstairs terrace.

A road to the left at the Marlin leads to the following hotels, some of the best at the beach: **Cabinas Espadilla** (private bath, heated water, fans, refrigerator, a/c, pool; $70-$90; with kitchen, $80-$110; 2777-0416; cabinasespadilla.com) has clean rooms in a tranquil garden atmosphere. Owned by the same family, **Hotel Playa Espadilla** (hot water, a/c, cable TV, phones, pool; $120-$160; with kitchen, $130-$180; breakfast included; phone/fax: 2777-0903; hotelespadilla.com), down the street on the left, has light, spacious rooms with tiled floors. There are tennis courts and a private nature reserve. Their very nice **Restaurant Puerto Escondido** is only for guests. Recommended.

La Posada Jungle Bungalows (private bath, hot water, ceiling fans, a/c, refrigerator, microwave, cable TV, pool, jacuzzi; rooms and bungalows, $60-$150; two bath/two bedroom house, $260-$270, including breakfast; children under 5 free; 2777-1446; laposadajungle.com, info@laposadajungle.com) have the unique distinction of being located right next to the exit of Manuel Antonio National Park. The monkeys don't seem to recognize the park boundaries so guests at this small, friendly lodge often are entertained by various forms of wildlife. The thatch-roofed bungalows are clean and comfortable and have porches with hammocks. Gathering places around the small pool and the breakfast patio make it easy to meet other guests. Breakfasts are generous, there's a pizza restaurant, and movies are shown on Thursdays. It's located next to the exit of the National Park, at the end of a bumpy unpaved street filled with cheap hotels.

GETTING THERE: By Bus: A direct San José–Manuel Antonio bus (2223-5567; $5) leaves the Coca Cola at 6 a.m., noon, 6 p.m., and 7:30 p.m., returning at 6 a.m., 9:30 a.m., noon and 5 p.m., with another return bus at 3 p.m. on Sundays. Buy tickets in advance on weekends and holidays and purchase return tickets as soon as you arrive. The Quepos ticket office is open Monday through Saturday, 7 a.m. to 11 a.m., 1 p.m. to 5 p.m.; Sunday, 7 a.m. to noon. This bus will pick you up at your hotel on its way from Manuel Antonio to Quepos, but you must be out on the road to flag it down. (Do not let anyone but the bus driver load or unload your baggage. Try to keep it with you if possible. Things have been stolen from the luggage compartment.) One driver on this route makes the trip in three hours, a fact that defies conventional concepts of space and time. We have heard of several people who have become quite religious on this bus. The bus will let you off at the airport near San José if you ask. The trip should take three and a half to four hours and cost about $5. (Watch out for pickpockets at the Coca Cola and in Quepos.)

Quepos–Manuel Antonio: From the southeast corner of the market, take a 20-minute bus ride (30 cents) seven scenic kilometers to the entrance of the park. They leave on the hour and half hour between 5 a.m. and 11 p.m. (check schedules at 2777-0263). Watch out for robberies in the tumult to get on this bus. A taxi to Manuel Antonio from Quepos costs about $4.

Quepos–Puntarenas buses leave at 4:30 a.m., 7:30 a.m., 10:30 a.m., 12:30 p.m. and 3 p.m., returning at 5 a.m., 8 a.m., 11 a.m. and 4:30 p.m. (three hours; $3). All of the above buses pass by Playa Esterillos, an hour north of Quepos.

Buses leave San Isidro de El General (2771-2550, 2771-4744) for Quepos at 7 a.m. and 1:30 p.m., passing through Dominical. They return from Quepos to San Isidro at 5 a.m. and 1:30 p.m.

Interbus (2283-5573; interbusonline.com) runs shuttles to Manuel Antonio from San José daily ($35). They also connect you to Monteverde, Guanacaste, Montezuma, and Arenal Volcano. Lynch Travel (2777-1170; lynchtravel.com, lyntur@racsa.co.cr) is their representative in Quepos. Lynch provides shuttles to Matapalo, Dominical, Uvita, and Sierpe. These private, air-conditioned buses are fast and comfortable.

By Car: The trip from San José is about three and a half hours if you take the Atenas turnoff and drive the narrow, winding road through the Aguacate mountains. This route is scenic and gives you a glimpse of rural life. You can buy sugarcane juice and fruit along the way. You can also take the Interamerican Highway to Puntarenas and then turn south, but you might be traveling with a line of trailer trucks.

By Air: SANSA has nine flights a day to Quepos during the high season (2290-4100, fax: 2290-3543; $50-$60 one way). Buy tickets at least two weeks in advance. SANSA also has Quepos–Palmar Norte flights. Check schedules at fly sansa.com. Nature Air (2299-6000, in North America: 800-235-9272; $60 one way, $120 roundtrip) has four flights to Quepos daily. Nature Air flights connect Quepos with Arenal, Tamarindo. Liberia, Palmar Norte, Puerto Jiménez, Golfito, Drake Bay and Limón. Check schedules at natureair.com.

MATAPALO

An hour south of Manuel Antonio along the bumpy Costanera Sur road is Matapalo, a small, quiet beach town set in the middle of a seemingly un-ending stretch of sand. One section of Matapalo is on the road, and its oceanside twin, with all the cabinas and restaurants, is a couple of kilometers away on the beach. The surf here is not what you would call gentle, but it is much less rough than it is at Dominical, about 15 kilometers farther south (see Southern Zone chapter). The firm beach at low tide is great for horseback riding or bike riding, and sea kayaks are for rent to explore nearby mangroves. At night the starlight is brighter than in more developed areas.

In the *pueblo*, enjoy good Tico food at **Soda Mango**.

At the beach road, across the little bridge south of the football plaza, **Express del Pacífico** serves French cuisine in a garden setting.

Dreamy Contentment (private bath, hot water, fan, a/c; $110-$240; 2787-5223; dreamycontentment.com) is a beach house and bungalows that sleep four to six. They invite visitors to "pause…reflect…rejuvenate."

El Coquito del Pacífico (private bath, hot water, ceiling fans, pool; $50-$70; phone/fax: 2787-5028; elcoquito.com) has spacious, bright cabi-nas with good screens and reading lamps and a beachfront gourmet restau-rant.

Down the road on the right 150 meters is one of the nicest places to stay or eat in Matapalo: **Albergue Suizo** (private bath, heated water, ceiling fans, some a/c; $30-$50; 2787-5068, 8382-7122; matapaloplaya.com). Rooms are spacious and clean. The Swiss owners serve tasty meals on their balcony.

Funky cabins with a French/Italian/Asian restaurant, **La Terraza del Sol** (private bath, cold water, fan; $20-$30; 2787-5081), a few hundred me-ters north, is open for guests only. The owner likes to have golf tourna-ments on the beach.

The **Jungle House** (private bath, heated water, fans, a/c, some kitchens, gym; $60-$70; $350 weekly; three-night minimum; phone/fax: 2787-5005, 8810-2040; junglehouse.com, jhinfo@junglehouse.com), offers cabinas and a six-bedroom beachhouse that sleeps 16. Its three night minimum gives guests "the opportunity to remember what the true human experience is about."

Next door, the **Bahari Beach Bungalows** (private bath, pool, jacuzzi, a/c option; 2787-5014; baharibeach.com, andrealudwig10@hotmail.com), owned by an Austrian and a Hungarian, has rooms ($60-$70) in the main building and luxury African tent bungalows ($80-$110) with porches and roomy baths. Their restaurant serves fresh seafood and good breakfasts.

El Castillo (hot water, kitchen; $70-$100, $220-$300 for the whole house; phone/fax: 8392-3460; elcastillo.net, dc@elcastillo.net), in the hills with awesome views of Playa Matapalo, offers rooms or rental of the whole house.

GETTING THERE: By Bus: Take a San Isidro bus from Quepos at 5 a.m. or 1:30 p.m., a Quepos bus from San Isidro at 7 a.m. or 1:30 p.m., or a Quepos-Matapalo bus at 10 a.m.

By Car: Drive south along the gravel Costanera Highway from Manuel Antonio, or north from Dominical (see Southern Zone chapter). Travel time is one hour from Quepos, half an hour from Dominical; ask about road conditions before you set out. Don't drive this road at night.

TWELVE

Southern Zone

Costa Rica's *Zona Sur*, or Southern Zone, encompasses the southern half of coastal Puntarenas Province (from Playa Dominical to the Osa Peninsula, to Punta Burica on the Panamanian border), as well as the mountainous southern half of San José Province and inland Limón and Puntarenas provinces, including Chirripó National Park and La Amistad International Park, which extends across the border into Panama. For hikers, naturalists, anglers, and those who want to get off the beaten track, this area has a tremendous amount to offer.

Despite its reputation nationally as a center of agroindustry (bananas, pineapples, palm oil, coffee), it has a larger percentage of national parks and forest reserves than any other region of Costa Rica. It also has the largest concentration of indigenous people, especially the Guaymis, Térrabas, and Borucas, centering around the towns of Buenos Aires and San Vito. The Southern Zone is also known for small, aesthetically designed nature lodges that fund private reserves where you can get up close and personal with monkeys, macaws, and dolphins.

LOS SANTOS

Los Santos is a mountainous region southeast of San José covered with well-groomed coffee farms. The higher reaches are cloud forest frequented by the beautiful resplendent quetzal, making this one of the closest quetzal-viewing areas to San José. From San José head toward Cartago, then up into the mountains on the Interamerican Highway toward San Isidro. The turnoff for Santa María de Dota is at El Empalme, 29 kilometers from Cartago. Stop to buy the tart apples and hard balls of sharp, white *palmito* cheese produced here. Or warm up with a cup of *agua dulce* and a hot *tortilla de queso*.

From El Empalme, continue down the road on the right to **Santa María de Dota** (11 kilometers). These mountains were the scene of the beginnings of the 1948 Civil War—the late Don Pepe Figueres' farm, *La Lucha Sin Fin* (The Endless Struggle), is located near Santa María. In the plaza is a monument to those who lost their lives in Costa Rica's battle to preserve the integrity of the electoral process.

For hikes through narrow mountain valleys and native oak forests, following rushing rivers and mesmerizing waterfalls, spend at least a day in **Copey**, seven kilometers uphill from Santa María. Its brisk climate at 7000 feet above sea level is refreshing, especially if you're feeling worn out from the lowland heat. Fish for your own trout lunch at **Pesca Río Blanco** (2541-1816) and buy crisp, local apples for dessert. Copey's old wooden **church** is a national monument.

Cafe Los Santos (wi-fi; open weekdays, 9 a.m. to 6 p.m.; weekends, 2 p.m. to 6 p.m.; 2546-7881) in **San Marcos Tarrazú**, six kilometers west of Santa María, serves decaffeinated coffee, a rarity in Costa Rica, along with 50 varieties of flavored coffee: orange, blackberry, honey and pollen, brandy—you name it! They have another branch in El Empalme on the Interamerican Highway at the turnoff to Santa María de Dota and Copey.

Santos Tour (2855-9386; santostour.net) will take you to an organic coffee farm (see pages 394–95). You can also pick your own strawberries, blackberries, avocados, and cherries at local farms through their tours. The Extreme Forest Tour in Providencia offers various innovations on the ubiquitous zipline canopy experience. They also offer an adventurous Jeep trip from Los Santos by back roads to Manuel Antonio.

This area is part of the **Cerro Vueltas Biological Reserve**, which borders Tapantí/Maciso de la Muerte National Park to the northeast and Parque Nacional Los Quetzales to the south. These protected areas are connected to Chirripó National Park and La Amistad International Park stretching down into Panama, making this the largest biological corridor in the country.

El Toucanet (private bath, hot water; $60-$80, including breakfast; children under 12 free; 2541-3045, 2541-3131; eltoucanet.com, reserve@eltoucanet.com) is a welcoming lodge in Copey. The big windows of its **restaurant** overlook a peaceful forest and a rushing mountain stream. They specialize in freshly caught trout. It can get chilly in these hills, so the cabins have thick blankets and the restaurant has a cozy sunken sitting area around a fireplace. Their new suites have great views and Jacuzzis. Owner Gary

Roberts gives a free guided tour every morning to search for the resplendent quetzal. From December to July, sightings are common just 15 minutes from the lodge. The rest of the year he will take you to a higher altitude to find them. They also offer a horseback tour with breathtaking views for experienced riders, a tour of a local coffee factory, or hiking in the cloud forest and *páramo*. It is one kilometer east of the Copey church. Recommended.

GETTING THERE: By Bus: You can catch the bus to Santa María from the Los Santos terminal in San José (Calle 21, Avenida 16 bis; 2221-7070, 2223-1002). Buses leave at 6 a.m., 9 a.m., 12:30 p.m., 3 p.m., and 5 p.m. and return to San José from the main square in Santa María six times a day. The trip is about two hours.

Copey has its own bus service now, leaving from Santa María de Dota. Check schedules at 2541-1449. A taxi from Santa María to Copey costs about $10.

To get to Copey without going through Santa María, take a San Isidro bus (Calle 16, Avenidas 1/3) to Cañón del Guarco, kilometer 58 on the Interamerican Highway. (You'll see the little yellow markers on the side of the road that tell you how many kilometers you are from San José.) From Cañón it's seven kilometers downhill to Copey. Santa María is another seven kilometers downhill.

By Car: Head east of San José on the Interamerican Highway past Cartago and drive toward San Isidro. At Empalme turn right toward Santa María, or continue to kilometer 58 and turn right to go directly to Copey. It takes about one and a half hours. If you drive up from Santa María, make sure you have four-wheel drive, or at least a powerful engine and high clearance.

To get to this area and avoid the hectic traffic of San José, go south of the international airport to Villa Colón and climb up to Palmichal de Acosta, where you can stay at Nacientes Palmichal. From there, find your way to San Ignacio de Acosta. Continue past the church to Vuelta de Jorco, where you turn right to go to San Gabriel and Frailes. From Frailes, follow signs to the Los Santos area: San Pablo de León Cortés, San Marcos de Tarrazú (where there is a bank with an ATM), and Santa María de Dota. The roads are nicely paved, and the churches and plazas of these charming villages are picturesque. Take a detour to see the views from the hillside village of San Isidro de San Pablo de León Cortés by taking a right turn before you enter San Pablo. It takes about three hours to drive from the airport to Santa María by this route. Recommended.

CERRO DE LA MUERTE

The Interamerican Highway, which becomes San José's Central Avenue, crossing the city from west to east, turns right at Cartago to connect the Central Valley with the Southern Zone. It winds into the mountains that surround fog-shrouded Cerro de la Muerte, the highest pass on the Interamerican Highway. This entire area is part of the Cerro Vueltas Biological Reserve, mentioned above.

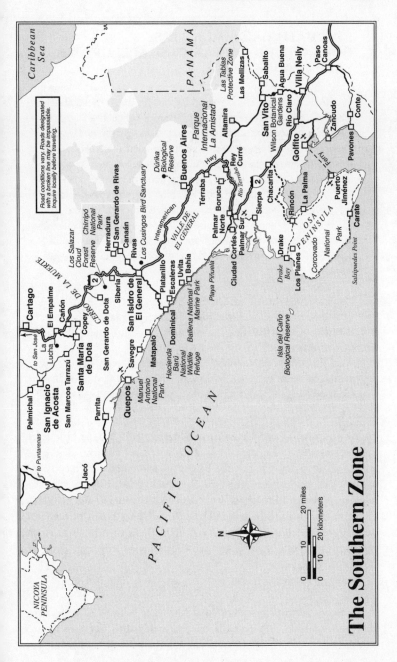

Road conditions vary. Roads designated with a broken line may be impassable. Inquire locally before traveling.

Caribbean Sea

PANAMÁ

Las Tablas Protective Zone

Las Melizas

Parque Internacional La Amistad

Durika Biological Reserve

Buenos Aires

Altamira

San Vito

Wilson Botanical Gardens

Sabalito

Agua Buena

Villa Neily

Paso Canoas

Conte

Río Claro

Golfito

Zancudo

Pavones

Los Salazar Cloud Forest Reserve

Chirripó National Park

San Gerardo de Rivas

Herradura

Canaán

Rivas

Los Cusingos Bird Sanctuary

Rey Curré

Térraba

Río Térraba

Palmar Norte

Boruca

Sierpe

Chacarita

Rincón

La Palma

Puerto Jiménez

Carate

OSA PENINSULA

Corcovado National Park

CERRO DE LA MUERTE

Cartago

El Empalme

Cañón

Copey

Siberia

San Gerardo de Dota

San Isidro de El General

Platanillo

Escaleras

Uvita

Bahía

Dominical

Matapalo

Ballena National Marine Park

Playa Piñuela

Ciudad Cortés

Palmar Sur

Los Planes

Drake

Drake Bay

Isla del Caño Biological Reserve

Subsequides Point

to San José

La Lucha

Santa María de Dota

San Marcos Tarrazú

Savegre

Quepos

Manuel Antonio National Park

Hacienda Barú National Wildlife Refuge

Palmichal

San Ignacio de Acosta

Parrita

Jacó

to Puntarenas

Interamerican Hwy

VALLE DE EL GENERAL

PACIFIC OCEAN

NICOYA PENINSULA

N

20 miles

20 kilometers

10

0   10   20

The Southern Zone

INNOVATIVE COMMUNITIES: SOL COLIBRÍ—ORGANIC, SHADE-GROWN, FAIR TRADE COFFEE

This area, situated at 5000 to 6000 feet above sea level, is known in coffee circles as Tarrazú, world famous for its 100 percent Arabica coffee with 100 percent Strictly Hard Bean quality.

There is much interest in fair trade, shade-grown, and organic coffee, but these terms do not all imply each other. *Fair trade* means that coffee producers are paid fairly for their products. *Shade-grown* means that trees grow among the coffee bushes in the traditional manner, providing habitat for birds and wildlife. However, growing coffee in the shade makes it hard to deal with *ojo de gallo*, a disease that affects the leaves of the plants, so minimal amounts of chemicals are usually used to treat the disease. This "almost organic" shade grown coffee is called *cafe ambiental* in Spanish.

In the Los Santos region, you can visit farms that produce Sol Colibri coffee, which is certified organic by Costa Rica-based Eco-Logica; certified shade-grown by the Smithsonian Migratory Bird Center, and certified fair trade by the Fair Trade Labeling Organization.

Sol Colibrí (2240-1424, 2541-1960; solcolibri.com) was started in 1995 in Dota-Tarrazú by Arturo Segura and Shelley Gillespie, whose intention was to simply grow good organic cof-

As you wind around **Cerro de la Muerte**, you'll see the lush vegetation become stunted and then diminish. When taking this trip, dress in layers and try to go early in the day, before fog and rain reduce the visibility to zero. This can happen even in the dry season. Landslides are also a very real danger during heavy rains. If you are cold in your car and intimidated by the driving conditions, imagine how Costa Ricans hiking or driving ox carts must have felt before the road was built. That's why this area is called "Mountain of Death." Several high-altitude mountain lodges are on or near Cerro de la Muerte.

Quetzals Paradise (private bath, heated water; 2200-0241, 2771-4582; quetzalsparadise.com) virtually guarantees that you will see quetzals in their reserve between November and May. The Serrano Obando family guides are intimate with the birds' hangouts and habits, but even if you're unlucky, the guided hike is lovely and punctuated with curiosities: huge

fee. But, as Arturo told us: "Coffee is the second most traded commodity in the world after oil. As we entered the coffee market we found a system that manipulated the farmer, disregarded the environment, and isolated us in one area of the coffee economy. Prodded by the challenges of working in this system, we decided to find the most direct way to connect our coffee with the consumers."

Today Sol Colibrí unites over 1800 small family cocoa and coffee farms in DIRECT trade so that they receive tangible economic benefits from their hand-crafted labor of love. As grower, processor, exporter, importer, and distributor, Sol Colibri eliminates the intermediaries, giving its members the economic means to become educators and stewards in their own communities while delivering the classic taste of Tarrazú.

You can tour Arturo Segura´s coffee farm with **Santos Tour** (2855-9386; santostour.net).

Sol Colibri's partnership with U.S.-based Tortuga Coffee (www.tortugacoffee.com) provides a straightforward, effective way for organizations, schools, and others to raise money through easy-to-use online coffee sales. Each sale generates a significant donation ($4/bag of coffee and $1/bag of cocoa powder) to the organization of the customer's choice as well as a donation to support the leatherback turtle restoration and other environmental projects in Costa Rica sponsored by the EcoTeach Foundation.

cipresillo trees that naturally hollow out in their old age, and marine fossils in the rocks beside one of their creeks. Most visitors spend the night in the comfy, heated cabins because quetzal sightings are most likely in the early morning, but you can also stop in for a guided tour. The former managers of Mirador de Quetzales, Jorge Serrano and his family, have now started their own lodge, They offer a nocturnal hike ($60 including dinner and breakfast). To get there, go one kilometer west after you turn off the Interamerican Highway at marker 70.

PARQUE NACIONAL LOS QUETZALES

One of Costa Rica´s newest parks, the 5000-hectare Los Quetzales ($10; 2200-5354) protects the ancient high altitude oak forests that are home to the amazing birds it is named after. The ranger station is at kilometer 74 of the Interamerican Highway across from Chespiritos Restaurant. Trails are

INNOVATIVE COMMUNITIES: COOPESAVEGRE—PRESERVING THE BEAUTY OF PROVIDENCIA

In 1998 the Government of Spain launched a far-sighted program to preserve the watershed of the Savegre River, deemed one of the purest rivers in Latin America. The extensive oak forests of Alto Savegre had long been familiar to the Spanish as the source of the oaken casks used to age their famous wines. Most of the *campesinos* who lived in the high forests made their living from turning ancient oaks into charcoal, until the Costa Rican government stopped the practice in the 1970s.

Around the turn of the century, a Spanish delegation visited 36 communities, from the river's headwaters in Providencia down to where the Savegre meets the sea south of Manuel Antonio National Park. They built simple suspended bridges to help people get around in this steep mountainous area, and trained many *campesinos* to be environmental advocates. Today these efforts are bearing fruit as many of their trainees manifest their commitment to this beautiful river in a number of interesting projects throughout the watershed. Two of them are described here. This is one of the few regions in Costa Rica that is actively working on a zoning plan.

Restaurante Las Cascadas del Savegre (2226-6376; coope_savegre@yahoo.com) serves well-prepared fresh trout as part of a elegant four-course meal. The welcoming exterior decorated with hanging flower baskets and the clean design of the interior are unexpected in this isolated mountain village. Owner Juan Francisco Aguero takes off his chef's hat and leads you on a short,

still being developed. For now you can take the 3.5-kilometer Ojo de Agua trail into the forest and walk back to the ranger station on the Providencia road. You can gaze at the mighty forests of Parque Nacional Los Quetzales from the villages of Providencia, 13 kilometers west of the ranger station, and San Gerardo de Dota (entrance at kilometer 80 on the Interamerican).

Ten kilometers south of the ranger station, on the Intermamerican Highway, is the *páramo* section of the park. Because of the nature of the *páramo*, there are no trails, but the stunted vegetation means you won't get lost.

SAVEGRE TREK **Coopesavegre** (2226-6376; info@coopesavegre.com) can take you on a six-day, five-night trek starting on the paramo at 11,350 feet above sea level and hiking down to San Gerardo (7150 feet). The next

fascinating tour of **Providencia**, to see the ecologically run coffee processing plant, the waterfalls in the crystalline river, and La Piedra, the cave where the first *campesino* settlers stayed after discovering this glorious area. The tour, lodging and three great meals cost around $50-$60/person. Recommended.

Albergue Las Cascadas, about a kilometer down the road are simple and clean ($20/person, including breakfast; contact info above). They rent a new two-bedroom house for $60-$70.

Armonía Ambiental (shared baths, heated water; $40/person, including meals and tour; 2226-6376; coope_savegre@yahoo. com) has fantastic views of 14 mountains and the rich oak forests of Parque Nacional Los Quetzales. For breakfast, Doña Noire serves artistic arrangements of the various tropical fruits grown on her farm. When we were there, cala lillies were in bloom, which lent a touch of elegance to the humble charm of her dining area. Accommodations are in her home or in a new cabin up the hill with great views.

In this pristine mountain village, as in most gorgeous rural areas, there is no garbage disposal facility. Doña Noire addresses this problem with creativity and enthusiasm. She and her family stuff plastic soda bottles with more plastic, and use them as building materials. She makes planters out of old bleach bottles and washing machine innards, and builds garden terraces out of tin cans. Her enthusiasm is contagious. Volunteers are welcome at Armonia Ambiental, as are vegetarians. The family can take you on hikes or horseback rides in the forest above their farm. Armonía Ambiental is located a couple of bumpy kilometers beyond Restaurante Las Cascadas. Recommended.

day, you hike to Providencia (5688 feet). The third day has an eight-hour hike up to 6250 feet, descending to La Chaqueta at 2300 feet, The fourth night is spent at El Brujo Tent Camp at 800 feet. On the fifth night you arrive at El Silencio before marching into the sea at Playa El Rey, part of Manuel Antonio National Park, on day six. The trip can also be done by horseback. The whole six-day trek costs about $400 including naturalist guide, lodging, and meals, and offers many opportunities for birding, fantastic vistas, refreshing dips in the river, and visiting communities along the way. You have to be in good shape to do this rigorous but rewarding trek.

SAN GERARDO DE DOTA   San Gerardo de Dota, a narrow, pristine mountain valley at 6900 feet, has become a mecca for birders, hikers, and trout fishers. Be prepared—the weather is crisp at this altitude and it gets downright chilly at night. The cloud forests here are famous for sightings of the beautiful resplendent quetzal.

El Jilguero (open daily, 9 a.m. to 10 p.m.; 2200-5913) is a bar/restaurant/souvenir shop at the entrance to San Gerardo (kilometer 80 on the Interamerican Highway) that offers Thai, Argentine, Caribbean, and Middle Eastern food as well as a warming woodstove. If you arrive on the bus, you can use their phone to call your hotel in San Gerardo or to arrange taxi transport down into the valley (about $5).

Soda El Junco (open daily, 7 a.m. to 8.p.m.; 2740-1059), one kilometer toward San Gerardo on the left, offers trout fishing and will cook your catch in its cozy restaurant.

Cabinas y Senderos Las Cataratas (private bath, heated water; $60-$70, including breakfast; 2740-1065; cataratas.tk) 3 kilometers from the entrance to San Gerardo on the right, are attractive individual bungalows set around a trout pond and looking out into the forested hills of Parque Nacional Los Quetzales. Some rooms have fireplaces. Their nicely designed restaurant specializes in steak and trout. There are nature trails to waterfalls. Recommended.

Comida Típica Miriam (open daily, 6 a.m. to 8 p.m.; 2740-1049) is next on the left. Doña Miriam is very sought after for her good home cooking. She has a cute little cabin (private bath, heated water, electric heat; $20-$40; 2740-1049) downhill from the restaurant that looks out into the lush forest, and a plainer two-bedroom cabin as well.

Dantica Lodge (private bath, hot water, electric heaters, jacuzzis, satellite TV, some kitchens; $130-$220; suites with fireplaces, $160-$180; honeymoon package, $190-$210; including breakfast; children under 12 free, ages 12 to 17 half-price; 2740-1067, fax: 2740-1071; dantica.com, info@dantica.com) is on a mountaintop four kilometers from the Interamerican Highway with incredible views of the forested hills of Los Quetzales National Park. Their private cloud-forest reserve is ideal for birding. Two examples of the creative, stylish touches found in anything they design: the tabletops in the breakfast room are glass panels suspended over a layer of roasted coffee beans; as the sun warms them, the whole room smells of coffee. Antique Colombian colonial doors and wrought iron work add a historic touch to the clean lines of the spacious rooms and baths. The newest rooms are down a long path through the forest (they take your bags there for you) with even more awesome views of the ancient oak forests. Their Latin American crafts shop offers one-of-a-kind examples of the best contemporary indigenous art from many different countries. Recommended.

The **Trogon Lodge** (private bath, hot water, restaurant, cable TV; $90-$140; 2293-8181, fax: 2239-7657; grupomawamba.com, info@grupo mawamba.com) has duplexes of dark-stained wood overlooking lovely flowering gardens next to a stream where you can catch your dinner. One and a half kilometers of trail lead through their primary-forest reserve. The lodge offers horseback trips and has its own **canopy tour**.

Cabinas El Quetzal (private bath, solar-heated water; $50-$60/person, including meals; phone/fax: 2740-1036; cabinaselquetzal.com), down the road, is a good low-cost alternative. They can show you around the area and put you in contact with neighbors who rent horses. The dining room has a beautiful river view.

Savegre Mountain Hotel (private bath, heated water, restaurant, bar/lounge; 2740-1028, fax: 2740-1027; savegre.co.cr) has comfortable rooms ($150-$170, including meals) and junior suites with bathtubs and fireplaces ($200-$220, including meals). Over 170 bird species have been observed from the 16 kilometers of hiking trails here. It hosts the Quetzal Education Research Complex in partnership with Southern Nazarene University in Oklahoma. Students who come to study quetzals share information with local residents and visitors through a series of public talks at the hotel. They offer horseback riding, waterfall, coffee, and fly-fishing tours. Be sure to make reservations; the lodge is quite popular.

Los Ranchos (private bath, hot water; $60-$70, children half-price; 2740-1043) has cute two- and three-room bungalows with kitchens and balconies looking out onto a pond in a peaceful, park-like garden. There are boats, barbecues, fishing, campgrounds, and tent rentals ($8/person). It's probably quieter to stay there during the week. They offer a two-day cloud-forest tour for $70 including meals and lodging. Recommended.

Suria Lodge (private bath, heated water; $70-$80, including breakfast; 2740-1004; suria-lodge.com, suriacabins@racsa.co.cr) has comfortable rooms in a garden setting and a trail to a waterfall.

GETTING THERE: By Bus: Take a San Isidro bus (see below) and ask to be left at the "*entrada a San Gerardo*" at the 80-kilometer mark on the Interamerican Highway. San Gerardo is nine kilometers downhill from there, a scenic two-and-a-half- to three-hour walk. A shuttle bus from San Jose will also drop you off at the entrance to San Gerardo (shuttleosa.com).

By Car: If you are driving from San José, follow the directions in "Getting There" for San Isidro de El General, and turn right at the 80-kilometer mark. Make sure your vehicle has a powerful engine since the road is extremely steep and narrow.

ON THE WAY TO SAN ISIDRO

LOS SALAZAR CLOUD FOREST RESERVE   The Salazar family owns a 2000-hectare cloud forest reserve near the village of Siberia, at kilometer 99 on the Interamerican Highway. They offer a two-day **cloud forest tour** including meals and lodging for $50-$60. **Cabinas El Páramo** (private bath, heated water, kitchens, electric heaters; $30-$100; 2226-6376; coope_savegre@yahoo.com) are individual bungalows nestled in a cloudforest garden where it's easy to see hummingbirds. The lodging have a rustic charm and homey decor; some can sleep up to ten people. This region supplies mushrooms to San José´s gourmet restaurants. You can sample native mushroom dishes at **Restaurant El Páramo**, a short walk from the cabins.

Coopesavegre (2226-6376; info@coopesavegre.com) offers a three-day cloud forest birding tour with overnight stops is Providencia, San Gerardo, and Siberia.

Several roadside cafeterias on the Cerro specialize in quick *comida típica* for bus passengers. The classic **La Georgina**, in Villa Mills at kilometer 95, serves a wide variety of local treats. They have hummingbird feeders, trout ponds, and orchids. They also rent basic rooms with electric blankets (private bath, heated water, TV; $15-$20; 2770-8043) and new, larger cabins with fireplaces and kitchens ($30-$40). On a rare clear day you can see Volcán Irazú to the north and Chirripó to the south.

At kilometer 119, 20 minutes before arriving in San Isidro, the friendly **Valle del General** offers a panoramic view and well-prepared, inexpensive *comida típica*. This area is famous among birders for sightings of the white-tailed emerald hummingbird, red-headed barbets, violet sabrewings, and scaled antpittas, as well as tanagers, woodcreepers, warblers, and vireos. They offer birding tours with an experienced guide ($125-$150, including meals and lodging; half-day tour for $50/person, four person minimum) and a six-cable **canopy tour** ($25). On a hillside below the restaurant are eight cute, comfortable rooms with balconies (private bath, hot water; $50-$60, including breakfast; 8384-4685, 8836-6193, fax: 2772-2727; vistadelgeneral.com, admin@valledelgeneral.com).

SAN ISIDRO DE EL GENERAL

When the fog clears as you descend from Cerro de la Muerte, the **Valle de El General (Perez Zeledon)** offers beautiful flowers and a lovely climate. For more information about this area, see turisur.com.

The bustling, fast-growing town of **San Isidro de El General** is the gateway to Chirripó National Park and the southern Pacific beaches of Dominical, Uvita, and Tortuga. The clean public market in San Isidro is a delight, offering an array of beautiful fruits and vegetables, and good, inexpensive places to eat.

Birders will be interested in a visit to **Los Cusingos Neotropical Bird Sanctuary** (open 7 a.m. to 4 p.m. by appointment only; closed Monday; 2253-3267; cct.or.cr; admission $10, children $5) in the foothills southeast of San Isidro. This is the former home of renowned ornithologist Alexander Skutch, co-author of *The Birds of Costa Rica* and many other works based on his lifetime of nature observation. The lovely gardens were designed by his wife, Pamela Lankester, of the famous Lankester Gardens in Cartago. Both are now deceased and the 78-hectare sanctuary is administered by the Tropical Science Center in San José.

On San Isidro's central plaza, the **Restaurant/Bar Chirripó**, at the hotel of the same name, is a favorite for local gringo residents. **El Tenedor** (closed Monday; 2771-0881) serves Italian food down from the central plaza, 75 meters toward the Hotel Iguazú on the second floor. Locals have recommended **Restaurante Mexico Lindo** (2771-8222) for tasty Mexican food at reasonable prices. You'll find Mexico Lindo inside the Centro Comercial Pedro Perez Zeledon on the south side of the Plaza.

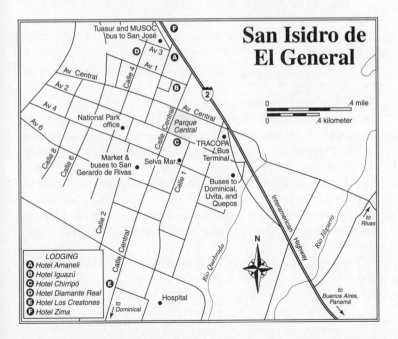

San Isidro de El General

LODGING
- **A** Hotel Amaneli
- **B** Hotel Iguazú
- **C** Hotel Chirripó
- **D** Hotel Diamante Real
- **E** Hotel Los Crestones
- **F** Hotel Zima

La Reina del Valle (2771-4860; lareinadelvalle.com), on the west side of the plaza, is the traditional place to go for great *bocas* and local food. It has unique views of the goings-on in the plaza from its light, airy dining room and its second-floor bar.

Kafé de la Casa (2770-4816) is an art gallery that serves light meals on garden tables and often has live music. It's half a block west of Hotel Amaneli.

Saveur de France (open 7:30 a.m. to 7 p.m., closed Sunday; 8994-9909) in the Centro Comercial Los Betos, is owned by a French couple who make genuine brioche, croissants, and other delightful pastries. You can order a filling goat-cheese and ham baguette sandwich, and treat yourself to a *torte au Cointreau* for dessert.

Selva Mar (2771-4582, fax: 2771-8841; exploringcostarica.com, selva mar@ice.co.cr), around the corner from Hotel Chirripó, is a travel agency committed to ecotourism. They will also help you make reservations for any lodges listed below and will arrange domestic flights and car rentals. They specialize in one- to five-day treks up Chirripó, and in the Paso de la Danta Biological Corridor and Corcovado (chirripo.com).

SEPA (2770-1457, fax: 2771-5586; spanish-school-costarica.com, info@spanish-school-costarica.com) offers one- to three-week Spanish instruction combined with tours, homestays, or environmental volunteer work.

BTC Internet (2771-3993), in the shopping center on the south side of the plaza, has internet connections. You can also make telephone calls from the ICE, two blocks north of the Parque Central. There are ATMs at the Banco de San José and Coopealianza.

LODGING   There are several clean and inexpensive hotels in town. Near the bus stops and close to the Interamerican Highway you will find the relatively noisy **Hotel Amaneli** (private bath, heated water, wall fans, some TV; $10-20/person; 2771-0352) and the quieter **Hotel Iguazú** (shared bath, $10; private bath, heated water, wall fans, cable TV; $20-$30; 2771-2571). **Hotel Zima** (private bath, hot water, fans or a/c, pool; $20-$40, 2770-1114, 2770-8394; hotelzima@hotmail.com) in a quieter area on the east side of the highway, is fresh and new with a nice swimming pool. **Hotel Chirripó** (hot water, fans, cable TV; with shared bath, $15/person; with private bath, $20-$30/person; 2771-0529) is right on the plaza.

The nicest place to stay in town is the imposing new **Hotel Diamante Real** (private bath, ceiling fans, a/c, oversized jacuzzis in suites, phones, wi-fi, restaurant, conference room; $50-$70; 2770-6230, fax: 2770-6250; hoteldiamantereal.com, info@hoteldiamantereal.com), with excellent mattresses and amenities. It's just 100 meters from the MUSOC bus station.

Hotel Los Crestones (private bath, hot water, ceiling fans, a/c, cable TV, wi-fi, restaurant, conference room, pool; $60-$70; 2770-1200, fax: 2770-5047; hotelloscrestones.com, info@hotelloscrestones.com) is clean and airy. It's on the southwest side of the stadium in San Isidro, near the road to Dominical.

Six kilometers south of San Isidro, on the left, is the large, comfortable **Hotel del Sur** (private bath, hot water, fans or a/c, phones, cable TV, pools; $50-$70, including breakfast; 2771-3097, fax: 2771-0527; hoteldelsur.net), with well-tended gardens, tennis and basketball courts, playground equipment, large conference rooms, a casino, and a good restaurant.

Albergue de Montaña Talari (private bath, solar-heated water, screens, refrigerator, restaurant, pool; $50-$60, including breakfast; children 5 to 10 half price; phone/fax: 2771-0341; talari.co.cr, talaricostarica@gmail.com) is in a lovely setting on the banks of the Río El General, six kilometers (15 minutes) from San Isidro toward Chirripó National Park. It's known for good birding. Birding tours are available.

At **Montaña Verde**, near Rivas, you can learn about organic coffee farming and visit a *trapiche*, where brown sugar is made. The farmers of Montaña Verde have a lodge (shared bath, cold water; $20-$30/person, including meals) where you can stay and get to know the community. Participants in their "voluntourism" program lend a hand with sustainable agriculture and community projects. Volunteers work 25 hours a week, stay in the lodge and are responsible for their own food. Optional trips for volunteers include: climbing Chirripo, visiting the indigenous community at Boruca, or visiting Manuel Antonio, Corcovado, or Puerto Viejo on the Caribbean. Contact them through ACTUAR (2248-9470; actuarcostarica.com, info@actuarcostarica.com).

GETTING THERE: By Bus: Comfortable buses leave San José for the three-hour trip to San Isidro from the spiffy MUSOC station (on Calle Central, Avenida 22, across from Maternidad Carit; 2222-2422) every hour from 5:30 a.m. to 5:30 p.m. Buy tickets in advance, especially on weekends and holidays. Buses back to San José leave hourly.

By Car: Follow San José's Avenida Central toward Cartago, then follow signs to San Isidro. There is a tricky spot just before Cartago where you should continue straight ahead on a smaller road toward San Isidro instead of following the freeway left into Cartago. The trip is a precipitous 125 kilometers, and takes three hours. Do not try to rush this trip because there is almost always some delay on this part of the Interamerican—road work or an accident; also it can be very foggy and misty in the afternoon. To get to Rivas, for Talari and Montana Verde, take the uphill turnoff to the left, just past the bridge south of San Isidro and continue 10 kilometers to Rivas.

CHIRRIPÓ NATIONAL PARK AND ENVIRONS

San Gerardo de Rivas and **Herradura** are small mountain villages at the entrance to Chirripó National Park. Most people stop here on their way to the famous Cerro Chirripó, but even if you are not up to climbing the mountain, the scenery in this area is beautiful and birds of all kinds are abundant. Not to be missed is the wood sculpture of Rafael (Macho) Elizondo of El Pelícano (see below). This prolific artist sees birds, people, and animals in wood and stone, and does what is necessary to bring out what he sees. He does not sell his *artesanía*, but sometimes trades with other crafters. Highly recommended.

Narrow gravel roads follow the Chirripó Pacífico river and the neighboring Río Blanco through scenic valleys lined with vegetable, coffee, and dairy farms, perfect for invigorating day hikes. You can see quetzals halfway up the mountain; it's best to go with a guide who can show you where they nest. **Herradura Hot Springs** (8391-8107; admission $3, children $1), in a lovely natural setting is half a kilometer up the road to Herradura, then 20 minutes uphill through the pastures. The bath-like temperature is maintained with a trickle of cold water from another stream above. Any of the hotels listed in this section can provide you with specific directions and guides for exploring this verdant area.

LODGING   **Río Chirripo Retreat** (private bath, heated water, jacuzzi, wi-fi; $510/person per week, including meals; 2742-5109, 8858-9885; rio chirripo.com, frank@riochirripo.com) welcomes yoga, wellness and other groups (minimum eight people) to its 12-acre center overlooking the beautiful river that gave it its name. There's a solar-heated pool, and an open air yoga deck. Vegetarian cuisine is served at the temple-like lodge, which has a fireplace for chilly nights.

El Pelícano (shared baths, heated water, TV, gallery, pools; shared bath $10-$20; cabins that sleep two to six, $30-$70; 8332-5050, phone/fax: 2742-5050; hotelelpelicano.net, info@hotelelpelicano.net) has wood-paneled rooms with comfortable beds and valley views above a restaurant high on a hill. The entrance to the lodge is up a steep hill paved with rocks; it would help to have a car with fairly high clearance.

Cabinas Marín (shared and private baths, heated water; $20-$30; 2742-5091; ciprotur@racsa.co.cr), next to the ranger station, have nine rooms behind their *soda/casa/pulpería*.

Posada del Descanso (shared bath, heated water, laundry service; $7-$12; private bath, $20-$30; 8369-0067, 2742-5061; marlaequ@costarriense.cr), 400 meters toward San Gerardo from the ranger station, can give you a lot of information and can take you on tours of the area, including the family's own *finca*.

Roca Dura (camping $5, shared bath, $7-$10; private bath, heated water, $20-$40; 8363-7318; luisrocadura@hotmail.com) is a funky multistory *cabina/soda* built on top of a giant boulder overlooking the river. It's right in town, across from the soccer field.

Albergue Urán (shared bath, heated water, $10; cabin with private bath, $20-$30; 2742-5004, phone/fax: 2771-1669) is the closest lodge to the trailhead, located 2.5 kilometers beyond the National Park ranger station. They have a store where you can buy what you will need on the mountain and a laundry service. Their restaurant serves tasty Tico food.

CLIMBING CHIRRIPÓ   Chirripó means "Land of Eternal Waters." It is regarded as sacred land by the local indigenous people, who do not venture up the mountain. The area is magnetically charged. Watches and compasses can be affected. Then there are the *nímbolos*, or dwarves, that play tricks on you up there. The old rangers have lots of stories. The trek up Chirripó can be painful, tiring, frustrating, and freezing, but it's so satisfying to reach the summit, which is really the top of this part of the world, being the highest peak in southern Central America at 12,503 feet. A climb up Chirripó, with only one day at the summit, will take a minimum of five days, including transportation to and from San José.

Making reservations for lodging within the park: Reservations to hike Chirripó are hard to come by. Only 35 hikers are allowed in the park each day, making it very difficult to get a space. In addition, reservations can only be made on May 1 and November 1 each year. Most reservations are snapped up by companies that run hiking tours to Chirripo. Due to cancellations, you can sometimes find a space by presenting yourself at the ranger station in San Gerardo (open daily, 6:30 a.m. to 4 p.m.; 2742-5083) a few days before you want to hike. For up-to-date information, contact Selva Mar (2771-4582; chirripo.com, selvamar@ice.co.cr).

Kingfisher

If you can get in, charges per person include $15 for two days, plus $10 per night for lodging in the *albergue* near the top of the mountain. Each extra day costs $10 admission and $10 for lodging. The *albergue* has two bunk beds with vinyl-covered mattresses and four security boxes in each room. There are shared baths. You can rent blankets, sleeping bags, and camping stoves and gas for camping stoves at the top. There is potable water, but you have to bring your own food.

To prevent fires, only stoves can be used, and only within the *albergue*. Smoking is not allowed in the park, only at the lodge in permitted areas.

Porters: There is an association of local men who will lug your backpack and equipment up the mountain. This will probably make your hike a lot more enjoyable. To arrange for *porteros*, you must get to San Gerardo the day before you plan to hike and ask around to find who's available, or contact Selva Mar (2771-4582; chirripo.com, selvamar@ice.co.cr) to arrange a porter for you. This service is not for hikers with inferiority complexes— just as you're struggling up another hill halfway up the mountain, you will meet the man who hauled up your stuff whistling gaily down the trail. Payment is made when you arrive in San Gerardo de Rivas.

Guides: Trails are well-marked, so there's no problem in going alone, but there are many advantages of going with a bilingual guide. You learn more about the history, legends, wildlife, and plants of the area. You don't have to make any arrangements yourself, and don't have to carry anything. While other tired hikers are struggling to boil water with their campstoves at the top, you'll be treated to gourmet meals prepared by someone experienced in high-altitude cooking. Make reservations at least two months in advance.

Check-in: To climb Chirripó, check in at the ranger station, near the final bus stop in San Gerardo de Rivas. It's open 6:30 a.m. to 4 p.m. If you want to leave before 5 a.m., as we did, check in the day before. Don't start any later than 8 a.m.—start earlier if it's raining or windy. You cannot enter the park after 10 a.m.

What to bring: The summit area is above timberline, so once you get there you can always see where you are as long as inclement weather and fog do not envelop you. Watch out for lightning and falling trees. Be sure to bring:

- A water bottle, at least one liter per person, to replenish all the liquid you'll lose sweating.
- Warm clothes and a warm sleeping bag. It gets very cold at night— between -5°C (23°F) in the windy dry season and 3°C (37°F) in the rainy season. Bring or rent extra blankets. I slept in a Polarguard sleep-

ing bag with one blanket inside it, another on top, another underneath, all my clothes on, and a friend beside me. I was almost warm. You can rent blankets and sleeping bags at the top.

• Snacks for the hikes. Dried bananas and peanuts are good for energy when you're climbing. Carrots proved to be our lifesaver on the Cuesta de Agua. They quench your thirst and give you something to do slowly and steadily as you climb that never ending hill.

• A kerosene or alcohol burner to cook your meals. Building fires in the park is not allowed. You can rent camping stoves at the top.

• A poncho to keep you dry during the daily multiple rain showers. Veteran Chirripó climbers warn against getting wet during the hike. It might seem okay while you are heated up on the trail, but it can be dangerous when you get to the top.

• Waterproof shoes, with gaiters in rainy season.

• Hiking poles.

• Flashlight.

• Map and compass.

• Binoculars and a camera (200 ISO film) or batteries and chargers for digital.

GETTING THERE: By Bus: The 5:30 a.m. San Gerardo bus leaves from 150 meters south of San Isidro's Central Park; the 2 p.m. bus leaves from the bus terminal near the market. The trip takes about 90 minutes. When asking which of the many buses to take, specify San Gerardo de *Rivas*, because there's another San Gerardo. To be able to start your hike before dawn, arrive a day early and spend the night in San Gerardo de Rivas. The 10:30 a.m. bus from San José will get you to San Isidro in time to catch the 2 p.m. bus to San Gerardo. If you miss the bus, a taxi will take you to San Gerardo for about $20-$30. Buses leave San Gerardo for San Isidro at 7 a.m. and 4:30 p.m.

By Car: It's about 45 minutes from San Isidro to San Gerardo de Rivas. Take the paved road, which you'll see going uphill on your left just south of San Isidro, after the second bridge (there's a small sign for Parque Nacional Chirripó). It's 9 kilometers to the town of Rivas. San Gerardo de Rivas is 11 kilometers on good gravel roads from there.

PASO DE LA DANTA BIOLOGICAL CORRIDOR

Danta is the Spanish word for Baird's tapir, the largest land mammal in Central America. The tapir's closest relatives are the horse and rhino. The tapir's most unusual feature is its prehensile nose, which it uses to eat leaves, much like an elephant uses its longer trunk. The tapir has a stocky body and short legs. Though it weighs 200 to 400 kilos, it is very agile and elu- sive and is mostly nocturnal in areas where it is hunted. Tapirs make dis- tinctive trails through the forests they inhabit. The Paso de la Danta Biological Corridor seeks to bring the endangered tapir back to the Fila Costeña, the mountain range that rises up from the coast between the Río Savegre, south of Quepos, and the Río Térraba near Palmar Norte. Tapirs now exist only in the Osa Peninsula and in the high mountains of La Amistad International Park. The Paso de la Danta hopes to connect these two habitats, increasing the tapir's chances of survival. Within the biological corridor, lo- cals have already sighted mono titis, spider monkeys, scarlet macaws, white hawks, and ocelots—species that had been believed to be extinct in the area.

Headquarters for the biological corridor are at the office of ASANA (asanacostarica.com), a grassroots conservation organization founded in 1987. The 130,000-hectare biological corridor encompasses 55 communities, with a total of 10,000 inhabitants.

During the August to December turtle nesting season, local communi- ties patrol Playa Matapalo, Playa Burú, Playa Dominical, and Playa Bal- lena. They have accompanied 50,000 baby turtles into the sea in the last five years. Visitors who are seriously interested in turtle conservation may accompany volunteers and park officials on their nightly patrols. Seeing turtles is not guaranteed.

DOMINICAL

The scenery along the Costanera Sur Highway south of Playa Dominical is reminiscent of California's Big Sur coast—with lush tropical vegetation, of course. The Costanera is destined to become the major north–south route through Costa Rica, connecting Puntarenas with Ciudad Cortés in an easy couple of hours. The gravel road between Manuel Antonio (Quepos) and Dominical, although it can be driven throughout the year, is still unpaved, but the road between Dominical and Cortés is fully paved. Residents usu- ally travel here through Cerro de la Muerte and San Isidro, rather than us- ing the bumpy Quepos–Dominical road. The Dominical area is already being carved up into condos and villas.

The area has numerous beaches, many with rough waves and strong currents. Swimming at the long beach at the village of Dominical can be dangerous, though surfers love it. On the other hand, the warm, reef-pro- tected waters of Ballena National Marine Park, half an hour's drive to the south, are perfect for swimming and snorkeling. The small beaches near Dominicalito, one kilometer south of town, are also safe for swimming.

Southern Expeditions (2787-0100; southernexpeditionscr.com) offers scuba diving, snorkeling trips to Ballena National Park and Isla del Caño, daytrips by land and boat to Corcovado National Park, challenging sea kayaking at Las Ventanas (see below), and river kayaking through Hatillo mangrove swamp north of Dominical.

The area's numerous and spectacular waterfalls provide a refreshing break from the sea level's sweltering climate. **Don Lulo's Cataratas Nauyaca** (closed Sunday; 2787-8013, fax: 2787-8137; cataratasnauyaca.com; $45) takes you on horseback from Platanillo, a small town between San Isidro and Dominical, to two beautiful waterfalls with a large swimming hole. Breakfast, lunch, and a snooze in a hammock are offered at Don Lulo's ranch. The two private biological reserves in the area offer even more to do. (See description below of Hacienda Barú.)

About half an hour before Dominical, on a curve between the villages of Tinamaste and Platanillo, **La Choza de Alejo** serves Mexican food and seafood. Their modern, spacious rooms (private bath, hot water, fans, refrigerator, pools; $60-$80; with jacuzzi, $110-$120; dominical.biz/lachoza dealejo/index.htm, lachozadealejo@dominical.biz) have balconies with a distant view of the ocean and pretty gardens with a waterfall. Alejo and his family are thoughtful and genial hosts, the showers and mattresses are good, and, at 2000 feet above sea level, the nights are cooler than at the beach. In Platanillo, the **Restaurant El Barú** offers good roast chicken and grilled meats.

Finca Ipe (2787-8130; fincaipe.com, info@fincaipe.com), 15 minutes down the road, is a biodynamic organic farm that produces food, medicinal herbs and tinctures, and essential oils. They rent finely crafted, open, airy houses ($220-$250/week) with valley and ocean views. Their six-room Bamboo House can be rented for seminars. Recommended.

As you approach Dominical from San Isidro, you follow the peaceful **Río Barú**. If you go right instead of left to cross the bridge into the village, you'll come, in about a kilometer, to the area's only gas station, where you can buy tide tables, fishing supplies, film, maps, and the *Tico Times*. They also repair flat tires.

A bit farther north, **Hacienda Barú National Wildlife Refuge** offers many activities on their 830-acre private reserve. Their **Flight of the Tucan** canopy tour has eight cables with spans that range from 20 meters (65 feet) to 91 meters (296 feet), where you reach velocities of up to 35 kph (22 mph) between the 15 different takeoff and landing platforms, some on the ground and some in trees. The tour is set up to show how the primary forest forms layers of canopy so you can find out first-hand what the word biodiversity means. You will learn and observe more about nature on the Flight of the Toucan than on most other canopy tours. If you don't want to zip, you can ascend over 105 feet to a platform suspended in the canopy of a magnificent tree and just observe. Another tour involves camping in a tent on a platform in a jungle clearing. This gives you a good opportunity to look for nocturnal mammals. There is also a beautiful trail through the jungle to the beach.

The book, *Monkeys Are Made of Chocolate*, is a fascinating series of essays and stories by Jack Ewing, founder of Hacienda Barú, recounting his experiences and observations from 30 years of tropical living. He began farming rice and cacao and raising cattle on Hacienda Barú in the early 1970s, then started noticing how trees connecting forest patches allowed monkeys, birds, and finally sloths to repopulate the area. Now the monkeys harvest the cacao trees, and Hacienda Barú has become a center for learning about nature, both for tourists and the communities within the Paso de la Danta Biological Corridor. You can buy *Monkeys Are Made of Chocolate* and many other natural gifts at the shop in the reception building at Hacienda Barú.

Hacienda Barú Lodge (private bath, solar heated water, fans, kitchen, pool, restaurant; $60-$70, including breakfast; children under 10 free; 2787-0003, fax: 2787-0057; haciendabaru.com, info@haciendabaru.com), consists of three-room cottages with screened porches close to the reserve and about 400 meters from Playa Barú on a lovely jungle trail. Salads at their restaurant are organic, and their menu has vegetarian items.

SURFING AND RAFTING   Dominical is an important surfing destination (see crsurf.com, a Dominical-based web page), and most of the *cabinas* on the beach in the town itself are designed to attract surfers, complete with blaring rap music. Even without a car, you can get to several places on the bus that offer more peace and quiet than the town.

Green Iguana Surf Camp (8825-1381, 2787-0157; greeniguanasurf camp.com) offers surfing and survival Spanish lessons, taught by bilingual Costa Ricans for adults and teens.

Dominical Surf Adventures (8839-8542, 8897-9840; dominicalsurf adventures.com) offers surfing, canyoning, hiking, kayaking, and rafting, plus yoga and massage. They will take you to the Class II and III rafting on the Río Savegre. The closer Guabo river has Class II and III and one Class V rapid, which only experts can do. But the two trips are appropriate for kids over 10 if they portage the Class V rapid. They run a Class III and IV trip to the Brunca river for those 12 and over. They do kayaking trips to Ventanas and the Islands of Ballena National Park.

SPANISH **Adventure Education Center** (2787-0023, in the U.S.: 209-728-8344; adventurespanishschool.com) combines surfing and Spanish, as well as offering classes in Medical Spanish and courses for families. Students can get to know the country by studying at their Turrialba and Arenal campuses as well. They also provide a two-week, chaperoned Spanish, surfing, and adventure program for teens (teenspanish.com).

SERVICES The **Dominical Visitor Center** (2787-0232, 8820-0989; tourgal@gmail.com) rents cars, motor scooters, and bicycles, and helps with hotel and tour reservations. There are several **internet cafés** on the main street.

There are public phones in town at Cabinas DiuWak and by the soccer field in front of Restaurant San Clemente (see below). To use them, you must purchase a phone card at San Clemente.

The **Plaza Pacífica** shopping center, just south of the entrance to town along the Costanera, includes a souvenir shop with a selection of clothing and gifts from the world around, a well-stocked supermarket open 8 a.m. to 6 p.m. daily, and a branch of the **Banco de Costa Rica**.

LODGING AND RESTAURANTS Dominical itself is not a particularly charming beachside village, but it is where most of the lodging and restaurants are concentrated.

A few minutes upriver from the village of Dominical is the **Villas Río Mar Resort** (private bath, solar hot water, ceiling fans, refrigerator, phone, internet; $80-$170; children under 5 free; 2787-0052, fax: 2787-0054; villas riomar.com, info@villasriomar.com) with pool, jacuzzi, mini-gym, tennis court, a conference center, and a spa. The thatched bungalows have spacious porches with mosquito-net curtains and a terrace sitting area with hammocks.

Another half-kilometer up the river road, you will come to a narrow hanging bridge over the Barú. We wouldn't recommend driving over it since it swings and groans under the weight of a car, but it is quite beautiful and makes a nice stroll from Dominical.

Jazzy's River House (private bath, hot water, kitchen; $70-$80, including breakfast; dominical.biz/jazzys) rents a fully equipped house near the river in town. The upstairs sleeping area is open to nature, with one double and two single beds with mosquito nets. It's behind the vegetarian restaurant, **Maracatú**.

San Clemente Bar & Grill has inexpensive Tex-Mex specialties; pool tables, surfing videos, and a satellite TV define the ambience. There is also a public phone.

Nearby is **Posada del Sol** (private bath, heated water, wall fans, screens; $40-$50; two-bedroom apartment with kitchen, $60/day, $300/week; phone/fax: 2787-0085; posadadelsol@racsa.co.cr), clean and pleasant, and with its own well-water supply.

Veering right at the Y in the road will take you to several cabinas in front of the best surf break on the beach. **Cabinas DiuWak** (private bath, heated water, ceiling fans, some a/c, laundry, phones, jacuzzi, internet, restaurant/bar; standard and deluxe rooms, $80-$150; bungalows and suites, $150-$180, including breakfast; 2787-0087, fax: 2787-0089; diuwak. com, diuwak@racsa.co.cr) and its bar/restaurant, **Tulu** featuring pub food, seafood and pasta. **Tortilla Flats** (private bath, heated water, hammocks, ceiling fans or a/c; $30-$50; phone/fax: 2787-0033; tortillaflatsdominical. com) has good grilled sandwiches and seafood. **Cabinas San Clemente** (private bath, heated water, ceiling fans; shared bath, $10/person; with fans or air conditioning, $30-$60; 2787-0026, fax: 2787-0158) are fairly nice oceanfront rooms for surfers and backpackers.

Antorchas Camping (2771-0459; campingantorchas.net), a block inland from the corner of Cabinas San Clemente, has camping space with bathrooms ($8/person, includes bedding), safe parking, kitchen facilities, hammocks, surfboard rentals and a basketball court. They also rent basic rooms ($10/person), and rooms with a private bath ($18).

Coconut Grove (private bath, hot water, fans, a/c, some kitchens, pool; $60-$90; houses, $110-$130; no children under 10; 2787-0130; coconut grovecr.com, info@coconutgrovecr.com), a kilometer and a half south of Dominical, is near a nice beach. They have thoughtfully designed individual cottages and two beach houses. There's a small pool and hammocks with an ocean view, and a certified yoga instructor gives classes every day. Recommended.

Costa Paraíso Lodge (private bath, heated water, ceiling fans, a/c, kitchens, wi-fi; $100-$140; 2787-0025, 2787-0340; costa-paraiso.com, info@ costa-paraiso.com) is quiet and secluded. Picturesque rock formations on the beach in front of the hotel form a lagoon; nearby beaches, protected by a reef, are safe for swimming. The tastefully decorated cabinas are designed with natural ventilation and there is a lovely *rancho* with hammocks near the water.

GETTING THERE: By Bus: A bus leaves the Empresa Blanco terminal (2771-4744), just off the Interamerican Highway in San Isidro, for Dominical every day at 7 a.m., 9 a.m., 1:30 p.m., 4 p.m., and 10:30 p.m. Buses leave Quepos for Dominical at 5 a.m., 6:30 a.m., 9:30 a.m., 1:30 p.m., and 5:30 p.m. Buses leave Uvita for Dominical at 4:30 a.m., 5 a.m. 10 a.m. and 1 p.m. and 5 p.m. The San José–San Isidro–Dominical route is the most efficient. Buses leave San Isidro for Dominical at 7 a.m. and 1:30 p.m., arriving an hour later. You can also take the three-hour San José–San Isidro bus (see San Isidro section earlier in this chapter) and get a taxi to Dominical for $30-$40.

By Car: Dominical is about an hour from San Isidro on a paved road. Follow the signs through San Isidro. If you are coming from Quepos ask about road and bridge conditions before leaving. The Quepos-Dominical trip takes about an hour and a half on a bumpy gravel road.

ESCALERAS AREA

About three kilometers south of Costa Paraíso, a road to the left climbs steeply up to the Escaleras area. Several lodges, cooled by mountain breezes and affording breathtaking views of the Pacific, can be found here. The road is an inverted U; the other end meets the Costanera a few kilometers down the road. Access is often only possible in a four-wheel-drive vehicle; most of the lodges will pick you up in their own vehicles, if you prefer.

Shelter from the Storm (private bath, hot water, a/c, fans, kitchens, phones, wi-fi, pool; $110-$290; 8287-8262; shelter-from-the-storm.net, daryl@shelter-from-the-storm.net) has spacious, well-appointed villas that look out over the sea from the Escaleras hills. With their wide verandas strung with hammocks, and their stunning ocean and jungle views, Shelter from the Storm is a great place to relax and enjoy. Recommended.

The beautifully designed **Necochea Inn** (shared bath, hot water, ceiling fans; $80-$100; private bath, $120-$150, including breakfast; 2787-8072, 8395-2984; thenecocheainn.com, info@thenecocheainn.com) is the dream come true of a California artist who has decorated her comfortable B&B with antiques and original art. Two of the rooms have jacuzzis, and all rooms have balconies with views of forest and ocean. Breakfast is served on the deck near the small pool, and other gourmet meals are available on request. The lodge has many nice touches, like handcrafted mosaic counter-tops, stone bathrooms and a game room. Recommended.

Bella Vista Lodge (private bath, solar-heated water, ceiling fans, inter-net; rooms, $50-$70; cabins with kitchen, $80-$90; 2787-8069; bellavista lodge.com, information@bellavistalodge.com) has a beautiful view of the ocean from high atop the Escaleras road. Accommodations are simple but comfortable, and the lodge has a wide, breezy veranda. The two-bedroom house down the hill is probably quieter than the rooms in the main lodge.

Back on the Costanera, at kilometer 148, in the middle of the inverted U, there is a road heading up one kilometer to **Pacific Edge** (private bath, hot water, fans, refrigerator, pool; $60-$70; larger cabin with kitchen, $80-$90; no children under 12; 2787-8010; pacificedge.info, pacificedge@racsa.co.cr), which has individual rustic but comfortable cabins with broad, covered porches and a fantastic view. The cheery owners, a British-U.S. couple, can arrange catch-and-release fishing trips with local fishermen. They have two observation towers. With advance notice they will pick you up from the bus stop on the Costanera, or in Dominical. Four-wheel drive is best. Recommended.

A few kilometers south, turn left, go uphill, then turn left again and take the right fork to *campesino*-owned **Cabinas Brisas del Mar** (private bath, cold water, a/c; $15-20; 2787-8008), small rooms with a terrific view of the ocean from the hotel's balcony and access to a 73-hectare primary forest reserve. Four-wheel drive is recommended.

GETTING THERE: By Bus: A bus leaves the Empresa Blanco terminal in San Isidro (just off the Interamerican Highway) daily at 9 a.m. and 4 p.m., arriving in the Escaleras area at 10:30 a.m. and 5:30 p.m. You can also take the 1:30 p.m. San Isidro–Quepos bus and get off in Dominical. If you are staying at one of the lodges on the Escaleras horseshoe, ask the management to help coordinate transportation from the coastal road. Schedules change, so be sure to check.

By Taxi: Taxis from Dominical to Escaleras cost under $10, from San Isidro it's $35.

By Car: The Costanera Sur road between Quepos and Dominical is still unpaved; it's in good condition, although the rough gravel is hard on tires. South of Dominical the road is paved. The San Isidro–Dominical road is paved, with a few potholes. The roads up to Escaleras are unpaved and require four-wheel drive.

BALLENA NATIONAL MARINE PARK

Ballena National Marine Park (2786-5392; admission $10) is one of Costa Rica's two marine parks. The first 50 meters inland from the high tide line are part of the park; the rest is ocean.

The park protects the largest coral reef on the Pacific side of Costa Rica and the Ballena Islands, where humpback whales are seen with their young between December and April and in September and October. Local boatmen like Chume of **Ballena Adventures** (8817-5435) can take you out to the reef for snorkeling, skindiving, fishing, dolphin watching, or birdwatching. Frigate birds, brown boobies, and ibises all nest on Isla Ballena. If it's sunny and hasn't been raining lately, snorkeling and skindiving can be rewarding. At low tide you can walk to good snorkeling spots off **Punta**

Uvita, the rocky point that spreads out like a whale's tail at the end of the sandy *tómbolo* near the park entrance. The water here is gentle and warm.

To the south, **Playa Colonia** is good for camping because you can drive right up to the campsites, and there are sinks, bathrooms, and showers. The road leading to Playa Colonia is about a kilometer past the second entrance to Bahía on the Costanera. There is a ranger station there and the beach is patrolled at night. *Tips:* Don't camp under a coconut tree—the coconuts can fall on your head. Bring your own toilet paper.

Eight kilometers south of Punta Uvita is **Playa Ballena**. The rocky half of the beach has a natural swimming pool at low tide and the other half is sandy. MINAE has its ranger station at this beach, and charges $10 admission. If you are not staying at La Cusinga Lodge (see p. 416), this is the best way to access the amazing **Playa del Arco**, one kilometer north of Ballena. Playa del Arco is divided in two by a small, forested point that has a beautiful natural tunnel that you can walk through at low tide, so know the tides before you start out.

South of Playa Ballena, is **Playa Piñuela**, a lovely little beach, where local fishermen moor their boats and sell their catch.

Kayakers and sightseers will be awed by the tunnels and caves of **Playa Ventanas**, just around the point south from Playa Piñuela. Over millennia, the sea has carved huge arches in the limestone cliffs that form the small bay. The other tunnels and caves offer plenty of chances for an adrenaline rush to jolt Class IV and V sea kayakers out of their tropical lethargy. **Southern Expeditions** (2787-0100; southernexpeditionscr.com) and **Domincal Surf Adventures** (8839-8542, 8897-9840; dominicalsurfadventures. com) will take you there. Wading is recommended over swimming at Ventanas, since the waves can be quite rough. During low tide you can walk halfway through the cave at the northern end of the beach; at high tide there is an awesome boom and a cloud of sea vapor as each wave hits the other opening of the cave and the water rushes through.

UVITA   Eighteen kilometers south of Dominical, you will see signs for **Oro Verde Nature Reserve** (2743-8072, 8843-8833; costarica-birding-oro verde.com) 3.5 kilometers to the left. They offer three-hour birding hikes ($30, including breakfast) and have an observation platform in the forest. Birders will find this trip rewarding for its wide range of habitats and altitudes; 310 species have been observed there, including many members of the trogon family.

Staying at **Rancho La Merced** is a great way to explore the area on foot or on horseback. Lodging is in a nicely decorated two-bedroom cabin in the hills (private bath, solar-heated water, fridge; $80/person, including meals and a birding tour; 2771-4582; rancholamerced.com, selvamar@ice.co.cr). Toucans were just hanging out in the lush garden next to the cabin when we were there. The cabin is located on the road to Oro Verde, but the reception is at Rancho La Merced's stables on the main highway opposite the road to Oro Verde. You can also be a "cowboy for a day" at their ranch. Recommended.

Hotel Tucan (hot water, ceiling fans, a/c, cooking area, wi-fi; in dorms, tents, hammocks or tree house; $6-$10/person; rooms with private bath, $20-$30; 2743-8140; tucanhotel.com, tucanhotel@yahoo.com) is a hip place to be, with hammocks strung in the open-air lounge, and large paper lanterns providing color and style. Rooms are around the lounge and restaurant, and there is a tree-house room in front. To get there, turn inland at the Banco de Costa Rica. Recommended for budget travelers.

Cascada Verde (private rooms, shared or private bath, $20-$30 double; dorms, $10/person; 2743-8191; cascadaverde.org, cascadaverde@gmail.com) welcomes guests into its communal experiment in sustainable living. Permaculture, cleansing vegetarian foods, body/mind healing, arts and crafts, and Spanish classes are all offered there. The yoga and meditation platform has a distant view of the sea. When we were there, the delicious scent of fresh basil and greens from their garden permeated the atmosphere. Volunteers ($100/month, three-month commitment) work four hours a day. They are two kilometers uphill from the Banco de Costa Rica in Uvita. Get there before dark so you can find your way.

Villa de las Aves (private bath, hot water, fans, a/c, screens, TV, fridge; 8838-3378; villadelasaves.com) has two luxurious villas ($170-$230, two-night minimum), each with its private outdoor jacuzzi, and one B&B room ($80-$90, including breakfast) on a secluded 17 acres in the hills to the east of Uvita. Their candle-lit **Chef's Table Restaurant** (open 6 to 9 p.m. Friday to Monday) features seasonal ingredients beautifully presented by the owner, a Cordon Bleu master chef. She gives gourmet cooking classes that last one to five days. To get there, take the first left after the Marino Ballena Restaurant. Turn left after two kilometers and follow signs. Four-wheel drive necessary. Recommended.

A few kilometers south, **La Cusinga Lodge** (private bath, solar-heated water, natural ventilation; rooms: $130-$170, including breakfast; children 5-11 half-price; groups of eight or more in bunk bed rooms with fantastic views, $70-$80, including meals; 2770-2549, fax: 2770-4611; lacusingalodge.com, info@lacusingalodge.com) is a beautiful rainforest reserve overlooking the ocean. The breezy cabins all have great ocean views, and the food is wholesome and well-prepared. All materials used in construction are natural and display their innate beauty. Rocks of all shapes, sizes, and hues inspire the architecture. There are not many coastal areas (besides Corcovado) where virgin forest comes right down to the beach as it does here, and visitors will be rewarded with many bird and wildlife sightings. There is a waterfall-fed swimming hole in the forest. A 20-minute hike on the Los Raices trail leads to beautiful Playa del Arco. La Cusinga is definitely a place for people who are self-sufficient and in good physical condition, and prefer a quiet environment. The owners have done just enough to make the buildings and trails comfortable and safe, without taking away from the direct experience of nature. For an engrossing recounting of cross-cultural experiences and conservation on this amazing piece of land, read Jon Marañón's *The Gringo's Hawk,* available at online bookstores or at La Cusinga's gift shop. Recommended.

BAHÍA   This is the closest village to the park, a couple of kilometers west of the Costanera (when traveling south, take either the first or second right after the bridge over the Uvita river). There are two internet cafés, a restaurant, and an ATM in the Don Israel shopping center on the Costanera. **Villa Hegalva** (private bath, cold water, table fans; $10-$20; 2743-8016) has clean rooms and a covered patio strung with hammocks. They allow camping in their yard for $3/person. Nearby, **Cabinas Dagmar** (private bath, heated water; rooms, $15; apartments, $20-$30; 2743-8181; cabinas dagmar@hotmail.com) offers rooms and small equipped apartments (a/c, fans, TV, refrigerator) on the second floor of a well-tended older building.

Cabinas Las Gemelas (private bath, cold water, ceiling fans, a/c option, TV; $20-$30; 2743-8009) are situated 150 meters north of the school.

Cabinas la Rana Roja (private bath, cold or heated water, fans, some a/c, refrigerator, communal kitchen, cable TV; $30-$40; 2743-8047, 8819-0697; cabinaslarr@hotmail.com) are clean, have good mattresses, and have plenty of room for families. They are on a corner 100 meters west of the soccer field.

SOUTH OF UVITA

Beaches and mangroves fill the area between Uvita and Ciudad Cortes. Kayak in the mangroves of the **Río Térraba** (2248-9470; actuarcostarica. com, info@actuarcostarica.com) with sharp-eyed local guides who will help you spot birds, iguanas, caimans, frogs and reptiles. After the tour, enjoy a delicious native lunch. This tour is owned and managed by thirteen local families who formed a cooperative in order to protect this habitat so necessary for the survival of local wildlife.

The French-Canadian area of Ojochal is off this stretch of the highway, across from Playa Tortuga. **Citrus Lounge** (2786-5175), 100 meters east and 100 meters north of the entrance to Ojochal, is a chic restaurant with an elegant menu: snails, saffron fish, duck with calvados, served at indoor or outdoor tables. They have a small gourmet store and often have live music. **Restaurant Exotica** (open 11 a.m. to 4:30 p.m., 6 p.m. to 9 p.m.; 2786-5050) serves superb French and international cuisine in the center of Ojochal. Recommended.

Mar y Selva Ecolodge (private bath, hot water, bathtubs, a/c, TV, wi-fi, pool, restaurant; $90-$110; 2786-5670; maryselva.com), 29 kilometers south of Dominical, offers spacious but homey bungalows and a 75-foot swimming pool. There are distant ocean views from the main house and a telescope for spotting whales. The restaurant serves organic food and there is an airy, light-filled yoga room. We were not able to visit, but it sounds like a great place for health conscious travelers.

Hotel Villas Gaia (private bath, hot water, fans, some a/c, restaurant, pool; $70-$90; family room for up to seven, $130-$140; 2786-5044, fax: 2786-5009; villasgaia.com, info@villasgaia.com) named for the Greek earth goddess, offers lovely *casitas* surrounded by lush tropical gardens. It's within walking distance of Playa Tortuga, and close to Playa Ventanas and the beautiful beaches of Parque Marino Ballena. They have a gourmet restaurant. Recommended.

GETTING THERE: By Bus: Buses leave daily at 9 a.m. and 4 p.m. from San Isidro's Empresa Blanco terminal (just off the Interamerican Highway), arriving in Bahia two hours later. From Quepos, follow the directions in the "Getting There" section for Dominical. Travelers from Quepos can intercept the San Isidro–Uvita bus in Dominical around 11 a.m. A private shuttle bus will also take you to Uvita (shuttleosa.com).

By Taxi: A taxi to San Isidro costs $30-$40, to San José, $140-$150.

By Car: The Costanera Sur between Dominical and Ciudad Cortes is paved and in good condition. The drive to Uvita takes about 20 minutes. To reach Dominical from San Isidro or Quepos follow the directions in the "Getting There" section under Dominical. Try a roundtrip circuit through the Southern Zone. You can drive one way from San José to Manuel Antonio, south along the coast to Dominical and Uvita, then north, through San Isidro, and over Cerro de la Muerte to get back to San José.

By Air: You can cut many hours from your trip by flying as far as Palmar Sur (about ten kilometers from Ciudad Cortés) and taking a bus or taxi the rest of the way to Uvita. SANSA (2290-4100, in North America: 877-767-2672, fax: 2290-3543; flysansa.com) and Nature Air (2299-6000, in North America: 800-235-9272; natureair.com) fly there daily.

OSA PENINSULA

The Osa Peninsula reaches out of southwestern Costa Rica into the Pacific Ocean. Historically it was one of the most remote areas of the country, unknown to most Costa Ricans. Now, nature-loving Ticos and foreign tourists are arriving in large numbers to explore the incredible richness of the peninsula. Its large virgin rainforests receive 150 to 230 inches of precipitation a year, and it hosts an incredible variety of tropical flora and fauna. In the Osa alone, 375 species of birds have been identified. This is about half the number of species in the whole United States. Of the eleven endemic freshwater fish species in Costa Rica, nine are found only in the Osa. Over 124 species of mammals live there, 58 of them bats. Within the Osa Conservation Area, which extends from Dominical to the Panama border, 34.5 percent of the land is protected. These protected areas are home to 28 endangered bird species and 13 endangered mammal species, like tapirs, scarlet macaws, spider monkeys, jaguars and pumas.

The biological richness of the Osa is due to the fact that three million years ago, part of the peninsula was an island. Later, during the last Ice Age, approximately 20,000 years ago, the high mountains to the north, in the Los Santos region, were frozen. The slow freezing process gave some plants and animals time to move to lower altitudes, where they remained after the ice had melted. So today's Osa has plants that originated at both low and high altitudes. The Osa contains the most extensive rainforests on the Pacific coast of Mesoamerica (between México and Panamá).

The 600-foot-deep Golfo Dulce, between the eastern coast of the peninsula and the mainland, holds biological riches that are just beginning to be known. Humpback whales and dolphins can be observed there, as well as on the Pacific side. The extensive mangrove swamps that line the coast are important nurseries for marine wildlife.

The peninsula has been the site of much ecological destruction by lumbermen, settlers, and gold miners. The creation of Corcovado National Park in 1975 and the cooperative work of both international and grassroots organizations has served to protect much of the region's natural wealth, but illegal logging, poaching, and even sport hunting, are still serious threats.

Many migrant farmers came to the peninsula after the all-weather road connected the peninsula with the mainland in the mid-1980s. Most new arrivals settled in the traditional way, by burning off all the forest covering their little plot of land and then cultivating or grazing cattle on it. This approach is productive for a very short period of time. Rainforest soil is quite poor when there's no forest covering it: once the trees are gone, the rainforest's self-fertilization by dead leaves, plants, and animals stops, and the soil becomes infertile. When it rains, the soil erodes and silt fills the rivers. Because there is little biomass left to absorb excess moisture, floods become a problem.

The Osa Conservation Area, Corcovado Foundation (corcovadofoundation.org), and the Nature Conservancy are working with local community groups to form a biological corridor that would link Corcovado, Piedras Blancas National Park northwest of Golfito, and the Sierpe-Térraba wetlands north of Drake Bay in order to insure a viable future for both the people and wildlife of the region.

Most visitors in the 1980s had to go on a hardcore mission to backpack through Corcovado National Park. But now there are many options for softer-core tourists who want to see the rainforest but want their strawberry-macadamia nut pancakes for breakfast, too. Most of the prime land for tourism, with the magnificent views, is owned by foreigners, mainly North Americans.

PALMAR NORTE AND SUR

Palmar Norte and **Palmar Sur**, while not tourist destinations in themselves, are the gateways to Drake Bay, the Osa Peninsula, and Golfito to the south. Also, if you have traveled down the Costanera to Ciudad Cortés, you can turn north in Palmar to visit Boruca, Térraba and the Dúrika Reserve, or cross the Río Térraba at Paso Real to continue south to the Altamira entrance of Parque Internacional La Amistad and San Vito (see below). You can also fly into the airport in Palmar and continue to the above destinations or head up the Costanera to Uvita and Dominical. The airport is in Palmar Sur, across the Río Térraba. Taxis are usually around when flights come in.

GETTING THERE: See "Drake Bay" section below for air, bus, and car directions to Sierpe and Palmar.

DÚRIKA BIOLOGICAL RESERVE   High in the Talamanca mountains above Buenos Aires is **Dúrika Biological Reserve** (2730-0657; durika.org, infodurika@durika.org), operated by a self-sufficient agricultural community. The 18,500-acre private reserve is a buffer zone for this section of La Amistad International Biosphere Reserve. The community's resident naturalist can lead hikes of one to five days through Reserva Biológica Dúrika and La Amistad, including a trek up Cerro Dúrika, a peak of over 11,000 feet, and a three-day trek visiting various indigenous communities.

As a response to poaching and illegal logging in their area, Dúrika members have been trained by the Public Security Ministry to be environmental police, with all the duties of regular police officers. The community has purchased adjoining farms to make a biological corridor for local wildlife, which needs to change altitude according to the season. Their **Center for Natural Therapy** offers acupuncture, homeopathy, and neural therapy as well as massage, hydrotherapy, and clay treatments. They have a dental office that specializes healing by removing amalgam fillings and replacing them with resin.

Accommodations (private or shared bath, solar-heated water, internet; $50-$60/person, including meals and tours of the farm) in the guest cabins are rustic but cozy. The views are amazing, the gardens are beautifully tended, and the fresh vegetarian meals and herbal teas are full of healing energy. Volunteers are welcome to share their expertise or learn in this pristine mountain environment.

GETTING THERE: Call the reserve as far ahead as possible so they can prepare for your visit. Take a Tracopa-Alfaro bus to Buenos Aires (5 a.m., 6 a.m., 8:30 a.m., and 2:30 p.m., Calle 14, Avenida 5; 2222-2666, 2223-7685; 4.5 hours); there are also buses from San Isidro every two hours. Once you are in Buenos

INNOVATIVE COMMUNITIES: TÉRRABA AND BORUCA

Térraba and Boruca are small indigenous villages cradled in a green valley in the southwestern part of Costa Rica. The surrounding countryside is beautiful—you can walk up the red dirt trails for views across mountains, valleys, and rivers.

Etnoturístico El Descanso (private bath, cold water, restaurant; $20-$30; 8825-3513, 2248-9470; info@actuarcostarica.com) has several simple thatch-roofed cabins in a peaceful setting. The owners, longtime leaders in the Térraba indigenous community, can show you how chocolate is grown and processed, or take you to a creek with a natural jacuzzi. The women etch elaborate scenes onto large, hollow *jícaras* (gourds) and make jewelry from native seeds.

At **Rincón Ecológico Cultural Térraba**, Paulino Najera (8848-9649) will take you on an all-day hike in the forest to learn about native medicinal plants and indigenous customs.

From December 24 to January 2, visitors can participate in Térraba's *Juego del Toro y la Mula*, going from house to house with villagers wearing masks representing power animals, drinking *chicha*, and dancing to the music of drums and flutes.

In **Boruca**, 12 kilometers up the road, the **So Cagru Women's Art Group** (shared bath, cold water; $30-$40/person, including breakfast and tour; 2286-5136, 2730-2453) offers lodging in

Aires, they will arrange for a taxi to pick you up and take you to the community ($80 for up to four people). Their office is near the entrance to town, 100 meters east, 400 meters south, and 25 meters west from the Banco Nacional in Buenos Aires.

By Car: It takes about 90 minutes to get to Dúrika from Buenos Aires. The last 3.5 kilometers are on very bad road. Try to get to Buenos Aires no later than 4 p.m. so you can reach the reserve in daylight. Four-wheel drive is necessary. You can make it in a regular car to Buenos Aires and take a taxi ($80) 18 kilometers to the reserve.

SIERPE

Sierpe is a steamy riverside village where you catch the boats to lodges near the river and to Drake Bay. The **Oleaje Sereno** (private bath, hot water, ceiling fans, a/c; $60-$70; 2788-1103; hoteloleajesereno.com, hotel oleajesereno@racsa.co.cr), located right at the dock, is very clean. They have a fenced parking lot and will watch your car for you for a nominal fee

traditional-style thatch-roofed huts. It used to be that only men could carve the colorful balsa wood masks that Boruca is known for, but now women carve them too. Boruca women are especially known for their weavings, done with yarn spun from cotton that grows only in this area. The cotton is dyed with natural tints, including a purple extracted from a terrestrial mollusk that lives on cliffs near the Térraba River delta. To obtain it, they scale the cliffs, locate the now-scarce shells, remove them from the rock wall, blow on the animals so they will spray their dye, and then replace them on the cliff for their next visit. That's true sustainability.

They will take you on a tour of their workshops. Their three-day *Fiesta de los Diablitos* begins on midnight on December 30.

These communities are being threatened by the construction of what could be Costa Rica's largest hydroelectric dam project.

GETTING THERE: By Bus: Buses leave Buenos Aires for Térraba at 11:30 a.m., and 2, 3:30 and 4:30 p.m. Ask the driver if the bus continues to Boruca.

By Car: The Terraba/Boruca turn off is about five minutes south of Buenos Aires on the Interamerican. Drive 4 kilometers west to the village of Térraba and turn left at the plaza, following signs to El Descanso. Boruca is about 12 kilometers up the road. When you get to the village, take the right fork and go 75 meters to So Cagru. Your car should have high clearance and a powerful engine.

while you go to Drake Bay. They also have a nice open-air restaurant next to the dock, and arrange fishing tours. **Sonia's** *pulpería* is the communications center for Sierpe, with telephones, faxes, radios, and more, for public use, plus an incredibly wide variety of items for sale.

On the Sierpe waterways: **Sábalo Lodge** (shared bath, $50-$80; private bath, $80-$90, including meals; children under 12 half-price; sabalo lodge.com, info@sabalolodge.com) is the vision of a North American couple seeking simple living in the jungle. You'll see plenty of wildlife from your hammock on the verandah. Their four-day package includes transportation from Sierpe, kayaking, hiking or horseback riding, a visit with a local family, and a boat trip to Playa Blanca, an isolated beach near the mouth of the Sierpe River. Meals at Sábalo Lodge feature organic tropical fruits, locally grown vegetables, and fresh fish.

Río Sierpe Lodge (private bath, solar-heated water, fans, spring, screens; $310-$530/person for three nights; children under 12 half-price; including meals, tours, and transportation from Palmar or Sierpe; 2253-5203, fax:

2253-4582; riosierpelodge.com, info@riosierpelodge.com), a good place for serious birders, naturalists, and anglers. Their packages include snorkeling, diving, or dolphin and whale excursions. Owner Mike Stiles is a bird expert with years of experience in the region, and particular knowledge of the birds that frequent the estuarine and primary forest systems near the lodge. Try to get one of the cabins that has a screened upstairs bedroom and jungle or river views.

DRAKE BAY

Drake Bay, purported to be where Sir Francis Drake anchored the *Golden Hinde* and set foot in Costa Rica in 1579, is on the northern coast of the Osa Peninsula, accessible by boat from Sierpe or by plane from San José or Quepos. Scarlet macaws and monkeys are easy to spot there as you hike along the trail above the rocky coves south of the Río Agujitas.

The bay is rich in marine life. Four types of whales visit the bay. All the hotels in the area will take you to see the dolphins, which seem to love to gather around boats, arcing out of the water and leaping high into the air. **Vida Marina Research and Conservation Center** (in North America: 831-345-8484; vidamarina.org, divinedolphin.com, info@vidamarina.org), specializes in tours to "enrich the deep connection that humans have with dolphins and whales." Their Wild Dolphin Encounters epitomize respect—the animals are never chased or fed, and the choice to interact is always their choice. Dolphins are not as easy to see when the seas are rough—so beware of going on a day when ocean waters may be choppy.

You can also spend a fascinating evening with biologist **Tracie the Bug Lady** (8382-1619; thenighttour.com, eyeshine@racsa.co.cr), who will lead you into the jungle with hand-held night-vision optics devices that cast an eerie green color on everything but allow you to see clearly in the dark without disturbing the animals. She and her partner teach you how to see the eye-glow from frogs and spiders, and explain the weird mating rituals of leaf-cutter ants and stick insects. You might even see a boa. It's well worth the $35 fee. She supplies you with boots and walking sticks. She also rents a beautiful house in the forest (8867-6143; drakebayholiday.com).

There is a nine-platform, six-cable zipline **canopy tour** ($45) in Drake. Your hotel can book it for you.

All the lodges on Drake Bay offer fishing trips and guided tours to Corcovado National Park and **Isla del Caño**, a small, round, forest-covered island about 20 kilometers off the coast that is thought to be the site of a pre-Columbian cemetery. Stones carved into perfect spheres can be found on the island; their significance is still unknown. **Snorkeling** and **scuba**

diving are especially good at Isla del Caño because the water is often clear in the dry season and five coral platforms surround the island. The lodges all lend out snorkeling equipment, and many offer PADI-certified diving programs. Kayaks are also available. **Corcovado Expeditions** (8833-2384, 8818-9962; corcovadoexpeditions.net) leads kayak, mountain bike, hiking, birding, and wildlife photography tours in the area.

Even though tourism in this area largely depends on dolphins, whales, coral reefs, and marine biodiversity, the offshore area between Corcovado and Ballena Marine Park is completely unprotected, except for the area surrounding Isla de Caño. These waters are unscrupulously exploited by shrimp boats, which operate at night, notoriously hauling up everything in their nets just to get the shrimp, and letting the by-catch die. Ask your hotel how you can help support the formation of a marine wildlife refuge in this area, and boycott shrimp whenever you see it on the menu.

GETTING AROUND: The most common way of getting to Drake Bay involves a 75-minute boat trip down the Sierpe River and across the river mouth to the open sea before you get to the lodges. The San Pedrillo entrance to Corcovado is about half an hour's boat ride south of Drake Bay, or a four-hour hike. It's a 40-minute boat ride from Drake Bay to Isla del Caño.

The lodges listed first are south of the village of Drake Bay. Drake Bay Wilderness Camp, Aguila de Osa, and La Paloma are clustered around the Río Agujitas where the main docks are. (They will lend you canoes and kayaks for exploring the Río Agujitas). The next seven are scattered along isolated beaches between Drake and the border of Corcovado National Park. While these more-remote lodges offer boat transportation, reaching them on foot from the Agujitas area is also possible at low tide. For instance, Marenco and Punta Marenco are 40 to 50 minutes by foot south of the Agujitas River. Poor Man's Paradise is a three-hour hike south of the Agujitas, and Campanario is one hour on foot beyond that.

Just south of the river are Las Caletas, a series of small coves bordered by rocky outcroppings. The trail goes up above the coves. It's a lovely hike, with plenty of chances to swim and snorkel if you want to. South of Marenco the landscape flattens out and the trail is sometimes on the beach itself.

Note: It really is smart to bring well-fitting rubber boots to this area. They give much-needed traction on the muddy trails, and can keep you dry through most stream crossings at low tide. Otherwise, sand gets in your wet sandals and rubs your feet—the same happens with wet sneakers. If you bring boots, be sure to bring several pairs of thick socks that extend above the rim of the boots. If you don't, the boots rub against your calves.

Don't expect to find an ATM or bank in this area. Bring cash for small purchases and find out in advance whether your hotel accepts credit cards. Most rates are all-inclusive so you don't need a lot of money here.

LODGING   Most lodges require a two-night minimum and offer packages including meals. Prices are for double occupancy. Check websites carefully for current information on the transportation options included in each package. For instance, some three-day packages include roundtrip air transportation from San José, others include roundtrip boat transportation from Sierpe, and others include only boat transportation from the Drake Bay airport.

On the north side of the Río Agujitas is **Aguila de Osa Inn** (private bath, hot water, ceiling fans; $770-$870/person for three nights, including meals, transfers from Palmar Sur, and tours to Corcovado and Isla del Caño; discount for children; 2296-2190, fax: 2232-7722, in North America: 866-924-8452; aguiladeosainn.com, info@aguiladeosa.com), with airy cathedral ceilings, Italian-tile baths, stained glass, and original art in all the rooms. The views and the gardens are stunning and the cuisine is excellent. Emphasis here is on sportfishing, but many other activities are offered as well. It's a climb to the rooms, so guests should be in fairly good shape.

Across the Río Agujitas is **Drake Bay Wilderness Resort** (solar- and gas-heated water, ceiling fans, internet; $770/person for three nights; $580/person with shared bath, including meals, kayak use, boat transport from Drake Bay airport, and two tours; discount for children; phone/fax: 2770-8012, in the U.S.: 561-762-1763; drakebay.com, drakebayresort@comcast.net), right at the mouth of the Río Agujitas with good American- and Tico-style food served in a breezy bar and lunch room overlooking the water, and plenty to do near the lodge. Snorkeling is good both right at the resort and ten minutes away by boat at Punta San Joseçito. You can relax in the giant tidepools at the far end of the property or in their saltwater swimming pool. There's a butterfly farm you can ride to on horseback or mountain bike, an hour and a half from the lodge. Sea-kayaking instruction is also offered, as well as an excellent dolphin tour.

Staying in the *ranchos* at **La Paloma Lodge** (private bath, solar-heated water, ceiling fans, balconies, pool; $1100-$1400/person for three nights, including meals, transportation from San José, and tours to Corcovado and Isla del Caño; children 12 and under 30 percent off; 2293-7502, fax: 2239-0954; lapalomalodge.com, info@lapalomalodge.com) is like waking up in the jungle. Perched high on a hill, the private two-story *ranchos* are surrounded by greenery and birds, with views of Drake Bay and Caño Island beyond. A winding staircase connects the two floors, and louvered wooden shutters open to let in air and light. Their tiled swimming pool offers spectacular ocean views. Free guided nature walks with staff naturalists were included when we were there; a guide took our 13-year-old son kayaking while the rest of us relaxed on our balcony hammocks. The airy dining room serves delicious food. Kayaks, canoes, boogieboards, and snorkeling equipment are free for guests, and there is PADI-certified scuba instruction. It's a short downhill walk to the beach. Three- to five-night scuba packages are also offered. Getting to La Paloma from the landing dock on the river involves a fairly steep 15-minute uphill climb, so it is not a good choice for those with heart problems or trouble walking. Recommended.

A 45-minute walk south of La Paloma brings you to **Marenco Beach and Rainforest Lodge** (private bath, cold water, fans; rooms and bungalows, $60-$80; children under 12 free; 2258-1919, fax: 2255-1346, in North America: 800-278-6223; marencolodge.com, info@marencolodge.com), one of the original ecotourism projects in Costa Rica. Cabins, high on a hill with private porches, look out at gardens that attract birds and butterflies, and at Isla del Caño beyond. Researchers are always in residence at Marenco, and double as naturalist guides. Their rates are per room, not per person, unlike many lodges in the area. Marenco Beach Lodge shares the view and the 500-hectare **Punta Río Claro Wildlife Refuge** with its neighbor, **Punta Marenco Lodge** (private bath, cold water, mosquito nets; $90/person, including meals; 8877-3535, 2234-1308; puntamarencolodge.com, pedro@puntamarencolodge.com), individual *ranchos* with one side totally open to the view, owned and operated by Pedro Miranda, the founder of the reserve, and his family. Their three-night package is $500/person, including meals, Corcovado, Isla del Caño, and Punta Rio Claro tours and transport from Sierpe. A half-hour hike from either lodge through a series of lovely rocky coves ends at the Río Claro, where a deep natural pool lends itself to a refreshing swim. Both lodges have wet landings and require an uphill hike to get to.

Poor Man's Paradise ($560-$620/person for three nights, including meals, tours, and air transport from San José or boat transport from Sierpe; 2771-4582, fax: 2771-8841; mypoormansparadise.com, selvamar@ice.co.cr) is a family-run project on isolated Playa Rincón, a three-hour hike (go at low tide only) or a 20-minute boat ride south of Drake. Cabins are simple and clean, with good mattresses (private bath, cold water, table fans), a common hanging-out area, and a platform with tents (shared bath, cold water). Farther back is the restaurant where Doña Carmen takes care of her guests as if they were family. Son Pincho specializes in low-cost sport fishing trips. They offer horseback riding and have a sheltered reef ideal for snorkeling at low tide. They do not have a dock, so be prepared for a wet landing.

Cabinas Orquideas (private bath, cold water; $75 per person, including meals; 8899-8995, in North America: 612-695-8282; bbb1007@hotmail.com), nearby, are owned by members of Doña Carmen's extended family. Two cabins overlook the ocean from the hills, three are in the rainforest, and one is on the beach. A two-bedroom beachhouse rents for $350 per night.

Proyecto Campanario (shared and private baths, cold water; 2258-5778, fax: 2256-0374; campanario.org, reservations@campanario.org) is a remote biological reserve and field station on a beautiful cove about a half-hour boat ride south of Drake Bay. It's the brainchild of Nancy Aitken, a high school teacher with a dream to help people understand the rainforest. There are tables and benches in the most beautiful parts of the reserve so you can spend time being quiet and listening to the forest. The no-frills field station provides bunkbed accommodations with shared baths downstairs. Large tents on platforms up the hill from the field station are more secluded and have private baths. Their three-night package ($430/person) includes meals and transportation from Sierpe plus guided trips to the reserve and Corcovado. They also offer a seven-day Rainforest Conservation camp, a ten-day course in Tropical Biology for students, and professional development programs for teachers. Internships require a three month commitment. Visiting Campanario is an educational, and inexpensive way to see this beautiful area. As one visitor said, "I have learned so much, not only about the rainforest, but about what it takes to live in such a serene, non-techno world."

Casa Corcovado (private baths, hot water, ceiling fans; 2256-3181, fax: 2256-7409, in North America: 888-896-6097; casacorcovado.com, corcovdo@racsa.co.cr; closed September 1 through November 15) is on the border of Corcovado National Park, a half-hour boat ride from Drake Bay. After a beach landing that has to be done at exactly the right gap in the waves, guests are transported straight uphill for a welcome cocktail at a simple but elegant screened bar with a great view of Isla del Caño. The bungalows are set back at the edge of the forest and do not have views. They are private and well designed, with good mattresses and spacious, tiled bathrooms. There are bungalows with two interconnecting suites and a screened porch, good for families. Another attractive open-air bar is cantilevered over the jungle where chances for bird watching abound. There is a spacious recreation room with videos and a library, and a fresh-water pool surrounded by jungle. Casa Corcovado is known for excellent service. Their three-night package costs $940-$1100, including meals, air transport from San José to Palmar, or boat from Sierpe to the lodge and trips to Corcovado and Caño Island.

DRAKE VILLAGE   North of Río Agujitas, toward the town of Drake (pronounced "Drah-kay" in Spanish, also known as Agujitas), are several places to stay. There is an administered public telephone at the *pulpería* about two-thirds of the way down the beach. There is a steep but not-too-slippery trail leading from the entrance to La Paloma Lodge down to a hanging bridge across the Agujitas river. It leads downhill on the other side, goes by Aguila de Osa, and takes you into the village. It takes about half an hour to walk to the *pulpería* that way. If you don't want to make the hike, you or your hotel can usually find someone to ferry you the short distance across the river from the hotels' dock.

Albergue Jinetes de Osa (shared or private bath, solar-heated water, ceiling fans; $70-$100/person, including meals, transportation extra; children under 12 half-price; 2231-5806, in North America: 866-533-7073; jinetesdeosa.com, reservations@jinetesdeosa.com) specializes in scuba diving, rents snorkel equipment, and can arrange inexpensive small-craft fishing trips in the bay. They also offer three-day diving packages ($650-$900) and adventure packages ($550-$710).

Halfway down the beach, an uphill road next to the *pulpería* leads you to **Cabinas Jade Mar** (private bath, cold water, table fans, mosquito nets; rooms, $15/person; cabins, $50; 8384-6681, 8845-0394; jademarcr.com, info@jademarcr.com), simple but very clean cabins run by a local family. You will really get a sense of life in this small beach town by staying here. They have a breezy, open-air dining room and provide tours and boat transportation all over the area; they also rent a two-room house near the beach that sleeps up to eight (kitchen, TV; $50-$80). Recommended.

At the end of the beach you'll see a road coming from the north and following a river inland. This is the Rincón–Rancho Quemado road, which could change the face of Drake forever if it becomes viable year-round.

If you wade across the river and scramble up the embankment and over the road, you'll see a steep trail that will bring you to **El Mirador Lodge** (private and shared bath, cold water, natural ventilation mosquito nets; $40-$50/person, including meals; 8387-9138, 8836-9415, in North America: 877-769-8747; miradordrakebay.com, info@miradordrakebay.com), rustic accommodations with a beautiful view of Drake Bay and nearby rivers and waterfalls. They have an organic garden and cook with a methane biodigestor. Recommended for budget travelers who don't mind the uphill hike. They also have **Hostel Bambu Sol** near the village.

LOS PLANES   Four kilometers uphill from Agujitas, in the village of Los Planes, a conservation organization started by two local women has converted a former park ranger station into **Tesoro Verde** (shared bath, cold water; $50-$60, including meals; 2248-9470; actuarcostarica.com, info@actuarcostarica.com), a charming inn with sunny rooms and access to their

12-hectare rainforest reserve. Staying at Tesoro Verde puts you in the center of village life, with plenty of opportunities for intercultural exchanges. This group's dedication to preserving the land and stopping illegal hunting and logging is impressive. You can hike to an isolated *finca* in the forest where Oldemar and his family will guide you to secluded waterfall pools, or take an hour's horseback ride to the Río Claro. Tesoro Verde lodge has its own canopy tour. They have tours to Isla del Caño and the San Pedrillo entrance to Corcovado ($469 for three nights, four days including meals, tours, and shuttle from San José). To get there, take the fork to the right at Cabinas Jade Mar in Drake and walk four kilometers, passing over a hanging bridge, to the village of Los Planes, or arrange a $5 taxi from Drake.

GETTING THERE: You should definitely make reservations and travel arrangements before you go to Drake Bay because crossing the river mouth is best done with the tides. Also, many lodges do not have their own docks, and landings need to be coordinated by captains and assistants experienced with each place. For these reasons it is best to let your lodge arrange transportation for you from San José, Quepos, Palmar, or Sierpe. You can get to Palmar by bus or plane. There is a shuttle bus (shuttleosa.com) that stops in Sierpe on its way to the Osa, or you can drive to Sierpe if you have a car (the Hotel Oleaje Sereno, next to the main dock in Sierpe, will watch your car while you are in Drake). Many travelers leave Drake Bay for the end of their trip, turn in their rental cars in Quepos and fly to Drake, or take Lynch Travel's 6:30 a.m. shuttle from Quepos to Sierpe (returns from Sierpe at noon; $35-$40; lynchtravel.com). They then fly or shuttle back to San José (shuttleosa.com). If you have a package deal, transportation costs are included, but, as mentioned above, be sure about which costs are included and from where. Each hotel has a different system.

By Bus to Sierpe: If you want to get there on your own, take the 5 a.m. TRACOPA bus to Palmar (Calle 14, Avenida 5; 2222-2666; $7). The trip takes six hours. After you get to Palmar, follow directions for boat travel from Sierpe, below.

By Car to Sierpe: At Palmar Sur on the Interamerican Highway, drive south through a maze of banana plantations to the town of Sierpe. Ask the banana workers for directions at every intersection (there are no signs and it's easy to get lost). From Sierpe, follow boat directions below. The Palmar-Sierpe trip takes about 20 minutes.

By Shuttle Bus to Sierpe: **Shuttle Osa** (8825-6788; shuttleosa.com) has daily shuttle buses from your San Jose hotel to Palmar Norte, Uvita, Dominical, and Puerto Jiménez.

By Car to Drake: A bumpy gravel road connects Drake with the Rincón on the Golfo Dulce. If you take the Interamerican Highway all the way to Chacarita and head towards Puerto Jiménez, you will come to the bridge in the town of

Rincón. Turn right and drive about an hour to Los Planes, then down to Drake. This is the road that has been facilitating logging operations north of Corcovado. It runs from Rincón to Rancho Quemado and on to Drake Village. It doesn't cross the Agujitas River, so you'd have to leave your car on the village side if you wanted to visit lodges to the south in Drake Bay. **Dona Emilse** will watch your car for $10/night. This road can only be driven by a high-clearance vehicle, and only in the dry season. Check with your hotel regarding road conditions and driving times.

By Bus and Taxi: A bus will take you from San José to Rincón, north of Puerto Jiménez (Transportes Blanco, Calle 12, Avenidas 7/9; 2257-4121; 6 a.m.; $6.50; eight hours). From there you can hire a taxi-truck to Drake Bay on the Rincón road, a bumpy 32 kilometers ($100). **Shuttle Osa** (shuttleosa.com) can also drop you off in Rincón.

By Air to Palmar: You can fly to Palmar with SANSA (2290-4100, fax: 2290-3543; $90-$100, one way; flysansa.com) or Nature Air (2299-6000, 800-235-9272; natureair.com; $100-$110). Pick up the flight in Quepos if coming from Manuel Antonio.

By Air to Drake: Nature Air (natureair.com) has two flights a day to Drake ($100-$110, one way). SANSA (flysansa.com) also has at least three flights a day to Drake ($90-$100, one way). Make sure that you have a jeep and boat transfer from the airstrip to your hotel.

PUERTO JIMÉNEZ

Puerto Jiménez is the largest town on the Osa Peninsula. People say its first inhabitants were prisoners sent away from the mainland with machetes and a warning never to come back.

Despite, or perhaps as a result of, its tawdry history, Puerto Jiménez is now the gateway to some of the most beautiful tourism projects in the country. Because the Osa was considered such a no-man's land, it opened to tourism much later than the rest of Costa Rica. The people who started tourism projects here did not do so to jump on the bandwagon, but because they had a vision that the beauty of the land could be the key to its preservation. The ecotourism projects in this area are principled, and are already seeing the effects of their efforts: scarlet macaws and harpy eagles are coming back. As in Drake Bay, you can probably see as much wildlife in the private reserves of these lodges, or from their terraces, as you can by going to Corcovado itself. And it has its positive effects on the local community: Don Alfredo Mesén, an employee of one of the lodges, heard that a neighboring *campesino* was about to cut the trees on his land—virgin forest. Don Alfredo suggested that in one year, his neighbor could make more money by guiding tourists through his forest than he could by cutting it down. The farmer took him up on it, and Señor Mesén sent him a steady supply of tourists from his beach hotel. At the end of one year the farmer was better off economically, and will be for years to come. Now other *campesinos* are calling the hotel, asking to be supplied with tourists.

We should not paint too rosy a picture, however: deforestation and poaching are still serious problems.

Cafénet El Sol (2735-5702) in the center of town has high-speed internet access. It has links to local hotels on its website: soldeosa.com. As you come into "downtown" Puerto Jiménez, it's at the end of the first block, on the left. It can make hotel, national park, and tour reservations for you or watch your luggage while you run errands. There is a lot of good information at **southerncostaricamap.com.** They sell a "green card" online that can get you discounts during your vacation.

El Tigre, just south of La Carolina on the main street, is a general store where you can change money, and stock up on food or camping supplies. They run a **collective taxi** service to Cabo Matapalo ($2.50) and Carate ($7) that leaves at 6 a.m. and 1:30 p.m. and returns at 8:30 a.m. and 4 p.m. every day but Sunday ($60 per carload at other times). There is a gas station at the southern end of Puerto Jiménez, where you turn right to go to Matapalo and Carate.

You can rent four-wheel-drive vehicles in Puerto Jimenez for $70-$120/day.

There is a full-service **Banco Nacional** in Puerto Jiménez.

You can observe **turtle nesting** at Playa Piro or Playa Platanares. Starting in August, you can see baby turtles scrambling to the sea if you go early in the morning. **Friends of the Osa** (osaconservation.org, seaturtles@osaconservation.org) welcomes volunteers for its turtle monitoring program from the June through December turtle nesting season. You can stay a week ($300) to several months ($900/month, including meals) training in data collection and longterm species monitoring. No experience and no Spanish is required. Volunteers live in beach houses near old-growth rainforest. Friends of the Osa also gives seminars in birdwatching and wildcat research.

You can arrange sea kayak trips or sunset dolphin watches at the downtown **Escondido Trex** (phone/fax: 2735-5210; escondidotrex.com, escondidotrex@hotmail.com) office in Restaurant La Carolina. Joel Stewart (2735-5569) of **El Remanso** (see Cabo Matapalo below) helps you climb 180-foot forest giants or rappel down waterfalls. **Bosque del Cabo** (2735-5206) has an observation platform high in the forest canopy that you can slide to on a cable. **Aventuras Tropicales** (2735-5195; aventurastropicales.

com, info@aventurastropicales.com) is located on the street leading to the kayak launch in the "gringolandia" district south of town. Alberto Robleto, owner and chief guide, is a Costa Rican biologist who now delights in offering tours of the Golfo Dulce and its mangroves, as well as hiking and biking tours.

Herrera Botanical Garden (8838-2314), on the Platanares road, has brought a lot of wildlife into the area by planting native trees and flowers. A self-guided tour on its 12 kilometers of well-manicured paths costs $5-$10. There are tree platforms and a great **camping** area.

LODGING   Right off the pier, with a back wall on the mangrove swamp (big bathroom windows provide almost an aquarium effect at high tide), are the **Cabinas Agua Luna** (private bath, hot water, a/c, cable TV, phone, refrigerator, restaurant; $60-$70; 2735-5393; agualuna@racsa.co.cr).

The North American–owned **Cabinas Jiménez** (private bath, hot water, fans; $50-$80, children under 7 half-price; some a/c; 2735-5090; cabinas jimenez.com, info@cabinasjimenez.com) are nicely decorated with carved headboards and Guatemalan bedspreads. The more expensive rooms have refrigerators, private decks, and water views. They are four blocks toward the water from the bus stop.

Away from the waterfront there are several inexpensive hotels and cabinas, all locally owned, with budget rooms. **Cabinas Carolina** (private bath, some a/c, cable TV; $20-$40; 2735-5696) is behind Restaurant Carolina on the main street. Walk to the next corner, turn left, and you will pass the **Hotel Oro Verde** (private bath, cold water, fans; $10/person; 2735-5241). Turn the next corner where the street dead-ends at the mangrove and you will find the **Hotel Bosque Mar** (private bath, heated water, fans, a/c, cable TV; $20-$40; 2735-5681). Return to Cafénet El Sol and continue one block farther and you will come to the bus station, the hub for budget travelers.

Cabinas Marcelina (private bath, heated water, fans, some a/c; $40-$50; 2735-5007; cabmarce@hotmail.com) are nicely tiled and decorated and have a pleasant yard. A few blocks down the main street from the gas station you will find **Cabinas Eilyn** (private bath, some heated water, fans, a/c, cable TV, internet; $60-$70, including breakfast; 2735-5465; cabinas eilyn@hotmail.com).

A block and a half from the airport, **La Choza del Manglar** (private bath, hot water, ceiling fans, a/c, screened windows, wi-fi; $60-$110, including breakfast; children under 5 free; ages 6 to 12 $5; 2735-5605, in North America: 888-467-3181; manglares.com, reservations@manglares.com) is set in four acres of mangroves and gardens. The cabins and restaurant have been decorated with bright tropical colors by two local artists. The large natural garden behind the inn shelters birds and wildlife. A retinue of tanagers, woodpeckers, monkeys, and raccoons often appears for breakfast.

Parrot's Bay Village (private bath, hot water, ceiling fans, a/c, wi-fi; bungalows, $120-$160; cabinas, $150-$200, including breakfast, welcome drink, and use of kayaks; house that sleeps six, $330; 2735-5180, in North America: 866-551-2003, fax: 2735-5568; parrotbayvillage.com, parrot bayvillage@racsa.co.cr) is a group of attractive, comfortable cabins on the beach on the far side of the airport. While the lodge has its own sportfishing program, it also welcomes families (babysitting service) and ecotravelers, rents kayaks, and arranges sea and land tours. Their restaurant and bar are very popular with locals and tourists. Across the road from the cabins is a nature trail into the mangroves, where you can see cayman, monkeys, egrets, and ibis ($330).

RESTAURANTS   **Agua Luna** (open 10 a.m. to 11 p.m.; 2735-5033), on the spit between the gulf and the mangrove, right near the dock, serves generous portions of Chinese food. The owner runs the cabinas of the same name (see above).

The open-air restaurant at **Parrot's Bay Village** is one of the more pleasant eating places in Puerto Jiménez. They offer an excellent bistro-style menu for lunch and dinner. **Restaurant Carolina** is a popular meeting place for expats in the center of town, and **Juanita's Mexican Bar and Grille** (2735-5056), next to Cafénet El Sol, serves California-style Mexican cuisine, and an all-you-can-eat breakfast buffet. Their bar is the town's most popular nightspot.

A wide variety of *sodas* offer breakfast as early as 5 a.m. so you can catch the 6 a.m. taxi to Corcovado. They offer inexpensive *casados* for lunch and fried fish for dinner.

Restaurant Il Giardino (open daily, 4 p.m. to 10 p.m.; 2735-5129) serves wood-fired pizzas, homemade pasta, and Italian wines in a garden setting with beautiful handcrafted furniture.

The **Jade Luna** (open Monday through Saturday, 5 to 9 p.m.; 2735-5739) is the creation of New York restaurateur Barbara Burkhardt. With only the freshest ingredients, flown in or purchased from local farms and fishermen, your casual fine-dining experience could start with appetizers like smoked trout, goat cheese tarts, or freshly made paté, move on to an authentic Greek salad, reach a crescendo with Cajun-blackened seafood or steak, and come to a smooth denouement with homemade ice cream or sorbet—all for a price of around $40-$50 for two. This stylish gourmet eatery is located 500 meters east of the airport on the road to Platanares.

See next section for nightlife at the Monochingo Bar on Playa Platanares.

GETTING THERE: By Bus: Take the Empresa Blanco bus from San José at noon ($7; Calle 12, Avenidas 7/9; 2257-4121). The trip lasts eight to ten hours. The bus passes through San Isidro at 3 p.m.—catch it one block south of the main bus station. Buses also leave San Isidro for Puerto Jiménez at 9 a.m. and 3 p.m.. The bus returns from Puerto Jiménez at 5 a.m, 11 a.m. and 1 p.m. If you are coming from some other point, intercept the Villa Neily–Puerto Jiménez bus at 6:30 a.m., 11:30 a.m. or 3 p.m. at Chacarita (Piedras Blancas), at the entrance to the Osa Peninsula on the Interamerican Highway.

By private shuttle bus: **Shuttle Osa** (shuttleosa.com) runs from your San Jose hotel to Los Santos, Dominical, Uvita, Sierpe, and ends in Puerto Jiménez.

By Car: Follow the Interamerican Highway to Piedras Blancas (Chacarita) and turn right. It can take as much as three hours to drive the 75 kilometers between Chacarita and Puerto Jiménez. The road gets totally destroyed by the huge lumber trucks that constantly traverse it, and by flooding during the rainy season. Rumor has it that the road will be fixed soon, but don't plan to drive here unless you check with your hotel on road conditions and driving times. Be really alert for bicycle riders along the Interamerican Highway. There are a lot of them, especially at dawn and dusk, and they don't have lights.

By Boat: An old launch leaves the municipal *muelle* in Golfito for Puerto Jiménez every day at 11 a.m., returning the next morning from Jiménez at 6 a.m. The enjoyable ride across the gulf takes an hour and a half. Dolphins often swim and dive alongside the boat. The super ferry from Golfito ($4) takes a half hour, and leaves Golfito at 10 a.m., 11 a.m, noon, 1 p.m. and 3 p.m. Zancudo Boat Tours (2776-0012) will take you from Zancudo to Puerto Jiménez for $30 for two.

By Air: SANSA offers two flights a day to Puerto Jiménez in the high season (2290-4100, in North America: 877-767-2672; flysansa.com; $90-$100, one way). Nature Air (2299-6000, in North America: 800-235-09272; natureair.com) flies to Puerto Jiménez three times a day ($100-$110, one way).

SOUTH OF PUERTO JIMÉNEZ

The following projects are located south of Puerto Jiménez, an area that is not serviced by public electricity. All of them rely on private generators or solar and candle power, so be sure to bring a flashlight. The phone numbers we give are where the lodges pick up their messages, so call for reservations as far ahead of your arrival as possible. Lodges in the area north of Puerto Jiménez are listed after those to the south.

PLAYA PLATANARES **Playa Platanares** is a long, peaceful beach on the Golfo Dulce six kilometers south of Puerto Jiménez, the best beach for swimming and bodysurfing in the area. Whales can be spotted there in October and November. Iguana Lodge funds a **turtle** protection project there, patrolling the beach nightly from May to November. **Volunteers** and donations are gratefully accepted. The 249-acre **Preciosa Platanares Wildlife Refuge** is a privately owned mangrove estuary, accessible by kayak, horseback, and footpath from the beach. The waves at Playa Platanares are gentle and safe for children, and all three of the following lodges welcome families.

Black Turtle Lodge (shared or private bath, hot water, solar fans; $160-$220, including meals; children $20-$50; 2735-5005; blackturtle lodge.com, info@blackturtlelodge.com), to the left at the beach, has individual raised bungalows with balconies at canopy level, and *cabinettas* that are closer to the ground. There is a shaded platform on the beach for hammocks and a large, beautiful screened yoga platform under the trees. The lodge offers yoga retreats and can host up to 20 people.

Iguana Lodge (private bath, solar-heated water, ceiling fans, wi-fi; children under 12 half-price; 8829-5865, 8848-0752; iguanalodge.com, info@iguanalodge.com), has rooms above bar/restaurant **La Perla** ($130-$140, including breakfast) and spacious cabins on stilts ($150-$180, including breakfast and dinner) so that each has an ocean view; the screened cabin walls are louvered so you can catch the breeze from any direction. There are two beds upstairs and two below, so it's a great place for families. Rooms are decorated with the owner's original artworks, and guests can watch her paint on the lodge's veranda. There is a lovely Japanese hot tub, and tasteful sofas and rockers make for a congenial sitting area. Meals, featuring freshly caught seafood and lots of veggies, are really special and served in a huge two-story *rancho* by candlelight. Tuesday is barbecue night. Next door, sister restaurant **La Perla** (also called **Monochingo**) is the place to go for **dancing** to live salsa music on Friday nights. Hammocks are strung between the palm trees in front. They also rent Villa KulaKula, a three-story, three-bedroom house next to the lodge ($520-$530 per night, three night minimum). The owners are very active in the community and can direct you to the most interesting things to do. Use of boogie boards and kayaks is free for guests, and there are bicycles for rent. Recommended.

CABO MATAPALO   As you head south of Puerto Jiménez, the road is bumpy and unpaved. If you are not a four-wheel-drive wizard, it's better to fly into Jiménez and let your hotel transport you out here, or take the *taxi colectivo*. **Playa Matapalo** is *the* surfing beach in the Osa, reachable by an unmarked but obviously well used road on the left as you climb toward Lapa Ríos. Pan Dulce Beach is the first beach you come to and the best for swimming; surfing lessons are given there. Matapalo Beach is for advanced surfers only. There are three waterfalls in this area, one of which is used for rappelling. There is also a huge strangler fig tree that you can climb up inside. Horseback riding on the beach is another favorite activity here. There are many vacation houses for rent in Matapalo; see soldeosa.com/matapalo.htm. Yoga retreats are given by **Tierra de Milagros** (tierrademilagros.com)

Buena Esperanza (2753-5531) is a restaurant and bar just after the Río Carbonera on the left, about 15 kilometers south of Puerto Jiménez. It's the only restaurant between there and Carate. They also rent colorful open-air cabins (shared bath, cold water; $25/person).

The locally owned **Osa Vida** (shared bath, cold water, communal kitchen; $20-$30/person; 2735-5719), 200 meters from the surfer's haven, Playa Matapalo, has simple, palm-roofed, screened rooms with fans and reading lamps.

Lapa Ríos (private bath, solar-heated water, natural ventilation, screens and mosquito nets, pool; $250-$330/person, including meals, transport from Puerto Jiménez, and two of their guided tours; 2735-5130, fax: 2735-5179; laparios.com, info@laparios.com) is a luxury resort on a 1000-acre reserve containing primary and secondary rainforest. Thatch-roofed bungalows dot the side of a hill, at the top of which is a spacious restaurant. Up a tall spiral staircase is an observation deck with a beautiful view of the Golfo Dulce. The rooms are tastefully designed with wide private balconies. Each balcony has a shower surrounded by lush foliage so you can bathe outside while enjoying the view. Guests can learn about medicinal plants from a local shaman, visit waterfalls in the reserve, take a night hike, learn to surf, or visit the calm beach at the bottom of the hill. Monkeys, toucans, and macaws are often visible from the elegant restaurant terrace, which hangs over the jungle high above the sea. Lapa Ríos, one of the first hotels to gain the highest rating on the government's Certification of Sustainable Tourism, gives a free "sustainability tour" in which guests learn about solar water heating, wind-up flashlights, methane production from an underground biodigestor, and salt purification instead of chlorine in their swimming pool. The tour ends with a friendly visit with the head cook to get the local point of view. The management recommends against bringing children under 5 for safety reasons, though they offer family and many multi-day packages. Recommended.

The land owned by the next two hotels is also a wildlife refuge.

Bosque del Cabo (private bath, hot water, solar electric, fans, spring-fed pool; $150-$200/person, including meals; children under 12 half-price; cell phone: 8381-4847, phone/fax: 2735-5206; bosquedelcabo.com, reservations@

bosquedelcabo.com), a few kilometers farther down the road and left down a mile-long driveway through the forest, has a spectacular view of the ocean from above Playa Matapalo at the very southern tip of the Osa Peninsula. You can walk or take a horseback ride down to the beach, where there is a beautiful waterfall pool, or slide Tarzan-like on a cable to a wildlife observation platform 110 feet up in a *manú* tree in the middle of the forest. You can wander the trails on your own, looking for monkeys and sloths, or call on the resident naturalist to guide you. Ten chic, tropical-style individual bungalows are perched at the edge of a semi-circular cliff overlooking the sea. They are spacious, with porches and unique outdoor showers decorated with creative mosaic work. Mosaic outdoor tubs let you relax in the water's warmth while gazing at the stars. Screened and louvered windows allow you to adjust the natural air flow inside the room. There are several more bungalows with garden and jungle views. The restaurant serves good international food and is receptive to vegetarians. Three houses are available for a weekly rental of $2000-$2700/week, meals not included. With advance notice, they can arrange a taxi from Puerto Jiménez for $25 each way. Recommended.

Just after the entrance to Bosque del Cabo is the long driveway down to **El Remanso Rainforest Beach Lodge** (private bath, hot water, natural ventilation, restaurant/bar, spring-fed pool; $130-$170/person, including meals; 2735-5569, fax: 2735-5126; elremanso.com, info@elremanso.com), owned by Belén Momeñe of Spain and Joel Stewart, a North American who runs tree-climbing and waterfall-rappelling adventure tours from their property. They met while working on Greenpeace's boats. The four spacious bungalows are designed for those who like quiet and privacy, and are decorated with delightful murals of angels. One has water views. There is a house that sleeps ten. Meals feature fresh seafood and exotic fruits. The beach is a ten-minute walk downhill. You can take a zipline to a platform in the forest with a picnic breakfast at 5 a.m. for bird observation. They offer a three-night active package for $970, including meals, tours, and domestic flights, as well as personal coaching, wildlife exploring and drawing retreats. Closed October and November. Recommended.

GETTING THERE: It takes about an hour to get from Puerto Jiménez to Cabo Matapalo. Your hotel can arrange taxi transport for about $25 per car. Note that you shouldn't try to drive down Bosque del Cabo's driveway if it starts to look mucky; leave your car by the side of the road and walk the rest of the way. You can take the 6 a.m. or 1:30 p.m. *taxi colectivo* from Jiménez and get off at Matapalo.

CARATE The road gets better after Lapa Ríos, continuing an hour through pleasant cattle country to the Río Aguas Buenas, which sometimes becomes too deep to cross in the rainy season. You can ask the local taxi driver to arrange for horses to meet you at the river if it looks like crossing on foot is impossible. Carate is another eight kilometers after the river.

Just before you get to Carate, you'll see **The Lookout** (private or shared bath, solar hot water, pool; $120-$180/person, including meals; discounts for children; 2735-5431, in North America: 815-955-1520; lookout-inn.com, info@lookout-inn.com). It offers bungalows in a hillside garden about an hour by foot from the La Leona station. In addition to the rooms in the lodge, there's, a "monkey house," two tiki huts, and a "Swing Inn," a private open air treehouse, with a huge deck and three hammocks. Their popular bar has great ocean views, as do the rooms in the lodge, the observation deck and the hot tub.

Luna Lodge (private bath, hot water, fans, pool; $140-$180/person, including meals; in secluded one-room tent, $80-$90/person, including meals; discounts for children; 8380-5036, in North America: 888-409-8448; lunalodge.com, information@lunalodge.com), on a mesa high above the Carate River, is a wonderland of waterfalls and wildlife, with individual bungalows, rockers on the porches, and its own version of the open-air shower. The "hacienda rooms" near the restaurant are for those who want to feel more protected from nature and who don't want to hike up to the bungalows. Its Wellness Center hosts yoga, massage, and creative visualization, with classes at their spacious, elegant yoga studio overlooking the jungle and sea. Meals are made from fresh fruits and vegetables grown at the lodge's organic gardens. Luna Lodge borders Corcovado, but its lofty elevation makes for cool, comfortable nights. It's located two and a half kilometers north of the Carate airstrip up a long, muddy, and bumpy road.

La Leona Lodge (cold water, spring water pool, screened windows; $60-$90/person, including meals; children 4 to 10 half-price; 2735-5704, fax: 2735-5440; laleonalodge.com, laleona@racsa.co.cr), on the beach, is a tent camp with six kilometers of trails going to two lookout points. Some tents have adjacent garden baths; others have shared baths. Their restaurant, **Jardines de Mar**, faces the beach and is the last place to eat before you enter the park.

GETTING THERE: There is no public bus service south of Jiménez. Taxi-trucks leave from Supermercado El Tigre in Puerto Jiménez daily at 6 a.m. and 1:30 p.m. ($7/person to Carate). If you wish to go later in the day, it costs $60 per taxi to Carate. In the rainy season, if the Río Aguas Buenas is too high, the truck only goes to the river, and you have to hike the remaining eight kilometers to Carate. The truck/taxi driver or your hotel can arrange for horses to meet you at the river. There is no problem crossing the river in the dry season.

By Car: The gravel road south of Puerto Jiménez is passable only for four-wheel-drive vehicles in the rainy season. It takes about two hours to get to Carate. Check with your hotel about current road conditions and driving times.

By Air: To get from Puerto Jiménez from San José or Quepos, take SANSA or Nature Air.

You can charter a five passenger plane for about $450 from Puerto Jiménez to Sirena from Alfa Romeo Aero Taxi (2735-5353; alfaromeoair.com; seven-minute flight) the company most familiar with the zone. They have offices near the airport in Puerto Jiménez.

NORTH OF PUERTO JIMÉNEZ

The locally owned **Río Nuevo Lodge** (shared bath, cold water; $50-$60/person, including meals and transportation from Puerto Jiménez; children under 15 half-price; children under 7 free; 2735-5411, fax: 2735-5407; rio nuevolodge.com reserve@rionuevolodge.com) is a lovely tent camp at the juncture of three rivers. The home-cooked food is very good and the gardens are tended with *cariño.* This is a little oasis, truly off the beaten track. It is accessible by a turnoff about ten minutes north of Puerto Jiménez, but let them take you there—you have to ford several rivers and cross a hanging bridge in the process. From Río Nuevo, you can take the path less traveled in a nine-hour hike that ends in Carate and spend the night at a gold-miner's house. Recommended.

A few kilometers north of Puerto Jiménez and eight bumpy kilometers inland is the village of **Dos Brazos**. **Bosque del Río Tigre Sanctuary and Lodge** (private or shared bath, cold water, natural ventilation, mosquito nets; $130-$140/person, including meals; $170-$180/person, with unlimited guided birding; discounts for children under 12; 2735-5062, 8383-3905, in North America: 888-875-9453; osaadventures.com, info@osaadventures. com) is a 31-acre private reserve just beyond Dos Brazos. Owned by Abraham Gallo and Liz Jones, a hospitable Tico-gringa couple who are ardent rainforest and birding enthusiasts, the lodge has an open design that makes electric fans unnecessary. Mosquito netting protects sleeping guests from wayward insects. The second floor of the lodge contains four corner rooms (shared bath), separated from each other by an attractive reading area, well-stocked with natural history books and identification guides. There is also a secluded riverside cabin (private bath) surrounded by lush foliage. Meals, personally supervised by Abraham, are a point of pride—delicious, wholesome, and gourmet. Quality birding binoculars are available to guests to help them get the most from their fascinating hiking and birdwatching expeditions. To get there by car, take a clearly marked turnoff four kilometers north of Puerto Jiménez, and follow the road eight kilometers to Dos Brazos. Make a left at the concrete bridge at the entrance to town. Follow signs to the lodge. In the dry season you may be able to drive across the river to the lodge. In the rainy season leave your car at a nearby *soda*. They will show you the best place to wade across the Río Tigre (it's about two feet deep). Liz and Abraham can arrange for a taxi to meet you at the airport or bus stop. It is best to make reservations at this small lodge before you come. Recommended for birders.

There is a collective taxi service to Dos Brazos. Ask for current schedules.

Birding is great at the Swiss/Tico-owned **Suital Lodge** (private or shared bath, hot water, fans, mosquito nets; $50-$70; children under 12 free; 8826-0342; suital.com, lodge@suital.com), 17 kilometers east of the town of Rincón. The rustic cabins have verandas for hummingbird watching. This 70-acre reserve's well-marked trails take you to the shore; the sea here is gentle for kayaking.

GOLFO DULCE

On the Golfo Dulce, between the Osa Peninsula and the mainland, the *costa* is *rica* indeed: lush vegetation; breezy, rocky beaches; deep, green waters. There are several ecotourism projects set on the eastern rim of the gulf, which really make the area worth visiting. Because all the lodges are isolated and accessible only by boat, prices are per person, including meals and sometimes transportation from Puerto Jiménez.

Dolphin Quest (rustic *ranchos*, shared baths, natural ventilation; with double occupancy, $100-$120/person in private *ranchos*; camping, $50-$60, including meals; children under 6 free; ages 7 to 15 half price; dolphin questcostarica.com, dolphinquest@email.com), located down the beach from Golfo Dulce Lodge, is a laidback farm where you can explore the jungle, help with gardening, ride horses, kayak, snorkel, or look for dolphins. It's definitely for people who are comfortable with alternative lifestyles. They are interested in hosting retreats and workshops in their large, open-sided, cement-floored, thatched *rancho*.

Casa Orquídeas is a beautifully landscaped private botanical garden overlooking the sea. Longtime residents Ron and Trudy McAllister take you on an hour's tour of the garden, where you can see what the spices and fruits in your kitchen look like on the vine—and taste them if they're in season. You'll see ginger, vanilla, black pepper, cinnamon, cacao, cashew, mango, avocado, and papaya, as well as tons of beautiful orchids and familiar houseplants in their native habitat. Tours begin around 8:30 a.m. Saturday through Thursday, $5 per person (four-person minimum, not including transport). All the nearby lodges plus Zancudo Boat Tours (see below) will take you there.

Playa Nicuesa Lodge (private bath, solar hot water, fans, mosquito nets, resident yoga/massage thearapist; $160-$190/person, including meals and transport from Puerto Jimenez or Golfito; children ages 6 to 12 $90-$100; two-night minimum stay; 2258-0704, in North America: 866-348-7610; nicuesalodge.com) is a unique ecotourism opportunity on the Golfo Dulce. The 2800-foot main lodge, with its massive beams, is reminiscent of a woodsy lodge in Maine, but it's open to nature on all sides. The rooms are very well done, with molded plaster open-air bathrooms that add such a charming, creative touch to the hotels of the Osa. Some of the cabins have two bedrooms, ideal for families; others are more secluded for honeymooners. The water on this part of the gulf is protected and lake-like, good for kids. Their dock is the perfect place to see bioluminescence at night. Trails into the rainforest behind the lodge are flat and comfortable for walking. Snorkeling is good at nearby shallow reefs, and the use of kayaks is free for guests. The very creative chef and the friendly local guides make this a good place to get to know the Costa Rican staff as well as the North American owners. "The Edible Landscape" is the theme of one of their vacation packages: learn to forage in the rainforest for your dinner! Readers that have stayed a week say there is plenty to do. They also offer the entire premises for retreats or workshops for up to 20 people. Recommended.

CORCOVADO NATIONAL PARK

In the 1970s, scientists realized that the Osa Peninsula was one of the richest, most diverse tropical areas on earth. The tremendous rainfall, remote location, and variety of unique habitats (eight in all, ranging from mountain forest to swamp), made protection from development imperative. Fortunately scientists won the battle against lumbermen and other proponents of rainforest destruction, and the 108,022-acre national park was founded in 1975.

Since then, the park has been the site of much scientific research, and biologists have identified at least 500 species of trees, 285 birds, 139 mammals, 116 amphibians and reptiles, and 16 freshwater fishes. The rainforest canopy reaches higher than anywhere else in the country, due to the abundant rainfall and low altitude.

Besides its ecological wealth, the area has an interesting human history as well. Some of the best-known and most notorious inhabitants of the national park have been the *oreros* (gold panners). The *oreros* are independent, solitary types who know the peninsula like the backs of their hands.

During their heyday, they sifted for their fortunes in the streams and rivers of Corcovado National Park, camping in crude lean-tos and hunting wild animals for food. They would only venture out to Puerto Jiménez once in a while to sell their gold nuggets to the Banco Central's special gold-buying office there. But in the mid-1980s, due to massive unemployment in the region, the gold panners' numbers grew so large that their activity started causing real destruction. The silt from their panning was filling up the rivers and the lake in the park's basin. In 1986, the park service and the Costa Rican Civil Guard physically removed all of the gold panners, promising them an indemnity for their lost jobs. After a year without payment, the *oreros* camped out in protest in the city parks of San José until the government came through with the checks they had promised. Many *oreros* are back in Osa, panning in the forest reserve that borders Corcovado. Even though their activity is destructive, the park service has decided to let it continue rather than risk the panners retreating into Corcovado.

VISITING CORCOVADO If you would like to have an experienced guide, zoologist Mike Boston of **Osa Aventura** (2735-5758; osaaventura. com) leads customized trips. There are three ranger stations at which you can enter Corcovado National Park: San Pedrillo, La Leona, and Los Patos. You can camp at any one of these entrances (park admission $10, plus $4 for camping). The most famous ranger station is La Sirena, connected only by trail to the other stations. La Sirena is the only one with dorm-like accommodations and a kitchen that prepares three meals a day. In order to stay and eat at La Sirena, you must make reservations one month in advance (see below).

San Pedrillo is about half an hour by speedboat from Drake Bay. All the Drake Bay lodges offer one-day guided tours to San Pedrillo. Camping is allowed ($14, admission included). If you want to hike to Sirena, this is not a good place to enter. There are three river mouths to cross in the 25 kilometers between San Pedrillo and Sirena, and all crossings must be done at low tide to avoid encounters with sharks or crocodiles. The distances be-

tween the rivers make it impossible to cross them all at low tide in one day. So the San Pedrillo entrance is best for a one-day tour by boat from Drake, and not recommended for hiking without a knowledgeable guide.

To get to **La Leona**, it's two hours of bumping along in the back of the truck-taxi to Carate, then a 45-minute hike (3.5 kilometers) along the beach. The truck-taxi, or *taxi colectivo*, leaves Puerto Jiménez daily at 6 a.m. and 1:30 p.m. ($7/person), or you can leave at any hour in a plusher SUV taxi for $60. You can camp at La Leona ($14) without making reservations if you bring your own food. However, you DO need reservations in order to hike from La Leona to La Sirena station and stay overnight in the dorm rooms. And you do need a permit to camp there. If you don't want to camp but want to explore Corcovado for the day from La Leona, it makes the most sense to stay overnight at one of the lodges in Carate, La Leona Tent Camp Lodge being the closest to La Leona station. Don't swim here—there are sharks and the current is strong.

CARATE–LA LEONA–SIRENA   The walk from La Leona to Sirena spans 16 kilometers and takes five to seven hours. It is almost entirely along the soft sand beach. You must do it at low tide, because you walk around a couple of rocky points covered at high tide. Many people do the beach hike at night in order to avoid the sun.

First you come to a rusted shipwreck at Punta Chancha, with huge engines scattered around the rocks. A bit later you reach **Salsipuedes** (Get-out-if-you-can) **Point**, which has a pretty cave hollowed out of the coast. At some of the rock points there are trails that cut inland for a few hundred meters. The best way to find them is to start looking as soon as the coast seems impassable. The Salsipuedes trail gives you a break from the soft sand for a kilometer or two, but coat yourself up with repellent before starting into the jungle.

There are many monkeys along this trail. You will probably see scarlet macaws singing raucously and winging awkwardly through the sky. *Pizotes* (coatimundis) also come to the coast frequently. After you cross the Río Claro, cut in either on the Sirena trail or at the airstrip a bit farther down.

LA PALMA–LOS PATOS–SIRENA   The third entrance to Corcovado is **Los Patos**, on the eastern border of the park, accessible from the town of La Palma, north of Puerto Jiménez. You have to cross the Río Rincón 26 times before you get to Los Patos from La Palma. Horses are available for rent ($20-$30) in the village of Guadalupe, just outside La Palma. Taxis from Puerto Jiménez to Los Patos cost $60-$80; from La Palma, $40-$50. There are buses several times a day between Puerto Jiménez and La Palma. It's a 20-kilometer hike from Los Patos to Sirena. Hikers are not allowed to

leave Los Patos later than 11 a.m., so start off early. Since there is no public transportation to Los Patos, but there is the truck-taxi that returns to
Puerto Jiménez from Carate at 8:30 a.m. and 4 p.m., it makes more sense
to enter Corcovado at Los Patos and come out at La Leona if you want to
hike for several days.

A boon for hikers is the new, locally owned **Danta Corcovado Lodge**
(private and shared baths, heated water, fans, kitchen facilities; rooms, $40-
$60/person, including breakfast; camping, $5-$10/person; 2735-1111, phone/
fax: 2735-1212; dantacorcovado.net, info@dantacorcovado.net), three kilometers southwest of La Palma and eight kilometers northeast of the Los
Patos entrance. There are screened, covered platforms for tents, comfortable, well-ventilated wooden rooms, and more private bungalows farther
back in the forest, all with whimsical decorative touches. Meals are served
family-style. They rent horses, run tours to the nearby Guaymi indigenous
reserve, and do night tours around their lagoon, looking for caimans and lu-
minescent mushrooms. Recommended as a good staging area for your hike
to Corcovado.

Reservations: If you plan to use this route, you must make reservations
one month in advance. The best way to do it it through the webmaster at
soldeosa.com. He will make all arrangements for you for $25, no matter
how many are in your party. This service is well worth it. He will have your
permits delivered to your home before you leave for Costa Rica so that you
don't have to go south to Puerto Jiménez and then make your way back north
to La Palma and Los Patos. Contact him at reservations@soldeosa.com.

The worst stretches of the whole trip are immediately before and after
Los Patos, where the trail can be swampy and slippery, especially in the
rainy season.

When you enter the park at Los Patos, there are five kilometers of steep
trails through high mountain forests, then fifteen kilometers of flat walking
in low, dense rainforest to the research station at Sirena. The trail is clearly
marked, but at some river crossings you have to check up- or downstream
for where the trail takes off again. Some of the rivers can be thigh-deep in
the rainy season. Don't do this walk at night. Most snakes are nocturnal,
and they like water. Don't cross the rivers in sandals.

Be careful not to walk into biting spiders, whose webs span the trail;
bring repellent and plenty of patience for the horseflies. On the way you
might see frogs, morpho butterflies, and monkeys, and perhaps the tracks
of tapirs and ocelots.

Sirena is a 15-bed research station populated by ecotourists and biological researchers who are mostly from the United States or Europe. Do not

bathe in the ocean because there are sharks; there are crocodiles in the nearby Río Sirena. You can rent canoes at the station ($20).

These beaches are infested with *purrujas*, invisible biting insects that leave itchy welts that seem to never go away. Do not plan to hike or camp here alone—it's a jungle out there.

Additional things you will need to bring for a comfortable stay include:

- a tent with good screens if you are camping
- a lightweight sleeping bag or a sheet or two—bedding is not provided
- a mosquito net—they are not provided
- at least two types of insect repellent, in case one doesn't work
- sunscreen
- several changes of polypro clothing, with long pants and long sleeves to protect you from sun and bugs
- a wide-brimmed hat and a bandanna
- a rain poncho or umbrella
- a towel
- a flashlight
- candles and matches
- a Swiss Army knife
- plan to carry all the water you will need (at least four liters of water or more); water in the park is not potable and the river water is salty
- snacks—a generous supply in case you're delayed on your way to one of the park's stations
- binoculars
- one pair of good hiking boots that will stand up to getting wet, and a pair of tennis shoes. Sandals are not recommended because of the danger of snakes. River crossings should be done in hiking boots, and the sneakers can be worn when you're between treks
- rubber boots
- several pairs of long socks
- a clothesline

GOLFITO

The port town of Golfito has a gorgeous setting—lush, forested hills surrounding a deep bay on the Golfo Dulce with the misty outline of the Península de Osa in the distance.

The town is stretched along one main road squeezed between the gulf and the mountains. Virgin forest blankets the mountains, which have been made into a wildlife and watershed reserve.

The northern part of town is the Zona Americana. United Fruit administrators once lived in this neighborhood in big wooden houses on stilts, surrounded by large lawns and gardens. The southern part of town is called the Pueblo Civil and is a noisy collection of bars, restaurants, and hotels. There is an ATM at the Banco Nacional on the far side of the soccer field.

Many Central Valley shoppers visit the **Depósito Libre**, a huge outdoor mall north of town. These air-conditioned shops filled with *electrodomésticos* (household appliances) and luxury items were created in an attempt to boost the economy after United Fruit left in 1985.

Cataratas Avellan (admission $5; meals, $6; 8397-8318; avellancr.com), six kilometers north of the Deposito on a dirt road, has primary forest, trails to a 90-foot waterfall and a zipline canopy tour ($20).

For an interesting ethnobotanical experience in this area, visit the **Paradise Tropical Garden** (2789-8746; paradise-garden.travelland.biz), the project of Robert Beatham, affable former United Fruit manager. There you will get to see, touch, taste, and smell a variety of tropical fruits and learn about plant lore while learning about the history and future of the zone. It's in Río Claro, where you turn off for Golfito on the Interamerican Highway. On your way from the north, take a road to the left just before the bridge over the Río Lagarto. Tours are usually given in the morning. Make reservations in advance.

LODGING AND RESTAURANTS   In our humble opinion, the best places to stay and eat are outside the town.

La Casa del Arbol Bed and Breakfast ($80-$90, including breakfast and gourmet dinner; 2741-1131; casaarbol.com) at kilometer 45 on the Interamerican before the turnoff to Golfito, is the project of a French-Canadian family, filled with the owner's paintings and sculptures. One room is built in a tree.

Seven kilometers before the entrance to town, in a grassy orchard with cabins and camping spots, is **La Purruja Lodge** (private bath, cold water, ceiling fans; $40-$50, including breakfast; children under 12 free; phone/fax: 2775-5054; purruja.com, info@purruja.com). The rooms are very clean, all in a beautiful setting. Breakfast and dinner are served at the lodge, and the owners provide tours to see crocodiles and caves nearby. It's a great place to stay with kids, because it's away from the road with lots of room to run around. Buses to Golfito pass in front every half hour. Recommended.

At **Chalet Suizo Tropical** (closed Monday; 2775-5352; chaletsuizo-tropical.com) next door, a Swiss chef serves up gourmet cuisine in a charming tropical setting.

In another kilometer, you'll come to **Margarita's Rancho Grande** (2775-1951), known for *comida típica* cooked over a wood fire, as well as filet mignon and *sopa de mariscos*.

GETTING THERE: By Bus: Golfito buses leave the Alfaro–Tracopa station (Calle 14, Avenida 5; 2222-2666, 2221-4214) at 7 a.m. and 3 p.m., and cost $9. They return at 5 a.m. and 1:30 p.m. It's an eight-hour trip. Or you can take any Zona Sur bus to Río Claro—that's the turnoff to Golfito. Villa Neily–Golfito buses pass through Río Claro hourly. It's a half-hour trip from the highway to Golfito. Buy your return tickets as soon as you get to Golfito.

By Car: Follow the Interamerican Highway from San José to Río Claro and turn right. The trip takes about seven hours. If you want to do the trip in two days, San Isidro de El General or the coast south of Playa Dominical are good places to stay overnight. Going to Golfito is a good way to avoid the bumpy road to Puerto Jimenez.You can drive paved roads Golfito, turn in your car there, and take the Superlancha. It leaves at 5 a.m., 10:30 a.m., noon, 1:30, and 4 p.m., and gets to Puerto Jimenez in half an hour.

By Air: You can avoid the long, winding (though scenic) bus ride by flying SANSA to Golfito (2290-4100, in North America: 877-767-2672, fax: 2290-3543; $90-$100 one way). Check schedules at flysansa.com. Nature Air (2299-6000, in North America: 800-235-9272; $100-$110 one way) also flies to Golfito. Check schedules at natureair.com.

PIEDRAS BLANCAS NATIONAL PARK In 1991, the President of Costa Rica declared 14,000 hectares in the Esquinas Rainforest, on the eastern side of the Golfo Dulce, a national park. The land is blanketed by lush virgin forest. There are many endemic species of plants and animals. It is also a refuge for migratory birds.

Esquinas Rainforest Lodge (private bath, heated water, ceiling fans; $90-$120/person, including meals; discount for ages 5 to 10; phone/fax: 2741-8001; esquinaslodge.com, esquinas@racsa.co.cr) is a cluster of well-appointed duplexes, kept cool because three of the four walls have large, screened windows. There's a chlorine-free, stream-fed pool surrounded by beautifully landscaped gardens and trails through primary forest. The reception area, library, and restaurant are in a large building topped with a locally woven palm roof. Horseback riding, mountain biking, kayaking, and dolphin-watching tours are all available from the lodge. All profits from the lodge are used for improvement projects proposed by the people of La Gamba, a village near the park entrance.

GETTING THERE: By Car: Drive toward Golfito as far as Villa Briceño, at kilometer marker 37 on the Interamerican Highway. Make a right, and follow signs for five kilometers on a gravel road that has several small wooden bridges without guardrails. If you take the Golfito bus or fly to Golfito, a taxi to the lodge costs about $20. There is a mountainous back road that will take you from Golfito to Esquinas in about 15 minutes in the dry season. **Senderos Cataratas Avellan,** mentioned in the Gofito section, are also in La Gamba.

ZANCUDO

Playa Zancudo, on a strip between the ocean and the Coto River, is one of the Zona Sur's most popular beaches during the dry season. The fine black-sand beach stretches for miles, and the surf is mostly gentle. This safe beach is ideal for families with children. The southern section of Zancudo offers good surfing, with beach breaks in both directions. Because it is relatively unknown, there is no line-up.

The mangroves along the Río Coto and the Atrocha canal connecting Zancudo with Golfito serve as a safe nursery for the area's rich fishing grounds. **Zancudo Boat Tours** (2776-0012; loscocos@loscocos.com) offers scenic kayak trips along the Río Coto to view birds, crocodiles, monkeys, and otters ($45). Trips to Casa Orquídeas botanical garden (see above), and the Osa Peninsula are available as well. It's only $60 for two people to go by boat from Zancudo to Puerto Jiménez—a pleasant way to arrive at the gateway to Corcovado; it's $15/person (minimum $40) to go to or from Golfito. Andrew Robertson, a transplant from the U.K., is ZBT's witty and entertaining captain.

LODGING   Hotels and cabinas are plentiful, and a better value than those at many other Costa Rican beaches. We'll describe our favorites in order from north to south. If you drive, reverse the order. If your boat lets you off at the public dock, turn left on the main road to get to the cabinas listed below.

The restaurant/bar at **Cabinas Oceano** (private bath, heated water, ceiling fans, a/c, screened windows, mosquito nets, TV; $70-$90, including breakfast; 2776-0921; oceanocabinas.com, info@oceanocabinas.com), 50 meters from the Zancudo supermarket, serves pancakes and waffles for breakfast, good *ceviche,* and will pack picnic lunches. Their two cabins are set in well-manicured gardens near the beach.

The locally acclaimed **Macondo** (open noon to 3 p.m. and 5:30 p.m. to 9:30 p.m.; 2776-0157; macondo-hotel.com, info@macondo-hotel.com) is a second-floor Italian restaurant that overlooks the mangrove estuary. They have six rooms (shared bath, heated water, ceiling fans, a/c; $40-$60) and a small pool.

La Puerta Negra (open for dinner only; 2776-0181) is a small Italian restaurant with lots of character, owned by excellent chef Alberto. He makes his own bread and pasta, which he serves in his herb garden near the beach. He rents a cabin for $30-$40.

The owners of Zancudo Boat Tours also operate **Cabinas Los Cocos** (private bath, heated water, table fans, kitchens; $60-$70; weekly and monthly rates available; 2776-0012; loscocos.com, loscocos@loscocos.com), about two kilometers or a 20-minute walk south of the municipal dock. Los Cocos consists of four individual houses, two of which are reconditioned banana company cabins, with big decks overlooking the ocean, and two thatch-roofed *ranchos*, one with a loft that sleeps four. They are quiet, private, and shipshape. Bikes, kayaks, and boogieboards are available for guests, They also rent three beach houses ($700-$750/week). Recommended.

Next door, **Cabinas Sol y Mar** (private bath, heated water, ceiling fans, wi-fi; $30-$50; 2776-0014; zancudo.com, solymar@zancudo.com), with cabinas and a restaurant, offers horseshoe and volleyball tournaments, and surfboards for rent. The cabins have good air circulation. There is camping space available (bring your own tent, $3/person) and a house for rent ($800/month).

Cabinas y Restaurante El Coloso del Mar (private bath, heated water, screened windows, fans, wi-fi; $30-$60; 2776-0050; coloso-del-mar.com, info@coloso-del-mar.com) has quiet beachfront and garden rooms. Its restaurant offers local and international cuisine, and sometimes live music and dancing.

Four kilometers from the center of town is **Oasis on the Beach** (private bath, hot water, fans, some a/c, refrigerator, screened windows, internet; $50-$90; 2776-0087; oasisonthebeach.com, reservations@oasisonthebeach.com) with individual elevated cabins, and rooms in a two-story villa. Its breezy restaurant/bar is open for breakfast, lunch, and dinner and features weekly pizza and movie nights. The hotel provides bikes and boogie-boards for guests and offers dune buggy rides into town. The cabins are well appointed and very comfortable. Surfing is good here. **Los Tres Amigos** (2775-0123), down the street, sells clothes, sandwiches, and familiar U.S. groceries. They have the only gas station in town.

GETTING THERE: By Car: If you have a four-wheel-drive vehicle, driving is usually possible, and the trip from Golfito takes between one and two hours. Locals say that the trip can be done in a regular car in the dry season, but it's always best to have a high clearance. Look for the Rodeo bar at kilometer 14 of the Río Claro–Golfito road, and turn south. Fifteen minutes later on paved road you come to an old-fashioned barge that takes about five minutes to ferry you across the

Coto River, provided that it isn't dead low tide. The ferry shuts down at 6 p.m., so be sure to get there before dark. In another half hour you'll get to the place where the road goes south to Pavones and north to Zancudo. There are signs in most crucial places. It's good to ask directions as often as possible. When in doubt, turn right.

By Boat: The *Macarela,* a public ferry, $5), leaves the municipal *muelle* in Golfito around noon, Monday through Friday only. Since the schedule depends on the tide, the ferry will take either the Atrocha (mangrove canal shortcut, only possible in high tide) or the ocean route (beach landing; you have to walk ashore). The trip takes 40 minutes. Not for people with a lot of luggage. The easiest way to get to Zancudo is with Zancudo Boat Tours (2776-0012; $15/person, $40 minimum); they take you to your hotel so that you don't have to walk 30 or 40 minutes in the hot sun—and it is hot!

By Taxi: A land taxi costs about $40 from Golfito.

PAVONES

Pavones is highly publicized in surfer magazines for having the longest wave in the world but we have heard that this legendary wave only occurs about ten times a year, usually between April and September. When it does happen, expect rides more than a minute long, and over 150 surfers in the water, especially in June and July. This wave is for experts only.

It is a beautiful area, much more lush and green than Zancudo, and there are some delightful places to stay. The area is now attracting nature lovers, bird watchers and aficionados of tropical flowers and fruits. Dr. Bob Bacher, a tai chi teacher with 40 years of experience, organizes trainings and retreats through **Tai Chi Vacations** (taichivacations.com, chenti@mac.com) centered in Pavones, where you can learn this ancient "inner" martial art for health, long life, and inner peace. **Shooting Star Yoga Studio** (8393-6982; shootingstarstudio.org) offers yoga and karate classes. **Sea Kings Surf Shop** (2393-6982) rents surf equipment and bikes, arranges tours, and has **internet** access.

The **Manta Club** is owned by an Israeli couple who are surfing aficionados. They film the surfing every day at Pavones and show the videos at night, often as a prelude to DVD movies, while admiring surfers eat their shish kebab and falafel. The vegetarian **Café de la Suerte** in the center of town is also popular and rents a cabin ($40-$50, including breakfast).

Mira Olas (private bath, heated water, fans, mosquito nets, hammocks, kitchens; $30-$50; $150-$240/week; children under 12 free; 8393-7742; miraolas.com, miraolas@hotmail.com) are several private cabins on a hill full of fruit trees. One is rustic, another is "Jungle Deluxe," and "La Mod-

INNOVATIVE COMMUNITIES: ALTAMIRA, GATEWAY TO LA AMISTAD INTERNATIONAL PARK

The National Biodiversity Institute, Inbio, has spent several years training local guides in the Altamira area, and now there are two community-based lodges there that can supply you with guides and help you set up your trip. Make reservations at least two weeks in advance in order to be able to get entrance permits and secure guides. Harol Lescano is one of the only bilingual guides. Bring your own sleeping bag.

ASOPROLA (private bath, heated water, internet; $20-$30/ person, including meals; 2743-1184; eco-index.org/ong/asoprola-cr-esp.html, asoprola@yahoo.es or 2248-9470; info@actuarcosta rica.com) is a friendly lodge ten minutes from the entrance to La Amistad International Park. You know you are in for a treat when you see the bus stop at the entrance, a Gaudiesque structure with round windows, every inch of which is decorated in with delightful mosaics. Their **Restaurante Arco Iris** glows from floor to ceiling with more mosaics, including mosaic trees that hold up the roof. Cupboard doors in the cooking area are made of translucent green wine bottles cut in half, creating a beautiful bamboo pattern. When we were there the restaurant was full of young volunteers adding their own designs to the walls and floor. The force behind this abundance of creativity is Pancho. You can hike to his rainforest reserve through ASOPROLA's fields of organic coffee, sugar cane, and pineapple. He has developed an anti-erosion system for building trails that uses recycled tires, as well as an innovative signage system throughout the area (see below). **Volunteers** are welcome to work in the school or at the lodge. Recommended.

erna" has heated showers. Monkeys and birds are frequently seen there. The *finca*, owned by a U.S.-German couple, is accessed by a dirt road heading a quarter mile inland from the fishermen's co-op at the entrance to town. It's great for couples or families who like peace and quiet, and is an easy walk to the river or the beach. Recommended.

South of town are several places to stay, described in order of appearance. To get there, go back a quarter mile to the fish co-op and turn inland. Turn right at the supermarket and cross the bridge over the Río Claro.

An attractive, spacious bed and breakfast built on a hill overlooking the sea, **Casa Siempre Domingo** (private bath, heated water, fans, a/c; $80-

Cerro Biolley (shared bath, heated water; $40-$70/person, including meals and tours; 2248-9470; actuarcostarica.com, info@actuarcostarica.com) is the only coffee processing plant in Costa Rica that is owned and operated by women. Guests can tour their prize-winning *beneficio* and pick coffee with them during the September to January production season. At other times of year they will take you hiking in their rain forest reserve, and can arrange a longer hike to **Sabanas Esperanza**, high plains surrounded by mountains of virgin forest within La Amistad International Park, where you might see the tracks of jaguars or tapirs. You can stay inexpensively in their homey lodge and enjoy their great country cooking. **Volunteers** stay with local families or at the lodge. Recommended.

GETTING THERE: By Bus: Take the 5:45 a.m. Tracopa bus (2290-1308) from San Jose to Las Tablas de San Vito. Another bus meets that bus at the Las Tablas turnoff on the San Vito road and takes you to Altamira and Biolley.

By Car: Take the Interamerican Highway about 20 minutes past Buenos Aires. Turn left to cross the Río Térraba at Paso Real, and drive toward San Vito for about 15 minutes. Pancho has designed the signage for the whole area, so when you get to Las Tablas, the turnoff for Altamira on the San Vito road, you will see a strange cement tree, hung with round mosaic signs framed by old bicycle tires. Turn left at the signs. In about half an hour on gravel roads you will see signs directing you to ASOMOBI to the left. Five minutes more and you will be in Altamira. The park entrance is another 5 bumpy kilometers straight ahead. In Altamira a sign directs you to ASOPROLA, on kilometer to the right.

$90, including breakfast; 8820-4709; casa-domingo.com, heidi@casa-domingo.com) is owned by a couple from Cape Cod, and has a fantastic view. You should have a car to stay here.

One and a half kilometers south of town are **Cabinas La Ponderosa** (private bath, hot water, ceiling fans, some with a/c; $60-$130/person; children under 10 $5; $20/person for meals; 8824-4145, in the U.S.: 954-771-9166; cabinaslaponderosa.com, info@cabinaslaponderosa.com), which are well-designed and completely screened-in. There is a volleyball court, full-size basketball court, and a large, screened game room with satellite TV, ping pong, foosball, and hammocks. They have a two-bedroom villa that sleeps up to six ($200, four night minimum). All accommodations can be rented for retreats or workshops for $3600/week (25 guest limit). Recommended.

Four and a half kilometers south, high on a jungle-covered hillside, is **Tiskita Lodge** (private bath, pool; $120/person, including meals; phone/fax: 2296-8125, fax: 2296-8133; tiskita-lodge.co.cr, info@tiskita-lodge.co.cr). The rustic but comfortable cabins all have superb ocean views and are cooled by sea breezes. Agronomist Peter Aspinall has planted more than 125 varieties of tropical fruits from around the world here, which attract many birds and monkeys. Peter has been working on re-establishing the scarlet macaw population. Today you can see and hear dozens of pairs of these large, colorful birds throughout the region. Guided nature walks are available and trails wind up and down the mountain backdrop in this 800-acre reserve. A 65-foot waterfall and swimmable ponds are close to the cabins. Three-night packages ($835/person) include meals and guided walks but not transportation. Tiskita is closed September 15th to October 15th.

GETTING THERE: By Bus: A bus for Pavones leaves at 10 a.m. and 3 p.m. every day from the *bomba* in Golfito, returning at 5:30 a.m. and 12:30 p.m. daily. A taxi to Pavones costs $50 to $60, depending on how far south you're going.

By Car: It takes a little over an hour to get from Zancudo to Pavones, with gorgeous views on the way. It takes about an hour and a half to get to Pavones from Golfito. As with Zancudo, look for the Rodeo Bar at kilometer 14 of the Río Claro–Golfito road, and turn south. The section up to the Río Coto is paved. Cars cross the river on a ferry contraption ($1.25 for car and driver, 15 cents for each passenger). The ferry shuts down at dark, so don't get stuck there. Roads south of the river to Pavones are gravel or dirt, It's good to have a high-clearance vehicle. You will probably want to ask directions frequently.

PARQUE INTERNACIONAL LA AMISTAD

Parque Internacional La Amistad extends over the Talamanca mountains from the southern border of Chirripó National Park down into Panama. It is the largest park in the country (599,000 hectares), and its Panamanian counterpart is more than three times larger. Comprising eight life zones, La Amistad is one of the richest ecological zones in Central America. The United Nations has declared the park and its neighboring reserves and protected zones a World Heritage site and has given it the status of Biosphere.

Preliminary surveys indicate that two-thirds of the country's vertebrate species are found in this park. It is an extremely important refuge for animals that require large areas in order to hunt, forage, and reproduce, like the jaguar, margay, and puma.

The official gateway to La Amistad is the **Altamira** entrance (2200-5355; admission $10; camping $5; bunks at ranger station, $6). The ranger station is a 20-kilometer (one hour) drive up a gravel road from a turnoff about 15 minutes down the road to San Vito. Once you get to Altamira there are beautiful views, a campground with tiled bathrooms, a covered cooking area with picnic tables and bunk bed accommodations in the ranger station (bring your own sleeping bag). They have an exhibit of all the insect, butterfly, and moth species that are found in the park.

Sendero los Gigantes del Bosque is a circular hike that takes about two hours. Along the trail, the plants, trees, brooks, and the forest itself speak to visitors through a series of 13 natural history stations.

A three-day guided trek to the **Valle del Silencio,** 14 kilometers from the Altamira station, is the main attraction for serious hikers. You can do a one-day hike to **Casa Coca,** where you might see the tracks of nocturnal jungle cats. On the three-day hike, you spend the night at Casa Coca, then visit Valle del Silencio the next day, returning to spend the night at Casa Coca. No matter how adventurous you feel, don't undertake the trip without a guide. It's very easy to get lost, and hikers have died from hypothermia and falls in the slippery, precipitous terrain. Camping in this area is most enjoyable in the dry season (January through April).

SAN VITO

Founded in the early 1950s by immigrants from postwar Italy, **San Vito** is in a high, mountainous valley with an invigorating climate. The town of 45,000 has a strong sense of its roots, with good Italian restaurants and gelato parlors. **Pizzeria y Restaurante Lilliana** (2773-3080), 50 meters west of the park, is a popular place run by an Italian family.

Two spurs off the Interamerican Highway lead to San Vito. From the north, cross the Térraba River on the Paso Real bridge, and drive 38 kilometers up the fertile backbone of the Coto Brus. This is the route the bus takes from San José. From the south, take the Villa Neily-San Vito road, built by the United States in 1945 during World War II as a strategic protection point, because the area is due west of the Panama Canal. The road rises so sharply that, in 20 minutes, Villa Neily's sweltering heat is forgotten in the cool misty mountains above San Vito. Views are spectacular, but the road is so winding that you should really pull over to enjoy the vista.

Halfway between San Vito and Wilson Botanical Gardens is the unique **Finca Cántaros** (open Tuesday through Sunday, 9 a.m. to 5 p.m.; 2773-3760; fincacantaros.com; admission $1). The *finca* consists of grassy picnic grounds with a pond (camping $5) and panoramic views; a renovated historic farmhouse with a children's reading room; and a gift shop with high-quality, hand-painted ceramics, Boruca and Guaymi woven goods, and delicious orange-guava jam, among other things, all at reasonable prices. Proceeds from sales of the handicrafts, both locally produced and brought from other areas of the country, go toward staffing the reading room. Recommended.

LODGING   **Hotel El Ceibo** (private bath, hot water, cable TV, bar, balconies; $40-$50; 2773-3025, fax: 2773-5025) is very clean and by far the most comfortable in town. The rooms in the back have views. The hotel has a good Italian restaurant. It is behind the Municipalidad, right in the center of town.

WILSON BOTANICAL GARDENS   San Vito's main attraction is undoubtedly **Las Cruces Biological Station** and **Wilson Botanical Gardens**, 5.4 kilometers uphill from town on the Villa Neily road. This floral wonderland is fascinating for lay visitors and the botanically inclined alike. Its astonishingly diverse collection was gathered from around the world and designed by the original owners, Robert and Catherine Wilson, with help from the great Brazilian horticulturist Roberto Burle-Marx. The garden is now owned by the Organization of Tropical Studies, a consortium of U.S., Latin American, and Australian universities.

One could spend days on the self-guided tours through the garden's 25 acres of cultivated sectors—trails are dedicated to heliconias, bamboos, orchids, lilies, gingers, palms, and ferns, to name a few. Nine kilometers of trails in the 632-acre forest reserve offer mountain vistas, overlooks of the rainforest canopy, and hikes to the lovely, rocky pools of the Río Java. The gardens' bird list of 330 species includes some aquatic species of the nearby San Joaquín marsh.

Day visits cost $24 for a full day, $18 for a half-day; child, student and researcher rates are available. Lodging is in comfortable cabins with balconies (private bath, heated water; $80-$90/person, including meals and a guided walk; children 5-12, $30-$40). Some units are wheelchair accessible. There is library and video room for rainy afternoons. Regular guided tours leave at 8 a.m. and 1:30 p.m.; special birding tours start at 5:45 a.m. You must make reservations before you visit (2773-4004; ots.ac.cr.edu. travel@ots.ac.cr). Recommended.

GETTING THERE: By Bus: Buses to San Vito leave San José at 5:45 a.m., 8:15 a.m., 11:30 a.m., and 2:45 p.m. from Tracopa (Calle 14, Avenida 5; 222-2666; $8.50). It's a six-hour trip. Buy tickets in advance, and call to make sure of the times. Most of these buses pass the botanical gardens after a stop in San Vito. Check with the driver.

A taxi from San Vito to Wilson Gardens is about $3.

By Car: The San José-San Vito trip takes five hours: two and a half hours to San Isidro, after which the road straightens out a bit, then one and a half hours to the Rio Térraba bridge, then another hour on the paved but pot-holed road to San Vito. Be sure not to miss the turnoff to the bridge at Paso Real, 15 kilometers after Buenos Aires. You'll see the river on your left, then you'll pass the bridge down below before you see a small sign indicating the road to San Vito. Once in San Vito, turn right onto the main street and follow it 15 minutes more to the botanical gardens.

ISLA DEL COCO

Isla del Coco (Coco Island), 500 kilometers off the Pacific Coast, boasts 200 dramatic waterfalls, many of which fall directly into the sea. It was made into a National Park in 1978, and declared a UNESCO World Heritage Site in 1997 because of the richness of its flora and fauna. Because the island is uninhabited, animals there are not afraid of humans. The fairy terns find humans so interesting that they hover about them curiously.

Although its geological origin remains a mystery, scientists believe Isla del Coco is a volcanic hot spot at the center of the Cocos tectonic plates.

The Coco Island finch is a subspecies of the finch endemic to the Galápagos Islands that prompted Darwin's questions about evolution. Several species of birds, lizards, and freshwater fish found on the island have not been seen anywhere else on earth. Whereas on mainland Costa Rica there are so many species that the behavior of each is highly specialized, on Isla del Coco individual birds of the same species will have different feeding habits—very interesting from an evolutionary standpoint. Some 77 non-endemic species, mainly seabirds, can also be observed.

European sailors probably first discovered the island in the 1500s. Many early visitors were pirates who rested and restocked fresh water there during expeditions. They named the island after its many coconut palms, but apparently enjoyed the coconuts so much that there are almost none left today. Passing boats installed pigs, deer, and goats on the island to provide meat for return voyages. With no predators, these animals now constitute the majority of the wildlife there.

There are tales of buried treasure on the island. The Portuguese Benito Bonito, "The One of the Bloody Sword," is said to have buried his fabulous treasure there. Also during the early 19th century, at the time of Peru's wars of independence from Spain, the aristocracy and clergy entrusted their gold and jewels to Captain James Thompson, who promised to transport their riches to a safe port. Thompson disappeared with the loot and is supposed to have hidden it on Isla del Coco. Although many treasure hunters have searched the island, no one has found anything yet.

Hunting for gold doubloons might not be rewarding at Isla del Coco, but scuba divers find it rich in natural treasures. The ship **Sea Hunter** (2228-6613, in North America: 800-203-2120; underseahunter.com, info@underseahunter.com) takes divers to the island for ten days of heavy-duty diving. Several sailboat companies in Guanacaste offer trips to Coco.

To get direct information on Coco National Park, contact the Area de Conservación Marina Isla del Coco in San José (2258-7295; acmic.sinac.go.cr).

Appendix

LIVING IN COSTA RICA

RESIDENCY

Tourists may own vehicles, property, and businesses in Costa Rica, and may generate income from their own companies, but the Immigration Department does not look kindly on this arrangement long-term. After a few renewals of your visa—obtained by leaving the country and coming back in—you should apply for residency. Securing permanent residency in Costa Rica is a complicated and increasingly difficult process but still easy in comparison to other countries, and required if you plan to live here for more than a few months.

Do not plan to make your residency application yourself unless you have plenty of patience to deal with lines, national holidays, lunch breaks, misunderstandings, offices that have moved from where they were a month ago, impossible-to-find phone numbers, and so on. If you have comfortable shoes and love to meditate or read novels while waiting in line, you'll find *trámites* (bureaucratic machinations) just your cup of tea. If you are nervous and impatient or have fallen arches, you will suffer. Of course, you can have a professional handle this for you.

Potential residents will want to visit the **Asociación de Residentes de Costa Rica** (Avenida 4, Calle 40, San José; 2233-8068, 2221-2053, fax: 2233-1152; arcr.net, arcr@casacanada.net). Their website is a great resource for learning about current immigration policies. The association's contracted specialists will see potential residents through the lengthy approval process for *pensionado* or *rentista* status.

Christopher Howard of **Relocational and Retirement Consultants** (liveincostarica.com) offers tours through different parts of the country for prospective residents.

WAYS TO WORK

The Costa Rican government doesn't want foreigners taking jobs from Costa Ricans. Therefore, most foreigners are not allowed to work unless they are performing a task that Ticos cannot do. But with some thought, you might be able to discover a skill you have that will help you establish temporary residency (*residencia temporal*). Qualified teachers are needed at the English-, French-, Japanese-, and German-speaking schools in San José. English teachers are often needed by the various language institutes. The National Symphony needs musicians; the *Tico Times* needs reporters. You would be surprised at how many gorgeous, isolated ecotourism projects need bilingual people with managerial experience—many educated Ticos are not willing to live so far from "civilization."

Doctors, lawyers, architects, and engineers are plentiful here and are protected by powerful professional associations that make entry difficult for foreigners.

LEGAL ADVICE

If you live here and have a business or buy land, sooner or later you will need to hire a lawyer. Legal fees vary greatly. Some very good lawyers charge more because they know that what they do is far superior to the run of the mill. If you have the money, it is worth every penny to have a good lawyer here.

You can educate yourself about Costa Rican laws at costaricalaw.com. There you will find updated information on real estate transactions, corporations, residency and immigration, commercial transactions, banking and finance, powers of attorney, environmental laws, copyrights, trademarks, worker's compensation, automobile regulations, taxation, social security, labor legislation, and much more.

REAL ESTATE AND INVESTMENTS

According to an article in the *Tico Times*, ". . . the potential investor in Costa Rica should beware of *all* glib, 'fact-filled,' English-speaking promoters flogging *anything*, whether it's gold mines, beach property, condominiums, agribusiness, or mutual funds. Costa Rica has long been a haven for con artists whose favorite targets are trusting newcomers. This doesn't mean, however, that legitimate investment opportunities don't exist. Investors here, like everywhere else, are advised simply to move cautiously, ask lots of questions, and check with well-established, reputable companies before parting with any money. That way, investors can be confident of making a good choice."

Know that any land within 200 meters of the high tide line on the beach is public and cannot be legally owned. You can "buy" it and build on it only after meeting a series of prerequisites and dealing with the local municipality and the Ministry of the Environment.

Owning land and houses anywhere in Costa Rica can transform it from paradise into living hell unless you follow a few rules of thumb: Hire a lawyer you trust before undertaking any transaction. Always place deposit money in an escrow account; never give it to the seller or the seller's attorney. Beware of being an absentee landlord or business-owner. It doesn't work.

The **American Chamber of Commerce of Costa Rica** (open daily, 8 a.m. to 5 p.m.; Sabana Norte, 300 meters to the northeast of ICE; 2220-2200, fax: 2220-2300; amcham.co.cr, chamber@amcham.co.cr) publishes a monthly magazine, *Business Costa Rica*, with information on economics, finance, legislation, and other related topics. Also, be sure to read *Potholes to Paradise* by Tessa Borner.

HEALTH CARE

The Social Security system makes low-cost medical care available to those who need it, but its clients must deal with long lines, short appointments, and delays lasting months between referral and delivery for X-rays, ultrasounds, operations, and other diagnostic treatment services. Doctors also have their private practices in the afternoons. See Health Vacations in Chapter Three for an idea of current medical costs. Well-qualified alternative medicine practitioners such as acupuncturists, homeopaths, chiropractors, and massage therapists are also available in Costa Rica and charge less than their northern counterparts. Check the *Tico Times*. Homeopaths are listed in the phone directory.

There are several English-speaking chapters of AA, CODA, and NA in Costa Rica. They list meetings in "Weekend" section of the *Tico Times*.

Long-term nursing home care is much less expensive here than in North America. **Finca Futuro Verde** (fincafuturoverde.com) in Rincon de Salas, near Grecia in the Central Valley offers several rooms for seniors and are building one-bedroom garden apartments for assisted living.

One thing that few retirees take into consideration is that in Costa Rica it is illegal to refuse life-supporting devices such as respirators.

RESOURCES

See our guide to Costa Rica on the internet at the beginning of Chapter Three. Also, check out *Potholes to Paradise* by Tessa Borner.

RECOMMENDED READING

BIOLOGICAL CORRIDORS

Ewing, Jack. *Monkeys Are Made of Chocolate*. Dominical, CR: 2003. Available at haciendabaru.com. A fascinating collection of essays by a North American naturalist about wildlife and forest regeneration at Hacienda Barú, where he has lived, farmed, and philosophized for several decades. Lots of good information about biological corridors.

ECOTOURISM

Honey, Martha. *Ecotourism and Sustainable Development: Who Owns Paradise?* 2nd ed. Washington, D.C.: Island Press, 2008. Definitive analysis of the issues surrounding ecotourism and sustainable tourism certification by an expert.

HISTORY AND CULTURE

Bell, John. *Crisis in Costa Rica: The 1948 Revolution.* Austin: University of Texas Press, 1971. History of the 1948 civil war.

Biesanz, Mavis, Richard, and Karen. *The Costa Ricans*. Prospect Heights, IL: Waveland Press, Inc., 1988. A sympathetic portrayal of traditional Costa Rican culture.

Biesanz, Mavis and Richard. *The Ticos: Culture and Social Change in Costa Rica.* London: Lynne Rienner, 1998. A fun-to-read look at Costa Rican culture Doña Mavis, who observed Ticos from the 1940s until her passing in February 2008.

Borner, Tessa. *Potholes to Paradise: Living in Costa Rica: What You Need to Know*. Port Perry, Ontario: Silvio Mattacchione, 2001. A frank, very readable account of the experiences of several families and their ups and downs as immigrants. Full of practical advice.

Marañón, Jon. *The Gringo's Hawk.* Eugene, OR: Kenneth Group Publishing, 2001. An engrossing and beautifully written autobiography of a North American who has lived in Costa Rica since 1972, with nuanced recounting of his struggles as an environmentalist and great portraits of local people.

Palmer, Paula. *What Happen: A Folk-History of Costa Rica's Talamanca Coast*. San José: Zona Tropical, 2005. A revised edition of the classic oral history of the Afro-Caribbean Talamancans.

Palmer, Steven Paul and Molina Jimenez, Ivan. *The Costa Rica Reader: History, Culture, Politics.* Durham, NC: Duke University Press, 2004. This brings together newspaper accounts, histories, petitions, memoirs, poems, and essays written by Costa Ricans, designed to reveal the complexity of the country's past and present, and showing how Costa Rican history challenges the idea that current dilemmas facing Latin America are inevitable or insoluble.

Ras, Barbara. *Costa Rica: A Traveler's Literary Companion.* San Francisco: Whereabouts Press, 1994. An excellent English translation of short stories by Costa Rica's best writers.

NATURAL HISTORY

Botanica Editors. *Botanica's Orchids: Over 1200 Species.* San Diego, CA: Laurel Glen Publishing, 2002.

Carr, Archie. *The Windward Road: Adventures of a Naturalist on Remote Caribbean Shores.* Gainesville: University Press of Florida, 1979. The book that inspired the worldwide turtle conservation movement.

Colesberry, Adrian. *Costa Rica: The Last Country the Gods Made.* Guilford, CT: Globe Pequot Press, 1993. Coffee table classic of travel writing with photographs.

DeVries, Philip. *The Butterflies of Costa Rica and Their Natural History.* Princeton: Princeton University Press, 1997. A color-filled volume about butterflies.

Fogden, Michael and Patricia. *Hummingbirds of Costa Rica.* San José: Zona Tropical, 2005. Gorgeous photographs of hummingbirds and the flowers they like to feed on by experts who have been studying them for decades. Fascinating information in an accessible style.

Forsyth, Adrian and Miyata, Ken. *Tropical Nature: Life and Death in the Rain Forests of Central and South America.* New York: Touchstone, 1995.

Franke, Joseph. *Costa Rica's National Parks and Preserves: A Visitor's Guide, Second Edition.* Seattle, WA: Mountaineers Books, 1999.

Garrigues, Richard and Dean, Robert. *The Birds of Costa Rica, a Field Guide.* Zona Tropical, 2007. Written and illustrated by longtime birding guides, this book weighs much less than the two-pounder by Stiles and Skutch, so it's much easier to carry into the field. Notes on habitat, behavior, key identifying marks and calls are all noted opposite a picture of each bird, as well as the best months and locations in which to see them. Recommended.

Haber, Zuchowski and Bello. *An Introduction to Cloud Forest Trees,* second edition. Puntarenas, CR: Mountain Gem Publications, 2000.

Henderson, Carrol L. *Field Guide to the Wildlife of Costa Rica*. Austin: University of Texas Press, 2002. Excellent guide.

Inbio. The Institute of Biodiversity has many bilingual guides on everything from bromeliads to cacti, beetles to whales. Order at inbio.ac.cr under Inbio Editorial.

Janzen, Daniel, ed. *Costa Rican Natural History*. Chicago: University of Chicago Press, 1983. The undisputed bible of Costa Rican ecology, with 174 biologist contributors covering almost everything there is to know about the subject. Entertaining and well-written. Also published in Spanish.

Leenders, Twan. *A Guide to Amphibians and Reptiles of Costa Rica*. San José: Distribuidores Zona Tropical, S.A., 2001.

Nadkarni and Wainright. *Monteverde: Ecology and Conservation of a Tropical Rain Forest*. New York: Oxford University Press, 2000.

Reid, Fiona. *A Field Guide to Mammals of Central America and Southeast Mexico*. New York: Oxford University Press, 1997.

Skutch, Alexander. *Trogons, Laughing Flacons, and Other Neotropical Birds*. Texas A&M University Press, 1999. Costa Rica's master birder, who passed away in 2004 at age 99 and was the author of 25 other books, describes the behavior of the trogon family, which includes the resplendent quetzal.

Stiles, Gary F., and Alexander Skutch. *A Guide to the Birds of Costa Rica*. Ithaca, NY: Cornell University Press, 1990. *The* birder's guide to Costa Rica. Illustrated by Dana Gardner. See companion audiotape, below.

Wainwright, Mark. *The Natural History of Costa Rican Mammals*. San José: Distribuidores Zona Tropical, S.A., 2003. A beautifully illustrated guide.

Zuchowski, Willow. *Tropical Plants of Costa Rica*. San José: Zona Tropical, 2006. A guide to 430 plants with 540 photos, yet small enough to take into the field.

PERIODICALS

amcostarica.com. A daily English-language online periodical.

The *Tico Times*. The best way to keep up with what is happening in Costa Rica. Apdo. 4632, San José; 2258-1558, fax: 2233-6378; tico times.net. Delivered around the world in print and online.

AUDIO FIELD GUIDES FOR BIRDERS AND NATURALISTS

The Cornell Laboratory of Ornithology's Library of Natural Sounds has several audiotapes that can help you identify birds and animals in the wild at **Wild Birds Unlimited** (877-266-4928; sapsuckerwoods.com), the gift shop of the Cornell Lab of Ornithology.

Costa Rican Bird Song Sampler has the songs of 180 bird species arranged by habitat. A booklet provides the page and plate numbers for the species as they are found in *A Guide to the Birds of Costa Rica* by Stiles and Skutch (see "Books," above).

Sounds of Neotropical Rainforest Mammals is an audio companion to the book *Neotropical Rainforest Mammals* by Louise H. Emmons. Disc One features primates, Disc Two has all other mammals.

Voices of Costa Rican Birds: Caribbean Slope, a two-CD set containing 225 species, the largest compilation available.

Voices of the Cloud Forest, a CD of sounds from a day in the Monteverde Cloud Forest Biological Reserve. Sounds of cloud-forest denizens are identified at the end.

Index

Lodging Index

Dining Index

Notes from the Publisher

An alert, adventurous reader is as important as a travel writer in keeping a guidebook up-to-date and accurate. So if you happen upon a great restaurant, discover a hidden locale, or (heaven forbid) find an error in the text, we'd appreciate hearing from you. Just write to:

Ulysses Press
P.O. Box 3440
Berkeley, CA 94703
www.ulyssespress.com
e-mail: readermail@ulyssespress.com

It is our desire as publishers to create guidebooks that are responsible as well as informative. We hope that our guidebooks treat the people, country, and land we visit with respect. We ask that our readers do the same. The hiker's motto, "Walk softly on the Earth," applies to travelers everywhere . . . in the desert, on the beach, and in town.

You're already helping!

Simply by purchasing *The New Key to Costa Rica*,
you have helped preserve Costa Rica's environment

Would you like to do more?

At Ulysses Press, we believe that ecotourism can have a positive impact on a region's environment and can actually help preserve its natural state. In line with this philosophy, we donate a percentage of the sales from all New Key guides to conservation organizations working in the destination country—in Costa Rica, our environmental partner is the Resource Foundation.

The Resource Foundation, a nonprofit membership organization founded in 1987, is working through its Costa Rican affiliate, Arbofilia (Asociación Protectora de Árboles), to improve agricultural productivity and assist low-income rural families, while at the same time protecting natural resources and promoting conservation.

The target area is near Carara Biological Reserve, in the central part of Costa Rica, on the west coast near the Pacific Ocean. From an ecological standpoint, the area lies between the northern limits of the South American tropical rainforests and the beginnings of the dry forests of Mesoamerica. It has a number of major rivers that supply water for many important communities in the Central Pacific region.

Ulysses Press encourages you to further support this organization. For more information, or to make a donation, contact:

The Resource Foundation
P.O. Box 3006
Larchmont, NY 10538
phone/fax: 914-834-5810
e-mail: resourcefnd@msn.com

HIDDEN GUIDES

Adventure travel or a relaxing vacation?—"Hidden" guidebooks are the only travel books in the business to provide detailed information on both. Aimed at environmentally aware travelers, our motto is "Where Vacations Meet Adventures." These books combine details on unique hotels, restaurants and sightseeing with information on camping, sports and hiking for the outdoor enthusiast.

PARADISE FAMILY GUIDES

Ideal for families traveling with kids of any age—toddlers to teenagers—Paradise Family Guides offer a blend of travel information unlike any other guides to the Hawaiian islands. With vacation ideas and tropical adventures that are sure to satisfy both action-hungry youngsters and relaxation-seeking parents, these books meet the specific needs of each and every family member.

Ulysses Press books are available at bookstores everywhere. If any of the following titles are unavailable at your local bookstore, ask the bookseller to order them.

You can also order books directly from Ulysses Press
P.O. Box 3440, Berkeley, CA 94703
800-377-2542 or 510-601-8301
fax: 510-601-8307
www.ulyssespress.com
e-mail: ulysses@ulyssespress.com

HIDDEN GUIDEBOOKS

____ Hidden Arizona, $16.95
____ Hidden Baja, $14.95
____ Hidden Belize, $15.95
____ Hidden Big Island of Hawaii, $13.95
____ Hidden Boston & Cape Cod, $14.95
____ Hidden British Columbia, $18.95
____ Hidden Cancún & the Yucatán, $16.95
____ Hidden Carolinas, $17.95
____ Hidden Coast of California, $18.95
____ Hidden Colorado, $15.95
____ Hidden Disneyland, $13.95
____ Hidden Florida, $19.95
____ Hidden Florida Keys & Everglades, $13.95
____ Hidden Georgia, $16.95
____ Hidden Hawaii, $19.95
____ Hidden Idaho, $14.95
____ Hidden Kauai, $13.95
____ Hidden Los Angeles, $15.95
____ Hidden Maine, $15.95
____ Hidden Maui, $14.95
____ Hidden Miami, $14.95

____ Hidden Montana, $15.95
____ Hidden New England, $18.95
____ Hidden New Mexico, $15.95
____ Hidden Oahu, $14.95
____ Hidden Oregon, $15.95
____ Hidden Pacific Northwest, $18.95
____ Hidden Philadelphia & the Amish Country, $14.95
____ Hidden Puerto Vallarta, $14.95
____ Hidden San Diego, $14.95
____ Hidden San Francisco & Northern California, $19.95
____ Hidden Seattle, $14.95
____ Hidden Southern California, $19.95
____ Hidden Southwest, $19.95
____ Hidden Tahiti, $18.95
____ Hidden Tennessee, $16.95
____ Hidden Utah, $16.95
____ Hidden Walt Disney World, $13.95
____ Hidden Washington, $15.95
____ Hidden Wine Country, $13.95
____ Hidden Wyoming, $15.95

PARADISE FAMILY GUIDES

____ Paradise Family Guides: Kaua'i, $17.95
____ Paradise Family Guides: Maui, $17.95

____ Paradise Family Guides: Big Island of Hawai'i, $17.95

Mark the book(s) you're ordering and enter the total cost here ⇨

California residents add 8.75% sales tax here ⇨

Shipping, check box for your preferred method and enter cost here ⇨

❏ BOOK RATE   **FREE! FREE! FREE!**

❏ PRIORITY MAIL/UPS GROUND   cost of postage

❏ UPS OVERNIGHT OR 2-DAY AIR   cost of postage

Billing, enter total amount due here and check method of payment ⇨

❏ CHECK   ❏ MONEY ORDER
❏ VISA/MASTERCARD _____ EXP. DATE _____

Name_____Phone_____

Address _____

City_____ State _____ Zip _____

Money-back guarantee on direct orders placed through Ulysses Press.

ABOUT THE AUTHOR

Beatrice Blake has been living or traveling in Costa Rica for more than 30 years. In 1985, she rewrote *The Key to Costa Rica*, which her mother, the late Jean Wallace, had originally published in 1976, and has been updating it every other year since then. Beatrice enjoys helping people plan their vacations (www.keytocostarica.com/costaricaconsults.htm) and is an expert in community-based ecotourism. She lives near Brattleboro, Vermont.

ABOUT THE PHOTOGRAPHER

David Gilbert, the photographer of the color insert, began his relationship with photography at an early age when his grandfather gave him an ancient Nikon. Fifteen years later, his interest has grown into a way of life: he has chronicled California, Costa Rica, the Southwest, Ecuador, Mexico, Nicaragua, and Peru with his camera. A graduate of Brooks Institute of Photography, David regularly shoots for travel and nature publications. He currently resides in Berkeley, California.

ABOUT THE ILLUSTRATOR

Deidre Hyde is an illustrator working out of Costa Rica. A graduate of the University of Reading, England, with a degree in Fine Arts, her work has taken her throughout Central and South America, West Africa, and Italy. Her main focus is on conservation themes and she works closely with conservation groups such as the World Conservation Union. Hyde is painting for conservation.